Burma:
Insurgency and the Politics of Ethnicity

Martin Smith

Zed Books Ltd
London and New Jersey

Burma: Insurgency and the Politics of Ethnicity was first published by Zed Books Ltd, 57 Caledonian Rd, London N1 9BU, UK, and 165 First Avenue, Atlantic Highlands, New Jersey , 07716, USA.

Cover design by Andrew Corbett.
Laserset by Selro Publishing Services, Oxford.
Printed and bound in the United Kingdom by Billing and Sons Ltd, Worcester.

US CIP is available from the Library of Congress.

British Library Cataloguing in Publication Data

Smith, Martin
Burma: insurgency and the politics of ethnicity.
I. Title
959.105

ISBN 0-86232-868-3
ISBN 0-86232-869-1 pbk

Contents

Glossary of Burmese Terms

Athin	Association
Bo	military commander
Bogyoke	supreme commander
Dacoit	robber, brigand
Dobama Asiayone	'We Burmans' Association
Duwa	traditional Kachin headman or ruler
Hutladaw	royal court
Ka Kwe Ye (KKY)	government defence militia
Khun	Shan royal rank
Kuomintang (KMT)	Chinese nationalist party, led by Chiang Kai-shek
Lakh	100,000
Mahn	form of address to Pwo Karen male
Manao	Kachin victory celebration
Minlaung	Pretender
Myosa	a junior prince/ruler in the Shan, Karenni States
Mujahid	Muslim fighter in Islamic holy war
Myothugyi	Ruler
Nai	form of address to Mon male
Pongyi	Buddhist monk
Pyi Saw Hti	government village militia
Pyi Thu Sit	government people's militia since the 1960s
Sangha	Buddhist order of monks
Sanad	treaty granted to Shan, Karenni rulers by British
Sai	form of address to young Shan male
Saw	form of address to Sgaw Karen male
Sawbwa (Saopha)	hereditary prince or regent in the Shan, Karenni States
Sawke	traditional Karen headman
Sayadaw	Abbot
Sitwundan	irregular government militia in late 1940s
Thakin	master
Tat	army, militia
Tatmadaw	Burmese Army
Thugyi	Headman
U	form of address to adult Burman male
Yebaw	comrade

Acronyms and Abbreviations

ABFSU	All Burma Federation of Students Unions
ABKO	All Burma Karen Organisation
ABPO	All Burma Peasants Organisation
ABSDF	All Burma Students Democratic Front
ABSU	All Burma Students Union
ABTUC	All Burma Trade Union Congress
ADA	Arakan Defence Army
ADSUB	Alliance for Democratic Solidarity Union of Burma
AFO	Anti-Fascist Organisation
AFPFL	Anti-Fascist People's Freedom League
AIO	Arakan Independence Organisation
AIR	All India Radio
aka	also known as
ALO	Arakan Liberation Organisation
ALP	Arakan Liberation Party
ANLP	Arakan National Liberation Party
ANC	Arakan National Congress
ANUO	Arakan National United Organisation
APLP	Arakan People's Liberation Party
ARIF	Arakan Rohingya Islamic Front
ASSPO	All Shan State Peasants Organisation
BIA	Burma Independence Army
BNA	Burma National Army
BSPP	Burma Socialist Programme Party
BWPP	Burma Workers and Peasants Party
CAS	Civil Affairs Service
CC	Central Committee
CCP	China Communist Party
CDP	Chin Democracy Party
CIA	Central Intelligence Agency
CNF	Chin National Front
CNLP	Chin National Liberation Party
CNUO	Chin National Unity Organisation
CNVP	Chin National Vanguard Party
CPA	Communist Party of Arakan
CPB	Communist Party of Burma
CPI	Communist Party of India
CPM	Communist Party of Malaya
CPSU	Communist Party of the Soviet Union
CPT	Communist Party of Thailand
CRDB	Committee for the Restoration of Democracy in Burma
DAB	Democratic Alliance of Burma
DNUF	Democratic Nationalities United Front
DPNS	Democratic Party for New Society
DSI	Defence Services Institute
DSO	Democratic Students Organisation
EC	Executive Council/Committee

FAA	Frontier Areas Administration
FACE	Frontier Areas Committee of Enquiry
FEER	*Far East Economic Review*
FNDF	Federal National Democratic Front
GCBA	General Council of Burmese Associations
GSC	General Strike Committee
IAPG	Independent Arakenese Parliamentary Group
IOR	India Office Records
KAF	Kawthoolei Armed Forces
KCO	Karen Central Organisation
KGB	Kawthoolei Governing Body
KIO/KIA	Kachin Independence Organisation/Army
KKY	Ka Kwe Ye
KMLF	Kawthoolei Muslim Liberation Front
KMT	Kuomintang
KNA	Karen National Association
KNDO	Karen National Defence Organisation
KNLA	Karen National Liberation Army
KNLC	Karen National Liberation Council
KNLP	Karen/Kayan New Land Party
KNPP	Karenni National Progessive Party
KNU	Karen National Union
KNUF	Karen National United Front
KNUP	Karen National United Party
KPLA	Kawthoolei People's Liberation Army
KRC	Karen/Kawthoolei Revolutionary Council
KRF	Kokang Resistance Force
KSNLF	Karenni State Nationalities Liberation Front
KYO	Karen Youth Organisation
LC	Leading Cell
LID	Light Infantry Division
LDC	Least Developed Country
LDP	League for Democracy and Peace
LNO	Lahu National Organisation
LNUP	Lahu National United Party
MIS	Military Intelligence Service (*aka* Defence Services Intelligence)
MFL	Mon Freedom League
MNDO	Mon National Defence Organisation
MNF	Mizo National Front
MPF	Mon People's Front
NCNA	*New China News Agency*
NDF	National Democratic Front
NDUF	National Democratic United Front
NEC	North-East Command
NLA	Nationalities Liberation Alliance
NLC	National Liberation Council
NLD	National League for Democracy
NMDO	National Mon Democracy Organisation
NMSP	New Mon State Party
NNC	Naga National Council
NNSC	Naga National Socialist Council
NSCN	National Socialist Council of Nagaland
NSH	Noom Suik Harn
NUF	National/Nationalities United Front
NUFA	National Unity Front of Arakan

NULF	National United Liberation Front
NUP	National Unity Party
PA	People's Army
PBF	Patriotic Burmese Forces
PCP	People's Comrade Party
PDF	People's Democratic Front
PDP	Parliamentary Democracy Party
PLA	Patriotic/People's Liberation Army
PNF	Palaung National Force
PNO	Pao National Organisation
PPP	People's Patriotic Party
PRP	People's Revolutionary Party
PSLO/P	Palaung State Liberation Organisation/Party
PVO	People's Volunteer Organisation
PYF	Patriotic Youth Front
RBA	Revolutionary Burma Army
RC	Revolutionary Council
RF	Red Flag
RNA	Revolutionary Nationalities Alliance
RPF	Rohingya Patriotic Front
RUSU	Rangoon University Students Union
RSO	Rohingya Solidarity Organisation
SEATO	South East Asia Treaty Organisation
SLORC	State Law and Order Restoration Council
SSA	Shan State Army
SSAE	Shan State Army East
SNUF	Shan National United Front
SSIA	Shan State Independence Army
SSNLO	Shan State Nationalities Liberation Organisation
SSPP	Shan State Progress Party
SUA	Shan United Army
SUF	(Rangoon University) Students United Front
SURA	Shan United Revolutionary Army
SSWC	Shan State War Council
TNA	Tailand National Army
TNP	Tribal National Party
TRC	Tailand Revolutionary Council
TUC(B)	Trades Union Congress (Burma)
UKL	Union Karen League
UKO	Union Karen Organisation
UMP	Union Military Police
UNDP	Union Nationals Democracy Party
UNF	United Nationalities Front
UNLD	United Nationalities League for Democracy
UPNO/UNPO	Union Pao National Organisation
UWSA	United Wa State Army
VOPB	Voice of the People of Burma
WACL	World Anti-Communist League
WNA	Wa National Army
WNC	Wa National Council
WNO	Wa National Organisation
WPD	*Working People's Daily*
WSC	Workers and Services Council
YMBA	Young Men's Buddhist Association
ZNF	Zomi National Front

Chart 1: Insurgent Organisations at Time of CPB Mutinies, March 1989

Name	Leader	Nos.[1]	Support	Operational Areas
ABSDF	=Tun Aung Gyaw	1000	Largely Burman, Mon	Kachin-Karen-Kayah-Mon-Shan States
NUFA				
-AIO	*Kyaw Hlaing	30	Rakhine	North Arakan
-ALP	*Khine Ye Khine	70	Rakhine	Rakhine State, Karen State
-ANLP	*Maung Sein Nyunt	30	Rakhine	North Arakan
-CPA	*Maung Han	100	Rakhine	Rakhine State
-TNP	*Pa Di Phru	30	Kamui, Chin, Marung	Arakan Hill Tracts
eARIF	Raschid Ba Maung	150	Rohingya Muslim	North Arakan
CNF	*J K K Thang	200	Chin	North Chin/Kachin State
CNLP	Win Maung	20	Chin	North Chin/Rakhine State
CPB	Ba Thein Tin	15000	Various[2]	Shan-Kachin-Rakhine, Tenasserim
CPB-RF	Thaw Da	30	Burman, Chin, Rakhine	North Arakan
KIO	*#Brang Seng	8000	Jinghpaw, Maru, Lashi, Lisu	Kachin State, N Shan State
KNU	*Bo Mya	6000	Sgaw, Pwo, Pao	Karen State, Tavoy, Thaton, Toungoo
KNPP	*Saw Maw Reh	500	Kayah, Kayan, Bre, Shan	Kayah State
KSNLF	#Nya Maung Me	150	As above	As above
KNLP	#Shwe Aye	200	Kayan, Kayah, Pao	Karenni, SW Shan State, Pyinmana
LNO	*Paya Ja Oo	100	Lahu (Nyi, Na, Sheleh)	SE Shan State (Monghsat)
-Abi Faction	Thein Myint	100	As above	As above
NNSC	Muivah	400	Naga	Naga Hills - India
NNC	A.N. Phizo	200	Naga	As above
NMDO	Nai Pagoeman	100	Mon	Mergui
NMSP	*Nai Shwe Kyin	1500	Mon	Mon State, Karen State
PSLP	*Kyaw Hla	500	Palaung	NW Shan State (Namhsam)
PNO	*Aung Kham Hti	500	Pao	SW Shan State
PPP	=U Thwin	70	Burman	Karen State
SSNLO	#Tha Kalei	500	Pao, Shan, Kayan	SW Shan State
SSPP	*# Sai Lek	2500	Shan, Palaung etc.	Northern/Central Shan State
TRC	Khun Sa/Jemg	3000	Shan, various hill-peoples	S, SW Shan State, Loimaw
WNO	*Maha San	200	Wa	SW Shan State
WNC	Ai Hsiao-hsu	500	Wa	S Shan State

Notes and Key:

1 Figures are approximate. They are the number of armed regulars or village militia the fronts could support. Most groups have trained considerably larger numbers than can be armed at any one time.
2 The CPB has mainly ethnic Burman members. Its PA consisted largely of ethnic minority recruits, especially Wa, Akha, Shan, Kachin and Chinese.
* NDF members, most of whom also belonged to the DAB (=)
# Alliance with CPB

The above were active armed insurgent groups in 1989. Most were confined to underground and guerrilla operations. Only the CPB, KIO, KNU, KNPP, NMSP, PSLP, PNO, SSNLO, SSPP and TRC controlled large base areas or 'liberated zones'. Other smaller groups generally train and shelter in their camps. Both Naga factions have their headquarters on the Burma side of the border, but operate mainly on the Indian side. There are also several other groups politically active in the border areas which have no or little armed strength but which also circulate anti-government propaganda.

Chart 2: Insurgent United Fronts

Pro-CPB

People's Democratic Front (1949-58) ★
Communist Party of Burma (White Flag)
Communist Party of Burma (Red Flag)
People's Volunteer Organisation - White
   Band (later People's Comrade Party)
Arakan People's Liberation Party
Revolutionary Burma Army (1949-50)

National Democratic United Front (1959-75)
Chin National Vanguard Party (1959-63
   -absorbed into CPB)
Communist Party of Burma (White Flag)
Karen National United Party
Karenni National Progressive Party (1959-69)
New Mon State Party (1959-69)
Shan State Nationalities Liberation
   Organisation (joined 25-7-74)

*All Nationalities Peoples' Democratic Front
(1989-present)*
Communist Party of Burma
Shan State Nationalities Liberation
   Organisation
Karenni State Nationalities Liberation Front
Kayan New Land Party
Democratic Patriotic Army

Other All-Burma Fronts
National United Liberation Front (1970-4)
Chin Democracy Party
Karen National Union
New Mon State Party
Parliamentary Democracy Party (later
   People's Patriotic Party)

Democratic Alliance of Burma (1988-present)
All eleven NDF Members (see right) except
   KNPP
All Burma Students Democratic Front
All Burma Muslim Union
All Burma Young Monks Union
Committee for the Restoration of Democracy
   in Burma
German-Burmese Association (from 1989)
General Strike Committee Rangoon (1988-9)
Muslim Liberation Organisation
Overseas Burma Liberation Front
Overseas Karen Organisation
People's Liberation Front
People's Patriotic Party

Democratic Front of Burma (from 1990)
All DAB members (see above)
National Coalition Government of Burma

Ethnic Nationalist
*Democratic Nationalities United Front
   (1956-8)*
Karen National Union
Karenni National Progressive Party
Mon People's Front
Pao National (Liberation) Organisation

Nationalities Liberation Alliance (1960-3)
Kachin Independence Organisation
Kawthoolei Revolutionary Council
Karenni National Progressive Party
Noom Suik Harn - Shan National United
   Front

United Nationalities Front (1965-6)
Karen National United Party
Karenni National Progressive Party
Kayan New Land Party
Shan State War Council
Zomi National Front

Nationalities United Front (1967-75)
Karen National United Party
Karenni National Progressive Party
Kayan New Land Party
New Mon State Party (1965-9)
Pao (from 1966 - as SSNLO from 1969)
Zomi National Front

Revolutionary Nationalities Alliance (1973-5)
Karen National Union
Karenni National Progressive Party
Kayan New Land Party
Shan State Progress Party

Federal National Democratic Front (1975)
Arakan Liberation Party
Karen National Union
Karenni National Progressive Party
Shan State Progress Party

National Democratic Front (1976-present)
Arakan Liberation Party (as NUFA from
   1988)
Chin National Front (joined 1989)
Kachin Independence Organisation
Karen National Union
Karenni National Progressive Party
Kayan New Land Party (resigned 1977)
Lahu National United Party (till 1984): LNO
   from 1987
New Mon State Party (joined 1982)
Palaung State Liberation Party
Pao National Organisation
Shan State Progress Party
Wa National Organisation (joined 1983)

★ The PDF of the 1950s was effective only in Arakan but the term PDF is still used to describe communist fronts.

*The above are the major insurgent alliances formed with the intention of developing a
'United Front' strategy. Their effectiveness has varied considerably; several have existed
contemporaneously. Only the PDF, NDUF, NULF, NDF and DAB made any real impact.
There have also been many local alliances, too numerous to mention.*

MAP 1

Map of Burma at time of 1989 CPB ethnic mutinies

MAP 2

Major Ethnic Groups of Burma

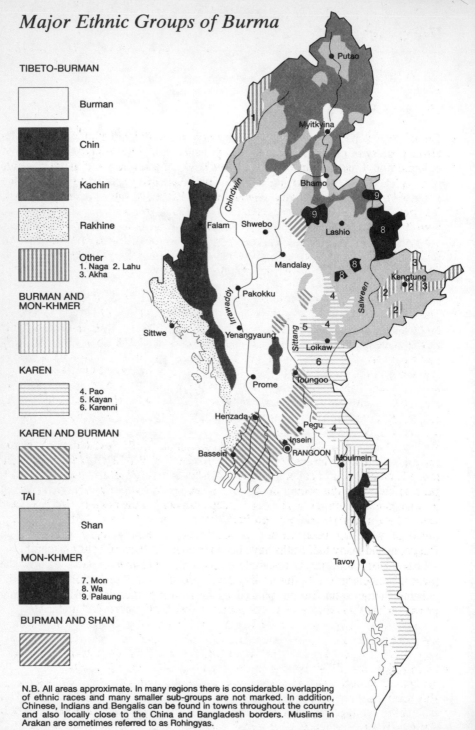

TIBETO-BURMAN

Burman

Chin

Kachin

Rakhine

Other
1. Naga 2. Lahu
3. Akha

BURMAN AND
MON-KHMER

KAREN

4. Pao
5. Kayan
6. Karenni

KAREN AND BURMAN

TAI

Shan

MON-KHMER

7. Mon
8. Wa
9. Palaung

BURMAN AND SHAN

N.B. All areas approximate. In many regions there is considerable overlapping
of ethnic races and many smaller sub-groups are not marked. In addition,
Chinese, Indians and Bengalis can be found in towns throughout the country
and also locally close to the China and Bangladesh borders. Muslims in
Arakan are sometimes referred to as Rohingyas.

Foreword

Out of deep respect for Burma, a country rich in cultural and ethnic diversity but also a country of considerable untapped potential still suffering the distortions of colonial rule, I had begun working on this book long before the traumatic events of the great democracy uprising of 1988. But it had always seemed likely that the country was a sleeping volcano which, by definition, was one day likely to erupt. Yet out of all the ideas, speeches and slogans thrown up in such a tumultuous period, one expression above all was to strike an immediate chord, as for all those who heard it, when in her first public appearance before ecstatic, cheering crowds on the Shwedagon hill on 26 August, Aung San Suu Kyi, the daughter of Burma's great independence hero, Aung San, spoke of the need for Burma's 'second struggle for independence.'

It had always been my intention to put forward and try to explain the largely unrecorded struggles of Burma's diverse ethnic peoples through the era of colonial rule and a near half century of war and civil strife. Whether a solution is now at hand or whether the bitterness engendered over the past three years is only paving the way for future decades of conflict remains unclear. But as the country, like much of the communist and socialist world, now pauses on the threshold of a new era, the time seems particularly right to take a step back into the past and begin a new reassessment of Burma's long and inconclusive history of both armed and political struggle which has so far failed to create a cohesive national identity for this deeply troubled land.

Most of the information contained in this book is the result of journalistic research, conducted largely in the years 1982-90, in which repeated trips were made back and forth between London, Burma and South-East Asia. Early on it became clear that this would be a very difficult task. Not only is there a paucity of documentation on the years since independence, but the country has remained isolated and in a state of deep conflict. Moreover, with a few notable exceptions, much of what has been written is inaccurate, especially under the BSPP in Rangoon, and many half truths have been repeated for want of better research.

I have tried, therefore, to assemble a coherent, documented history of how the present political crisis in Burma has developed through a re-examination of the existing literature on Burma, backed up by as many interviews with the living protagonists as possible and the collection of first-hand reports and materials.

The India Office in London is a good starting point for the colonial administration, but is no substitute for the important archaeological and anthropological field-work that still needs to be done. The writings of Josef Silverstein, David Steinberg, Robert Taylor and Bertil Lintner, who all generously shared their ideas, throw interesting light on the contemporary scene. But otherwise, due to the extensive notes (which are at the end of the book) I include no bibliography. The notes contain much original information on issues the research uncovered but for which there is no room in the main narrative. I have frequently had to rely on oral testimony for long-distant events. Accurate dates and statistics, in particular, were a constant problem. None the less any errors will be my own, but I hope such detailed notes will allow other students and writers to pursue all these issues further. Burma is a highly literate country with proud educational traditions, but after the political upheavals of the last half century vital research in far too many areas is only just beginning.

Finally, the list is too long to thank all the people who have helped in the writing of this book. Sadly in Burma today it is still not safe to mention individual names. None the less, despite the country's isolation and the xenophobic sounds that sometimes emanate from Rangoon, I have had nothing but encouragement, hospitality and advice from all the Burmese peoples, of all ethnic races, I have encountered on my many trips around the country and through the 'liberated zones'. All thought it important that this story was told. Skaw Ler Taw and Max McGrath, who sadly both died before the book was completed, were a particular inspiration. But for all my many friends in Burma, it is better for now to say a collective thank you.

My grateful thanks, too, to Adrian Cowell, Wolfgant Trost and Jeffrey and Joan Smith, as well as to Robert Molteno of Zed Books for his enthusiasm, patience and advice, and to Selina Cohen for her careful editing.

But above all, my deepest gratitude is due to my wife, Susanne, who accompanied me on many arduous journeys and without whose constant encouragement and support the book would not have been possible.

Martin Smith 1991

PART ONE
THE ROOTS OF CONFLICT

1

The Burmese Way to Stagnation and the Crisis of 1988

For many years opponents of Burma's longtime military leader, Gen. Ne Win, had been warning they were waiting for D-Day, the date on which he finally stepped down from power. But even so, the sheer scale and ferocity of the demonstrations and riots that broke out across the country following Ne Win's announcement on 23 July 1988 to a stunned, emergency meeting of the ruling Burma Socialist Programme Party (BSPP) in Rangoon that he was indeed preparing to leave the stage, took even some of the most seasoned Burma watchers by surprise and were to reverberate for weeks around an astonished world.

In 26 years of Ne Win's unique *Burmese Way to Socialism* Burma had become one of the most isolated and hermetically sealed countries in the world. Outside visitors were few, tourists allowed seven day visas only and movement was restricted to Rangoon, Mandalay and a handful of other tightly controlled towns close to the central plains. But those few who did enter the country were invariably charmed. Many likened their journey to taking a step back in time into a fairytale land caught in a time warp. Foreign diplomats, faced with what was regarded as a hardship posting, instead came to regard themselves as members of a privileged and exclusive club. And, despite the all too obvious poverty, to many on the political left Burma was a perfect and romantic vision of a non-aligned, Third World country developing under its own steam. For political scientists and jet age tourists alike, the quaint, crumbling decay of Rangoon made a welcome contrast to the high-paced bustle of Bangkok, Singapore and other neighbouring Asian capitals. And if the attentions of agents of the shadowy but omnipresent Military Intelligence Service (MIS) were sometimes oppressive, well that was just another price that had to be paid. Misty-coloured picture books of the land of smiles, pagodas and saffron-robed Buddhist monks today grace many a coffee table in the West.

Three months, four administrations and 10,000 deaths later the myth of this idyllic Burmese Shangri-La lay shattered forever. Yet Ne Win's warning in his resignation speech could not have been clearer: 'When the army shoots, it shoots to hit.'[1] The transformation in international perceptions was equally dramatic. The regime of Burma's new military strong man, Gen. Saw Maung, who seized power in a bloody coup on 18 September, was to become as internationally reviled as the military juntas of Pinochet's Chile or Haiti under the Duvaliers. The governments of the USA, Great Britain and Burma's two largest creditors and aid donors, West Germany and Japan, all cut off aid in immediate protest at the shooting of scores of unarmed demonstrators. Nor were there any indications the Soviet Union or China would step forward to fill the vacuum as the country teetered on the brink of collapse. The scale of the killings, witnessed by many foreign diplomats in Rangoon, have cast a pale shadow over the country from which it will take many years to recover.

However, for the foreign media, excluded from the country for so many years, keeping track of the explosive events of the year was to prove a near impossible task. The crisis of 1988 had crept up virtually unnoticed in the world outside and, with very few exceptions, news and commentary always lagged two or three steps behind. For several months reports of student-led protests over shortages of essential goods and spiralling rice prices had been circulating. But it was only in March of that year that the world first took note of their growing momentum. Ostensibly the first spark was trivial. A 'town and gown' brawl, which began outside a teashop in the Rangoon suburb of West Gyogon on 12 March and continued into the next day, ended with a policeman shooting dead a young student, Maung Phone Maw, from the Rangoon Institute of Technology (RIT). Then in the following days, as students took to the streets in protest, a number of attacks were reported on government-owned buildings and property.

The government's reply was astonishingly severe. As tanks were brought into the streets the security forces, led by the feared Lon Htein riot police, clamped down with horrifying force and an estimated 100 civilians were killed; 41 of these were students who suffocated to death in a prison van deliberately driven around the city for two hours on the short way to Insein gaol. According to one who survived, Thu Yein, a third-year Rangoon University mathematics student, they died a gruesome death; as many as 120 young people, most already suffering the effects of tear-gas smoke, were crammed into a space meant for less than half that number.[2] Having initially produced a whitewash report in which only two deaths were admitted, it was to take the government four months to acknowledge this barbaric act and the Home Minister, U Min Goung, was eventually forced to resign.[3] But many Rangoon residents were still clearly shocked by the brutality of the military's behaviour. Dozens of detainees were beaten or tortured and a number of female workers and students allegedly raped. One eyewitness I spoke to, a retired but internationally respected politician from the 1950s (he has requested anonymity), even saw students being forced by soldiers into the Inya Lake near his home where a number disappeared, presumed drowned; others escaped in panic through his garden. Later this incident became known as the 'White Bridge' massacre.

The violence of the army's response and the government's abrupt closure of all colleges and universities may have cowed the student demonstrators, but not for long. Soon after the campuses reopened in early June, the protests resumed. Classes were again disrupted as students at Rangoon University and RIT began demanding the release of their arrested colleagues, the reinstatement of the hundreds who had been expelled, and the right to set up an independent student union (something expressly forbidden under the 1974 Constitution of the ruling

BSPP). In response, on 20 June the Education Ministry announced Rangoon University would be closed down again.

The following day students began an impromptu march from the Institute of Medicine's Prome Road campus into the city. On the way they were joined by dozens of monks, workers and high-school students in a crowd which had swollen to an estimated 20,000-strong by the time it reached the city centre. This time, as clashes broke out, the security forces opened fire and several demonstrators were killed; later in the day six policemen were also reportedly murdered as the crowds fought back with home-made weapons and rioting spilled over into the Rangoon suburbs.[4] Again the government responded by closing down all colleges of higher education and a dusk to dawn curfew was imposed in Rangoon. The next day the police cordoned off and cleared the ancient Shwedagon Pagoda, Burma's holiest shrine and historically the symbolic centre for political protest in the city, which the students had temporarily occupied. This may have succeeded in dampening down the protests in Rangoon, but on 23 June there were the first reports of large gatherings and disturbances in Mandalay, Moulmein, Taunggyi and a number of other provincial towns outside the capital. In Pegu alone 70 people were feared dead after more serious rioting broke out.[5]

Into July the country lived on a knife's edge. Rumours were rife. But the government's crack-down and the restrictions on movement only exacerbated the worsening shortages of supplies in the shops, and the prices of essential goods, such as cooking oil and medicine, continued to rocket dramatically. The price of rice, for example, always the touchstone for political protest in Burma, was estimated to have risen by 400 per cent since the start of the year alone. Then on 12 July emergency measures had to be introduced in Taunggyi, Shan State, after clashes between the Buddhist and Muslim communities (allegedly provoked by the authorities) raised more memories of the violent communal disturbances that had bedevilled Burma in the past. (In Maungdaw, Arakan State, news had been suppressed in mid-May of a number of fatalities in similar disturbances.) The next outbreak of protest was to have an even greater psychological significance for the BSPP's aging chairman, Gen. Ne Win, now in his 78th year. On 22 July martial law was imposed in his home town of Prome, 160 miles north of Rangoon, after six days of rioting despite an existing curfew and ban on all public gatherings. The alarming scale of these mounting demonstrations may have forced Ne Win's hand or it may have hurried him into the early announcement of a decision already taken. But it was against this worsening backdrop that over 1,000 of the party faithful gathered in Rangoon at the end of July for the historic emergency Congress of the BSPP.

Ne Win's resignation, however, was not the only surprise awaiting them. Not only did he also announce he was quitting the party as well (and calling for several of his senior colleagues, including his long-time deputy and heir apparent, Gen. San Yu, to step down with him) but he proposed a national referendum to vote on the question of a return to a multi-party system of government. This revolutionary suggestion was to predate by a year the democracy movement in China and the tumultuous events which swept the one-party states of Eastern Europe in 1989 and saw the downfall of such equally hard-line rulers as Romania's Ceausescu and East Germany's Honecker.

That night Ne Win's motives were the subject of much speculation in the Rangoon tea shops, but few were surprised when the BSPP Congress immediately voted down his remarkable proposal. That Burma should remain a one-party state had long been the main article of faith of the BSPP and was enshrined in Article 11 of the 1974 Constitution. Indeed the very manner in which this controversial proposal was so cavalierly introduced (and as quickly disposed of) suggested to many observers that the whole process was prearranged to clear an orderly way for his chosen successor, Brig.-Gen. Sein Lwin, another military strong man very much in his master's mould.

The announcement, however, may well have been Ne Win's crowning error. As the people flooded back into the streets, the call for the restoration of multi-party democracy was to become the main rallying cry for the, as yet, unfocused protest movement and the main target of their anger was the hated Sein Lwin, dubbed the 'butcher of Rangoon' for his role in the bloody suppression of the March demonstrations. Indeed an older generation of university graduates now recalled it was Sein Lwin, then a junior officer, who had ordered troops to open fire on student demonstrators on the Rangoon University campus in July 1962, shortly after the military coup which brought Ne Win to power. Dozens were killed in a stubborn but forlorn protest which ended with troops blowing up the Students Union building. It was the same Sein Lwin, others remembered, whose troops entered the campus in the 1974 disturbances surrounding U Thant's funeral, where they terrorised students before restoring government control.

This time the main centres of protest continued to be in Rangoon and Mandalay. But in the coming days, in what leaders of the democracy movement insist was a genuinely spontaneous uprising, mass protests erupted in a staggering array of towns across the country, including Moulmein, Tavoy, Mergui, Pegu, Toungoo, Sittwe (Akyab), Minbu, Pakokku and even Myitkyina in Burma's far north.

All the time Burma's young student leaders were gaining in confidence. Sein Lwin's declaration of martial law on 3 August was immediately followed by the call for a general strike. On 4 August masked speakers addressed crowds, several thousand strong, near the Sule Pagoda in Rangoon's main central area and called for the ousting of Sein Lwin, the release of all political detainees, the restoration of democracy and an end to human rights abuses.[6] A new mass demonstration was called by the students for the auspiciously chosen '8-8-88', a news item picked up by Christopher Gunness, the BBC's Dhaka correspondent, and re-reported to electrifying effect in a country starved for years of any real internal news coverage. Across the country workers laid down tools and took to the streets. Having for several days taken a less aggressive approach in a bid to defuse the situation, the government's response was to be its most draconian yet. In Rangoon alone doctors were later to put the death toll as high as 3,000 in what rapidly became a blood-bath as troops repeatedly opened fire on demonstrators. (This huge figure has never been confirmed; on 20 August State Radio claimed 'only' 112 dead and 267 wounded were actually brought to hospitals.) Similar shootings were reported in many other towns across the country. Even in the sleepy provincial town of Sagaing, State Radio announced 31 people were killed and 37 wounded after troops opened fire on a crowd allegedly trying to take over a police station (survivors put the true death toll at 327 in one of the worst massacres of the summer as demonstrators were mown down in carefully planned 'killing zones' around the town).[7] Further south in Bassein 30 civilians, including boys as young as 13 and 14, were killed as police and troops, using armoured carriers, broke up a 5,000-strong demonstration.[8] Nor was the violence entirely one sided. As government buildings and installations came under increasing attack, it was reported that three policemen in Rangoon's working class Okkalapa district had been beheaded by the mobs.[9]

Now clearly losing control of the situation, the BSPP old guard was forced into a desperate ploy. On 12 August after a brief but bloody interregnum of just 18 days, Sein Lwin resigned, his place being taken one tense week later by Dr Maung Maung, a lawyer and writer who had studied in the west and was virtually the only non-military man ever to have served in the higher ranks of the BSPP. In a bid to win time Maung Maung announced a new strategy and what at first appeared to be a far more conciliatory approach. An eleven-man Commission, headed by Tin Aung Hein, a civilian lawyer, would be set up to tour the country to investigate the 'people's genuine opinions on the prevailing political, economic and public administration conditions.'[10] Their report would then be delivered to the People's Assembly by the end of September for discussion. 'The fire of anger,' said Dr Maung Maung in a television address, 'can be extinguished with the cool waters of love and compassion.'[11]

Three days later Rangoon Radio added that the Commission would specifically be looking at the issue of multi-party democracy. This, however, failed to stop the protests; as student leaders pointed out, there was still no mention of elections or a referendum and all powers of decision making still effectively lay with the BSPP. Already on 16 August lawyers on the influential Rangoon Bar Council had issued a statement pledging their support for the 'people's movement'.[12] Then on 22 August tens of thousands of demonstrators, chanting slogans calling for a referendum on multi-party democracy, again poured into the streets of Rangoon in support of the students' call for a national general strike. In Mandalay an even larger crowd, estimated at over 100,000-strong, was reported to be on the march, marshalled by Buddhist monks; other large marches were held in Monywa, Prome, Sittwe, Taunggyi and Moulmein. In Sittwe, for example, where 50,000 people paraded through the streets waving red banners (the colour chosen by students as the symbolic colour of democracy), BSPP administration totally collapsed and party officials were pulled out in front of the crowds by students wearing red arm bands and made to confess their sins. Only in Moulmein did the security forces hit back after protesters tried to seize the Customs Office, and an estimated 58 students and monks were killed in a joint naval/army attack by night on the Strike Centre at the Kyaiktok Pagoda.[13]

The following day in Rangoon, encouraged by the military's failure to respond (news of the Moulmein massacre was suppressed), even larger crowds, including doctors and lawyers in their working gowns, office workers, writers, musicians, actors and even army veterans, took to the streets. The main focal point for their demonstrations was the Rangoon General Hospital where many of the victims of the earlier shootings had been taken and, in one particularly notorious incident, troops had opened fire, hitting several nurses. Here doctors and medical students formed a Supervision Committee of Students to try and coordinate activities with other strikers and a 'democracy wall' briefly flowered. This was immediately covered with comic posters denouncing Ne Win, Sein Lwin and the army hard-liners.

The BSPP government now made what at the time appeared to be another major concession. On 24 August, on a day which saw the largest demonstrations yet and thousands of government office workers joining the marches under banners identifying their Ministries, martial law was lifted and Dr Maung Maung announced a special BSPP Congress would be convened on 12 September. The main purpose of the Congress would be to decide whether to hold a referendum to choose between a one-party and multi-party system of government. Leaving little doubt on which way he expected party members to vote, Maung Maung made it clear that if the Congress decided against the referendum, he and the other top party leaders would resign.[14]

Once again, however, this failed to satisfy supporters of the democracy movement which in five short months had achieved a remarkable momentum of its own. Still no obvious leaders had emerged, but in the general excitement the previous demand for a national referendum was virtually forgotten and many activists instead urged the country to go straight to the polls. To oversee and organise these elections another spontaneous demand emerged, that the BSPP should step down completely and be replaced by an interim coalition government. With the BSPP now apparently on the run, the more optimistic already believed this was just a matter of time, while the more militant were already talking of putting Ne Win, Sein Lwin and the ruling military clique on trial.

People's Power and the Democracy Summer
There now followed just over three weeks of unbridled euphoria and the most astonishing display of people's power. This gave both an indication of the long-felt frustrations and untapped potential of the new opposition movement, but also the first warnings of the grave dangers that lay ahead.

Certainly to the outside world, at least, it appeared for a brief moment that the government was indeed caving in. Many foreign diplomats believed Ne Win was making desperate preparations to flee the country. Apparently confirming the BSPP's capitulation, on 26 August Rangoon Radio announced that everybody arrested in connection with the unrest since 3 August (reportedly 2,750 people) had been released. And as troops began pulling back from the streets and returning to barracks, Strike Centres and People's Committees, consisting of monks, students and workers, sprang up in dozens of towns and villages across the country to take over the local administration and speed up the distribution of food and supplies to the needy. In many towns barricades, manned by volunteers armed with home-made weapons, were set up around public buildings and old-timers began recalling the great national liberation protests of the 1920s, 1930s and 1940s when similar patriotic crowds, in the same spontaneous alliance of students, monks and workers, had repeatedly forced the colonial authorities to back down. Farmers and their families from the countryside crowded into the towns, and everywhere pictures of Aung San, the hero of the independence struggle, were on prominent display. The same infectious enthusiasm reached even the press, long under tight government control. State Radio continued to function as the military's mouthpiece, but many newspapers carried front-page stories detailing the demands and actions of the democracy movement.

It was only at this late point that the first leaders of the new opposition felt it was safe to emerge publicly. However, it was also to be immediately obvious that the democracy movement was by no means united. After 26 years of military government this, perhaps, should not have been surprising. One of the most damaging legacies of Ne Win's dictatorial rule was that not only had no successors been groomed or rival parties allowed to function, but all opponents or dissenters, both inside and outside the party, had been ruthlessly quashed. Even some of his closest associates had routinely been imprisoned. For example, as recently as 1983 Brig.-Gen. Tin Oo, then BSPP general-secretary, and Col. Bo Ni, Home and Religious Affairs Minister, both of whom were former heads of the National Intelligence Bureau, had been gaoled for life on alleged corruption charges.[15]

But now in the summer of 1988 there was to be a remarkable explosion of new political forces. Spearheading the democracy movement were the students who had been leading the anti-government protests from the very beginning. Their organisation, however, was still very loose. Nationally the students were generally referred to under their historic name, the All Burma Students Union, and this, in theory, maintained informal contacts around the country. This partly explains the speed with which the protests had spread. The students, despite their suppression under Ne Win and the BSPP, were still a much admired section of the community and this can be dated back to the celebrated Rangoon University strike of 1920 from which Burma's national liberation movement had grown. Even Ne Win himself had first come to prominence in the student protests at Rangoon University in the 1930s.

However, in the summer of 1988, with the virtual halting of all road and rail traffic around the country, communications were still difficult and individual student organisations were to all intents and purposes having to act independently. As a result various local associations and unions were formed under a variety of different names and leaders. On the national scene the best known of these was the All Burma Federation of Students' Unions (ABFSU), set up in Rangoon on 28 August with a claimed 50,000 membership and led by the near mythical Min Ko Naing (an assumed name meaning Conqueror of Kings), in reality, Paw U Tun, a third-year zoology student from Rangoon University. Other prominent figures on the 119-man ABFSU Organising Committee who have since continued to play a leading role in the democracy movement include the joint-secretary, Winn Moe, whose late father had been a Foreign Office official, and the general-secretary, Myo Than Htut, a Rangoon University physics graduate who is today better known as Moe Thee Zun (June Hailstorm). The three were childhood friends. However, still nervous of possible repercussions (and wisely as it turned out) the students took the clever precaution of giving the same name to many of their public spokesmen and at different moments there appeared to be any number of different 'Min Ko Naings' active in the city.[16]

Close to the students, and especially in many up-country towns, were the Buddhist monks, historically in the forefront of political protest in Burma and without doubt the most respected single group in the country. Like the students, Burma's estimated 150,000 monks were hardly a united force, but many monasteries had their own grievances against the government and a number of leading abbots had been upset by a BSPP campaign (long overdue in the view of many citizens) in the late 1970s, masterminded by Sein Lwin, to weed out corrupt officials and bring the clergy under closer central control. During this campaign many dissident monks had been disrobed. Since the protests began in June a number of monasteries, such as the Thayettaw in Rangoon and those of the *Yahanpyo* (Young Monks Association) in Mandalay, had been providing safe houses in which students could hold meetings, and some 30 to 40 monks had reportedly been shot in the demonstrations preceding Sein Lwin's downfall. Now throwing off any restraint hundreds of monks, many armed with sticks, came out onto the streets to help the new People's Committees keep law and order, and both leaders of the opposition movement and many soldiers and government officials were to welcome their appearance.

None the less, in many towns organisation of the People's Committees still remained extremely informal. It was a revolution that had not been planned and, other than the vague demand for democracy, had no clear ideological basis. To bring some sense of organisation to the growing political confusion, at the end of August a General Strike Committee (GSC) was formed to try to bring student, monk, teacher, doctor, writer and worker leaders from the country's key industries, including the dockyards and railways, together in one front. Over 100 GSC representatives, claiming to represent 50 Strike Committees and a remarkable 10,000 new unions and associations from around the country, met for several days in Rangoon in early September. But with transport links now totally cut, its activities were effectively confined to Rangoon, Mandalay and a few larger towns.[17] Its most obvious achievement was the continued mobilisation of vast mass rallies in Rangoon, which were echoed in several other towns. The Electrical Engineers Union, for example, agreed to keep emergency water and electricity supplies running, but stopped or sabotaged all other services, including work at the Syriam oil refinery. The country was now at a virtual standstill.

The next activists to reveal themselves were the leaders of the different political coalitions and parties which had belatedly begun to emerge. For many students, however, there was a large element of political opportunism and 'Johnny-come-lately' about most of these. Indeed, given the scale of the uprising, there were to be surprisingly few new faces at all. For suddenly in late August a long list of almost forgotten names from the past began to reappear in quick succession, and Western diplomats and journalists found themselves having to dip into their history books to identify just who was who.

First came the surviving political leaders from the short-lived era of parliamentary democracy in the 1950s. These were headed by the 81 year-old former prime minister, U Nu, who had been Burma's leader through most of the years from independence in 1948 until overthrown and imprisoned by Ne Win in 1962. A deeply religious man undoubtedly popular with the monks, U Nu had for some years been quietly travelling the country lecturing on Buddhism and gathering large crowds wherever he spoke. Still working closely with him were several of his former colleagues including Bo Hmu Aung, a former speaker of the Union Parliament and a member of that historic band of *Thirty Comrades*, including Ne Win, who had travelled to Japan with Aung San in 1941 to begin armed training for the anti-British uprising.

Then came the army dissidents led by 70 year-old retired brigadier-general, Aung Gyi, Ne Win's former deputy and his main co-conspirator in the 1962 coup. In early 1988 Aung Gyi had penned a series of letters to Ne Win which were highly critical of the BSPP, and these widely circulated letters had done much to encourage the students in the early wave of protests. As a result, Aung Gyi had been arrested during Sein Lwin's 18 days in power and was only released on 25 August, to a tumultuous welcome from the crowds. Another popular figure now to surface was retired general, Tin Oo, a former army Chief-of-Staff and Minister of Defence (no relation to the former Intelligence chief, Tin Oo), who had been imprisoned in 1976 for apparently failing to report a plot on Ne Win's life. After his release under amnesty in 1980, Tin Oo had studied law and now, during the exuberant mass rallies in Rangoon, was quickly to build a reputation as an articulate and persuasive orator.

But even the new names appeared to have the same striking historical connections. On 26 August a 43 year-old expatriate, Daw Aung San Suu Kyi, Oxford educated and married to a British academic, who happened to be in the country visiting her ailing mother, addressed a huge 500,000-strong rally on the slopes of the Shwedagon hill and was to become the instant darling of the crowds and the immediate focus of the Western media's attention. In her they saw another Cory Aquino (Philippines) and Benazir Bhutto (Pakistan), both of whom had unexpectedly emerged in the 1980s to sweep to power in popular people's movements against equally tyrannical regimes. What distinguished Suu Kyi, of course, was the name of her father, the founder of the modern Burma army, Aung San, who had been assassinated when she was just two.[18] Suu Kyi was quickly supported by a close circle of intellectual advisers, including well-known writers, artists and lawyers such as U Win Tin, U Aung Lwin and U Tun Tin, who had long been secret but bitter critics of the BSPP.

However, Aung San was not the only famous name to reappear. A number of sons and daughters of other prominent figures from the past also started to come forward. These included Daw Cho Cho Kyaw Nyein, daughter of U Kyaw Nyein, the late leader of the defunct Socialist Party, and Dr Tin Myint U, son-in-law of the late UN secretary-general, U Thant, who was working with political exiles abroad. But though perhaps nobody realised it at the time, probably the most powerful of all was Ne Win's own favourite daughter, Sanda Win, a doctor with the army rank of major.

From the very beginning, though on paper their objectives appeared much the same, the fledgling opposition was divided. A general understanding did exist that these prominent figures could afford to take the kind of public risks that were likely to be too dangerous for others. But none the less two main factions emerged, one headed by U Nu and the other built around the individual personalities of Aung Gyi, Tin Oo and Aung San Suu Kyi. To the consternation of many students it appeared that many of the personal rivalries, which had overshadowed party politics in the democratic era of the 1950s, were coming to the fore again.

In their defence it can be argued that these were heady days. With the BSPP government still widely expected to collapse at any moment (something nobody would have dared suggest even six weeks earlier) the stakes were extremely high. It was impossible to predict with any certainty what would happen from one day to the next. Hundreds had already been killed and the situation remained extremely volatile. Whether in Rangoon or Mandalay or amongst the expatriates and exiles in Bangkok or London, it was not hard to meet many who proclaimed themselves the future ministers or saviours of Burma. But next to the students there were few prepared to put in the hard political graft.

Mistakenly, as the ABFSU and GSC continued the street protests, the two 'political veteran' factions followed largely different paths. While Aung Gyi's followers worked at winning the support of the military (and Aung Gyi despite his public criticisms of the BSPP never accused Ne Win directly), U Nu, still a wily political operator despite his advancing years, played a far more provocative hand. On 28 August, in defiance of the constitutional ban on political parties, the first meeting was held in the Bahan suburb of Rangoon of the League for Democracy and Peace. With U Nu as patron, on the League's 20-man Executive Committee were Bo Hmu Aung and Mahn Win Maung, a former president of Burma, and a number of other prominent national figures from the 1950s, including the retired army officers, Brig.-Gen. Aung Shwe, Col. Saw Myint and Bo Khin Maung, who was also a former Industry Minister. Tin Oo, too, was initially a member of this committee.[19] Like Aung San Suu Kyi, U Nu began giving frequent telephone interviews to journalists calling from abroad, particularly the BBC whose nightly Burmese-language broadcasts were avidly listened to by huge crowds across the country. Indeed in many towns gongs were sounded to warn of the hour of the impending broadcasts. For Burmese citizens and foreigners alike, it was an astonishing moment of *glasnost*.

However, despite the increasing confidence of the opposition leaders, many other observers felt a growing sense of unease. Despite their retreat, Dr Maung Maung and the BSPP leaders still had not stepped down. Ne Win was still in the wings. And as the country veered towards the brink of breakdown (anarchy was the word on many people's lips) there was a growing vacuum in the national administration. Clearly conditions like this could not persist indefinitely. Perhaps the first to recognise this were the foreign embassies which began the quiet evacuation of family dependants and non-essential staff. But now, too, many of the same old-timers, who had happily been recalling the great days of Burma's national liberation struggle, began to warn of the deep traumas of 1948, the year of Burma's independence, when the country had fallen apart under the combined weight of rebellion and army desertions. Indeed, as the first reports of soldiers and airmen joining the demonstrations began to come in, such dire predictions were to gain some credibility, especially when Tin Oo claimed in a BBC interview that the opposition movement now had the support of 60 per cent of the army.[20]

However, comparisons with 1948 were something U Nu was anxious to avoid. 'The situation is quite different,' he told me. 'There is a lot more order now. Everything is under the control of the monks. They have set up administrative committees and are taking charge.'[21]

It was at this critical moment that once again the extraordinary ignorance of much of the world media was to be revealed. As headline writers first began to pencil in the threat of impending 'Civil War', many editors very belatedly appeared to discover that not only did Burma already have over 30,000 ethnic and communist insurgents but many of these had been in armed rebellion since the earliest days of Burma's independence. Indeed one of the very reasons given for Ne Win's seizure of power back in 1962 was the military's determination to keep these insurgent movements at bay. And though, under the BSPP, they had largely been penned back in the rugged mountains surrounding the central Irrawaddy plain, between them they still operated in or loosely controlled anywhere between one quarter and one third of the country. Vast areas of Burma had long been strictly off-limits to foreign visitors, except for the intrepid few who had crossed in illegally from abroad.

In September 1988 a quick scan was to reveal that these insurgent organisations, still numbering some 25 groups in all, could largely be divided into two major blocs, one headed by the Communist Party of Burma (CPB) and the other by the National Democratic Front (NDF), an alliance of ten ethnic minority armies demanding the formation of a federal Union of Burma. (See Charts 1 and 2.)

The first to suggest any involvement was the CPB, the oldest political party still active in Burma and, with some 15,000 men under arms, the single largest insurgent force. In its first official, though notably belated, comment on 28 August the CPB's Central Committee issued a statement, subsequently broadcast on the party's rebel radio station close to the Chinese border, identifying the CPB with the aims and objectives of the opposition movement and extending 'its praise and congratulations to the students and people on their victories.'[22] The real degree of the CPB's influence is very much open to question (and will be examined more fully later on), but certainly after the coup the Saw Maung regime was to try and play up the CPB's role for its own political purposes. But at the time a number of diplomatic sources and senior opposition leaders confirmed what they saw as the CPB's growing influence behind some, at least, of the Rangoon and Mandalay demonstrations.[23] For the most part, however, they were referring to veteran, long surrendered communists, such as Thakin Tin Mya or Bo Ye Htut, coming out of retirement and a small CPB cell, the 4828 Regional Committee, which had been in secret contact with a handful of RIT and Rangoon University students from the very beginning. As a result virtually all the leaders of the democracy movement have since remained adamant that the CPB's role in actually fomenting the uprising was minimal.

Meanwhile U Nu, who had himself briefly led the insurgent Parliamentary Democracy Party along the Thai border in the early 1970s, held out the olive branch of peace talks (if elected) with the ethnic minority NDF, several of whose members, including the Karen National Union (KNU), he had been allied with in his jungle days. Indeed in early August, following the first outbreak of shootings in Rangoon, a number of students had already arrived in KNU territory adjoining the Thai border and held informal talks with NDF leaders. More young people followed from Moulmein in the aftermath of the massacre on 22 August, and a secret delegation was sent by the ABFSU after its formation at the end of the month. The arrival of these predominantly ethnic Burman students was not something the staunchly nationalist NDF leaders had expected. But having gone on the military offensive in support of the democracy movement during Sein Lwin's brief reign, the different NDF armies decided to suspend large-scale operations and instead try to establish contacts with the emerging political parties in the cities. For military hardliners in Rangoon, still largely confined to barracks, any such conciliation was completely out of the question and exactly, as it soon transpired, the kind of provocation they had been looking for.

These, however, were not the only issues now muddying the waters. By early September the country was in a state of paralysis. Transport had ground to a virtual halt and flights in and out of the country, except for a few emergency shuttles, had ceased altogether. In many areas food, medicine and other essential goods were in desperately short supply and most workers and strikers had not received any pay for weeks. Inflation had reached dizzying heights. A tin of condensed milk, for example, was selling for 120 kyats (£12 at the better, official exchange rate), half the average worker's monthly wage, and many families were having to rely on their friends and relatives for charity.

It was against this background that around the country there were increasing reports of robberies, looting and mob violence. There is no reason to doubt that many of these stories were true. But from the very beginning leaders of the opposition movement were to allege that a deliberate campaign of 'dirty tricks' had been hatched. All parties pointed accusing fingers in exactly the same direction, i.e. at the hated Military Intelligence Service (MIS) and ruling BSPP.

Certainly, since Dr Maung Maung's announcement of the BSPP Congress in September there had been an ominous silence from Ne Win's military old guard who had retired into their heavily defended quarters around the Inya Lake suburb of Rangoon. Here they continued to keep close counsel behind locked doors and this was to lead to persistent rumours (probably leaked deliberately) that Ne Win and Sein Lwin were preparing to leave the country. In fact nothing could have been further from the truth.

Later a report was to surface, first published in the newspaper of the ABFSU at the beginning of September, of a secret meeting attended by senior BSPP leaders at Ne Win's residence on 23 August, the day before martial law was lifted. Those who first read it thought it must be a forgery, but it ran so closely parallel to what subsequently ensued that, though some doubts must remain, many observers today believe it is authentic.[24]

According to this document, it was agreed that the defeat of the opposition movement was absolutely dependent on the continued loyalty of the army or *Tatmadaw* to the BSPP.[25] At the same time, it was argued, if a multi-party system were introduced it would 'negate the role' of the military and the many *Tatmadaw* veterans who had given their 'lives and limbs' for the country. Their aims were thus synonymous and a new tactical strategy had to be drawn up 'to crush the opposition'. The first step would be to separate the students from the masses; the second to 'annihilate the student leaders and hardliners.' To do this military personnel would be secretly sent out throughout the country to create conditions of such lawlessness that 'the masses and business community will come to depend on the armed forces for protection'; then as the chaos continued, people would soon realise the 'aimlessness and confusion of a multi-party system.' Sooner or later this would pave the way for a coup, the only question being one of timing. If the country continued its rapid slide into anarchy the military takeover would be quick; if not, efforts would have to be stepped up. Criminal elements would have to be let loose and allowed to go on the rampage.[26]

But of the greatest importance in any scenario, the report argued, was that the *Tatmadaw* be back in charge again during what it was recognised would be a period of transition, which could well mean an interim government or the holding of a referendum or multi-party elections. This would not matter, for once in control the students should already have been isolated from the masses, and, with the photographic evidence it was now gathering, the MIS would be able to pick up all the student leaders, writers and film stars who were leading the democracy movement.[27]

This sketch analysis has proven astonishingly accurate. As if on cue, at the end of August some 9,000 prisoners were suddenly released from seven different prisons in a variety of chaotic circumstances which have never been adequately explained. On 26 August Rangoon Radio reported that apparently spontaneous anarchy, including riots, fires and shootings, had broken out in several prisons across the country. In the confusion 513 prisoners escaped from Insein gaol while another 57 were killed. Meanwhile 1,600 prisoners escaped in a mass breakout from Sittwe gaol (eyewitnesses say cheered on by the townspeople) where six more inmates were killed, and another 100 escaped from Bassein gaol. In the following days further rioting was reported at Katha, Bhamo, Myaungmya and Mandalay gaols in which the authorities admitted there were many more casualties. Yet, despite this apparent mayhem, the government chose this moment to release from Insein gaol another 4,805 prisoners said to be nearing the end of their sentences.[28]

Intentionally or otherwise, the simultaneous release of so many prisoners, including many of the country's most hardened criminals, was yet another explosive ingredient to add to the fast deteriorating situation, and their release coincided with a marked escalation in violence. Though in many towns leaders of the Strike Committees insisted administration was now well organised, on State Radio there were daily reports of looting and attacks on government warehouses. For many observers there was great mystery over just who was carrying out these raids. In Rangoon many of the disturbances centred on the workers' quarter of Okkalapa. But here many local residents claimed not to know the identities of the gang leaders. Rumours began to circulate that the robberies were being instigated by MIS agents, a charge denied on Rangoon Radio on 6 and 7 September, but repeated by Aung San Suu Kyi on Britain's Channel Four television the same day. Eyewitnesses, confirming Suu Kyi's allegations, reported seeing army units carrying away large stocks of food and supplies from government warehouses and leaving the doors open for looters. The boldest raid was on the local offices of the UN Food and Agriculture Organisation on 8 September, the only reported attack on foreign property, while several times men in uniform were seen carrying away cash boxes from branches of the Union Bank of Burma.

Whoever was responsible, such accusations and counter accusations only served to inflame tensions and in this worsening atmosphere much of the violence appeared increasingly irrational and vicious. A number of unidentified corpses with stab wounds were fished out from the Inya Lake and several MIS agents were murdered by enraged mobs, some after trials before the monks. In one particularly gruesome episode, three suspected government agents, including one woman, who were allegedly caught trying to poison the water supply to Rangoon Children's Hospital, were beheaded and their heads put on public display. Army leaders later claimed that over 100 people, including 30 members of the security forces, were killed by demonstrators during the uprising.[29]

Despite the mounting violence, opposition leaders continued to claim the situation was still well under control. Foreign diplomats, however, clearly saw matters differently and as the weekend of 10/11 September 1988 and the scheduled BSPP Congress loomed closer, the evacuation of family dependants was urgently hurried up.

It was, thus, largely to try and put a stamp of normality on proceedings that U Nu, who more than any other leader appeared to recognise the dangers in letting the situation slide, made his most dramatic move yet. After a secret approach by Winn Moe of the ABFSU, on 9 September U Nu announced the formation of a rival government, with a 25-man Cabinet and himself as prime minister, in a letter circulated to foreign embassies. Elections, he claimed, would follow one month later. Twenty-six years after the coup which had toppled him from power, U Nu's tone was exultant: 'I have exercised my (constitutional) right at 9 a.m. this morning. I have taken back the power which Gen. Ne Win has robbed from me. From this hour, sovereign power no longer rests with Gen. Ne Win. It has come back into my hands, and I announce this fact with joy.'[30] U Nu, however, was to make a serious error in not first discussing this move more closely with the ABFSU students and other leaders of the democracy movement and in the coming days, as the rift between opposition leaders widened, he was roundly condemned on all sides for political opportunism. 'Simply preposterous' was Aung Gyi's reaction to the news.[31]

In the event, U Nu's declaration served as little more than a distraction and, by bringing the special Congress forward two days, BSPP leaders ensured the meeting went through without any serious mishap, albeit in a Parliament building surrounded by barbed wire and troops. In what again appeared to be another major concession to the opposition movement, 75 per cent of the party delegates in attendance (968 out of a possible 1,080) voted for the introduction of a multi-party system of government; and, in apparent recognition of the strength of feeling in the country, they abandoned any plans to hold a referendum on the subject.[32] It was announced that a new civilian Commission, headed by a veteran civil servant, U Ba Htay, would be established to oversee the holding of elections and these could be held within three months, if conditions permitted. But Dr Maung Maung's tone was also notably tougher. Warning that attacks and threats against BSPP officials must now cease, he issued a stern declaration: 'The time has now arrived to restore law and order all over the country.'[33]

None the less, on paper at least, it appeared for a moment that the BSPP was now bowing to the inevitable and had given in to the opposition's demands. Certainly this was the initial reaction of several foreign governments. Instead, opposition leaders, taking up the cry they had repeated all summer, once again claimed it was 'too little, too late.' Pointing out the enormous difficulties they would face in contesting the first multi-party elections in the country in nearly three decades, they argued that the opposition would be at a considerable disadvantage in competing with the BSPP. Not only would the BSPP be organising the elections but, with the backing of the army, it would be the only party with a countrywide infrastructure and organisation. Indeed, as many political veterans warned, elections had only been held on three occasions since independence, in 1951/2, 1956 and 1960, and each time amidst scenes of great confusion and controversy.

The new demand of the opposition movement was the immediate resignation of the BSPP and the formation of a neutral interim civilian government to organise the promised elections. 'It's some progress but it's not satisfactory,' was Aung San Suu Kyi's verdict. 'They haven't promised an interim government. It seems the elections will be held under the present government and that makes us all doubt that they can be free and fair.'[34] On 13 September, Aung Gyi, Aung San Suu Kyi and Tin Oo, who were generally regarded as the most moderate of the opposition leaders, did meet with the Election Commission, but warned that 'since the country and the people have completely lost confidence in the government, they can neither accept nor trust a commission formed by the government.'[35]

The strikes thus continued, but there was now to be a marked hardening of attitudes. Much of the carnival atmosphere from the great marches of the previous week had disappeared. On 12 September large crowds once again took to the streets of Rangoon to reject the BSPP's plans. But this time students were seen passing out leaflets in the name of the ABFSU calling on the people to make this the last day of peaceful protests, while at Rangoon General Hospital students and monks embarked on a hunger strike. Meanwhile in Mandalay and several other towns similar large marches were reported.

SLORC and the Saw Maung Coup
On reflection, as these mass protests continued, the next few days were to be the calm before the storm. With fresh troop movements seen around the city, it was clear army commanders were making quiet preparations. In the early hours of 14 September, in one of several trial runs, troops overran the Strike Centre at Kyaunggon, 65 miles west of Rangoon, and arrested 200 people. Recognising these warnings, many student leaders began drawing up plans to go underground.

Others were still very confident and, in a surprise raid on 17 September, several dozen activists, accompanied by young monks, took over the top floors of the Ministry of Trade building where security personnel had been keeping watch and took away their arms and uniforms. The same day the CPB issued on their rebel broadcasting station an appeal, welcomed by many veteran communists and left-wing leaders in the cities, for a military ceasefire, the overthrow of the BSPP, talks between all opposition parties, and the holding of multi-party elections.[36]

But perhaps what was finally to force the army's hand was the increasing appearance in the streets of young military personnel marching in support of the opposition's demands. At first these were junior airforcemen from Base 502 at Mingdalon on the city's edge but later growing numbers from the navy and different army units stationed around the city. Many, through their work, had close contacts with democracy activists at RIT and Rangoon's Workers' College, where a particularly militant Students Union had taken control. Pictures of these uniformed and smiling soldiers, splashed on newspaper front pages around the world, were to give the impression of a regime which had lost control completely. Meanwhile, frustrated at the failure of their elders to agree plans for the interim government (they had wanted Aung Gyi, Aung San Suu Kyi, Tin Oo, U Nu and the former *Thirty Comrade*, Bo Yan Naing, to declare an emergency administration to hold elections), radical activists from the ABFSU and the GSC called a meeting for the afternoon of 18 September at Rangoon University's Convocation Hall. Here they proposed to force the political pace by declaring their own parallel government, made up of strike committees and workers' unions. They took their vote at 3.30 p.m.

Thus finally, at 4 p.m. on 18 September, just seven days after the BSPP had voted to usher in a new era of democratic reform, Ne Win's military old guard struck. Clearly the plan to use Dr Maung Maung as a civilian leader had failed. Though widely described in the foreign media as a 'coup', it was more obviously a change of faces or, as one diplomat put it, 'a reshuffling of the pack.' The new strong man and chairman of the State Law and Order Restoration Council (SLORC) was Gen. Saw Maung, the army Chief-of-Staff and Minister of Defence, and very much a loyal subordinate of Ne Win and his protégé Sein Lwin. And though in his first press statement he promised multi-party elections would still go ahead, Saw Maung also made clear the army's first priority would be 'to restore law and order and peace and tranquillity.'[37] It was a theme later much embellished by Brig.-Gen. Khin Nyunt, the head of Military Intelligence, who swiftly emerged as the real brains behind the regime.

Whether the country was indeed on the brink of collapse (and many activists still dispute this) it was immediately clear the army's intention was to crush the opposition democracy movement once and for all. If the people had really believed Saw Maung's promises, they would have rushed out to welcome the troops. Instead they took to the streets in protest. Equally significantly, it was also clear that, whatever wild predictions had been circulating about army mutinies and desertions, all the key commanders had stayed loyal.

As the 10 p.m. curfew imposed by the new regime approached, troops began firing warning shots over the heads of students and demonstrators who had gathered in the streets. In self defence many had armed themselves with primitive weapons including wooden spears, knives and *jinglees* (sharpened bicycle spokes which can be fired from catapults). Most scattered at once, but at midnight there were still large crowds reported at Rangoon University and the General Hospital.

'The change in atmosphere in the space of a few hours was frightening,' reported one of the few Western journalists in the city. 'Earlier in the day, opposition leaders were talking buoyantly of an interim government being within reach, ending 26 years of rule by the Burma Socialist Programme Party.... Students were jubilant as they marched through the streets, calling for democracy.'[38]

There now followed several days of scenes of the most horrific violence and countrywide bloodshed much of which, given the tight reporting restrictions enforced, has remained unrecorded.[39] In Rangoon, in the first three days alone, 1,000 people including schoolgirls, monks and students, were reported to have been killed. As army units moved through the city breaking up Strike Centres, eyewitnesses spoke of seeing monks trying to stop the killings by surrounding attacking soldiers. 'Many students are being mowed down. Can't anything be done?' one reporter telephoned in tears to the *Associated Press*.[40]

Some of the most shocking scenes occurred outside the US Embassy where troops from the 33rd Light Infantry Division (LID) took careful aim and shot into a crowd of 1,000 students who had been peacefully demonstrating outside. Here they naively believed the army would not dare open fire.[41] These terrifying moments were captured by an amateur video cameraman and later shown to horrified audiences across the world. Subsequent broadcasts on State Radio depicting those killed as 'destructive elements' only deepened a growing sense of outrage amongst many diplomats. Saw Maung himself later claimed only 15 demonstrators had been killed, though he did add that 500 people he described as 'looters' had also died.[42] In other parts of the city, however, students and other civilian activists did fight back and in Tamwe district hand-to-hand fighting was briefly reported. Outside Rangoon some of these battles were fierce, but in most cases the young guards of the Strike Committees were no match for heavily armed troops.[43] To break up the Strike Centre in the southern town of Tavoy, for example, schoolchildren who fled with their teachers in terror reported that the local army commander, Lt.-Col. Myint Thein, shot dead U Pan Kyaw, a middle school headmaster and secretary of the local Democratic Front, at point blank range in full view of the townspeople. Four other bystanders were killed by troops who opened fire on the crowd.[44]

But if the army's first object was to drive the protesters from the streets and drive a wedge between the students and the rest of the opposition movement, it was cynically successful. The death toll in the year's violence is today generally estimated to have passed the 10,000 mark. The true numbers, however, will never be known, for in another tactic learnt on the insurgent battlefields, troops routinely carried away and disposed of the bodies of all the dead and wounded. And in the following weeks as the military clampdown continued, gathering information about those who had disappeared was to become a near impossible task. Strict nighttime curfews were enforced, gatherings of more than five people banned, and all schools and universities remained closed. An entire year in the education of Burma's children was to be lost. 'People are living in a state of fear,' said one Amnesty International spokesman. 'It might seem remarkable. Many people have lost relatives. We even have films of some of the shootings. But as yet no one has been able to draw up any kind of accurate list of those killed or arrested.'[45]

Confusing the numbers of those missing, another 10,000 students and political activists from the cities, including lawyers, doctors, soldiers, monks and teachers, fled to liberated zones controlled by the country's diverse rebel armies, some into

CPB-controlled territory in the Shan State and the Tenasserim Division but the great majority into areas held by the ethnic minority NDF. An estimated 2,000 of these (largely from Mandalay, Lashio and Upper Burma) took sanctuary with the Kachin Independence Organisation (KIO) and Shan State Progress Party in the mountains of the far north, but most headed for the nearby jungles in the southeast. Here in the Dawna Range some 6,000 took refuge with the Karen National Union and New Mon State Party. Many immediately began armed training. Their determination was to impress even the most battle hardened of KNU veterans. 'They are really keen to fight,' said KNU Central Committee member, Skaw Ler Taw, a British army veteran from the Second World War. 'To them there is no other way to destroy military rule and achieve true democracy and peace in the country.'[46]

Other NDF leaders were initially more cautious about the sudden influx of so many young Burmans and not just because of historic racial antagonisms. Warned Brang Seng, chairman of the KIO, 'No one can turn into a guerrilla fighter overnight. Many could well be killed. It would be better if other countries took pity on their plight and helped them travel abroad to finish their studies.'[47]

This, however, cut little ice with student leaders intent on revenge. Before going underground a number, including ABFSU leaders Min Ko Naing and Moe Thee Zun, had agreed to stay behind in the cities to try and set up new political networks. On 20 September six soldiers were reportedly killed by one student cell in Moulmein, which had already returned from the border with weapons. But most of the better known leaders of the Strike Centres and demonstrations felt they had no choice but to take sanctuary and try to regroup. Scattered in small groups in malaria infested jungles across the country, they faced formidable obstacles in establishing contact with other democracy activists they had hardly known even in the heady days of August. But, with NDF help, on 5 November 50 representatives from some 18 groups were finally able to get together to form an umbrella organisation, the All Burma Students Democratic Front (ABSDF), with a 21-person Central Committee, chaired by a veteran student activist from the 1970s, Tun Aung Gyaw, at the KNU base of Kawmoorah on the Thai border.[48]

Initially, other than support for a return to multi-party democracy and a deep distrust of the Saw Maung regime, the ABSDF had no clear ideology. But many students, still deeply shocked by the brutality of the army's behaviour, claimed they had nowhere else to turn. Said 17 year old Ma Sein, a female high school student from Rangoon:

> Any elections they hold will be a farce. The only reason they haven't arrested U Nu, Aung San Suu Kyi and the other well known leaders is because they still care about international respectability. But they know who the real leaders of the protest movement are. They have photographs and they have names. Many have already been killed or forced to flee. They'll come for the rest of us when they are ready.[49]

Saw Maung's strategy, student leaders claimed, was clear. By depicting Burma's crisis as essentially a question of law and order, the Burmese army or *Tatmadaw* hoped to legitimise their hold on power, drive the opposition underground and marginalise the fledgling democracy movement as a political force. This view was supported by U Nu who refused to disband the new government he had declared and accused the army of carrying out a campaign of 'revenge on the people' in the name of law and order.[50]

Within weeks, however, it was already clear that the new regime was even more calculating than this. Few doubted that behind the scenes the 77 year-old Ne Win was still pulling the strings, but executive power had now been handed over for the first time to a new generation of younger officers, including his daughter, Major Sanda Win, the army Vice Chief-of-Staff, Lt.-Gen. Than Shwe, and MIS chief, Brig.-Gen. Khin Nyunt. For many opposition leaders, this largely faceless generation, the first graduates of the élite Defence Services Military Academy set up in 1954 and the first to study in the West, had represented the hope of their revolution. But now it appeared increasingly unlikely that they would break ranks. Painfully the realisation began to dawn that the Burma army of 1988 was very much the creation of Gen. Ne Win and not its founder, Aung San, as so many opposition leaders had mistakenly assumed.

It was Sanda Win and Khin Nyunt who were widely credited with running a sophisticated, though often wildly inaccurate, propaganda campaign in the national press, which was once again brought back under tight government control. In Ne Win's Burma misinformation had long been the rule of the day, but following Saw Maung's takeover these efforts were redoubled. Previously the BSPP had only rarely responded to criticism in the Western press and given only few and fleeting details of the insurgencies, but now Rangoon Radio and the *Working People's Daily* began working overtime. Frequent denunciations of the *Voice of America* and the BBC, which (largely through telephone interviews) had graphically carried news of the uprising all summer, were backed up by highly coloured accounts of the students' travels and their meetings with NDF leaders. The students, it was claimed, listened only to the BBC which, in turn, was loudly accused of supporting the ethnic insurgents. Brig.-Gen. Kyaw Ba, chief of the Northern Command, even went so far as to say that news reports by the BBC had made the situation so unstable that the army had no choice but to seize power.[51]

The culmination of this fevered and paranoid campaign came with the hurried publication of a series of highly contradictory books which alternately blamed the democracy uprising on the 'conspiracies' of the CPB, the 'sky full of lies' (i.e. the foreign media) and 'traitorous cohorts abroad' (i.e. rightists).[52] At no point were the political grievances of the opposition or the widespread hatred of the BSPP admitted, and individuals such as Nay Min, a lawyer gaoled for 14 years for the 'crime' of reporting to the BBC, were variously described as both 'leftists' and 'rightists' without apparent embarrassment. With the promise of new studies to reveal the true role of the army in saving Burma, it was clearly an attempt to rewrite history. 'A Fascist Disneyland', was the considered response of one foreign diplomat.

But perhaps the most striking departure in these new explanations in the state media, which until then had undoubtedly been one of the world's most turgid and dull, was the attention paid to the country's insurgencies. Indeed, the very day after Saw Maung seized power, Rangoon Radio accused the CPB of exploiting the situation and ran reports of the seizure of CPB materials in both Rangoon and Loikaw. Suddenly, after years of playing down the insurrections, it was as if Burma were a land in flames. This picture was reinforced by near daily accounts of battles with different insurgent armies across the country.

The new priority the military gave these little known wars was revealed by Lt.-Gen. Than Shwe as early as 30 September in an address to graduates of an army cadet training course, where he described the insurgencies as 'the biggest obstacle to the country's development.'[53] The students in the mountains, too, were now described as part of the insurgent underworld. Officially they would be welcomed back and widespread publicity was given to a steady stream who did return (an initial deadline of 18 November for amnesty was extended to the end of the year and then forgotten); but there were also reports of the deaths of a number of students in rebel action.[54] On 21 October, for example, battles were reported in six of Burma's seven ethnic minority states as well as fighting or arms seizures in three of the country's seven divisions (Tenasserim, Sagaing and Pegu).[55] The three largest battles were with the CPB in the eastern Shan State where on 25 September a 1,500-strong CPB assault force briefly captured Mong Yang town; with the Kachin Independence Organisation along the main Myitkyina-Bhamo road; and with the Karen National Union around the strategic outpost of Mae Tah Waw on the Thai border, which the KNU captured at the end of October after a month long battle. Here some 50 students joined KNU units in the final stages of the attack. Both the NDF and the CPB confirmed several hundred casualties (killed or wounded) on both sides but denied there was anything particularly exceptional about the scale of the year's battles. As they pointed out, such jockeying for position at the end of the rainy season had long been a near annual, though largely unreported, event.[56] But the army's message this year could not have been clearer. As the arrests and fighting continued, slogans in the *Working People's Daily* continued to warn: 'It should not be forgotten that the *Tatmadaw* is the life of the nation.'

Whether the army had really crushed the opposition movement was, of course, as yet unclear. But with many of the leaders of the democracy uprising forced underground, certainly the first stage of the army's plan to restore its authority had been completed. The next problem was to get the people back to work. For weeks, across the country reports of soldiers shooting 'looters and destructive elements' on sight were to continue, but a deadline of 3 October for government personnel to return to their offices was, after a slow start, generally adhered to.[57] None the less, after the upheavals of the previous months, the economy remained in a parlous state and still on the brink of collapse, a prospect heightened by the cut-off in aid from all Western countries, including Burma's largest creditors, West Germany and Japan.

It was at this point that SLORC's new Minister for Trade, Col. Abel, in what was at first widely perceived as a cynical bid to restore international confidence, announced a complete about turn in economic strategy and a new 'open door' policy to open up the country to foreign investment and trade. SLORC officials later claimed, probably correctly, that this was a continuation of the reforms intended by Ne Win at his resignation in July. But given the continued volatility in the country and doubts over the military administration (the leaders of SLORC were all members of the last BSPP government) there were few immediate takers.[58] Instead the regime, breaking years of isolation, embarked on a crash programme of selling abroad precious natural resources, including fishery rights, gemstones, timber and oil concessions, for desperately needed revenue and foreign exchange. This search for cash had been given a new urgency since the salaries of soldiers and many civil servants had been doubled in the immediate aftermath of the coup as a precaution to ensure their continued loyalty.

At this desperate moment the regime was to be helped by a number of highly opportunist timber deals struck with businessmen in neighbouring Thailand, where years of uncontrolled tree felling led in January 1989 to a total logging ban to prevent further soil erosion and flooding. Their go-between with Gen. Saw Maung was no less a personage than the Thai army commander-in-chief, Gen.

Chaovalit, the first foreign leader to recognise the new regime, despite widespread criticism in his own country. Indeed many of the forests under negotiation were still in rebel held areas.

Undeterred, Saw Maung now pushed ahead with preparing for the promised elections. Despite a nighttime curfew and a ban on meetings of more than five people, new political parties were invited to come forward to register with the Election Commission. At first there was a trickle. Within days it became a flood. If the opposition had appeared divided in August, the situation quickly reached farcical proportions. Eventually 234 parties, replete with patrons, party officers and executive committees, had registered, and all with virtually identical aims and objectives. The Burma Democratic Party, the National Peace and Democracy Party, the United Peace Democracy Party, and the Real Democracy System Party are just four names picked at random. The list appeared endless. Again there was a surprising paucity of new faces and a strong whiff of political opportunism, though many parties privately admitted they had been formed simply for extra petrol and telephone allowances and to get around the strict ban on public meetings. But to decipher just who was who, once more journalists and diplomats found themselves leafing through their history books and fading press clippings. Two versions of the Anti-Fascist People's Freedom League (the main political coalition from the 1940s and 1950s) were formed, but without the AFPFL's long-time leader, U Nu, who remained patron of the League For Democracy and Peace (LDP) he had set up in August. (Somewhat ambiguously, however, several leading members of the LDP, including Bo Khin Maung, disappeared underground to turn up with U Nu's son, U Aung, on the Thai border where they set up their own insurgent front, the Alliance For Democratic Solidarity Union of Burma.)

Other famous names from the 1950s now began to emerge including Aung San's older brother, U Aung Than, who set up his own party, the People's Democratic Party, along with Thakin Lwin and other former supporters of the pro-communist Burma Workers and Peasants Party. Some of the other parties were even more extraordinary. Perhaps the most remarkable was the Unity and Development Party set up by 83 year-old Thakin Soe, once one of the country's most feared revolutionaries, who after leading the insurgent Red Flag communist movement for over two decades had been captured in 1970 and sentenced to death. But now even the People's Volunteer Organisation (PVO), initially set up after the Second World War as an association for wartime veterans before itself going into rebellion, was reformed. Forty years later, just what the PVO's role would be in the Burma of 1988 was very unclear. But certainly Saw Maung was quick to use the apparent confusion to justify his own hold on power: 'With such a proliferation of political parties, no caretaker or interim government can be formed. Such a demand for interim government is a step backward. It amounts to destabilising the situation which has just become stable and to recreate disturbances.'[59]

Elections, Saw Maung continued to assert, would still go ahead, but it was soon obvious that only a few parties would have any real credibility. Of these the most obvious contender was the National Unity Party (NUP), formed on 24 September, which was, in fact, the former BSPP disguised in new clothes without any serving military members. Allied to the NUP were a number of smaller satellite parties made up of former BSPP supporters, such as the Kachin State National Democratic Party, which it was presumed had been formed to ward off ethnic nationalist aspirations.

However, of the opposition movement from August only a few real contenders were left, including the LDP of U Nu and Bo Hmu Aung, which was still popular with an older generation who remembered the 1950s, and the National League for Democracy led by Aung San Suu Kyi, Tin Oo and Aung Gyi. Critically, the NLD managed to win the support of the ex-army Patriotic Old Comrades League, chaired by Aung Shwe, which had criticised U Nu's declaration of a provisional government and, from the beginning, most observers were convinced that the NLD would win any freely held election handsomely. The NLD survived one damaging split in December when Aung Gyi, making vague accusations (frequently repeated by SLORC) of the NLD being infiltrated by CPB supporters, left to form his own Union Nationals Democracy Party and, in early 1989, Suu Kyi and Tin Oo began attracting vast crowds in defiance of martial law restrictions as they began to tour the country. But perhaps the most poignant new party was the Democratic Party For New Society (DPNS) formed by Moe Thee Zun and a number of ABFSU leaders who decided to stay behind to test the political waters. (By agreement, while other student leaders regrouped in rebel held areas, the ABFSU chairman, Min Ko Naing, remained in hiding with supporters in Rangoon and Mandalay and tried to keep the ABFSU alive until his capture the following year.) Allied with the NLD, the DPNS rapidly built up a mass youth following in Rangoon and, according to Moe Thee Zun, was intended as a pressure group to make sure the democracy ideals and sacrifices of 1988 were not forgotten by compromise with SLORC.[60]

How any of these groups could hope to compete with the vast machinery of the NUP, which inherited the buildings, property and registration lists of the BSPP, was by no means clear and most party leaders continued to assert that their registration with the Election Commission did not imply any trust in SLORC. Few observers doubted that the army's aim was gradually to force through a coalition of all these different political forces and identities into one or two manageable blocs in apparent opposition to the NUP as the time of the elections approached. Privately army leaders asserted elections would only go ahead when the NUP could be assured of at least 75 per cent of the vote. Indeed at no time was it made exactly clear what the election was for, a Constituent Assembly, it appeared, rather than government, meaning the army would still remain in power.

Nothing was more suggestive of the cosmetic reforms the army leaders were keen to force through in advance of any 'democratic' election than the sudden, international renaming of the country as *Myanmar Naing Ngan* (Union of Burma) in June 1989 and the Burmanisation of most public names and titles. Far from being a move to show that Burma was a multi-racial country, as was claimed, ethnic minority leaders angrily pointed out *Myanmar* was simply the historic ethnic Burman name for Burma. Just as the streets of Rangoon had been spotlessly cleaned and the buildings whitewashed in the aftermath of the coup, SLORC appeared to believe it could wipe the slate clean by a few ornamental adjustments to names and places.

An even more sinister development was the forcible relocation during 1989/90 of thousands of working class city dwellers from towns across the country, including Rangoon, Mandalay and Taunggyi, into the malaria infested countryside. Here they were resettled in isolated and ill prepared new towns. Ostensibly, they were squatters being rehoused under well-organised slum clearance schemes, but in reality many were well-established communities in the strategic heart of the country that had played a leading role in supporting the democracy uprising. They were to pay a heavy price for their support. Diplomats, who were initially kept well away from the new towns, estimated as many as 500,000 civilians were moved under armed guard and dozens of elderly people and children died. Even the tourist town of Pagan was cleared in April/May 1990 and the 5,200 inhabitants abruptly moved, in what they believed was a bid to cut all contacts between locals and foreigners to a minimum.

But amidst all these changes, perhaps the most astonishing was the way Ne Win's military creation, the BSPP, which had dominated Burmese national life for a quarter of a century, was so casually dropped, and without any explanation. Indeed all military or security personnel (and many other employees of state organisations) were now banned from belonging to any political party at all. Yet, most ambiguously, the army leaders who had brutally crushed the democracy movement but now promised elections and open trade, were all Ne Win loyalists to a man.

It did not take long for the regime's logic to be revealed. With the charade of BSPP rule having come to a disastrous and embarrassingly inept end, it soon became clear that Ne Win's supporters, who undoubtedly would have faced purges (or worse) had the uprising succeeded, were now trying to reserve for themselves the neutral, arbiter role in Burma's uncertain future. For most this hardly implied any great change of political course. One only has to look at some of Burma's neighbours (Bangladesh, Thailand, Pakistan and Indonesia) to find countries which are democracies in name, but in which the military, in different guises, continues to have the dominant and usually final say.

Eventually the date of May 1990 was set for the proposed elections, but notably in this new arrangement there was no place either for the country's diverse insurgent fronts (an offer of peace talks by the NDF was publicly rejected) or for the students now underground who had led the democracy movement from the beginning. All were forbidden by law from registering with the Election Commission, so the real political picture in Burma was hardly complete. One immediate result was a steady escalation in army operations against the KNU, where most ABSDF students were training. Several of the opposition leaders still at liberty in Rangoon, including U Nu and Aung San Suu Kyi, continued to assert that a peaceful solution could still be found through the creation of a new interim coalition government to supervise the elections. But already in November 1988 the deteriorating political scene had been polarised further by the declaration of a provisional, parallel government, the Democratic Alliance of Burma (DAB), in KNU territory, including leaders of the NDF, the ABSDF, the General Strike Committee, the All Burma Young Monks Union and political exiles from abroad.[61] The elections would go ahead with, in effect, two declared governments in the country, each committed to the annihilation of the other; and bomb blasts at the Syriam oil refinery and Rangoon City Hall in mid-1989, which resulted in five deaths, were a reminder of the insurgents' ability to carry the war well away from the jungle war zones.

Complicating matters even more at this precarious moment and conjuring up the image of a country that was finally falling apart was the sudden collapse during early 1989 of the armed forces of the insurgent CPB on which the army was still trying to blame the democracy uprising. Between March and May an estimated 15,000 troops from the CPB's People's Army, who controlled vast areas of the mountainous north-east, mutinied to form several new ethnic Wa, Shan and Kokang ethnic rebel armies. Some of these forged immediate ceasefires with the

Burmese army while others held talks with the DAB, leaving the immediate future even more politically uncertain.

Few observers, then, were surprised when, as the anniversaries of the democracy uprising and Martyr's Day (the commemoration of Aung San's death) approached, the military began its second political clampdown. With the country under martial law and foreign journalists and tourists still largely excluded, over 7,000 common criminals were unexpectedly released from gaol during July and, according to diplomats, an estimated 6,000 political activists across the country rounded up in their place. To deal with these cases new military tribunals were set up with only three possible penalties: death, life imprisonment and three years hard labour. At least 2,000 of those arrested were from the main opposition party, the NLD, whose leaders Aung San Suu Kyi and Tin Oo were both put under house arrest, Tin Oo later receiving three years in gaol with hard labour.[62] The NLD was not at this time proscribed, though a number of other parties (mostly accused of pro-CPB sympathies) were, including (temporarily) the DPNS, whose leader, Moe Thee Zun, had already escaped to KNU territory where, a few months later, he was elected the ABSDF's new chairman. 'Yes, there will be elections,' predicted one ambassador in Rangoon, 'but only when all the opposition leaders are in gaol.' A few weeks later his prophecy looked to have come true when U Nu and several leaders of the LDP, who refused to dissolve their own 'provisional government', were placed under house arrest.

Amidst this second wave of arrests SLORC felt confident enough to reopen the schools, albeit with troops in attendance and after parents had signed forms guaranteeing their children's good behaviour. But the decade still ended with the gates around all universities and colleges of higher education (where the democracy movement had started) still firmly shut.

In just one year, therefore, the stage had come full cycle and Burma had returned to virtually the same divisions that had existed at the beginning of the uprising. Of course nobody seriously expected things ever to be quite the same again and if Ne Win's *Burmese Way to Socialism* was not exactly buried, it was most certainly dead. And yet on the surface little had changed. The army remained in power, insurgents were active in the jungles and Burma's fledgling political parties were still struggling to come to terms with the aspirations of the people. It is the kind of statement that could have been written in 1968 or 1958, or even 1948, the year of Burma's independence, for that matter.

Then dramatically, in a surprise twist when it was least expected, in an address on 9 January 1990 to what he said would be the last meeting of senior army commanders before the promised elections, Saw Maung vowed that the army would stand by the election result and hand over to the elected government. In the future, he pledged, in what appeared to be a veiled warning to the assembled officers, the army would stick to what it was good at, namely fighting insurgents and defending the country's independence.[63] After the events of 1988/9, which he described as 'once a century', political problems would be left to politicians. Tantalisingly, he then left open the prospect that the insurgencies, which he accepted were 'political' questions, could be settled, without army interference, by negotiations by the future civilian government.[64] Given the bizarre circumstances in the country, with hundreds of opposition leaders still in gaol and the countryside ravaged by fighting, it seemed a forlorn prospect and a more ambiguous speech than ever. But it once again signalled, just as a new era appeared to be dawning, that Burma's deep political crisis could still turn in any direction.

Least Developed Country Status: The Background to Collapse
Thus belatedly foreign governments began to ask the kind of questions that had
needed asking all along. What had prompted the crisis of 1988 and the extraordinary violence of that year? How could such a potentially prosperous country have
come to such a state of total collapse? How much control had the Ne Win regime
ever really had over the country and its diverse peoples? Who were these half-
forgotten leaders of these little-known parties that were now once again emerging? Who were all these communist and ethnic insurgents and why had these
conflicts gone on so long? Could they now seriously challenge the power of the
army? And what, if any, were the possible solutions?

Answering the first of these questions at least is not difficult and needs to be
dealt with straight away. Even for the most casual visitor to Burma it should not
have been difficult to detect the warning signs. Clearly underlying the remarkable
bravery of the protest movement was a deep resentment at over two decades of
brutal political suppression by the ruling BSPP and the Military Intelligence
Service (MIS). But undoubtedly the trigger that finally brought Burma's long-
suffering citizens into the streets was the shambolic and fast deteriorating state of
the national economy which, by 1987, had brought the country to the brink of
domestic and international bankruptcy.

Part of the government's chronic economic difficulties could indeed be blamed
on the crippling costs of these long-running wars with various communist and
ethnic insurgents, which had continued virtually uninterrupted since 1948. Too
often regarded as a peripheral problem, these almost forgotten wars had long
legitimised the military's hold on power and contributed to the siege mentality of
successive governments in Rangoon. In 1988, in a country with no external
enemies, defence spending was generally estimated to be sapping up some 40 per
cent of the national budget and, equally importantly, these widespread insurgencies continued to deny the government access to many of the areas richest in
timber and mineral resources in the entire country.

But most economic analysts were already long agreed that the major share of
the blame had to be lain on a quarter century of gross economic mismanagement
by the ruling BSPP and Ne Win's whimsical *Burmese Way to Socialism*. An
idiosyncratic blend of Marxist, Buddhist and nationalist ideology, it had seen
Burma decline from a country once regarded as amongst the most fertile and
mineral rich in Asia to one of the world's ten poorest nations. This had starkly
been brought into perspective by Burma's admittance to Least Developed Country
status at the United Nations in December 1987. Indeed, so humiliating was this
news that it took the government four months to announce the decision to its own
people. But with an average per capita income of just $200 per annum, an exter-
nal debt in excess of $4,000 million and foreign exchange holdings of less than
$20 million, Burma was now officially categorised alongside such other major
recipients of international charity as Chad, Ethiopia and Nepal. A further warning
came in March as the first student protests started, when Burma's largest aid
donor, Japan, threatened to cut off all financial assistance unless the BSPP
quickly introduced substantive economic reforms.

If any doubts still remained, the threadbare nature of the BSPP's record had
been painfully exposed shortly afterwards in Aung Gyi's series of carefully
worded letters to his former mentor, Gen. Ne Win. Whilst not disavowing his
socialist beliefs, Aung Gyi characterised Burma's position in the international
community as 'almost a joke' and called for immediate change.[65] The impact of

these letters, which were copied and widely circulated around the country, was electric and such criticism, coming from within the army's own ranks and from one of Ne Win's former supporters, was the more devastating. Aung Gyi was quickly arrested. But the evidence is still damning. At the time of Ne Win's coup in 1962, official rice exports were up to some two million tons per annum. In 1988, despite a doubling in production, they were virtually nil.[66]

This still leaves the question of how this breakdown had been allowed to happen in a country of such abundant potential. Again, despite the paucity of reliable information, it was not difficult to pinpoint reasons for this dramatic collapse. Though a civilian government in name, the BSPP administration radiating out from Rangoon down to the township and district levels remained dominated by serving or retired army officers. Most had built their careers in fighting Burma's diverse insurgencies and this, in part, explains the apparent callousness with which the *Tatmadaw*'s tactics of the insurgent battlefields were brought back to the streets of Rangoon in suppressing the students' protests. Indeed, widely accused of some of the worst excesses were the 22nd and 33rd LIDs, hurriedly redeployed to Rangoon from the Karen front for the capital's defence.

Few administrators had the experience, let alone the training, to deal with the complexities of running the highly centralised system of economic planning and production demanded by Ne Win's one-party rule. Worse still, insulated by a cosy system of perks, which included extra rations and privileged access to imported goods sold at subsidised prices, senior army officers were always protected from the worst exigencies of Burma's precipitate decline.

The reality for the majority of Burma's 40 million population, however, had long been quite different. In fact there were drastic shortages of essential everyday goods, such as medicine, petrol, textiles and even bicycles. The shortfall could only be smuggled in from abroad. This in turn spawned a thriving black market trade in raw products, such as rice, teak, cattle, opium and jade, spirited out of the country to pay for these expensive imports. Ironically, the major beneficiaries from this illicit trade were the very insurgent movements the BSPP government was fighting. Taxes on this constant flow of goods, much of which passed through rebel held territory, provided the bulk of funds with which they financed their struggles. The scale of the trade is today vast and impossible to calculate, but an unofficial World Bank estimate in early 1988 put the annual value of this two-way traffic at a remarkable $3 billion, or some 40 per cent of Burma's total Gross National Product, leading one bank consultant to comment on the eve of the uprising that 'economic statistics in Burma are a modern day fairytale.'[67]

However, if the government had for many years been able to rely on the underlying fertility of the country and the ingenuity of its people, by the mid-1980s all the indications were that this had changed. In August 1987, amidst growing shortages of rice and essential spare parts for industry, Ne Win was forced to make his first public admission of mistakes, and the first tentative steps to relax restrictions on the production and sale of several goods, including rice, were announced.[68]

This, however, was followed in September by the 'demonetisation' of the Burmese currency, the second time in three years the government had resorted to this drastic measure which, in effect, made immediately worthless all the larger currency bills in circulation. For many observers there was even a slightly comical aspect to this bizarre move as the demonetised bills were each time replaced with newer and ever more awkward denominations, of 15, 35 and 75 kyat, then 45 and 90 kyat. Many believed that Ne Win, whose temper was notorious, was going senile or following wild astrological predictions. (The 75 kyat note was introduced in Ne Win's 75th year; the number 9 (4+5) is Ne Win's lucky number and frequently recurs in government announcements. The 1990 elections, for example, were scheduled for the 27th (2+7) May, on the 4th Sunday in the 5th month, 1990.) Indeed this was confirmed by one of Ne Win's few foreign friends, who broke off all contact with him after a bitter argument over the second demonetisation (Ne Win claimed it was meant to bankrupt black marketeers): 'He is the last great Asian despot and really believes he has saved Burma from corruption by the outside world. The trouble is he is no longer capable of rational thought. He only believes in omens and there are only two kinds, good ones and bad ones.'[69]

But in a country living so close to the subsistence level the result of these demonetisations could not have been more serious. Thousands of ordinary citizens lost their savings overnight, precipitating the first serious outbreak of anti-government demonstrations in over a decade and this, in turn, led to the eventual explosion of anger in March 1988. A common sentiment expressed by so many supporters of the democracy movement that year, whether students, workers, farmers or teachers and other government employees, was that now they had nothing else to lose.

This brief synopsis, however, does scant justice to the scale of the social and political problems now facing Burma as, at the end of the 20th century, it embarks on a new chapter in its history. Rather it provides the necessary but alarming springboard to take a step back in time and begin a re-examination of the many complex causes which, four decades after independence, have brought the country to the edge of such bloodshed, despair and disaster.

2

The Peoples of Burma: A Historic and Ethnic Background

As has often been remarked, the first thing colonial rule denies a people is their history. The full British occupation of the land which has become modern Burma lasted just 62 years, but the new Republic of the Union of Burma which came into being on 4 January 1948 bore little resemblance to any nation or state from the historic past. The power and authority of the Burman kings and the central courts at Ava and Mandalay had been destroyed. The economic hub and the political centre had been moved to Rangoon and the Delta region of Lower Burma. And the institutions of political power bequeathed to the new nation were an ill-fitting suit of clothes modelled on the loose pattern of British parliamentary democracy. Simply establishing a new central political authority was the first priority.

Moreover, now to be incorporated into the new Union were the Frontier (or Excluded) Areas, thousands of square miles of rugged hill tracts and loosely independent mini-states, covering over 40 per cent of the total land area. These were also home to diverse ethnic minority peoples, largely as wary and ignorant of the new government in Rangoon and historically as little affected by any government on the central plains as they had been by the remote era of British rule. British rule had done little to reduce historic tensions between the peoples of hills and plains and much of this territory lay uncharted and little known. Several hundred miles of border remained entirely undemarcated. It is largely in these remote ethnic minority areas that insurgent movements have remained most firmly entrenched since independence, as attempts by successive governments to extend authority into the hills have met with resistance. One Wa nationalist leader from the remote Shan substate of Ving Ngun today claims (and with some justification) that it was neither their Shan neighbours, nor the British colonial rulers, nor even governments in Rangoon since independence, that finally brought to an end the traditional independence of the Wa chiefs, but the insurgent Communist Party of Burma (CPB), which first 'invaded' the state in the late 1960s.[1]

The tasks of political integration facing the government of Burma's first premier, U Nu, were formidable. From the beginning the central government was under armed challenge. Independence came with the smaller break-away Red Flag faction of the CPB of Thakin Soe already underground. Three months later the mainstream White Flag faction of the CPB and, next to the Socialist Party, the best organised political party in Burma at the time, followed the Red Flags underground and launched an all-out offensive to seize power. The start of the CPB insurrection was then the fuse for mass mutinies from the police and armed forces.

From this disastrous beginning the situation continued to deteriorate rapidly. At the beginning of 1949 the rebellion of the Karens broke out in south-east Burma and, buoyed by the wholesale defection of Karen units in the fledgling Burma Army, the Karen National Union (KNU) began its long bid for an independent Karen State. As fighting raged across the Delta and into Upper Burma, rebellion swiftly spread to other restive minorities, the Mon, the Karenni, the Pao and the Kachin, while in Arakan in the north-west, where the level of insurgency had never really subsided since the end of the Second World War, not only Red and White Flag communists but ethnic Rakhine and *Mujahid* separatists, as well as various militia and dacoit gangs, all contributed to a complete breakdown in law and order.

Faced with insurgency on such a bewildering scale, the embattled Union government in Rangoon was to struggle on for 14 years from one political and constitutional crisis to another, interrupted briefly, in 1958-60, by the 'military caretaker' government of Gen. Ne Win. This, however, very much proved to be a trial run. In March 1962, as determined Shan and Kachin separatist movements gained momentum across the north-east, Ne Win seized power in a military coup and finally brought to an end the brief era of parliamentary democracy.

Full attention was now turned to the military defeat of the rebels and, following the breakdown of peace talks with many of the insurgent leaders in Rangoon in 1963, this took on an added impetus. It was not, however, until 1974 that a new constitution was introduced and the one-party rule of the Burma Socialist Programme Party (BSPP) and Ne Win's unique *Burmese Way to Socialism* were ratified by a national referendum. But by the time of the CPB mutinies in 1989, 27 years after the coup and 41 years after Burma's independence, the scale of insurgency, if largely pushed back into remoter border regions, had scarcely declined. Both the CPB and the KNU remained underground and in control of extensive 'liberated' zones, while no less than 25 other armed groups, ranging in size from the 8,000-strong Kachin Independence Army to the 30 guerrillas of the Arakan Independence Army, continued to offer armed opposition to the central government (see Chart 1). Dissidents from virtually every ethnic and political group have taken up arms against the central government at some stage since independence. Even U Nu and several of his colleagues from the first independence government took to the jungles for a brief period in the late 1960s and early 1970s and, allied with the KNU and its former ethnic insurgent opponents, launched their own short-lived rebellion. In short, insurgency has remained endemic and, in many areas of Burma, the armed struggle virtually a way of life.

To explain such a diverse and often changing kaleidoscope of insurgencies presents many difficulties. Most commentators have tried to make a basic distinction between political insurgents, largely the CPB, and the various ethnic nationalists. However, in practice such distinctions are ambiguous. In over 40 years of armed conflict, the ethnic and political insurgencies have crossed at so many points that it has become impossible to deal with any of the insurgent movements in complete isolation.

On the one hand, broadly separatist aims have been held by many of the ethnic fronts, but the struggles of the ethnic minorities, too, have been characterised by deep political divisions and debate, and many fronts have continually split into pro- and anti-communist factions. When not fighting with the CPB, ethnic fronts have usually been allied with it. Linking many of the ethnic fronts with the CPB in the rebel underground has been the Maoist strategy of a united front (see Chart

2), which today remains a key element in the struggles of most revolutionary groups. Its comparative failure is undoubtedly a major reason behind the insurgents' perennial inability, despite often considerable military strength, to topple the central government.

Seen from another viewpoint, ethnic minority leaders often contend that the CPB merely represents an alternative face of Burman nationalism.* It has long been accepted that the overthrow of any government in Rangoon might well mean the replacing of one Burman-dominated government with another. But while it would obviously be wrong to try and explain the long struggle of the CPB in simply ethnic terms, there are important areas in which the CPB, too, can be seen as representing a nationalist viewpoint. Not only is the CPB the oldest active political party in Burma, but it is the only party that can profess to surpass the revolutionary legitimacy and tradition of anti-colonial/anti-fascist struggle claimed by the two other important post-war national parties, Aung San's Anti-Fascist People's Freedom League and Ne Win's BSPP. The CPB's role in Burma's own national liberation struggle is thus indelible.

In recent years even this basic ethnic distinction between the CPB and the minority rebel fronts has, however, become confused. The contradictory situation had been reached by the time of the 1989 mutinies where, while the leadership of the CPB remained predominantly ethnic Burman, most of the recruits to the CPB's 15,000 strong People's Army were ethnic minority, largely hill tribe Wa and Akha. Indeed, ever since the fall of the CPB's last strongholds in the Pegu Yomas of central Burma in the mid-1970s, the CPB's remaining 'liberated zones' had largely been located in the ethnic minority areas of north-east Burma, i.e. in the Kachin State and, more importantly, in the Shan State. Today the very outcome of the CPB's long, but failing, insurrection is inextricably wound up in the continuing struggles of the minority peoples. Several thousand Burman democracy activists, who fled the cities to take up arms in the aftermath of the 1988 coup, have joined the ethnic forces of the National Democratic Front (NDF) in the eastern mountains. In a further dramatic development in December 1990, their numbers were augmented by newly elected members of Parliament from the National League for Democracy (NLD). Burma's cycle of insurgency was once again complete.

The starting point, then, for any study of Burma's diverse insurgencies must be a brief look at Burma's complex ethnic background, followed by an examination of the era of British rule. It was from the convulsive events of the British era that most modern political movements were to emerge and ultimately to result in conditions of such chaos at independence in 1948.

An Ethnic Overview
The population of Burma today stands at some 42 million, double the estimated figure at independence. Under the 1974 constitutional reforms the map of modern Burma shows seven divisions, largely populated by the Burman majority, and

---

* The terms 'Burman' and 'Burmese' are confusing and are often used interchangeably. But generally 'Burman' is used to refer specifically to ethnicity and 'Burmese' to nationality, i.e. someone could be ethnic 'Shan' but a 'Burmese' citizen. The introduction by SLORC of the Burman term 'Myanmar' for 'Burma'/'Burmese' in 1989 has yet to become widely accepted colloquial usage and is not used here.

seven ethnic minority states, the Chin, Kachin, Karen, Kayah, Mon, Rakhine (Arakan) and Shan. This, however, gives the deceptive appearance of an easy symmetry to what is undoubtedly one of the most complex ethnic mixes in the world. Over 100 languages have been identified in Burma. The 1931 census, the last available to attempt to give any kind of detailed ethnic breakdown, distinguished 44 ethnic sub-groups amongst the Chin alone.[2] In a population of 14,647,497 the census, in a set of figures many minorities believe are deeply flawed, put the major ethnic families such as the 'Burman', including Rakhine, at approximately 65 per cent; the Karen at just over 9 per cent; the Shan at 7 per cent; the Chin and Mon some 2 per cent plus each; the Kachin, Palaung-Wa and Chinese at just over 1 per cent each; and the 'Indian', many of whom have since left Burma, at around 7 per cent.[3]

Present-day statistics are even more contentious. No reliable figures have been collected or released since independence and those that are published appear deliberately to play down ethnic minority numbers. This is particularly true of the Karens, probably Burma's second largest ethnic group, though when real peace returns a careful survey would be needed to distinguish the exact Karen, Shan and Burman populations. The 1931 census, for example, calculated the total Karen population of Burma, including the various related sub-groups such as Pao and Kayah, at 1,367,673, but when during the Second World War the Japanese conducted their own survey, they came up with a figure of 4.5 million.[4] The difference, in part, can be attributed to British survey methods, which would have recorded many Buddhist Karens as Burmans, but it is also due to the sheer inaccessibility of many Karen-inhabited areas in the eastern mountains and the number of Burmese-speaking Karens in the Delta. Today most neutral estimates calculate the Karen population at some three to four million with another 200,000 living across the border in Thailand. By contrast, at the time of the 1988 democracy uprising the BSPP government did not put the Karen population at even two million, while leaders of the KNU today estimate the true number of Karens, in line with the growth in Burma's population, at some seven million, including Paos (Taungthus), Kayans (Padaungs) and Karennis.[5]

By the same token, leaders of the other main ethnic minority communities estimate the Shan and Mon populations at approximately four million each, the Buddhist Arakanese (Rakhine) at 2.5 million, the Muslim Arakanese (sometimes known as Rohingyas) at one to two million (many of whom are now living in exile), the Zo or Chin at two to three million, Kachin at 1.5 million and Palaung-Wa at one to two million.[6] All figures, particularly the Mon, need treating with great circumspection, being projections based largely on ancestral records or regions of habitation, rather than on an accurate count of present-day communities. It is impossible, therefore, to compare one set of figures for accuracy against another. Intermingled in different communities across the country there are also an estimated one million Chinese, Tamils and other minorities of Indian origin.

A more accurate enumeration of racial statistics, however, would in itself do little to illuminate the complexity of ethnic politics in modern-day Burma. Few regional divisions are racially exclusive. Indeed, of the ethnic minority states, the Chin, Kachin and Karen are, strictly speaking, just collective names for the various ethnic sub-groups within each state, which have only become widely accepted terms of political identity within living memory, while the Kayah, Mon, Rakhine and Shan are the names of only the majority ethnic groups in each territory. Certainly in the diverse ethnic insurgencies which have plagued Burma since independence, traditions of cultural and political independence have continued to be claimed by minorities not identified in even the present political structure. Ethnic Naga and various Muslim fronts, for example, remain active in the north of Burma, while in the strife-torn Shan State various Pao, Kayan, Palaung, Wa, Kokang and Lahu armed forces all continue to pose as serious a challenge to the Shan rebel fronts as to the central government. In fact, even the 20 or so ethnic sub-groups of the Karens are represented by four different armed nationalist movements today, the mainstream Karen of the KNU (predominantly Sgaw and Pwo), the Karenni of the Kayah State, and the Pao and Kayan of the Shan State, and these, too, have been beset by ideological and factional differences.[7]

With the rapid spread of Burmese over the last century, language is another confusing denominator for ethnic identity. Certainly in Great Britain, where Gaelic and Welsh are little spoken today, the widespread use of English has done little to dampen nationalist enthusiasms amongst the Scots, Irish and Welsh. Nor do the majority Burmans, who are still generally agreed to make up an estimated two-thirds of the population, necessarily form one distinct or homogeneous political bloc. Much of the Burman population in Lower Burma consists of assimilated Mons and Karens. Moreover, elsewhere in Burma there exist several distinctive dialects and local sub-groups, such as the Intha and Danu and, in many areas, regional loyalties still run very deep. It is certainly no coincidence that since the fall of the CPB's Pegu Yoma base areas, the CPB's only remaining footholds in predominantly Burmese-speaking areas have been in the Rakhine State (where determined separatist movements remain active) and in the Tavoy-Mergui districts of the old Tenasserim Division of Lower Burma. Here traditions of Tavoyan independence and the short-lived Tavoyan rebellion of the 18th century are still remembered. Indeed villagers in the CPB's small southernmost liberated zone still refer to their Burman cousins as the Pagans (i.e. people from Pagan), with the distant echo of the ancient capital and an age long gone by. And it is not only the CPB that has sought to work on such feelings of estrangement. When in the late 1960s U Nu's Parliamentary Democracy Party turned to the jungles to launch its own armed rebellion, the chosen starting point was the same disaffected south-east where, amongst the uneasy mix of Tavoyan, Karen, and Mon inhabitants, little sense of loyalty to the central government had been established.

That such remarkable ethnic diversity should exist in Burma is perhaps not so surprising. The deep mountain ranges and north-south running valleys of Burma's several great rivers, the Irrawaddy-Chindwin, the Salween, and the Mekong, have since time immemorial proven the natural routes of migration to a constant flow of peoples from the high plateaux of Central Asia. But though geographically squeezed between the two great neighbouring powers of India and China, the rugged horseshoe of mountains surrounding the central Irrawaddy valley has historically proven a formidable barrier, as much to rulers trying to unify Burma from within as to any invading armies. The result has been a constant meeting and intermingling of peoples across the centuries, which has led to a pattern of cultural exchange and adaptation of almost infinite kind. Before the first British annexation, the Lower Delta, which is now regarded as part of the Burman heartlands, was also a frontier region of malaria-infested mangrove swamps and dense forest inhabited by different ethnic peoples.[8] Burma's comparative seclusion was thus near total.

But if Burma has often been called an anthropologist's paradise, the complete untangling of its complex ethnic past is a task still to be accomplished. Historians are generally agreed that the earliest inhabitants of modern Burma still recognisable today are the Mons of Lower Burma. They are the descendants of Austro-Asiatic (Mon-Khmer) peoples who once occupied much of South-East Asia and from whom today's hill tribe Palaung (Ta-ang) and Wa inhabitants of the Shan State are also distantly descended. The first Karen and Chin settlers were probably the next to move down into central Burma before the main body of ethnic Burman migration occurred into Upper Burma in the 9th and 10th centuries AD. In the wake of these migrations the existing inhabitants were presumably either absorbed or pushed deeper into remote mountains and forests. Others like the Pyu (or P'iao), who left evidence of a highly developed civilisation, simply disappeared. At about the same time, the first Shans began moving through the river valleys of the far north-east as part of a major ethnic Tai migration into South-East Asia. The present ethnic picture was completed by the migration of various tribes, largely Tibeto-Burmese in origin, into the remote mountains of the north-east, the last probably being those of the various Kachin sub-groups. It is a movement that still goes on, for various hill tribes, such as the Lisu and Akha, continue to move down into Thailand.

It was largely amongst the diverse Mon, Burman, Arakanese and Shan valley kingdoms that recorded history began. But it was more on the basis of city-states than of a nation that any political structure was to develop. Power was to oscillate between the various kingdoms with great frequency. Occasionally a powerful monarch, such as Anawrahta, the Burman ruler of Pagan in the 11th century, would achieve ascendency and establish a system of patronage over various satellite kingdoms; at other times power would fragment and influence gravitate in new directions. Thus the 14th and 15th centuries have been called the Shan centuries; in the early 16th century, Mon civilisation in Burma probably reached its peak under the Mon kings of Pegu. There has even been speculation that the 18th century was the Karen century.[9] At the same time there is undoubtedly a strong ethnic Burman imprint on much of Burma's history; the dynastic kingdoms of the three great Burman rulers, Anawrahta in the 11th century, Bayinnaung in the 16th and Alaunghpaya in the 18th, some 700 years apart, greatly shaped the Burmo-centric form of much of the surviving historical record. On the eve of the first British annexation during the Konbaung dynasty founded by Alaunghpaya, the Mon and Arakanese kingdoms were finally overrun and the authority of the court at Ava extended to borders approximating the shape of present-day Burma.

Of the various hill peoples few records remain. Certainly many of the surviving legends suggest a wandering, nomadic past as far removed as possible from the authority of the central valley kingdoms. Powerful monarchs on the plains usually tried to impose taxes or raise levies in the hills and the hill peoples frequently became caught up in the many regional wars. Slave raiding, too, was commonplace. Indeed certain of the distinctive customs of the hill peoples (such as the giraffe necks of the Kayan women on the borders of the Shan/Kayah State, or the distinctive tattoos of the northern Chin) are believed to have developed as much as a way of distinguishing themselves from the valley peoples (in order to prevent such abductions) as any symbol of group identity. But though many of the hill peoples share a similarly wandering past and practise a similar *taungya* (slash and burn) style of agriculture, most generalisations about them are hazardous. They developed an extraordinary variety of distinctive cultures, many of which survived well into the 20th century. These ranged from the complex clan systems of the Kachin hills to the strictly endogamous marriage customs of the Karen, from the head-hunting Animism of the Nagas and Was to the staunch Buddhism of the Pao and Palaung. But, in general, political authority rarely extended beyond the level of the village or village circle and, where it did, as in the Karenni states or ethnic Palaung substate of Tawngpeng, it was usually modelled (largely in name only) on the kingdoms in the valleys below. Administration was essentially self governing (any central control was indirect) and it was a system with which the British rulers were to interfere little. The result has been the survival of strongly independent, or what nationalist leaders describe as anti-central and anti-feudal, traditions amongst many of the hill peoples, which have seen frequent expression in the political turbulence of the last 42 years.

It must be stressed, however, that many important details of Burma's ethnic past are still conjecture. Deep controversies continue over many long-past events. A chance archaeological find could still turn many cherished beliefs on their head. For example, most contemporary histories persist in identifying the modern Shans with the ancient Kingdom of Nanchao in China's modern-day Yunnan Province, whereas more careful studies point to the real rulers as ethnic Lolo, whose modern-day descendants are the hill tribes, Lahu and Akha.[10] Burman writers, too, have come routinely to identify the long-lost Pyu as the first proto-Burmans, whereas Pao nationalist leaders today claim this identity for themselves. Even the mysterious Gwe, who dramatically descended from the eastern hills to play a decisive role in supporting the last great Mon uprising at the southern city of Pegu in 1740 AD, led by the *Minlaung* (Pretender) Smin Dhaw, and then as suddenly disappeared, have been variously identified by puzzled historians as Karen, Shan, Lahu or Wa.[11] The evidence of Mon and Burmese chronicles strongly suggest a Karen identity, most probably Pao or Kayah.[12] But Mon villagers I have interviewed have a far more straightforward explanation. Refuting the suggestion by Western academics that Gwe is a lost word of ethnic identity, they claim it is simply a corruption of the Mon word 'Gweh' or 'Gwere' meaning 'friendly', as in 'Gweh Karen' or 'Gweh Shan'. The 'Gwe' were therefore simply Smin Dhaw's allies.[13]

But in general, in the highly charged atmosphere of ethnic conflict which has divided Burma since independence, all too many interpretations betray singularly contemporary points of view. With much of Burma off limits, simple academic studies have been impossible, but political leaders and modern scholars alike have been keen to establish historic identities commensurate with contemporary political situations. Suffice to say, interpretations of Normans and Saxons in mediaeval Britain on the basis of modern views of French or German ethnicity would prove an equally speculative venture.[14]

The era of British rule has increasingly been blamed for this confusing record of ethnic relations in Burma. It was during this brief period that much of the information was gathered and many of the reports written on which most contemporary accounts and perceptions are largely based. The various colonial administrators and scholar-missionaries, typified by the 'colonial builder cum scholar cum adventurer', Sir James George Scott, would usually try to label peoples on the basis of perceived differences in language and culture, largely with an eye to future annexations.[15] While the basic ethno-linguistic categories still in use today are British in origin, many of the British methods of survey proved unsatisfactory in Burma. In the various government censuses and reports there were constant shifts in criteria for what was deemed an ethnic group. As one frustrated British official noted in an appendix to the 1931 census, 'some of the races or tribes in Burma change their language almost as often as they change their clothes.'[16] Simply asking the question 'mother tongue' as opposed to 'language ordinarily used in the home' produced a dramatic 61 per cent increase in the Mon population of Burma between the censuses of 1921 and 1931.[17]

Not surprisingly, many ethnic minorities still believe that no true census of the real ethnic populations in Burma has ever been taken. In the 1921 census there were only speakers of Burmese recorded in Mergui district, whereas by 1931 over 100,000 speakers of Merguese had suddenly appeared.[18] If such distinctions had remained theoretical it might not have mattered, but British rule, with its built-in distinctions between ethnic races (particularly between the valley and hill peoples), ossified many of these perceived differences and ensured that different races remained on largely different roads to political and economic development.

In recent years, however, and in particular since the pioneering studies of Edmund Leach in the Kachin hills, greater stress is placed on similarities in language and custom and the evidence of inter-cultural borrowing.[19] In general this has produced more understandable results. It has been demonstrated, for example, that the persistently independent political identity of the Karenni, who by any definition are ethnic Karens, came about more by the assimilation of the political system of their Shan neighbours to the north than by any lost historical tradition.[20]

This line of argument has, however, led some scholars into increasingly fanciful expositions on the nature of ethnicity in Burma. At one extreme this is represented by speculations such as 'do the Karen really exist?'[21] While possibly rhetorically stimulating to armchair theoreticians, such accounts, largely written from the highly misleading perspective of neighbouring Thailand, where there is a small Karen population, do little to understand the persistence of the Karen rebellion; nor do they acknowledge the very real grievances of the different ethnic minorities or the attempts by several to secede. It is after all the Karens and Kachins of Burma who, of all the people in South-East Asia once considered tribal (a highly pejorative term in the modern political world, much beloved in the tourist industry) have sustained longest their dream of creating independent nation states. At worst such writers give comfort to governments in Rangoon, which have long since set course on what ethnic leaders allege is a straightforward policy of 'Burmanisation of the minorities'. It is, thus, not only politicians who have long since abandoned the optimistic 'unity in diversity' politics of Aung San at independence. 'Ethnic politics is the obverse of the politics of national unity,' was the very starting point of one study on Burma's complex ethnic problems by the American political scientist, Robert Taylor.[22]

Historians have also followed this trend. Various studies suggest that strictly mono-ethnic societies have probably never existed in Burma's history. Not only did the kingdoms of the Burman, Arakanese, Shan and Mon rulers follow the same principles of kingship and Theravadha Buddhism (introduced originally by the Mon), but the very composition of the central courts, or *Hutladaw*, frequently reflected the precepts of a plural, poly-ethnic society. For example, important commanders in Smin Dhaw's Mon rebellion at Pegu in the 18th century were ethnic Burman, while many of the troops in the Burman armies despatched from Ava to quell the rebellion were ethnic Mon.[23] The very use of politico-ethnic terms (such as Burman, Karen, or Shan) in interpreting Burma's history is called into question. But again care must be taken when placing such evidence in a modern context. This is not so much suggestive of any one unified tradition in Burma's history, but rather that political movements have usually reflected a regional/poly-ethnic character and that this is a pattern that continues to the present. For example, in the fierce, set-piece battles along the Karen front since 1984, Arakanese volunteers have fought on both sides, though interviews with various participants suggest it would be foolish to read any exact principles of ethnicity into what was for most soldiers more simply a matter of political or economic choice.[24]

Again, in the ranks of the KNU are many Burmese-speaking Karens from the Delta who speak little or no Karen, while in the Burmese Army are Karens from the hills, for whom Burmese is very much a second language. And perhaps most confusedly of all, when delegations from the KNU and CPB met in 1985 after a ten-year interval, leaders from both parties (U Soe Aung, central committee member of the KNU, and Kyaw Mya, Politburo member of the CPB) were in fact ethnic Rakhine, with both men taking some pride in this fact. The safest interpretation, then, would be that perceptions of race are just one determinant in political-social behaviour.

Since independence governments in Rangoon have not, however, been concerned with such anthropological niceties. Rather, the priority has been to establish the idea of a common Burmese identity shared by all the inhabitants of modern Burma. 'There is hardly any other nation more homogeneous than the people of Burma,' claimed Thakin Mya in his presidential address to the Constituent Assembly in 1947. 'Economically and geographically our country is an indivisible unity.'[25] In ethnic terms, this has meant a subtle emphasis on the distant Tibeto-Burmese origins of many ethnic groups. It is a policy which, it can be argued, has met with some success with the Chin, 'who are historically, geographically and ethnically Burmese,'[26] but not with the Maru, Azi and Lashi of the Kachin State (identified in the 1931 census as part of the Burma group), many of whom have come to identify with the separatist aims of the Kachin Independence Organisation (KIO). Indeed one of the most notable successes of the KIO, by comparison, has been its ability to forge a united nationalist movement amongst the several ethnic sub-groups of the north-east, despite government attempts to depict it simply as an ethnic Jinghpaw movement.

The sheer scale of the obvious ethnic differences in Burma today then clearly limits the use of this argument. Instead greater stress is usually put on the shared historical experiences of the different ethnic races. It is a theme taken up in the preamble to the 1974 Constitution, 'We the people residing in the Socialist Republic of the Union of Burma, have throughout history lived in harmony and unity sharing joys and sorrows in weal and woe,' and is constantly returned to by politicians and historians alike. President San Yu's speech at the 38th Union Day Rally in February 1985 struck a familiar refrain: 'The Socialist Republic of the Union of Burma is a country where people of different nationalities live together. Throughout the history of Burma, people of all nationalities have joined hands and taken a unified stand in the anti-imperialist struggle, the national liberation movements and in the tasks of building a socialist society.'[27] After seizing power in 1988, the new state Law and Order Restoration Council of Gen. Saw Maung, while dropping all references to socialism, kept the same language and historical aspirations, virtually word for word intact.

History books are increasingly being rewritten. In *Burma's Struggle against British Imperialism* by Daw Ni Ni Myint (the wife of Gen. Ne Win), it is taken as axiomatic that opposition to the British annexation sprang from one source and one Burmese identity. Once the lowlands and the Burmans had fallen, the flag of Burmese nationalism was taken up, in turn, by Shans, Kachins and Chins.[28] While resistance did indeed move into the hills, such a hypothesis underestimates much conflicting evidence, not least the scale of the rebellions which broke out in the Shan and Karenni hills as several ethnic groups took advantage of the weakness of the Avan court (caused by the British invasion) to launch serious uprisings of their own. Since 1988 further books have been planned by SLORC in conjunction with Ni Ni Myint, who has been put in charge of the Historical Research Commission at Rangoon University, and these have continued to paper over racial differences and to whitewash the role of Ne Win and the Burmese Army. Linking the national liberation movement of the 1920s and 1930s, and the anti-Japanese resistance and independence struggle of the 1940s, to the same political time continuum, Ne Win's *Tatmadaw* is projected as simply the modern embodiment of all national aspirations. 'The *Tatmadaw* in all its historical glory shall continue to fight and annihilate all enemies,' boasted the *Working People's Daily* in October 1988, less than three weeks after the Saw Maung coup.[29]

None the less, despite the contentious nature of the evidence, there are other historians, both Burmese and non-Burmese alike, who have apparently accepted this line of argument. Michael Aung Thwin, for example, has even tried to identify Aung San and Ne Win as only fourth and fifth in line respectively of the great unifying Buddhist rulers since Anawrahta with the recognised *kamma* sufficient to 'reunite' the country.[30]

It is a view of history the ethnic nationalists bitterly dispute. 'There is undoubtedly no community of language, culture or interests between the Shans and the Burmese save religion, nor is there any sentiment of unity which is the index of a common national mind,'[31] claimed the Shan State Independence Army in a 1959 publicity statement. The KNU alleges that, 'throughout history the Burmese have been practising annihilation, absorption, and assimilation (3 As) to the Karens.... The Karens are much more than a national minority. We are a nation.'[32] The Arakan Independence Organisation takes a different approach and allies the plight of Burma's forgotten ethnic minorities with other disenfranchised 'nations' in the post-colonial world, such as the Kurds and Eritreans, defining them as 'hidden colonies'; it accuses modern governments of trying to promote 'Official Nationalism, a new method of colonisation'.[33] And though the mainstream White Flag CPB has always argued for the territorial unity of modern Burma, various communist fronts, too, have often shown sympathy for the separatist cause. In the Rakhine State the Communist Party of Arakan, which broke away from the Red Flags in 1962, similarly justifies the need to wage a separatist struggle: 'A nation which has been annexed into an Empire, if it does not get back its sovereignty, is still under the colonial yoke and is still a colonial nation.... The struggle of Arakan is a struggle against the Burmese colonialists.'[34]

And whatever the placatory rhetoric of governments and politicians in Rangoon since independence, perceptions of race have remained an extremely sensitive issue. Burma today has some of the most extreme citizenship laws in the world. Full citizenship is, in theory, confined to those who can prove they had ancestors resident in Burma before the first British annexation in 1824. Non-Buddhists have always been regarded with great suspicion and in 1978 Burma was the scene of one of the largest refugee exoduses of modern times. Over 200,000 Muslims from Arakan fled into neighbouring Bangladesh after the heavy-handed government *Nagamin* (King of Dragons) census operation to check identity cards got badly out of hand amidst widespread reports of army brutality and murder. In 1979 Ne Win, despite his own mixed Burman-Chinese lineage, gave a rare public expression to these views:

> Today you can see that even people of pure blood are being disloyal to the race and country but are being loyal to others. If people of pure blood act this way, we must carefully watch people of mixed blood. Some people are of pure blood, pure Burmese heritage and descendants of genuine citizens. Karen, Kachin and so forth, are of genuine pure blood. But we must consider whether these people are completely for our race, our Burmese people: and our country, our Burma.[35]

It is worth noting then that as successive governments have grappled with the problem of national unity, loyalty to the concept of any 'national' government in Rangoon has hardly prevented thousands of ethnic Burmans taking up arms against the central government since independence. Nor has Buddhism, which over 80 per cent of the population follow and the government has on occasion been able to use to some effect against the 'godless' communists, proven a much greater basis for national unity. Criticism, too, has often been made of the largely Christian leaderships of the KNU and KIO which have both been accused of being, like the CPB, under alien influences. But of the eleven members of the NDF (a loose alliance of ethnic insurgent organisations formed in 1976 which today looks to the West for its federalist model), Buddhism is undoubtedly one of the strongest tenets in the political identity of no less than five member organisations, namely the Shan, Mon, Arakanese, Pao and Palaung (see Chart 2). Indeed Buddhist *pongyis* (monks), such as U Seinda, the first leader of the Arakan rebellion, and Aung Kham Hti, today president of the Pao National Organisation, have played as important a role in the ethnic minority struggles as did the itinerant *pongyis* in the developing national liberation movement of the 1920s and 1930s. Today in many areas the network of monasteries or *pongyikyaung* provide a vital link in the rebel underground and saffron-robed *pongyis* remain familiar figures at many insurgent bases in the 'liberated zones'.

Statistically, nationalist leaders allege, the 43 years since independence have served to disguise the true form and scale of Burma's ethnic problems. Anthropological and scientific field studies have been virtually non-existent. Those that have been allowed, such as F.K. Lehman's study on the Karenni in the 1950s, have been politically motivated, i.e. to justify the ethnic and political separation of the rebellious Karens from their supposedly peaceful cousins, the Karennis. Indeed, in 1951 the dozen or so sub-groups of the Karennis were confusedly renamed in Rangoon as Kayahs to terminate their Karen lineage.[36] In 1989, the Karens were also officially renamed by SLORC as 'Kayins', a name ethnic nationalist leaders reject as strongly as they do the historic Burman term for their country, 'Myanmar'.

Moreover, by the deliberate manipulation of figures, which are only rarely released, the ethnic Burman population has apparently continued to grow rapidly with the departure of the British and Indian communities, while the birth rates of most minority races (and not just the Mons and Karens) have inexplicably slumped. For example, whereas the Burman population in 1973 was estimated by one calculation to have more than doubled, from 9.5 million in 1931 to 20 million, no explanation was given as to why, according to Rangoon, the ethnic Shan population had grown much more slowly, from just over one million to 1.6 million.[37]

The result, intentionally or otherwise, has been the continued marginalisation rather than integration of the minorities; evidence for this can be seen in the continuing political violence and civil war. Today ethnic minority languages are rarely taught or even used beyond fourth grade in schools, while few economic development projects have ever been located in the ethnic minority regions. By any denominator (economic, educational or political) the minorities have been hugely disadvantaged.

Burma's Changing Frontiers
Lastly, it should be noted that, though Burma enjoys a natural geographic isola-tion, emphasised by successive governments since independence, influential ethnic and political relations have historically never been confined simply to the races inhabiting Burma today.[38] Burma's vast borders and boundaries have always been ill defined. It was growing conflict along the northern frontier with India that first brought the British into Burma. Today the area remains one of considerable ethnic confusion as various militant ethnic Naga and Mizo/Chin nationalist movements continue their activities on both sides of the border, often in tandem. In the south, wars with the kings of Siam continued across the centuries with territory and prisoners regularly exchanging hands. The Tavoy-Mergui districts were again in Siamese hands as late as 1792. Today the traveller heading across the Thai/Shan border will still find any immediate ethnic changes largely imper-ceptible; the first predominantly Burmese-speaking towns are over 100 miles away. Indeed, during the Second World War the Shan sub-states of Kengtung and Mong Pan were handed over by the Japanese to the Siam government to little apparent local protest. And, after independence, a general Thai, if not govern-mental, sympathy for the struggle of their Shan ethnic cousins (and to a lesser extent of the Karen and Mon, small numbers of whom also live across the border) has without doubt greatly aided the different insurgent movements based along the border.

But the shadow hanging over all has always been China. Chinese influence over Burma, whilst somewhat overestimated in Chinese records, has always been deeply felt ever since the fall of Pagan to the Mongol armies of Kublai Khan in 1287 AD. Over the centuries Chinese armies were often to invade and, though always pushed back (sometimes by Shan and sometimes by Burman rulers), at the court in Beijing Burma was usually regarded as subject and tribute was some-times paid. And though politically this influence has always been lightly felt (the vast barrier of the mountains proving too great an obstacle) in human terms the border has remained only loosely accepted. Throughout the era of British rule China laid claim to much of the remote border region and Chinese migrants and adventurers, as well as local Kachin, Shan, Wa, Lahu, Akha and other hill peoples, continued to move back and forth across the unmarked frontier.

At the beginning of the Second World War the Japanese War Ministry's initial plan was to transfer large areas of Upper Burma to the nationalist government of Chiang Kai-shek.[39] Then, after independence, the new communist government in Beijing produced considerable alarm in Rangoon by producing maps in which vast amounts of north-east Burma were included in China. Indeed, it was not until 1960 that a border was finally agreed, but this has not marked the end of Chinese influence across the 2,100 km. border. Armed Kuomintang remnants, who first crossed into the Shan State in 1949/50, have continued to play a surprisingly important role in insurgent politics in the state, while the CPB, which in its early years had shown a marked orientation towards India, from the late 1960s took control of much of north-east Burma with both material and ideological support from across the Chinese border. There remains a large ethnic Chinese population in Burma; such prominent figures as Ne Win, San Yu and Aung Gyi are all of mixed Chinese ancestry, and Chinese remains a commonly spoken language, especially in the Shan State. This has often created confusion (and not only among outside observers) about the true ethnic identity of insurgent groups. In 1985 talks between one of the major Shan separatist fronts (the Tailand Revolutionary Council) and the KNU foundered when Karen leaders continued to insist that leaders of one faction, Khun Sa's Shan United Army, many of whom are a distinctive Shan-Chinese admixture from the Loimaw and Kokang areas, were not real Shans at all, but ethnic Chinese.[40]

Thus the picture to emerge from Burma's complex ethnic history is one of a pattern of ethnic relations in a state of constant flux, politically, socially and culturally. Certainly the general ethnographic map can be simplified; the ethnic races in Burma today can be broadly classified into four major groups, the Tibeto-Burmese, the Tai, the Karen, and the Mon, rather than the apparent *reductio ad absurdam* of the British era. At the same time the survival of such a remarkable array of distinctive dialects, languages and cultures into the late 20th century has served to strengthen the belief of many minorities in their historic independence. According to the veteran Naga leader, A.N. Phizo, 'it is amongst people who have never been subjugated that there is the greatest variety of language and dialects. Only subjugated people learn a common language.'[41]

And again, though it can be argued there existed in many areas a tradition of adaptation and mutual accommodation between the ethnic races which perhaps gave little hint of the instability that was to follow after independence, any control by the central kingdoms over the vast hill tracts was largely nominal and usually exercised more through feudatory relations than territorial conquest and assimilation. Undoubtedly, then, whatever the shared aspects of culture and history, until the eve of British annexation there survived in many areas strong regional and ethnic traditions of independence. And it was these that British rule and the very manner of the British annexation were to amplify. Whatever unity did exist was shattered.

3

'Order without Meaning': British Rule and the Rise of the National Liberation Movement

Nation building was never a British priority. The British annexation of Burma was piecemeal and always peripheral to the main British concern which was India. Rather, the twin motives were of security and profit, and colonial administrators were to display a destabilising readiness to trade territory. Concerns over security after a series of disputes along the frontier with India were what led to the annexation of Arakan and Tenasserim in the first war of 1824-6. The initial plan was to offer (or sell) Tenasserim back to the Siamese who had occupied the Tavoy-Mergui districts till shortly before. Manipur and Assam, which were seized at the same time, are today included in modern India. Then, with criticisms mounting from traders over obstructions from the court at Ava, Lower Burma was added in the second campaign of 1852/3 in one of the most 'casually undertaken' wars in colonial history.[1] Soon, however, as a series of expeditions increasingly indicated that a back door to the hidden El Dorado of China would not easily be found, enthusiasm began to cool. It was only when the growing threat of rival French influence on the court at Mandalay became apparent that the forcible annexation of Upper Burma was engineered and, in January 1886, Burma finally incorporated into the British Empire, not as an independent new colony but as a province of India.

Attention was now turned to securing the unknown frontiers. In the same haphazard fashion armed columns were cautiously dispatched into the hills. A particular anxiety was the reaction of China, which the colonial government in India was anxious not to provoke. Explained the viceroy, Lord Dufferin, to Sir Charles Crosthwaite to whom the task of pacification had fallen, 'feel your way and when you come against anything hard, pull back.'[2] China, however, was at the time rather more preoccupied with Tibet and eventually gave up claims to Bhamo and territory east of the Irrawaddy, which the British had at first been ready to concede, in return for an agreement of British non-interference in Tibet.[3] Perhaps not just coincidentally, it is in many of these Trans-Salween areas that until the 1989 mutinies the CPB was most firmly entrenched.

Siamese troops, too, were at first invited in to occupy Karenni territory east of the Salween River until the threat of continued Karenni protests forced a change of mind. But even with the cooperation of Britain's potential rivals for territory, pacification did not prove an easy task. For several years expeditionary columns continued sweeps across the hills. Serious resistance was met with in the Kachin and Chin hills and parts of the Shan states. Indeed the northern Hukawng valley was not brought under British control until the late 1920s; route marches into the remote Wa and Naga hills, mapping out the unknown terrain and little-known peoples, were still continuing until the very eve of the Japanese invasion.

The borders that eventually came to be pencilled in can be seen to have been decided as much by British and French colonial interests as by historical precedent. This has taken on a critical significance in the second half of the 20th century. No doubt, viewed from the distance of Calcutta, London or Paris, the remote and thinly populated mountain ranges along the southern Yunnan plateau appeared convenient buffers to any conflict over rival interests. But as elsewhere in South-East Asia, the choice of natural boundaries such as rivers and their remote mountain watersheds, which are the natural roads and thoroughfares of the region, has proven a major impediment to the development of peoples suddenly cut off on either side of international frontiers. Many of Burma's minorities are today divided across such international borders. The once free-roving Akha and Lahu of the Shan State, for instance, instead find themselves increasingly isolated in small pockets between the modern borders of Burma, Laos, China and Thailand and four very different political and economic systems. And it is not only the hill peoples of Burma who have been so affected. The origins of the hill-tribe Hmong and Mien rebellions which have broken out across Thailand, Laos and Vietnam over the last 40 years can be traced to very similar causes, but have been similarly overlooked in virtually all accounts of regional communist and national liberation movements.

The Structure of Colonial Government
As the annexation progressed, the establishment of a system of administration to cope with the newly acquired territories followed in equally piecemeal fashion. Again the priorities were simple: a minimum of inconvenience and a basic requirement that annexed territories raise sufficient revenue to pay for themselves. A very lopsided system riddled with inconsistencies thus developed. In October 1886, as British forces still struggled to quell resistance on the central plains, Lord Dufferin wrote to the secretary of state for India in London, Viscount Cross, outlining the policy he intended to follow in the hills:

> The Shans, Kachins and other mountain tribes live under the rule of hereditary Chiefs, whose authority is generally sufficient to preserve order amongst them. Here, then, we have to deal not with disintegrated masses as in Burma Proper, but with large organised units, each under the moral and administrative control of an individual ruler. If we secure the allegiance of these rulers, we obtain as far as can be foreseen most of what we require and all the premonitory symptoms give us reason to hope that this will not be a difficult task.[4]

Already the basic distinction between the hills and plains, which was to become the hallmark of British administration, had been made. On the central plains, with the abdication of the last Burman king, Thibaw, nothing less than the complete dismantling of the powers of the *Hutladaw*, or Court, was envisaged. The monarchy was abolished and in 1888 a new system of administration was introduced (largely following the existing practice in India) and the old township or circle units and the powers of the local *Myothugyis*, or hereditary rulers, broken up. Instead authority was devolved to individual headmen (*thugyi*) for each of Burma's 17-18,000 village tracts. It was a system that never gained real acceptance in the rural countryside. In the towns, meanwhile, a start was made in trying to introduce British administrative and educational institutions.

By complete contrast, however, once British supremacy had been acknowledged, in the vast hill tracts there was to be remarkably little interference with the rule of the traditional rulers and chiefs. Indeed the Shan and Karenni *Sawbwas* (*Saophas*) and Kachin *Duwas* were to maintain what are usually described as their royal or feudal positions until even after Burma's independence. Perhaps most anomalously of all, the Karenni states were never even included within the borders of Burma but, in theory, retained their nominal sovereignty until Burma's independence in 1948. But it did fulfil the basic British requirement of being a cheap system established, as Dufferin ordered, 'at least possible cost' and with which minimum interference was needed. A 'thin red line' of commissioners and their deputies were by and large able to cope. On the eve of the Second World War there were just 40 members of the Burma Frontier Service administering the entire Scheduled Areas.[5] Today, given the complete breakdown in central control, this figure seems astounding.

From the British perspective, the obvious shortcomings of this system were at first obscured by the rapid development of rice production in the Lower Delta, which increasingly became the main focus of British interest. With the clearing of vast areas of the Lower Delta, any anxieties over the basic self sufficiency of Burma were dispelled as rice exports rocketed, from 162,000 tons in 1855 to two million tons in 1905/6.[6] Much of this rice was destined for India, justifiably earning Burma the nickname, 'the bread-basket of India'. Indeed by the 1920s, with annual exports passing three million tons, Burma had become the world's largest exporter of rice. But inevitably this dependence on India, which was a major source of resentment to the growing nationalist movement, became a problem for the British civil servants posted to Burma, who faced difficulties arguing the 'case for Burma'.[7]

Gradually a distinctive and separate form of administration for Burma began to evolve. Under a series of reforms, beginning with the Morley-Minto reforms of 1909 and ending with the Government of Burma Act in 1935, a limited form of Home Rule was introduced. But the eventual separation of Burma from India under the 1935 Act did not occur until 1937 and, as it turned out, only one election to the new legislature was ever held. As will be seen, this secondary position to India was to have serious implications for the development of the national liberation movement in Burma.

Even more crucially, these reforms did little to address the very real problems of political representation posed by Burma's complex ethnic background. The convenient distinction in rule between the hills and plains that had evolved during the process of annexation came to be encoded in law. There were many odd anomalies. Burma remained divided into two distinct areas, namely Ministerial Burma, or the old Burma Proper, and the Frontier Areas, which became known as the Scheduled or Excluded Areas. For Ministerial Burma there was a parliament to which there were elections and a limited form of local democracy, though matters such as defence and external affairs remained the exclusive preserve of the governor. But the concept of communal representation, bitterly opposed by many Burman politicians, was allowed in seats reserved for certain minorities, the Karen and immigrant Chinese, Indian and Anglo-Burman.[8] Yet (and somewhat inconsistently) there was to be no separate representation for the Mons of Lower Burma; the question of seats for the Southern Chin (and Muslims), briefly considered in 1932, was ruled out.[9] In the light of the later failure of ethnic Chin and

Mon rebel groups to take real root in these districts, many observers might consider this a significant decision. By contrast, the Karen areas, which enjoyed separate representation, became early centres of the KNU insurrection. Interestingly, religious communalism in Burma, though it should not be underestimated as a smouldering political force, has never developed into anything like the scale of problem it has become in other parts of the old British India Empire; the single exception has been north Arakan, where Muslims form a distinct majority constituency in several districts along the Bangladesh border.

Meanwhile the vast hill tracts of the Frontier Areas remained directly under the governor. Comprising the Karenni and Shan states, the Salween district and arbitrary chunks of the Arakan, Chin, Kachin and Naga hills, they made up over 90,000 square miles of territory and well over a third of the total land area of British Burma. Here, under the loose supervision of the local residents of the Burma Frontier Service, all civil, criminal and financial affairs continued to be administered by the hereditary rulers and chiefs. But again there were many odd inconsistencies. While most of the 'backward tracts' were left in a state of sleepy isolation, in the Shan states, which were considered more advanced, a Federal Council of Shan Chiefs was formed in 1922 which was to become an important forum for representing Shan and *Sawbwa* interests. Then, in a belated attempt to redress some of these inequalities, the Frontier Areas were themselves divided into two categories, Part I or Excluded Areas and Part II or Partially Excluded Areas. The Part II Areas were, in turn, divided into two groups, one with the right to elect members to parliament and one without.[10] The map of Burma thus swiftly became a curious patchwork of oddly different administrative islands. The Kachin hills, for example, remained entirely under Part I of the Scheduled Areas but the small enclaves around Myitkyina and Bhamo, where there was also a small Shan/Burman population, were placed in Part II and with rights to electoral representation in Rangoon. Not for nothing, then, has Michael Aung Thwin dubbed the British pacification, 'Order without Meaning'.[11]

It was not only the methods of British administration that were critically to affect the development of national aspirations. Under the *pax Britannica* there were considerable movements of peoples, which resulted in significant changes in the ethnic composition of many parts of Burma. Vast areas of the Lower Delta were cleared, then rapidly filled as large-scale Burman immigration from the dry zone to the north accelerated a process already begun under the Konbaung dynasty. In many areas the indigenous Mons and Karens were swamped. An 1856 census for Henzada district had calculated that nearly half the population were ethnic Mon (Talaing); but in the 1911 census, out of a total population of 532,357, only 1,224 described themselves as Mon, of whom only 399 could speak Mon and not even 50 write it.[12] Undoubtedly this process was accelerated by the preference the British gave the Burmese language in these areas.

From many hill areas, too, there was a general movement, though on a lesser scale, of peoples to the plains. But without doubt, from the viewpoint of the Burman majority, by far the most serious development was the steady immigration of labour from India. By 1931 the Indian population had already passed one million, out of an estimated total population of 14,650,000.[13] Over half the population of Rangoon was Indian and many government departments were entirely Indian staffed. But it was, in particular, the activities of a caste of landowners and *chettyar* money-lenders of Indian descent (greatly contributing to the growing impoverishment of rural farmers during the world economic recession of the late 1920s) that were to cause most resentment. This, in turn, fuelled the growing tide of Burmese nationalism and political consciousness during the 1930s. Violent anti-Indian riots broke out in 1930 and again in 1938 in which hundreds (mostly Indians) lost their lives.[14] In the great Saya San rebellion, which raged across the rural countryside in 1931, it was again Indians who bore much of the anti-British resentment.[15] The Chinese (and allegedly Karen) community was also on occasion the target of such attacks and these incidents served only to enhance the racial character of developing political movements. Popular cartoons of the time show Burmans squeezed out of their own country by a motley crowd of 'guests', i.e. Europeans, Chinese, Hindus and Muslims. Eventually, during the Second World War, an estimated 500,000 Indians fled Burma, chased out by the young nationalists of the Burma Independence Army; and untold thousands died in one of the darkest passages of Burma's history.

Missionaries, the Karens and Ethnic Minority Rule
Not surprisingly, critics of the period of British rule have laid much of the blame for such incidents on the effects of the British policy of divide and rule. Certainly it is not difficult to find evidence to support this view. Even before the first annexation, the British authorities had been giving shelter to Bo Khyun Pran (King Bering) and his resistance fighters from Arakan and, at first, appeared to be aiding and encouraging Mon rebellion against their Burman rulers. Then throughout the era of colonial rule the British were to persist in the preferment of recruits from the ethnic minorities into the armed forces. Local Karen villagers served as guides for the British Army in the wars of 1824/5 and 1852/3, and Karen troops played a vital role in the suppression of rebellions in Lower Burma in 1886 and again in the Saya San rebellion of 1930-2. As late as 1939 there were only 472 Burmans in the British Burma Army, as compared with 1,448 Karens, 886 Chins and 881 Kachins.[16]

The advent of American, British and other European Christian missionaries also certainly proved a powerful stimulus to the development of non-literate minorities, such as the Kachin and Karen. For many isolated Karen communities, which had suffered great losses and hardship in the wars between the Burman and Siamese kings on the eve of the British annexation, the missionaries' offers of literature, health care and religion appeared to provide a very real hope for national salvation. As early as 1830 the American Baptist, Dr Wade, using the Burmese alphabet (on the grounds that any Karen who could already read would read Burmese), had put the Sgaw Karen language into writing. In 1841 another missionary, Dr Mason, established a Karen newspaper in Tavoy, *The Morning Star*, which, despite a brief interruption during the Second World War, was, until it was forcibly closed down shortly after Ne Win seized power in 1962, Burma's longest running vernacular newspaper.[17]

Though today perhaps only one sixth of all Karens are Christians (most Karens are Buddhists or Buddhist Animists), Christian education had a dramatic impact; mission schools sprang up across Lower Burma as tens of thousands of Karen villagers moved from their remote forest homes into the towns (including Bassein, Henzada, Tharrawaddy, Insein, Rangoon, Toungoo and Moulmein) from the Irrawaddy Delta to Tenasserim. In 1875, the Baptist (later Judson) College was founded in Rangoon and, nicknamed Karen College, it swiftly became an important centre for the spread of Karen nationalist ideas. In 1881, pre-dating the Young Men's Buddhist Association (YMBA) by over two decades, the Karen National Association (KNA), the forerunner of the modern-day KNU, was formed. Though the Karen national movement hardly developed at as rapid a pace as the YMBA, the KNA showed the same broad cultural concerns. Established by Christian Karens, it was open to all Karens regardless of religion or location; its aims were to promote Karen identity, leadership, education and writing and to bring about the social and economic advancement of the Karen peoples.[18]

Set against this more benign socialising influence of the Christian Churches is the fact that many writings of the early missionaries were expressed in highly nationalistic terms, often reflecting an unhelpful ethnic bias, perhaps even a sense of frustration with the Buddhist majority amongst whom they made little progress. A number of missionaries, inspired by Karen legends of a single god, *Y'wa*, a Garden of Creation and a Golden Book, were driven on in the mistaken belief that in the Karens they had discovered one of the lost tribes of Israel.[19] Mass conversions to Christianity later took place amongst the Chins and Kachins without any of this nationalist fervour; but describing the Karen role in the suppression of the 1886 Burman rebellions, the American missionary Dr Vinton was positively enthusiastic:

> I never saw the Karen so anxious for a *fight*. This is just welding the Karens into a nation, not an aggregate of clans. The heathen Karens to a man are brigading themselves under the Christians. The whole thing is doing good for the Karen. This will put virility into our Christianity.... From a loose aggregation of clans we shall weld them into a nation yet.[20]

When the Karen rebellion broke out many years later, in 1949, writers and missionaries such as Vinton's correspondent D.M. Smeaton, author of the *Loyal Karens of Burma*, were bitterly accused by the U Nu government of having deliberately sown the seeds of racial and religious conflict.[21]

Burman conversions to Christianity were, by comparison, minuscule; schoolchildren in Burma are today taught that the Christian Churches represented just another branch of the colonial armoury, the three Ms, missionaries, merchants and military.[22] But such an interpretation plays down the diversity of Churches, the fact that many were quite beyond British control and the difficulties this caused both the minorities and the colonial administration. In 1883, for example, fighting broke out between Karen villagers on the Karenni-Toungoo borders with Roman Catholic priests and Baptist missionaries supporting rival sides and in 1948 this long-running Baptist/Catholic feud provided the final spark for the outbreak of the Karenni uprising.[23]

At the same time a dangerous resentment (which has never really gone away) was to grow amongst many Burman nationalists, who were suspicious of the close relationship the alien missionaries were developing with many Karen and, later, Kachin and Chin communities. Ethnic assertiveness and the expression of ethnic minority views became equated with the divisions of colonial rule. 'In order to separate them culturally from the Burmese,' claimed U Ba Swe, president of the Socialist Party and prime minister of Burma (1956/7), 'they converted the Karens to their religion and also created a separate literature and privileges for them.'[24] This distrust was fuelled by the Karen role in the colonial army and, it can be argued, has until today prevented an objective assessment of any ethnic minority cause, including the Buddhist Shans and Mons. In harking back to the colonial experience, ethnic nationalists are regarded as stooges and separatists whom it is automatically presumed are being instigated by some foreign power (such as the US, China or Thailand). Even in 1987, despite the remarkable ideological journey of the Karen nationalist movement, which has included experiments in communism, capitalism and united fronts with every other nationality in Burma, the state-controlled press was still accusing the KNU of simply 'invoking their old owner-masters and craving for colonial servitude, yearning for their distant relative over and above their own mother.'[25] The KNU, for its part, replies by taking up the same theme and accuses 'Burman chauvinists' of seeking to return the Karens and other ethnic minorities to the conditions of 'slavery' which existed before the British invasion.[26]

Clearly colonialism did immense damage to inter-communal relations; the appearance of preferential treatment for different ethnic groups did, without doubt, bring about a widely varying response to British rule. While obvious exceptions can be found, such as the Arakanese *pongyi*, U Ottoma, the Mon lawyer, U Chit Hlaing, and the CPB's Bengali theoretician, Goshal (also known as* Thakin Ba Tin), it was largely amongst the Burman majority, resentful of British rule and the subordinate status of Burma to India, that the push for independence began. At the same time, on the more positive side, the involvement of such ethnic-minority politicians could be regarded as the first signs of a genuine Burmese nationalist movement in the modern sense. Certainly from the 1920s onwards, in many areas of the Lower Delta it becomes increasingly difficult and pointless to try and pinpoint Mon/Burman ethnicity in developing political movements. Many inhabitants from this area today, including many senior government officials, would claim a mixed Mon/Burman ancestry.

The consequences of the piecemeal nature of British rule were to have equally serious, though largely overlooked, implications for the minorities. Whatever the belief, still widespread today, about the British favouring the ethnic minorities, British rule in fact did little to advance minority aspirations.[27] The Karen, politically the most persistent and articulate in their desire for independence and political representation, were divided into five different administrative districts between Ministerial Burma and the Frontier Areas; rough lines were driven through Karen-majority zones against the expressed opposition of Karen leaders and spokesmen.[28] The Kachin *Duwas* and chiefs who made the trek down to Rangoon in 1925 to put the case for their separation from Burma were accorded a polite reception but little else. It was long accepted by colonial officials that the political separation of the Zos as Chins or Mizos between Burma and Assam was artificial and that they should be reunited in a new 'North-East Frontier Province' to 'have a fair chance in the self-governing India of the future,' but no action was taken.[29] And the governor tried to block Shan leaders coming to London to represent their views at the Burma Round Table hearings of 1931.[30] In the main the political stage was left open, as it was again in the critical years after the Second World War, to the Burman politicians who were always to argue for the political integration of British Burma.

Moreover British reliance on traditional rulers in the Frontier Areas did little to advance the political development of the minorities. Far from cementing traditional relationships in society, British policy frequently had the opposite effect.

---

*   Henceforth abbreviated to *aka*.

What had often been fluid, mobile societies, usually with ample freedom to oust poor headmen or rulers, found themselves burdened with immovable tyrants, now sanctioned by British law. The British, too, were highly inconsistent in their political recognition of ethnicity, especially in the Shan states, where ethnic Shans made up perhaps only half the total population but were always favoured as rulers of the more than 40 sub-states. These varied wildly in size from Kengtung which, with an area of 12,400 square miles, made up a fifth of the total land area, to the 24 square-mile valley at Kyong, which had just 2,500 inhabitants. Racial distinctions were only loosely acknowledged. Ethnic Was, though often described as Shans, were eventually recognised as royal rulers in three small principalities in the eastern Shan state and a Palaung dynasty was approved at Tawngpeng in the north-west. But while a Pao *Myosa* was appointed at Hsihseng (Hsahtung) in the south-west, the tens of thousands of Paos living in the adjoining substates, like the Lahus and other local minorities, were nominally left under Shan rule.

In the best traditions of British empire building, a 'school for the sons of the Shan chiefs' was established in 1902. Bizarrely run along British public-school lines, it forged an even greater division between the new aristocracy and its subjects, though it did later produce a number of able administrators. In the southern Shan states, in particular, the rules of several *Sawbwa* families were distinguished by remarkable corruption. Indeed, in the 1936-8 period the Kayan villagers of the small substate of Mongpai rose up to throw out one particularly inept ruler, but were to get little British support. Without doubt, behind the Pao and Kayan rebellions that have continued on and off since independence has been a residue of resentment against their treatment by the Shan *Sawbwas* under the British administration. Little attempt was made to build any democratic institutions through which these grievances might be voiced. An experimental model-village project begun at Sinlumkaba in the Kachin hills in 1937 was very much the exception. This was to have serious implications at Burma's independence (when most of the ethnic minorities were ill prepared to represent their case) and is reflected, in part, in the intense revolutionary politics of many nationalist movements since independence.

Equally serious for the minorities was the economic neglect of the Frontier Areas. With rice production booming in the Delta and timber and oil extraction also proving increasingly profitable from the turn of the century, there was little incentive to invest funds in the development of the hills. What did develop were single industries, often dependent on imported labour from India and deemed sufficient to cover basic administrative costs; in the Shan states these included a tea factory at Namhsam and the lead/silver mines at Bawdin and Namtu; in the Karenni states wolfram mines at Mawchi (at one stage the world's largest); and a sugar mill at Sahmaw in the Kachin hills. Until the upheavals of 1988-90, it was a picture of economic development little changed in the 40 years since independence. What changes in economic production there have been (and there have been remarkably few) occurred largely in the Delta and the Burman heartlands.

And yet, despite the lack of planning, as a handful of roads and railways slowly worked their way into the hills in many areas there were significant changes in the pattern of trade, which did strengthen ties between the hills and plains. The northern Shan states, for example, which had previously traded largely across the border towards China, now began to move more produce to the west to Burma Proper. This situation has many parallels in the French annexation and administration of Indo-China, in which Laos, and to a lesser extent Cambodia, were regarded as the natural protective buffers and reservoirs of untapped resources for the main French interest, which was coastal Vietnam. Similarly little attempt was made to develop these areas, yet they were to emerge from the colonial era physically, if not psychologically, inside the orbit of Vietnam; this has resulted in the resumption of historic regional power struggles over sovereignty and zones of influence, involving both China and Thailand, which are yet to be resolved.

The picture that emerges from the British administration of the hill tracts is not so much one of benign paternalism as of chronic neglect. Noel Stevenson, director of the Frontier Areas in the frantic years after the war, who was much criticised by the independence movement for his support of the minority cause, stands out as one of the few British officers aware of the seriousness of the deteriorating situation. In October 1944, with the end of the war in sight, he wrote to the Royal Anthropological Institute in London to lambast the almost total lack of British knowledge of the Frontier Areas and its peoples. Warning that the events of the Second World War had 'increased a hundredfold the ancient animosities between the hills and the plains,' he asked:

> Can we become successful co-planners with the hill men to guide their future if we do not start by knowing their existing way of life? Obviously not, unless we accept the original Bolshevik thesis that total revolution is the only road to progress. Where then do we stand? Books on Burma written by trained social scientists are conspicuous by their absence from the Institute's library. The official files of the past 50 years have disappeared in the defeat of 1942. On what basis then will our future plans be laid? Against what background of recorded knowledge shall we frame our perspective?[31]

Stevenson's solution was to introduce a programme of anthropological and scientific studies. In the circumstances, it was probably already too little and too late.

The Revival of Nationalism: 1885-1930

If the British had neglected the aspirations of the ethnic minorities, they also appeared to have totally underestimated the strength of the growing nationalist movement amongst the Burman majority, or, indeed, even to have distinguished it from the growing lawlessness in Burma Proper, which came to characterise the latter years of British rule. It is doubtful whether British rule ever gained much acceptance amongst the Burman majority. The attempt to build British-style institutions and a western-style democracy had received only a luke-warm response. Elections, if not deliberately boycotted, were treated with widespread apathy. And, though in the late 1930s there was some semblance of the development of western-style political parties, at independence in 1948 the older generation of politicians who had served in the colonial government were swiftly bypassed and forgotten. The young nationalists, nearly all Marxists, who led Burma to independence in 1948, had their political education in the national liberation movement of the 1930s and the anti-fascist resistance of the Second World War.

It is against this background that the radical traditions of most of Burma's postwar political parties, both above- and underground, need to be understood. Burma since independence is, after all, that rarity, a country in which successive governments have been regarded as left wing, but in which the principal political opposition has come from the left. The origins of the main national parties, from the CPB to Ne Win's BSPP, are deeply rooted in anti-colonial/anti-fascist resistance.

Even many of the new parties formed in the aftermath of the 1988 democracy uprising, from the National Unity Party (NUP) to the National League for Democracy (NLD), while supposedly marking a change of political direction, continue to claim the same broad anti-imperialist traditions.

Resistance to British rule did not end with the abdication of King Thibaw. For several years spontaneous rebellions continued across much of the Lower and Upper Delta. Though British records tend to speak of the leaders as bandits and dacoits, many were in fact former *Wuns* and *Myothugyis* and officials of the dissolved central court, or *Hutladaw*. Buddhist *pongyis*, too, played a leading role. It would appear that with the collapse of the central court leadership had naturally devolved to surviving representatives of the old political élite. Eventually the last traces of armed resistance were crushed by the forces under Sir Charles Crosthwaite's command, but not before some 30,000 troops had been brought in to complete the task.[32]

But this hardly marked the end of political opposition. Like national liberation movements elsewhere in South-East Asia, the first signs of a national resurgence appeared in the revival of a broad cultural movement. Already in the late 1890s Buddhist societies had begun to appear in Mandalay and several towns in Lower Burma and, in 1906, the Young Men's Buddhist Association (YMBA), modelled on the Young Men's Christian Association, was formed. In part these societies, popular with students, replaced the role of the Buddhist *Sangha* (order of monks) whose authority in traditional areas, such as education, had begun to decline without any official sanction from the new British rulers. Within ten years some 50 branches had sprung up across Burma. But while it was over religious issues (such as the footwear controversy) that the YMBA first began to attract attention, it was not for long confined to such a narrow field. In 1917 the YMBA sent a delegation to the Chelmsford-Montagu hearings in Calcutta to ask for Burma's separation from India. Then, in 1920, the YMBA organised a boycott of elections to the Indian Legislative Assembly and Council of State at Delhi.[33]

The transformation from cultural movement to national movement was apparently complete with the strike at Rangoon University, which began on 5 December 1920, just four days after the passing of the British-sponsored University Act. This controversial reform firmly tied university education in Burma to colonial administrative interests, the English language and the model of India's Calcutta University. There was widespread public support for the students' demand for national schools, free from British control, which would teach Burmese language, literature and history. Even more significantly, as the American historian Josef Silverstein notes, the protest marked the students' entry as a potent force in national politics and this date is still commemorated as Burma's National Day.[34] 'We believe that at this juncture,' claimed the Students' Boycott Council in a statement that has inspired future generations of students, 'nothing can save the nation but a proud and indomitable stand on the part of Young Burma, with the whole-hearted cooperation of the Burmese people.'[35]

The YMBA was now largely superseded by the formation of a General Council of Burmese Associations (GCBA), which worked to broaden the scope of the nationalist movement, but crucially failed to win support from the ethnic minorities. In the countryside the GCBA was, however, able to link closely with the *wunthanu athins* (national associations) that had begun to mushroom in villages throughout Burma Proper. Increasingly they began to challenge the authority of the village *thugyi* or headmen on whom the British administration was largely dependent. Shadow administrations were set up in some areas in an ominous precedent of the rural insurgencies that were to break out after independence. Rural violence became increasingly commonplace, especially in Tharrawaddy district, and many *athins* were outlawed by the government. The movement gained its first martyr with the death in prison of the *pongyi*, U Wizara. However, this rural movement was for the most part uncoordinated and was eventually to culminate in the great Saya San rebellion of 1930-2, which was brutally but effectively quashed (see Chapter 5).

At this stage Burma's close association with India created problems for the political direction of the nationalist movement. At first the main faction, led by U Chit Hlaing and supported by the *pongyi* U Ottoma (who was also a member of the Indian National Congress), favoured separation from India. Taking the lead from the Indian National Congress, it led the largely successful boycotts of the elections of 1922, 1925 and 1928.[36] However, after the Simon Commission in 1928 advocated the separation of Burma from India its leaders changed tack, for they were fearful of losing the political benefits the Indian National Congress appeared to be winning in India. Joining forces with a smaller faction led by Dr Ba Maw, who was to be the wartime head of state under the Japanese, they stood for the 1932 elections as the Anti-Separationist League. Another smaller faction, led by such founder members of the YMBA as U Ba Pe and U Maung Gyee, continued to push for separation and contested elections under various titles, including the 21 Party, the Home Rule, the Nationalist and the People's Party.[37] Only a third and much smaller faction, representing business and minority (predominantly Indian, Chinese and Eurasian) interests and headed by Sir J.A. Maung Gyi's Progressive or Independent Party, worked with the British and, despite a poor showing in the elections, was initially preferred to office.

The KNA and the Development of Ethnic Minority Parties
Discussion of ethnic-minority questions largely came under the remit of the governor and the Frontier Areas Administration, but the KNA, the only well-organised indigenous minority party in Ministerial Burma, was also generally supportive of the British, though reports of difficulties with the Karen community, including two *Minlaung* uprisings in the 19th century, were generally glossed over.[38] Crucially, the colonial government did little to investigate, recognise or reconcile the rising tide of Karen nationalism and this was to leave an explosive situation at Burma's independence.

Like the YMBA, the KNA developed largely in response to British plans for administrative reform in Burma. But dominated by a small group of educated Sgaw and Pwo Karens, mostly teachers and lawyers from Bassein, Rangoon, Insein, Moulmein and Tavoy, the KNA faced constant difficulties in being taken seriously as the sole representative of Karen interests in Burma, especially in the Frontier Areas. Virtually all the KNA leaders were Christians, several of whom had studied in Britain, the USA and the West, and it was in fact not until 1939 that the KNA sought to rectify its apparent lack of organisation in the Buddhist community by forming the Buddhist (also Burma) Karen National Association.

The KNA was, however, determined in its representation of the Karen cause. At the Chelmsford-Montagu hearings in India in 1917, it, the only equivalent party representing minority interests, had antagonised the YMBA by arguing that

Burma was not 'yet in a fit state for self-government' since it was 'inhabited by many different races, differing in states of civilisation,... religion and social development' which it might take years of 'strenuous training under British governance' to rectify.[39] But three years later, with the prospect of Home Rule being granted, the KNA changed its position and its chief spokesman, the lawyer Sidney Loo Nee, submitted a criticism of the 1920 Craddock Reforms in which he argued that the Karens, as Burma's second largest indigenous race, should have their interests and identity protected by separate electorates and thus 'advance step by step along with the Burmans'.[40] Despite strong Burman objections, the KNA won this argument and, following the Whyte Committee of Enquiry, the Karens were granted five (later twelve) seats in the Legislative Council of 130 (later 132) members.[41]

As the Burmese national liberation movement gathered momentum during the 1920s, KNA leaders began to object that communal representation, in itself, was not enough. Though the Karen population was not marked by the same rate of assimilation as the Mon, Karen language and culture were felt to be under increasing threat and the numbers of Karen-speakers in the Delta began to decline rapidly. KNA leaders felt that Karen interests, particularly in the schools and judiciary, were taking a secondary position to Burman.

In 1928 came the first proposal for the creation of an independent Karen State by the widely regarded 'father' of the Karen nation, Dr San C. Po, the most prominent of the Christian Karens who had studied in the West. That year Po described his vision in a book, *Burma and the Karens*, published in London: 'It is their desire to have a country of their own, where they may progress as a race and find the contentment they seek.... "Karen Country," how inspiring it sounds!'[42] The model he envisaged was loosely akin to Switzerland or Great Britain, where he compared the Burmans, Karens, Arakanese and Shans to the English, Welsh, Scots and Irish. The Karen he allied with 'Gallant little Wales', but, stressed Po, 'the present-day ideal is self-determination.'[43] This still remains the KNU's basic demand. In the same year Karen leaders supported Po's proposal to the Simon Commission for the creation of a Karen State in the Tenasserim Division. If this was not granted, Po warned, 'it is greatly to be feared that a new group or generation of Karen extremists or obstructionists will arise.'[44]

But while the British generally looked favourably on the Karens (they were the only 'native' minority accorded communal representation in the legislature), such pleas largely fell on deaf ears.[45] Indeed of all Burma's minorities, the Karens were to suffer the most from the arbitrary reforms of British administration during the 1920s and 1930s. The complicated spread and ethnic diversity of the Karen population were always to count against KNA aspirations and, though in 1947 the British did briefly consider this, KNA claims of a pan-Karen nationality amongst the various Karen sub-groups were never recognised. Karen-inhabited areas remained divided between Ministerial Burma, Parts I and II of the Scheduled Areas, the Karenni states and the south-west Shan states.

British records do show an awareness of Karen anxieties and, as a token gesture, in 1938 it was agreed to set aside one date each year for the Karen New Year. Today this date is celebrated in Karen villages on both sides of the battle lines. But the major British concern was always with Ministerial Burma. Here it was felt that Karen interests, both of the Delta Karens and those in the eastern mountains, would best be served by building up Karen representation on a numerical

basis; in addition to the preference for Karen volunteers in the colonial police and
army, in the late 1930s a number of KNA leaders were appointed to government
and (by Dr Ba Maw) to Cabinet office. The Karen-majority districts of the
Frontier Areas, by contrast, were regarded as uneconomic backwaters, not necessarily separate from but rather behind the plains in terms of both civilisation and
political and economic development.[46] An important principle thus developed,
which has had a lasting impact. If an area could be considered a plains area, even
if it were predominantly Karen, it had to be included in Ministerial Burma.

The result was an abrupt line drawn along the western edge of the eastern hills,
effectively dissecting the Karen population and bearing only a passing resemblance to local geography, politics and economics. The only areas in which Karen
territory or independence were explicitly recognised were amongst the most
backward, i.e. in the Karenni states and Pao state of Hsihseng, where local Karen
chieftains, like the Shan rulers, had been recognised as *Sawbwas* and *Myosas* in
the process of annexation.

Though primarily intended as a short-term measure, these divisions ultimately
did much to weaken the Karen case and their importance today cannot be underestimated. Though their names may be different, the same divisions exist on the
map of modern Burma, continuing to fuel a deep sense of Karen under-represen-
tation. The present Karen State, for example, includes rather less than 25 per cent
of the Karen population of Burma. Chin and Kachin leaders claim they have
similarly lost strategic tracts of lowland territory over the years, which are
naturally needed for the economic advancement of their peoples. But the British
decisions did fit in with the general belief and demands of the mainstream nationalist movement. 'Buddhist Karens have always identified themselves with the
Burmese and have never asked to be classified as a separate race,' claimed the
People's Party in 1933.[47]

Unlike the Burmese nationalists, the KNA, true to the judicial training of many
of its leading members, adopted a strictly legalistic approach towards challenging
its British rulers; throughout the 1930s it put forward a series of claims, based
largely on the administrative anomaly of the Karenni states (which technically lay
outside British Burma), for the creation of a similarly independent 'Karen Free
State or Republic' in the eastern hills. This, it was believed, could then be
expanded to include other Karen-majority areas of Burma. Various supporting
claims and petitions were put in to the governor from KNA supporters in the
Salween and Toungoo districts of the Frontier Areas and much attention was
given to trying to elevate the traditional Karen headmen or *Sawkes* to the same
status as the Karenni *Sawbwas* to the north.[48] Indeed one KNA petition from
Salween in 1938 was backed up by the signatures of 101 chieftains in the
district.[49]

The colonial administration, too, recognised the legal inconsistencies in
Karenni's continued separation from Burma. But despite no fewer than 12 official
enquiries into Karenni's political status between 1873 and 1939, no action was
ever taken.[50] Nor did the British ever accede to KNA demands. Throughout the
1930s the entire question of Karen separation or independence was completely
overshadowed by the Burmese national liberation movement and the growing
political ferment on the plains.

Other ethnic minorities, such as the Mons, Kachins, Chins, Nagas and Shans,
now claim that their territories were also dissected by the divisions of British rule,

but, as modern political movements, most, including those of Ministerial Burma, did not emerge until after the Second World War. For example, ethnic Mons, such as U Chit Hlaing and Sir J.A. Maung Gyi, achieved leading positions in the Burmese nationalist parties, and only in 1937 did a group of Mon *pongyis* and intellectuals, headed by U Chit Thaung, a government chemical engineer, form the All Ramonnya Mon Association. With cultural and religious aims very similar to the early KNA and YMBA, leaders of the insurgent New Mon State Party today consider this the forerunner of the present nationalist movement.[51]

Similarly, while prominent Arakanese leaders, such as U Ottoma and Sir Paw Tun, a pre-war prime minister, were working with the mainstream Burmese political parties, an ethnic Rakhine movement was also slowly stirring. In 1909 a Scholarship Association was formed in Akyab and, by the end of the First World War, local Rakhine organisations had proliferated across the territory under such names as the Association for Awakening and the Patriotic Association. One of these, the Arakan Association, wrote to the British government demanding the appointment of a secretary of state for 'neglected Arakan' and, together with another group, the Rakhapura Association, headed by the post-independence leader, U Aung Zan Wai, attended the 1921 Congress of the GCBA in Mandalay. In the 1930s the Rakhine members of parliament were loosely grouped together in the Arakan Party and, in 1938, under pressure from leading Buddhist monks, the various Rakhine associations agreed to merge into the Arakan National Congress. But it was not until May 1940 in Pauktaw that the Congress finally met at a conference attended by a Burmese nationalist delegation from the *Dobama* movement, headed by the communist leader, Thakin Soe. In the same year the renowned *pongyi* and future insurgent leader, *Sayadaw* U Seinda, who had been leading the nationalist calls, established the quasi-Buddhist Central Auwadasariya Organisation, from which the armed nationalist movement rapidly grew.[52]

All these ethnic Mon and Rakhine parties were formed largely as a result of concern over the continued decline in the public expression of their languages, culture and traditions in Burman-majority areas, and their fears were hastened by the rapid advances made by the national liberation movement during the 1930s. The one notable exception was the small Chin National Unity Organisation (CNUO), formed in 1933 in Mindat in the southern Chin hills by U Vamthu Mawng, a former soldier in the Burma Rifles, who called for the political reforms of Ministerial Burma to be introduced to the Chin peoples.[53] In 1934 Mawng's representatives made contact with Burman political leaders in Rangoon and, as a result of later nationalist agitations, several CNUO leaders, including Mawng, were imprisoned by the British. Though the CNUO, later superseded by the United Chin Freedom League, clearly had little influence amongst the many Chin sub-groups in the mountains in the interior, Mawng himself became a popular choice with Burman leaders and was appointed the first Chin Cabinet minister at independence in 1948; at the 1951 general election, however, he was decisively rejected by his own people.

The Dobama Asiayone, Aung San and the Resort to Arms: 1930-41
The activities of these ethnic minority politicians have left little more than a foot-note in the historical records of the British; at the time they were completely overshadowed by Burman nationalist leaders. For while leaders of the Anti-Separationist League, the Home Rule Party and other early nationalist parties

generally worked, like the KNA, within the system, at the beginning of the 1930s a new generation of radical young nationalists surfaced, who were eventually to lead Burma to independence. In May 1930, in the wake of the anti-Indian riots, the *Dobama Asiayone* (We Burmans Association) was formed in Rangoon. At first, lacking any real programme or ideology, the *Dobama* was largely another nationalist consciousness-raising front. Its members, mainly students and intellectuals, marked their first appearances with patriotic songs and speeches and addressed each other with the title, 'Thakin' (lord or master), to show that they, the people, were the real rulers of their country. Writing 20 years later the CPB's early theoretician, Thakin Thein Pe (*aka* Thein Pe Myint), characterised the early days of the YMBA movement as 'religious nationalism' and the beginnings of the *Dobama* as 'narrow nationalism'.[54] But it was from this small beginning that the first political vanguard movement in Burma was to develop, and it was to take off with a rapidity that few could have foreseen.

Taking inspiration from the Saya San rebellion which raged in the countryside, the ultimate aim of the Thakin movement was nothing less than Burma's independence. But without doubt the historic success of the Thakin movement was to bring together and organise in ten short years the different and largely unpoliticised sections of the community, including students, peasants and workers. In 1930 an All Burma Youth League was established and contacts made with the Rangoon University Students Union (RUSU), which had been formed the same year. In 1933 the first trade unions in the Burma Oil Company were formed and, during 1934, the Thakins were active in various rural agitation campaigns.[55] Then, in the second strike at Rangoon University in 1936, a new and highly capable class of Thakin leaders surfaced, including two, Aung San and U Nu, who were eventually to mastermind the drive to Burma's independence. Ostensibly the strike, which was largely dismissed by the colonial authorities at the time, began after the RUSU secretary, Aung San, was expelled for publishing anti-British articles in the student magazine *Owei* (Peacock's Cry). Then, when U Nu, the RUSU chairman, followed this up with a series of anti-British speeches, he too was expelled. But for three months, in a dramatic outburst of nationalist feeling, students camped out at the Shwedagon Pagoda and, as the protests spread to Mandalay, the All Burma Students Union (ABSU) was formed.[56] (Subsequently *Owei*'s name was changed to that of *Khut Daung*, the Fighting Peacock, the emblem of ABSU, which was again much in evidence in the street protests of 1988.)

As demonstrations mounted throughout 1938, variously known as the 'year of strife' or the year of the numerically auspicious '1300 (Burmese era) Revolution', the Thakins began to pop up everywhere — in the 11-month strike in the oil fields at Chauk and Yenangyaung (where Thakin Soe was especially active) and in the long march of striking workers on Rangoon. Thakin leaders, such as Aung San, Nu and Hla Pe (later Bo Let Ya) from the *Dobama* executive, toured the country making speeches and raising funds. As the demonstrations increasingly turned to violence, hundreds, including the new ABSU and RUSU student leaders, Thakins Ba Hein and Ba Swe, were arrested. At another university strike in Rangoon in December the first student martyr, Aung Kyaw, was killed and several injured during a charge by mounted police. In February the following year another 17 people were killed during a demonstration, led by Buddhist monks, in Mandalay when police opened fire on the crowd.[57] Without doubt the frequently invoked

'spirit of 1938' was a powerful motivating force in the upheavals of 1988 affect-
ing, as it did, all the same sections of the community.

Increasingly the growing influence of Marxism on the Thakin movement
became apparent. The Thakins had always read widely; books as diverse as Sun
Yat-sen, Rousseau and various Sinn Fein and Fabian tracts were all later
mentioned by Thakins as early popular texts. Marxist writings had apparently first
been introduced into Burma in 1932 by Dr Thein Maung on his return from the
Burma Round Table Conference in London. In the same period in England
another Thein Maung (a state scholar) made what was probably the first Thakin
contact with the international communist movement when he met with another
overseas Burmese student, Oo 'Ashin' Kyaw, who attended meetings of the British
Communist Party and the League Against Imperialism. The young journalist Tun
Pe also used money bequeathed by Saya San to buy books recommended in
Pandit Nehru's *Impressions of the Soviet Union*. But it was only with the foundation of the *Nagani* (Red Dragon) Book Club by Thakins Nu and Than Tun in 1937
that Burmese-language translations of the Marxist classics were for the first time
widely circulated.[58] But if Marxism came comparatively late to Burma it was to
have a deep and immediate impact. Like Ho Chi Minh and the Vietnamese
communists a decade earlier, the left in Burma came to Marxism (and thus
Leninism) via the colonial question; Marxist analysis was undoubtedly very much
in tune with the experiences of the young Thakins in the nationalist movement.
For the moment, however, the expression of these ideas was influenced by the
more reformist united-front strategy adopted by the Comintern in the mid-
1930s.[59]

In the light of later developments, it is important to emphasise that, though little
commented on at the time, two factions in the *Dobama Asiayone* were now to
emerge, the larger and more influential of which was led by Kodaw Hmaing (born
1876), co-founder of the *Dobama* and a much respected veteran of the nationalist
movement. This group included Aung San, Than Tun and Nu whose shared
interest in Marxism, initially aroused through Marx's explanations of imperialism
and colonialism, was to lead in the late 1930s to a growing interest in socialism
and a broader international outlook. The other was more simply nationalistic
(with some overt right-wing leanings) and was led by Tun Ok and the *Dobama*'s
other co-founder and former RUSU president, Ba Sein. Both broke away from the
mainstream *Dobama* in 1938. Amongst their followers was a little-known postal
clerk, Shu Maung, who had reputedly left Rangoon University in 1930 without
completing his degree. But in 1941, now known as Ne Win (Brilliant like the
Sun), he was to leap to national prominence; it was with this nationalist grouping
that Japanese agents were first to make contact. (Commentators have also
suggested that national socialism, in the early war years at least, was to hold some
fascination for several leading members of the Kodaw Hmaing faction, in particular Aung San who visited Japan. However, any influence was clearly short
lived.)

None the less, despite these differences, under the growing influence of
Marxism the realisation of the importance of forming new and broader mass
organisations and political fronts was immediate. In 1936 a small Fabian league
had split from the *Dobama* to try to introduce Fabian socialism by parliamentary
action. The mainstream *Dobama* itself formed a new organisation, the *Komin
Kochin* (One's Own King, One's Own Kind), and won three seats in the legisla-

ture, but these tactics remained incidental to the main struggle. In January 1939, with the Thakins again taking the lead, the All Burma Peasants Organisation was formed and the groundwork laid for the All Burma Trade Union Congress (ABTUC), which came into existence a year later in January 1940. The declared aim of both organisations, again reflecting the impact of Marxism, was the building of a socialist state in Burma.[60]

Then on 15 August 1939 six men, Thakins Aung San, Soe, Ba Hein, Hla Pe (*aka* Bo Let Ya), Ba Tin (Goshal) and Dr Nath, gathered in a small room in Barr Street in Rangoon for the historic founding meeting of the Communist Party of Burma (CPB). (Thakin Than Tun, though he remained in close counsel, did not join at this stage.) As with many insurgent movements since independence, there has been continuous confusion over which of so many secretive and cell-like gatherings were informal meetings and which were official. Different participants have later attributed different decisions to very different times and places. Indeed the colonial authorities at first seemed to be unaware of the CPB's formation (the party was only proscribed in February 1941), apparently believing that the only communist groups active in Burma were small cells operating in the Bengali community. This no doubt explains, amidst the confusion of the war in Europe, the failure of British Intelligence to respond. But the CPB's veteran chairman, Ba Thein Tin, remains adamant that it was at this clandestine meeting that the twin decisions were first taken to launch a broad-based communist movement and a national anti-imperialist front; it is this date the CPB has always celebrated as its founding anniversary. The six inaugural members were each designated a specific task; Aung San, secretary-general; Soe, mass organisation; Ba Hein, student affairs; Let Ya, treasurer; Ba Tin, party organisation; and Dr Nath, librarian.[61]

With the exception of Thakin Soe, who died in 1989, these men have all long since passed away (only Ba Hein and Soe died of natural causes). Now even CPB veterans and archivists have difficulty providing documentation of the party's early history, conducted as it was against the backdrop of war. But, according to several scholars, it was at this initial meeting that the CPB's basic manifesto was first drawn up. This little-changed statement was surprisingly precise in its objectives. Defining Burma as a 'semi-colonial and feudal country which had to pass through two revolutionary stages,' namely of 'national liberation' and of 'socialist revolution', the CPB called for the commencement of armed struggle.[62]

Perhaps the most intriguing insight into the exact circumstances of the CPB's formation comes from the political scientist, Robert Taylor, who documents the growing influence of the Communist Party of India (CPI) and the Comintern, which had both previously appeared to regard Burma as a backwater of India. This may well provide the best explanation for the apparent clarity of vision of the CPB's founders. The Thakins' first contacts with the CPI had been made by Thein Pe Myint and Bo Let Ya while both were students in India in 1936; when Thein Pe returned to Burma in early 1938 he was accompanied by the Bengali communist, B.N. Dass.[63] Amongst the Bengali community in Rangoon even closer ties were maintained by the Burma-born Bengali, Thakin Ba Tin, through the Bengal Province Committee of the CPI. (In the early 1930s British police had quickly crushed attempts to set up a similar network in the Chinese community, linked to the South Seas Communist Party in Singapore.)[64] According to Taylor, who relies largely on Thein Pe's recollections, the catalyst that led to the CPB's formation was the arrival from India in mid-1939 of the CPI representative,

Purandu (or Niranda) Dutt. He had come at Thein Pe's invitation and, after clearance from the Comintern, tried to bring together two existing Marxist study groups in Rangoon, one Indian and one Burman. Indeed of the six founder members of the CPB, two, Ba Tin and Dr Nath (a graduate of Rangoon Medical College), were of Bengali extraction. Following the mass exodus of Indian immigrants during the upheavals of the war, the influence of the Indian community in national politics was much diminished (except in business) and, after Ne Win's coup, it was virtually nil. But evidence of the importance of this early Indian role could be seen in the series of strikes by Bengali-dominated docker and labour unions in Rangoon during 1940/1, in which Ba Tin, who in 1940 was elected president of the Rangoon Sawmill Workers Union, played a prominent part.[65] These were to keep the colonial authorities busily preoccupied right up to the eve of the Japanese invasion. Other Indian members whom CPB veterans now claim were influential in the CPB's organisation of the trade union movement were the ABTUC leaders, S. Mukerjee (Pyu Win) and Rajan (Aung Naing).

Shortly after the formation of the CPB, the People's Revolutionary Party (PRP, also sometimes known as the Burma Revolutionary Party), the forerunner of the post-war Socialist Party, was formed, though exact details are uncertain. The CPB was later to claim that the PRP was another early communist front aimed at broadening the anti-colonial resistance; certainly the PRP contained a number of prominent CPB supporters. Along with the future leaders of the Socialist Party, Thakins Mya, Nu, Ba Swe and Kyaw Nyein, the PRP's founders included Aung San, Hla Pe (Let Ya) and Ba Hein from the CPB, Thakin Chit, who later became vice-chairman of the CPB, and Hla Maung (Bo Zeya), the CPB's future Chief-of-Staff.[66] At this stage there was considerable interchange between these new fronts and the unions; Aung San himself later admitted to having joined and left the CPB twice.[67] But from this point on, with the formation of the first revolutionary Marxist parties, the Thakin movement was to take on a markedly more radical line of action.

In this highly politicised atmosphere and with the probability of Burma being drawn into the Second World War growing ever more likely, the decision to launch armed struggle was now inevitable. The young radicals looked in every direction. By the end of 1939 several Thakins, including Nu, had visited Chunking in China to have talks with the nationalist government of Chiang Kai-shek and, whilst there, had tried unsuccessfully to make contact with the China Communist Party (CCP). The CPB, too, made its own unsuccessful efforts to contact Mao Zedong (see Chapter 6). Then, in March 1940, a *Dobama* delegation, headed by Thakins Aung San, Than Tun and Ba Hein, travelled to India to attend a meeting of the Indian National Congress and met several leaders, including Gandhi, Nehru and Chandra Bose, as well as officials of the CPI. Nehru, in particular, was to make a deep impression on the young *Dobama* team. But it was Japanese agents, already underground in Burma, who offered the more immediate prospect of arms and training.

The first step on the road to war had been the formation in October 1939 of the Freedom Bloc. This was an alliance of the *Dobama Asiayone* (Kodaw Hmaing faction), the ABSU, politically active monks and the *Sinyetha* (Poor Man's Party) of Dr Ba Maw, formed to try and increase pressure on the British to recognise the right of Burma's independence. It was a symbolic but vital pact which, for the first time, brought together the two (intra- and extra-parliamentary) wings of the national liberation movement. Aung San and Dr Ba Maw were appointed secretary and *Ahnashin* (president-dictator) respectively. A consummate politician and former opponent of the *Dobama*, Ba Maw had been Burma's first prime minister, serving until February 1939, and he was to bring to the young radicals' cause a new level of middle class support.

In September 1939 Ba Maw approached the Japanese consulate in Rangoon and his emissary, Dr Thein Maung, travelled to Tokyo to sound out the Japanese government about support for a nationalist uprising.[68] Early the next year Ba Maw, who had begun to display increasingly dictatorial tendencies and a frequent recourse to Burmese mythology in his public speeches, which disturbed many young Thakins, proposed preparing underground resistance forces and sending selected men abroad for military training.[69] But the clearest plan for the future uprising, as Ba Maw later conceded, was outlined in early 1940 by Aung San, who had by now emerged as the nationalist movement's leading agitator and spokesman. Born in 1916 at Natmauk in the Magwe district, into a family he described as well-to-do gentry, Aung San came to personify the aspirations of the young intellectuals now taking over the lead in the nationalist movement.[70] In 1939 he was arrested briefly for conspiracy to overthrow the government by force. Following his release, he again proposed the strategy of a countrywide campaign of strikes, demonstrations and anti-tax drives, backed up by escalating guerrilla activity, to bring down the British administration.[71]

Meanwhile, the Ba Sein/Tun Ok faction of the *Dobama*, which had refused to join the Freedom Bloc, had made its own contacts with the Japanese consulate and, in early 1940, discussed with the naval Intelligence officer, Lt. Kokubu, the possibility of sending volunteers to Japan for training.[72] Ba Sein, in particular, strongly supported Japanese militarism. But even the PRP was now to make contact with the Japanese, despite the objections of Ba Hein and the party's CPB supporters. In August 1940, in Rangoon, Thakin Mya and Dr Thein Maung met the Japanese secret agent, Col. Suzuki, who shortly afterwards masterminded the formation of the Burma Independence Army (BIA). Amongst the ideas they discussed was the plan to build up supply bases along the Siam border in preparation for a Japanese-backed uprising.[73]

Throughout these secret discussions the Freedom Bloc was keeping up pressure on the British authorities with a series of mass independence rallies staged across the country. This finally prompted the colonial government in the middle of 1940 to begin the wholesale arrest, under the Defence of Burma Rules, of leaders of the *Dobama* and the Freedom Bloc. Amongst those detained were Dr Ba Maw and Thakins Nu, Than Tun, Soe and Kyaw Nyein. This, however, hardly had the intended effect; several later said that their imprisonment at this stage had played an important part in their political education. Ba Sein, too, was arrested when he tried to slip into Siam with the help of his Japanese contacts.

Two men, Aung San and Hla Myaing (Bo Yan Aung), escaped on the Norwegian freighter, the *Hai Lee*, to Amoy in China. There is still some dispute over the exact purpose of Aung San's mission. He said he had an open brief; Dr Ba Maw said his trip was prearranged with the Japanese consulate; others, including the CPB, say he was trying to contact the CCP.[74] But whatever the original plan, in November 1940 the two men were discovered in Amoy by an agent of the Japanese *Kempeitai* (Secret Police) and, on 12 November, just over one year after Aung San had helped found the CPB, the two men voluntarily flew on to Imperial Japan, where they were met at Haneda Airport by Col. Suzuki himself. Here was a clear illustration of what the Czech scholar, Jan Becka, called their 'pragmatism' and of the difficulties the young Thakins faced in their quest for independence in a fast-changing world.[75]

At Col. Suzuki's suggestion Aung San drew up what was to become known as his Plan for Burma's Independence, or Blueprint for a Free Burma, in which he outlined his future vision of a unified and independent Republic of Burma.[76] Tactfully, to assuage Japanese doubts over his political leanings, he added this could now be brought about with Japanese assistance and as part of the Japanese Greater East Asia Co-prosperity Sphere. This fitted in well with the requirements of the Imperial Army's Supreme Command, now anxious to close the Burma Road from Lashio to Kunming in Yunnan, which they blamed for prolonging the war in China.[77] As a result a special Intelligence unit, the *Minami Kikan*, was formed under Col. Suzuki with two objectives, to close the Burma Road and to support the national uprising. *Minami* agents were immediately dispatched to Bangkok to build up supply networks and depots along the Siam border, while plans were made to bring 30 volunteers to Japan for training as military leaders. For this purpose, in March 1941 Aung San secretly returned with a *Minami* agent on a Japanese freighter to Burma to help recruitment and to explain the Japanese plan to his Thakin colleagues. It was not a difficult task. Following the arrest of the *Dobama* leadership, few Thakins now had any doubts about the wisdom of accepting Japanese aid.

Between March and July 1941 Aung San and the *Thirty Comrades* quietly began to slip away to Japan for armed training. So secret were these preparations that, according to Ne Win's biographer, Dr Maung Maung, Shu Maung (Ne Win) and the other members of the Ba Sein/Tun Ok *Dobama* faction were surprised to meet Thakins from the Kodaw Hmaing group on board ship.[78] But once in Japan these factional differences were largely forgotten and by the end of the year, after completing an arduous training camp on Hainan Island, they had travelled back to Siam. Within a month they had recruited over 3,500 volunteers along the border.[79]

Finally, on 28 December, the Burma Independence Army (BIA) was formally inaugurated. The same day the *Thirty Comrades*, each taking a new *nom de guerre*, held the traditional *thwe thauk* (blood-drinking) ceremony in Bangkok. This involved sipping blood, drawn from their arms, mixed with liquor in a communal silver bowl as a pledge of eternal loyalty and comradeship. Most striking was their youth. They had an average age of just 24 years.

Three days later the first BIA units began to enter Burma in the wake of the Japanese Fifteenth Army. They received a rapturous reception from the Burman majority. Most of Burma's ethnic minorities, however, remained ominously silent. Whatever was left of the *pax Britannica* was finally and forcefully shattered. Virtually no one was to remain untouched by the traumatic events of the next four years.

4

War and Independence: 1942-8

For a whole generation of Burmese of all classes, races and political beliefs, the Second World War was without doubt the major formative political experience. Burma was devastated as the armies of two colonial powers trampled across its soil. Few areas escaped unscathed. What the invading Japanese army did not destroy, retreating British soldiers burnt down in a calculated 'scorched earth' policy.[1] Three years later the pattern was repeated in reverse as the British 14th Army re-entered Burma from the north. The British and Japanese were not the only foreign forces fighting inside Burma; nationalist Chinese armies and various American units under Gen. Stilwell's command continued operations across much of the north-east throughout the war. Describing the Chinese army's treatment of the Kachin, one Frontier Service officer was moved to write: 'War is war, but it would be difficult to find a parallel of human suffering to that endured by the peaceful, loyal and simple Kachins of Burma at the hands of the Chinese.'[2]

As fighting swept to and fro across Burma it was virtually impossible for anyone to stand aside; it is largely in the perceptions of this war, so shortly before Burma's independence, that many of the revolutionary traditions developed which have fuelled over 40 years of insurgency.

The BIA, CPB and AFPFL Uprising

For the Burman majority the war marked nothing less than the start of a major and ultimately successful uprising for national independence. The *Thirty Comrades* and the Burma Independence Army (BIA) first fought on the Japanese side in the belief that Burma's independence, declared on 1 August 1943, would be their reward. In the Cabinet of the wartime head of state, Dr Ba Maw, served several of the key Thakin leaders who were to lead Burma's major political parties after the war. These included Thakin Than Tun of the CPB, Thakin Mya of the Socialist Party and Thakin Nu, Burma's first prime minister. Even the one non-Burman in the Cabinet, Thaton Hla Pe, played a part. He led the Pao insurrection that broke out in 1949 and was still leading his insurgent followers in 1975 when he died of ill-health in rebel-held territory.

Once the illusory nature of Burma's independence became clear, another resistance movement was launched. A new underground front, the Anti-Fascist Organisation (subsequently known as the AFPFL or Anti-Fascist People's Freedom League), was formed in August 1944 at a meeting of CPB, PRP and BNA (Burma National Army, the renamed BIA) leaders in Pegu.[3] Then, with the allied armies already converging on the Irrawaddy Delta, a second major uprising was launched, this time against the new Japanese rulers, which became an important factor in the swift conclusion to the allies' Burma campaign. On 27 March 1945 BNA units disappeared underground and turned on their Japanese instructors. Pressed on all sides by the allied forces and now harried by guerrilla attacks in the rear, Japanese lines of supply and communication in the Lower Delta swiftly began to break down. By 2 May Rangoon had fallen, with BNA units symbolically moving into the city two days in advance of the first allied troops. BNA forces continued to harass the retreating Japanese army and BNA leaders were later to claim to have inflicted some 16,000 casualties, including over 12,000 killed and 4,000 wounded.[4]

For all the successes of the anti-fascist resistance, the AFPFL essentially remained a united front in which several organisations played an important part. Of these, at least during the war years, the CPB without doubt played the most effective role, both politically and militarily. Its hand had been behind many of the key political and organisational decisions taken. Following the united-front line advanced by Georgi Dimitroff at the Seventh Comintern Congress in 1935, it was the Insein Manifesto written by Thakins Soe and Than Tun in Insein gaol in July 1941 which, against the prevailing opinion of the *Dobama* movement, first identified world fascism as the major enemy in the coming war and called for temporary cooperation with the British and the establishment of a broad allied coalition that should include the Soviet Union. The national liberation struggle, it was argued, would be resumed after the defeat of fascism.[5] Initially this line was ignored by the mainstream nationalist movement which, following Aung San, at first placed some faith in the Greater East Asia Co-prosperity Sphere rhetoric of the Japanese, though only a small faction under Dr Ba Maw showed any fascist leanings.

Thakin Soe, however, was to remain underground throughout the war, leading a perilous existence travelling between the Lower Delta and Arakan organising resistance and training cadres. Thakin Than Tun, now Minister for Land and Agriculture in the wartime Cabinet, remained in close contact, passing on Japanese Intelligence and publishing and circulating CPB material. In wartime conditions the CPB thus gained much valuable organisational experience. It rapidly expanded its membership and, in January 1944, at a secret meeting near Dedaye in the Delta, successfully held its First Congress chaired by Thakin Soe.[6]

Another high-ranking CPB official, Thakin Thein Pe, found his way to India in July 1942 and made contact with the British Burma government-in-exile. Though distrusted at first, he was eventually able to placate British fears to become the key link between British Intelligence and the anti-fascist resistance.[7] As a result training was given to some 70 volunteers (many of whom later joined the CPB) who made their way out to India and, towards the war's end, some 3,000 arms were dropped to the AFPFL resistance.

The CPB's influence was again critical in March 1945 when the decision to begin the anti-Japanese uprising was reached. It was the CPB's proclamation, *Independence Statement No. 4: The Time To Revolt Has Come*, the last of Thakin Soe's four wartime directives, issued on 27 February on the eve of the AFPFL's fateful meeting in Rangoon, that outlined the main tactical and organisational principles of the anti-Japanese resistance. CPB commanders and commissars already held many of the key positions in the resistance zones. Indeed the communist commander of the BNA's north-west military command, Bohmu Ba Htoo, hurried away early from the AFPFL meeting to order his units against the Japanese on 8 March, three weeks in advance of the main AFPFL uprising (and to considerable effect).[8] Soviet scholars estimate that units under CPB control inflicted as many as 50 per cent of all AFPFL casualties on the Japanese army and ended the war with nearly 40,000 resistance fighters under their control.[9] Speaking at the Second Congress of the Communist Party of India (CPI) in February 1948 Than Tun was in no doubt about the CPB's pre-eminent role: 'It is to the eternal glory of our Party that it is our Party which initiated, organised and led the anti-Japanese resistance, bringing it to a successful conclusion.'[10] Till today no CPB propaganda would be complete without reference to the revolutionary lessons learnt during the war.[11]

War and the National Minorities

The Burmese nationalist movement did not defeat the Japanese on its own. The ethnic minorities played an equally important role. But perhaps most cruelly in the light of the ethnic conflict which has divided Burma since independence, this is where things began to go badly wrong. In the many bitter convolutions of the war the different ethnic groups often came to stand on opposing sides. The Karen troops in the British Burma Army remained loyal to the British, as they had done in 1886 and in the Saya San rebellion of 1930-2, and suffered grievously as a consequence.

Tensions began to rise as soon as the first BIA troops re-entered Burma. The BIA was predominantly Burman. But while it was again the Indians who bore the brunt of the communal hostilities which broke out, many atrocities were reported in Karen villages, especially in Papun district in the eastern hills, where a number of Karen elders were taken hostage and executed, and in outlying rural areas of the Delta. No final figures have ever been tabulated of Karen casualties, but in Myaungmya district alone the official report put the Karen death toll at over 1,800 and recorded the destruction of 400 Karen villages.[12] In one notorious incident, 152 men, women and children were brutally murdered by the BIA, including the pre-war Cabinet minister, Saw Pe Tha, and his family.[13] For many terrified Karen villagers, the assassination of Pe Tha had a particularly grim irony. In 1938, in response to what many Karens believed were improving relations with their Burman neighbours, Pe Tha had joined the other leaders of the Karen National Association, Sir San C. Po, Sidney Loo Nee, Thaton Hla Pe and Thra Shwe Ba, in issuing an appeal for national unity to the Karen people on the eve of the first Karen New Year's Day. As they put it: 'Progressive in thinking, constructive in planning, and courageous in living, we can share responsibilities with other communities for the making of a united people.'[14]

The death of Pe Tha and the many violent massacres of the war have never been forgiven or forgotten by Karen leaders. According to another KNA leader, Saw Tha Din, who was a member of the Karen Goodwill Mission to London in 1946 and a future leader of the Karen insurrection: 'How could anyone expect the Karen people to trust the Burmans after what happened during the war — the murder and slaughter of so many Karen people and the robbing of so many Karen villages? After all this, how could anyone seriously expect us to trust any Burman government in Rangoon?'[15]

There can be little doubt that there were unscrupulous local politicians who used the opportunity to settle old scores. But today survivors (and also from Arakan where similar attacks were reported on Indian and Muslim villagers) are adamant that members of the Thakin movement did much to instigate these incidents. The Karens were clearly regarded as potential fifth-columnists, a view confirmed in a report in December 1942 by the new home secretary, U Paing, to the prime minister, Dr Ba Maw, in which he gave two reasons for the killings, the 'excesses' of the BIA and the 'loyalty of the Karens towards the British'.[16] Though Burman leaders such as Aung San, Than Tun and Thakin Soe worked to try and calm the situation, it was already too late and many old fears, lying largely dormant during the era of British rule, were instantly revived. Saw Tha Din, who led a KNA delegation to Rangoon to plead for help from Col. Suzuki (*aka* Minami), the Japanese commander of the BIA, today remains convinced that but for the swift Japanese intervention, Karen casualties could have been far worse.[17]

Nor did Dr Ba Maw help the situation by trying at first to ignore the Christian KNA leaders and instead work only with representatives of its Buddhist wing, the BKNA. It was, in fact, not until 1943 that, realising the BKNA's limitations, he asked Christian leaders to set up a new front, the Karen Central Organisation (KCO), and a KNA leader, Thaton Hla Pe, an ethnic Pao, was appointed Minister of Forests and the veteran Karen nationalist, San C. Po, a member of the Privy Council. After this, on 13 August 1943, Tokyo Radio reported that the Karen-Burman strife had ended.[18] Eventually two Karen battalions under San Po Thin and the Sandhurst-trained Hanson Kyadoe joined the BNA in the Lower Delta, though only after meetings with Aung San, Than Tun and Ne Win had convinced them that Aung San was preparing to turn the BNA against the Japanese.[19]

These, however, were Delta Karens trapped by the Japanese occupation. The majority of Karens and their close Karenni cousins joined rather more enthusiastically with British underground forces, which had remained in contact throughout the war. Hundreds of others made their way out with the British to India. Over 12,000 weapons were supplied to them by air-drop (more than four times the amount supplied to the AFPFL), which they were to turn with considerable effect on the retreating Japanese forces in 1945. Karen and Karenni guerrillas were later estimated to have killed over 12,500 Japanese troops retreating through the eastern hills.[20] Theoretically they were now fighting as BNA allies, but much damage had already been done and many Karens had started to plan for independence. Four years later most of these Karen units were to go straight into rebellion and virtually the entire present leadership of the KNU saw military service on the British side in the Second World War. Even more significantly, the Karen forces were made up of both hill and plains Karens, i.e. Buddhists, Christians and Animists without distinction. 'If this war has awakened and aroused nationalism,' warned the KNU in 1947, 'it has not left the Karens untouched or asleep.'[21]

The Kachins and Chins, too, for the most part, remained loyal to the British; parts of the Kachin hills, along with remote areas of the Naga and Chin hills, were the only districts of Burma not to have fallen to the Japanese. Various Kachin, Naga and Chin levies performed invaluable service for the allied armies; only U Vamthu Mawng's small Chin force in Kanpetlet and in the Pakokku hill tracts, later much lionised by the Burmese press, joined with the BNA for the AFPFL uprising.[22]

For the Kachins, in particular, the Second World War brought an extraordinary political awakening. Indeed for a few brief moments in 1945 the sleepy airfield at Myitkyina was by some estimates the busiest in the world. But, ominously, doubts were raised over the BIA's wartime behaviour which did not bode well for the future. The best known Kachin commander, Naw Seng, was to lead his troops into rebellion with the KNU in 1949 before embarking on what was perhaps the most remarkable career of any of the insurgent leaders. After leading the short-lived Pawng Yawng uprising of 1949/50 he returned to Burma from China in 1968 as commander of the CPB's North-East Command.[23]

The situation amongst the Shans was even more confusing. Though the Shan states (with the important exception of Kengtung and Mong Pan which were given to Siam) were joined by treaty to Burma in 1943, Shan nationalists today believe that Japanese recognition, following the British precedent, of the traditional Shan *Sawbwas* as the rightful rulers of the hills and a prohibition on armed Burman units from entering their territory, are further proof of the historic independence of the Shan peoples. Indeed, it has even been argued that the ease with which sovereignty over a large part of Shan territory was handed over from a colonial administration in Rangoon to their Thai cousins in Bangkok only confirms the political separateness of the Shans from Burma.[24] None the less, a number of Shans served with the allied forces, while towards the end of 1944 Bo Kyaw Zaw trained one Shan company as a separate unit within the BNA.[25] But, in general, most Shans, like the Was, Akhas and other local hill peoples, preferred to try and sit the war out in their remote highland homes.

Of all the ethnic minorities, it was in fact only in Arakan that the local Buddhist Rakhine population cooperated wholeheartedly with the BIA/AFPFL, though, significantly, the Muslim population worked with the British, especially the underground V Force and, as a result, there were serious Muslim/Buddhist clashes during the war. But here, too, the role of the Arakanese nationalist movement has been much overlooked, largely submerged as it is in most contemporary accounts of the CPB and the AFPFL. A spontaneous and independent uprising of the Arakanese Defence Army (the Arakan branch of the BNA) on 1 January 1945 helped the allied forces clear Arakan of Japanese forces even before the main AFPFL uprising at the end of March. There was later great resentment over the actions taken by the British military administration, known as the Civil Affairs Service (Burma), in disarming the Arakanese resistance. Several top leaders, including the Arakan Defence Army chief, Bo Kra Hla Aung, were arrested and, in 1947, even before independence, the most famous of these, the *pongyi* U Seinda, took many of his old resistance fighters underground to lead the movement for an independent Arakan State. Meanwhile, in the far north a separatist Muslim *Mujahid* movement plotted to take the old Mayu Division out of Arakan and into the newly created Muslim state of East Pakistan. Today, over 45 years on, the same insurgent divisions persist.

Thus, out of these diverse wartime experiences markedly different perceptions were to surface. In a sense all had emerged as victors. Burma had been briefly united, even if only in name. The leaders of the AFPFL, the CPB and the BNA, as well as the ethnic minorities, had gained first-hand experience of leading their own peoples. At the same time some worrying precedents had been set. With the British continuing to recruit ethnic Kachin, Karen and Chin battalions while the Japanese-trained BNA remained predominantly Burman, the war had been fought along largely racial lines.[26] This was reflected in the emerging political movements. Perhaps even more ominously, the wartime experience led many young nationalists of very different political belief and persuasions to realise the potential of armed struggle in the political upheavals to come. Many of the campaigns and battles that have raged across Burma since independence have eerie echoes of the campaigns of the war.

The Battle for Independence, CPB-AFPFL Splits and the Death of Aung San
As the war came to an end the British government was slow to wake up to the new realities in Burma. The idea that it should become self-governing in some form (the model of Switzerland was often mooted) was generally accepted in principle, but no concrete plans were made. The first draft plan, the *Blue Print for Burma*, an unofficial policy document produced in November 1944 by a group of young Conservative MPs and approved by the exiled governor Sir Reginald Dorman-Smith, envisaged the reintroduction of direct rule for a 'reconstruction period' of up to six years, but concluded that the Frontier Areas 'should not form part of the proposed Burmese dominion until such time as they clearly express a desire to join it.'[27] The first official statement of British policy, the White Paper of 17 May 1945, accepted eventual self-government for Burma with dominion status within the British Commonwealth, possibly within three to four years, but wanted the Frontier Areas to remain under British government control 'until such time as their inhabitants signify their desire for some suitable form of amalgamation with Burma proper.'[28] But nowhere in these documents was the scale of the country-wide uprising or the role of the AFPFL acknowledged. Indeed Dorman-Smith at first appeared to try to work with only pre-war politicians, such as Paw Tun and U Saw, who were now largely discredited and had little influence in the war-ravaged countryside. The request by an AFPFL delegation to visit London was rejected and Dorman-Smith was to persist to the end of his tenure as governor in considering to bring Aung San to trial for his role in the execution of a Muslim village headman in Thaton during the war, a move which would no doubt have had the most serious consequences.

Now faced with the task of restoring order, the British military, by contrast, had little doubt about the depth of nationalist feeling. Reports filtering back from the front acknowledged not only the degree of support the AFPFL forces enjoyed but also their true objectives. Warned Lt.-Gen. Slim, commander of the Fourteenth Army, in May 1945: 'It is my opinion that the young Burman of today regards us merely as a lesser evil than the Japanese. His real ambition is to be quit of all foreign rule and to establish a Burmese government for this country.'[29]

Perhaps more than any other leading post-war British figure, Lord Mountbatten, supreme allied commander of South-East Asia, recognised the rising tide of Asian nationalism and the inevitability of independence for Britain's Asian colonies. With responsibility to a far larger theatre of war than the Burma campaign, he was well aware of the dangers of continuing to place too much reliance on the indigenous (largely Indian) forces under his command. He recognised it was only a question of time before the British would have to give way.

A rift was thus to develop with Dorman-Smith over the treatment of the AFPFL. Having already accepted the principle of dropping arms to Karen guerrillas, Mountbatten decided to support and arm the AFPFL's uprising. Then, at the war's end he afforded recognition to the BNA and offered what in effect turned out to be a general amnesty.[30] After presiding over the victory parade in Rangoon in June 1945 he met three of the key men of the hour, Gen. Aung San, commander of the BNA, Col. Ne Win and Than Tun, general-secretary of the AFPFL, and, promising independence within three and a half years, concluded an outline agreement on the absorption of the BNA (now to be renamed the Patriotic Burmese Forces, PBF) into the new Burma Army. This agreement was finalised in September 1945 at the Kandy conference at which Dorman-Smith still refused to negotiate directly with Aung San. At this point, and much to the surprise of the British, Aung San turned down the offer of a high-ranking military appointment to enter into the political arena.

But if Mountbatten brought to Burma a fresh eye and an awareness of issues beyond the confines of Burma, he was also to make one more crucial, though perhaps unwitting, decision. By immediately recognising the role of the national liberation movement and allowing Aung San centre stage (Churchill, by contrast, called Aung San a 'traitor rebel leader'[31]) Mountbatten took much of the ground away from the communists. Aung San, though he remained close to CPB leaders, had begun to distance himself from the communist movement and to maintain a broadly nationalist position. It is tempting to make comparisons with Indo-China and Vietnam. Where similar recognition was not accorded Ho Chi Minh and the national liberation movement in the anti-Japanese resistance. The Vietnam Communist Party was later able to retain control over the political direction of the nationalist movement, but in Burma, as British historian Hugh Tinker puts it, 'as early as May 1945 the political future was decided virtually in favour of Aung San and the AFO [AFPFL].'[32] The AFPFL at first refused the offer of positions on the Governor's Executive Council, claiming instead the right to nominate members as it chose. But once the AFPFL finally took up these positions in September 1946, a move bitterly denounced by the CPB and one which precipitated the CPB's final break with the AFPFL, the AFPFL's domination of all political dealings with the British government was complete.

However, for the present, even if the British had accepted the inevitability of Burma's independence, freedom was still not in sight. AFPFL leaders recognised that independence might yet have to be won. Aung San and the AFPFL were to engage in a steady game of political brinkmanship to ensure there was no last-minute hesitation on the British part. Mass rallies and meetings continued to be staged up and down the country. The basic demands of the AFPFL were first outlined at a mass meeting at the Naythuyein Hall in Rangoon in August 1945.[33] In Arakan, meanwhile, Aung San allegedly wrote to U Seinda's resistance fighters, who were refusing to lay down their arms, supporting their decision 'to fight the British as guerrillas'; for tactical reasons, he explained, in central Burma the AFPFL would cooperate with the British.[34] In November another impressive mass rally, estimated to be the largest ever held in Burma, was staged at the Shwedagon Pagoda in Rangoon. British officials even believed one mass rally at the Shwedagon in January 1946 might signal the start of a general armed uprising.[35] Then, with the British apparently hesitating over the incorporation of the PBF into the Burma Army, Aung San again upped the political tempo by reforming BNA veterans into a loose paramilitary organisation, the *Pyithu Yebaw Tat*, known in English as the People's Volunteer Organisation (PVO). Wearing uniforms and openly drilling in public, the PVO greatly contributed to the escalating pressures on the British government. By independence it had swelled to an irregular force of over 100,000-strong which, in the insurgent turmoil of the 1950s, was to have a bizarre rebel life of its own.

By this time the growing rift between the CPB and the AFPFL was becoming obvious. The CPB's apparent hesitation at this stage has been the subject of much conjecture and its leaders have long since admitted to a series of tactical errors which were to cost it much valuable ground. At the war's end the AFPFL leadership was largely divided between three groups (the CPB, the People's Revolutionary Party, and a loose nationalist faction under Aung San), with the CPB probably having the edge in party organisation. But from here on, there was to be a growing divergence between the CPB leaders and their old comrades from the Thakin movement. Within a year the Socialist Party, re-formed in September 1945 from the PRP, had replaced CPB officials in nearly all key positions. Indeed for the first few months after the war, the Socialist Party appeared to take the more militant line towards the British. In the light of the serious splits in both the CPB and the AFPFL, which were now about to occur and which had grave implications for the communist movement in Burma, it is worth looking at subsequent events in closer detail.

The starting point for the CPB's troubles was its Browderist line of peaceful evolution adopted before the end of the war at its Second Congress in Rangoon's Bagaya Road in July 1945. This strategy had first been advocated in a policy document, *Toward Better Mutual Understanding and Greater Cooperation*, written by Thakin Thein Pe in India, where he had again been working closely with the CPI and its chairman, Joshi. Browderism followed an interpretation of world trends by the American Communist Party leader, Earl Browder, who, taking confidence from the advances national liberation and communist movements appeared to have made during the war, believed armed struggle would no longer be necessary. World fascism and imperialism, he argued, were being so weakened by the war that progressive political change, including national independence, could now be brought about by constitutional methods. In his address to the Congress, the party chairman, Than Tun, also took heart from the success of the Labour Party in the British general election, which he interpreted as a victory for the working people of Great Britain.[36]

There can be no doubt that the CPB's decision arose from its confidence in the party's leading role in the AFPFL. Of all the nationalist leaders probably only Than Tun, a former schoolmaster, stood next to Aung San, his brother-in-law, in terms of national prestige, a position the British had been quick to recognise. 'It was clear,' wrote Aubrey Buxton, 'that he was the thinker behind Aung San and the AFO [AFPFL].... Aung San referred to him repeatedly for his point of view.'[37] CPB officials retained influential positions across the country in both the AFPFL and PBF. At the end of the war the CPB had been able to increase recruitment considerably, particularly from PBF volunteers now being demobbed. So confident were they of their position that in June CPB leaders invited PRP followers to apply individually to join the CPB. (A previous attempt to merge the CPB and PRP into a united front, 'The Vanguard of the Revolution', in October 1944 had ended in failure.[38]) Failing that, they warned PRP leaders not to obstruct the programme of the AFPFL HQ. But in the context of the time the CPB's actions now seem remarkably conciliatory. Resolutions passed at the Congress called for full cooperation with the British and, if necessary, the surrender of arms. Only CPB commanders in the field raised any objections. For the first time, too, the one-man style of leadership of Thakin Soe, now replaced by Thein Pe as CPB secretary-general, came under fire.[39]

As a result a disastrous split in the communist movement was soon to develop with reverberations still felt today. In September 1945 Thakin Soe and fellow Politburo member, Ba Tin, travelled to India for talks with the CPI. Here Browderism was already under attack. Thakin Soe, who had apparently acquiesced to the peaceful evolution line at the Second Congress, now returned to

Burma convinced that the only way to achieve independence was through armed struggle. At a stormy CPB CC meeting on 22 February 1946, Thakin Soe denounced the reformist tactics of the CPB and urged it to give up its collaboration with the AFPFL and instead concentrate on leading and organising a revolutionary uprising of the working class. At the end of the meeting seven CC members defected with Thakin Soe to form a new breakaway party that came to be known as the Red Flag CPB (a term reputedly coined by Thakin Soe himself).[40] The other 19 CC members remained solidly behind Thein Pe and Than Tun. Ever the man of action, Thakin Soe immediately led the Red Flags underground and rapidly began to expand their activities, setting up their own local administrations in the rural districts of Pyapon, Pakokku, Tavoy and Arakan, all of which later became major centres of the Red Flag insurrection. By July his party was declared illegal and the Red Flags' long insurgency had begun.

The main White Flag faction remained above ground, officially at least, though by the week a more aggressive stance became clearly apparent.* CPB leaders now claim that by 1946 the Browderist line had been abandoned, though the evidence does not always back this up. Certainly the CPB's hand was behind many of the more violent protests that broke out. In one CPB-sponsored mass demonstration at Tantabin in June 1946, four people were killed when police opened fire on the crowd. In the countryside, meanwhile, Red Cultivators' unions were established and recruits enlisted from the PVOs. Here the activities of the Red Flags and White Flags often overlapped and many communist sympathisers appeared to be members of both groups. Hard-pressed British officers later admitted, to a mounting background of rural violence, that it was often impossible to distinguish Red Flag, White Flag, PVO or plain dacoit.

Inevitably strains in the AFPFL leadership became apparent. Vital to the success of peaceful evolution was the CPB's continued ability to dominate the AFPFL. During July and August 1946, however, the long simmering dispute over the AFPFL leadership broke into the open, with Aung San and the Socialist Party winning the day and, it would appear, carrying the majority of the AFPFL coalition with them. At the end of July Than Tun was forced to resign as general-secretary of the AFPFL, a post he had held since its inception, and was replaced by the socialist, U Kyaw Nyein. Than Tun was later blunt in his self-criticism: 'Owing to our shortcomings and weaknesses, we were outmanoeuvred.'[41]

Aung San had now built up a formidable power base inside both the Socialist Party and the AFPFL, as well as his private army, the PVOs. It was also clear that the deepening split in the CPB, compounded by its vacillation in 1945, had lost it much of its previous authority in the country. As the CPB acknowledged 40 years later in its Third Congress Report: 'The fruits of victory gained during the resistance against the Japanese fascists were therefore surrendered: armed units were

---

* While Thakin Soe always appeared happy with his party's militant Red Flag name, the term White Flag was more a convenient colloquial label to distinguish the two factions, generally avoided by White Flag leaders who insisted they were the true CPB. In this account, therefore, the title CPB, unless specified otherwise, will always refer to the mainstream White Flag party. The much smaller Red Flags will always be referred to separately. There has also been a tendency by Burmese governments, as well as Western writers, to refer to the White Flags as the Burma Communist Party or BCP and the Red Flags as the CPB. But this distinction is artificial and is rejected by communist leaders as too suggestive of a Burman racial orientation.

disbanded, a large quantity of arms were given up, and base areas were abandoned. The revolution in Burma suffered serious setbacks because of this revisionist line.'

During September the rift with the AFPFL continued. The final spark was Aung San's decision to take up the longstanding offer of seats on the Governor's Executive Council. During September the country had been paralysed by yet another round of demonstrations and strikes, which had begun with the police but had soon spread to government civil servants, students and oilfield workers. Though the original strike was ostensibly over pay and conditions, it was clear that both the socialists and communists were directing a political confrontation with the British authorities from behind the scenes. Aung San now used this breakdown to squeeze concessions out of the new governor, Sir Hubert Rance, who had arrived on the last day of August. Rance immediately took the decision that Dorman-Smith had hesitated to make, appointing Aung San, the AFPFL's nominee, counsellor for defence on the Executive Council (EC). The other AFPFL representatives now immediately agreed to join the EC. On 28 September a new eleven-man EC was named which for the first time included six AFPFL nominees, Aung San also being named deputy chairman, the same position Nehru had been granted in India. These posts were equivalent to ministers in the pre-war Cabinet and Aung San now became the effective prime minister. Only one CPB member was nominated, the largely discredited Thein Pe, the original instigator of the CPB's Browderist line, who was shortly to be forced into a six-month leave from the CPB for 'self-study and re-thinking'.[42]

Rance, however, received the response he wanted. On 2 October, with the AFPFL's apparent intervention, the strikes were called off. The CPB's reply was immediate and vitriolic. Its leaders accused the AFPFL leadership of a sell out and the communist-dominated All Burma Trade Union Congress immediately launched a new wave of strikes. The AFPFL responded with its own mass demonstrations and on 12 October its EC voted to expel the CPB. Ten days later the rift widened when, amidst growing acrimony, Thein Pe resigned from the Governor's Executive Council and bitterly denounced Aung San and the other EC members for surrendering 'to British duplicity'.[43] The split became final at a protracted meeting of the AFPFL Supreme Council in Rangoon from 1-3 November at which one CPB speaker after another accused the AFPFL leadership of acquiescing to British designs. After a curt final speech from Than Tun, the CPB members walked out.[44] It was then left to U Nu, the future prime minister, to propose the motion expelling the CPB. From this point on the Socialist Party nominees, Kyaw Nyein, Nu, Ba Swe and Thakin Mya (assassinated in July 1947) dominated the AFPFL and held virtually all the key positions in the first post-independence government.

With the break, British Intelligence immediately reported an increase in underground CPB activity, both Red Flag and White Flag, so much so that the ban on the Red Flags was lifted for a while since it was felt to be lending the rebels romantic appeal. Thakin Soe, who had been arrested on 31 October, was released on 11 November in an attempt to quell an outbreak of demonstrations. But he immediately disappeared underground again and remained bitter in his denunciations of both Aung San and the British.

The White Flags, meanwhile, still appeared ambivalent. At a CC meeting at the end of December, the CPB acknowledged criticism from the Indian Communist

Party for its Browderist line and the following month first discussed its future slogan, 'the final seizure of power'. None the less many communist supporters still appeared to believe that they could regain the AFPFL leadership. The building of a new 'Democratic Front based on AFPFL-Communist Party unity, without the collaborating bourgeois leadership' remained the central White Flag strategy until the outbreak of the CPB insurrection in March 1948.[45] CPB propaganda was mainly directed at the 'collaborators' on the AFPFL's EC. But the most virulent criticism was reserved for the two 'rightists' on the EC, U Ba Pe and Tin Tut. It was this that led the CPB, after initially denouncing the elections, to field 25 junior candidates in the April 1947 elections to the Constituent Assembly. Aung San, who also shared the CPB's concern over the emergence of rightist parties, met with CPB leaders to discuss the allocation of seats. The idea was for the CPB to oppose right-wing candidates, but eventually this logic led it to oppose some AFPFL candidates as well. According to the CPB's manifesto: 'Those who love the AFPFL should vote for communists because it means building a real AFPFL. Your votes will make the rightist leaders weak.'[46] In the event, both Ba Pe and Tin Tut were elected and the CPB won only seven seats in its Toungoo, Yamethin and Sandoway strongholds. Of the 182 electoral seats available in Burma Proper, 171 were won by the AFPFL coalition, mostly by socialists and PVOs.

Behind the scenes the White Flag CPB was now beginning to step up underground activities in several of its former wartime rural base areas, where arms had not been surrendered and activists were preparing for any eventuality. In March 1947 a major police/army operation, codenamed Operation Flush, was launched in the hills above Pyinmana, which remains a symbolic centre for the White Flag insurgency. In a striking rehearsal of counter-insurgency campaigns after independence, the commander of units of the new Burma Army making its first appearance was Col. Ne Win. CPB Politburo member, Ba Thein Tin, who had travelled to London for the British Empire Conference of Communist Parties, alleged that the government's aim was to shatter 'communist influence before elections to the All Burma Constituent Assembly'.[47] Meanwhile, in an address to a vast rally at the Cultivators' Union Congress in Pyu on 8 March, Than Tun himself publicly confirmed that the CPB 'was fighting the British Imperialists' and urged Aung San to reunite with the masses to overthrow the British.[48] Real freedom, he argued, would only be achieved by revolution and he called for the non-payment of rent, the forcible ploughing of new fields and the breach of forest laws. During the Congress, a CPB booklet, *Towards the Seizure of Power*, was openly circulated. Operation Flush, which resulted in dozens of casualties, did not end till May but, as British Intelligence noted, communist influence in the area was 'by no means eliminated'.[49]

Whether full-blown hostilities would have broken out before independence must remain a speculative question. But the devastating assassinations of Aung San and five Cabinet colleagues on 19 July 1947 clearly came as a severe jolt to the CPB. Than Tun, in particular, was devastated. According to one eye-witness, he stormed into the British club in Rangoon and began smashing glasses.[50] There are several unresolved mysteries about the murders. The pre-war prime minister, U Saw, who had previously enjoyed British support, was later tried and executed for his alleged role. Others have pointed their fingers in other directions, including at British Intelligence or a corrupt faction within the new Burma Army, claiming it inconceivable that Saw, amidst such tight security, could have planned the attack alone. Certainly his behaviour was remarkably nonchalant for a man apparently trying to seize power.[51]

The CPB itself was convinced the murders were part of an 'imperialist plot'. One reason for the strength of this belief became clear a few months later when CPB Politburo member, Ba Tin, revealed that at the time of his assassination Aung San had been talking to CPB leaders again about the formation of a new AFPFL/CPB united front. Just six days before he was killed, in what proved to be his epitaph speech in Bandoola Square, Rangoon, Aung San publicly alluded to his own growing political doubts by calling on the crowd to be 'united and disciplined' in the hard years ahead 'whether you have a communist government or a socialist government'.[52] Allegedly disappointed at the results of the Nu/Attlee talks which had just finished in London, Ba Tin claimed that Aung San was considering giving his support to a general strike the CPB was preparing for 15 August.

> Imperialism estimated that if things were allowed to take their own course, the rising would develop under communist initiative and the tempo of the united upsurge would be so powerful that Aung San could not be in a position to check it or sabotage it from within. That is why they decided to take no risks and kill Aung San.[53]

Now, according to Ba Tin, at a time ripe with revolutionary possibilities, the CPB was to make yet another crucial mistake. 'If we had acted *independently* of Thakin Nu and led the masses to mass protest actions, and called for an AFPFL-CP united front to take over power to avenge the murders and repel the British, the situation would have changed immensely in our favour.' Instead the CPB allowed itself to be sidetracked by drawn-out negotiations with U Nu, whom the governor had asked to succeed Aung San. The CPB in effect continued its conciliatory line. At a CC meeting on 30 July it adopted the new slogan, Turn the Provisional Government into a Real One. Behind this was the expectation that the CPB would be readmitted to the provisional government. But without doubt there was a very real fear that, with independence looming, further disturbances would only jeopardise the British withdrawal from Burma. According to Ba Tin, at a critical moment the CPB had again failed to inspire and lead the masses: 'We were panicked by the murders and we immediately went on the defensive.' From the end of July until October the CPB continued with talks that brought it no nearer to office. Only on the eve of independence, with the completion of Ba Tin's historic thesis, *On the Present Political Situation in Burma and Our Tasks*, did the CPB's future revolutionary line come out into the open.

The Expression of Ethnic Minority Fears

British attention was now focused on the CPB/AFPFL and the national liberation movement, but the ethnic minorities and hill peoples, who had generally stayed loyal to the British throughout the war, were largely neglected. Perhaps critically, unlike the AFPFL and CPB, the hill peoples never threatened to back up their cause with anti-British violence. (The one nationality force to attack the British in 1945/6, U Seinda's Rakhine guerrillas in the remote forests of central Arakan, came under the remit of Ministerial Burma and was not distinguished from other armed bands in mopping up operations at the end of the war.) But in view of the scale of the ethnic insurgencies which were soon to break out and the many warnings offered, the apparent lack of official British recognition at the time is all the more remarkable. As with the CPB, the seeds of future conflict were being sown.

At the end of the war British officials sent the minorities conflicting signals about their future intentions for Burma. Throughout the war individual British officers, especially in the underground services and in the various levies in the hills, had made promises and pledges of support to the Karen and Kachin troops under their command. Though still widely remembered today, these promises ultimately meant very little indeed. At the insurgent Karenni National Progressive Party headquarters, a copy is still kept of a plaque left behind by British officers from Force 136 commemorating the activities of the Karenni resistance in the Mawchi area. At the end of the war these promises seemed to be guaranteed in the *Blue Print for Burma* and the Government White Paper, both of which indicated that no decisions would be made on the Frontier Areas and their peoples without their full consent. Right up to independence, the hill peoples, particularly the Karens, continued to believe that, whatever the state of British negotiations with the AFPFL, they still had the ultimate right of self-determination. This is still the most contentious issue between the ethnic nationalists and the central government and explains, in part, the repeated failure of later peace negotiations.

It was from the Karens, who were the most closely intermingled with the Burman majority, that the first indications of serious political disagreements came. In September 1945, following a mass meeting of 'liberated Karens' in Rangoon, a Karen memorial for the creation of a United Frontier Karen States, which would include the entire Tenasserim Division as well as the Nyaunglebin subdivision of Pegu district and territory in Siam stretching as far as Chiang Mai, was sent to London but went unanswered.[54] Signed by Saw Tha Din, Saw Ba U Gyi and the leaders of the Karen Central Organisation (KCO) and addressed both to the British government and Conference of United Nations, the memorial explained that they expected this Karen 'Home Land' would eventually be expanded to incorporate the already 'excluded' Salween district in the Frontier Areas and their 'blood-brothers' in the Karenni states. Two months later, however, another KCO statement pledged the Karens' ultimate goal, once this state had been formed, was still 'federation' with 'our moderate and considerate Burmese brothers sympathising our national aspirations in the achievement of a Federated Dominion of Burma'.[55] But still worrying the KCO was the age-old fear of absorption by the Burman majority: 'The last three and a half years have shown us what can and most inevitably will happen to a small race or nation in the absence of a protecting power.' Therefore, for this federation to succeed, the continuance of British or Commonwealth protection was envisaged.[56]

The following April a mass meeting of Karens in Toungoo repeated the demand for a Karen state with the addendum that the form of government for this new territory should 'not be lower than that to be given to Burma'.[57] Again no official reply was forthcoming from a Labour administration in London preoccupied with the AFPFL/CPB and the rather more turbulent events in several other of Britain's overseas colonies. As in the 1930s, it was felt that Karen interests were sufficiently protected by Karen representation on the Governor's Executive Council, though it was sometimes recorded that at these meetings the Karen representatives, outnumbered by Burmans, would sit in sullen silence.[58]

Dissatisfied with the lack of response, a four-man Karen 'goodwill delegation' of trained lawyers (Saw Tha Din, Saw Ba U Gyi, Sidney Loo Nee and Saw Po Chit) travelled to Britain in August 1946. In London there was again no encouragement for any separatist demands.[59] But if the Burma Office recognised the seriousness of the situation that was developing, no action was taken. Valuable time was thus lost and perhaps the last opportunity for any kind of meaningful discussion was gone. From the end of 1946 there was an increasing divergence between Burman and Karen political leaders which was to erupt in violence soon after independence.

Meanwhile, in the thinly populated Karenni states, which had still not been incorporated into British Burma, the warnings of the strength of nationalist feeling were equally ominous. In September 1946 a United Karenni Independent States Council was formed and at the year's end a flag-day was celebrated with patriotic speeches.[60] By the middle of 1947 the faction of the Karenni leadership under U Bee Tu Re, which was soon to go into rebellion, had unilaterally declared the independence of the Karenni states. This action was supported by Karen leaders in the Delta who, harking back to the KNA's strategy in the 1930s, believed that the legality of the Karenni case lent weight to their own cause.[61]

Similar demands were being made by their more numerous cousins, the ethnic Paos, both in the Shan State, where a group of Pao *pongyis* were organising the *Pao Long Bu* (Pao Solidarity), which was to form the basis of the first Pao nationalist party after independence, and in Thaton district, where Pao, Sgaw and Pwo community leaders were working closely together. On the day of the full moon in March 1947, just as the Pao movement was gaining momentum, Pao villagers marched in traditional dress to the Shwe Sayan Pagoda in Thaton, to demand to be known in future government reports by their Karen name, Pao, instead of the Burmese, Taungthu. This date is still celebrated as Pao National Day by the insurgent nationalist movement. Once again the British turned a blind eye.

The Shans and Kachins, who were entirely under the Frontier Areas Administration (FAA) and thus less touched by the political unrest on the plains, cautiously watched the situation. Though their principal political spokesmen were still largely the traditional *Sawbwas* and *Duwas*, they appeared keen to protect their independence and resented the AFPFL's attempts to organise in the hills. In discussions with British officials, Kachin representatives raised the possibility of amalgamating with China, and the Shans with Siam. The Kachins, in particular, were concerned about the territorial integrity of a future Kachin State (Kachin-majority areas, including the state capital, Myitkyina, had been carved into different districts by the pre-war British administration) and the threat of armed struggle was briefly raised. In January 1946 a great victory *Manao* (festival) was celebrated at Myitkyina to which the governor Dorman-Smith was invited though not, in a pointed snub, Aung San and the AFPFL because of 'their connection with the BIA'. Aung San then put out a press release declining 'an invitation which was never sent', thereby raising Kachin hackles still further.[62]

But, in general, both the Kachins and Shans had a wait-and-see attitude to the situation and were prepared to enter into any negotiations conducted in good faith. In March 1946 the Shan *Sawbwas* sponsored a conference at Panglong to discuss the future of the Shan states, to which representatives of the Chin, Kachin and Karen were invited. Though little of any substance was achieved, the anti-British diatribe of the one AFPFL politician to attend, U Nu, was ill-advised and considerably raised the political temper.[63] The speech of U Saw, later executed for his role in Aung San's assassination, was better received. A message from the governor was also read out which was largely a restatement of White Paper

policy. Of the other speakers few records survive. Chin delegates warned that they
were in no position to talk 'too roughly to Burma, upon whom they rely for
food.'[64] But the mood of the conference was perhaps best summed up by a declaration of the Kachin elders. Refuting U Nu's criticism of the British, they asked:

> What have the Burmese public done towards the hill peoples to win their love and
> faith? It was through the influence of a section of the Burmese public who, while
> saying that we all belong to the same race, blood and home, called in our enemies, the
> Japanese, that the hill peoples have suffered miserably during those dark years that
> followed.

But they did hold out some hope:

> For the hill peoples the safeguarding of their hereditary rights, customs and religions
> are the most important factors. When the Burmese leaders are ready to see this is done
> and can prove that they genuinely regard the hill peoples as real brothers equal in every
> respect to themselves shall we be ready to consider the question of our entry into close
> relations with Burma as a free dominion.[65]

Another request was for a 'back door' road from the Frontier Areas through a
separate Karen State via Papun and Moulmein to the sea. This would have
reduced the economic dependence of the Frontier Areas on the central plains. To
this day no such road has been constructed. But on the positive side, as far as the
British were concerned, was the formation of a United Burma Cultural Society
with Sao Shwe Thaike, the Yawnghwe *Sawbwa*, as chairman and U Saw as
secretary.

Contacts between the hill peoples and the AFPFL slowly improved. One
important intermediary was the Kachin Sama *Duwa*, Sinwa Nawng, who,
uniquely amongst the Kachins' predominantly Christian leaders, was a Buddhist
whose father had reputedly been killed while leading the spirited resistance to the
British in the Sama region at the turn of the century. Staunchly anti-British,
Nawng had followed in his father's footsteps, raising local Kachin levies to work
with the BNA during the Second World War. Another BNA ally, U Vamthu
Mawng, who attended the AFPFL's historic Naythuyein conference in 1945, was
credited by Burman leaders with performing a similar placatory role in the Chin
hills. As a reward, both men were appointed Cabinet ministers in the first AFPFL
government in 1948.

Another pragmatic voice was that of the *Sawbwa* of the predominantly Pao
substate of Hsihseng (Hsahtung), Sao Khun Kyi, who tragically died of a stroke
on the brink of independence. Representing the Pao minority in a Shan state (with
almost feudal powers he reportedly refused to use), Khun Kyi strongly believed in
political bridge building through discussion to prevent the national minorities
being swallowed up by the Burman majority.

It was as a result of the influence of traditional minority leaders like these that in
November 1946, at the AFPFL's urging, a Supreme Council of the United Hills
Peoples was formed with Sao Shwe Thaike, who was also to become Burma's first
president, elected president. But an ominous practice was becoming evident.
Whereas AFPFL leaders were in near continuous consultation with British
officials, minority leaders, still relying on the guarantees of the White Paper, were
continuing to petition London and the FAA directly. As a result there were very
real misconceptions developing over British policy in Burma.

It was H.N.C. Stevenson, now director of the FAA, who was to sound the warnings. In June 1946, predicting the very real possibility of a Karen rebellion, he urged far more serious treatment of Karen demands and called for a proper census of the Karen population. His intention, he said, was to forestall 'letting things drift to the point of Karenistan' (i.e. secession) by creating a Karen territory inside the Frontier Areas. His predictions proved ominously correct. Fortifying the Karen now was:

> the knowledge gained in four years of guerrilla war — that if they go all out for their demands they have the guts, the skill, and the allies (the northern tribes) necessary to wrest them from the Burmese by force, if other means will not prevail. The only thing that restrains them is the belief that we will repay their loyalty by giving them a homeland. I have come to the regrettable conclusion that the present Karen quiescence means simply that they refuse to quarrel with us. But when we go, if go we do, the war for the Karen State will start.[66]

Stevenson was criticised by British and Burman observers alike; in Burma today his name stands high in the pantheon of colonial demonology. That the AFPFL should have dogged his footsteps is not surprising, for there was a not unreasonable fear that any hesitation on the part of the British in granting the Frontier Areas independence would adversely affect the Burman drive for freedom. Moreover, a severely truncated Burma (with the Karen demanding the whole of the Tenasserim Division and the Shan, Kachin and Karenni all showing signs of considering a future outside Burma) would have left a skeletal and much reduced new nation. The watersheds of all the main rivers would have lain in countries outside Burma whose political reliability could no longer be counted on. There was also concern that giving serious concessions to the Frontier peoples and Delta Karens would only encourage the growingly restive Mon and Arakanese to increase their own political demands. The situation was fraught with possibilities. The worst (but by no means impossible) scenario would be for the British to create a separate dominion from the Frontier Areas where they would remain and for years to come try to exert leverage on the plains.

The reaction of the Burma Office is less understandable. There was little support for Stevenson amongst a very inexperienced new generation of colonial officers; the war had decimated the ranks of the pre-war administration. Only D.B. Petch, the commissioner of the Tenasserim Division, came out in public support of the Karen demands and was, like Stevenson, bitterly criticised by the AFPFL.[67] British civil servants' decisions invariably reflected the Labour government's desire to find as quick and smooth a way to Burma's independence as possible. The time for political experiment was past. Nor should it be forgotten that the negotiations leading up to independence were overshadowed by the even more convulsive transitions to independence of India and Pakistan, which were of far greater concern in London. When at one particularly delicate moment a minute paper concerning the odd anomaly of the Karenni states landed on PM Attlee's desk, he reacted with great irritation: 'It should be obvious to the Burma Office that at a time when we are considering the future of the Indian states it is most inopportune to deal with this question.' 'Petulant,' added one civil servant.[68]

From the safe distance of London, government officials completely underestimated the depth of feeling amongst the minorities. 'Abysmally ignorant,' was Stevenson's description many years later of his colleagues at the Burma Office.[69] Worse still, when conflicting reports did arise, they suppressed the news and concealed it from both Parliament and the British public.[70] In Parliament there were still politicians, not least Winston Churchill, yet to be reconciled to the independence of Britain's colonies. Perhaps the best indication of civil servant feeling was expressed by L.B. Walsh-Atkins, principal at the Burma Office:

> The phrase 'homogeneous Karen area' may sound superficially innocent and attractive, but it is submitted that it has most undesirable potentialities particularly when one considers how it might be interpreted by the government of Burma among whom are some whose concern and enthusiasm about the undoubted merits and deserts of the non-Burmese peoples of Burma may perhaps lead them to lose sight of the wood in their concentration on the trees.... We shall, it is submitted, be betraying this wider responsibility if we lend ourselves to facile talk about 'race' and encourage the spread to Burma of this plaguey 'nationalism'; in short, that we must do nothing to promote, and whatever we can do to avoid, the Balkanisation of Burma.[71]

Caught between his critics in the AFPFL and the Burma Office, Stevenson eventually resigned in frustration at the end of 1946. But 45 years on the problem of the minorities appears to have become remarkably personalised. Stevenson's departure changed very little; it merely removed from the scene one of the best informed and most knowledgeable voices. Stevenson had never argued for the dissection of British Burma, but rather had tried to find a more gradual and equitable way to eventual integration. As director of the FAA he was only too aware of the consequences of the neglect of the Frontier Areas during the era of British rule. After his resignation he was to protest:

> I have never been other than what I proclaim myself to be, that is, a believer in and propounder of the unpopular (in the hills) theme of a United Burma, an ex-officio spokesman who had tried for over long to secure a medium through which the hill men can speak for themselves the unpleasant truths which have made some of my opinions so unpopular.[72]

Certainly Stevenson's stream of reports and recommendations bear this out and, as perhaps the last alternative proposals for the hills, are worth closer examination. He was deeply critical of the lost opportunities in the era of British rule. He decried the lack of real economic analysis or coordination between the Frontier Areas and Ministerial Burma. Indeed he found no real figures had ever been kept of the volume of trade between the hills and plains. His solution was simple: 'I believe that the multiplication of and strengthening of the economic relations between the hills and the plains will be the shortest and most inexpensive route to a unified Burma.'[73]

In this view Stevenson has many surprising allies. Aung San, who was one of his most persistent critics and frequently quoted Lenin and Stalin in his discussion of the minority question, identified the same priorities in his *Blueprint for a Free Burma* written in Japan:

> the essential prerequisite is the building of one unified nation. In concrete terms it means we must now bridge all gulfs now existing through British machinations between the major Burmese race and the hill peoples, the Arakanese, the Shans and unite all these peoples into one nation with equal treatment unlike the present system which divides our people into 'backward' and 'administered' sections. All the natural barriers that make mutual associations and contacts shall be overcome, for instance, by construction of effective modern communications such as railways and roads.[74]

Soviet scholars followed the same theme: 'Lenin considered the main feature in the forming of a nation to be the consolidation of economic ties between the previously isolated territorial groups of the country's population, and the merging of local markets in a common national market. The common national market takes shape, of course, within the political boundaries of the state and not within separate ethnoi.'[75]

Even after his departure, Stevenson continued to warn London of the grave situation: 'At the time I left Burma the Karens were I believe under the impression that something was being done for them in London.... I feel it is necessary that it should be made abundantly clear to them that all action rests with them and that *nothing* is being or can be done by London.'[76]

Tragically this was never done. Right up to independence Karen leaders continued to petition the British government directly and to try and bypass the AFPFL. Crucially the KNU, established in February 1947 and by far the most influential of all the Karen political organisations, boycotted both the Governor's Executive Council and the elections to the Constituent Assembly, which devised Burma's new Constitution. The vacancies were usually filled by AFPFL protégées whose standing in the Karen community was often negligible. Even some of the more respected ones, such as San Po Thin and Kyaw Sein from the Karen Youth Organisation (KYO), eventually rebelled. But by then a section of the Karen leadership had long given up any hope of a negotiated settlement. Many KNU veterans today admit that by that stage they had already resolved to take up arms after independence come what may and had started preparations even before the British left. Independence thus came with the Karen question unresolved and the KNU, like the Red Flag CPB, already outside the political mainstream.

Panglong and the 1947 Constitution
With the arrival of the new governor, Mountbatten's old deputy, Maj.-Gen. Rance, at the end of August 1946, British policy underwent a significant change and took on a new urgency. By agreeing to AFPFL demands and its historic accession to his Executive Council, Rance found himself swiftly outmanoeuvred. While the strikes were called off, the AFPFL issued a new memorandum, 'Proposals for the Immediate Demand of a Fuller Measure of Self-Government', which to all intents and purposes now appeared as a statement of EC policy. Rance immediately informed London, 'the White Paper is now out of date.'[77] Attlee took this up in a speech to Parliament at the end of the year in which he promised that political developments in Burma would keep in step with India. Only Churchill's voice was raised in objection at this 'extraordinary haste'.[78]

Throughout 1947 events continued to move with the same dramatic speed. On 2 January Rance cabled Pethwick-Lawrence at the Burma Office about a completely new approach:

> We should start with the premise that there is only one Burma and that the part known as Ministerial Burma and that known as the Frontier Areas are merely parts of the whole. They have been one in the past and they must remain one in the future so that our ultimate aim is always a united Burma in the shortest possible time.[79]

Aung San and a delegation of Burman leaders now proceeded to London for the series of historic meetings with the British government which were to result in the Attlee-Aung San agreement of 27 January. It was not a unanimous decision. Two of the delegation, U Saw and Thakin Ba Sein, refused to sign the final declaration and, back in Burma, Than Tun and Thakin Soe denounced the agreement.[80] In view of its historic significance, it is worth noting that no delegates were present from the ethnic minorities. The two Karen representatives on the EC were simply not invited. From the Frontier Areas Kachin and Shan leaders cabled warnings that they would not regard any agreement as binding.[81] Questions were raised in the British Parliament, for by now the situation was becoming increasingly untenable for the British government. Reports from Burma warned of the increasing inability of the British military to control the situation for much longer. British officials believed there was a very real possibility of an AFPFL/CPB uprising should the discussions fail. Aung San was widely believed to have set a deadline for 31 January for the talks to succeed. Indeed during the talks some 850 Red Flag CPB supporters, led by Thakin Soe, stormed and occupied the Secretariat building in Rangoon.[82] Intelligence officers warned that any delay would only play into the CPB's hands. Advised one report: 'There is no other course than to grant demands at once.'[83] Cabled Rance: 'AFPFL is the only horse to back.'[84]

Though no exact timetable was laid down, the Attlee-Aung San agreement set out what was to be the course of events leading up to Burma's independence. In April elections would be held to a Constituent Assembly to determine the future Constitution. In the meantime the AFPFL-dominated EC would function as an interim government. Significantly, there was no longer any mention of any separate Frontier or Karen states; and though in private Attlee continued to insist that the Frontier Areas be 'fully consulted' and not coerced into the future Union, he appeared to accept all Aung San's guarantees.[85] Aung San argued what had always been the AFPFL position, i.e. that it was only British machinations that had kept the peoples of Burma apart (he pointed a finger at Stevenson) and in a much quoted speech declared the way to the future:

> We can confidently assert here that so far as our knowledge of our country goes, there should be no insuperable difficulties in the way of a unified Burma provided all races are given full freedom and the opportunity to meet together and to work without the interference of outside interests. So far as we are concerned, we stand for full freedom of all the races of our country, including those so-called Karenni states, and we hold strongly the view that no such race and no regime in our country should now be denied the fruits of the freedom that must shortly be achieved by our country and our people.[86]

The question now was to put these views to the test.

An opportunity afforded itself at the second Panglong conference in February 1947. A complete account of what actually took place at Panglong has yet to be written, but it was largely on the basis of this meeting that the principle of the formation of a Union of Burma was agreed; any lingering British doubts about the ability of Aung San and the AFPFL to mediate with the Frontier leaders were satisfied. Aung San did much to allay fears about the unequal treatment of the Frontier peoples in a future Union. In a famed saying, which has since become a byword among ethnic nationalists, Aung San assured: 'If Burma receives one kyat, you will also get one kyat.' In the final Panglong agreement of 12 February, 23 representatives from the Shan states, the Kachin hills and the Chin hills signalled their willingness to cooperate with 'the interim Burmese government'. A representative of the Supreme Council of the United Hills Peoples would now be appointed to the Governor's Executive Council and the Frontier Areas brought within the 'purview of the Executive Council'. But this would not mean the ending of the Frontier Areas' traditional self-rule. Clause Five guaranteed: 'Full autonomy in internal administration for the Frontier Areas is accepted in principle.'

There were, however, several serious shortcomings. Representatives of the Karen and Karenni were again conspicuous by their absence. Four Karen observers did attend but took no part in the proceedings. Nor were there any Arakanese or Mon delegates from Ministerial Burma, or elected representatives of other minority peoples from the Frontier Areas, such as the Pao and Wa; they were all bypassed by the agreements reached. But many observers still considered the 'spirit of Panglong' more important than any specific details and the anniversary of the Panglong agreement is still celebrated as Burma's Union Day. But in the rebel 'liberated zones' these celebrations have long had a very hollow ring. Ethnic leaders claim that their last residue of goodwill for the Panglong agreement dissipated when Ne Win seized power in 1962 and tore up the 1947 Constitution. Indeed, amongst the dozens of political leaders Ne Win arrested was Sao Shwe Thaike, the Yawnghwe *Sawbwa* and ex-president of Burma (1948-52), who more than any other ethnic leader worked to gain minority agreement at Panglong. Never forgotten by the Shan people, his youngest son was shot and killed by a soldier on the night of the coup, while Shwe Thaike himself died in military custody shortly afterwards. Clearly a new Panglong agreement will one day need to be reached to restore the spirit of Union.

The inadequacies of the agreements reached at Panglong swiftly became apparent after independence. On the eve of the conference Chin, Kachin and Shan leaders met and agreed on a number of united demands, including the same political rights and privileges as the Burmans, the continued right of political autonomy and the right of secession from the proposed federation. But after a week of hard bargaining a number of individual agreements were reached. The exact chronology of these pacts and understandings is still unclear.[87] Some were made at Panglong, others finalised later. But the general terms of these agreements were to resurface in the Constituent Assembly and ultimately in the Constitution adopted on 24 September 1947. The result was a Constitution as lopsided and riddled with inconsistencies as any treaty drawn up in the era of British rule. In short, it was a recipe for disaster.

As Josef Silverstein points out, though the Constitution made no mention of the words 'federal' or 'federalism', it was clear that this was its main intention.[88] Power was to be divided between Burma Proper and the ethnic states. Though Burman representatives would predominate in both Houses, Burma was to have a bicameral legislature with a 125-seat Chamber of Nationalities and a 250-seat Chamber of Deputies. The Shan states were to be reconstituted as one, with the extraordinary right of secession (Articles 201-6) after a ten-year trial period, a right apparently adapted from the Constitution of the Soviet Union. A 50-man State Council, whose members would also serve in the Union Parliament (25 in each House), would become the supreme legislative body for the state but at the local level 33 of the hereditary *Sawbwas* would retain their traditional powers and could not be removed. The Karenni states were similarly to be reconstituted as one with the same right of secession. The Kachins, however, apparently abandoned this right in return for the inclusion in the new Kachin State of the two major towns of Myitkyina and Bhamo. A 19-member Kachin Council would be established whose members would similarly be represented in Parliament but, in deference to the pressure of Burman AFPFL activists in the towns, half of these had to be non-Kachins. But in the Kachin-majority hills the traditional headmen and *Duwas* would again be allowed to continue their administration.

The Chins, who were politically quiescent, ethnically divided and always ready to acknowledge their dependence on Ministerial Burma, ended up without even a state; instead they were formed into a Special Division, with few of the political privileges of the Shans and Kachins. The new Chin Council would only be advisory.

Even more inconsistently, in a complex set of arrangements the final designation and status of a Karen territory and political rights were left to be decided after independence, while the Mon and Arakanese of Ministerial Burma, who were also about to go into rebellion, received no distinctive recognition at all. Indeed throughout 1947 there were mounting reports coming in from Arakan (where Rakhine nationalists led by the charismatic *pongyi*, *Sayadaw* U Seinda, frequently merged with Red Flag guerrillas) that the rebellion had already begun. British officers preferred to label it 'dacoitry'. The evidence, however, was over-whelming.

The Threat of Insurrection: Arakan, KNDOs and MNDOs

Historically, the most glaring of all the 1947 Constitution's many failings was its muddled attempt to resolve the Karen question. But even before the British left, in the largely unreported experience of Arakan there were also clear warnings of the dangers of the political centre in Rangoon seeking to impose solutions on the national minorities without taking full account of their opinions. For this reason, the events in Arakan deserve closer examination.

The Rakhine nationalist movement had developed along three diverging lines: a small pro-British parliamentary wing led by Sir Paw Tun and U Kyaw Min, which later did surprisingly well in the elections of the 1950s; the pre-war Arakan National Congress (ANC) led by U Aung Zan Wai, an AFPFL EC member close to Aung San; and a militant nationalist faction led by U Seinda, which broke away from the ANC in November 1945 to form the Arakan People's Liberation Party (APLP).[89] Zan Wai, admitting his own errors, later put much of the blame on Aung San for the depth of these schisms. Having earlier encouraged U Seinda's armed resistance, in March 1946 Aung San toured Arakan with an AFPFL EC delegation, including Thakin Mya and Zan Wai, and, at a secret meeting in Minbya, convinced ANC leaders headed by *Sayadaw* U Pyin-nya Thi Ha not to waste time trying to reform local ANC branches shattered by the war but to dissolve the party and join the AFPFL as individuals.[90] Arguing that the time set for Burma's independence at the Naythuyein conference (January 1948) was running out, the 'urgency of the situation', he told them, called for a 'united national organisation'. They unanimously agreed and the ANC was formally dissolved into the AFPFL in 1947.

According to Zan Wai, however, far from hastening national unity, they soon found that they had left the door open to the 'interference of Burma Proper' in the 'peaceful political arena of Arakan'.[91] Despite heated arguments with Thakin Mya, U Kyaw Nyein and the AFPFL leaders in Rangoon, the socialist and communist parties from the AFPFL coalition (which were in fierce competition with each other) sent teams into Arakan to recruit young nationalist leaders — with the most disastrous results. Wrote Zan Wai:

> The consequence of their activities was such that the success achieved by the ANC in uniting the whole of Arakan in the struggle for independence was torn asunder, and there ensued factions carrying flags of sundry colours - red, white, yellow, etc. At a

time when we had just started to build a new state, a new nation, a new people, sections of progressive young people of a national minority, of Arakan, suddenly confronted each other as mortal enemies.[92]

The Arakanese leaders' mistake, Zan Wai later accepted, was not to reorganise the ANC first and then affiliate to the AFPFL. As a result political unity in Arakan was entirely dependent on the faction-ridden AFPFL, which many Buddhist Rakhine and Muslim leaders had already rejected. The scale of their error became clear within months, when the CPB's expulsion from the AFPFL at the end of 1946 broke the fragile consensus that bound Rakhine nationalists and wartime veterans to the AFPFL (most local Muslims were organising separately) and caused the nationalist movement to shatter. Some forces joined U Seinda's APLP, some the local-defence PVOs under Bo San Tha Kyaw and Nyo Htwan, some the Red Flags led by Seinda's erstwhile ally, *Bonbauk* (bomb thrower) Tha Kyaw, who had originally been recruited by the Socialist Party, and still others the White Flag CPB led by present-day Politburo member, Kyaw Mya.

Through all these upheavals Zan Wai's smaller AFPFL residual rump was forced to remain conspicuously silent in Rangoon. Overnight Ramree Island, Sandoway and Gwa, which was evacuated after the police station was burnt down, became communist strongholds and the AFPFL buildings were occupied. From 1-3 April 1947 an All Arakan Conference, attended by 700 delegates and watched by an estimated 60,000-strong crowd, was called by U Seinda and *Bonbauk* Tha Kyaw in Myebon to reconcile these differences and a temporary Arakan Leftist Unity Front was formed. But Aung San, who joined other delegates, including U Ba Swe of the Socialist Party, made little impression in addressing the audience. British Intelligence reports confirm eyewitness accounts that the crowd shouted slogans not only against the British, the elections, the police and the army but also against Aung San, who was accused of a sell-out in London. The popular cry now was for revolution and for Arakan's independence.[93]

The main strategy agreed by the Arakan Leftist Unity Front was a patriotic campaign for the non-payment of rent, loans and taxes. Feelings were running especially high amongst wartime veterans and farmers in the countryside, where the economy had yet to recover from the devastation caused by the war. Within weeks the no-tax drive had swept across the Arakan countryside from Akyab to Sandoway, where a White Flag communist, U Aung Myat, was elected to the Constituent Assembly. Personal criticism of Aung San, too, was beginning to mount. But the Unity Front itself began to fracture badly following the arrest in May of U Seinda who, now openly advocating violence, had led a 3,000-strong mob in an attempted break-out of prisoners from Ramree gaol.

The result was even greater turmoil with strikes across Arakan by hundreds of local headmen, mass *pongyi*-led demonstrations, and repeated attacks on police stations, granaries and warehouses by different guerrilla bands. Dozens of casualties were reported, largely on the rebel side, as each insurgent force began trying to set up its own shadow administration in the districts. Red Guard guerrillas under Red Flag commanders, Tha Kyaw and Aung Lin, were particularly successful. In many areas the most obvious consequence of these attacks was a complete breakdown in law and order, despite the committal of 7,000 troops (mostly Gurkhas, Punjabis and Burmese police) by the British to quell the revolt. Officials were unable to move without a heavily armed guard. In miniature, it was a warning of the chaos that was to follow in the country at large after independence.

More damagingly, the strength of the military crack-down led to the growing estrangement of many local inhabitants from Aung San and the AFPFL, who were publicly accused of calling in the troops. Notably, too, Rakhine intellectuals and *pongyis* in Rangoon, supported by the pre-war prime minister, Sir Paw Tun, lent their voice to demands for the release of U Seinda, for recognition of the histori-cal independence of Arakan (before the Burman invasion of 1784), and, not unreasonably, for the immediate formation of an autonomous Arakan State with the same rights as the Shans and Kachins.[94]

The groundswell of protests failed to move AFPFL leaders in Rangoon and up to his death Aung San's position remained surprisingly ambiguous. While 'in principle' claiming to accept Arakanese demands for statehood, in drafting the Constitution he argued against Zan Wai and the Arakanese MPs, telling them that pushing their demands now would 'create the impression of disunity' and might even 'delay the declaration of independence'.[95] Once again he got his way, leaving everyone more confused than ever. Eventually questions were asked in the British House of Commons about the state of 'lawlessness' in Arakan. In reply ministers were specifically advised by the Burma Office not to mention a particularly prescient Reuters report, which had just warned: 'The trouble in Arakan is essen-tially a rebellion for the separation of Arakan, but communist agitators and dacoit bands have infiltrated into the movement.'[96] Against this troubled backdrop, a fast-growing campaign by Muslim activists for the creation of an Islamic 'frontier state' in the Muslim-majority districts of north Arakan was completely lost sight of.[97] Again in their haste, both the British and the AFPFL were to leave behind a time-bomb ticking in Arakan, which, Muslim and Rakhine nationalists argue, could easily have been defused by discussion.

The most remarkable omission of all from the 1947 Constitution was a Karen State. The entire question of the Karens, probably the largest and certainly the most restive of the minorities, was left to be settled after independence. No real definition of Karen ethnicity or Karen territory was made. In the absence of any agreement (and the KNU, which had boycotted the election, was refusing to take part in these discussions) complicated provision was made to create a future Karen State out of the Salween district, the Karenni State and adjacent Karen-majority areas (if and where the inhabitants agreed). This new state would have the same status as the Shan State (Article 180), but the right of secession, which had been granted to the Karenni and Shan states, was expressly ruled out for the Karens (Articles 178, 201-6). Should these arrangements prove unsatisfactory, an alternative proposal had been inserted into the Constitution which, instead of a Karen State, allowed for the creation of a special region to be known as Kawthoolei (Kawthulay). This would include the Salween district and adjoining Karen-majority areas determined by a special commissioner (Article 181). Until these issues could be resolved the interests of all Karens in Burma, including those of the Delta who made up the great majority of the Karen population, would be represented by a number of separate political rights, including 22 reserved seats in the Chamber of Deputies (including two from Karenni), a Karen Affairs Council and a Karen minister who would have control of all administrative, educational and cultural affairs relating to Karens.

The political inconsistencies towards the Karens did not end here. In recognition of their historically strong legal position, in addition to the right of secession, the

Karennis and Shans were allowed to continue their traditional *Sawbwa* rule. But the question of another Karen sub-group, the Kayan in neighbouring Mongpai in the Shan State, was left unresolved and remained an administrative headache throughout the 1950s, finally bursting into open rebellion in 1964 shortly after Ne Win seized power. Even more damagingly, despite many warnings virtually no discussion was given to the far more numerous Paos who were to take up arms with the KNU in 1949.

In final judgement of the 1947 Constitution, cynics could argue that the different rights granted ultimately depended on the minorities' individual bargaining powers and that these owed more to the haphazard nature and legal quirks of British rule than to any genuine national aspirations. Shan and Karenni *Sawbwas* (*Saophas*) had been granted *Sanads*, a form of charter given to the Indian maharajahs, but the Kachin *Duwas*, Chin *Matus* and Karen *Sawkes* had not, while the Mon and Arakanese communities enjoyed no separate political representation at all. The contradictions and ambiguities of the Constitution therefore satisfied no one and were to lead from one debilitating argument to another throughout the 1950s. In the early 1960s U Nu finally accepted the need to create Mon and Arakan states, but only with the Ne Win coup and the introduction of the totalitarian 1974 Constitution was the first ever attempt made to standardise the political administration of Burma. Now, after the democracy uprising of 1988, as Burma stands on the threshold of its third Constitution since independence, there clearly remain questions of enormous historical complexity to be redressed.

Many of the inadequacies in the 1947 Constitution were overlooked in the general euphoria of the time. After Panglong the position of Aung San and of the AFPFL had been considerably enhanced in British eyes. Aung San had originally led British officials to expect little from the meeting. Though it was only an agreement with some of the Frontier peoples (and only some leaders at that) it was interpreted in London as the basis for an agreement with all. From here on the governor's reliance on the AFPFL and its spokesmen was near total. Conflicting views continued to be put to the British government, but the governor would usually accept the AFPFL's interpretation; and where contradictory evidence still got through, it was either ignored or suppressed.

Nowhere was this more obvious than in the British handling of the Karen case. Right up until the British departure, memorials and petitions from Karen communities, still trusting in the protection of British rule, continued to pour into the colonial government. Today they are forgotten, simply gathering dust on the shelves of the India Office in London.[98] But with the failure of the 1946 Goodwill Mission to London, Karen leaders had decided it was time to take action for themselves. The Attlee-Aung San agreement made the following January, again without any Karen representation, only furthered the deepening sense of gloom.

The political tempo now began to gather pace fast. From 5-7 February 1947, as Aung San and the AFPFL leaders prepared for Panglong, 700 delegates from all the existing Karen parties (the KNA, the Baptist KNA, the Buddhist KNA, the KCO and its youth wing, the KYO) gathered at the Vinton Memorial Hall in Rangoon for an All Karen Congress. Here they agreed to merge together into a new organisation, the Karen National Union (KNU). The tone they set was notably sharper; resolutions were passed calling for a separate Karen State with a seaboard, the continuance of racially exclusive Karen units in the armed forces, an increased number of seats (25 per cent) in the Constituent Assembly based on a Karen population figure of four million, and a new ethnic census of Burma.[99] A deadline of 3 March was set for a favourable reply, a date the British government let come and go without any clear answer.

While the Karen elders still refused to stage any confrontation with the British, the KNU now began a series of spoiling tactics, a move Karen leaders today concede may well have been a mistake of historic proportions. On 4 March, Saw Ba U Gyi, the young Oxford-educated barrister who had been elected KNU president, resigned his post on the Governor's Executive Council. His place was immediately taken by San Po Thin, who had earlier been one of the most enthusiastic supporters of the KNU's boycott tactics. This was one of several acts of political opportunism which were to earn San Po Thin the KNU's undying enmity. 'I don't even want to see his face,' said Saw Ba U Gyi later.[100]

Despite the KNU's repeated warnings, British officials still failed to grasp the seriousness of the worsening situation during the Frontier Areas Commission of Enquiry (FACE) of March/April 1947. Set up as one of the conditions of the Attlee-Aung San agreement, the FACE, unlike the Panglong conference, was to hear testimony from all the peoples of the Frontier Areas. However, the freedom of the enquiry, chaired by Lt.-Col. D.R. Rees-Williams, had already been effectively proscribed by the Panglong agreement and was confined to discussion of the Frontier Areas, where few Mons and Arakanese and perhaps only 20 per cent of the Karen population of Burma actually lived. On the eight-man committee were four Burmans, three from the AFPFL and the fourth, Tin Tut, was Aung San's chief adviser (an ethnic balance one Karen delegate, Saw Marshall Shwin, objected to in a stormy exchange of words).[101] Ironically, in the 1930s he had played in the same college football team in Rangoon as Ne Win, but, according to Shwin, who was tortured by the Japanese after being turned in by the BIA: 'There were no hard feelings then; but that was before the war.'[102]

The EC counsellor and his deputies selected at Panglong were three of the four minority committee members. The fourth, Saw Sankey of the KNU, became one of the main leaders of the Karen rebellion. But at the time he did not publicly dissent from the enquiry's conclusions, later alleging he had been in constant danger of his life. The British saw this as yet another example of Karen prevarication; Sankey's colleagues today say he had no choice.[103]

On virtually every topic, testimony was bewilderingly wide. On being asked what future administration he would like in the Wa states, one Wa representative replied, 'We have not thought about that because we are wild people.'[104] But the AFPFL were by and large able to dictate the proceedings to their advantage and the final report largely echoed the details of the Panglong agreement. Whereas the Burmese independence movement was represented by just one voice (the AFPFL's), over 50 often conflicting groups were called from the hills, highlighting their poor state of political preparation and development. In the case of the Karens, in particular, very unrepresentative testimony was accepted, a fact John Leyden, Stevenson's successor at the FAA, later admitted.[105] AFPFL enthusiasts, anxious that any delay in a Karen settlement might cause the British to stay in the Frontier Areas after independence, induced a delegation of hill Karens of dubious legality from the Salween district led by Saw Lu Lu, to appear to counter the evidence of Marshall Shwin and the earlier official Karen delegates who had largely reiterated the resolutions passed by the KNU Congress in February. None the less, Lu Lu's word (asking to 'come into Burma as a district') was accepted, which only added to many Karens' growing sense of grievance.[106]

Even today a reading of Karen testimony at the FACE gives clear warning of the growing racial antipathy and inter-communal violence about to break out. The future prime minister U Nu, for example, accused the KNU of being used by the British Conservative Party and Church 'to obstruct the march of AFPFL to independence', while Mahn James Tun Aung of the KNU accused ethnic Burmans of attempting 'to exterminate the Karen people'.[107] Setting a clear precedent for the future, the AFPFL persistently questioned the right of out-of-district Karens to represent the Frontier Areas and, as Rees-Williams, much to the KNU's dismay, wrote in the *Sunday Times* on his return to Britain, this led to some very confusing arguments.[108] KNU leaders still see this as a convenient get-out. 'Confused? It suited the British to be confused,' claimed Saw Tha Din.[109]

Despite its obvious political eclipse, the KNU still pressed on with its boycott of the Constituent Assembly elections. So effectively was this boycott organised that in Toungoo district only 6 per cent of the constituency voted and in Bassein district only 5,370 of over 14,000 possible votes were cast.[110] But while this protest was intended to show the depth of the KNU's support, it effectively removed the main nationalist voice from the many critical debates to come. The 26 seats reserved for Karens were taken by 20 candidates from the KYO and six independents, including two from Karenni.

In view of the important intermediary role the KYO was now to play, it needs to be stressed that it was not simply a pro-AFPFL front, as is often assumed. It did, however, produce a handful of early Karen leaders, including Mahn Ba Khaing (assassinated with Aung San in July 1947) and Mahn Win Maung, a future president of Burma, who were to work closely with the AFPFL. But other KYO leaders, such as San Po Thin and Mahn Kyaw Sein, later joined the insurrections.

The KYO and KNU disagreed over the status and territory of a Karen State. Smith Dun, an ethnic Karen briefly appointed Chief-of-Staff of the Burma Army at independence, later wrote that, 'the KNU was asking for the best part of Burma while the KYO was asking for the worst.'[111] It was less simple than this, but generally the KYO was more respectful of Burman demands. Formed in October 1945 as the youth branch of the KCO, the KYO showed an early interest in socialism, culture and education, and later affiliated with the AFPFL. Prominent amongst its supporters were veterans of the BNA who, after their wartime experience, argued that the rights of the Delta Karens could only be preserved by finding some form of accommodation with the Burman majority. At the same time the KYO's proposals, modelled (like Aung San's) on the Constitution of Yugoslavia, were tinged with a strong nationalism. They included demands for the protection of Karen language and culture in Burman-majority areas of the Delta and the creation of a Karen Autonomous State from the Karen-majority areas in the east, and with the important right of secession from the 'free Burma federation'.[112] On this basis the KYO was able to build up a sizeable following in several towns in the Delta. Though it later gained some influence among Karen officers in the Burma Army who saw themselves as the protectors of the peace, the KYO never managed to organise the hill Karens in the east and in this lay a major weakness. The KYO never rivalled the KNU for countrywide support.

Thus, as the Constituent Assembly continued its deliberations without them, the leaders of the KNU, like the communists, began making their own preparations for independence. Many Karen communities believed another outbreak of attacks on Karen villages was inevitable with the British departure. Indeed, since the beginning of 1947 arms training had already begun in many Karen villages in the Delta in response to what KNU leaders alleged were PVO provocations. Then, at the end of May, as Red Flag and PVO violence continued, instructions were sent from KNU headquarters in U Loo-Nee Street, Rangoon, to district party organisers to set up their own local defence militia.[113] Formally inaugurated on 17 July 1947 as the Karen National Defence Organisation, these KNDOs, as they came to be known, are still the backbone of KNU military organisation and have frequently been copied by other insurgent groups elsewhere in Burma.

The first to follow the KNDOs were supporters of the Mon Freedom League (MFL, later Mon United Front), established with Nai Shwe Kyin (*aka* Nai Ba Lwin) as its first chairman in Moulmein in August 1947. Angered at the failure of Mon candidates (including Shwe Kyin) in what they claim were rigged elections to the Constituent Assembly, the MFL allied with the KNU and began organising peasant, worker, women and youth unions, as well as a paramilitary wing, the MNDOs, commanded by Nai Hla Maung.[114] Another faction, the United Mon Association, had earlier been set up by Mon Po Cho, who had boycotted the elections, but both parties agreed on a united set of demands for the immediate establishment of a Mon State in conferences at Kamawak and Pa-auk, Mudon, before the end of the year.[115]

Meanwhile, KNU leaders were establishing underground contact with sympathetic units in the Burma Army, in which Karen troops had been reconstituted as three battalions of Karen Rifles. The key organiser was Saw Ba U Gyi's right-hand man, Saw Sankey, who had been the KNU representative at the FACE. The mostly Karen-staffed Signals Section was an important link in his underground Group X network.[116] No sooner had the transmitters closed down at the end of the day's business, than they started humming again as KNU sympathisers exchanged news of the day's developments; the KNU was able to keep this important line of communication open until the insurrection finally began in January 1949.

Having been outmanoeuvred at the FACE hearings in April by U Nu and AFPFL leaders, the KNU's disillusionment with the AFPFL was finally complete in September when the signature of another unofficial Karen representative from the hills, Saw De Ghai, was accepted on a copy of the draft Constitution. In retaliation, De Ghai was assassinated by the KNU soon after the Karen rebellion began. Likewise, in the case of the Karenni states, where one faction in the Karenni leadership (allied with the KNU) was still refusing to work with the AFPFL, similar manoeuvrings took place. When the first two Karenni representatives selected to the Constituent Assembly, U Bee Tu Re and San Thein, refused to take their places, a new delegation suddenly materialised in Rangoon, headed by the AFPFL activist U Sein. Privately British officials doubted their credentials, but again took no action.[117]

The result of these intrigues was that the KNU and the Karenni U Bee faction continued to prepare for armed struggle. Even as late as October 1947, with the British still exerting pressure on U Nu, the AFPFL Cabinet was prepared to offer the Karen a state that would have included the Karenni State, the Mongpai substate, the Salween district and the Part II areas of the Thaton, Toungoo and Pyinmana hill tracts.[118] A Karen Affairs Council was planned for the Delta Karens. Such a gesture would be considered generous today, but by then it was too late. The KNU was demanding much of the Delta as well, including the whole of the Irrawaddy Division and the Insein and Hanthawaddy districts. This controversial demand probably lost the KNU its last chance of any goodwill from the British government. At least officially, the KNU still pursues its claim to this mixed Burman-Karen territory. But according to Skaw Ler Taw, one of the veteran KNU leaders responsible: 'Our aim was to take up a position of strength first. We believed we could always negotiate later.'[119]

On 3 and 4 October, 600 KNU delegates from across Burma gathered in Moulmein in sombre mood for the Second KNU Congress, held under the slogan, Righteousness Exalteth a Nation. Also in attendance were Pao and Mon *pongyis* and representatives who were shortly to launch their own uprisings with the KNU. Wide-ranging motions were discussed and it was agreed to present the Karen case to the United Nations.[120] But the man listened to most intently was the KNU's future strategist, Mahn Ba Zan, who lectured on military organisation.

In a last desperate attempt the KNU sent Prime Minister Attlee a booklet to distribute to the British Parliament, which repeated the demand for an independent Karen State in a federation of Autonomous National States in Burma.

> It is a dream that Karen and Burman can ever evolve a common nationality, and this misconception of one homogeneous Burmese nation has gone far beyond the limits and is the cause of most of the troubles and will lead Burma to destruction.... Karen and Burman belong to two different racial origins [and] to two different civilisations. To yoke together two such nations under a single state, one in numerical minority and the other as a majority, must lead to growing discontent and final destruction.[121]

Further warnings of political violence came from other parts of Burma. In early November the defence minister, Bo Let Ya, hurried to Arakan where Red Flag and Rakhine guerrillas from the APLP had begun a huge move out of the countryside to attack the towns. A 700-strong force was believed to be operating in Akyab district alone.[122] In December, further north at Dubbro-Chaung village, Buthidaung, hundreds of supporters of the popular Muslim singer, Jafar Hussain (*aka* Jafar Kawwal), many of whom had secretly stockpiled their weapons at the end of the war, declared the formation of the Mujahid Party and pledged themselves ready to begin battle for an Islamic state. Meanwhile the White Flag's leading theoretician, Ba Tin, was putting the finishing touches to his revolutionary thesis.

As the hours to Burma's independence ticked away the situation deteriorated fast. With the Red Flags already underground and the KNU making military preparations, the prospects were far from good.

5

Insurgency as a Way of Life

In September 1945 Lord Mountbatten met the youthful leaders of the wartime resistance at Kandy in Ceylon. At this meeting were leaders of the AFPFL and the Patriotic Burmese Forces (the former BNA), as well as representatives of the Karen and Arakan resistance. Their mission was to discuss the formation of a new Burma Army. If in the insurrections which have divided Burma since independence it has often seemed that insurgency has developed a life of its own, an examination of the subsequent careers of the participants is revealing. Though the war was over, half (including Mountbatten) were eventually to meet violent ends in a variety of different circumstances.

For the PBF:

Bogyoke Aung San (Commander-in-Chief) — assassinated July 1947.

Bo Let Ya (deputy Commander-in-Chief) — deputy Prime Minister 1947-8; Commander insurgent PDP from 1970; killed in battle with KNU 1978.

Bo Ne Win (Group Commander) — Army Commander-in-Chief from 1949; head military caretaker government 1958-60; led military coup 1962; Burma president and BSPP chairman; retired 1988.

Bo Zeya (Chief-of-staff) — Commander 3rd Burma Rifles; went underground 1948; CPB Chief-of-Staff and CC member 1950s; mission to China 1953-5; head of CPB delegation 1963 peace parley; killed in action 1968.

Bo Kyaw Zaw (Zone Commander, Pegu) — leading *Tatmadaw* brigadier in campaigns against KNU and KMT in early 1950s; sacked for pro-communist sympathies 1957; supporter of NUF 1957-62; went underground 1976; now CPB CC member.

Bo Maung Maung (Zone Commander, Penwegon) — director Defence Services Military Academy 1950s; member military caretaker government 1958-60; ambassadorial duties from 1961; retired.

Bo Zaw Min (*aka* Kyaw Win) (Staff) — *Tatmadaw* major 1950s; retired.

For the AFPFL:

Than Tun (Gen.-Sec.) — led CPB underground 1948; assassinated 1968.

U Ba Pe — arrested for conspiracy against government 1954; released 1958; retired.

Saw Ba U Gyi (Karen) — founding chairman KNU 1947; led KNU underground 1949; killed in action 1950.

Ahko Nyo Htwan (Arakanese) — Cabinet minister 1948; later ambassador to Australia.

From their wartime experience came the military and organisational skills that later led most to choose armed struggle as the main means of fighting for their political beliefs. Than Tun and Bo Zeya went underground with the CPB in 1948; Saw Ba U Gyi launched the KNU insurrection at the beginning of 1949. Bo Let Ya, a founder member of the CPB, however, only followed Burma's first prime minister, U Nu, into the jungle in the late 1960s; while nearly three decades passed before Kyaw Zaw eventually joined his colleagues in the CPB-liberated zones. Facing them all this time were many of their old comrades-in-arms, including Ne Win and Maung Maung. Indeed Ne Win was the only one to achieve power by armed means alone. (Ironically Mountbatten, too, met a violent end, assassinated in 1979 by an IRA bomb, an incident many wartime veterans in Burma remember with some poignancy.)

This personal element is undeniably important in understanding the extraordinary durability of Burma's diverse insurgencies. Since the early 1950s different government spokesmen have taken great care to avoid using the term 'civil war', preferring to label their armed opponents as 'bandits' or 'racist saboteurs', or at best as traitors skulking round in remote mountain hideouts.* In a typical speech on Union Day 1988, shortly before being named Ne Win's successor, Gen. Sein Lwin alleged: 'They kidnap local youths and force them into their ranks. They demand protection money, rob, collect taxes, smuggle out precious resources, sell drugs and falsify truths to discredit the State.'[1] But missing from this kind of analysis is any acknowledgement that many of the veteran leaders of the insurgencies, such as CPB chairman, Ba Thein Tin, or KNU CC member, Saw Thein, were once personally known to Ne Win and were close friends of the leaders of the *Tatmadaw*. Moreover, this personal element was amplified among a new generation of military leaders by the outbreak of the Shan and Kachin rebellions in the late 1950s, when many high-school and university graduates went underground. It is thus not unusual, even today, for commanders on rival sides to know one another. This situation reached its peak in the early 1970s when several other heroes of the national liberation movement, including the *Thirty Comrades* Bo Yan Naing and Bo Hmu Aung, joined U Nu and Bo Let Ya in the rebel underground. For a lasting peace to come, a good deal of spilt blood will have to be forgiven.

But such personal rivalries alone cannot account for the sheer scale of Burma's insurgencies. Armed struggle, as events in 1988 again demonstrated, is a consistent and often spontaneous way of expressing political opposition. As diverse rebel movements continue to rise and fall with bewildering frequency, in many parts of rural Burma insurgency has become a way of life. Many of the basic conditions for this breakdown in law and order can be found in Burma's complex ethnic past; the rise and fall of so many different armed movements is less haphazard than first appears. In the absence of any stable or recognised central authority, various traditions (some of which are unique to Burma) have come into play. It is on these traditions, still adhered to well into the late 20th century, that many insurgent movements have, often unwittingly, been able to build.

---

*   There has also been much argument over the words 'insurgent' and 'rebel' which most armed opposition groups reject as pejorative, implying their struggles are unlawful. Many prefer the American term 'freedom fighter'. Here I prefer to use the term 'insurgent', implying the intention to overthrow a government or seize power by armed means.

The Traditions of Rebellion

Burma is a predominantly rural society. Even Rangoon today, under the still-pervasive influence of Ne Win's sleepy *Burmese Way to Socialism*, functions more as a collection of small villages and townships than as the bustling Asian capital its 2.5 million population would suggest. And though generally led by intellectuals, the various rebellions are essentially rural rebellions based on the rural peasantry, whether of the Burman majority or the ethnic minorities.

The formation of local *Tats*, or pocket armies, is well established among the peasantry of Lower and Upper Burma and for centuries village raiding was something of a local sport. Using this tradition to their advantage through a flexible system of political patronage, the Burman (or Mon or Arakanese) kings would quickly raise levies for their military campaigns. But this same tradition was often turned against them when *Minlaung* pretenders challenged the throne. In such wars local loyalties were usually decisive. The British abolition of the monarchy and *Hutladaw* (Royal Court) did not kill the tradition. While British records describe the rebel bands which sprang up across the country in the late 1880s as 'dacoits', there is evidence that they expressed a political voice. Every Burmese schoolchild is taught that *Myothugyi*, Bo Min Yaung, the grandfather of Burma's independence hero, Aung San, was the legendary leader of the anti-British resistance movement. Even in this century some villages in Upper Burma have been known as *myin* (cavalry) or *thenat* (musketeer) villages, indicating their recent military duties and service.[2] As many writers observe, the Burman people have long been proud of their martial traditions.

Levy service was also well established among the minority peoples of the hills. Kachin, Chin and Shan recruits periodically came down from their upland homes to serve in the armies of the Burman (or Mon) kings, a tradition the British twisted to their advantage in the colonial administration of Burma. Intra-village raiding was also very much a feature of life in the hills and, when not feuding with each other, ethnic groups in the Kachin and Karenni hills often raided villages in the valleys and plains. Indeed one reason the British moved to annex the hills was 'the protection of the plains'.[3] Such raids were usually led by local headmen or chiefs. In the vast highlands of the Shan states the situation was (and is) more complicated. In this case the ruling Shan *Sawbwas* (*Saophas*) usually called up village levies for their campaigns (in the manner of the Burman kings); they continued to claim this right into the 1950s, even after Burma's independence. Local headmen and chieftains thus became well practised in the art of raising and training troops at short notice. Much of Shan history over the centuries was marked by continual warfare with Burman kings or rival Shan dynasties as various families and alliances strove to achieve ascendancy. One such Shan alliance, the Limbin confederacy, made a bid to overthrow King Thibaw on the eve of the British invasion and was only suppressed with difficulty as the British moved into the hills.[4]

Not surprisingly, the Shan princes served as a model to many other ethnic groups in the hills, particularly the Wa, Pao, Palaung and Karenni, who fashioned their own (though not racially exclusive) substates along the lines of the Shan rulers. The Burman and Mon kings also exerted influence over their ethnic neighbours. The *Minlaung* pretenders, who over the centuries frequently tried to seize the royal throne, served as an inspiration to many less advanced groups and communities, especially the millennial sects of the Lahus and Karens, which combined Buddhist, Animist and, later, Christian prophesies in their quest for a semi-divine deliverer or saviour. Indeed one such Karen-led *Minlaung* rebellion against the British broke out in the Shwegyin hills in 1856.[5]

Despite the semblance of colonial order in Rangoon, the *pax Britannica* hardly touched the volatile social conditions in the countryside. In the largely unadministered Frontier Areas, there was little interference with the rights of traditional rulers and headmen (whatever their status) and, though rarely reported, spontaneous uprisings continued throughout much of British rule and were often expressed in just such historic forms. For example, during 1917-19 Thado and Haka chiefs in the Chin hills led a local anti-British rebellion which was violently crushed and, as late as 1938, 80 heads were taken in one battle during an outbreak of intra-village raiding in the Naga hills.[6] During 1936-8, ethnic Kayan villagers in the small Shan substate of Mongpai also rose up to overthrow their Shan ruler and resisted British attempts to reintroduce *Sawbwa* rule. Even after the return of the British and the supposed restoration of law at the end of the Second World War, a large dacoit gang (of 60 men) was still reported to be active raiding villages along the Karenni borders.[7]

What really showed such historic traditions were not yet dead was the great Saya San rebellion, which broke out in Lower Burma in December 1930. Saya San's movement, led by a former *pongyi* and described by the British historian Hugh Tinker as a 'medieval outburst', followed a traditional political and religious pattern.[8] Most of the organisers were political *pongyis* who worked closely with local *wunthanu athins* (national associations).[9] In early 1930 a small army of Saya San's followers, known as the *Galon* Army, began training in the Pegu Yomas east of Tharrawaddy with only 30 guns between them. (The *Galon* was a mythical eagle accredited with destroying the dragon, *Naga*, now identified with the British.) At the outbreak of the rebellion, hostilities spread so fast the British were taken completely by surprise. Within seven days 1,500 supporters (many tattooed and protected by superstitious amulets) had gathered in the district. In the following weeks the rebellion spread rapidly across the countryside, first to Yamethin, Pyapon, Bassein and Henzada, then further north to Prome and Thayetmyo, where the British authorities were finally able to prevent any further escalation.[10] While many of the rebel bands were disorganised and included criminal elements, there is little doubt that Saya San was able to recruit disaffected landless farmers and villagers to his cause, just as any *Minlaung* pretender to the throne might have done in the past. Only in April 1932 was the rebellion finally suppressed. But small groups dispersing into the Pegu Yomas demonstrated their capacity to survive in remote forest hideouts; it was a clear warning of the rural insurgencies to come. The final human toll was high: when the rebellion was finally crushed the British had inflicted 3,000 casualties (dead and wounded) and arrested over 8,000 villagers.[11]

The Saya San rebellion was a great inspiration to the young Thakins in the *Dobama Asiayone*. While there is little evidence of a direct link with the Thakins in the cities (politicians U Saw and Dr Ba Maw defended the *Galon* rebels), the challenge posed to the British administration by armed resistance did not go unnoticed. The first paramilitary *Tats* were established at the end of 1930. At the *Dobama* conference in 1935 they were organised into the *Dobama Ye Tat* (*Dobama* Army) which, in 1936, became the *Bama Let Yon Tat* (Army of the People of Burma).[12] As the war approached, the *Tats*, composed largely of students and workers, increasingly became an everyday part of the political scene in Burma. Two pre-war prime ministers, Dr Ba Maw and U Saw, formed pocket armies of their own: U Saw's army took the name *Galon Tat* to commemorate his defence of the *Galon* Army prisoners.

With the Second World War came a vast escalation in military knowledge and a massive influx of modern weaponry and supplies. Many Burman leaders who dominated the national stage after independence received their first military training from the Japanese Imperial Army. Three of the *Thirty Comrades*, Bo Let Ya, Bo Yan Naing and Bo Hmu Aung, who later joined U Nu's insurgent Parliamentary Democracy Party, trained and infiltrated back into Burma's Tavoy-Mergui districts through southern Thailand. Nearly 30 years later they repeated the same journey as they returned to their former stamping-grounds. Even Ne Win, who spent much of the last four decades directing his own creation, the modern Burma Army (*Tatmadaw*) against the Karen National Union in south-east Burma, re-entered the country in 1941 through Karen villages along the frontier, which have since remained at the centre of the Karen insurgency.

Another four of the *Thirty Comrades*, Bo Zeya, Bo Ye Htut, Bo Yan Aung and Bo Kyaw Zaw, were later to play a leading role in the CPB insurrection while yet another, Bo La Yaung, led the People's Volunteer Organisation (PVO) underground in 1948. Eight more of these much-revered comrades died or were killed during the Second World War, while two more, Bo Min Gaung and Bo Setkya (who also went underground after the 1962 coup), went on to join the Socialist Party and served in the AFPFL government, joining the fight against insurgency in the early years of independence. But most observers believe Bo Ne Win was the most profoundly influenced by his training in Japan. Many years later, completely ignoring the important role played by the minorities in the war, he confirmed what many ethnic nationalist leaders had long been alleging — the deliberate Burmo-centric political shaping of the army that had begun under the Japanese. 'Our *Tatmadaw* emerged from the crucible of the independence struggle, through the BIA, BNA and the BPF[PBF].... In the case of the Navy and the Air Force, we had to make use of personnel left by the British as the nucleus for our forces. We had to reorientate such personnel to see our point of view.'[13]

The few ethnic Burmans who trained or served with the British in the wartime resistance were similarly eclipsed. When the *Tatmadaw* seized power in 1962, all but three of the seats on the Revolutionary Council were given to former BIA men. Ne Win's critics maintain that the influence of the wartime experience and training under the Japanese was what gave BSPP rule its distinctly national socialist (some say fascist) tinge. The armies of India and Pakistan, with which the *Tatmadaw* has often been compared, owe nothing to the Japanese and grew entirely from the epoch of the British Empire.

The Second World War also provided a crucial military training ground for the ethnic minorities. Kachin, Karen and Karenni volunteers, many of whom made their way out to India, received intensive training in conventional and guerrilla warfare before returning to Burma in regular allied divisions, or parachuting behind Japanese lines in such famous undercover units as Force 136, Wingate's 'Chindits', or Merrill's 'Marauders'. Today the exploits of these forces have become the stuff of legend in the eastern hills, none more so than the story of Capt. Seagrim, 'Grandfather Longlegs', the first British levy commander with the Karens who, in a vain attempt to prevent reprisals against Karen villagers, voluntarily gave himself up and went to his death, along with many of his former Karen soldiers imprisoned in Rangoon.[14]

With the wholesale mutiny of the Karen Rifles and one regiment of the Kachin Rifles in 1949, these units took their wartime arms and experience directly underground; many of the lessons learnt during the arduous campaigns of the Second World War have since become standard practice among the armed opposition.[15] The KNU's military wing, the Karen National Liberation Army (KNLA), is still run along British lines and visitors to its bases today are awoken to the wartime bugle-calls of the British Army.

Similarly, when in 1961 the Kachin Independence Organisation (KIO) began its insurrection led by Zau Seng, a former Intelligence officer in the American 101 Force, many British and US army veterans were called out of retirement to train a new generation of Kachin volunteers. In fact until 1979 English was the KIO's main language of command. A number of other insurgent leaders across Burma also had their first military experience with the British. Hpalang Gam Di, CC member of the CPB, is a former Kachin levy, while Saw Maw Reh, veteran founder of the Karenni National Progressive Party (KNPP) and president of the National Democratic Front, once served as a bombardier in the British Army. But this influence is most obvious in the ranks of the KNU. In 1984 all five KNLA brigade commanders and all four brigadiers, including KNU president, Bo Mya, were veterans of British units from the Second World War.

Thus from the war came considerable military knowledge. Immediately afterwards the traditional *Tats* were again much in evidence. By 1947, besides Aung San's PVO, seven other parties had set up *Tats*: the White Flag and Red Flag factions of the CPB, U Saw's *Galon Tat*, Ba Sein's *Dobama*, Ba Maw's *Maha-Bama*, the Students' Revolutionary Front and the Indian National Congress. Of these the PVO was by far the largest. The same year Karen and Mon nationalists made their first moves to create their own local defence militia, the Karen National Defence Organisation (KNDO) and its Mon counterpart, the MNDO, both of which still survive in south-east Burma's rural areas. Meanwhile, in Arakan various armed communist, nationalist and Muslim forces were being formed. Many of them had fought during the war and their remnants, led by another wartime veteran, Maung Sein Nyunt, are still operating along the Bangladesh border.

With the outbreak of the insurgencies came the introduction of Mao Zedong's strategies of *Protracted War* and *Guerrilla War*. Both these booklets have provided essential reading to successive generations of guerrilla commanders throughout the world who have been inspired by the successes of Mao's Red Army in China and the national liberation movement in Vietnam. From a largely unplanned and spontaneous beginning, by the early 1950s the White Flag CPB's military strategy was based more or less entirely on Mao Zedong's works.

Mao's influence was not, however, confined to the communist movement. The KNU had copies of his writings as early as 1949 and, through the 1950s, this led to the Karen nationalist movement's ideological drift to the political left and, ultimately, to a series of damaging factional splits. Such divisions were later echoed by smaller nationalist fronts, including the Karenni, Mon, Pao and Chin. Even the Shan State Army (SSA), established in 1964, and its political wing, the Shan State Progress Party (SSPP), were later to split over this ideological dilemma, with military commanders in the field generally more sympathetic to

Mao Zedong's thought. Even today, though after the experiences of the last 40 years many ethnic nationalist movements in Burma are extremely wary of the CPB and of communism, adapted versions of Mao's *Protracted War* are used in most insurgent training classes, though usually without the communist component.

Amidst the political chaos which has been enveloping Burma since independence and the better-organised struggles of groups such as the CPB, KNU, KIO and SSPP, many spontaneous uprisings, echoing the upheavals of earlier centuries, continue to erupt and to frustrate the central government and insurgent fronts alike. Though most of these movements began as local self-defence militia, as a reaction to the highly politicised nature of armed conflict in Burma, several have developed into surprisingly dynamic political movements. In a study of peasant rebellions, *Why Men Rebel*, T.R. Gurr identifies three basic conditions for spontaneous uprisings: relative deprivation that can be blamed on the government rather than the local élite; intense discontent amongst ordinary people but not the élite; and the loss of a population's economic security.[16] Without organisation and the participation of the local élite, such uprisings, he believes, are likely to remain localised and thus doomed to failure. But, unless they are quickly crushed before being able to enlist new support, they can escalate into what he calls an internal war.

Burma has had many such internal wars. Perhaps the best example came from the insurgent Kayan nationalist movement, which came into being in 1964 in the south-west Shan state of Mongpai in the wake of the emergency demonetisation measures introduced by Ne Win's Revolutionary Council. These made all 50 and 100 kyat notes worthless overnight and effectively robbed poor hill farmers of all their savings. Led by Bo Pyan, a local Catholic headman from Pekon township who had made his name with arms dropped by the British in the anti-Japanese resistance, the uprising began as the latest in a line of largely spontaneous Kayan peasant rebellions dating back to the 17th century.[17] This time, following immediate suppression by the *Tatmadaw*, the uprising could well have petered out without further ado. But, with an influx of new blood led by a Kayan student from Rangoon University, Shwe Aye (*aka* Nyaint Lu Tha), and with armed support from the KNU, KNPP and CPB, though small (200-300 strong), the Kayan New Land Party has grown into a determinedly persistent armed force along the Shan/Kayah borders, resisting all blandishments to merge forces from its Karen and Karenni cousins and the CPB. (After many years of retirement, Bo Pyan rejoined the party when the 1988 democracy uprising was crushed.)

Such disturbed conditions still prevail, particularly in the previously unadministered Frontier Areas of the Shan State. One of the significant successes of the KNU and KIO movements has been their ability to form viable, centralised political fronts out of such chaos. The KNU in south-east Burma and the KIO in the north-east have for many years controlled vast liberated zones with their own regional governments, education departments and armies among peoples and subgroups that were never politically united under the British. The failures of the CPB and SSPP (undoubtedly the most political of all the various ethnic fronts in the Shan State) are thus all the more striking. In early 1991 more than ten different armed ethnic groups continue to patrol and tax their own territories inside the state.[18] The spontaneous Lahu rebellion which broke out in late 1972, for example, was led by the Lahu's elderly spiritual man-god, Pu Kyaung Long, and was at first subdued by the *Tatmadaw* with heavy loss of life. But, following the example of other insurgent groups, it soon developed into a more ideological movement, the Lahu National United Party (LNUP), with one faction eventually going over to the CPB and another, led by the old man's son, Paya Kya Oo, building up a new group, the Lahu National Organisation, in the southern Shan state. (When a similar millennial movement amongst the Karens, the *Telakhon*, led by another man-god, the *Phu Chaik*, took up arms against the *Tatmadaw* in south-east Burma in 1967, it was quickly suppressed by the KNU, which executed its leader. See Appendix.)

Local loyalties are also strong amongst the majority Shans, but since the internecine assassinations of various rival leaders, a united Shan independence movement remains very much a pipe-dream. The faction of the Shan United Army under Khun Sa (*aka* Chan Shi-fu), for example, though able to expand its territory, retains its strongest following among the local inhabitants of the remote valley of Loimaw in the Mong Yai substate, where his family, who migrated from China in the 18th century, became *Myosas*. Similarly, though for 20 years the CPB occupied much of the region, strong nationalist feelings continued to be expressed by the Chinese-Shan Kokangese of the Kokang substate and a variety of insurgent forces were formed by other local leaders, such as Lo Hsing-han, Pheung Kya-shin and Jimmy Yang MP, brother of the last Kokang *Sawbwa*. After the 1962 coup, Rangoon University educated Jimmy Yang forcibly raised his own insurgent Kokang Resistance Force, much as any other feudal lord might have done in the recent past. Significantly, the ethnic mutinies which led to the mass breakup of the CPB's People's Army in 1989 began in Kokang. Chao Tzang, son of Sao Shwe Thaike, the Yawnghwe *Sawbwa*, was another Shan 'royal' who played a leading role in the insurrections, while Chao Nor Far from the Palaung royal house of Tawngpeng, the ethnic Wa, Maha San, from Ving Ngun, and the Karenni ex-Force 136 officer, Sao Shwe, from Kyebogyi were rebel leaders from minority *Sawbwa* families.

Successive central governments have not failed to recognise this reality. They, like the insurgents, quickly realised when the set-piece battles of 1948-50 began to peter out that organisation would be the key to the war in the countryside. Thus where governments have failed to break down traditional loyalties, they have not hesitated to try and win local rebel leaders to their side. A succession of different local militia have been formed, from the Territorial Army or *Sitwundan* in 1948 to the *Pyu Saw Hti*, modelled on Israel's settlement defence system, in 1955. (According to legend, *Pyu Saw Hti* was a warrior-prince who reigned in the 2nd century AD.)

The *Ka Kwe Ye* (KKY) units, begun in 1963 after Ne Win's coup, were particularly notorious and did much to take the steam out of the fast-rising Shan separatist movement. Local leaders such as Khun Sa, Lo Hsing-han and the Wa prince, Maha San, were allowed to keep their arms and continue policing and taxing local trade so long as they gave no support to the separatist cause. Though clearly helping to bring about the further fragmentation of the Shan nationalist movement, this ultimately did little to reduce the overall scale of insurgency; instead it stretched the credibility of the Ne Win regime since most of the legalised groups had become heavily involved in the opium trade. The scheme was abandoned in 1973 following international protests and KKY units were ordered to disband. But many leading KKY commanders, including Maha San and Lo Hsing-han, simply crossed over to the rebel side. After being captured and sentenced to death, Lo Hsing-han was quietly released in 1980 to work on the side of the government; he re-emerged publicly in 1989 to play a leading role in fomenting the CPB mutinies.

The *Tatmadaw* used similar tactics to try and divide other insurgent organisations. In late 1984 some 130 troops from the LNUP were reorganised as a local defence force in the Mongton area after surrendering with their leader, Paya Ja Oo. It proved a short-lived experiment. Within a year they had slipped back underground with their weapons once more to fight the *Tatmadaw*. Paya Ja Oo is by no means the only insurgent leader with such a chequered history. Both the vice-president of the Tailand Revolutionary Council (TRC), Khun Sa, and the KNU president, Bo Mya, once served in local defence militia. After the 1989 split in the CPB, the Burmese Army was quick to make a deal with several of the breakaway leaders, including the local rebel commander, Pheung Kya-shin, who in one short year went from 'opium warlord' to 'Kokang elder statesman' in the Rangoon press. As the State Law and Order Restoration Council (SLORC) turned attention to the challenge posed by the NLD and the new democracy parties in the cities, the KKY programme appeared to be very much back on the political agenda for Burma in the 1990s.

The methods used by Ne Win and his government's armed forces to combat the insurgencies (and their relative strengths and weaknesses) are assessed in greater detail later on. The extraordinary diversity of the various political forces that take up arms has often made it impossible for Rangoon to concentrate its resources and military strength on any single foe. If the AFPFL had only had the CPB and KNU to face in the 1950s, when fighting was still concentrated around the major towns and cities, a settlement to the war could possibly have been forced far more quickly. And since the 1960s and early 1970s, when the war front was being pushed back into the hills, the plethora of insurgent armies in the Shan, Kachin and Kayah states has made the entire north-east region a veritable minefield for government troops faced with attack from every possible side. At the same time, if the broad spread of these insurgent forces has generally been considered an asset to the rebel cause, their sheer scale and variety must also count as a major reason for their failure to achieve their political goals. Fierce wars, largely unreported in the outside world, have also been fought on the rebel side.

Disparaging comments have been made, particularly in Rangoon, about the relatively small size of some of the ethnic armies. Over the last few years in Arakan, for example, ethnic armies have wilted and splintered under the constant onslaught of army pressure, but it has not brought any kind of political settlement to the area. The state of siege mentality that exists in many other parts of the country is still evident across much of the north-west. To be effective as an anti-government force, an insurgent organisation does not need to control safe base areas and liberated territories. For example, since the early 1970s the Irish Republican Army in Northern Ireland is estimated to have had a maximum of 200 gunmen active at any one time (most living quietly within their own communities, undetected by British security forces), but their impact on daily life in Ireland is incalculable. Relatively small armed groups, such as the Palaung State Liberation Party, the KNPP and the (Muslim) Rohingya Patriotic Front, have had equally disturbing impacts in their own communities over the past few decades and, without a final political settlement to the war, this state of affairs could well continue.

Perhaps the study that most closely defines the social conditions in which such endemic insurgencies flourish is one that makes no actual mention of Burma: *Bandits* by the Marxist historian Eric Hobsbawm. He argues that 'social banditry... is one of the most universal social phenomena known to history, and one of the most amazingly uniform.'[19] Picking random examples over the last two centuries from around the globe (China, Colombia, Indonesia, Sardinia, Turkey), he draws up a persuasive list of specific conditions that can cause so many popularly supported, though usually small, rebel movements to arise. All his criteria fit Burma exactly: peasant, rural societies; tribal or kinship societies 'familiar with raiding'; 'unsettled and unpacified regions, especially those inhabited by minority peoples'; 'remote and inaccessible areas', especially near frontiers or where authorities from one district to the next have little knowledge of each other; times of 'pauperisation and economic crisis'; communities threatened with the destruction of their 'way of life'; and large numbers of marginalised free-men (outlaws) such as soldiers, deserters, ex-servicemen and landless labourers.[20] This does not, however, mean that such rebels are merely robbers or express no political voice. As Hobsbawm points out, 'banditry at such times may be the precursor or companion of major social movements such as peasant revolutions... the social bandit [is] a special type of peasant protest and rebellion.'[21] Many insurgent leaders would argue that such is the case in Burma today. (See Appendix for a note on millenarianism which Hobsbawm believes is a historical accompaniment to social banditry.)

It is important to emphasise that not all the violence following the British departure from Burma can be blamed on the activities or ideologies of different insurgent groups. Clearly conditions were ripe for social upheaval: there was a complete collapse in law and order with countless, unrecorded dacoit bands springing up across the country. By 1957 Burma had the highest murder rate in the world. According to official statistics described by a senior police officer as only 'half the story', in the first nine years of independence there were at least four recorded murders every day, making a total of 11,979 known deaths.[22] These figures did not include insurgent-related deaths which were recorded separately and were far higher. No wonder many groups the government repeatedly described over the years as rebels, such as the Pao National Organisation in the strife-torn hills around Taunggyi, see themselves as the protectors of their people rather than the instigators of violence. They have genuine and popular support from local villagers who see the rare *Tatmadaw* patrols as simply another agent of conflict.

The Economics of Rebellion
A further factor needs to be mentioned in explaining the continuing vitality of Burma's insurgencies. Apart from full Chinese support for the CPB for a decade (1968-78) and CIA-instigated financial assistance to U Nu in the early 1970s, all the armed opposition movements have had to be largely self-supporting. In the face of the 190,000-strong *Tatmadaw*, which took a stranglehold on national life with the declared aim of annihilating all resistance, this would at first appear to have been a remarkable feat.

At least in the early years finding fresh supplies was not a problem. Vast stockpiles of arms and ammunition had been built up during the Second World War and many weapons hidden. In the 1950s, with the central government under pressure from all sides, insurgent commanders were usually able to replenish their armouries by raids on military barracks and stores, often helped by the defection of soldiers and police from the government side. Security was really only tightened for the first time and full weight put behind the military's attempts to crush the insurgencies during Ne Win's military caretaker administration of 1958-60. Ne Win's success at this time no doubt encouraged him to believe that, with the country allegedly sliding back into chaos in 1962, a military government unfettered by civilian restrictions could solve this intractable problem once and for all. In fact nothing was further from the truth. Ironically the 1962 coup gave many of the insurgencies a new lease of life.

Ne Win's thinly disguised Burmanisation policies and attempt to create a submissive one-party state in a country of such obvious ethnic and cultural diversity pushed many hitherto little affected sections of the community into the insurgents' camp. But it was above all his extraordinary *Burmese Way to Socialism* and attempt to build a reconstructed socialist economy, isolated from the outside world, which was to prove his undoing. If Ne Win had pursued any other course, the situation would undoubtedly have been very different today.

Though seeing some progress, the democratic era of the 1950s was marked by widespread corruption and poor production.[23] But after 1962 ill-conceived attempts to create monopolies of restricted goods such as rice and salt and the hasty nationalisation of virtually every sector of the economy caused a sudden shortage of essential goods and an urgent demand for consumer products which had all but ceased to enter the country. Then followed the mass exodus of some 300,000 Indian and 100,000 Chinese merchants and traders out of the country. In many areas the local economy collapsed as traditional avenues of supply and demand came to an abrupt end. There was now only one source of supply: the black market. Slowly goods began to be smuggled illegally into the country from abroad, from Malaysia, China and East Pakistan, but to begin with mostly from Thailand. To pay for this trade, travelling in the opposite direction were unprocessed agricultural products and minerals, such as cattle, rubber, rubies and teak, which fetched far higher prices on the world market.

The importance of this trade, much of which still passed through insurgent-held territory in the early 1990s, cannot be underestimated, both as a symbol of Burma's economic decline and the insurgents' ability to run their own governments. For many years Western economists, placing too much reliance on fanciful reports and statistics produced in Rangoon, downplayed its significance. But as Burma's crisis worsened in the mid-1980s, attitudes changed. In 1988 a World Bank consultant, astounded by the virtual disappearance of any rice that year for official export, estimated that as much as $3,000 million or 40 per cent of the GNP annually changed hands on the black market.[24] These figures are no surprise to the few outsiders who have travelled in rural Burma or the long-suffering Burmese people for whom trading on the black market has long been a national way of life. Explained one Thai Intelligence officer with long experience of cross-border trading: 'Many people, when they hear figures quoted in millions, are very sceptical. They look at the vegetables, cheroots and cattle, which are all most people see trickling across the border, and think the trade can't be very large. What they forget is the high value of goods like jade, teak, rubies and opium which pass through largely unnoticed.'[25]

There are undoubtedly individuals, including government officials, who have made personal fortunes from this unregulated trade. Army officers on duty in the Shan and Kachin States have for years lined their pockets by privately dealing in rubies and other precious stones. But in countless interviews with more everyday smugglers making the dangerous trip to and from the different borders, I invariably found that simple stories of human hardship were usually the motivating factor: a farmer selling a buffalo to raise money for black-market medicine desperately needed for a sick relative, or a labourer carrying a wheel or motor parts to repair a broken engine. Such people have no access to the thriving black-market businesses in government-controlled towns; even teachers usually give extra private coaching to supplement their meagre incomes.

This trade has become the armed opposition's lifeblood. Local taxes in rebel-held areas produce sufficient food or income for daily subsistence, but the 5-10 per cent levies on black-market trade raise the cash to buy black-market arms and ammunition. The ability to control this trade generally reflects the insurgents' individual strengths; most are extremely adept at protecting and controlling their own trade routes. Local trade wars between rival armed groups and battles over strategic passes and strongholds have led to frequent charges of warlordism, which the insurgents vehemently deny even though they are not without some truth. Over the years most groups have been able to secure their own sources of income: jade for the KIO; teak, cattle and luxury consumer goods from Thailand for the KNU; medicine and rice for the Muslim Rohingyas and the Rakhine nationalists in Arakan; and opium for many of the groups in the Shan State, especially Khun Sa's TRC. Indeed, with an annual opium crop that has swept past the 1,000 ton mark, it is quite likely, as the experience of Colombia and Peru (cocaine) and Afghanistan (opium) has shown, that even with a political settlement, the twin problems of banditry and insurgency may well exist in north-east Burma for many years to come; the international narcotics market fuels its own wars. (The CPB, which until 1989 controlled vast areas in the Shan State, had diverse sources of revenue, but is not untainted by the charge of involvement in the opium trade since it, too, taxed farmers cultivating poppy fields.)

The result of this thriving, privately controlled black-market trade is that, while in the 1950s many groups depended for their survival on political organisation and close cooperation with local villagers, since the 1960s most insurgent groups have been able to build up relatively large armies, which in some cases have far exceeded their real political abilities. Faced with insurgency on such a scale, the *Tatmadaw* has simply been unable to cope and long ago settled instead for a policy of gradual attrition. Generally speaking, military analysts calculate, for any chance of success in fighting a guerrilla war government forces need a ten to one ratio in their favour. But in Burma, with combined insurgent forces over the last four decades standing at between 25,000 and 30,000 armed regulars, it is not hard to see why progress has been slow.

How the economic reforms the Saw Maung regime has promised since the 1988 coup will affect the situation is for the moment unclear. It is notable that one of SLORC's first moves has been to try and destroy the insurgents' financial base by attacking border strongholds and stepping up official trade with its neighbours. In response insurgent groups have broken into smaller cells and tried to disrupt the trade by attacking roads, bridges, railway lines and government installations in the towns. None the less, the early indications suggest the *Tatmadaw*'s new strategy has hit many insurgent armies hard; unlike the *Tatmadaw*, they all have to try and survive without any external support. In late 1990 in areas where ceasefires with rebel forces had been agreed, SLORC even began proposing massive road-building and border development programmes with United Nations aid in Rangoon's first apparent recognition of the economic basis of insurgency.

The changing political climate, the SLORC ceasefires and, despite the continuing repression, the victory of the National League for Democracy in the 1990 election also open up the real possibility of country-wide peace talks and negotiations. But until now the irony has been that the *Tatmadaw* has frequently been outgunned in guerrilla warfare by opposition forces with better Chinese (AK47s) and American-made weapons (M16s, M79s, mortars, rocket launchers). During the Indo-China War black-market weapons were plentiful and are still (mostly as a spillover from the Cambodian conflict) easily available, at a price, on the international arms market. The *Tatmadaw*, though, has largely depended on weaponry made under licence in Burma from the West German company, Fritz Werner. But captured G2 and G3 automatics are heavy (with a tendency to jam) and are most certainly a second choice for all insurgent armies.

Significantly, until the Saw Maung coup the *Tatmadaw* made little use of the air. The BSPP government did possess a small airforce and 20 or so helicopters donated by the US under an anti-narcotics programme. But after several were shot down in the early 1980s they were only rarely used in battle. In 1990, with funds from the emergency sell-off of natural resources, SLORC bought a fleet of new aircraft, reportedly including 12 F-6 or F-7 fighters from China, but the government still does not possess the financial reserves to risk or repair damage. The *Tatmadaw* has also made much less use of mechanical transport than might be expected. Very few new roads have been built; others, such as the Ledo Road, have been lost to the jungle. As a result, in front-line battle zones the *Tatmadaw* has frequently had to rely on human porters to carry supplies. This, in turn, has led to persistent allegations of gross human rights' abuses. It is also an exceedingly antiquated way of fighting a well-trained and armed enemy in terrain ideally suited for guerrilla warfare. The result has been that, though there have been one or two largescale *Tatmadaw* operations each year and occasional battles involving several thousand troops (with the CPB, KIO and KNU), most of the fighting has long been characterised by small skirmishes and guerrilla strikes.[26]

The Victims of War

The human cost has been very high. As with other government statistics, after the tens of thousands of casualties in the open civil war of 1948-52, there has been a certain symmetry to official *Tatmadaw* battle reports, with the government usually claiming the deaths in battle of an average 2,000 insurgents each year against the loss of some 500-600 government troops.[27] Insurgent leaders, however, more than put these figures in reverse. For example, since 1980 the KNU has estimated government casualties on the south-east front alone as running at over 1,000 deaths a year; and, to quote an earlier figure, in 1977 the CPB estimated *Tatmadaw* casualties at 1,735 dead and 2,336 wounded in clashes with the CPB's People's Army.[28] But all these are military casualties and I suspect that civilian casualties are just as high. Few reliable records have been kept but the KIO claims to have recorded the verifiable deaths of 33,336 civilians at the hands of government forces in the years 1961-86; for its part, in the first nine months of 1965 alone, the *Tatmadaw* claims to have 'crushed' 4,500 Kachin insurgents.[29]

Under present circumstances it is impossible to verify any of these claims or statistics, but a figure of about 10,000 deaths a year nationwide from the insurgencies over the last four decades is probably fairly accurate, though with some much higher annual fluctuations. Tragically, the carnage in the cities in 1988 probably gave that year one of the highest figures since early independence. SLORC chairman, Gen. Saw Maung, showed a touch of self-defensiveness when, in an astonishing moment of openness after the coup, he revealed that, in 1989, 28,000 families in Burma were receiving pensions for soldiers who had 'fallen' since 1953 and 40,000 for disabled veterans.[30] Of civilians, defence militia, insurgents, the thousands who had died before 1953 or those whose pensions had been discontinued or refused, he gave no figures at all. But, in an admission that political optimists believe may mean that the *Tatmadaw* is finally facing up to the scale of Burma's human disaster, he added that the true death toll 'would reach as high as millions, I think. Indeed, it really is no good'.[31]

Cynics argue that Ne Win and the *Tatmadaw* high command, though starting off as the defenders of Burma, have long since needed the insurgencies to justify their hold on power. It can be said that the real political struggle in Burma since independence has been a battle between the various new 'democracy' forces (from the AFPFL, NLD and CPB to the KNU and KIO with their various demands for free speech, federalism and communism) against the might of Ne Win and the country's military strong men. By the same argument, this closeted and predominantly Burman group of soldiers, invoking fanatical blood loyalty and the traditions of such great all-conquering monarchs as Alaunghpaya and Anawrahta, have simply put the clock back and embarked on a new era of military conquest in the mountains and countryside to reimpose a historical central authority.

Whatever the justification, the results have been the same. Though little seen and reported in the world outside, the death toll in four decades of constant fighting has been appalling. Compared to the much larger conflagrations in the region, these wars may have seemed relatively small, but in the end the cost has been just as devastating. Much of the fighting has centred around small rural communities, especially in the ethnic minority states. Yet, though the government has had its successes, no side has been able to win decisively. In Burma there have been no political victors. In the process millions of homes, families and lives have been shattered and, in many areas, the national economy has remained paralysed at a level even lower than it was under the British. To travel writers on the tightly controlled Rangoon-Pagan-Mandalay tourist loop, it might indeed look like a land lost in time, but in reality Burma has long been in a deep decline.

It is necessary to have this background picture before going on to examine in more detail the course of the different insurgent movements. Since much of Burma has remained officially off-limits, it is absolutely vital to keep in mind how the insurgencies have actually looked on the ground.

PART TWO
INSURRECTIONS IN THE
PARLIAMENTARY ERA

6

The 'Final Seizure of Power': A Country Goes Underground

> 'The history of our Party can be described as basically a history of armed struggle.'
> (Statement of CPB CC at its 45th founding anniversary, 15 August 1984)

Few countries have had a more perilous transition to independence than Burma but, overshadowed by the terrifying scale of the racial and religious bloodbath in neighbouring India, its trauma passed by little noticed by the outside world. Independence arrived with the Red Flags of Thakin Soe and various Arakanese and *Mujahid* guerrillas already in the field. It then took less than three months for the insurrection of the CPB's mainstream White Flag faction to begin.

Key protagonists on all sides now agree there was a tragic inevitability about the outbreak of fighting. In the wake of Aung San's assassination, personal and political relations between the wartime comrades deteriorated rapidly during the latter half of 1947, despite the CPB's apparently conciliatory line towards U Nu and the 'bourgeois' AFPFL leadership. If during these critical months the CPB's position had appeared surprisingly ambivalent towards both the British and the provisional AFPFL government, communist leaders today contend that it was because underlying their uncertainty was the conviction that the British would not really leave. Many still felt it might yet be necessary to fight. As a result, they argued, the unity of the CPB, the AFPFL and all other patriotic forces had to be maintained at all costs.

When it became clear during the second half of 1947 that the British were indeed preparing to pull out, attention began to focus on the Nu-Attlee Treaty of October 1947 and a bitter row developed over the terms and true definition of Burma's independence. Communist leaders described it as a fake, a sham and as keeping Burma in a servile, semi-colonial state: an opinion the CPB still holds.[1] As the CPB's general-secretary, Thakin Than Tun, explained in March 1948:

Behind this facade of sham independence the old colonial social order is retained. British imperialism continues its domination, though the form has changed. Imperialism did not hand over power to the national bourgeoisie until it was sure the national bourgeoisie had given up the path of opposition and that it was going to use the power so transferred not against imperialism but against the people.[2]

The main target of the CPB's hostility was the Let Ya-Freeman Defence Agreement, appended as an annex to the main Nu-Attlee Treaty, under which a British military training mission would be allowed to remain behind in Burma for an initial period of three years. Equally controversially, it also provided for the possibility of a future military alliance with Britain. This the CPB took as both evidence of British intention to subvert the future sovereignty of Burma and proof of U Nu's final capitulation. On National Day, 8 November 1947, U Nu called for a new Socialist Party-PVO-CPB coalition, but when talks failed he denounced the CPB in a nationwide broadcast 'as treacherous as the song of sirens'.[3] CPB leaders, he alleged, had already secretly ordered their followers to begin collecting arms. None the less, the effectiveness of the CPB's campaign against the Nu-Attlee Treaty, which gained widespread credence in Burma at the time, was reflected in the government's continued reluctance to join the British Commonwealth of Nations. This contrasted sharply with both India and Pakistan and was the first evicence of the isolationism which characterised the foreign policies of virtually all political parties in Burma during the 1950s and 1960s.[4]

On the Present Political Situation: The CPB's Thesis of Armed Insurrection

The CPB's future revolutionary strategy was outlined in Thakin Ba Tin's historic thesis, *On the Present Political Situation in Burma and Our Tasks*, drawn up in December 1947 and reputedly discussed at a CPB Central Committee meeting in Rangoon on 18-19 February 1948. While not yet ruling out any hope of isolating U Nu, Bo Let Ya and the socialist leaders, U Ba Swe and U Kyaw Nyein, in the collaborationist AFPFL leadership, Ba Tin warned that much of the CPB's thinking during 1947 had been misguided: 'We totally forgot the Leninist principle that the imperialist bureaucracy and state machine cannot be taken over and run in the interest of the people; on the contrary it has to be smashed.'[5] No transition to socialism, he argued, would be possible under an imperialist-backed bourgeois-landlord government. The CPB faced a clear choice, either intensify the struggle while 'the forces of revolution are strong and undefeated' or passively wait until the AFPFL government is ready to launch civil war on its own terms.[6]

Since Ba Tin's thesis formed the cornerstone of the CPB's militant political philosophy well into the 1950s, it is worth examining in detail. In reviving the slogan, 'the final seizure of power', from the CPB's January 1947 CC meeting, Ba Tin urged the party to step up a propaganda campaign to expose the fraudulent nature of Burma's independence and the complicity of U Nu's supporters and to build up a new 'fighting united front from below'.[7] The key elements of the CPB's political programme, he argued, should be a 'national rising to tear up the treaty of slavery'; the immediate nationalisation of all British and foreign assets; the abolition of all forms of landlordism and debt; the dismantling of the existing state bureaucracy and its replacement with a people's government; and, finally, alliances and trade agreements with 'democratic China, fighting Vietnam and Indonesia' and other democratic countries resisting 'Anglo-American imperialist domination'.[8] To carry out this planned national rising the CPB would follow a

twofold strategy: an escalating campaign of strikes by workers and state employees in Rangoon and other government-controlled towns, while in the countryside
new liberated zones defended by Red Guards would be built up and militant
PVOs trained in partisan warfare.[9]

There has since been considerable controversy over the exact timing and thinking behind Ba Tin's thesis. CPB leaders now discount suggestions by Western
writers that he completed his paper after attending a Communist Party of India
(CPI) CC meeting in Calcutta in early December 1947. In fact in the mid-1960s
Ba Tin was one of the first victims of the CPB's own mini Cultural Revolution
and the CPB's veteran chairman, Thakin Ba Thein Tin, today describes the thesis
as only Ba Tin's 'personal views'.[10] But whether or not Ba Tin actually attended
the Calcutta meeting, in late 1947 it became known that at that meeting the CPI,
under Ranadive's new leadership, had decided to abandon its own 'united front'
compromise with the Indian National Congress and instead adopt a line of armed
revolution to overthrow the Nehru government.[11] This has led to speculation that
the CPB's decision to launch its own armed struggle so shortly afterwards was
made under the influence of the CPI and, by implication, on the instruction of the
international communist movement. Such speculation, heightened by government
propaganda, continued to mount after CPB Politburo members, Thakins Than Tun
and Ba Thein Tin, attended the Second CPI Congress in Calcutta in February
1948 and the CPB's student leader, Aung Gyi, visited the grandly titled Conference of Youth and Students of South-East Asia Fighting for Freedom and Independence, also in Calcutta, the same month.[12] Many Western writers saw the
almost simultaneous outbreak of communist uprisings in Burma (March), Malaya
(June) and Indonesia (September) the same year as final, conclusive proof of
'orders from Moscow' and an internationally coordinated communist conspiracy
in the region.[13] Today Ba Thein Tin completely rejects these charges:

> There is not an iota of truth mooted in the western newspapers that the armed revolu-
> tion in Burma and other SEA countries were inspired and instigated by the Youth
> Conference or by the advice of the CPI. These items in the western press are brazen
> lies to discredit our party. As everybody knows, the civil war in Burma broke out
> because the ruling class of Burma attacked our party and the people by force of arms
> and not vice versa.... Probably, there may be certain influences exerted from the inter-
> national communist movement within our party. However, all the lines and policies
> adopted by our party at various stages of our revolution are entirely decided by our
> party. No other parties are responsible for that. Hence we are entirely responsible for
> all of them.[14]

Though there was certainly a general orientation away from the CPI and
towards the China Communist Party (CCP) in the late 1940s (the CPB has
become particularly close to the CCP since the 1960s), CPB policy
pronouncements frequently contained the same staunch nationalism, even xenophobia, as most other political movements in Burma.[15] With the later exception of
China, CPB contact with other international communist parties has always been
spasmodic; there was hardly any at all at the time of the outbreak of the insurrection. Unlike Indo-China there were no communist leaders, such as Ho Chi Minh,
with wide experience of the Soviet Union and the communist movement in
Europe.

Contact with the CPI had been established by Thein Pe Myint in 1936 (see
Chapter 3). Indian communists and CPB leaders, particularly Thein Pe and Ba

Tin, the CPB's Burma-born Bengali theoretician, maintained intermittent contact through the Second World War and into 1947. In 1941 the CPB also sent a young intellectual, Aye Ngwe, into China to ask for aid from Mao Zedong and the CCP, but he remained cut off by the war. In 1943 Thein Pe briefly met Zhou Enlai in China and returned to India with translations of CCP material and Mao Zedong's book, *New Democracy*. (Linking Burma's independence struggle with those of India and China, Zhou described the alliance of other communists in Burma with the Japanese as amazing and wrong.[16]) In September 1945, CCP CC member, Teng Fa, talked to Thein Pe on a stop-off in India and Fa advised him to start preparing for armed conflict with the British.[17]

But the CPB only really participated in an international communist forum for the first time in February 1947, when Ba Thein Tin and Aung Gyi visited London for the British Empire Conference of Communist Parties. Aung Gyi subsequently travelled on to Czechoslovakia and visited several other European countries, but with minimal impact back home.

Nevertheless, as American historian Frank Trager points out, explicit in both Ba Tin's thesis and Than Tun's subsequent address to the CPI Congress was the CPB leaders' recent study of the 'theory of the Sixth Congress of the Communist International, i.e. the left revolutionary strategy of the Comintern's third period, 1928-34' and the decisions of the first Cominform meeting held in Poland the previous September.[18] Their language clearly paraphrased the so-called Zhdanov line, named after the speech by the Cominform's Soviet delegate, Andrei Zhdanov, who, echoing Stalin, divided the world into two major blocs: the imperialist, anti-democratic camp led by the US and the anti-imperialist, democratic camp led by the Soviet Union. Zhdanov warned that, though severely weakened by the war, the countries of the imperialist bloc were now trying to regain control of their pre-war colonies, either by handing over power to 'collaborationist national bourgeois' regimes (India, Burma) or by trying to crush national liberation movements, such as those fighting the Dutch in Indonesia or the French in Vietnam.[19] As a result, Ba Tin explained, in October 1947, immediately after the Cominform meeting, the CPB began its own study class on the 'theory of colonial revolution'. Linking the 'fate of the Burmese revolution' to other revolutionary movements in India and South-East Asia, Ba Tin argued that a 'special responsibility' had now fallen upon the CPB. By uprooting the 'disease of reformism' both in itself and the AFPFL government, the CPB 'could be the initiators of a new revolutionary upsurge and an uprising which is bound to lead to similar developments in the neighbouring countries'.[20]

But, as other commentators point out, the speech of the Cominform's Yugoslav delegate, Edvard Kardelj, was more likely to have ultimately proved decisive.[21] Kardelj argued that the working class in former colonies could only hope to achieve victory through armed seizure of power, not by compromising in united fronts with the national bourgeoisie. Thus, independently or otherwise, with the CPB CC's discussion of Ba Tin's thesis in February 1948 and its apparent acceptance of this analysis with its implicit rejection of reformism, the stage was set for armed confrontation. 'Comrades,' Than Tun exhorted the Second CPI Congress, '1948... will decide the fate of the liberation movements in South-East Asia.'[22]

It is futile, then, to try and decide who fired the first bullet. CPB leaders have always maintained that their resort to arms in 1948 was essentially a defensive measure. But in Calcutta, while claiming to be trying to avoid civil war, Than Tun had already made clear the CPB's willingness to use force:

> We have more than a *lakh* [100,000] of class conscious militants who have military training, many of whom have had experience of partisan warfare and who can be swung into action whenever the occasion demands it. We also have *lakhs* of workers, peasants and common people behind us.... We are prepared to return two blows for every blow struck against us — smash the imperialist-feudal-bourgeois combine — establish real independence, a people's democracy and a lasting peace.[23]

The CPB's Armed Struggle Commences

As if on cue, from February 1948 another wave of CPB-backed strikes in the All Burma Trade Union Congress (ABTUC) began to grip Rangoon. Spreading from the Burma Oil Company, mass walk-outs by workers, reputedly orchestrated by Ba Tin, paralysed Steel Brothers, the timber mills, the dockyards of the Irrawaddy Flotilla Company and dozens of other small companies and industries around the city. Communist leaders were also encouraged by an exuberant mass rally of the All Burma Peasants Organisation in mid-March in the CPB stronghold of Pyinmana, where farmers were celebrating the end of the harvest; a cheering 75,000-strong crowd, addressed by Than Tun and Ba Tin, passed resolutions supporting the strikers and 'Arakan freedom fighters' battling the AFPFL government and called for the smashing of 'fascism (AFPFL) by all possible means'.[24]

The Red Flag guerrillas' increasingly violent activities around the country did not help government fears. Thakin Soe was arrested on 10 March and, as more Red Flag leaders were picked up over the next few days, documents outlining a communist plan to seize Rangoon by force were captured. There was still considerable interchange between Red Flag and White Flag ranks (Red Flag Politburo member, Thakin Tin Mya, for example, joined the White Flags the following year) and government officials became utterly confused over the real scale of the CPB threat.

Convinced that the White Flags were planning to revolt as the anniversary of Resistance Day approached, on 25 March U Nu ordered the arrests of Than Tun and the CPB leadership. He was stopped for a moment by the first of several interventions by the People's Volunteer Organisation (PVO), which proposed making one more attempt to reunite the Red Flags, White Flags, PVOs and socialists. Faced with the threat of the PVO's withdrawal from his fragile AFPFL coalition government, U Nu had no choice but to comply and two days later even declared that if these talks were successful (i.e. against his better judgement they agreed on unity), he would resign.[25] On the same day, however, at a mass Resistance Day rally organised by the CPB in Bandoola Square in the heart of Rangoon, Than Tun made his most militant speech yet; he was later quoted in the government press as saying that he would have the Bagaya (a communist stronghold in Rangoon) 'overflowing with the blood of socialists'.[26] This immediately prompted U Nu to reissue orders to arrest the CPB leaders. But when the police arrived at CPB headquarters on the Bagaya Road in the early hours of 28 March, they found that Than Tun and his colleagues, allegedly tipped off in advance, had already slipped away. Over the following days some 350 CPB activists were picked up in Rangoon, but by this time Than Tun's party was already in Pyinmana calling out its armed supporters, a decision CPB chairman Ba Thein Tin says was taken by the CPB Politburo before leaving Rangoon. Thus, after less than three years as a legal, above-ground party, the CPB's long insurrection had finally begun.

The CPB's initial campaign, directed from the White Flags' main strongholds in the rural countryside between Pyu and Yamethin in central Burma, was largely concentrated in Pegu, Myingyan and Bassein districts and the Lower Delta. Through April and into May CPB guerrillas seized police stations, captured small towns and villages, and destroyed government supply lines and communications.[27] By mid-May, however, as the army began to take back the first CPB positions, many observers felt the CPB's offensive was in danger of petering out.[28]

'Leftist Unity' Talks: Mutiny Spreads to the Army and PVOs

At this moment the CPB was boosted by the first of a series of desertions and defections from the government side; this gave its campaign a dramatic boost and, within months, brought the AFPFL government to the brink of collapse.

The first group to come over was Aung San's former private army, the PVO, which since his death had been a largely rudderless force. At independence the PVO was estimated to have between 100,000 and 800,000 supporters, with the lower figure generally regarded as the more accurate.[29] Originally Aung San had intended to integrate some 10,000 of these wartime veterans into the police and armed forces; the rest would be helped to return to civilian life through a programme of land redistribution and farming cooperatives. But following his assassination PVO leaders insisted on retaining their paramilitary formations and the PVO increasingly took on the character of a national political party. With widespread rural support and countrywide organisation rivalling the Socialist Party's, it quickly became an important part of the AFPFL's umbrella coalition, especially in view of the CPB's increasingly vociferous opposition; 44 PVO representatives were elected to the 255 seat Constituent Assembly (in many areas the PVOs also marshalled the elections) and three, Bo Po Kun, Bo Sein Hman and Bo Hmu Aung, were appointed to U Nu's Cabinet.

This led both the CPB and the Socialist Party to try and win the PVOs over to their side. The Socialist Party made the first bid. In October 1947 it agreed in principle with PVO leaders to the formation of a new coalition party to be known as the Marxist League.[30] Under the agreement the PVOs would disband immediately after independence. But Independence Day came and went with many PVO district leaders, jealous of giving up their most obvious source of power, refusing to hand in their weapons. This was the first clear intimation of the problems the central government would have with paramilitary formations and warlordism throughout the 1950s. At the end of January a similar plan to form another coalition party, the Aung San League, also failed because local PVO leaders again refused to disband what were, in effect, their own private armies.

By this stage two main factions had emerged; the larger, known as the White Band PVO because of its distinctive arm bands, had pro-communist sympathies and was led by Bo La Yaung (one of the former *Thirty Comrades*) and Bo Po Kun; the other, led by another of the *Thirty Comrades*, Bo Hmu Aung, was closer to the Socialist Party and became known as the Yellow Band PVO. (For these generally left-wing sympathies the PVOs were sometimes called 'green communists'!) Having interceded on the CPB's behalf at the end of March, in early May the PVOs again demanded that the prime minister, U Nu, open negotiations with the CPB.

This hastened the introduction of U Nu's Fifteen Point Leftist Unity Programme, which was, he conceded, initially an attempt to win back the PVOs and outflank the communists. It also set the tone for much of the AFPFL government throughout the 1950s; in this first draft can be seen the shape of Burma's future *pyidawtha* (welfare state) programme, which was introduced in 1952. Land and any monopolising foreign trade interests were to be nationalised, government administration democratised and any foreign aid that compromised Burma's independence rejected. At the same time various health, educational and welfare programmes would be introduced.[31]

The most controversial suggestion was also the last, Point Fifteen, which proposed forming a Marxist league composed of socialists, communists and PVOs to 'propagate the writings of Marx, Engels, Lenin, Stalin, Mao Tse-tung, Tito, Dimitrov and other apostles of Marxism'.[32] This proposal received much criticism at home and abroad (the British and American press accused U Nu of having gone over to communism) and it was quickly dropped. Later it disappeared even from government accounts of the events, with the draft now referred to as the Fourteen Point Programme.

Nor were the PVOs or communists impressed. The White Band PVO called for round-the-table peace talks with the CPB in which the communists would be regarded 'as equals with the PVO and the AFPFL', while the CPB ruled out any talks with the 'current leaders' of the government.[33] U Nu, meanwhile, was adamant he would not negotiate with any group still in active revolt, a position maintained by all governments through the long years since.

Matters finally came to a head in mid July. With the government already racked by unrelated factional feuds, which saw U Nu briefly resigning and the deputy prime minister, Bo Let Ya, Foreign Minister, U Tin Tut, and Socialist Party chairman, U Ko Ko Kyi, all leave the Cabinet, an emergency Leftist Organising Council meeting was called in Rangoon to find a solution to the war. In attendance were all the main Socialist Party, PVO and army leaders (including Gen. Ne Win, Bo Zeya and Bo Ye Htut), the dissident communist Thein Pe Myint, who had refused to go underground with the CPB, as well as the CPB CC member, Bo Thein Dan, trade union leader and former *Thirty Comrade*, Bo Yan Aung, and the Red Flag's military commander, Bo Aung Min. (The latter three were especially released from gaol.) After far-ranging discussions which touched on the likelihood of the impending Karen uprising, three points were finally agreed on as the future basis for national unity: the acceptance of the Fifteen Point Programme; a left coalition government including the Socialist Party, the PVO and both factions of the CPB; and a united Burma Army free from racial distinctions.[34]

After the meeting Bo Thein Dan and Bo Yan Aung were sent to the CPB's jungle headquarters to pass the proposals on to Than Tun and the CPB leadership; Aung Min was also released but later joined the White Flag CPB. This was as far as the peace process went. With U Nu delaying any move that would admit the CPB to government and a new dispute breaking out over the army leadership, restive White Band PVO units, caught in fighting between the CPB and the government, began to turn their guns against the army. On 28 July Bo Po Kun and Bo La Yaung ordered the rest of their White Band supporters underground and with them went an estimated 4,000 men under arms, or 60 per cent of the PVO's main fighting force. Across the country thousands more irregular PVO militia followed in sympathy. It was, the AFPFL government charged, 'a stab in the back'.[35]

The government's troubles did not end here. The PVO defection triggered off a series of mutinies by communist sympathisers in the Union Military Police (UMP) and fledgling Burma Army which, like the PVO, had lost much of its sense of direction in the aftermath of Aung San's death. In mid-June a battalion from the Sixth Burma Rifles went over to the communist side in Pegu district. In quick succession, on 9 and 10 August 1948, the First Burma Rifles stationed in Thayetmyo and the Third Burma Rifles in Mingdalon joined them. Their commanders, Bo Zeya and Bo Ye Htut, were both former *Thirty Comrades*, standing next only to the Karen, Gen. Smith Dun, the army Chief-of-Staff, and his deputy, Ne Win, in army seniority. Indeed shortly before going underground, Bo Zeya had approached U Nu (apparently with Smith Dun's approval) with the suggestion that he (Bo Zeya) be made Defence Minister rather than Ne Win.[36]

These defections, which included experienced army officers such as Bo Thet Tun, Bo Soe Maung and Bo Sein Tin, had a dramatic impact. They marked a major revival in the CPB's fortunes and these men became the key architects of the CPB's military strategy in the early 1950s. The First Burma Rifles made an immediate strike down the road towards Rangoon, but was stopped in an ambush by troops still loyal to the government near Letpadan, while the Third Burma Rifles, harried by aerial strikes all the way, moved north to join them. In the coming months the army's unopposed control of the skies was to prove vital to the government's survival; but both mutinous regiments were eventually able to re-group in Prome where they were temporarily reorganised into a new force, the Revolutionary Burma Army.

Thus by August 1948, within eight months of independence, there was complete chaos. Most of Arakan was in the hands of various Red Flag, White Flag, PVO-UMP, Rakhine and *Mujahid* guerrilla bands, while vast areas of central and Lower Burma, including the strategic towns of Yamethin and Prome, had fallen under CPB or PVO control. Fighting had reached the suburbs of Rangoon; 88 out of 311 police stations in the country were reported to be in rebel hands, while in the countryside ferries and trains had virtually ceased to run.[37]

As if this were not enough, in August the government was further rocked by the outbreak of fighting in the Karenni State, quickly followed at the beginning of September by the seizure of the southern cities of Moulmein and Thaton by Karen and Mon ethnic nationalists giving the first warning of their growing military muscle.

In the light of the ethnic rebellions about to break out, it is ironic that through these turbulent months the government was only saved by the continued loyalty of the Chin, Kachin and Karen regiments in the Burma Army, especially the six battalions of the Kachin and Karen Rifles, of which four were themselves to go into revolt in early 1949.[38] The appointment, as a symbolic token of goodwill at independence, of the Karen officer, Gen. Smith Dun, as commander-in-chief of the Burma Army and another Karen, Saw Shi Sho, as Air Force chief, did much to ensure the continued loyalty of the ethnic minority troops under their command. The Karen and Kachin Rifles recaptured Prome, Thayetmyo and much of the Pyinmana area from the CPB in fierce fighting in the strategic heart of Burma during the latter half of 1948, which gave the government time to reorganise its disintegrating military command and (perhaps even more importantly as it soon transpired) to prepare secretly for the outbreak of war with the Karen National Union.

Racial Tension: Background to the Karen Rebellion

Though attention in Rangoon was focused on the CPB and the day-to-day fortunes of U Nu's precarious coalition government, independence swiftly dispelled the notion, still commonly held amongst ethnic Burman leaders, that the KNU was a British-inspired invention which would fade away with their departure. The KNU had never accepted the provisions for a Karen State under the terms of the 1947 Constitution. As early as 3 February 1948, the KNU's chairman, Oxford-educated lawyer Saw Ba U Gyi, wrote to U Nu repeating the Second KNU Congress' controversial manifesto of October 1947, including the demand for Karen territory in the Delta, and setting a deadline of just one month for the government to agree.[39] To back this up, the KNU organised a day of protest on 11 February and, despite government attempts to block the demonstrations by closing roads and stopping traffic, Karen leaders claim as many as 400,000 KNU supporters took to the streets in dozens of towns and villages across the country. Carried at the head of each procession were banners bearing the mottos that have since become the four main slogans of the Karen revolution; these words still adorn the walls of all schools and administrative buildings in KNU-controlled territory:

Give the Karen State at once — Independence
For the Burmese one kyat and the Karen one kyat — Equality
We do not want communal strife — National Unity
We do not want civil war — Peace.

Though U Nu did not officially reply, the campaign forced the AFPFL government to acknowledge the KNU's growing organisational strength. In early March U Nu held a series of meetings with the Minister for Karen Affairs, San Po Thin, and with leaders of the Karen Youth Organisation who had been elected to Parliament; but after that they were very much pushed into the background.

U Nu now offered to meet Saw Ba U Gyi and the KNU leadership. Before the meeting, 500 delegates from Lower Burma gathered in Rangoon on 3 March for the Third KNU Congress. Opinion was divided over meeting the AFPFL. Most representatives spoke against accepting U Nu's invitation. In his Congress address, Saw Ba U Gyi himself warned that the government was unlikely to agree to their demands, adding to great applause: 'If they use diplomacy, we too must use diplomacy, but this time we won't talk about requesting our state but about having it.'[40]

The talks, however, merely accentuated the great gulf between the KNU and AFPFL government. U Nu claimed the Karen State was already provided for under Articles 180 and 181 of the Constitution. If the KNU wanted to extend these areas, it must enter Parliament and amend the Constitution. Far from asking 'rupee for rupee' with the Burmans, the Karens, U Nu argued, by getting the right of a state in the east and separate political privileges for the Delta Karens, were already getting 'half a rupee more'. To this Saw Ba U Gyi replied that the Karens had not yet received even 'one anna'.[41] No agreement was reached. At the end of the talks U Nu released a statement outlining Karen demands and accusing the KNU of attempting to set up a parallel government in Karen-majority areas. The government already had evidence, he claimed, that far from surrendering illegally held arms, KNU sympathisers were trying to increase supplies through black market purchases. In the volatile context of the times, his tone was ill chosen. A section of the vernacular press in Rangoon seized upon these accusations and, through 1948, played a provocative role in inciting communal tensions.[42] Even veteran KNU leaders concede that U Nu was most likely only trying to warn of the dangers of a communal explosion, a view supported by the fact that, despite the failure of the talks, Ba U Gyi and U Nu remained in close counsel until the eve of the Karen uprising.

The outbreak of the CPB insurrection and army-PVO mutinies overtook the tenuous discussions. Despite U Nu's accusing words and the Rangoon government's obvious vulnerability, Karen troops stayed loyal to the army's high command throughout these traumatic months. Tragically, the success of these Karen and Kachin troops (who after all were only obeying Rangoon's orders) in battle with the CPB-PVOs stirred up resentment in the local Burman population and, sadly, increased the rapidly worsening racial tensions.

Nor was the KNU, as U Nu alleged, entirely blameless. As outlying Karen villages came under attack, local KNDO units, claiming they feared a repetition of the massacres of the war, began to take over hundreds of district and village administrations. This, KNU veterans insist, was primarily a defensive measure. KNDO activities were coordinated from U Loo-Nee Street, Kemmendine, Rangoon, where training seminars were organised in the KNU compound by the first KNDO commander, Mahn Ba Zan, a former headmaster from Maubin. Two organisational zones were set up, the 'Delta' under Saw Hunter Tha Hmwe, a pre-war school inspector, and the 'Eastern' under the lawyer Saw Sankey, who had been the KNU representative on the 1947 Frontier Areas Commission of Enquiry. In areas where Karen villages were few, KNDO troops were drafted in to augment numbers; arms were distributed by a secret courier service organised by KNU sympathisers in the Karen Rifles.[43]

In other areas local Karen militia (like many PVOs, Red Flags and CPB supporters) operated beyond any central authority. Most Delta respondents blame neither the CPB nor the KNDO for the increasing outbreaks of inter-communal fighting from the middle of 1948. But, as in the confusion at the end of the Second World War, it was often hard to distinguish between the many armed bands roving central and Lower Burma. There were no fixed battle-lines, banditry was rife and there was an undeniably racial character to much of the intra-village raiding. There were no doubt guilty parties on all sides. The most notorious Karen dacoit leader was Saw Seaplane, whose parents had reputedly been murdered by the BIA in early 1942. In mid-1948, after being sprung from gaol by his followers, he launched a reign of terror in Pyapon district with a series of revenge attacks. The official government account of the Karen uprising, *The KNDO Insurrection*, attributes many of these incidents to the KNDO, which its veterans bitterly deny.[44] They do, however, admit to a raid on the Maubin treasury which, they say, was carried out under Tha Hmwe's orders; 40 *lakh* kyats were taken and the money distributed to local KNDO units to buy arms.

Whoever was to blame, all parties now realised the very real danger of a full-scale communal war. To avert this tragedy U Nu and Saw Ba U Gyi together toured the Lower Delta and, at a mass meeting in Pyapon, Ba U Gyi publicly announced the KNU would never use force in pursuit of its demands. While government criticism of the KNDO continued, U Nu agreed to allow a number of local KNDO units to arm themselves against the CPB and White Band PVOs. The government's position was still precarious. The most striking example of this new-found trust was in the no-man's land south-west of Rangoon where KNDO units, in response to a request from Smith Dun (and with U Nu's permission), were asked to recapture Twante from the CPB and guard the Twante Canal, the vital waterway linking Rangoon and the Irrawaddy River.[45] This they successfully accomplished, but in the confusion of those days the release of this news was again badly handled and many Burmans, seeing KNDO units move into position on Rangoon's doorstep, believed the Karen insurrection had already begun.

Meanwhile in the forgotten Karenni State nationalist fighting had already broken out. On 9 August 1948, following a factional Baptist-Catholic split in the Karenni leadership, the Mya Leh village headquarters of U Bee Tu Re, who had championed the separatist cause during the independence negotiations with the British, were attacked in a surprise pre-emptive strike by the UMP's 13th regiment. U Bee was taken prisoner and brutally murdered shortly afterwards, for which Karenni nationalists have never forgiven Rangoon. The result was a dramatic polarisation in political support across the state as hundreds of villagers led by the young Kyebogyi *Sawbwa*, Sao Shwe, took up arms against the AFPFL-backed administration of the Kantarawaddy *Sawbwa*, Sao Wunna. Ironically, both men were former comrades-in-arms in Force 136. The state was immediately placed under martial law and, in this remote backwater, the government was able to keep the lid on news of the scale of the fighting for several months. But this is the date the insurgent Karenni National Progressive Party (still led by Sao Shwe's former lieutenant, Saw Maw Reh) commemorates as the beginning of the Karenni nationalist uprising. 'The Karenni people are trying to wrest power from the Burma Union government by armed force,' reported one government despatch reaching Rangoon.[46]

Against this confused background, with still no concessions to the demand for an independent Karen State, Karen militants made their first move. On 1 September, under Saw Sankey's orders, combined KNDO-Karen UMP forces seized control of Thaton and Moulmein, Burma's third largest city, followed a few days later by Shwegyin and Kyaukkyi in the hills to the north. (Local units from the KNU's Mon ally, the MNDO-Mon United Front, led by Nai Shwe Kyin and Nai Hla Maung, also took part in the seizure of Moulmein.) The action was ostensibly a response to the breakdown in law and order across the country, but veteran KNU leaders now concede it was a poorly executed attempt to gain ground before what many believed was an inevitable outbreak of hostilities. It was certainly a calculated strike. With KNDO units holding the only road links and the CPB controlling most of the area between Thaton and Pegu to the north, the entire Tenasserim Division was cut off from Lower Burma and could only be approached by boat across the Gulf of Martaban. But the move was badly coordinated (reflecting the KNU's still weak organisation) and after just four days the vital seaport of Moulmein was handed back to the Second Kachin Rifles, who were allowed to land from the sea. Missing were five *lakh* kyats taken from the treasury and some 200 arms which had been distributed to local KNDO and MNDO units.

The Accusation of British Involvement

The handling of the Moulmein occupation remains a matter of considerable sensitivity among the nationalist leadership; argument continues over whether handing it back was a gross strategical error or whether at the time the KNU was still committed to working through the due processes of the law. Many Christian

Karen elders and pastors schooled in British traditions felt uncomfortable with the mantle of a revolutionary. But according to Mika Rolly, from the beginning a member of the underground cell, Group X, liaising between the Karen Rifles and Saw Sankey, who actually ordered the occupation, there was another more urgent motive, namely to take a seaport to land arms expected from British sympathisers.[47] Other KNU leaders, including Saw Tha Din, who on Saw Ba U Gyi's instructions negotiated the town's return (and with Nai Shwe Kyin was later imprisoned by the government for his pains), now claim they were unaware of any such plot. From this it can only be concluded that Saw Ba U Gyi himself was not fully informed of the plan, a view with which Rolly concurs.[48]

But there was a British plot, though in the light of subsequent publicity it was much smaller than is popularly believed. It cost the Karens dearly and reinforced the lingering image of the KNU as an unpatriotic, pro-British front. At the critical Leftist Organising Council meeting in July/August 1948, as Socialist Party, PVO, army and CPB officials were urgently discussing how to stop the fighting between the CPB and the government, the discussion had turned, somewhat inevitably, to the threat of Karen rebellion. Delegates described the KNU 'separatist' movement as an 'imperialist plot' and agreed that in the coming months the 'main weapon that the imperialist (British, American and Burmese) would use was the Karen revolts to be led by the KNU and KNDO'.[49]

Not for the first or last time had the left in Burma totally failed to understand the political aspirations of the Karen nationalist movement; the call for leftist unity to head off this perceived imperialist conspiracy was, not surprisingly, a dismal failure. Successive Labour and Conservative governments in Britain continued to supply arms to the AFPFL government even after the British Military Mission was ordered out at the beginning of the Karen uprising; the Let Ya-Freeman Defence Agreement was formally abrogated only in January 1954. None the less, the decisions of the Leftist Unity conference (followed shortly afterwards by the discovery of a small British gun-running plot) signalled a hardening of attitude towards the Karen question by army and Socialist Party leaders, which was to have serious repercussions by the end of 1948.

If ever the much-awaited British plot was to succeed, it was now. But instead of involving the British government or opposition Conservative Party as had been feared, the instigator was an ex-Force 136 adventurer, Col. Cromarty-Tulloch, who had parachuted into the Karenni hills during the war to organise local resistance. At the war's end Tulloch returned to Britain with a letter of accreditation from the Karen Central Organisation authorising him to represent Karen interests until their delegates could arrive. In the hills today many nationalists believe his motives were not entirely altruistic and think he discovered something during the war, possibly gold, for which he was determined to return. Certainly his private actions bore this out. Promising to be back one day, he left a suitcase of money (probably the remains of his Force 136 funds) with the Karenni leader, Sao Shwe, with instructions to start building a new road from Kyebogyi to the important mineral mines at Mawchi.

Back in London Tulloch actively supported the Karen cause, writing articles and organising meetings for the short-lived Friends of the Hills Peoples of Burma, which were attended by a number of prominent Burma veterans, including postwar governor, Dorman-Smith, and ex-FAA director, H.N.C. Stevenson.[50] But most drew the line at his more ambitious plans. In mid-1948 he travelled to

Calcutta with the apparent intention of sailing on to Moulmein with a boatload of arms and ammunition. Another Force 136 confederate, Alexander Campbell of the *Daily Mail*, made it to Rangoon, but the plot was uncovered and he was arrested and deported, leaving Tulloch stranded in Calcutta unconvincingly protesting his innocence.[51] Of the Tulloch group only Revd Baldwin, a Karen-speaking Seventh Day Adventist minister, who himself had been deported by the British shortly before independence, is known for certain to have made it back into Burma. Crossing over the border from Thailand at the beginning of the Karen insurrection, Baldwin worked in the KNU's Foreign Relations Department until his death from blackwater fever near Kamamaung in 1951. Written on his grave-stone is the epitaph: 'Here lies one who loves the Karens.'[52] In the early days of the insurrection there were also a handful of other Britons and Anglo-Burmans caught up in the fighting, such as Captain Vivian, who had been imprisoned in Insein gaol for illegal arms trading, Bruce Humphrey-Taylor, a Burma Navy rating, and Michael Londsdale, a former forestry officer who helped set up the first Free Karen radio station in Toungoo. This was later to give the appearance of a rather larger conspiracy than ever really existed.

A young nationalist, Oliver Ba Than, who travelled to Britain with Baldwin, was Tulloch's link with the Karen underground. Rolly claims that Ba Than con-veyed the instructions from Tulloch that led Sankey to order the occupation of Moulmein; it was clearly a highly secret plan. Ba Than, like Sankey, was killed in the early days of the insurrection and, other than Rolly, few Karen survivors appear to have direct knowledge of the real details of the plan.[53] But H.A. Stonor, a Karen sympathiser and veteran of the Welsh Regiment, has confirmed the key details of the Tulloch conspiracy.[54] As part of the operation Stonor travelled to India where he was meant to link up with Tulloch, but when the plot was uncov-ered he travelled on to Thailand to find that the other members of the group had already given up and gone into hiding. Tulloch was later arrested and imprisoned in Britain on unrelated fraud charges; he was so afraid of being assassinated by Burmese agents that he refused bail while awaiting trial. It was perhaps the Karens' misfortune to become involved, however unwittingly, with such a man. At his trial the judge described him as 'a champion of lost causes'.[55]

The Regional Autonomy Enquiry, *Sitwundan* and Outbreak of Fighting
If the whole debacle was to end in confusion, at least it hastened the commence-ment in October 1948 of the much-delayed Regional Autonomy Enquiry Commission, which had been provided for in the Constitution to investigate Karen claims. In response to continuing signs of ethnic restiveness elsewhere in Burma (particularly war-torn Arakan where fighting with *Mujahids*, U Seinda's Rakhine nationalists and the CPB-PVOs continued) this was now expanded to include Mon and Arakanese claims. The 1948 Commission was far more repre-sentative of ethnic minority interests than the FACE of 1947 had been. On the 28-man committee were six Karens, including Saw Ba U Gyi, Mahn James Tun Aung and Saw Tha Din of the KNU, six Mons, five Arakanese, seven Burmans, and four other representatives of frontier people. But the result was equally incon-clusive. In a long recount of Karen history, the KNU repeated the need for a Karen homeland, to be known as the Independent Karen State, where Karens could 'develop socially, politically, educationally, and economically on their own lines and claim the right of self-determination'.[56] It also repeated its controversial

demand that the state include Karen-majority areas of the Irrawaddy Delta. But one olive-branch was held out: 'Attainment of this objective will not, of course, shut out the possibility of what will always be regarded as the ultimate goal, namely the Common Federation of all the Peoples of Burma.'[57] Another significant new claim put to the Commission and appended to the main KNU declaration was a pledge by the KNU and two Mon nationalist fronts, the United Mon Association and the Mon United Front, to work for a joint Mon-Karen Independent State in the areas of Tenasserim they were both claiming. This agreement arose because ties between Karen and Mon leaders in the Moulmein area grew closer; it was the first clear statement of KNU recognition that the territories they were claiming were not racially exclusive.

Though perhaps no one realised it at the time, this was to be the last public airing of the Karen case. Amidst bitter fighting with the CPB, however, it served as little more than a distraction. The Commission only finally reported in February 1949, after the Karen rebellion had begun; the KNU immediately rejected its recommendations for Karen statehood from an extended Salween district within the Union. The hearings, if a reminder was still needed, only served to emphasise the deep divide between Burman and Karen leaders and even U Nu, nicknamed Karen Nu in government circles for his allegedly pro-Karen views, was to argue, 'I am 100 per cent in disagreement with the present creation of separate states (for Mons, Karens and Arakan).'[58] Most worryingly, at no time did KNU or AFPFL leaders begin to find a common language to resolve what were clearly entrenched political positions. Each side lectured the other and the KNU representatives withdrew from the Commission soon after giving their testimony.

In December 1948 communal relations again took a marked turn for the worse. As in the Second World War, observers tried to apportion equal blame for the increasing outbreaks of racial violence, but the evidence is overwhelming that the Karen community came off very much the worse. The deteriorating atmosphere can partly be attributed to the First Karen and First Kachin Rifles' decisive defeat of the CPB in their Pyinmana strongholds in mid-month. By all accounts Karen and Kachin troops were ruthlessly efficient as they swept through CPB-controlled villages. For many PVOs and BIA veterans who had successfully come through the Second World War and the independence campaign of 1945-7, the sight of Karen and Kachin troops, whom many still regarded as stooges of the British, inflicting defeat on their fellow countrymen was particularly galling.[59]

From the confused tangle of events that followed it is impossible to extricate any real logic or sequence. Disaster followed disaster. KNU leaders today allege the AFPFL government had already embarked on a sinister anti-Karen programme, code-named *Operation Aung San*, to quash the nationalist movement. No copy of this plan exists today and over the years its scope and scale have been considerably embellished. Karen leaders appear to be referring to an army document captured at Meiktila in 1949, which summarised KNU aims and history and had a detailed breakdown of the Karen population in Burma (including its towns, army units, government departments). KNU archives record it as a plan 'to nip the uprising in the bud' and suggest KNU contacts with other ethnic minority leaders, especially the Kachins and Chins, had also been investigated.[60] This, however, is hardly proof of the army's intention to carry out an anti-Karen pogrom.

None the less, the evidence seems to confirm that by the end of 1948 army contingency plans for a Karen uprising were already well underway, though it is questionable whether by the time fighting began the government was much better prepared than the KNU. Certainly, even before the KNDO occupation of Moulmein, the government had good reason to doubt KNU intentions. As early as June 1948, when the collapse of the U Nu government was expected daily, KNU leaders say they met secretly with Dr Ba Maw and Thakin Ba Sein, two of the few leading non-AFPFL politicians still active in Rangoon. Among other things, they wanted to know whether this faction would help set up a coalition government if the KNDO/Karen Rifles took control of Rangoon. KNU general-secretary, Thra Tha Htoo, passed the gist of these discussions on to La Bang Grong of the Kachin National Congress, whose support the KNU was anxious to win. Inevitably these talks came to the attention of the pro-AFPFL Kachin Cabinet minister, the Sama *Duwa* Sinwa Nawng, who warned U Nu. The KNDO occupations of Moulmein and Thaton in September would only have added to government fears and, in November, Sinwa Nawng again repeated his warnings with the ominous words: 'Delay will mean disaster.'[61]

Thus in the second half of 1948, following closely on the heels of the decisions of the Leftist Organising Council meeting in Rangoon, the government began secretly preparing for the possibility of an armed confrontation with the KNU. With the army still largely dependent on its Kachin, Karen and Chin regiments in the war with the CPB, U Nu started to form local auxiliary defence groups, known as the *Sitwundans*, for deployment at the rear. By the end of the year over 100 such territorial units had been formed, largely from supporters of the Yellow Band PVOs and Socialist Party. Many were poorly trained and disciplined and it was these *Sitwundans* (which soon outnumbered the Karen UMPs and KNDOs) rather than the Burma Rifles that created most of the trouble.

Karen leaders still insist these units were working to a secret military agenda, but the evidence is circumstantial. U Nu had set 31 January 1949 as the date for the final formation and training of the units, perhaps not coincidentally the date fighting officially began.[62] Significantly, command of the *Sitwundans* was not given to Karen army Chief-of-Staff, Smith Dun, whom the Leftist Unity conference had pinpointed as a likely imperialist collaborator, but to his deputy, Maj.-Gen. Ne Win.[63] Karen leaders also read a sinister significance into the assassination of Cambridge-educated U Tin Tut, the one member of U Nu's Cabinet with a distinguished background in the British colonial administration, in a mysterious bomb explosion on 18 September 1948. Tut had resigned as Foreign Minister the previous month to become inspector-general of Auxiliary Forces with the rank of brigadier. Though various parties have been accused, including the CPB and a number of different political rivals, no one has ever admitted responsibility for his murder.

It was noticeable from the beginning that the *Sitwundans* adopted a different approach towards the KNDO units, which Smith Dun had employed against the CPB. (As Karen leaders point out, the KNDOs were outlawed in February 1949 just four days after the Karen rebellion began, while the CPB was not declared illegal until 1953.) As they moved into position the *Sitwundans* and local UMPs began ordering the KNDOs and ethnic Karen UMPs to surrender their arms. Many refused and immediately deserted with their weapons. In several areas fighting broke out with both the *Sitwundans* and KNDOs claiming to be operating in the government's name. The Cabinet appeared to back the *Sitwundans*, while the Rangoon press loudly interpreted the Karen delegates' resolution to the Fourth

KNU Congress in Bassein in October 'to accept responsibility for safeguarding lives and property in Karen-majority areas' as a challenge to government authority.[64] The Socialist Party meanwhile again mooted the idea of negotiations with the PVOs and CPB to form a joint front against the KNU, while the wealthy businessman and trustee of the Shwedagon Pagoda, Sir U Thwin, led an unsuccessful mission to make peace with Bo Po Kun and the White Band PVOs.

At this convulsive moment the terrifying prospect of a repetition of the BIA-Karen conflict of the Second World War once again raised its ugly head. The worst incident occurred in Palaw, Mergui district, on Christmas Eve 1948. Apparently aware that the local Karen UMP force had just been disarmed, *Sitwundans* threw hand-grenades into a church killing 80 Christian Karens at worship. Another 200 Karens were reportedly killed in similar attacks on nearby villages.[65] These were not isolated incidents. Throughout January 1949 sporadic, apparently motiveless attacks continued. One mid-month massacre left over 150 Karen villagers dead after auxiliary UMPs led by former PVO Cabinet minister, Bo Sein Hman, raided a Karen village in Taikkyi township.[66] (Sein Hman was killed shortly afterwards directing aerial operations against CPB-PVO positions near Tharrawaddy.) In retaliation, KNDOs again reportedly raided the treasury at Maubin in the Lower Delta; Ne Win's regiment, the 4th Burma Rifles, responded by burning down the American Baptist Mission school.[67] And accusations of government dirty tricks were not confined to the Karen community. Following the assassination of the Karenni leader, U Bee Tu Re, in August, a number of Mon nationalist leaders were killed, allegedly by government agents, including Nai San Thu who was gunned down in front of the Palace Cinema in Moulmein. Such attacks proved counter-productive and only ensured the Mon and Karenni resistance movements gathered pace with the KNU.

Meanwhile several hundred *Sitwundan* troops moved into position around the Karen quarters at Insein, nine miles from Rangoon, where local KNDOs had already raided the armoury. During the day they withdrew, but returned at night to set up road-blocks and begin sporadic sniper and mortar fire into the Karen quarters. Within days reports of similar incidents began to flood into KNU headquarters in Rangoon from Karen communities across the Delta.[68]

Saw Ba U Gyi and Saw Sankey now moved from Rangoon to Insein to set up new operational headquarters. Their first order was to call in KNDOs from outlying districts to protect the Karen quarters. At first there were only 80 KNDO troops in Insein, but by the time fighting began the garrison had grown to a force of 400, including a number of women volunteers. Meanwhile the press in Rangoon, with the notable exception of *The Nation*, continued to inflame public opinion with what historian Hugh Tinker, generally regarded as one of the most supportive of the U Nu government, called 'the wildest stories about "Karen provocation"'.[69]

At this critical juncture Saw Ba U Gyi asked the army's most prominent KNU sympathiser, commander of the First Karen Rifles, Col. Min Maung, to create a diversion. He immediately complied and on 27 January 1949 the First Karen Rifles seized control of Toungoo (astride the main Rangoon-Mandalay railway) and the small town of Tantabin nearby. The following day Pyu (25 miles south) was occupied, while 200 miles away in the western Delta, a KNDO force led by the naval mutineer, Saw Jack, unsuccessfully tried to capture Bassein in fierce fighting.

These desperate manoeuvres, however, only served to escalate tensions.
Through the night of 30 January, a barrage of *Sitwundan* mortar and machine-gun
fire poured into the Karen quarters at Thamaing and Ahlone in Rangoon, setting
dozens of houses ablaze. A last-ditch meeting between Saw Ba U Gyi and U Nu
(organised by Gen. Smith Dun who interceded with U Nu) was scheduled for
noon; but with the road to Thamaing now blocked the meeting was cancelled and
any hopes of a negotiated settlement instantly evaporated.[70] Fighting immediately
erupted on the roads around Insein; to all intents and purposes the Karen rebellion
had begun.

The most controversial remaining question concerns the manner in which the
army Chief-of-Staff, Smith Dun, was removed. In his autobiography, U Nu claims
his government tried to prevent Dun's resignation, but Dun's own memoirs paint a
very different picture.[71] Not only does he claim to have narrowly escaped assassination by government troops who opened fire on him, but alleges he was left with
no choice but to quit. He points the finger of guilt, though without mentioning his
name, very squarely at his 'deputy', Ne Win. It was his 'deputy', he says, who
directed the *Sitwundan* attacks on Thamaing. This, he wrote, he only found out
when he interceded with U Nu to try and stop the fighting. But the night before,
he now remembered, his 'deputy' had enigmatically warned him that: 'If only the
Karens had started two months ago it would be alright for them, not now.'[72]

With Smith Dun's forced resignation on 31 January 1949, followed by the
withdrawals of Air Force chief, Shi Sho, and the two remaining Karen Cabinet
ministers, the Karen community lost its last tenuous links with the AFPFL
government. A loyal officer to the last, Smith Dun refused to take up arms and
eventually retired with his family to Myitkyina in the Kachin State. News of his
ousting, however, brought the immediate wholesale defection or internment of
Karen units in the army and police and plunged the country into even greater
political and ethnic chaos.

The Catastrophe of Civil War and Emergence of Ne Win's Tatmadaw
The early development of the CPB and Karen insurrections is dealt with in more
detail in the following chapters. But it is impossible to overestimate the impact of
the KNU uprising. In Smith Dun's graphic words, the KNDOs and Karen mutineers went through the country 'like a dose of salts' in the successful race for
Maymyo and Mandalay.[73] In the south local KNDO units backed by well-
equipped army units seized control of dozens of towns, briefly overran Mingdalon
Airport, the AFPFL's main link to the outside world, and at one stage pushed to
within four miles of Rangoon.

It is important to remember that, despite the insurgents' remarkable gains during
this period, the Rangoon government ultimately survived and later even claimed a
victory of sorts. Provocative as they may have been, the *Sitwundans* achieved an
importance few could have foreseen, for once the KNU insurrection began the
AFPFL withstood an even more devastating series of desertions from the army
than had occurred with the CPB. Not only did the three regiments of Karen Rifles
go over to the KNU, but the First Kachin Rifles, led by Naw Seng, whom Ne Win
ordered to march on the KNU capital at Toungoo, swapped sides to join forces
with the KNU and to lead the advance on Mandalay. Subsequently they turned
north-east, driving right through the centre of the Shan State to capture Lashio
and to begin the short-lived Pawng Yawng rebellion of 1949/50.[74]

Overnight the political map of Burma disappeared under an extraordinary mosaic of insurgent colours. At one stage in April 1949, just three months after the Karen rebellion began, towns as far apart as Pakokku (Red Flag/White Flag CPB) and Henzada (White Flag CPB), Mandalay, Toungoo, Thaton, Einme and Twante (KNU), and Minbu and Magwe (PVO) had fallen to the rebel side. Thousands of prisoners taken in the earlier fighting were released. In the country-side armed ethnic Mon, Karenni and Pao nationalists also declared their own governments and turned their guns on the army. Meanwhile, as the Fifth Burma Rifles were rushed back from north Arakan where they had at last seemed to be getting the better of the Muslim insurgency, Jafar Kawwal's *Mujahid* fighters flared back into new life and seized control of most of the north-west frontier.

Perhaps the most remarkable battle was fought at Insein, nine miles from Rangoon, where Saw Ba U Gyi and the KNU garrison held out into late May through a 112-day siege. A strike by the All Burma Ministerial Services Union brought work in government offices across the country to a grinding halt and further complicated matters at this desperate moment for the 'Six-Mile Rangoon government', as U Nu's Cabinet was disparagingly called. CPB activists from the ABTUC call it Burma's 'second general strike' (after the 1946 strike); the protest only ended when many of the workers' leaders were arrested. Not surprisingly, this complete breakdown in law and order gave the CPB's faltering campaign yet another boost and for several months the CPB regained control of the key towns of Pyinmana, Yamethin and Myingyan in central Burma.[75] Prome and Thayetmyo remained in joint CPB-PVO hands well into 1950, and An and Gwa in Arakan, where U Seinda's Arakan People's Liberation Party was still active, until as late as 1956 and 1958 respectively.[76]

It was a miracle the government survived. Critically, after some initial hesitation, the Chin Rifles for the most part remained loyal. No reliable casualty figures from the battles of this era have ever been produced. Much of the fighting was characterised by opportunist strikes and guerrilla skirmishes rather than pitched set-piece battles, but untold tens of thousands were killed, wounded or made homeless. Across Burma towns and villages were swollen with refugees flooding in from the war-torn countryside. In a highly conservative estimate in 1952, Prime Minister U Nu put government casualties alone at 3,424 dead, including 1,352 army personnel.[77] This total, however, takes no account of civilian casualties or the many fatalities on the rebel side: 60,000 dead and over one million homeless in the first two years of the insurrections may well be the final toll.[78]

The effects of the insurrections on the fragile economy of the newly independent country suffering the ravaging consequences of the Second World War were, in the long run, equally debilitating and have left physical and psychological scars from which Burma has never recovered. In early 1951 U Nu calculated the total cost of the insurgencies at a crippling '322 crores rupees' (then about £250 million); he described the human cost as 'inestimable', but such figures give little indication of the near total collapse of the national economy.[79] Through the 1950s a largely pro-government media and small international press corps, which rarely ventured beyond Rangoon, uncritically reported one government victory after another, but gave little indication of the slow rate of recovery or of the insurgents' still widespread rural support and control.[80] In the midst of this destruction, insurgent 'no-rent' and land redistribution programmes seemed attractive to many farmers. The Ye-Tavoy-Mergui coast road was reopened only in 1958, ten years after fighting began; the first batch of timber logged in the Chin hills did not safely navigate the Chindwin and Irrawaddy Rivers down into Rangoon (a commonplace journey in British days) until the end of 1959. Oil production, too, was badly hit. It took until August 1953 to recapture the important oilfields at Yenangyat from the CPB/PVOs; even then, in 1955 output was still 80 per cent lower than pre-war levels.[81] Perhaps most damagingly of all, rice production and business have never recovered. In 1959/60 annual rice exports finally reached two million tons, but this was still far short of the pre-war average of over three million tons. Since then they continued to fall to the nadir of virtually nil in 1988.[82]

At the end of 1949 the government was further shaken (if indeed that were possible) by the unexpected incursion into the Shan State of several thousand heavily armed Kuomintang (KMT) remnants from Yunnan Province in the aftermath of the communist victory in China. In the early 1950s this led to a near full-scale war along Burma's remote Shan and Kachin State borders, with Gen. Li Mi's exile KMT army appearing to enjoy full American backing. As a result, in 1953 the AFPFL government turned to the United Nations for support and terminated all American aid in protest.[83]

With the insurgent Pao National Organisation and local PVO or CPB forces controlling much of the western Shan State, relations with the indigenous Shan population also became severely strained when thousands of government troops were rushed in to ward off the KMT's advance. Eventually, on 1 December 1952, the state was placed under martial law. Many Shans compared the behaviour of the government's predominantly Burman troops unfavourably with that of even the KMT's rampaging army, which was a major factor behind the outbreak of the Shan rebellion in 1958/9.[84] Perhaps most alarming of all, the KMT's threatening presence along the border for a brief moment raised the spectre of a military invasion from communist China. It was little wonder that successive AFPFL governments of the 1950s felt they had little choice but to turn in on themselves.

The manner in which U Nu's government survived back in 1948-52 needs emphasising, for it had important implications for the evolution of future political movements in Burma. Much of the political credit at the time went to the prime minister, U Nu, who, despite frequent threats to resign, appeared at times to be single-handedly keeping together a viable government coalition in Rangoon. At one stage virtually anybody still in Parliament was assured of national office; in April 1949, at what Nu later described as 'our darkest hour', he even survived the block resignation of all Socialist Party and Yellow Band PVO ministers from his Cabinet, a decision many observers wrongly interpreted as a move to hand the administration over to the CPB while he was up-country.[85] It is true that unofficial government contacts had been made with Than Tun over the possibility of peace talks and that the CPB had demanded the premiership and fresh elections. Indeed, in an apparent change of policy after international pressure, U Nu and Ne Win held unsuccessful talks with another insurgent leader, KNU chairman Saw Ba U Gyi, who came to Rangoon from Insein during April. But, in what was admittedly a highly confusing move at a highly confusing time, it is rather more likely the Socialist Party/PVO aim was simply to prepare the way for elections already scheduled for later that month.[86] These they naively hoped would peacefully end the civil war and the growing political chaos.

Clearly no elections could have been held then; Nu survived by enlisting six political independents (including Ne Win as his deputy) and seven ethnic minority representatives into his Cabinet. His firm response kept up the international pretence of a credible national government still in control of Rangoon; vital reinforcements of arms and supplies from Britain and India at the height of the insurrections brought timely relief. From this platform the AFPFL government later built up a position of some international respectability. The socialists and Yellow Band PVOs returned to the Cabinet in January 1950 and in 1953 the first Asian Socialist Conference was held in Rangoon. The following year the first meeting of the international Anti-Colonial Bureau was held in Kalaw. Leading on from the success of these meetings, Burma became an important supporter of the 1954 Colombo Powers Conference and the 1955 Bandung Conference.[87]

Underlying the AFPFL's fragile control of the country was, however, the growing strength of the army. Built around the uncompromising personality of the new army Chief-of-Staff, Gen. Ne Win, and the continued loyalty of his old regiment, the Fourth Burma Rifles, there emerged a new force, the *Tatmadaw*. A small nucleus of predominantly ethnic Burman army commanders began to dominate the national political stage, first through the military caretaker administration of 1958-60, and then more completely through the 1962 military coup and quarter century of one-party rule by the Burma Socialist Programme Party.[88] Among officers of the Fourth Burma Rifles closest to Ne Win were two veterans of his wartime BIA command in Zone Two of the Lower Delta, Brig. Tin Pe, who emerged in 1962 as the army's most influential Marxist ideologue, and Ne Win's deputy and co-conspirator in the 1962 coup, Brig. Aung Gyi, whose widely circulated letters so many years later did much to precipitate the crisis of 1988. Indeed Ne Win's first chosen successor, following his resignation in July of that year, was another veteran from the Fourth Burma Rifles, Gen. Sein Lwin, reputedly a member of the army patrol that ambushed and killed KNU leader, Saw Ba U Gyi, in 1950.

The *Tatmadaw*'s later predominance in Burmese national life must be seen against the background of the remarkable dangers and hardships of these years, the many deaths of comrades in battle and the belief that the army, above all, preserved the unity of the country. In a victory statement broadcast to the Burmese people after the fall of Rangoon in May 1945, Ne Win publicly claimed: 'The Burmese Army is not only the hope of the country, but its very life and soul.'[89] In October 1988, following the army's bloody suppression of the student-led democracy uprising, which for a brief moment threatened to repeat the upheavals of 1948/9, a military spokesman again proudly invoked the army's victories in the battles of those years with the ominous warning that the *Tatmadaw* 'continues to thrive on these fine traditions'.[90]

All this, however, refers to events some way in the future. It is now necessary to backtrack for a moment and consider why the CPB, the one party claiming to be trying to galvanise and unite opposition to the AFPFL, failed to seize power at what most observers would agree was undoubtedly the most opportune moment in its entire 52-year history. The CPB's failure stands in stark contrast to the experiences of communist parties in neighbouring China, Vietnam, Laos, Cambodia and Korea, all of which began (or resumed) their insurrections in the same turbulent post-war period and eventually came to power.

7

Failure, Retrenchment and United Fronts: The Communist Movement, 1948-52

Amidst the countrywide chaos and confusion of those early years, there was no one reason why the CPB should have failed in its bid for power; it was more a combination of overlapping factors (political, geographic, ethnic, military, economic and organisational) peculiar to Burma's complex history and social mosaic. Despite the acknowledged abilities of Than Tun, Bo Zeya and other communist leaders, there was no Ho Chi Minh to weld the many conflicting elements together into one dynamic, united movement. In this crucial respect comparisons with Vietnam are particularly apt. In Indo-China the Vietnam Communist Party managed to maintain its hold on the leadership and direction of the national liberation movement, often against overwhelming odds, through successive French, Japanese and American administrations. In China, the Communist Party was able to wrest the nationalist mantle from Chiang Kai-shek and the Kuomintang during the Japanese occupation. But in Burma the early British withdrawal undoubtedly took much of the nationalist political ground away from the communists.[1] The goal of building a broad 'people's democratic front' became (and remains) the main plank in the communist political strategy, but in newly independent Burma the CPB was only one of several competing leftist forces.

Parliamentary Democracy and the Enduring Influence of Marxism
The general public was no doubt confused by the bitter Red Flag-White Flag split; the continued prominence of the Socialist Party and the People's Volunteer Organisation (PVO) muddied the waters even further. The Socialist Party, which came to form the backbone of successive AFPFL Cabinets in the 1950s, took advantage of these divisions and sudden disappearance underground of so many leading CPB officials (including one of its own founder members, the ABTUC's Thakin Chit). It swiftly snatched and purged the leadership of the communist-dominated All Burma Peasants Organisation (ABPO) and built up its own organisation, the Trades Union Congress (Burma), to rival and eventually replace the CPB-backed ABTUC. This confusing political fragmentation on the left was further complicated by the Socialist Party's own split during 1950 into two factions, one led by U Kyaw Nyein and U Ba Swe who continued to serve in the AFPFL Cabinet (Ba Swe even replacing U Nu as prime minister in 1956/7) and the other by the trade union leaders, Thakins Lwin and Chit Maung, who formed a new organisation, the Burma Workers and Peasants Party (BWPP). Dubbed 'crypto-communists' or 'red socialists' in the Rangoon press, the avowedly Marxist-

Leninist BWPP, though always separate from the CPB but including such former communist sympathisers as U Ba Nyein, tried without success through various initiatives during the 1950s and early 1960s to bring the CPB back into the political mainstream and remained an important above-ground voice for communist ideas.

Though for many individuals socialist ideology undoubtedly served as a convenient cloak for business interests, for all these parties Marxism, if not Marxism-Leninism, was very much the *lingua franca* of the day. Through the People's Literature House on Merchant Street, Rangoon, and various bookstalls around the city, English translations of all the communist classics published in Moscow and Beijing (Marx, Lenin, Stalin, Mao Zedong) were widely available and were constantly studied by the country's young new leaders. Not until 1958, with the AFPFL's ambitious *Pyidawtha* (welfare state) programme already under way, did U Nu, a devout Buddhist, formally disavow Marxism at the Third All-Burma AFPFL Congress (the first in ten years); this in turn helped precipitate the final break-up of the AFPFL coalition.[2] Claimed U Ba Swe, one of the main instigators of the *Pyidawtha* programme, in a much quoted 1951 speech, which was to set the tone for successive AFPFL governments in the 1950s: 'Marxism is the guide to action in our revolutionary movement, in our establishment of a socialist Burmese state for workers and peasants. Our revolution can only be achieved with Marxism as a guiding principle.... Marxist theory is not antagonistic to Buddhist philosophy. The two are, frankly speaking, not merely similar. In fact, they are the same in concept.'[3] Apart from being determined to use Burmese methods based on Burmese conditions (unlike the communists whom he accuses of lamely accepting Soviet leadership), the political goals of the socialists he mentions in *The Burmese Revolution* appear remarkably similar to those of the CPB: the defeat of imperialism and the construction of a new Burma based on the principles of a people's democracy.[4]

This continuing and generally well-reported public debate undoubtedly softened the radical militancy of many in the small intellectual class who had led Burma's national liberation movement since the turn of the century. Though it took a few years to become obvious, with the British departure and the introduction, despite its many failings, of the *Pyidawtha* programme, the political climate in Burma had changed considerably. Wrote the historian John Thomson:

> The two main conditions of the pre-war period — imperialism and alien monopoly capitalism — which had attracted the Burmese nationalists to Marxism were thus largely reduced or on the way to becoming historical memories. And the lack of opportunities for graduates of Rangoon University, which had been the source of so much pre-war student discontent, was replaced by practically unlimited opportunity in the completely Burmanised government services.[5]

None the less, even if the mood had changed, one should not underestimate the serious challenge the CPB still posed and the deep influence the communist movement continued to exert on political life in the country. As Hugh Tinker said of the failure of the above-ground legal opposition to unseat the AFPFL coalition at the 1956 general election, 'the real opposition is, of course, the underground communists.'[6]

In view of the tentative political debate now beginning in Burma in the uncertain first light of a post-Ne Win era, it is important to emphasise that it is questionable whether the much-vaunted 'democracy era' of the 1950s ever really existed. Both general elections of the 1950s, as well as the 1960 election under Gen. Ne Win's military caretaker administration, were deeply flawed. The first 'rolling' election of 1951/2 took seven months to complete, with troops having to be rotated around the country to provide extra security for each region in turn. Even so, in both government and rebel-held areas many seats still went unopposed. Only one and a half million citizens of an estimated eight million electorate were actually able to vote and the final count produced the most undemocratic anomaly in which 60 per cent of the votes were cast for the AFPFL, which received 85 per cent of the seats.[7] Allegations of widespread intimidation and ballot-rigging again followed the 1956 election in which the BWPP, with the tacit approval of the CPB, formed an above-ground opposition alliance, the National United (or Unity) Front (NUF), and contested the election on a 'peace-ticket'. The NUF alliance won over 35 per cent of the votes cast, but again only a disproportionately small number of seats.[8]

Moreover, despite claiming countrywide organisation, the parties were little more than executive committees run by intellectuals in Rangoon, who rarely consulted their local committees or affiliates in the countryside. Most local MPs or party bosses, like many insurgent leaders, were little better than petty chieftains. Thus to carry out the daily business of Parliament, the AFPFL increasingly came to depend on individual bargains and agreements, of often labyrinthine complexity, with various political coalitions, particularly of elected ethnic minority representatives. The question of the creation of Mon and Arakan States, for example, became a controversial on-off issue throughout the late 1950s and early 1960s as U Nu successively offered, then withdrew, political inducements from ethnic minority leaders as he tried to win their support. With Karen, Mon and Arakanese insurgencies continuing, such behaviour merely eroded the 1947 Constitution's guarantees of ethnic autonomy and raised racial tensions even further.[9] Many above-ground ethnic parties, such as the Union Karen League, were simply absorbed by the AFPFL. Politically it may have appeared expedient, but it did little to address the urgent ethnic problems of the day; with ethnic minority issues reduced to little more than a side-show, a bitter legacy of resentment was building up which has never been fully dispelled.

Perhaps the most remarkable evidence of the CPB's enduring influence comes from Gen. Ne Win and the leaders of the *Tatmadaw* who finally seized power in 1962. In his damning 1988 indictment of the Burma Socialist Programme Party's (BSPP's) quarter century of misrule, Brig. Aung Gyi admits that at the time of the 1962 coup army leaders had no advance political plans other than 'to work on socialism as the basis'. Ne Win's chief insistence, echoing U Ba Swe, was that it be done 'with Burmese methods in a Burmese mode'.[10] Aung Gyi goes on to detail the stunningly simplistic way in which Ne Win's whimsical *Burmese Way to Socialism* evolved, with the startling revelation that the military's interest in socialism had in fact only begun in the mid-1950s with the realisation that the *Tatmadaw* 'should be able to fight the communists in ideology as well'. Aung Gyi claims to have presented a paper on this theme to a conference of battalion commanders at Meiktila in 1954/5, which the three men later 'assigned the duty' by Ne Win (Col. Saw Myint, former CPB member U Chit Hlaing, and U Saw U) used in 1962 as their guide-line in drawing up the BSPP's Bible, *The System of Correlation of Man and his Environment*, with which Ne Win was to rule the country.[11] But perhaps this is not so surprising. After all, the *Tatmadaw* had the task of defeating the CPB in the field and was only too aware of the scale of the challenge the CPB continued to pose.

Though the CPB failed in its initial attempt to seize power, it remained tantalisingly in the wings of Burmese politics throughout the 1950s, little recognised in the world outside, largely cut off from the international communist movement and generally maligned in the Rangoon press, but still the armed opposition force most likely to topple or replace the AFPFL. (The KNU, Mon, Karenni, Pao, Rakhine, *Mujahid* and other ethnic forces had broadly separatist aims which, with the key exception of the KNU, by definition posed little threat to Rangoon.) It is important, therefore, to examine the reasons for the CPB's continued weakness in closer detail and against this political background, for this was a time when the AFPFL government was often daily expected to fall.

The CPB Reorganises on a Revolutionary Footing
Of all the factors mentioned earlier (political, geographic, ethnic, etc.), the organisational was by far the most important, at least in 1948-50. Despite the CPB's growing militancy during late 1947 and early 1948, the White Flag CPB, like the KNU, was still not ready to launch a sustained armed challenge. Other than the general strategy outlined in Ba Tin's thesis, for a campaign of escalating civil disobedience in the towns backed by the creation of new liberated zones in the countryside few concrete plans had been made. Nor, despite Than Tun's claims of 100,000 'trained militants', was the real number of armed CPB supporters by any means certain. Estimates of the CPB's military strength in 1948/9 vary from anywhere between 4,000 and 25,000 troops and guerrilla combatants (the latter figure is also the usually accepted number of accredited party members), but in many rural areas the loyalty of *Tat-Ni* (Red Guards) and village militia had yet to be decided between the Red Flags, the White Flags and the PVOs, not to mention the different ethnic forces, *Sitwundans* and government home guards then under formation. With the Socialist Party and U Nu's AFPFL coalition having grabbed centre stage, the CPB had some way to go to rebuild the kind of national authority it had enjoyed at the end of the Second World War.

Today the CPB's chairman, Ba Thein Tin, insists the Politburo's decision to take up arms was a defensive measure following the 'ruling class' order from U Nu to arrest the CPB leadership 'down to the village cadres including members of the ABTUC, ABPO, youth, women and other mass organisations'.[12] (The CPB was not, however, officially declared an illegal organisation until October 1953.) The Politburo's decision to fight 'for the very existence of our party' was then confirmed by an underground meeting of the CPB CC in Rangoon in early April and confirmed by the full plenum of the CC, which assembled at Kyauk Kyibawk village, Pyu township, 120 miles north of the capital the following month. After this, the CPB's mobile party headquarters was moved to the Pyinmana-Yamethin area of central Burma where it remained, ever on the move, until the mid-1970s, sometimes moving further north into the Three M triangle (Mandalay-Meiktila-Myingyan) or, in the 1950s, across the Irrawaddy River into the southern Chin hills, but mostly in the forests and foothills running down both sides of the Sittang River valley.

Only in October 1948, six months after the insurrection began, were CPB leaders from across Burma able to meet for the first time to assess the situation. At a meeting at Myet Kya Kone village, Pyinmana, three main resolutions were passed: to amend the CPB's basic programme and Constitution 'to suit the conditions of revolutionary civil war'; to accept Than Tun's report, 'Six Months of our Revolution'; and to approve the decision to carry out agrarian revolution through an experimental land redistribution programme.[13] As in areas under Red Flag control, debt was abolished and farming and trading cooperatives established. Then in a move approved by the next full CC meeting at Shwedawmyaung village, Lewei township, west of Pyinmana in February, it was decided to instruct the White Flags to begin a gradual transition towards the principles of Mao Zedong's people's war and to enlarge the CC to its present 35 members representing the whole of Burma. (The 1989 CPB CC consisted of 30 members, though several had for years been unable to visit the areas they represented.) Meanwhile, still following the Maoist model, in each region of the country, village, township and district cadres were to be elected who, in theory, would in turn elect their own CC representatives as the need arose.

The following month the first steps were taken to restructure the CPB's scattered armed forces, then still known by the same name as Mao's victorious Red Army in China, the People's Liberation Army (PLA). These were now reorganised along Maoist lines into three wings (the main force, mobile guerrilla forces and local people's militia) under the control of a central military commission.[14] Again in Maoist style, the command of each unit, even down to platoon level, would be shared between military and political commissars. This restructuring was completed on 1 September 1950 when the PLA and Bo Zeya's Revolutionary Burma Army (RBA) were formally merged into a single military force, the People's Army of Burma (PA), under a people's revolutionary military commission to give guidance in political and military strategy. Headed by Than Tun and Ba Thein Tin, the PA's senior command was dominated by former Burma Army officers, including Zeya, Ye Htut, Soe Maung and Sein Tin, while the leading political commissar roles were given to Thakins Chit (ABTUC), Zin (ABPO), Than Myaing (propaganda) and other underground organisers of the anti-Japanese resistance.[15] The PA's strategy was to build up local forces (whether CPB recruits, army mutineers or PVOs) into a national army, based on a regional command system.

Despite this political centralisation, the CPB's military organisation in the field had to be relatively loose, which often confounded military analysts of the war. Throughout this period various White Flag CPB armies and guerrilla forces continued to operate in areas of Burma as far apart as Arakan in the north-west and the Irrawaddy Delta close to Rangoon and Tenasserim in the south-east; the PA's tenth army, for example, operated in the Lower Delta. Hundreds more villagers were mobilised as local people's militia. But until the early 1950s the CPB's regular force consisted of just four main divisions, each with an estimated 1,000 men under arms: the first in the Myingyan district and the Dry Zone of Upper Burma under the ex-*Thirty Comrade* Bo Yan Aung, the second in the Monywa-Shwebo-Mandalay districts under Bo Hla Maw, the third in Yamethin-Pyinmana-Toungoo under Bo Ye Maung, and the fourth in the Shan State led by Bo Tha Doe. Their names, troop concentrations and exact zones of operation, however, changed frequently.[16]

The outbreak of the Karen, Mon and Pao uprisings during 1949 undoubtedly gave the CPB a considerable, if unwitting, boost. Like the PVO, the CPB was quickly able to recapture much of the territory it had lost in the fierce battles of

1948. However, as the country teetered on the brink of collapse, it soon became apparent that the CPB was only one of several players, albeit the best organised, in the field. In some areas fighting immediately broke out between the PA and the KNU, especially in the Delta where many Burman and Karen villages lay alongside one another. All sides, including the *Tatmadaw* and pro-government forces, were accused of reprisals against the civilian population. Warlordism became an endemic problem. 'Any man with three gunmen and a fish-pond could become a chief,' remembers Mika Rolly, a KNU leader in the Delta.[17] Fighting raged back and forth with many armed bands owing no allegiance to any particular party. In other areas the CPB found PVO, Rakhine or Red Flag forces blocking their way; it was this rather than ideological considerations that eventually forced communist leaders seriously to consider applying Mao Zedong's Leninist theory of the 'united front'.[18]

The Communist Theory of the United Front
In a country as ethnically diverse and politically divided as Burma, the theory of the united front has dominated the thinking of insurgent leaders on all sides for 40 years of armed struggle. Its unsuccessful application must, therefore, be considered a major reason for the insurgents' perennial inability to transform large troop numbers into military victory. As many insurgent forces were sometimes posted to protect their rear from attack by their rivals as their front from a *Tatmadaw* offensive. Certainly back in 1949, though no completely reliable figures exist, the government was heavily outnumbered by the different insurgent forces. Irregular village militia most likely numbered more, but contemporary estimates put the combined regular leftist forces at some 13,000, including 5,000 armed CPB, 4,000 PVOs, as many as 1,400 army deserters in the RBA, and 3,000 police mutineers, while the KNU, through the wholesale defection of Karen units in the army and Union Military Police (UMP), could call on about 7,000 trained troops.[19] Other ethnic forces like the *Mujahid* and Arakan People's Liberation Party (APLP) were hardly mentioned in the confusion of the time. By 1951 the Rangoon press was speculating that insurgent numbers in Burma had nearly doubled to 43,000 men under arms.[20] Against these formidable numbers U Nu later claimed, with only a slight hint of exaggeration, that his government had begun in 1949 with just one and a half trained battalions, or some 1,000 regular troops, backed up by a small number of UMP units and the local *Sitwundan* militia.[21]

Had these different insurgent forces joined together, the AFPFL government, despite its continued control of the sea and skies, would never have survived. The question, then, is why the CPB was unable to exploit conditions of such outright opposition to the central government as the communist parties were able to in neighbouring China and Vietnam. In the final analysis the answer may well be the sheer complexity of modern Burma.

In traditional communist ideology and from what the CPB today calls its 'Marxist-Leninist-Mao Zedong' viewpoint, the united front should in theory consist of an alliance of all progressive forces (including the peasantry, patriotic bourgeoisie, socialists and communists) during the revolutionary transition from feudalism or bourgeois democracy to the ultimate communist goal of a people's democracy based on the 'dictatorship of the proletariat'. According to Lenin, only committedly anti-communist forces are excluded from the united front.[22] The role of the Communist Party, the only true proletarian party, is to act as the 'vanguard party' of the revolution; other parties are regarded as inherently weak or likely to waver. To counteract the Communist Party's own organisational weaknesses or inability to seize power by itself, the united front has two additional functions: to allow the Communist Party to establish a mass base in the general population, and to concentrate all energies on fighting the people's main enemies: imperialism, feudalism, capitalism and their agents.

In a further refinement in the late 1930s, when Chinese communists joined Chiang Kai-shek and the Kuomintang, Mao Zedong recognised that the intense patriotic feelings aroused by the Japanese invasion were a stronger rallying force in the country than the largely agrarian class warfare the Red Army was then waging. In these years the CCP, riding the nationalist wave, made some of its most rapid political advances. This led Mao to develop his two-stage theory of revolution: the first 'united front' or 'national liberation' stage of what he now termed 'national democratic' revolution against imperialism and feudalism (an expression which has a particular resonance for Burma's ethnic minorities); and the second transitional phase when, still employing the same united front tactics, the Communist Party leads the final transformation of society to socialism.[23]

Mao's analysis proved extremely apposite. Amongst Asia's communist parties, the ones that successfully harnessed the national liberation cause (China, Korea, Vietnam, Laos and Cambodia) eventually came to power. 'To subordinate the class struggle to the present national struggle against Japan,' wrote Mao, 'such is the fundamental principle of the united front.'[24]

In essence, the united front is a political tactic running concomitantly with the armed struggle (if indeed it is necessary to take up arms); achieving victory thus means the Communist Party combining with both above- and underground opposition forces. When, as in 1948-50, social conditions in Burma were similar to those in Vietnam and China, such a distinction did not present a problem for the CPB. Communist sympathisers and CPB cadres remained secretly active in many above-ground organisations and were frequently outspoken. In December 1949, for example, Aung Win of the ABTUC, speaking at the Trade Union Congress of Asian and Australasian Countries in Beijing, publicly supported Ba Tin's definition of Burma's 'fraudulent' independence and called for the violent overthrow of the AFPFL government.[25] Then in May 1950 Thakin Lwin, in protest at the AFPFL's decision to accept British aid, urged the affiliation of the TUC(B) to the communist World Federation of Trade Unions.[26] For a time, too, in addition to a host of locally produced CPB publications and magazines, such as the Upper Burma party headquarters' journal, *Revolution*, and the central party headquarters' *Red Star*, communist views regularly surfaced in such popular national newspapers as the *Kyemon* in Rangoon and the *Ludu* in Mandalay.

But with the continuing civil war, increasing militarisation of society and disappearance underground of many of the CPB's leading army and union organisers, much of the CPB leadership's time and energy had to be concentrated on dealing with other insurgent groups.[27] Across the country 'taking to the jungles' almost became a national pastime. Older CPB cadres in their fifties and sixties, formerly underground activists in trade unions, civil service departments and other organisations in the towns, have told me how the increasing risk of arrest gradually forced them underground to join their comrades in the rural 'liberated zones'. In fact since the military coup of 1962 the CPB has never been able to regain any real foothold in the cities.

Thus eventually during 1949/50, Than Tun and the CPB leadership abandoned their lone 'final seizure of power' strategy of 1948 and turned their attention to forming Burma's first insurgent united front. (In 1950/1 the CPB also sometimes called for a united front with the government against the KMT 'invaders', but neither CPB nor AFPFL leaders appear to have considered this a realistic proposition.) It was significant that, like the Socialist Party with whom they had refused to compromise, they played down the volatile ethnic question and instead concentrated on working with their ideological fellow-travellers, the Red Flags and PVOs, with whom their forces had sometimes violently clashed. Since both continued to receive widespread, though often highly confusing, publicity in the press at home and abroad throughout the 1950s, it is necessary to comment on both in some detail.

The Red Flags
Despite Thakin Soe's headline-grabbing activities, the Red Flag CPB was always a somewhat peripheral force. This owed much to the personality of its permanent general-secretary, Thakin Soe, a charismatic if dogmatic leader who built up around himself a loyal band of followers, including a number of women whom the Rangoon press, which has always shown a predilection for sexual innuendo, disparagingly referred to as 'devotees'.[28] At various stages Thakin Soe denounced most international communist movements; it often appeared he believed the Red Flags were the only true practitioners of Marxism-Leninism in the world. Though hardly reflecting his real views, this earned him the epithet 'Trotskyist', the usual communist appellation of the time for 'opportunist'.[29] Though they were to change in nature, the Red Flag/White Flag differences clearly ran very deep. As early as the British Empire Communist Conference in London in February 1947, Ba Thein Tin presented a report on the Red Flag movement which denounced Thakin Soe as a 'phrase-mongering left extremist'.[30]

None the less, throughout the early days of the insurrections, following the release from Tharrawaddy gaol of Soe (and the APLP leader, U Seinda) by Bo Zeya and the army mutineers, White Flag and Red Flag leaders, both at district and national levels, tried to work together and, until the mid-1950s, armed clashes between the two parties were rare. Red Flag cadres and armed units were active in small pockets throughout the Tenasserim Division, in much of Lower Burma and even around Rangoon. But the main Red Flag strongholds were further north in the rugged country and mountains between Pakokku and Minbu, in the lower Chin Division and in the Arakan Yomas where they had to compete for space in some of the country's poorest and most backward areas with the White Flags, PVOs, ethnic Rakhine APLP and Jafar Kawwal's *Mujahids*. (After Kawwal was assassinated by rivals in October 1950, leadership of the *Mujahid* movement fell to his better-known successor, Cassim, who was frequently denounced in the Rangoon press.)

Here in Arakan in the months before independence, popular Red Flag leader Aung Lin recruited *Bonbauk* Tha Gyaw and several hundred supporters, mostly intellectuals, from its peasant-backed ally, the APLP. On his way across the Arakan Yomas to Red Flag headquarters in the east in 1953, Aung Lin was killed (along with another CC member, Min Lwin) by Chin villagers; the Red Flags took savage revenge for the attack. The following year Tha Gyaw took over the local Red Flag leadership but soon became embroiled in fighting with yet another insurgent force, the PVOs. Peace talks were held with the PVO's Chief-of-Staff, Bo Htein Lin, who travelled up from central Burma, but after fighting broke out again, in which his young baby was killed, Tha Gyaw was dismissed by the Red Flag CC. Disillusioned, he surrendered to the government with 80 armed followers at Minbya in 1955 (after secret talks with U Ba Swe and U Kyaw Nyein) to fight back, his former comrades say, against the PVOs.[31]

The eventual surfacing of the nationalist Marxist movements, the Arakan National Liberation Party and the Communist Party of Arakan (CPA), in the Red Flag's last Arakan strongholds in the early 1960s brought about the effective demise of the Red Flag movement as any kind of serious military threat. In late 1960, under constant army pressure and with 250 camp followers, Soe was forced to shift his headquarters into the forest near the coastal town of Myebon, 40 miles south-east of the divisional capital, Sittwe (Akyab). The last straw, according to the present CPA chairman, Maung Han, who defected with Kyaw Zan Rhee and dozens of other local Red Flag officials in disgust, was Soe's clumsy attempt to replace ethnic Rakhine commanders with Burman officers from the Red Flag's central staff.[32] Ironically it was Kyaw Zan Rhee, the CPA's founder chairman, who had guided Soe's party across the mountains to safety in Arakan.

As a result of this territorial squeeze, the Red Flags (unlike the White Flags, PVOs and KNU) always faced serious shortages of arms and ammunition. Party supporters were more numerous, but in those early years, the Red Flag's real troop strength probably never exceeded 3,000 men under arms. By 1948 only one battalion of government troops had defected to join them. The movement was badly hurt, too, by a damaging split following the Red Flag's Second Conference in May 1953 at Wakya Yekywar village near Myaing, Pakokku. (The Red Flag's First Conference was reputedly held in the Delta at Thuhtaygoon village, Twante, during 1949/50 after Soe's release.) Here a critical report by Thakin Soe on Than Tun and the White Flag leadership over the White Flag/Red Flag split was accepted over the objections of two district party leaders, Tun Sein and Ko Htoo, who urged both sides to accept some responsibility. Following the Congress, the Htoo-Sein clique broke away with some 500 followers to form the New Democratic Party (sometimes also known as Burma's Third Communist Party), which operated for several years close to Red Flag base areas in Pakokku and Yaw townships and parts of the Lower Delta. In the mid-1950s there were a number of clashes with local Red Flag (and White Flag) forces in which some troops on both sides died. Eventually these differences were patched up and by the late 1950s the Htoo-Sein clique once again appeared to be operating as a faction, albeit a fast disintegrating one, of the Red Flag 'mother-party'. Their disappearance was complete with the surrender in December 1962 of the last 50 of these breakaway remnants, now going under the name, Workers United Party.[33] Claiming to support the political programme of Ne Win's Revolutionary Council, they were some of the very few insurgents actually to lay down their arms and come in after Ne Win seized power.

From 1953, when Thakin Soe introduced a party reorganisation programme known as the Selection of Party Cadres, other activists also began to drift away. In the 'liberated zones' many Red Flags accused Thakin Soe of replacing experienced party officials with simple yes-men and of trying to build his own personality cult. Outside Arakan Soe was increasingly left with a small band of experienced organisers, including his then wife, Ma Ngwe Zan, and fellow CC members Kyaw Win, Myint Aung and Ne Dun. By the end of 1958 *Tatmadaw* commanders estimated Red Flag military strength had fallen to just 750 armed followers and, 18 months later, in what was clearly an underestimate to justify the hardships of the military caretaker administration, a mere 209.[34] A few months later a military spokesman put Red Flag numbers at over 500 again, while *The Nation* reported one Red Flag force of 300-strong operating in the Yaw area alone.[35] While reflecting the Red Flags' steady decline, such fluctuating figures also demonstrate the continued volatility of the situation and the ability of insurgent groups to arise phoenix-like from the ashes.

However, what the Red Flags may have lacked in numbers they more than made up for in militancy. Accusations and counter-accusations of atrocities against the civilian population have been made by all sides in the 40 year war (often justifiably), but more often than not they were about the Red Flags. 'We dare to fight, we dare to kill, we dare to die,' ran a popular Red Flag slogan of the day. In one particularly notorious incident in 1960, Red Flag guerrillas led by former BIA commander Myint Aung allegedly executed 74 villagers from Sinzwe village, Htilin township, in the eastern Chin hills for allegedly collaborating with the *Tatmadaw*.[36] Similarly, though the Red Flags and White Flags resembled one another in structure through a Politburo and Central Committee system, in the field the Red Flags were always the more extreme. Whereas the White Flags advocated a policy of 'land to the tiller' and land redistribution, the Red Flags introduced immediate collectivisation. Entire villages were mobilised as 'people's militia' and landowners and Buddhist monks forced to relinquish their powers and land or risk being shot.[37] Radical 'red cultivator unions', no-rent campaigns and attacks on prisons, rice-granaries and police stations were very much the staple tactics of the Red Flag offensive.

Though in the countryside the Red Flags acquired a reputation for ruthless behaviour which ultimately did little to win the hearts and minds of the rural peasantry, one of the many ironies of their continued existence was the support Thakin Soe was able to win from a surprising number of intellectuals and middle-class workers (including civil servants, teachers, lawyers and students) still living in towns under government control. The Red Flags were, in effect, permanent testimony to the CPB's previous mistakes. This stemmed not only from continuing criticism of the CPB's Browderist line in 1945/6, which caused the Red Flags' original defection, but also from the originality and verve of Thakin Soe's prodigious intellectual output. A key figure in the 1938 oilfield strike, a distinguished wartime resistance leader and former president of the AFPFL, Thakin Soe was without doubt one of the more remarkable communist theoreticians of his generation.

Born in 1905 in Moulmein, as an employee of the Burma Oil Company during the 1930s he translated many Marxist terms into Burmese. Though his writings and speeches often contained highly idiosyncratic interpretations, the Red Flag faction, perhaps due to Soe's romantic appeal, maintained a surprisingly effective underground network (largely unnoticed by journalists and government officials) in many towns across Lower and Upper Burma. Many books and pamphlets in the Rangoon bookshops by such authors as Maung Tha Yar and Lin Yone Ni were rumoured to have originated from Red Flag sources or presses. One famous political tract, which was legally published but which former Red Flags are adamant was secretly written and put together under their auspices, was *Marxism and the Renegade Krushchev* by Thakin Pe Htay, a Red Flag CC member and adviser to the Red Flag's Youth Front (Burma) organisation, who had surrendered.[38]

Red Flag sympathisers led by Ko Yu, presently a CC member of the National League for Democracy, were highly active throughout the 1950s at Rangoon University. The above-ground Youth Front also ran a highly effective campaign organising peace rallies and putting up wall posters in dozens of towns and villages across the country. The Red Flags even claim to have had a secret supporter in parliament, 'Pakokku' Tin Shwe. But the best known of Soe's alleged sympathisers was former CPB member, U Chit Hlaing, who was selected to attend an international youth fair in Helsinki in the early 1950s and later visited Paris where he wrote about his travels. He surprisingly emerged in 1962 as one of the BSPP's leading theoreticians. As a result many believe that the intervention of ex-Red Flag CPB supporters of the BSPP, like U Chit Hlaing, Thakin Tin Mya and Daw Saw Mya, later earned Soe a reprieve from his 1973 death sentence. In recent years Soe was even a frequent house guest of Ne Win; one of the many curious sights of 1988 was the re-emergence of Soe, the former scourge of parliamentary democracy, so shortly before his death in 1989, as patron of the Unity and Development Party, one of the very first of the legal new 'democracy' parties to be formed in the aftermath of the Saw Maung coup.

Though they had less contact with ethnic minority insurgents, Thakin Soe (reputedly of Mon ancestry himself) and the Red Flag leaders were regarded as more sympathetic to the ethnic nationalist cause than their White Flag rivals. While the White Flags advocated the centralised model of China with autonomous regions for the minorities, the Red Flags accepted a system of independent 'people's republics' (the Karen People's Republic, the Arakan People's Republic) on the Soviet model and with the important right of secession. (Soe, however, was a great critic of what he called Krushchev's revisionism.) Again, whereas the White Flags kept quiet over the Chinese invasion of Tibet, Thakin Soe bitterly denounced Mao Zedong's action. (Ironically, in 1949 the Red Flags had sent CC member, Thet Tin, another veteran of the 1938 oilfield strike, to China to try and enlist Mao's support, but in China he changed sides and returned to Burma in 1963 as part of a White Flag delegation.)

Thus, though their numbers were low, for many years Red Flag cadres could cross safely from one part of the country to another through ethnic rebel-held areas. Then relations became soured, first with the KNU over Soe's continued efforts to build up a Red Flag Karen New Land Party among Karen villagers in the Delta, which the KNU decisively crushed; then with Rakhine nationalists in Arakan over the imposition of centrally appointed leaders. Many local Red Flags claim they were already angry about Soe's conciliatory line towards the *Tatmadaw* and U Nu government at the Red Flag's Third Conference in September 1961.[39] Red Flag remnants remained active into the early 1970s; I have met die-hards, led by veteran CC member, U Thaw Da, who refused to surrender and are still in the forests of Arakan. But the Rakhine split, combined with serious losses in their Pakokku strongholds at the end of the 1950s, meant the real beginning of the end for the Red Flag cause. 'In a certain sense,' John Badgely correctly predicted in 1969, 'the Red Flags echo the rebel tragedy of a century ago, when Burman guerrilla fighters fought along the fringes of the Arakan Yomas and Chin hills against the British for a quarter of a century before they were extinguished.'[40]

The People's Volunteer Organisation

The other leftist party with which the White Flag CPB had to deal was the PVO. Though little written about and largely ignored by political commentators, the PVO, or People's Comrade Party, as the rebel White Band faction became known, presented the White Flags with a permanent problem, which was much more troubling than the Red Flags. Of the 44 PVO representatives in the 1947 Constituent Assembly, only four were returned in the 1951 election; most of the rest had gone underground.[41] As a result large areas of Burma, including Minbu and several other major towns along the middle reaches of the Irrawaddy, fell under its control. But though on the surface relations between PVO and CPB leaders seemed good, there were very few areas in which the CPB could eventually take over from the PVO administration. Serious differences existed between the two parties.

The PVO's goals were avowedly socialist (even sometimes communist), but whereas the CPB wanted to establish a peasant revolution led by the working class, the PVO's roots lay solidly with the peasantry and what CPB cadres called the 'kulak' class. Its leaders, such as Bo Po Kun and the Arakan PVO leader, Bo San Tha Kyaw, came from the military and the wartime BIA, and their followers took underground with them a considerable quantity of arms and ammunition. With these they were able to defend great swathes of the rural countryside throughout the 1950s, especially west of the Chindwin, in the central Irrawaddy plain and Arakan. Though little reported in the Rangoon press its troop numbers were formidable. In Arakan alone PVO strength is today estimated by former supporters at some 3,000 men under arms and much of An township, for example, remained under loose PVO-APLP-CPB control until 1956. Here they sometimes joined in military operations with U Seinda's APLP, which also consisted largely of ethnic Rakhine wartime veterans and, between them, they effectively blocked *Tatmadaw* operations across much of the division.

Those who lived under PVO rule (even former PVO members I interviewed) seem unable to explain exactly what it was the PVOs believed they were fighting for. There was clearly a considerable amount of political opportunism. Many BIA veterans expected political status and positions as rewards for their wartime service and were unwilling to see politicians, many of whom had spent the war in the cities, taking over. None the less, because of their education and training, many PVO officers were widely respected in their own communities and it was noticeable that the *Tatmadaw* rarely launched large-scale operations against PVO territory. Military efforts were more usually directed against the CPB, KMT, KNU, the Mon People's Front and other ethnic rebel forces. For example, one leading rebel PVO commander, Bo Gamani, helped the AFPFL against the KNU and, until he surrendered with his men in 1956, was able to operate with apparent impunity in the Insein area just ten miles from Rangoon.[42] Former *Thirty Comrade*, Bo La Yaung, who had led the PVOs underground in 1948, also freely surrendered in the early 1950s; he later became a prominent figure in the aboveground opposition party, the National United Front, and, after the 1962 coup, in the BSPP Trade Ministry.

Zimbabwe, Mozambique and Angola are other examples of post-colonial countries in which wartime guerrillas have had difficulty adjusting to civilian life. But perhaps the clearest statement of PVO views came from the People's Comrade Party (PCP) after its leader, Bo Po Kun, and 29 CC members 'entered the legal fold' at Mandalay in August 1958. Arguing Burma was still under 'threat from the imperialists', the PCP pledged to continue the struggle for a communist state:

> Our policy is anti-imperialist. We disapprove of profit-making. We wish to set up a socialist economy.... Socialist nations are peace-loving nations. When they have to fight or go to war, it is because they are driven to it by the denial of justice on the part of others. When we were in the jungle, we created a people's army, set up a proletariat and a national united front. We were partially successful. Our greatest success was in the field of administration. Our People's Administration Committee was conspicuously successful. In our territory there was no dacoity, murder or rape. As a proletarian party we were able to resolve our differences.[43]

Interestingly, though the above-ground PCP made little mark, the PVO's former Chief-of-Staff, Bo Htein Lin (the ex-*pongyi* Tun Sein), joined U Chit Hlaing, the NUF's U Ba Nyein, and Brig. Aung Gyi and Bo Tin Pe from the *Tatmadaw* as part of a small group entrusted by Ne Win with the historic task of developing the *Burmese Way to Socialism*. And again in 1988 the PVO, now reformed by a handful of aged veterans led by Bo Nyunt Maung, Bo Aung Naing and Bo Ohn Tin, became another of the many forgotten anachronisms to reappear amongst the extraordinary political parties that suddenly mushroomed that year.

The First United Fronts
Against this backdrop, by the end of 1948 it was clear to the CPB's military and political leaders that if they were to have any chance of overthrowing the AFPFL by armed force, they would have to find some way of working with other insurgent progressive forces in a leftist unity front. It was a task they never really accomplished. The CPB's first attempt to form a joint front was the People's Democratic Front (PDF), set up in Prome, 150 miles north of Rangoon, in March 1949, shortly after the town was recaptured by combined CPB, RBA and PVO forces led by former MP, Bo Kun Zaw. Here, as in Pyinmana and a string of other rebel-held towns in the heart of Burma, joint Soviet administrations were set up (Prome with its broadcasting station serving as the PDF capital). But other than the eventual RBA-CPB integration of September 1950, the PDF made little progress. Than Tun, much to the chagrin of many communist sympathisers, resolutely rejected any alliance with the Red Flag 'renegades' or above-ground socialists and was, at first, equally opposed to any dealings with the KNU. It was, critics argued, the result of the CPB's inexperience. But in this determined, independent stand could also be seen the beginnings of an inflexibility, pride and belief in the Communist Party, which the CPB's rivals say has dogged the CPB in its relations with other political parties ever since. Complained the former CPB secretary-general, Thein Pe Myint, to the Indian communist leader, Comrade Dange, in October 1950:

> It is asserted that the only proletarian party is the CPB. Than Tun is acclaimed together with Marx, Lenin, Stalin and Mao Zedong as the proletarian leader. Leadership of Than Tun must be accepted. Leadership of the CPB must be accepted. Without question! The CPB seems to think that for the leadership of the proletariat to prevail in the revolution it is enough to cleverly expound, to loudly proclaim and to boldly assert. I think otherwise. The leadership of the proletariat had to be worked for.... Empty assertions of the CPB for leadership meet counter accusations for leadership from PVO, the Red Flag and the socialists.[44]

This argument resulted in an impasse during a time of major battles with government forces in which the PVO and CPB maintained separate administrations; this, as Thein Pe warned, inevitably led to armed clashes between trigger-happy troops on both sides. In heavy fighting, following disagreements at the PDF conference in Prome on 12 March 1950, the PVOs drove the CPB out of Thayetmyo and this left the door open for the *Tatmadaw* to recapture Prome, 30 miles south, in May 1950. After this debacle local ceasefires were arranged and various new PDF fronts formed in different parts of Burma throughout the 1950s.[45] The best known was the Tripartite Alliance Pact, signed by Than Tun, Soe and Bo Po Kun on 1 October 1952 at Alaungdaw Kathapa village on the Chindwin River near Monywa, north-west of Mandalay, amidst scenes of great rejoicing. Various sports contests and dancing performances by Red Star theatre troupes were put on in celebration.[46] Under this agreement three joint PLA commands would be set up: the Eastern (Shan, Kachin States and central Burma) under the White Flags; the Western (Chin hills, Arakan) under the PVOs; and the Southern (Delta, Tenasserim) under the Red Flags, each with a military strength of 1,500 troops. After overthrowing the AFPFL, their objective was to form an interim government to oversee the holding of new elections.

Subsequently PDF or tripartite meetings were held in Pakokku and Monywa districts during 1955 and 1956 and attended by Than Tun, Soe and Bo Ohn Tin (PVO). They discussed common political problems (including the Htoo-Sein clique) and agreed to step up agitation amongst rural farmers behind the CPB's recently adopted 'peace and unity' programme.[47] But though the name People's Democratic Front is still frequently used in CPB propaganda, as an effective countrywide front, the PDF died with the fall of Prome. The purpose of most later agreements was simply to demarcate territory and lay down terms of cooperation. Only in Arakan, where central government control had collapsed completely, did the CPB work at all closely with the PVOs. Here PDF administrations, consisting of the CPB under Maung Tu and present-day Politburo member, Kyaw Mya, U Seinda's APLP, and the PVOs led by Bo San Tha Kyaw (son-in-law of the AFPFL Minister for Minorities, U Aung Zan Wai) and the war hero, Bo Kra Hla Aung, effectively ran many townships until the mass surrenders of 1957/8. On occasion these local councils also included Red Flag supporters, though not the *Mujahids*; and Than Tun, Soe, Bo Ohn Tin and other rival communist leaders continued to meet frequently on their constant journeys across the country. In these discussions, ignoring both the ethnic nationalists and other worker parties in the cities, such as the BWPP with whom they were also in contact, Than Tun declared the White Flags, Red Flags and PVOs Burma's only true Marxist-Leninist parties.[48]

But talks aimed at effecting any kind of national reconciliation always broke down. During one White Flag/Red Flag/PVO conference in 1952, for example, after Than Tun proposed a joint military strategy to win 'victory within two years', Thakin Soe denounced as 'leftist adventurism' moves by the White Flags to replace PA commanders with officers from farmer backgrounds as part of their increasingly Maoist orientation.[49] Ineluctably the White Flags and Red Flags were moving towards what many commentators later referred to, somewhat inaccurately, as their respective pro-Chinese and pro-Soviet positions. Moreover only one important PVO leader, Bo Nyunt Maung, eventually joined forces with the CPB but he, too, surrendered with the PVOs at the end of the 1950s.

Finally, in late 1950, with efforts to work with their leftist rivals already breaking down, CPB leaders belatedly turned their attention to the KNU and the ethnic Pao, Mon and Karenni rebel forces which, together with the KNU, had taken control of much of Lower Burma and the rugged mountains along the Thai border in the remote south-east. In Indo-China, where the US government had invested vast amounts of money, time and effort trying to build up anti-communist 'Montagnard' hill-tribe forces in Vietnam and the ethnic Hmong *Armée Clandestine* of 'General' Vang Pao in Laos, it remains a matter of conjecture just who won the battle for the hearts and minds of the region's diverse ethnic races. But at crucial moments Ho Chi Minh, Gen. Giap and the Pathet Lao were all successfully able to play the ethnic minority card. In many remote highland areas both the Vietminh and later the Pathet Lao were entirely dependent on ethnic minorities, some loosely related to ethnic cousins across the Burma border, for recruits and vital military support.[50] Certainly in Burma, too, the CPB eventually accepted the pivotal importance of the ethnic question. In 1969 one CPB spokesman in China proclaimed: 'In Burma, there are more than 100 minority nationalities, many of whom are carrying out armed struggles. The CPB holds that the question of the minority nationalities is a special problem of the revolution in Burma. The correct handling of this question is the key to seizing victory of the revolution.'[51]

The CPB's critics, however, have always maintained there has been a considerable gap between CPB rhetoric on the nationalities question and actual practice. In his famous Calcutta speech in 1948, Than Tun publicly acknowledged 'the heroic struggle of the people of Arakan', 'the struggle of the people in Shan States for the overthrow of the feudal autocracy', and 'the honest desire of the Karen masses for self-determination'.[52] He went on to warn that the Karen movement was being weakened by its 'reactionary feudal leadership', a judgement shared by AFPFL leaders who feared the British government might yet use the KNU to destabilise the new Union. This analysis more than any other clouded the CPB's early dealings with the KNU and other nationalist movements. It in fact took until the Zin-Zan Agreement of November 1952 for an effective ceasefire to be reached, and another six and a half years (until the National Democratic United Front of 1959) for a military alliance to be agreed. Political questions were put on a back-burner. Thus, in effect, the civil war in Burma continued from three sides: the AFPFL, the communists-PVOs, and the ethnic nationalists. In the 1950s, by far the most important of these was the KNU.

The Battle For Kawthoolei: The Spread of Ethnic Rebellion

After the British left Burma, the Karen nationalist movement rapidly disappeared from centre stage in most international and domestic press reporting. The same omissions are notable in the few political histories of the era. In part, this was because the KNU had objectives which, in the main, were incidental to the mainstream course of political events in Burma, i.e. it has always been more concerned with the ethnic right of self-determination than with the overthrow of government in Rangoon. But this is not to underestimate the considerable challenge the KNU continued to pose. Of all the insurgent movements his government faced, U Nu described the KNU as the most 'formidable'.[1] This, however, was hardly a reflection of the KNU's still weak political organisation, but more a commentary on the number of troops it could call into action which, as U Nu admitted, put his government into 'unprecedented straits'. During early 1949 towns as distant as Einme and Insein in the Delta, Mandalay in the north, and Nyaunglebin, Thaton and Kawkareik in the south-east all fell to the KNU. Indeed Papun and several towns in the eastern mountains were held well into the mid-1950s.

Equally large areas of the country fell to the CPB-PVOs. But though CPB troops and cadres could still move easily through the Delta and into Rangoon, its main 'liberated areas' always lay further north in the Burman-majority heart of the country. Well supported in countless Karen communities across Lower Burma, it was thus KNU troops who for many years posed the most immediate military threat to U Nu and the embattled AFPFL government in Rangoon. In view of the damaging effect the KNU's offensive had on the psyche and perceptions of Burmese military and political leaders in the beleaguered capital, its early campaign deserves close examination. At the time the KNU and its growing number of ethnic allies were simply accused of being racists, separatists, fifth-columnists and imperialists. But as Burma enters the 1990s with the KNU and over a dozen other ethnic insurrections still continuing, none of the underlying political issues that brought the KNU into revolt have been resolved.

The Insein Siege and the Mutiny of the Karen/Kachin Rifles

Though the writing had long been on the wall for the eventual outbreak of fighting, veteran KNU commanders now admit that in the beginning they were outmanoeuvred by U Nu and the new army Chief-of-Staff, Ne Win. The starting date for the Karen uprising was not of their choosing. Both sides immediately recognised, however, that for the KNU to annex an independent Karen homeland in south-east

Burma, much depended on the swift seizure of Rangoon. They came remarkably close, which no doubt explains the particular antipathy many Burmese nationalist leaders feel for the Karen cause.

The crucial battle (and what probably turned out to be the most important in all the 40-year insurgencies) was fought at Insein, nine miles north of Rangoon, in early 1949 (see Chapter 6). Here following the outbreak of fighting on 31 January, the KNDO garrison guarding the Karen quarters quickly overran the rest of the town, including the warehouses and rice-granaries along the Hlaing riverside. Scouring the countryside for arms and ammunition, another KNDO force briefly seized control of Mingdalon Airport, four miles to the east, and removed the guns from three Spitfires caught standing on the runway. The aircraft were not, however, destroyed and KNU commanders were later to rue the decision to concede aerial power so casually to the government. None the less, for a brief moment the road to Rangoon lay open and KNDO units pushed as close as four miles from the city before being held up by a scratch force of pro-government militia, including army regulars, *Sitwundans*, Gurkhas and PVOs rushed in to defend the capital.

Critical for the KNU now was military support from other Karen forces, particularly the three regiments of Karen Rifles. On 27 January the First Karen Rifles, led by Col. Min Maung, had already seized control of the mixed Karen-Burman town of Toungoo in the Sittang River valley, 160 miles north of Rangoon, and were now contronted by government troops on the roads north and south. So on the first day of battle the KNU president, Saw Ba U Gyi, in Rangoon made wireless contact with the Second Karen Rifles in Prome and asked for their help. However, their officers, refusing to believe that the Karen army Chief-of-Staff, Smith Dun, had been replaced by Ne Win, fatally hesitated (see Chapter 6). It then took several days to call in their troops from outlying districts where most were still on operations against the CPB. In this vital breathing-space the government moved quickly to disarm and intern units of the Third Karen Rifles stationed 250 miles further north in Maymyo and Mandalay.

Once the Second Karen Rifles was assembled, caution was thrown to the wind. Disregarding advice to travel through the countryside via Henzada district, where local KNDO militia were already in control, a force of 2,000, including Karen Union Military Police and Forest Guards with their families in tow, set off down the main road towards Insein. But 30 miles south on the open road near Nattalin the convoy came under aerial attack. Though casualties were few, the strike had a disastrous effect on morale and many of the families surrendered along with their regimental commander. The remaining troops scattered. Several hundred melted into Karen villages along the Hlaing River to the south from where a handful eventually made their way into Insein. The rest headed eastwards across the Pegu Yomas highlands towards Toungoo.

Attention now focused on Toungoo in the east. Advance units of the First Karen Rifles had already pushed down from Toungoo as far south as Pegu, 40 miles from Rangoon, before being blocked. Prudently, Ne Win kept the Fourth Burma Rifles, the one force he felt he could rely on, back in the Delta to protect the capital; instead he ordered the First Kachin Rifles down from Pyinmana to retake Toungoo. Selected to lead the first attack was a young company commander, Naw Seng, a Kachin Levies veteran and holder of the British Burma Gallantry Medal, who had added to his military reputation in fierce clashes with the CPB during 1948. But Naw Seng only travelled as far as the first KNDO-controlled town,

Yedashi, before stopping to call for talks with Karen leaders. Later the government circulated rumours that he knew he was about to be arrested to face trial for atrocities committed against Burman villagers during the 1948 campaigns.[2] But this is scarcely conceivable; if it had really been the case, he would never have been entrusted with such an important mission. Naw Seng himself always made it clear he was unwilling to fight with the Karens who had served with him in the Kachin hills during the Second World War. Instead he returned to Pyinmana to lead the defection of virtually the entire regiment before heading back to Toungoo.

In Toungoo a War Council meeting of KNU, Karen Youth Organisation (KYO) and Kachin leaders now followed. They faced a choice: either strike south towards Insein and try to capture Rangoon, or head north to Maymyo and Mandalay, Burma's second largest city, where several thousand Karen troops and civilians were interned. No doubt a combined Karen/Kachin Rifles assault on Rangoon at this stage would have succeeded, but amongst KNU leaders, mindful of the massacres during the war and the recent atrocities at Palaw, there was an overriding fear of the fate of Karen prisoners. With the remnants of the Second Karen Rifles still supposedly moving to the relief of Insein, the decision was taken to turn north and, according to prisoners they freed, they arrived just in time.[3] But with this decision, the KNU lost its best chance of capturing Rangoon.

A motorised column under Naw Seng's command headed north at high speed, Pyinmana, Yamethin and Meiktila all falling in quick succession.[4] At Meiktila Naw Seng, in a famous stroke of military daring, commandeered two Dakota aircraft that had just landed and flew on into Maymyo on 21 February with just two platoons of Karen and Kachin troops, surprising the local garrison and releasing all the prisoners held there. Many joined him, though a significant number, including Smith Dun, refused. Buoyed by these new recruits and now attacking in a pincer movement, other towns in the north continued to fall rapidly: Kyaukse, Myingyan, Myitnge and, finally on 13 March, Mandalay, where some 3,000 PVOs had been armed for the town's defence.[5]

For a few desperate weeks chaos reigned as the CPB and rebel PVOs regained control of several towns hard won in the battles of 1948. More towns in the Delta and Tenasserim plain fell to the KNDOs, sometimes in collaboration with MNDOs, while the paralysing strike by the All Burma Ministerial Services Union broke out in Rangoon (see Chapter 6). In the midst of this confusion, U Nu happily accepted a ceasefire at Insein organised through the intercession of the British and Commonwealth ambassadors in Rangoon, and Saw Ba U Gyi travelled down to Rangoon for several days of talks with U Nu and Gen. Ne Win. Their intermediary was Bishop West, a trusted figure in the predominantly Christian Karen community in Insein.

KNU survivors from Insein now dispute the government's version of events; far from suing for surrender, they believe they entered the talks from a position of strength.[6] At the time, they point out, less than a quarter of the country was still under AFPFL control. They allege the government used the ceasefire as a delaying tactic to bring up fresh supplies and reorganise defences around the town. Both sides agree, however, that some initial progress was made. On 6 April Saw Ba U Gyi and Ne Win signed a preliminary treaty granting an amnesty to Karen troops who had joined the rebellion and allowing Karen civilians to keep weapons for their own protection. But when Ba U Gyi radioed these details to other KNU leaders, two leading KNDO commanders, Saw Hunter Tha Hmwe and Saw Aung Sein, sent back a new set of proposals, including demands for an immediate general ceasefire in Burma and government acceptance of the right of all insurgent organisations to hold on to any territories they occupied for the duration of the peace talks. These conditions U Nu and Ne Win rejected and on 9 April 1949 fighting flared up with renewed vigour.[7] It was over ten years before both sides sat down at the same table again.

With the breakdown of talks military attention swung back to Naw Seng and his joint Karen/Kachin force in the north of the country. Having failed to persuade any more units to defect from the other Kachin Rifle regiments, Naw Seng set off with a 2,000-strong force from Mandalay to the south with the avowed intention of capturing Rangoon by 1 May 1949. This time government forces were better prepared and he had to move more cautiously. His commanders discussed passing through the Shan State to avoid ambush, but it was agreed the support of the Shan *Sawbwas* could not be counted on. Instead Naw Seng split his troops into two columns and skirted along the western edge of the Shan plateau. Around Thazi, where a Chin battalion had taken up position, the column was held up for several days. Further south as they passed through Pyinmana, they were harried by CPB guerrillas. Then, after passing through Toungoo, a fierce battle broke out at Nyaunglebin where the Second Burma Rifles had dug in. The town fell after several days heavy fighting but over 40 of Naw Seng's Kachin followers died in the process. With supplies and ammunition running perilously low, the embattled column struggled on to Daik-u where again they found government forces had taken up position. With discretion the better part of valour, Naw Seng pulled his troops back to Toungoo where a makeshift Karen capital had been established.

With Naw Seng's thrust blunted, the tide at last began to turn the government's way. By 17 April Maymyo had been recaptured; then, on 24 April, Mandalay, where a CPB-PVO administration had taken over on Naw Seng's departure. For U Nu's beleaguered government these were important military victories, allowing attention to be concentrated on the siege at Insein where fighting was still continuing. Here, too, the situation had improved dramatically and, bit by bit through April, government forces began to capture KNDO positions around the town. Into May the situation for Karen defenders, still unrelieved and fighting on their very doorstep, grew increasingly desperate. By contrast, the relief in Rangoon was tangible. Each evening office workers would travel nine miles from the capital to take pot-shots at the Karen lines. Eventually, on 22 May, after a 112-day siege, a tactical retreat was made; the KNDOs quietly pulled back across the Hlaing River and slipped away into the countryside. Behind they left over 200 casualties, sick or wounded; but the final death toll from the Insein battle, which ran into the hundreds, has never been calculated.[8]

Reconstruction of the KNU and the Pawng Yawng Rebellion
All was not lost for the KNU, however, and optimism remained high. Much of the Lower Delta, including large sections of road, river and railway, was still under KNDO control. And though disorganised, virtually the entire mountain border region to the east, including the Karenni State, was in KNU or sympathetic ethnic nationalist hands (Mon, Karenni and Pao). Contemporary photographs show heavily armed Karen troops in full battle-dress; Second World War veterans were confident they could defeat any 'Burman' army. According to U Soe Aung, then a

young KNDO organiser in Henzada: 'We thought we would win within two to three years. We never thought we would be in the jungle 40 years later.'[9]

From its capital at Toungoo the KNU now launched its first political campaign. On 20 May, two days before the fall of Insein, the formation of a Karen State in KNU-controlled territory between Toungoo and Daik-u was declared.[10] On 14 June, after Saw Ba U Gyi's arrival, an emergency meeting was called and, for the first time since fighting began, KNU leaders tried to assess the situation. Like most early KNU conferences, the meeting was poorly attended. Only local KNU delegates from Toungoo, Thaton and Nyaunglebin were able to come; there were no representatives from the Delta. None the less, a number of decisions were taken which had an important bearing on the development of the war. These included the reorganisation of all the military forces under KNU control, now renamed the Kawthoolei Armed Forces (KAF), into two divisions along the lines of the KNDOs, the 'Delta' and the 'Eastern', under 'Gen.' Min Maung's command. When the meeting ended a statement over the Free Karen radio station announced to the world the establishment of a provisional Kawthoolei* government at Toungoo with Saw Ba U Gyi as the first prime minister.[11]

To break the military deadlock it was decided to launch a new offensive, again under Naw Seng's command, but this time to the north-east into the Shan State. With local KNDOs and Sao Shwe's nationalist forces already in control of Loikaw and Mawchi in the Karenni State and Pao militia in the Shan State openly stating their sympathies, the road to the north lay open. On 13 August 1949 Taunggyi fell to a combined assault by Karen, Karenni, Pao and Kachin soldiers and a considerable quantity of money and arms was captured. Here, however, there was a surprise parting of the ways.

Officially, Naw Seng carried on alone with his Kachin troops to begin the short-lived Pawng Yawng rebellion among Kachin villagers in the northern Shan State. He was highly confident. On 15 November 1949 the Pawng Yawng National Defence Force was formed near Kuktai with two military brigades (the first east of Kuktai and the second to the west); these were planned to instigate the spread of the rebellion across the hills into the Kachin State. But despite early military successes, including the capture of Lashio and Namhkam on the China border, it soon became clear that many Kachins, especially in the Burma Army and Kachin State, did not support armed struggle at this stage. Naw Seng also accused *Tatmadaw* commanders of sending predominantly Kachin troops to try and crush his movement. Eventually, after secret talks with a number of prominent Kachin leaders who stood on the AFPFL side, including Brig. Tang Ji and the *Duwa* Sinwa Nawng, in April 1950 Naw Seng crossed over into China and exile with some 300 followers.[12]

Veteran Kachin leaders privately say that, long before his exodus to the north, Naw Seng had been growing increasingly frustrated with KNU officers whom he believed were deliberately keeping him short of arms and ammunition. None the less, into exile with Naw Seng went some 50 Karen followers who returned with

---

*   There is some uncertainty over the exact origins of the name Kawthoolei. The term first surfaced after the war and is a word-play with several possible meanings. Veteran nationalists usually explain it as 'the country burnt black', i.e. the country which must be fought for (Kaw = country, thoo = black, lei = bare), but it is also often described as 'flowery' or 'green' land. The 'thoolei' is a green, orchid-like plant common in the eastern hills.

him to Burma nearly 20 years later, including Tun Tin, a future CC member of the CPB. At the same time he left behind with the KNU several Kachin soldiers, including his young lieutenant, Zau Seng, who a dozen years later became the first president of the Kachin Independence Organisation. But with Naw Seng's departure, the war of rapid mobile offensives with 'spectacular gains and losses' of territory came to a halt; not until Naw Seng's return as head of the CPB's North East Command was fighting on such a fluctuating scale seen again.[13]

For the KNU, the military and political reorganisation begun in June was now urgent. Radio contact was maintained between KAF units spread over a distance of some 300 miles from Bassein district in the western Delta to Loikaw and Myawaddy in the eastern hills, but no real tactics or plan of campaign had been established. As a temporary measure, in September 1949 an emergency Civilian Affairs Service (Kawthoolei), based on the post-war British CAS (Burma) in which many Karen officers had served, was established to administer KNU-controlled areas. Under this Kawthoolei Military Administration, as it became known, all political organisations were abolished; temporary standing orders were signed by Joshua Poo Nyo, a veteran of the India Civil Service and secretary to the post-war Frontier Areas Administration. But this could not disguise the mounting difficulties KNU organisers faced. In many ways the KNU's problems echoed those of the CPB which at the same time was trying to establish its own 'liberated' administration. While a solid nucleus of experienced commanders from both Force 136 and the British Army were directing military operations, few of the civilian administrators now caught up in the fighting had much taste for the war ahead. Veteran KNU leaders admit that before the rebellion began the KNU was really only effectively organised in Rangoon, Bassein and a handful of other major towns with sizeable Karen populations. In most rural areas KNU organisation was still negligible. And by the end of 1949, with stocks of heavy weaponry and ammunition running down, the very character of the war was changing fast. KAF commanders warned they would be unable to defend towns on the plains in conventional fixed-position warfare for much longer. The fall of Nyaunglebin in February 1950, Toungoo on 19 March, and the CPB's immediate loss of Pyinmana, 60 miles north, just ten days later, only served to emphasise their warnings.

A group of younger KNU leaders from the Delta now began drawing up plans for a complete restructuring of the KNU. This group, led by 38 year-old barrister Saw Ba U Gyi, included the KNDO's three regional commanders, Saw Sankey, Saw Hunter Tha Hmwe and Mahn Ba Zan. All were Christians, English-speaking and veterans of Force 136. To gain approval for their plans, Saw Ba U Gyi called a full KNU Congress, the first since the outbreak of fighting, which finally began on 17 July 1950 in Papun, the new KNU capital. This time virtually all the eastern hill districts, including Tavoy-Mergui, were represented, and Saw Sankey and Mika Rolly led a delegation of KNU leaders from the Delta who crossed over the Sittang River for the meeting. Also invited were representatives from the Indian community and rebel Mon and Karenni delegates, but both these movements were still in a formative stage and were yet to have a significant impact on the political scene.

Despite this broad attendance, the Congress ended inconclusively. The meeting analysed and approved the 'three ways of gaining independence' laid down by Saw Ba U Gyi: 'by voluntary gift, by the fight of the KNU, and by force of circumstances' and what have since become known as Saw Ba U Gyi's 'four principles of the Karen revolution':

There shall be no surrender.

The recognition of the Karen State must be completed.

We shall retain our own arms.

We shall decide our own political destiny.[14]

At the end of the Congress these were broadcast in Karen, Burmese and English over the Free Karen radio and, to this day, remain the cornerstone of KNU political demands. But on the thorny question of political reorganisation which, according to Congress secretary, Skaw Ler Taw, was the principal aim of the Congress, there was little progress; Saw Sankey was forced to withdraw his motion in the face of fierce opposition from military commanders who wanted to continue with the emergency CAS (Kawthoolei) and build up military organisation in each district first.[15] The most articulate opposition came from delegates from Thandaung-Leythoo in northern Toungoo, led by a military commander, Alfonzo, and Saw Ba Lone, a pre-war member of the Legislative Council, both of whom were formerly members of the AFPFL-affiliated KYO. Here the KNU had yet to be established and the district was controlled by the Toungoo mass organisation and the 200-strong Lion Force Battalion. Most of their leaders were ethnic Gekho-Bwe Karens, while the KNU supporters from Toungoo town, including Gen. Min Maung, were Paku Karens. Saw Ba U Gyi and the majority of the KNU leadership from the Delta, on the other hand, were Sgaw Karens, while Mahn Ba Zan was a Pwo Karen. Eventually in 1952 most of the Lion Force Battalion surrendered and only then was the KNU able to begin organising in the Toungoo hills. But it was a problem symptomatic of the chaos the KNU faced in the early years. Similar problems were encountered in Thaton district throughout the 1950s, where the Thaton No. 5 brigade mass organisation had been established, and the KNU only began organising in this area after 1953 when the Thaton brigade formally joined the KNU.

In the face of such sustained opposition, KNU leaders had to settle for a number of compromise resolutions eventually passed by the Congress. To replace the ineffective CAS (Kawthoolei) a new civilian council, the Kawthoolei Governing Body (KGB), was set up; it was agreed to begin KNU political training classes in each district and to open agricultural and marketing cooperatives in villages under KAF control. In return, to satisfy KAF commanders, a number of adjustments were made to regional military zones. But the Congress Report notes that at the end of the Congress Saw Ba U Gyi, recognising the failure of his plans, privately assigned the task of improving KNU construction in the east to three of his most trusted organisers, Saw Sankey in Thaton and Moulmein, Skaw Ler Taw in Nyaunglebin, and Mika Rolly in Toungoo, Papun and Mawchi.[16]

The tentative gains of the Congress were, however, now overshadowed by a disaster which shook the KNU movement to its very foundations. The Congress minutes record Saw Ba U Gyi's last words as, 'I am now going to pull a political stunt.' Exactly what he had in mind, he never revealed. But a few days later, on 12 August 1950, travelling in a small party through the hills near Hlaingbwe close to the Thai border (presumably *en route* to Bangkok and into contact with the outside world) Ba U Gyi and Sankey were trapped in a *Tatmadaw* ambush and killed. Ba U Gyi's body was taken to Moulmein and put on public display before reputedly being secretly thrown by soldiers into the sea. Not only would there be no martyr's grave, but his body would never lie on Burma's soil. The death of Sankey was no less damaging and their loss was a shattering blow at a critical stage from which it took the KNU many years to recover.[17] While in his earlier days Ba U Gyi enjoyed something of a playboy reputation, many observers (British, Burman and Karen alike) who worked with him in the long negotiations on the post-war Governor's Executive Council believed he had grown considerably in stature as a political figure and was the one KNU leader capable of uniting the Karen movement and building bridges with the AFPFL in Rangoon. One man who admired him was the former British governor, Dorman-Smith, who wrote to *The Times* lamenting his death:

> Saw Ba U Gyi was no terrorist.... I, for one, cannot picture him enjoying the miseries and hardships of a rebellion. There must have been some deep impelling reason for his continued resistance.... The major tragedy is that Burma is losing her best potential leaders at far too rapid a rate. Aung San, U Saw, Saw Ba U Gyi, U Tin Tut, all have gone.[18]

In sombre mood a handful of military and political leaders from the KNU's Eastern Division met in Mawchi on 21 September to choose Ba U Gyi's successor. Their first choice was the ethnic Pao, Thaton Hla Pe, a pre-war MP who had served as Minister of Forests in Ba Maw's wartime Cabinet. But Hla Pe had moved to the south-west Shan State at the beginning of the insurrection to help the fast-spreading Pao rebellion and sent back a message declining the offer. As an interim choice, Joshua Poo Nyo again took up the leadership, but his autocratic methods ensured that he proved a short-lived choice. Finally, to resolve the leadership question, on 9 January 1951 Gen. Min Maung called another full KNU Congress at Lumbu village near Toungoo. Again the meeting was handicapped by the absence of Delta representatives and this time it was decided not to elect a new president but to replace the leadership post by an executive committee, drawn from the KGB, with Hla Pe as chairman and the KAF commander, Min Maung, as his deputy. Hla Pe, however, again refused to come down from the Shan State and Min Maung declined on the grounds that he was too busy with military affairs. Instead he sent a message to the Delta leaders asking them to nominate one of their number as chairman. Eventually Saw Hunter Tha Hmwe, the KNU's most stirring orator and organiser, was chosen but he in turn sent a letter saying he was still too busy to leave and asking another former headmaster and Force 136 veteran from Toungoo, Skaw Ler Taw, to represent him until he arrived.

Thus for eight months during some of the heaviest fighting in the civil war the KNU was without effective leadership; only in December 1954 did Tha Hmwe finally cross over to the Eastern Division to take up his post. In the meantime much of the day-to-day responsibility for the KNU's central political organisation fell on Skaw Ler Taw, who, many years later, remembered this period as one of the most difficult the KNU ever faced.[19] Against the backdrop of war, the KNU now embarked on the difficult task of trying to integrate ethnically and politically the 20-odd Karen sub-groups, something never attempted before, not even during the British occupation. Even today the term 'Sgaw Karen' could apply equally to a Burmese-speaking Rangoon University graduate, born and brought up in Bassein in the Delta, or an illiterate, Animist hill-tribesman in the Dawna Range who has never even met an ethnic Burman.[20]

The KNU was short of neither men nor arms. Like the CPB and PVOs, it had access to large stockpiles of small arms left over from the Second World War and, though ammunition was always in short supply, sufficient could usually be purchased on the black market or captured in raids on army outposts. In 1950 the KAF could nominally call on some 15,000 men under arms and guerrilla units were still expanding. But these forces were hardly integrated. Not only were there rivalries between the KNDOs and 'professionals' from the Karen Rifles, but in many areas local territories were strictly demarcated. Armed clashes were not unknown. Indeed in some districts Karen forces had to be deployed facing government troops, the CPB or PVOs at the front and each other to the rear. Taxation in particular was chaotic and, like the CPB, the KNU was confronted with the endemic problem of banditry. According to Skaw Ler Taw: 'Of all the problems the KNU faced (military, political or financial) "warlordism" was the greatest.'[21]

Parliament's Disposal of the Karen Question
While the KNU was still grappling with these problems the AFPFL government, heartened by the socialists' return to the Cabinet in 1950, moved quickly to neutralise what was left of the above-ground Karen movement. As described in Chapter 4, the 1947 Constitution was riddled with inconsistencies on the complex and unresearched subject of Karen representation in Parliament. Alternative provision had been left to create either a Karen special region or a Karen State in the eastern hills. In the meantime a Karen Affairs Council and a Minister for Karen Affairs would represent Karen interests, including those of the more numerous plains Karens, with reserved seats for Karens in Parliament. By contrast, their Karenni cousins, who technically could be included in the new Karen State, were granted the right of secession and the continuance of traditional *Sawbwa* rule. The Kayans, on the other hand, were temporarily left inside the Shan State, while the Paos were given no political status at all.

The AFPFL now proved itself as adept as the British in the tactics of divide and rule and used legal ambiguities to drive deep wedges into the Karen nationalist movement. The first problem concerned the historical anomaly of the Karenni State which had so baffled the British. Here, with the outbreak of fighting in August 1948, the government had faced a twofold dilemma: on the one hand of trying to quash the last vestiges of the Karenni's historic sovereignty and separatism while, on the other, of attempting to prevent the Karenni *Sawbwas* from joining their rebellious Karen cousins in the KNU. The situation had since become considerably more complicated by the large influx of KNDOs into the state after the Karen insurrection began and, as a result, in the field the nationalist forces of the Kyebogyi *Sawbwa*, Sao Shwe, and the KNDOs were virtually indistinguishable. Eventually in 1951 in the midst of fighting, a contrived and ingenious solution was found and quickly passed into law with the renaming of the Karenni State as the Kayah State. This, at a stroke, both got rid of a name synonymous with Karenni independence and created a clear, though insupportable, racial distinction between the Kayah inhabitants of the state and Karen sub-groups elsewhere in Burma. The Kayah are, in fact, only the largest of the dozen ethnic sub-groups within the state and there is no ethnic basis whatsoever for the continued usage of the name Kayah as a term of regional ethnic identity. Present-day members of the Karenni National Progressive Party, who include Kayahs, Kayans, Pakus, Sgaws and even Pwo Karens and Shans, simply ignore the appellation. Undeterred, the government even invited Western anthropologists into Burma to try and prove this distinction really existed.[22] The results hardly backed up their claim, but government statistics today still preserve this fiction.

Meanwhile, no action was taken on the question of the various Karen sub-groups in the Shan State, where the rebellion of an estimated 300,000 Paos, led by Thaton Hla Pe and Bo Chan Zon, another British army veteran, was in full swing. Having initially begun as a *pongyi*-backed uprising against excessive taxation and persistent abuses of power by the ruling Shan *Sawbwas* (especially Sao Num of Laikha), the Pao nationalist movement was now being aided and abetted by a number of Karens, including Bo Special and his brother, Tha Kalei, sent up by the KNU to help.[23] In theory the Paos, as ethnic Karens, might have demanded inclusion in any new Karen territory, but like the Karen sub-groups in the small Mongpai substate, which was 90 per cent Kayan-Yinbaw and had the right of accession to the Karenni State, they were simply ignored.

Finally there remained the contentious issue of the territorial demarcation of a Karen State. When the Regional Autonomy Enquiry Commission eventually reported in February 1949, it recommended, as expected, the least radical of the various proposals considered (see Chapter 6), i.e. the formation of a Karen State by enlarging the Salween district to include adjoining Karen-majority areas delineated by a boundary Commission. In October 1951 this was accepted in principle by constitutional amendment, but the Karen community now found there was an additional price to be paid. U Nu, in particular, had grown increasingly critical of the separate political rights of the Delta Karens, who were not included in the new state, and urged Karens in a forceful speech before Parliament to choose between 'the Karen State or the minority rights. It is absolutely impossible to choose both.'[24] He saw minority rights as a real Pandora's box of troubles if applied to other minorities (like the Chins and Lahus) elsewhere in Burma; the very principle he described as a 'divide and rule' invention of the 'imperialists'.[25] With no one to oppose him, U Nu got his way and the result was a halving of the reserved Karen seats in the two houses of Parliament, from 44 to 22.

Thus in September 1952, following more or less exactly the British administration's haphazard divisional borders, legislation was passed adding the Kya-in, Kawkareik, Hlaingbwe, Paan and Thandaung districts to the Salween district in the east to create the new Karen State. At the time virtually all these areas were under KNU control; even today much of this territory lies within KNU 'liberated zones'. But for many Karens this greatly reduced 11,600 square-mile backwater of mountains and forests, with a capital at the then village of Paan, was final proof that the AFPFL's tactics since 1945 had been to isolate and squeeze out the Karen cause all along. If the Karens were ever to be allowed to develop economically, culturally or geographically as a people, the new borders made little sense and, as KNU leaders angrily pointed out, there was no seaport. While in the Shan and Kachin States there were very mixed ethnic populations which included Burmans and other minorities, for the Karen State a large, mixed Karen-Mon-Burman population was clearly not regarded as admissible by the AFPFL. With a population estimated at 578,354 in 1956, it probably did not incorporate even one quarter of the total Karen population in Burma.[26] Even Hugh Tinker, one of U Nu's greatest admirers and the KNU's most scathing critics, suggested expanding the state to include Thaton, Amherst and Toungoo districts with a capital at Moulmein. In 1956 he wrote: 'There is room for a more generous policy towards the Karens.... An expanded Karen State would still leave over half of the Karen community outside its territory in the Delta districts, but such a move would provide unmistakable evidence that the central government intended to give the Karens their full share in the national life.'[27] It was an error which convinced many Karens that the government in Rangoon lacked sincerity. The same borders were followed by the BSPP government and, even in the 1990s, are yet to be reviewed. This partly explains the continuing supply of recruits to the nationalist cause from districts all over Burma. To ensure a lasting peace a new Karen State or system more representative of Karen aspirations will one day have to be found. Instead of attempting the impossible (to delineate exact territorial or racial boundaries) it is perhaps time to return to the idea of building a strong, multi-ethnic political and economic region of Tenasserim, which at various times between 1945 and 1948 KNU, AFPFL, Mon and British leaders all accepted as a possible solution. (The BSPP later created a Mon State with a capital in Moulmein, but this satisfied neither Mon nor Karen nationalist demands.)

By the same token the fate of the remaining above-ground Karen political parties needs to be mentioned, for this was to set an important precedent for the future of ethnic minority politics under the AFPFL. For the Karen population at large, both supporters and opponents of the KNU, the outbreak of the rebellion was nothing short of catastrophic. (Prominent amongst those who refused to join the KNU were Smith Dun, Mahn Win Maung, the future president of Burma, and BIA veteran, Hanson Kyadoe.) Besides the many killed, wounded or made homeless, thousands of Karen civil servants, soldiers and policemen were arrested and interned. Many others lost their jobs. Only in 1951 did the government feel confident enough to start reinstating a handful of Karens into the police and, in 1952, into the army, but the Karen community never regained its former influence in the military or government bureaucracy.

By this stage three main parties had emerged: the Union Karen League (UKL), president, Mahn Win Maung, based largely in the plains, included former KYO supporters, affiliated to the AFPFL; the Union Karen Organisation (UKO), president, Dr Hla Tun, based in the eastern hills; and the Karen Congress, which included ex-KNU supporters who had either not gone underground or later given themselves up.[28] In 1951 the Karen Congress briefly won control of the Karen Affairs Council, but later withdrew leaving the UKL and UKO to contest the field. However, like ethnic minority parties elsewhere in Burma, in the absence of any clear constitutional guarantees of regional autonomy, both soon became embroiled in Rangoon party politics and, as a result, subservient to AFPFL political and factional interests. By 1956 both had virtually ceased to exist. That year, with the final abolition of Karen reserved seats in the national Parliament, the AFPFL convinced UKL leaders to dissolve their party and stand as AFPFL candidates in the general election. Meanwhile in the Karen State to the east the UKO formally merged with the AFPFL. According to Silverstein, such incidents 'demonstrated how national interest transcended local interest and how the Union government and the national AFPFL eroded the guarantees and provisions of the Constitution.'[29] Within a few years this same fate had befallen most other ethnic minority parties in Burma and was a major factor behind the emergence of insurgent Shan and Kachin movements in the late 1950s (see Chapter 10).

Rapprochement with the CPB and the Zin-Zan Agreement

Though these developments were peripheral to the main battle being fought between the KNU and AFPFL, they go some way towards explaining the very real depths of political antipathy and the conviction of many Karen leaders that it was hopeless to expect anything from negotiation. The KNU's claim for Karen State territory in the Delta, initially begun as a casually played bargaining chip, was now elevated into a basic political demand; many leaders argued that force was the only way to achieve a solution. According to Bruce Humphrey-Taylor, then attached to the KAF Delta Command, the slogan now was 'all or nothing'; this led the American missionary, Dr Gordon Seagrave, whom the AFPFL had briefly imprisoned in 1951 for his alleged support for the Karen cause, to make his famous remark: 'The trouble was that the Karens demanded just too much.'[30] In the periodic government amnesties very few KNU, Karenni or Pao leaders came in.

In 1951 the KNU still controlled, albeit loosely, the majority of Karen-populated areas in the countryside, both in the Delta and in the east. Both *Tatmadaw* and KNU leaders recognised that the Delta would be the strategic battleground for the long-term success of the Karen rebellion and it was here that both concentrated their early efforts. In the Delta, unlike the sparsely populated mountains in the east, there were large villages, abundant food supplies and a constant stream of new recruits. And while by December 1950, with the capture of Einme and Pantanaw, the government had retaken the last major towns under KAF control, through 1951 the situation was still rather one of stalemate. Most of the Karen villages surrounding the towns remained under KNDO control and KAF units roved freely from Henzada to Pyapon in the Lower Delta, providing further confirmation of the scale and spread of the Karen population.

In the 1950s the KNU developed at different paces in the Delta and in the eastern hills, reflecting the different stages of development in the various Karen communities in Burma, but it was always the KNU's Delta leaders who led the way with reform. In December 1949 they made their first moves towards reorganising the KNU on a revolutionary footing. At a meeting called by Mahn Ba Zan at Ywathagone village near Bassein, it was agreed to divide the Delta Division into seven military brigade districts (extended to eight in 1956 when the Pegu Yomas were organised under a separate command) and to set up a civilian KNU administration in each district.* But the difficulty for Delta KAF units was that here they were fighting on their home turf in often exposed positions on the plains; and a change of *Tatmadaw* tactics in 1952 shattered the comparative calm. In early 1952, taking advantage of a steady decline in CPB activity in central Burma, Ne Win launched a major offensive, throwing in planes, gunboats and tanks against the KAF's No.1 brigade under Gen. Kaw Htoo (*aka* Kyaw Mya Than) in Tharrawaddy district, 60′ miles north of Rangoon. This mixed ethnic Pwo-Sgaw brigade was probably the KAF's strongest; it controlled most of the Karen villages on the plains between the Irrawaddy and Pegu Yomas and, from early 1949, effectively disrupted all traffic on the river. Once again meeting strong resistance, government troops began to burn down Karen villages and

---

*   No.1: Henzada-Tharrawaddy, No.2: Myaungmya-Pyapon, No.3: Maubin-Twante, No.4: Labutta-Bassein, No.5: Bogale and south to the sea, No.6: Insein, Prome, and western Pegu Yomas, No.7: Bassein.

destroy paddy-fields in a severe, but effective scorched earth policy which forced Kaw Htoo to order the main body of his troops to pull back into the Pegu Yomas. Several hundred others headed south. The government then immediately switched the offensive to the south-west against the KAF No.7 brigade in Bassein district and the No.2 around Myaungmya, where the same tactics were repeated. Again after initially fierce resistance in which several tanks were captured, KAF troops were forced to pull back, some into the Arakan Yomas, some into the Pegu Yomas, and others into the empty grasslands and mangrove swamps to the south. Here, hounded night and day by government troops, several leaders, including Hunter Tha Hmwe and Mahn Ba Zan, were lucky to escape with their lives.

As KNU units retreated deeper into the more remote forests and foothills they increasingly came into contact with small CPB units (both Red Flag and White Flag) taking shelter in the districts; faced by a common enemy, military commanders on both sides immediately recognised the futility of fighting each other.

Until then relations between the CPB and the KNU had been poor. From the earliest days of the insurrections, even before the Karen uprising, there were frequent clashes between KNU and CPB supporters. None the less, during the April 1949 peace talks, KNU president, Saw Ba U Gyi, demanded that all armed opposition forces, including the KNU and CPB, be admitted to government. Then after the fall of Insein in June 1949 the KNU sent an emissary, Saw Maung Lay, to the headquarters of the People's Democratic Front in Prome to discuss the formation of a joint anti-AFPFL front. But Than Tun denounced Ba U Gyi as a 'lackey of imperialism' and the KNU as the 'running dogs of imperialism'.[31] It was a critical error. A joint KNU/CPB/PVO offensive at this stage might well have led to the capture of Rangoon.

At first relations had generally been better with the much smaller Red Flags, especially with Thakin Soe who was a frequent traveller through KNDO territory. During 1949, however, Thakin Soe antagonised KNU leaders by setting up a rival Karen front, the Karen New Land Party (KNLP), which began organising in Karen villages around Red Flag strongholds in Pyapon and Hanthawaddy in the Delta and Amherst district in the east. Small cells were also active in Insein and Tharrawaddy and the KNLP embarked on a radical programme of land redistribution which, though popular with poor farmers, caused local KNU organisers a great deal of trouble. KAF commanders immediately moved to crush this upstart new movement, but only in 1955 was the KNLP destroyed and its leader, Po Gyan, forced to join the KNU.

There thus remained a deep distrust between KNU and CPB leaders and neither side moved decisively to stop the constant communal battles of those early years. Veteran KNU officers readily admit that their troops killed many Burmans, including CPB sympathisers, in what they now refer to as the racial war of 1948-51. Karen casualties, they claim, were equally high. However, there were local differences in the chaotic pattern of the fighting; for example, ceasefires were organised in the Bassein area, while in others, such as the Pegu Yomas, fighting continued with the White Flags, Karen commanders allege, receiving arms supplies from the *Tatmadaw* to ward off the KNU's advance. Significantly, the most senior army officer they accuse was the *Thirty Comrade*, Brig. Kyaw Zaw, who was finally dismissed from the army in 1957 for his alleged pro-communist sympathies.[32] After his removal Kyaw Zaw, a CPB member at the end of the Second World War, became a prominent sympathiser of the above-ground

National United Front and finally went into the jungles of Panghsang in 1976 to join the CPB.

Eventually, however, in 1952, as the AFPFL government continued to win back ground from both the KNU and CPB, a truce was called, the initiative this time coming from the CPB. According to the popular version of events, troops on both sides spontaneously stopped fighting after CPB cadres brought the body of one of their comrades, killed in a recent clash, into a KNU camp and implored leaders on both sides to stop the killings. The plea was successful. Until then most of the KNU/CPB contact had been through junior CPB officials in the Lower Delta. Senior White Flag leaders for the most part stayed in the CPB's main strongholds in the Burman-majority districts north of Henzada. But in November 1952 a high-ranking CPB delegation, headed by Politburo member, Thakin Zin, travelled into KNU-controlled territory to Anangon village, Thabaung township, to meet Mahn Ba Zan, the KNU's Delta leader. The result of their discussions was what became known as the Zin-Zan agreement, which established an effective ceasefire, a committee to discuss common problems and a Joint Operations Committee to coordinate future military campaigns.[33]

It was the beginning of a long, often antagonistic relationship which has followed the course of insurgent politics in Burma ever since. But with Mahn Ba Zan and the KNU leaders resolutely refusing to accept the CPB's leadership, it took several years for the political basis of this alliance to change and the military advantages to both sides were at first small. None the less, the series of meetings with CPB leaders now set in motion had a critical impact on Karen thinking at a time when many KNU leaders had already decided a complete change in tactics was needed if the Karen revolution was to survive.

The Formation of the KNUP and the KNU's 'Second Phase' Programme
The first English-language copies of Mao Zedong's *Protracted Warfare* and Liu Shao-chi's *On Inner Party Struggle* were brought to Toungoo by Ba U Gyi in 1949. These he had apparently been given by local PVO commanders during the siege of Insein. Most Karen leaders, despite their generally pro-British views, were familiar with other communist works, in particular Stalin's *Social and State Structure of the USSR* and the *National Question in the Soviet Union's 1936 Constitution*. These, like AFPFL and CPB leaders, they had studied in the run-up to Burma's independence. Now with the increasing contacts with the CPB, Burmese-language copies of Mao's *Protracted Warfare* and *Guerrilla Warfare* were widely circulated; they have, however, never been translated into Karen.

While the KAF's ability in conventional and guerrilla warfare had never been called into question, many of these new ideas, especially on party organisation, had an immediate impact. One theme, in particular, hit a common nerve among KAF commanders disillusioned by the military aid the British government was giving to the AFPFL. With the failure of the KNU to seize power in the set-piece battles of 1949-50, increasing numbers of educated Karens, especially ex-civil servants and career military officers, were beginning to surrender. Reports coming in from the brigade districts were frequently alarming. The very continuation of the armed struggle, many KNU organisers argued, had now become dependent on the rural farmers and forestry workers, who not only were feeding and sheltering KAF units but also had to bear the brunt of the fighting. This led Karen leaders into their first serious discussion of class analysis and a complete review of the goals and tactics of the KNU movement. According to Skaw Ler Taw, the reasons were compelling: 'Through our revolutionary experience we had found that the class characteristics laid down by Mao Zedong were to a certain extent true. Intellectuals waver very easily. Many of those who had joined surrendered within two years. Peasants, too, have some possessions and are not always reliable. Only the workers, who have nothing, could be relied upon.'[34]

With these views in mind a group of KNU leaders, summoned by Mahn Ba Zan, met at Weythaung village in the Lower Delta on 9 June 1953 to discuss ways, as U Soe Aung remembers, 'to preserve the Karen revolution'.[35] Their first solution was to copy the CPB and set up a new vanguard party, the Karen National United Party (KNUP). The role of the KNUP, according to Skaw Ler Taw, its long-time secretary-general, was 'to get the political leadership. The KNU would remain a mass organisation, the backbone of the revolution'.[36] Like U Soe Aung, Skaw Ler Taw was co-opted and this first cell of KNUP members consisted of 'hand-picked men, prepared to dedicate everything to the revolution'.[37] The KNUP was then formally inaugurated at a conference at Gayetau village, Maubin district, in September; approval of its establishment as the KNU's vanguard party was given at the main KNU Congress, the First National Congress, in November 1953 in Papun. Here several KNUP members, including present-day KNU CC members, Tin Oo and Maung Maung, travelled up through the mountains to explain the new line. A number of Mon and Karenni representatives were also in attendance.

While it took several years for this new strategy to evolve, it was at the KNUP's historic inaugural meeting at Gayetau that many of the principles of what became known as the KNU's Second Phase Programme were drawn up. The whole course of the Karen rebellion was restructured in a new language. The chaotic early years of spontaneous uprisings, communal clashes, local rivalries and warlordism were redefined as the 'first phase of the Karen revolution' and a series of policy goals were laid down for what KNUP leaders claimed would now be the successful 'second phase'.

There was considerable controversy later over this new line and much of the second phase ideology has long since been abandoned. But many of the second phase policies, especially in party and military organisation, have had a lasting impact on the KNU movement and were later studied and borrowed by other ethnic minority fronts elsewhere in Burma. Though no mention of communism or the CPB was made, the KNUP was supposed to fulfil the role of any other Marxist-Leninist vanguard party. According to Skaw Ler Taw, the first object of the Second Phase Programme was 'more or less centralisation'.[38] To achieve this, the KNUP lifted wholesale many basic Maoist organisational principles. The KAF, like the CPB's People's Army, was now reorganised along Maoist lines into three divisions (regular, guerrilla and village defence) and in the Delta a start was made on this restructuring in 1953. Though the KNU only officially adopted the second phase in 1956, during 1953 a tentative political platform designed to improve contacts with farmers and workers from all nationalities was laid down for the KNUP. This included a land reform programme and a foreign-affairs policy based on the principles of peaceful coexistence.

In the Delta KNUP cadre training classes began in late 1953 and some of the second-phase policies were introduced in the brigade districts. The first results were promising. The most notable success was the virtual eradication of warlordism, which had remained a lingering problem in much of the Lower Delta. In

warlordism, which had remained a lingering problem in much of the Lower Delta. In several districts, especially No.4 (Labutta) and No.7 (Bassein), there was enthusiastic support from local farmers; relations between KAF troops and local villagers, which had often been tense, began to improve dramatically. Fish farms that had been shut down for years started to reopen and the KNUP set up new agricultural cooperatives in KNDO-controlled villages. But perhaps most important of all, in areas of mixed Karen-Burman population, or where CPB/KNUP forces overlapped, there was support from local Burman villagers.

These advances were soon translated into successes on the battlefield. With finances now better centralised and the KAF more attuned to fighting a mobile guerrilla war, in 1954 and 1955 KAF units were able to infiltrate back into many of the areas lost in 1952. Attacks on government outposts and supply lines were stepped up and, in May 1955, a 200-strong guerrilla force was able to gather for an attack on Khalaukchaik on the opposite bank of the river from Rangoon.[39]

On the obverse side, there were also some counter-productive results. Christian pastors and Buddhist *pongyis* joined some of the earlier training classes without any apparent objection. But when a radical anti-religious movement developed within the KNUP, sensibilities were stirred up in both Buddhist and Christian Karen communities and, in some areas of the Delta, these still rankle. Like other ethnic minority parties, the KNU has always regarded the right to religious freedom as a key demand. Skaw Ler Taw put it down to their youthfulness: 'Most of the radicals had no practical experience, only theoretical. Though they spoke about the masses, they were in fact anti-mass. It showed whenever they went into villages. They would demand money and food as if it was their right.'[40] KNUP leaders were, however, slow to react and only tried to solve the problem in the early 1960s when it was probably too late. A clear warning of the KNUP's future difficulties had been fatally ignored.

Hill Karens, the Eastern Division and the KMT Invasion

Meanwhile, in the rugged hill tracts to the east, KNU leaders faced very different problems. At the beginning of the insurrection virtually the entire Karen-inhabited border region with Thailand fell into KNU hands, yet political progress here, among the predominantly Animist or Buddhist-Animist hill Karens, was much slower.[41] The entire region was chronically underdeveloped. There were few roads or schools, even fewer hospitals and much of the local administration was still run by traditional village headmen. Under the KAF's Eastern Division several brigades and mobile battalions were formed in the early 1950s, but their activities were poorly coordinated.* In front-line areas, such as Thaton and Toungoo, KNDO village defence units were set up, but in other areas, such as the Tenasserim valley in Tavoy-Mergui, the KNU did not begin to organise effectively among the remote hill Karen communities until the 1970s. Many of these eastern hill districts have still never come under the direct control of any Rangoon central government, whether British, Japanese or Burmese.

---

* The Eastern Division brigades took some time to evolve into the form by which they are known today, No.1: Karenni (disbanded 1956), No.2: Toungoo, No.3: Nyaunglebin, No.4 (now No.7): Paan-Papun, No.5: Thaton (surrendered 1964, remnants disbanded and reformed in 1966 as No.1), No.6: Dooplaya (Kawkareik south to Three Pagodas Pass and Tavoy-Mergui, which was reformed as No.10 Battalion in 1970).

the beginning of 1952 KNU leaders were confronted by political rivals of a very different hue, the exile units of Chiang Kai-shek's nationalist forces from China. Having failed in their first attempts to re-enter Yunnan, these scattered Kuomintang remnants swiftly became an army of occupation and forcibly took control of much of the eastern and southern Shan State, as well as parts of the Kachin State borders. Local Shan, Lahu and Wa villagers were press-ganged into service and, by the end of 1951, this KMT army had grown into a 12,000-strong force and spread as far as the Karenni borders where it now threatened to enter.

To head off this challenge the Kawthoolei Governing Body in Papun sent a three-man delegation, Skaw Ler Taw, Mika Rolly and Ohn Pe, to meet the KMT's Eighth Army commander, Gen. Li Mi, at his headquarters at Monghsat in the southern Shan State. Here some 2,000 KMT troops were undergoing training, but the Karen delegates were unimpressed. As Rolly remembers: 'They were trying to colonise the Shan State. They had occupied all the biggest houses in every village in the region.'[42] But they did have something the KNU had so far manifestly failed to get: foreign support. Planes were flying in and out twice a week, carrying arms when they landed and opium when they left. Most of these military supplies were coming from Formosa (Taiwan), but various American advisers were also openly walking about. His aim, Li Mi explained, was to use the Shan State as a springboard for the recapture of Yunnan and he urged the KNU to make a joint regional anti-communist alliance with the KMT. The KNU's Delta leaders had, however, already ruled this out, so Li Mi put forward a second plan, namely to send KMT troops through the Karenni State into the Toungoo and Thaton hills and, with KNU support, try to capture Moulmein and thus open a route to the sea. This way bulk supplies, artillery and other heavy weaponry could be brought in. In return, he offered to supply the KNU with small arms and ammunition immediately; on this basis his plan was accepted. At the time much of the Karenni State was still under the control of the KAF Eastern Division's No.1 brigade, but Gen. Li Mi was also able to conclude an agreement with the Karenni leader, Sao Shwe, who at first refused to meet him.

At least on paper, this new alliance appeared formidable; it overshadowed the Zin-Zan agreement between the CPB and KNU in the Delta and, in 1953, led to official Burmese government protests at the United Nations over the KMT's US-backed activities, most of which were being coordinated through Thailand.[43] In April 1953, for example, a *Times* correspondent in Thailand's second city, Chiang Mai, described it as 'in effect a rear base' for the KMT and a few weeks later discovered 1,000 well-armed KMT soldiers and 400 KNDOs freely strolling about in the western border town of Mae Sot.[44]

However, like many other unlikely pacts thrown up in the chaos of war, the KMT-KNU alliance soon proved a hopeless failure. The KMT had the military back-up to support such ambitious plans, but not the political resolve. KMT troops were poorly disciplined and universally despised by local villagers wherever they passed. From March 1952 some 2,500 KMT troops began crossing through the Karenni State and northern Thailand into KNU-controlled territory, pushing as far south as Thaton, Paan, Kawkareik and Karopi on the seashore, where they eventually linked up with the recently formed Mon People's Front.[45] But the first joint campaign in February 1953, timed to coincide with a major KMT offensive in the Shan State, exposed the obvious weaknesses of this uneasy marriage of convenience. A combined assault on the Karenni State capital,

Loikaw, was easily repulsed as were attacks on the neighbouring towns of Bawlake and Namphe in the following weeks. Moreover, according to Skaw Ler Taw, not only were few of the promised weapons ever handed over, but 'the KMT failed to defend positions and never paid for supplies. Whenever the enemy attacked, they would withdraw without telling anybody. We lost a lot of good positions that way.'[46]

Even worse was to follow for the KNU. The new threat in the east caused understandable alarm in Rangoon and forced the government for the first time to change the focus of its military operations away from central and Lower Burma. While this may have given hard-pressed KAF units in the Delta a short breather, it drew heavy *Tatmadaw* fire on the neglected hills. In May 1953 Hlaingbwe fell; in November, in an operation master-minded by Brig. Kyaw Zaw, the valuable mines at Mawchi also fell, thus depriving the KNU of a valuable source of income in an otherwise impoverished backwater. With KNU forces pushed back on the defensive, Kyaw Zaw did not now let up, despite the mass evacuation of 2,000 KMT troops under UN supervision at the end of the year.[47] In April 1954 Operation *Sinbyushin* was launched in the Salween district which, while failing to achieve its objective of capturing the KNU capital at Papun, brought under *Tatmadaw* control sufficient villages to hand over the illusion of power to the 'legal' Karen State government in Rangoon. Finally, in March 1955, in Operation *Aungtheikdi* (final victory), government forces successfully pushed up the narrow jungle road through the hills to Papun which, after six years in KNU hands, was abandoned without resistance.[48]

Thus, in the Eastern Division as in the Delta, Karen troops were forced to retreat into the hills and onto the defensive. KAF commanders and political leaders in both divisions agreed it was time to take long overdue stock of the situation.

Virtually blow for blow their experiences had mirrored those of the CPB. But while KNUP leaders in the Delta continued to develop the Second Phase Programme, the CPB launched a new strategy which, within three years, was to change the face of insurgent politics in Burma.

9

'Revisionism' and the 1955 Line: The Prospect of Peace

In 1952 the CPB leadership began a decade of highly ambiguous decision making, highlighted by its 1955 'revisionist' line, which was soon as bitterly condemned within the communist movement as the mistaken Browderist line of 1945. At a time when in Indo-China the Vietnamese communists could successfully mobilise 200,000 peasants into action for the great battle at Dien Bien Phu, these were the years, CPB leaders now argue, of wasted opportunities. Into the mid-1950s the *Tatmadaw*'s military concerns lay elsewhere, i.e. with the battle-hardened KNU forces in Lower Burma and the KMT remnants in the Kachin and Shan State borders. The AFPFL's anxieties were added to by these two unlikely partners linking up in their threatening new anti-Rangoon alliance which, through the activities of various shadowy American and (Taiwanese) Chinese agents, suggested the first real outside interference in Burma's internal affairs. The KMT threat was not really laid to rest until 1961 (scattered KMT veterans even now remain active in border regions), but throughout these years the CPB leadership appeared to have lost its way. Its dogmatic Maoist strategy of 'people's' or 'protracted' warfare is discussed later, but throughout the 1950s, while in the field CPB organisation took on an increasingly Maoist colouration, its leadership seemed unsure of what political strategy it should follow, whether at home or abroad.

The International Communist Movement

(A) China
Like other communist parties in the region, the CPB took heart from the communist victory in China; there was a definite feeling that history was on its side. But apart from the occasional statement of ideological solidarity, CPB leaders were disappointed by the lack of any real international commitment to their position in the spreading civil war in Burma from the two great communist powers, the Soviet Union and China.[1] This view of international communist neglect runs counter to that held by many American political analysts who, in the 1950s and 1960s, with their domino theory became obsessed with the idea of the communist (largely Chinese) export of insurrection in the region. These fears were frequently voiced. In 1953, US Secretary of State John Foster Dulles spoke of a 'gigantic conspiracy designed to overthrow our government by violence', while as early as 1950 the US Congress passed a resolution announcing the existence of a subversive 'worldwide communist organisation' committed to the establishment of a

155

'communist totalitarian dictatorship' throughout the world by any means 'deemed necessary'.[2]

For historical reasons the Communist International (Comintern) of the 1920s and 1930s had problems identifying Burma during the era of colonial rule; there was some confusion over whether it should come under the remit of India and the CPI. With independence, India and the CPI quickly faded to a distant memory. But the continuing caution in the Chinese, if not the Soviet, attitude to the CPB is less surprising. Since the communist victory in China, the CCP has always distinguished between 'party to party' and 'government to government' relations with other countries, a position the CCP still maintains.[3] The Union of Burma, the first Asian government to recognise the new People's Republic of China in December 1949, proved no exception to this rule, except for a brief period in the late 1960s when China-Burma relations hit rock bottom.

In the early 1950s Mao Zedong and the CCP leaders had other priorities as they struggled to reconstruct their war-torn country, but they were not unaware of the situation in Burma. Though in 1950 a major CPB military offensive, codenamed *Aung Zeya*, failed to establish a firm foothold in Burma's remote north-east along the Shweli River valley, through other small base areas in the Shan and Kachin States the CPB was, as early as 1949, able to establish regular cross-border contact with the CCP. In the years 1949-53 three high-level CPB delegations made the arduous journey across the mountains into China's Yunnan province: the first was led by *Yebaw* Aung Gyi, the next two included such leading party dignitaries as Politburo members, Thakins Ba Thein Tin and Than Myaing, PA commander, Bo Zeya, and CC member, Thakin Pu. In 1950 the CPB's glowing assessment of the radical changes being introduced by Mao in China were publicised in a 36-page booklet, *The First Year's Journey of the New Republic of China*, edited by U Ba Win, which predicted both the Chinese invasion of Tibet and the eventual alignment of Burma with China.

In these years 143 CPB cadres reached China, where they were well received; a number travelled on to Beijing to attend classes in Marxism-Leninism at the CCP's Higher Party School.[4] Others studied at the Nationalities' College in Kunming and the Marxism-Leninism School in Chunking. Five younger cadres, including present-day CPB general-secretary Khin Maung Gyi, were selected to go on to study in Moscow; Ba Thein Tin himself visited the Soviet Union several times (with the aid of a Chinese diplomatic passport) and even Hanoi in 1963 where he met Ho Chi Minh.[5] Another CPB member, Dr Min Hlatt, travelled on to make contact with the International Students' Union in Prague, where for a time he worked at the university. For CPB leaders China thus became an important door to the outside world; in Beijing during this period the CPB team also met other prominent communist figures in the region, including Chin Peng of the Communist Party of Malaya and communist leaders from Thailand, Australia and Indonesia. But despite accusations in the Rangoon press of Chinese backing for the CPB (largely based on a number of pro-CPB broadcasts, reportedly by Aung Gyi, on Beijing radio) full military support was not yet forthcoming.[6]

Of much greater concern to the Chinese authorities was the security of their vast borders and the KMT threat still on their doorstep. These after all were the years of the international cold war, the smouldering Indo-China conflict and the Korean War, in which China lost half a million men. The later border conflicts with the Soviet Union and Vietnam are better known, but it is worth mentioning that the adjoining border with India has still not, in the 1990s, been mutually agreed; an armed confrontation between Chinese and Indian troops over the old British McMahon line was narrowly averted as recently as 1986 after a Chinese troop incursion into Arunachal Pradesh, close to Burma's Kachin State border.

Even more worryingly for the AFPFL government, the new communist authorities in China at first appeared to be following KMT claims, still repeated in Taiwan today, for a 77,000 square-mile area of the Kachin hills north of Myitkyina; in the 1950s the Chinese Embassy in Rangoon sported maps in which vast areas of north-east Burma were included in China (see Chapter 2). Many Chinese still believe that much of the trans-Salween region and the north-east Kachin State belong more naturally to China. Into the 1960s a constant flow of Chinese (and Tai, Lahu, Lisu) migrants seeking work in Burma or Thailand provided further confirmation that local inhabitants were yet to accept the post-colonial frontiers.

But back in the early 1950s Chinese communist leaders were mainly concerned about the US-backed KMT remnants of Gen. Li Mi's Yunnan Anti-Communist National Salvation Army, which between 1951 and 1953 made four major attempts to re-invade China from strongholds along the Kachin-Shan borders. This threat, rather than territorial claims or any immediate support for the CPB, was what led troops from the People's Liberation Army (PLA) to cross over the undemarcated border and enter Burma. From 1952 to 1957 PLA troops remained ensconced across the border, largely in the Wa substate and remote corners of the Kachin State. But despite occasional clashes with Burmese government troops, only in 1956 were voices in Rangoon raised in protest and, even then, only after a vociferous campaign by the *Nation* newspaper.[7]

This low-key approach to a highly inflammatory situation and the gradual *rapprochement* with communist China was one of U Nu and the AFPFL's major successes. Their own war with the KMT, as well as the AFPFL's non-aligned position (evidenced by Burma's refusal to join SEATO, the South-East Asia Treaty Organisation), the rejection of American aid over continued US support for the KMT, and the AFPFL's contribution at the 1955 Bandung Conference, lessened outstanding tensions between Beijing and Rangoon. Diplomatic relations continued to improve steadily throughout the 1950s. In 1954 Zhou Enlai himself called in at Rangoon to meet U Nu on his return from the Geneva Conference on Indo-China; a joint communiqué was issued reaffirming the 'five principles of co-existence' between the two countries and the right of people 'to choose their own state system'. 'Revolution cannot be exported', they concluded.[8] The same year U Nu repaid the visit to China where he elicited the surprising assurance that Chinese leaders had no contact with the CPB. The following year Gen. Ne Win led a military delegation to Beijing where he was received by Mao; in 1957, against a background of growing political and cultural exchanges, a Chinese team returned the visit.

The undoubted high point in Burma-China relations came in January 1960 with the signing in Beijing by Ne Win and Zhou Enlai of a Boundary Agreement and a ten-year Treaty of Friendship and Mutual Non-Aggression. Ne Win still takes pride in showing his rare foreign house guests in Rangoon a fading black-and-white film clip of his historic visit. This he believed put him on a par with Chairman Mao and the other great Chinese leaders. 'Chairman' Ne Win was soon to become his favoured title.

Given the scale of China's earlier claims across the 2,100 km border, the eventual territorial exchanges showed a highly conciliatory Chinese position. Three Kachin villages commanding the Hpimaw pass and the remote Panhung-Panlao region of the Wa substate were 'returned' to China in exchange for the Namwam Assigned Tract which was given to Burma. Early the next year 20,000 PLA and 5,000 *Tatmadaw* troops launched a successful combined operation against the heavily fortified KMT stronghold at Mong Pa Liao near the border with Laos, precipitating (after U Nu had again enlisted UN support) the second major American-backed evacuation of KMT troops to Taiwan and the virtual dissolution of the KMT threat to China.[9]

But this by no means marked the end of the border story; ironically the Kachin border agreement, along with U Nu's insensitive attempt the same year to introduce Buddhism as Burma's official state religion, was the last straw for many Christian Kachin nationalists. This historic treaty, made over the heads of local villagers, was a major factor behind the sudden outbreak of the Kachin uprising, begun by the Kachin Independence Organisation (KIO) in February 1961.

So it is important to stress that, throughout this period of Chinese military involvement in Burma, the Chinese communists lent no real military support either to the CPB or to restive Kachin nationalists along the border. Moreover, the CPB's own attempts to build up base areas in ethnic minority villages in the northeast in the 1950s also met with little success. This again contradicts the widely accepted opinion of many Western counter-insurgency analysts that, by establishing ethnic minority 'autonomous regions' inside China in the early 1950s, the CCP was trying to annex South-East Asia by more subtle means.[10] In particular, the formation of what was incorrectly described as a Free Kachin State in Yunnan, where over 100,000 ethnic Kachins live, was seen as an attempt to win influence across the Burma border. To counter this move, in 1956 the AFPFL felt worried enough to hold an emergency conference at Lweje on the China border to hear grievances from local Kachin leaders.[11] But significantly, throughout these years the Chinese authorities kept Naw Seng's exile band of Kachin insurgents from the failed 1949/50 Pawng Yawng rebellion in Gweichou Province quite separate from the CPB's China team. Only in 1967, when relations between Beijing and Rangoon broke down completely, did Chinese leaders purposefully bring them together.

(B) The Soviet Union

If in the 1950s the CPB found little active encouragement from the CCP, the same could be said of its relations with the Soviet Union, even before the Soviet-Chinese split. Burma was never a Soviet priority, though in the 1950s there were frequent allegations of clandestine Soviet financial support through its Rangoon Embassy for local trade unions and the above-ground Burma Workers and Peasants Party (BWPP) and National United Front.[12] Well into the 1950s Soviet leaders stood by the decisions of the 1947 Cominform meeting and the communist-sponsored South-East Asian Youth Conference of February 1948. In 1953 the Soviet press was still chastising the AFPFL government for being 'a medley of right-wing socialist betrayers in Rangoon'.[13]

But, in many ways, through the efforts of U Nu, U Ba Swe and the AFPFL leadership, Burma was already developing into what the Soviet Union came to regard as a model Third World country, non-aligned, socialist and developing at its own speed. This was publicly confirmed for the first time in December 1955 on a week-long visit to Burma by Bulganin and Khrushchev, who made stridently anti-British/anti-colonial speeches which, like Zhou Enlai's on his earlier stopover, were loudly trumpeted by the AFPFL and Rangoon press as a snub to the CPB; their visit was followed by an upsurge in trading relations with the USSR and other communist bloc countries.[14] In response, Mr Nutting, the British Foreign Minister, accused the Soviets of launching an offensive in South-East Asia 'in the grand manner'.[15]

Dispiriting though the international communist response may have been, there is no evidence (despite the CPB's furious attacks on the 'revisionist' leadership of the Soviet Union's 'Krushchev-Brezhnev clique' after the Sino-Soviet split) that either the CPSU or CCP tried to pressurise the CPB into following their conciliatory lead. Certainly CPB leaders today deny this.[16] None the less this important shift in the communist movement's approach, particularly by the Soviet Union, towards the newly independent countries of the Third World had a key bearing on CPB thinking. 'Instead of attacking the "pseudo-independence" attained by bourgeois regimes,' wrote John Girling, 'the Soviet Union sought to capitalise on feelings of hostility to, or suspicion of, Western policy which influenced men like Nehru, Nasser and Sukarno.'[17] Burma, U Nu and the AFPFL's socialist leaders clearly fitted into the same category. At the controversial Soviet Twentieth Party Congress in February 1956, Khrushchev forcefully advocated this new line when, in a public departure from Leninist principles, he declared that war was 'not fatalistically inevitable', even where imperialism still existed.[18] Then, in his famed but much misunderstood definition of war before the Soviet Academy of Social Sciences in January 1961, Krushchev expanded on this theme by explaining he did not think 'natural' wars of 'national liberation' in colonial or post-colonial countries were cause for super power confrontation. Since he regarded the eventual triumph of socialism now inevitable, 'wars are not needed for this victory', he claimed.[19]

Signs of this vital shift in Soviet policy, which began before Stalin's death, had long been evident, most notably at the 1954 Geneva Conference. Later the new Soviet line became one of the underlying reasons behind the Sino-Soviet split. None the less, in Geneva, CCP leaders, who had been supplying arms to Ho Chi Minh and the Vietminh since 1950, supported Soviet pressure on the Vietnamese communists (fresh from their victory at Dien Bien Phu) to accept the partition of Vietnam along the 17th parallel. It was, commented Gabriel Kolko, the Communist Party of Vietnam's 'first major lesson on the nature and limits of proletarian internationalism, and its impact profoundly affected its conception of the world'.[20]

The same was undoubtedly true of the CPB. Contradicting its rhetorically independent stand, Ba Thein Tin confirmed to me that the CC's fateful decision to adopt the 1955 'revisionist' line was based on an analysis of 'both the internal and international situations' in the fast-changing world of the 1950s.[21] It was to have the most profound consequences.

Doubts over Strategy: The Background to Revisionism
Until 1954, though the CPB had made no startling advances, it had been able to protect many of its rural 'liberated zones'. With the Tatmadaw's main troop deployments against the KMT, the KNU and other ethnic nationalist forces in the south-east, the CPB's PA, through a campaign of constant harassment and guerrilla strikes (sometimes alone, sometimes in conjunction with local PVO or KNU

units) more than kept government forces at bay. From Arakan and Katha in the north of the country to Tavoy-Mergui in the south, ambushes of *Tatmadaw* patrols and attacks on trains and buses or remote government outposts and installations were honed down to a fine art.[22] The capture of CPB jungle camps or surrender of CPB supporters were always heralded as the beginning of the end of the CPB, but the reality was that in towns across the country (even on the edge of Rangoon where CPB guerrillas still operated), government forces rarely ventured beyond the town gates after dark. The forests, the mountains and the rural countryside still belonged to the rebels. Indeed extravagant rewards for the capture of Than Tun, Thakin Soe and other CPB leaders, which by the mid-1950s had reached an astounding 100,000 kyat per head, never found any takers, despite the promise of police protection for life.[23]

Belying the CPB's militancy, however, was a deep crisis within the party leadership. The difficulties were political rather than military and concerned the structure and organisation of the CPB's party apparatus. A particular concern was the quality and training of party members, a problem which has preoccupied the CPB leadership ever since and, many would argue, has never been resolved. Despite its continued mass appeal, in many parts of the country the CPB had always lacked a nucleus of trained organisers and administrators. Like the AFPFL or KNU, its national leaders were mainly intellectuals from middle-class or merchant backgrounds. Most had at least finished high school. Than Tun, for example, was a former high school teacher in Rangoon, so was Thakin Chit in Mandalay; even the PA's commander, Bo Zeya, was a former president of Rangoon University Students Union.[24] But despite their experience of political organisation in the *Dobama* movement, the Second World War and the struggle for independence, the transition to 'protracted warfare' and the harsh realities of jungle life, in a war now fought between their own peoples, proved no easy task.

To compensate for these deficiencies, in the early years of the insurrection CPB district organisers ran dozens of military and political training classes (using different Marxist-Leninist and Maoist classics) in a bid to improve the effectiveness of party organisation in the towns and the quality of CPB administration in the liberated zones. Annual crop taxes, sometimes running as high as 10 per cent of the total yield, were levied and farmers and workers were encouraged to contribute food to local PA units and subscriptions to the various CPB-backed peasant, women and youth organisations. But clearly not all cadres were up to the task. Urged Than Tun, whom even the Rangoon *Guardian* described as 'an abler politician and leader than many of the leaders who lead Burma today',[25] in a colourful speech at the 1950 People's Democratic Front (PDF) conference in Prome: 'You have become *Min* [officials, administrators] and you must behave like *Min*.... Just as ancient Moslem preachers did missionary work with the Koran held in one hand and a sword in the other, we will work with a good doctrine in one hand and a gun in the other.'[26]

After long argument, Than Tun's solution, reflecting the experience of China and acknowledging the setbacks to the CPB's urban organisation in the upheavals of 1948/9, was to follow Mao's example and try to strengthen the party's rural base by building up a revolutionary party organisation based on the rural peasantry. 'To rely on the peasants', explained Lin Piao, 'build rural base areas and use the countryside to encircle and finally capture the cities: such was the way to victory in the Chinese revolution.'[27]

For the CPB it was a pragmatic rather than ideological step. In Burma, as in China, the peasantry and rural proletariat are estimated to make up over 80 per cent of the total population. For Mao's strategy to succeed, the CPB had to win peasant support to fight on the communist side in the civil war; indeed from 1950, while accelerating its 'land to the tiller' programme of agrarian reform, the CPB began to promote troops from peasant backgrounds in the PA command. But such moves had their pitfalls. Ensuring a stable supply of rice proved difficult, especially since in many areas over-zealous party leaders short-sightedly banned the movement of paddy to government-held areas, causing the price to slump. In other areas party cadres redistributed land on an arbitrary basis, fuelling rather than solving family differences. There was also the recurrent problem of warlordism, which distracted local CPB organisers as much as the AFPFL, the PVOs and KNU.

By 1955, therefore, with the CPB's military offensive clearly having run out of steam and, even more worrying, young CPB supporters circulating some surprisingly frank criticisms of Than Tun himself, the CPB leadership was well aware that a serious reassessment of its goals and tactics was long overdue.[28] In a major policy review in early 1955, in which he conceded a number of recent military and political advances by the U Nu government, Than Tun outlined five main areas in which the AFPFL had been able to gain ground on the CPB:

The failure of the CPB 'to achieve a united front' on the left. (He blamed the Red Flags);

The failure of the CPB to 'offer effective leadership' to rebel minority groups like the Mons and Karens;

The 'extreme economic distress of the people' which had enabled the AFPFL to win support for its *Pyidawtha* programme;

The AFPFL's use of a religious revival in the country 'to dull the people's consciousness'; and

The popular support the AFPFL had won for its 'sham' neutrality between the two power blocs by rejecting American aid.[29]

Optimistically, he described these AFPFL gains as 'temporary'.

Against this unsettled background CPB leaders from across the country gathered in April-May 1955 at Than Tun's forest headquarters, then at Kwe-U camp, near Settotaya town, on the borders of Minbu and Pakokku districts, for the historic CC meeting at which the party's 'revisionist' or 'peace and unity' line was adopted. Controversy continues to dog this meeting. *Tatmadaw* propaganda still maintains that 'Thakin Ba Thein Tin and his group' sent the new strategy by wireless from abroad under the direct influence of a 'foreign Communist Party', i.e. the CCP.[30] CPB leaders say it was an internal decision. None the less, implicit in this new approach, as Ba Thein Tin himself acknowledges, was the CPB's analysis of the recent changes in the communist world.[31] The ripples in the waves of the communist movement, stirred up by Krushchev in Moscow, had now reached the remote outposts of the Burmese jungle.

A decade later the CPB's intellectual theoreticians, Ba Tin and *Yebaw* Htay, rather than the party's senior executive, Thakins Than Tun, Ba Thein Tin, Zin and Chit, carried most of the blame for the revisionist line. But, whoever was ultimately responsible, it completely altered the main thrust of the CPB's strategy of armed revolution. The '1955 line', or to give its full title, the 'Programme for Cessation of Civil War and Peace within the Country', not only acknowledged the possibility of peaceful communist evolution and called for increased efforts to broaden the United Front, but also allowed for the possibility of peace talks with the AFPFL. However, it was by no means intended, as CPB supporters stress today, to signify an end to the CPB's determination to continue the armed struggle. Rather in a hark-back to Ba Tin's 1947 thesis, it was drawn up as the basis for a new political drive in the towns behind an escalating campaign of strikes and demonstrations to back up the countrywide call for peace.

The 1955 Line: Success

(A) Above-ground Political Action and the Kodaw Hmaing Peace Committee
In historic terms the results of the 1955 line can be regarded as mixed, though CPB leaders today definitely regard it as an enormous setback, comparable to the worst errors of 1945/6. Certainly the CC's decisions, which were quickly relayed by wireless transmitters and couriers around the country, were at first well received by the population at large. A less dogmatic approach from the CPB was welcomed by the KNU, the Mon People's Front (MPF) and other insurgent nationalists with whom the CPB still frequently argued over territory. As will be seen, the 1955 line was a double-edged sword as far as the minorities were concerned, but it did lead within four years to the formation of the National Democratic United Front, the first and really only successful united front representing ethnic insurgent groups, including the Burman majority, which stretched right across central Burma.

Equally, many political activists in the towns supported the new line; this swiftly led to the first (and perhaps last) important conjunction in political strategy and ideas between the CPB and the different above-ground opposition parties. At this stage CPB cadres could still move relatively freely in and out of Rangoon and here the new strategy was implicitly accepted by the influential BWPP. This helped speed up the formation of the coalition National United Front (NUF), which on a 'peace ticket' platform gave the AFPFL a surprisingly close run in the 1956 election, despite widespread allegations of AFPFL ballot rigging. In many rural constituencies the CPB encouraged local farmers to vote for NUF candidates and, as a clear sign of the CPB's influence, the NUF's strongest showing was in central Burma around the CPB's major strongholds. Indeed in the months after the election many observers believed the CPB was neatly synchronising its bombing campaigns to coincide with NUF speeches in Parliament, where NUF MPs argued it was only AFPFL recalcitrance that was forcing the CPB to continue its armed struggle.[32]

As the CPB offensive gathered momentum, however, it was not the opposition NUF that emerged as the focal point of the peace movement, but the revered veteran nationalist, Thakin Kodaw Hmaing, co-founder of the *Dobama Asiayone* and 1954 winner of the Stalin Peace Prize. Now in his 80th year, Kodaw Hmaing was able to win widespread support for his own eight-man Internal Peace Committee. On at least one occasion the AFPFL leadership felt under enough pressure (after the assassination of U Ba Swe's father-in-law, allegedly by CPB guerrillas) to send EC members to see him in person to explain its refusal to negotiate with the CPB.[33] A constant stream of political visitors, prominent amongst them U Ba Nyein and Thakin Lwin from the BWPP and the dissident communist Thein Pe Myint, trod the path to his door, where the tactics of the peace movement were discussed at meetings attended in secret by CPB cadres and couriers. Then, in

1958, as the peace movement reached its peak, the AFPFL allowed the Peace Committee to speak publicly on the CPB's behalf and to commemorate the tenth anniversary of the outbreak of the insurrections with a series of mass peace demonstrations.[34] Indeed, 30 years later, Brig. Khin Nyunt, head of Military Intelligence, specifically cited their involvement in the peace protests of 1958 as one of the main reasons for arresting several older leaders of the 1988 democracy movement, including U Tun Tin of the National League for Democracy and Nyo Win of the People's Progressive Party.[35] While in most cases no real evidence was produced (though Nyo Win later spent a few years in the *maquis* with the CPB) the inference that they had been working for the CPB all along was clear.

That Than Tun established a direct line of communication with the Peace Committee does not mean that Kodaw Hmaing, though clearly on the political left, was a CPB supporter. A former CPB cadre present at several of these meetings described him as a 'radical democrat who liked to be subversive. That was his way.'[36] Significantly, this same cadre, as an underground CPB organiser in Rangoon, plays down the CPB's influence over the different peace lobbies of the time, including the BWPP and NUF: 'I don't think Than Tun or the CPB could have initiated the peace movement alone. It was more the time and the environment which were right.'

So it is important to reiterate that the public support the CPB won for its 'peace and unity' line from Kodaw Hmaing and BWPP Marxist leaders, such as Thakin Lwin, Thakin Chit Maung and U Ba Nyein, did not mean that the Communist Party controlled or manipulated them, as happened with left-wing fronts in Vietnam; rather, it reflected the continued diversity of the political left in Burma and a countrywide desire for peace. Most BWPP leaders, who say they were similarly inspired by the changes signalled by Krushchev in Moscow, had simply never agreed with the CPB's taking up arms against the AFPFL.[37]

Nor for that matter was the BWPP-backed NUF, which gained 37 per cent of the vote in the 1956 election, simply a CPB front as many commentators have alleged. Undoubtedly the NUF contained many communist sympathisers, especially in worker and peasant unions. But equally, an important part of the NUF's support came from the small but influential Justice Party, headed by Dr E. Maung, a former Supreme Court justice who, like many supporters of parliamentary democracy, argued that a united opposition presented the only means of overthrowing the AFPFL government. On this platform, both the BWPP and the NUF, despite their pro-communist designations in the Rangoon press, were able to win support from such unexpected quarters as the Burma Muslim Congress and the conservative Arakan National United Organisation.[38] Other member organisations of the NUF included the Youth Front of Burma and People's Unity Party of Thein Pe Myint, who now won a seat in Parliament.

The NUF thus represented, like the AFPFL of 1948 or many of the unlikely political coalitions forged in the democracy summer of 1988, a pragmatic alliance of different political factions and leaders who became necessarily adept at concealing their real intentions. The spectre of clandestine but omnipotent CPB organisers secretly infiltrating and subverting all above-ground political organisations in Burma is an image the *Tatmadaw* continues to conjure up even today, though increasingly unconvincingly.[39] But back in the 1950s, when such charges had a more justified ring, the CPB's influence in the parliamentary opposition was difficult to tie down. Generally it was easier to spot the activities of CPB organisers in the trade union movement. Despite the disintegration of the ABTUC into pro-AFPFL, Socialist Party, BWPP or Peace Committee factions, dozens of CPB cadres remained active, though for fear of arrest they, too, were forced to maintain a low profile.

(B) The Student Movement
One important section of the community in which the CPB's open influence was little disguised was among the students on the country's restive university campuses; for the modern historian the student movement remains by far the best example of the CPB's underground organisation. In the early days of the insurrections the government made surprisingly little effort to clamp down on CPB campus organisers. Indeed well into the mid-1970s, student activists from the towns would slip in and out of the liberated zones, attending CPB training schools, exchanging news and bringing supplies of medicine and other vital equipment. Clearly for U Nu and an older generation of politicians, who had begun their own careers on the university campuses of the 1920s and 1930s, crushing student dissent was a step they were unwilling to contemplate. Burma's radical student tradition, though for a time taken over by the CPB, ran very deep.

Until the eve of independence, both the All Burma Students Union (ABSU) and Rangoon University Students Union (RUSU) were under CPB influence; this was mainly due to Thakin Ba Hein, former ABSU leader, founder member of the CPB and, even today, a legendary figure among students. 'We must not merely study,' he once claimed, 'we must also join the great causes of our country. If the present struggle is against oppression, then we must also join that struggle.'[40] Ba Hein died of malaria in 1946 but, encouraged by the CPB's new student leader, Rangoon University history graduate, *Yebaw* Aung Gyi, RUSU students went on frequent strikes during the great anti-British demonstrations of the independence campaign. Then, in February 1949, RUSU students once again walked out of their classrooms in solidarity with the Ministerial Services Union strike, which paralysed the AFPFL government at the beginning of the Karen uprising. This time, however, many of their leaders were arrested, while others fled to the jungle camps of the CPB.

Following this clamp-down, the Democratic Students Organisation (DSO), a student front sponsored by U Kyaw Nyein and the Socialist Party, seized control of RUSU. Their term of office was characterised by frequent complaints of maladministration and, in 1952, after a narrow failure the previous year, a joint White Flag/Red Flag/BWPP student front, the Progressive Student Force (PSF), formed from an earlier Marxist study group, won control in the annual student elections. But the PSF's period of office only lasted one year; in the 1953 election the Socialist Party flooded the campus with outside supporters, thus ensuring another DSO victory. This clearly fraudulent ballot brought two months of campus unrest which, after an ill-timed government decision to cut the students' annual holiday by two weeks, erupted into what became known as the students' October Revolution. Pitched battles were fought around the university campus with the police using tear gas and live bullets.[41] As the protests spread to Mandalay and Moulmein, dozens of students were injured or arrested.

After this debacle, the socialist-backed DSO was largely discredited and a new joint White Flag/Red Flag/BWPP alliance, the Students United Front (SUF), dominated all RUSU elections, as well as those of the renamed All Burma Federation of Students Unions. The SUF survived five years in office, until the 1958 'military caretaker' administration, under the new National Security Law, arrested large numbers of pro-communist students; a number were exiled to the Coco Islands along with other CPB supporters and trade union activists. In 1960 the SUF was briefly able to resume its activities, but only until the 1962 military coup when Ne Win tried to crush the student movement once and for all.[42]

Throughout these years the student campuses remained a hotbed of political activism and an important outlet for CPB views. The smaller and always more secretive Red Flag faction ran its own cells and won seats on the student councils; the bitter Red Flag/White Flag disagreements of their elders in the jungles rarely broke out into the open on campus. Exploiting what became known as the 'Two F' system (i.e. students were allowed three years of exam failures before being expelled) students from all parties were able to ensure continuity in their political administration. But the White Flag students were always the most successful at underground organisation.

Former CPB student leaders ascribe their success to the formation of dozens of small cells and study groups, not all immediately recognisable as connected to the CPB but all allowing CPB supporters to air or elicit views. CPB organisers still specify that a political cell must have a minimum of three members and a maximum of 30. There were cells in each university department and hostel, day cells and night cells, and 'agitation' cells where students could practise their writing and oratory. The CPB's influence was not confined to university campuses. In 1956 the government banned all student unions from schools throughout the country because of the alleged activities of 'communist' agents.[43] This followed an extraordinary incident a few months earlier when, after some question papers were leaked, U Nu had to give way to student protests and pass *en masse* all 63,000 candidates taking that year's middle school examinations. Before U Nu backed down, a middle school student, Harry Tan, was shot dead by police and another wounded in demonstrations later blamed on the CPB.

The CPB's student supporters also featured in all street protests in Rangoon, whether addressing crowds on street corners or driving around town delivering speeches through loud-hailers from the back of jeeps, scenes unthinkable today. But party discipline was not strict. Students would intermittently drop out and disappear into the countryside, to return after training with the latest news from the war front. Sometimes there were weekend seminars at which CPB cadres from the liberated zones would suddenly show up in the city to deliver a speech or explain the new party line. Though all communist sympathisers were expected to have studied the *Communist Manifesto* and Stalin's *History of the Communist Party of the Soviet Union*, it was on student rather than ideological questions that attention was focused at these meetings.

Former student activists say that Lenin's *The State and Revolution* and *For a Lasting Peace: For a People's Democracy* (Cominform's official journal) were also popular reading; on campus there were endless debates on dialectical materialism. But most students remember Liu Shao-chi's *How to be a Good Communist* and *On Inner Party Struggle*, with his more pragmatic advice on secrecy and party organisation, as being the most influential. Romantic stories by Burmese writers with a discreet political message or novels with a proletarian feel were also voraciously consumed. The best known of these authors, Bhamo Tin Aung, frequently gave speeches on campus, though he was later imprisoned by both U Nu and Ne Win for his efforts.[44]

In the same way CPB cadres tried to organise in the trade unions; all CPB supporters were expected to start study groups in their work places. As a result countless small cells proliferated across the country, ensuring a steady supply of new recruits to the communist cause. Government departments were a particular CPB target.[45] If from afar the CPB's activities often appeared spasmodic or poorly coordinated, this was a reflection of its political success, for, at the heart of many of these underground agitation groups were secret CPB LCs (Leading Cells) of committed party members. In the 1950s their composition changed frequently, but some of the best known CPB organisers today were members of the RUSU LC: Ba Kaung, Hla Win and Dr Nyi Nyi, the latter two of whom later became senior BSPP officials, Soe Thein, a future university bursar who also joined the BSPP and several, including Aung Thein Naing, Kyaw Khin, Tin Tun, Ba Swe Lay, Hla Shwe, Hla Kyi and Maung Thet, who fled after the 1962 coup into the jungles, where a number subsequently died or were executed in the CPB's Cultural Revolution of 1967/8. Ba Swe Lay, SUF chairman in 1962, for example, is still remembered for pioneering the famous *'Totet'* or 'progressive' system of writing the Burmese alphabet popular on political wall-posters today. Another young man who joined them was Ba Khet, who later surrendered to co-author *The Last Days of Thakin Than Tun.*

These underground cells loyally supported the CPB's political line and energetically approved its 1948 'seizure of power', 1949 'united front' and 1955 'peace and unity' policies; and it was on the party's instruction that they worked with other student groups on campus, including the Red Flags and BWPP. Another LC was set up to coordinate CPB organisation in schools.

They had notably less success at winning over the growing number of ethnic student dissidents to their cause; in these years Kachin, Shan and other nationalist student leaders at Rangoon University were quietly preparing their own armed uprisings. Brang Seng, present-day chairman of the KIO, Zaw Mai, the KIO's Chiefof-Staff, Shwe Aye, chairman of the Kayan New Land Party, Khun Kya Nu (*aka* Hseng Suk), Sai Pan (*aka* Boon Tai) and Sai Hla Aung (*aka* Hso Lane), each a future president of the Shan State Progress Party, were all student leaders of this generation. But when they finally decided to go underground, they made contact with the KNU, not the CPB. CPB activists constantly tried to infiltrate and influence the Ethnic Students Federation and the many nationality associations on campus. At one stage they even successfully put up an ethnic Kachin, Nan Zin La, first for the post of SUF chairman, then as RUSU president; he later broke away from the CPB to join the socialist DSO and was bitterly denounced. So it is ironic that the CPB's best known student leader of the 1950s and 1960s who is still politically active is an ethnic Shan, Sai Aung Win, who after joining the CPB in the Pegu Yomas following the 1962 coup, became a full CC member at the CPB's Third Congress in 1985.[46]

The 1955 Line: ...and Failure
The peace movement and the continuing victories of the SUF student movement were the most obvious successes of the 1955 line; former activists in the cities insist that at the time they saw no contradiction between the CPB's past call for armed struggle and the new call for peace. Their reasoning was straightforward. Despite the violence of the CPB's rhetoric, the party's official position had always been that they were simply 'fighting to protect' themselves from attack. Similarly,

they welcomed the visits to Burma by Zhou Enlai and Krushchev, since they were thought to lend more weight to the international communist cause and, by implication, the CPB. Only the visit in January 1955 of the breakaway communist leader of Yugoslavia, Tito, aroused their ire.

However, these positive developments were soon outweighed by the negative. Much hinged on the controversial offer of peace talks which, as today, were a matter of extreme sensitivity. Throughout the 1950s the AFPFL continued to assert that the CPB was suing for peace in what the Rangoon press described as 'letters from the jungle'. These usually referred to repetitions of past CPB statements; while Ba Thein Tin now accepts that all proposals for 'internal peace negotiations' have come from the CPB (including those of 1963 and 1980/1), he is adamant that in the AFPFL era they were only made twice, in 1950 and 1955.[47] The 1950 proposals were largely lost sight of in the breakup of the PDF when the whole peace process might have carried more weight; it was thus the 1955 offer that attracted most attention.

One immediate result of the offer, clearly not expected by the CPB CC, was the first surrender in several years of a large number of CPB cadres and district organisers. In mid-1956 a proposal from Than Tun, in letters with a Rangoon postmark, was sent to every member of Parliament, calling on them to work together to end the civil war and announcing that the CPB was now ready to renounce armed struggle.[48] The logic of this offer, which was generally well received in the cities, was seen in a very different light in the liberated zones. Here the mood had not been helped by a series of massive *Tatmadaw* operations in early 1956 designed to encircle and ensnare insurgent leaders. Particularly hard hit were White Flag and Red Flag general headquarters base areas, then in Pakokku district west of the Chindwin-Irrawaddy rivers, by Operation *Aung Thura* (in which napalm was used) and the Delta base areas of the CPB, KNU and PVOs by Operation *Aung Theza* around Bassein in the south-west. Though all the key rebel leaders escaped, dozens of casualties were reported in the following months as the army employed the same tactics against insurgent strongholds around Tavoy-Mergui, Toungoo, Yamethin and Mandalay.[49]

If the party leadership was prepared to talk to its class enemies in Rangoon, was it surprising, Than Tun's critics argued, that many CPB soldiers now wavered on the need to continue the armed struggle in dangerous frontline positions? The first prominent cadre to surrender was *Yebaw* Tin Aye in April 1957, whom the CPB had sent into Rangoon as an underground intermediary to make contact with the government through the auspices of one of the former *Thirty Comrades*, Bo Let Ya. Then a successful businessman retired from politics, Let Ya had been a founder member of the CPB.

Undoubtedly the most damaging loss came later that year when Maung Maung, chairman of the Pyinmana district CPB and a former member of the Constituent Assembly, surrendered with over 200 cadres and troops. The importance of past defections had always been overestimated in Rangoon but this, for the first time since the early 1950s, was the surrender of a key party unit and, coming in the CPB's Pyinmana stronghold, was a worrying psychological setback to the whole party.

'Arms for Democracy': The 1958 Mass Surrenders

U Nu, who resumed as prime minister in 1957 after briefly handing over to U Ba Swe, once again displayed his consummate political skills. Whatever his public pronouncements, Nu had always resisted the idea of peace by negotiation. In 1949 he had agreed with Ne Win to talks with the KNU during the siege of Insein, but otherwise both men, while stating their willingness in principle to negotiate with the CPB, had ruled out talks with any group in armed conflict. In 1957 the response was still the same and the reasons clear. As Nu astutely recognised, with insurgents active in over half the country and in control of vast rural areas, any ceasefire would have legitimated the CPB's shadow government and resulted in a partition of the country on the lines of Korea and Vietnam. Indeed *Tatmadaw* leaders still insist that this was one of the main stratagems behind the CPB's 1955 peace proposals (and on the advice of China which had been involved in both these previous divisions).[50] While a plausible theory, there is no concrete evidence for it; neither the CPB nor the CCP have ever admitted it, though the potential was certainly there and many reminders can still be seen. Even today, in many rural areas of Burma it is possible to be introduced to two village headmen, the government's and the former CPB chief.

Far from being pushed onto the defensive by the CPB's peace offensive, U Nu now turned the political momentum back on the CPB. Adapting the CPB's 'peace and unity' slogan, Nu came up with his own call of 'arms for democracy' and with startling results. It can be argued that the CPB's conciliatory gesture towards the AFPFL had already undermined the revolutionary zeal of many front-line cadres. But at the same time U Nu was able to recognise and capitalise on the deep desire for peace in a country war-weary after almost two decades of near continuous death and destruction.

Previous amnesties in 1948, 1949, 1950 and 1955 had passed by largely unnoticed, but Nu's call this time met with an immediate response and, with the important exception of the KNU, was followed by a flood of insurgent surrenders around the country. The terms of individual peace agreements may have differed, but during 1958 over 5,500 armed insurgents officially 'entered the light' to be greeted at lavish welcoming ceremonies by government officials. Probably as many more simply returned home to their villages without first informing anyone.

The first group to come in (after three secret meetings) was the CPB's PDF ally in Arakan, the Arakan People's Liberation Party. Its leader, the *pongyi*, U Seinda, surrendered with over 1,000 followers at a reception attended by the deputy-prime minister, Thakin Tin, in Minbya at the beginning of the year.[51] The next major group was the Pao National (Liberation) Organisation (PNO), headed by wartime Cabinet minister Thaton Hla Pe and Bo Chan Zon in the south-west Shan State. Little noticed by the outside world, the PNO had grown rapidly in the early 1950s into one of the largest insurgent forces in Burma with 5,000 volunteers operating in four military regions in the mountains around Taunggyi and Inle Lake. It had good relations with both the KNU and CPB, though not the Shan *Sawbwas* and their militia, with whom it frequently fought. Uniquely for a rebel force in Burma, it also had an above-ground face, the Union PNO (UPNO or UNPO), formed in 1950, which had representatives in the towns and won several seats in Parliament in the 1950/1, 1956 and, later, 1960 elections. In 1956 a UPNO candidate and former insurgent commander, Bo Heing Maung, was assassinated, allegedly by pro-AFPFL rivals. None the less on 5 May 1958, after secret talks between Hla Pe and Brig. Aung Shwe organised by the UPNO leaders, U Pyu, a Panglong signatory, and U Kyaw Sein, 1,300 Pao guerrillas handed over a formidable arsenal of 2,500 weapons at a ceremony in Taunggyi presided over by Defence Minister U Ba Swe; in their nine-year campaign PNO leaders estimate that 3,000 lives were lost.[52]

Five days later, 400 members of a short-lived Shan State Communist Party (SSCP), formed in 1956 by CPB defector and present-day Shan leader, Gon Jerng (Mo Heing), surrendered at another elaborate ceremony held at Hsipaw in the northern Shan State.[53] The PNO and SSCP were then followed in July by another CPB ally, the MPF, led by Nai Aung Tun, which recorded 1,111 members as laying down their arms that year.[54] Only present-day New Mon State Party leader, Nai Shwe Kyin, who was away travelling in the Pegu Yomas, remained behind in the jungles with a handful of followers.

From the government's viewpoint, the most important group to surrender was undoubtedly the troublesome PVO; over 2,000 of its members reportedly gave up their arms and 'entered the legal fold' with their leader Bo Po Kun between July and October 1958. By comparison CPB surrenders were few: the government recorded that 800 White Flag supporters took advantage of the amnesty during the year, but it was still a damaging blow. Most of these cadres were in the Sittwe (Akyab) district of north Arakan under the local CPB commander, Maung Hla Sein, and this virtually demolished the party's base in one of its former strongholds. Here it took CC members Kyaw Mya, with 200 armed remnants in the north, and Thet Tun, who crossed the mountains with a guerrilla force from the east, several years to rebuild PA troop strength to its former levels.

After ten years of bloodshed the collective result of these mass surrenders represented a decisive step forward in the authority of the central government and a major setback to the rebel cause. While not all the 1958 surrenders can be directly attributed to the CPB's revisionist line (Mon, Rakhine and Pao leaders were all reputedly promised their own states in secret peace talks before they came in), in its official report at the 1985 Third Party Congress the CPB CC tried to take the blame.[55] Claiming that 11,650 armed volunteers of all nationalities were 'lost to the revolution' because of the 'political and ideological' confusion of the party's 'peace and unity' line, it was admitted for the first time that CPB membership had declined by 2,150 to just 2,000 registered members.[56] This resulted in the following months in a series of damaging military setbacks. The CC's historic verdict was damning:

> The 1955 line, in sum, reflected the abandoning of armed revolution, working within the framework of the law, serving the ruling class, and abolition of the party. Despite burying facts beneath wordy phrases that line turned its back on basic Marxist-Leninist principles and was revisionist in nature. The consequence of adopting that line was severe setbacks within the party as well as at departments where there was party leadership. It was a great setback for the party and the revolutionary forces.[57]

In the vehemence of this criticism can be seen part of the reasoning behind the violence of the CPB's swing, within just six years, to the extreme political left and to the eventual public executions of Thakin Ba Tin, *Yebaw* Htay, Bo Yan Aung and a number of other party stalwarts blamed for introducing the 1955 line.

Meanwhile, encouraged by the new mood sweeping the country, optimists in Rangoon dared to express the private hope that the 1958 surrenders had signalled the beginning of the end of political violence in the country. Nothing could have been further from the truth.

A Political Exception: The Continued Growth of the KNUP
Before going on to examine the collapse of the AFPFL government and the
astonishing events that followed in the second half of 1958, mention needs to be
made of the continued political revival of the KNU which, following the 1958
surrenders, was targeted in Rangoon as the *Tatmadaw*'s most dangerous military
foe. It was ironic that, in view of the CPB having claimed responsibility for the
insurgent setbacks of 1958, of all the ethnic parties in Burma at the time, it should
have been the KNU that was to move closest to the CPB and to approve most
strongly of its 'peace and unity' line. Yet the KNU was the least affected by the
1958 surrenders and U Nu's 'arms for democracy' call.

It must be stressed that the CPB had no control over the KNU or (at this time)
over any other ethnic movement, as was frequently, but highly misleadingly,
alleged in Rangoon. As today, the KNU determinedly followed its own path. Bit
in the mid-1950s Karen leaders embarked on a period of selective
experimentation with communist ideology which, though it had some initial
successes, ultimately brought about a disastrous political split in the KNU
leadership. This, in turn, presaged the later schisms in the Shan, Pao and other
ethnic movements of the 1970s and 1980s into pro and anti-CPB factions.

At the same time, many of the administrative and military reforms the Karen
National United Party (KNUP), the vanguard party of the Karen revolution, now
introduced in its ten-year helmsmanship of the KNU movement became a standard model for ethnic nationalist fronts elsewhere in the country. Even in the
1980s the political language of the KNUP was still setting the tone for many
ethnic insurgent debates. For both these reasons, the development of the KNUP
needs further explanation.

Whatever the KNUP's failings, in retrospect the years 1953-8 marked the only
real period when the Karen nationalist movement (east and west, above- and
underground) was in any sense truly unified. After the chaos of the early war
years, the KNU's political consolidation began in 1953 with the KNU's First
National Congress in Papun. Much of the discussion here centred on the KNU's
disintegrating alliance with the KMT, but time was found to approve the establishment of the KNUP as the Karen vanguard party and, at the end of the meeting,
to release a memorandum to the Thai government announcing the formation of a
new Kawthoolei Governing Body (KGB) Cabinet in Papun and formally notifying
its neighbours that the KNU would be seeking recognition from the United
Nations for a Kawthoolei Free State adjoining the Thai border.[58] The KNU
claimed to have 24,000 men under arms, in alliance with 4,000 volunteers from
the MPF.

The pace quickened during 1954 with the arrival from the Delta of the KGB
president, 45 year-old Saw Hunter Tha Hmwe. The first act of *Mooso Kawkasa*
(Ruler), as he became known, was to dismantle the ineffective KGB and replace it
with a new administrative body, the Karen Revolutionary Council (KRC), made
up of co-opted representatives from all the KNU's military brigade districts in the
Delta and Eastern Divisions. Then in 1955, following the fall of Papun, a Karen
penal code, based on the colonial legal system of India, was drawn up by Saw Po
Chit, the veteran KNA lawyer, who had earlier been imprisoned by the AFPFL.
With only a few minor adjustments, this code is still used in the jurisdiction of all

KNU-held areas today.

These reforms were merely a prelude to the KNU's controversial Second National Congress, held between 26 June and 11 July in the 1956 rainy season at the KRC's Maw Koo camp in the Papun hills. At this meeting, attended by 80 Karen observers and 70 KNU delegates, including Mahn Ba Zan and most of the KNUP Delta leadership, as well as several Mon, Pao and Karenni representatives, the KNUP's Second Phase Programme was formally unveiled and ratified. Mahn Ba Zan and the KNUP cadres praised the progress of the Second Phase Programme in the Delta and, in his opening address, even the Congress chairman, Hunter Tha Hmwe, who was not a KNUP member, spoke enthusiastically about the KNUP's village cooperative system. But the Congress minutes clearly show that the radical position the KNU now adopted went far beyond a few administrative reforms. In deference to other ethnic nationalities in KNU territory, many of whom (mostly Mons, Indians and Muslims) had joined the KNU, the political name 'Kawthoolei' replaced the ethnic name 'Karen' in most official titles. Four organisational wings were set up, the Kawthoolei People's Council, (KP) Military Council, (KP) Justice Court and the Kawthoolei Administrative Body (or KRC). Following the China model, the three divisions of the Kawthoolei Armed Forces were renamed the Kawthoolei People's Liberation Army (KPLA), the (KP) Guerrilla Force and the Karen National Defence Organisation; political commissars were appointed to each unit, though only after 1963 were they ranked senior to military commanders in the usual Maoist style.

It is over the exact political orientation of this new policy that the greatest confusion remains. KNUP theoretician, Skaw Ler Taw, described the second phase as 'more or less a communist strategy'; Marshall Shwin, the veteran KNA conservative from Shwegyin, as 'more than socialism, less than communism'.[59] Mahn Ba Zan, who drew up many of the Congress resolutions, usually described himself as a socialist and, like many of the KNU's other Christian leaders, was an admirer of Robert Owen. In the Congress resolutions, at least, the political goals of the KNU were defined in socialist terms: To set up a sovereign Karen State; to permit other nationalities to set up their own sovereign states; to set up a People's Democracy Federal Union based on the right of self-determination for every minority; and to set up a socialist state.[60] Though there was no official reference to the CPB or communism, the Congress record contains clear evidence of the influence of the CPB and Marxist-Leninist ideology. The Congress slogan 'peace within our country' closely echoed the CPB's 1955 'peace and unity' line and many of the KNU's objectives were now defined in contemporary Maoist terminology:

Main Enemy: imperialism and feudalism

Immediate Target: the AFPFL which represents those interests

Strength: the leadership of the working class, but the main strength will be the peasants, the backbone of the revolution, under the workers' leadership

Alliances: intellectuals, government employees, businessmen

Temporary Alliances: national bourgeois

Strategy: armed struggle as the main tool, agrarian revolution as the second

Military Strategy: protracted warfare

Agrarian Strategy: abolition of landlordism

Foreign Policy: peaceful coexistence.[61]

Thus in less than a decade the KNU's transformation from what the left in Burma once described as simply an 'imperialist plot' to a radical, communist-aligned movement was apparently complete. For the day-to-day administration of Kawthoolei, the Congress confirmed that the KRC, in which a newly elected committee of KNUP members predominated, would remain the supreme executive body. But with confirmation of the KNUP as the Karen vanguard party, the name KNU was eclipsed and did not resurface in common usage until the 1970s, when Mahn Ba Zan and Bo Mya, a hill Karen commander in the east, began the second major reformation of the KNU.

How far the Karen nationalist movement ever accepted the Second Phase Programme is still a matter of considerable controversy, but within ten years it caused a complete east-west split in the KNU. The 1953 and 1956 Congresses have disappeared from all KNU records; if referred to at all, it is as meetings of the KNUP. In the Eastern Division, in particular, few second phase policies were ever introduced. Indeed, immediately after the Congress, the KRC president, Tha Hmwe, sent a delegation to Bangkok to set up an underground Karen 'embassy' in a bid to win Western aid for the Karen cause. Here he later joined his men for a series of meetings with Thai, American, CIA, SEATO and KMT officials who made clear their disapproval of the KNU's improving relationship with the CPB; this fuelled Tha Hmwe's growing disillusionment with the KNUP and his eventual surrender in 1964 (see Chapter 11).

However, the importance of the Second Phase Programme as an attempt to synthesize Maoist and nationalist ideology cannot be underestimated. In the Delta and parts of the Toungoo hills the KNUP survived as a radical political force for another 20 years, often in the face of sustained *Tatmadaw* pressure. And while most KNUP ideology has long since been rejected, many key KNUP principles in areas such as military and tactical organisation remain standard KNU policy. Indeed over half the senior KNU leaders today are former KNUP members, including both vice-presidents, Bo San Lin and Bo Than Aung, KNU general-secretary, Padoh Ba Thin, and vice Chief-of-Staff, Tamla Baw.

The KNUP also had a considerable influence on the development of other ethnic insurgent parties in Burma. As a main objective of the Second Phase Programme, Karen leaders turned their attention to working with other insurgent groups. Interestingly, in view of the KNUP's closening ties with the CPB, the KNU's first attempts to set up a united front specifically excluded the CPB and only involved other national minority forces.

Until then inter-party relations were haphazard. In the early days of the insurrections, the KNU had sent a number of volunteers, including the Sgaw Karen brothers, Bo Special and Tha Kalei, to help Thaton Hla Pe organise the PNO in the Shan State, while a local Paku Karen soldier, Tawplo (*aka* Richman), was dispatched to advise the new Karenni leader, Sao Shwe, after U Bee Tu Re was killed. Both groups are closely related to the Karens; the dream of a pan-Karen state including the Pao, Kayan and Karenni has still not been ruled out. But the KNU, in line with its oft-stated belief in the right of ethnic self-determination for all Burma's races, had from the beginning acknowledged their legitimacy.

Meanwhile, to the south, the KNU gave military and financial support to a number of rebel Mon groups active along the Tenasserim plain, where Karen and Mon leaders had agreed (in depositions to the 1948 Regional Autonomy Enquiry) that a joint Karen-Mon state should be formed. Here, in March 1953, Karen leaders encouraged the formation of the MPF. Though local Karen commanders refused to allow MPF troops to move into the Thaton area, territory was redemar-

cated around Three Pagodas Pass and large MPF base areas successfully established in Mudon and Thanbyuzayat townships.[62]

The first moves to put these relationships on a more formal footing were made
after the KNU's First National Congress in November that year. In 1954 a young
KNUP cadre, Bo San Lin, was sent north to establish regular contact with Hla Pe
and Sao Shwe. Having married a local Karenni woman, he became the KNUP's
chief liaison officer for the next 20 years, travelling constantly between Pao,
Karenni and Kayan territory. At the time the KNU Eastern Division's First
brigade still operated in the west of Karenni. But on 29 July 1957, shortly after
Sao Shwe's death from malaria, with the KNU's help (in line with its continued
recognition of the historic independence of the Karenni State) the Karenni
National Progressive Party (KNPP) finally came into being and KNU military
activities in the state virtually ended.[63] The KNPP's general headquarters was set
up at Kwachi, in the mountains south of Mawchi, where it remained for many
years; the party's first Constitution was also drafted later that year.

From these contacts the first ethnic minority front, the Democratic Nationalities
United Front (DNUF), was formed in April 1956 at a meeting of Mon, Pao, Karen
and Karenni representatives, chaired by Mahn Ba Zan, at the KRC's Mewaing
camp in the Papun hills. It was basically a forum group for nationalities with a
view to forming a joint military front at a later stage. There were also plans for an
ethnic Intha group (organised by the PVOs) from the Inle Lake area and a Kadu-
Danu group from Katha district to join. In 1957 a DNUF presidium meeting was
held in the Pegu Yomas so that delegates from Arakan could attend, but none of
these groups was able to make the journey; and with the mass surrenders of 1958
the DNUF came to an abrupt end, clearing the way for the KNUP's full alliance
with the CPB the following year. (See Chart 2.)

A number of veteran leaders from other ethnic fronts who joined Karen leaders
in these critical meetings now freely admit that their discussions with Mahn Ba
Zan, Skaw Ler Taw and the KNUP ideologues had a deep impact on the political
direction of their own movements. Present-day insurgent leaders closely involved
with the KNUP throughout this period include Saw Maw Reh, president of the
KNPP and National Democratic Front, Tha Kalei of the Shan State Nationalities
Liberation Organisation and Nai Shwe Kyin, chairman of the New Mon State
Party.[64] The KNUP rather than the CPB was thus the first major conduit for
communist ideology to these parties, all of which took up strongly left-aligned
positions.

Within the KNU movement, however, objections to the Second Phase Programme were not slow to emerge. At the end of the 1956 Congress a KNUP
training course for Eastern Division leaders was held at Me Ni Kawn village,
Kyaukkyi township. Mahn Ba Zan lectured on the international situation, Skaw
Ler Taw on the second phase and Thara Pla Say on party organisation. In an extravagant speech on agrarian policy, Mahn Shan Phale alienated Buddhist and
Christian representatives by describing the Kyaikitiyo monastery in Thaton in
derogatory terms. Delegates from the Thaton fifth brigade, led by ex-*pongyi* Bo
Soe, then refused to attend the remaining classes and the meeting eventually had
to be abandoned. The fifth brigade, then the strongest of the KNU's eastern
brigades with 1,200 men under arms, now went very much its own way; in fact it
had never really been brought under central KNU control. And while it continued
to cause government forces considerable trouble, it also became notorious for

poor discipline. Bo Soe himself was later assassinated by his own men and the entire brigade eventually surrendered in 1964 under another equally notorious commander, Bo Lin Htin, along with the KRC president, Tha Hmwe.

Many of the same objections were voiced by veteran Christian elders who had led the nationalist movement from the early days of the KNA and in the next few years several surrendered.[65] Others, such as Marshall Shwin and Tha Din, stepped down from active day-to-day involvement in the KNU and retired with their families into the hills.

If these were clear indications of the difficulties to come, the adoption of the Second Phase Programme also coincided with one of the most successful eras of the Karen revolution. This, in part, can be attributed to the changing political situation in Burma which, under the U Nu and Ba Swe governments of 1955-8, was at its most fluid and open since independence. Like the CPB, the KNU was in a position to take advantage. With improving coordination in their rural base areas, KAF units were able to skirt across much of the Irrawaddy Delta, harrying government supply lines and attacking isolated outposts and installations. In the east, the KAF was still able to launch periodic full-scale assaults on Kawkareik, Papun, Thandaung, Thaton and other government-held towns. In March 1958, the state capital, Paan, was overrun, 'burnt and looted'.[66] Moreover, while the government continued to depict the KNU as an illegal 'bandit' organisation, the second phase was undoubtedly very much in tune with the political climate of the time. There was a widespread desire for peace and in many front-line areas government appointed 'peace guerrillas' were openly sympathetic to KNUP aims. Like the CPB, underground KNUP organisers were able to move freely in and out of the towns, recruiting supporters and setting up cells; in Rangoon the KNUP established its own contacts with the above-ground BWPP, NUF and its small affiliate, the All Burma Karen Organisation, which tried to introduce KNU demands into the national political debate.[67] At the university, meanwhile, the KNUP was able to begin organising amongst Karen and other ethnic minority students.

While there was never any real suggestion that the challenge of the KNU, CPB or, for that matter, any other insurgent organisation, provoked the grave political crisis of late 1958, Gen. Ne Win and the *Tatmadaw* hardliners undoubtedly viewed the growing collusion between insurgent organisations and their above-ground supporters with mounting concern. Indeed with the flood of rebel surrenders that year, it became increasingly difficult to distinguish between members of the insurgent and parliamentary opposition parties. It was this connection the army was now aiming to break, first through the short-lived 'military caretaker' administration of 1958-60, then, from 1962, through a quarter century of BSPP rule.

In fact it is this threat to national security that Ne Win loyalists, even after the 1990 general election, use as the main pretext for the *Tatmadaw's* right to intervene in national political affairs. Since the army's experiences in the disastrous civil war of the 1950s, so their argument runs, elected politicians cannot be trusted.

10

The Collapse of Parliamentary Democracy: Ne Win Seizes Power

With the key exception of the Karen insurrection, the 1958 mass surrenders should in theory have marked the beginning of a new era of tranquillity in the war-divided country. As it turned out, they by no means indicated the end of the political turbulence that year. Not for the last time Burma was about to be rocked by political upheavals from the least expected quarters and the year ended with the country under the control of the 'military caretaker' administration of Gen. Ne Win. Though handled through various legal channels and with the apparent approval of U Nu ('Power in Burma Thrust upon a Reluctant General?' headlined *The Times* newspaper in London) it was a military coup by any other name.[1]

Various theories have been put forward for the *Tatmadaw*'s unexpected seizure of power in 1958. Some have argued that Ne Win feared the many insurgents entering the legal fold might now be able to win power through the ballot box. Others have pointed to the downturn in the economy and the still chronic state of lawlessness in much of the country. The social consequences of Burma's dislocated history were clearly coming home to roost; warlordism, corruption and banditry were rife. This was brought into focus in March that year by the forcible disbanding of the much-heralded government defence militia, the *Pyu Saw Hti*, which in many areas were quite clearly out of control. Many units were now operating as little more than the private armies of local AFPFL or ABPO politicians and, after the unprovoked killings of a number of villagers in the Tenasserim Division, several had become quite indistinguishable from dacoit gangs.[2]

A warning that the insurgencies themselves were by no means at an end came with the dramatic news that the KNU had moved its Delta headquarters to within nine miles of Rangoon. In the background, too, was the first stirring of unrest in the Shan State, which under the terms of the 1947 Constitution had the right of secession after a ten-year period. This time was now up.

In his first statement to Parliament as prime minister on 31 October 1958, Ne Win touched on virtually all these reasons when he described the situation as 'closely approaching that sad spectacle of 1948/9'.[3] He also made it very clear that he was opposed to any further amnesties for insurgents and army mutineers; these, he insisted, must make some admission of guilt before expecting any leniency. Indeed, he warned that many former insurgents, especially CPB sympathisers and members of the People's Comrade Party (PCP, former PVOs), now preparing to contest parliamentary elections on a pro-communist platform, had only surrendered to try and take advantage of the changing political climate.

175

Combined with the 1958 surrenders, 40,000 ex-CPB and PVO supporters had now been amnestied since the insurrections began and they formed a potentially powerful bloc. For the first time, too, Ne Win pinpointed the activities of 'economic insurgents, profiteers and black marketeers' as the cause of Burma's financial malaise, a problem that has plagued the country ever since.

These were all difficulties Burma had learned to live with in a decade of conflict; on the insurgent front, at least, there were now grounds for optimism. So the answer for the success of Ne Win's military takeover cannot be found here.

There was, however, another reason. What made 1958 so different was the final split in April of that year of the AFPFL into two factions. At a stroke the narrow consensus that had bound U Nu and the leaders of the Socialist Party and *Tatmadaw* together was broken. In name a broad coalition, by 1958 the AFPFL and the men who had led Burma through the first troubled decade (U Nu, U Ba Swe, U Kyaw Nyein, Thakin Tin, Thakin Kyaw Tun, M.A. Raschid, Gen. Ne Win and Brig. Aung Gyi) had become a narrow administrative oligarchy. In the face of so many overwhelming military and political difficulties, they had by and large buried their ideological differences and built up a highly centralised system of administration in Rangoon. Each, meanwhile, had concentrated on developing his own power base in the country amongst the AFPFL's estimated 1,350,000 affiliated members: Ba Swe and Raschid, Trades Union Congress (Burma); Thakins Tin and Kyaw Tun, ABPO; Kyaw Nyein, Youth Organisation; U Nu, Education, Buddhist *Sangha*; Ne Win and Aung Gyi, the defence services.[4] This, as events soon showed, had manifestly failed to lay the foundations for a permanent multiparty system of government. Long-buried personal antipathies undoubtedly lay at the back of the split, which began over an apparently trivial incident, the choice of a new general-secretary for the AFPFL; U Nu wanted the ABPO leader, Thakin Kyaw Tun: Kyaw Nyein preferred Thakin Tha Khin. But when at the Third AFPFL Congress in January 1958 U Nu publicly turned his back on Marxism, he also unwittingly took the lid off the first real political debate in years over the nature and direction of government in Burma.[5] In many respects, then, the situation has striking parallels with the political crises of both 1948 and 1988.

Breaking into two factions, the U Nu/Thakin Tin group, which became known as the 'Clean' AFPFL, and the Ba Swe/Kyaw Nyein or 'Stable' AFPFL, which included most of the survivors of the 1936 Student Committee, there followed months of heated accusations and counter-accusations, including the arrest of dozens of supporters on both sides during the disbanding of the *Pyu Saw Hti*. Both sides frantically lobbied for support and ended up with the most unlikely bed-fellows. Indeed, in June, with the streets of Rangoon deserted and troops in defensive positions around the secretariat compound, the Nu/Tin faction survived one no-confidence motion in Parliament only by enlisting the support of the National United Front (NUF), which included the 'crypto-communists', the BWPP, with whom they had long been at loggerheads.[6] Any notion of there still being a distinct Socialist Party or movement in existence, gently guiding both the AFPFL and country, was shattered.

The following month, in another complete about-turn on policy, U Nu agreed in principle to the creation of new Arakan and Mon States in return for the support of the conservative Arakan National United Organisation and the insurgent Arakan People's Liberation Party (APLP) and Mon People's Front (MPF), now laying down their arms. Meanwhile, encouraged by the scale of these surrenders and as an apparent pay-off for NUF support, Nu continued to promote his 'arms for democracy' peace initiative with a new amnesty called for 1 August 1958.

Army die-hards saw these moves as opening the door to the communists. For many battle-hardened veterans the sight of U Nu, the peace maker, sitting on the parliamentary benches with NUF politicians in their sky-blue (the colour of peace) *longyis*, was particularly annoying. Secret communist sympathisers in the NUF were widely believed to be advising CPB leaders in the liberated zones every step of the way. Elections scheduled for later that year, ostensibly to resolve the AFPFL split, were widely seen as the door through which the communists would finally be admitted to government. Of the 45 NUF members then in Parliament (led by U Ba Nyein and the former CPB general-secretary, Thein Pe Myint) 29 were picked out as pro-communist activists; indeed charges had only recently been dropped against two MPs for alleged 'trafficking with rebels'.

Not entirely by chance, Than Tun, who earlier appeared to be turning cool on the prospect of negotiations, in a new series of 'letters from the jungle' chose this moment to renew the offer of face-to-face peace talks, to be organised by Kodaw Hmaing's Peace Committee. Various offers were reported over the year, but the CPB's platform consisted of just three main demands: 'national independence' and a clear-cut rejection by the government of the 'Anglo-American aggressive bloc'; legalisation of the CPB and release of all political prisoners; and the right of the CPB to contest elections on an equal basis with other parties.[7] Once these rights were guaranteed, Than Tun promised, the CPB would be ready to lay down its arms. Another controversial suggestion which surfaced, much to the alarm of many army officers, was the proposed integration of the CPB's People's Army (PA) with the *Tatmadaw* once peace had been established.

Whether the CPB really could have exploited the situation to such an extent must remain open to question; contemporary press reports were (and still are) somewhat paranoid about the communist threat. But back in 1959 even *The Guardian* editor, Sein Win, then regarded as one of the more objective analysts of the political scene, felt constrained to write: 'The AFPFL split was the biggest victory for the communists since their insurrection 11 years ago. It was an automatic victory without bloodshed, and the split paved the way for the communist ascension to power.'[8]

Sein Win's words gained widespread credence at the time. However, serious doubts have since been raised about his impartiality, especially when he resurfaced in 1988 with his long-time mentor, Brig. Aung Gyi, to support *Tatmadaw* allegations that CPB conspirators were manipulating the democracy movement and Aung San Suu Kyi's National League for Democracy. Indeed his 1959 work, *The Split Story*, was republished in updated form by the Saw Maung regime. U Nu in fact only ever appointed one NUF leader, the non-communist Dr E. Maung, to his Cabinet and instead appeared, in typically impulsive style, to be trying to string the NUF along while he assembled a new coalition government.

This uncertainty caused a further rift between the governing Nu/Tin faction of the AFPFL, the Swe/Nyein 'stable' faction and the army which, despite Ne Win's pledges of neutrality, appeared to be moving closer to the Swe/Nyein faction. Without doubt the main reason for this was the sensitive issue of peace talks with the CPB, which the NUF, now making use of its alliance with U Nu, became increasingly determined to pursue.

In August, as the situation deteriorated and suspicion, the curse of Burmese politics, continued to spread, the Union president, Mahn Win Maung, prorogued Parliament and all three sides started to engage in some dangerous shadow-boxing. The air was filled with rumours of coups and assassination attempts; fighting broke out between rival dockyard and railway union workers as both AFPFL factions competed for support. At one meeting in U Nu's Rangoon compound at the beginning of September, the AFPFL member for Hanthawaddy even reportedly declared the *Tatmadaw* 'public enemy number one' and the Swe/Nyein faction 'number two'; the insurgents, to the army's consternation, he put as 'a poor third'.9 Five days later, the day after Red Flag leader, Thakin Soe, submitted his own 24-page peace proposal, the NUF presidium unanimously accepted Than Tun's offer of a meeting with Kodaw Hmaing's Peace Committee.

Finally, in circumstances never adequately explained by any of the main pro-tagonists, at the end of September matters came to a head with a coup and counter-coup being only narrowly averted. While U Nu was away on a tour up-country, his supporters suddenly tried to flood Rangoon with all the armed units they felt they could rely on. This apparent *putsch* was led by two of his Cabinet ministers, Bo Min Gaung and Bo Hmu Aung, both former *Thirty Comrades* and Yellow Band PVO leaders. Significantly, they employed the Union Military Police (UMP), loyal remnants of the *Pyu Saw Hti* and local Forest Guards, who all came under the Home and Agricultural Ministries, but decided against using the army, navy or airforce which came under the Ministry of Defence.10 Two and a half battalions of UMPs were secretly brought into Rangoon and 10,000 *Pyu Saw Hti* were reported to be ready in the countryside between Rangoon and Prome. Even the PCP, which had only recently surrendered, had been enlisted on U Nu's side.

Whether it was their own bid for power or, as they claimed, a last-ditch attempt to avert an army coup, was quickly lost sight of amidst a bitter welter of acri-mony. Certainly on U Nu's return, Bo Min Gaung and Bo Hmu Aung warned him the army had planned a coup for the night of 22 September. But coup or no coup, the *Tatmadaw* appeared to have detected all the Nu/Tin faction's plans well in advance and that same day, to the confusion of the foreign press corps, several UMP units, including one from Taungdwingyi 280 miles to the north, were disarmed at army road-blocks as they advanced down the road towards Rangoon.

With this impasse reached, on 26 September U Nu, apparently bowing to the inevitable, suddenly changed course and agreed to hand over power to the army Chief-of-Staff, Gen. Ne Win. Ne Win now had the job of forming a new govern-ment until the next elections could be held. Conspicuously, nobody used the words *putsch* or coup, but as *The Nation* wryly commented, U Nu had again shown what a great statesman he had become by 'succeeding in keeping the word *coup d'état* out of references to the situation in Burma'.11 Only NUF and Rangoon University Students United Front supporters took to the streets in protest.

Four weeks later on 28 October, after months of what American historian Frank Trager calls 'shameful, demoralising campaigning' by both factions of the AFPFL, U Nu formally resigned in favour of Ne Win, who was elected prime minister by an uncontested vote.12 In his resignation speech, Nu, a cunning communicator to the end, left no doubt that he believed it was the army's mistaken 'fear' of a communist takeover (through a merger of the 'clean' AFPFL, NUF and Bo Po Kun's PVOs) that had finally brought his government down.13

Ne Win's brief was to prepare the country for elections within six months, but it took nearly three times as long for parliamentary government to be returned.

The Military Caretaker Administration: 1958-60

Surprisingly, international analysts and observers of very different political persuasions have described Ne Win's 'military caretaker' administration of 1958-60 as the most orderly and best-run government in Burma since independence. The *Tatmadaw*'s achievements over these years certainly encouraged Ne Win to seize power again in 1962, when serious differences between the AFPFL, *Tatmadaw* and, this time, ethnic minority leaders began to threaten Burma's fragile political consensus.

The caretaker administration was, in effect, a trial run. The restoration of law and order remained the public priority of the day and, as troops went about relocating squatter communities, whitewashing buildings and cleaning the streets, there were clear precedents for the army's actions in the aftermaths of the coups of both 1962 and 1988. At the same time Ne Win was meticulous in his observance of the letter of the law, even resigning as prime minister until the Constitution could be amended when elections did not go ahead after the scheduled six months. There were also some tangible gains on the economic front with rice production, though still well short of pre-war levels, topping four million tons again and exports reaching two million tons, which still remains the post-war high.[14]

For modern historians, the military caretaker administration's most important legacy was the continued development of a national political identity for the *Tatmadaw* under Gen. Ne Win. Brig. Aung Gyi dates this process back to 1954/5; the historian Josef Silverstein puts it even further back to 1951 and the foundation of the Defence Services Institute (DSI).[15] In *The National Ideology and the Role of the Defence Services*, published in 1960, three main objectives were set out: the restoration of peace and the rule of law, the consolidation of democracy, and the establishment of a 'socialist economy'.[16] Few observers were deceived by the civilian veneer of Ne Win's emergency Cabinet; all Cabinet posts, though nominally held by civilians, were backed up by the appointment of over 100 military officers, mostly in their 30s or 40s, to senior executive positions. Of these a third had served in the Second World War and 20 had begun their careers as long ago as 1941 with the Burma Independence Army of Aung San.[17] Prominent among these were Brig. Aung Gyi in charge of finance and Col. Maung Maung on the Central Security Council. At the same time a National Solidarity Association was established, initially recruiting members from serving or retired military personnel, to try and build up non-partisan support for the government, with each ward leader in the country authorised to form a local branch. Moreover, the DSI, which was originally set up to provide troops with consumer goods at subsidised prices, expanded rapidly during the caretaker administration to become the country's largest commercial institution, with interests in banking, shipping, construction, transport and other major businesses.[18]

However, it was an indication of Ne Win's priorities at the time (and a telling indictment of the continued impact of the civil war) that, in the army's official account of these years, *Is Trust Vindicated?*, Ne Win allowed the *Tatmadaw*'s record to stand or fall more or less entirely on its successes in the battle against insurgency. It was no idle boast. The virtually unlimited powers it now assumed untied the military's hands and allowed front-line commanders full rein in the field; there was an all-round tightening up in tactics. Backed up by a new system of local defence militia, the People's Reporters, or Bow and Arrow Corps, the army went on an all-out offensive in 16 military command districts across the country.

Not even the insurgents' elusive above-ground supporters in the towns were spared. Under the controversial Public Order Preservation Act, over 400 suspected CPB sympathisers were arrested, of which 153 were deported to the Coco Islands.[19] The best known of these were NUF leaders, U Aung Than (Aung San's brother), Bo Mya Thway and *Yebaw* Hla Win (MPs for Wakema and Rangoon South respectively), who, even from gaol, continued to try and push the NUF's 'peace through negotiation' platform.[20] The press, at the time one of the most free in Asia, also came under intense pressure; the *Botahtaung*, *Kyemon* and *Rangoon Daily* newspapers were closed down for suspected communist sympathies or alleged anti-army reporting and their editors gaoled.

Many of those deported were in fact fully-fledged CPB members and, as CPB veterans today admit, it was a serious blow to the party's urban organisation. The CPB's trade union cells were especially badly damaged. One immediate casualty of this, according to former CPB activists in Rangoon, was an end to the close rapport with the BWPP and NUF, both of which from 1960 had begun to show pro-Soviet leanings.[21] Some of those accused of CPB membership suggested high-level communist infiltration into above-ground parties other than the NUF. For example, the leader of the AFPFL 'clean' faction in Mergui, Maung Nyunt, was detained for allegedly helping CPB guerrillas set fire to the town when it was overrun by the PA some years earlier; to avoid arrest U Pe Nyunt, the AFPFL 'clean' faction MP for Bilin, but according to the army a full CPB member with the PA rank of major, disappeared underground with 15 armed followers when his cover was blown. After briefly taking sanctuary with the KNU, he was killed in action four months later on his way to CPB-held territory.[22] (Party veterans have never admitted his CPB identity, but mention two MPs, U Ba Nyin and U Maung Ko, whom they say were above-ground supporters.)

Buddhism as a Political Weapon

The *Tatmadaw*'s psychological warfare department also intensified its campaign of 'ideological warfare' against the CPB. The main thrust of its offensive was a booklet, the *Dhammantaraya* (Dhamma in Danger), which in a virulent attack on the 'godless' communists tried to mobilise the country and clergy against the CPB. Over a million copies were printed in the Burmese, Mon, Shan and Pao languages and, in a country over 80 per cent Buddhist, the mere act of distribution was considered a merit. A different edition was prepared in Burmese and Urdu for circulation among the Muslim community, while another book, *The Burning Question*, aimed at the Christian community and the Christian-led KNU, was distributed in Sgaw and Pwo Karen, Chin, Kachin and English.[23] The main source for the army's attack was the notebook of a young communist cadre (reputedly U Chit Hlaing), who in 1944 had attended some CPB training classes led by Thakin Soe, where some allegedly blasphemous attacks on the influence of Buddhism in Burma were made. 'Religion is the opium of the people,' Soe was quoted as saying. 'Buddhism is the enemy of the proletariat in Burma: it must be attacked at every opportunity.'[24] Similar statements were attributed to Than Tun; the White Flags and PVOs were accused of pillaging and destroying Buddhist monasteries.

However, while the CPB, like many other insurgent groups, undoubtedly often upset religious sensibilities, I am wary of reading too much into the effectiveness of such anti-communist campaigns, despite the public support claimed by the army at the time. All political parties, above and underground, tried to enlist the religious argument on their side in the civil war, but with very mixed results. U Nu, who hosted the Sixth World Buddhist Council meeting of 1954-6, probably made the most determined effort to win the Buddhist *Sangha* to his cause, including during his years with the Parliamentary Democracy Party in the rebel underground, but he was by no means successful. I have met many Buddhist *pongyis* (and Christian pastors and Muslim *mullahs*) on both sides of Burma's present battle lines and, as they go about their duties, they usually appear ambivalent on the question of political ideologies. Undoubtedly one of the main virtues of *Theravada* Buddhism as practised in Burma is that, while nationalist in character, it is religiously tolerant and avoids dogmatic political strictures: Buddhism is the guide and an individual may be helped by teachers, but ultimately each person has to find his or her own way.

This apparent latitude on the question of communism rests uneasily today in the light of the 1988 upheavals, in which Buddhist monks played a leading role. After a quarter century of Ne Win's quixotic *Burmese Way to Socialism*, for a younger generation the words socialism and Marxism are virtually synonymous with corruption and maladministration. In the political climate of the 1950s, however, the Buddhist *Sangha* was not untouched by the highly fashionable impact of socialism and many monks, like many other Burmese citizens, became keen students of Marxism. Former monks say they were initially attracted by the Buddhist laws of change and Marxist discussion of materialism, which they saw as similar to Buddhist self-denial. In many monasteries too, monks and young novices are used to learning philosophical precepts by rote and, since there are no ideological strictures, Marxism with its moralistic slogans was seen as fitting easily into the same educational traditions. Burma is not alone in this. In Asia the Buddhist countries (China, Vietnam, Laos, Cambodia, Korea and Japan) have adapted to Marxism, Leninism and Western socialist philosophies, while amongst the Muslim nations the examples are very few, possibly only North Yemen.

Also, like Sri Lanka, Burma has a long tradition of militant politicised Buddhism (perhaps unusual for *Theravada* Buddhists). In modern times this dates back to the anti-British resistance of the 1880s and to the anti-colonial movement led by U Ottoma and Saya San in the 1920s and 1930s. As Bertil Lintner points out, the most striking example in Burma since independence is the left-wing Yahanpyo movement, popular among young monks in Mandalay; in the 1950s it was run along military lines and monks were permitted to keep weapons in their monasteries.[25] Also in the 1950s, Yahanpyo monks often turned up at fairs and public meetings to act as unofficial policemen. And in 1988 Burma's estimated 150,000 monks, including the long-suppressed Yahanpyo order, again took to the streets to police the great pro-democracy demonstrations. *Pongyis* organised many of the strike centres in Rangoon, Moulmein and Mandalay and, despite *Tatmadaw* allegations, most say they had long since abandoned any communist ideology.[26] The Thayettaw monastery in Rangoon was turned into a virtual fortress when it became one of the main centres of the democracy movement. Well into 1990 Buddhist monasteries and *Sangha* continued to keep alive the ideals of democracy long after the democracy protests and parties were crushed until they too came under attack.

To summarise, Burma's religious institutions have tended to reflect the great political struggles of the country at large and, as in neighbouring Thailand, Buddhism as a mobilising force has usually been prominent in the patriotic or nationalist movements of the time. This meant that, in a country as ethnically varied as Burma, monks and monasteries have also often played a vital role in supporting ethnic minority movements, particularly Pao, Mon, Rakhine and Shan. Generally this support has been moral or educational, occasionally financial or logistical. There is a long tradition in Burma of monks (usually novices) 'disrobing' to join various insurgent movements. Under present circumstances objective studies are impossible, but in Arakan (where I obtained first-hand personal profiles) a remarkably high number of senior insurgent leaders, including communists, were former *pongyis*. Most began their political careers in the 1950s and 1960s. Both Shwe Tha and Khaing Soe, CC members of the Communist Party of Arakan, hold theology degrees and are former teachers of the *Dhamma*; three CC members of the pro-Marxist Arakan National Liberation Party, Ba Saw Aung, Twan Re and Kyaw Than Oo, are ex-*pongyis*; virtually all the leaders, past and present, of the staunchly nationalist Arakan Liberation Party, such as Khaing Ye Khaing, Soe Naing Aung and Khaing Pray Thein, are also former monks.

So while the *Tatmadaw*'s religious campaign of 1958-60 undoubtedly had some success in mobilising anti-communist sentiment (reflected to some extent in U Nu's victory in the 1960 election), at the time the CPB's response was very low key. Through its Magwe district branch it issued a thousand copies of *Rip off the Mask*, a brochure reiterating its support for Buddhism, and reminded the country that its *Draft Program of Basic Tasks* guaranteed each individual the right to practise his or her religion, traditions, culture and language.[27] The CPB also accused the army of introducing a system of 'fascist military dictatorship' and of trying to cause a split between the communists and the *Sangha* by compromising Kodaw Hmaing's peace movement which, it claimed, both it and many Buddhist monks supported.[28]

However, if the Psychological Warfare Department's religious campaign can best be described as inconclusive, the *Tatmadaw*'s military campaign, which a compliant press widely publicised, was undeniably effective. Carefully censored reports of fierce clashes with a variety of White Flag, Red Flag, Karen, Mon, Shan, KMT and *Mujahid* insurgents appeared daily across the country. In these accounts the *Tatmadaw* invariably came out on top. Some of the heaviest fighting reported was in the Henzada, Bassein and Myaungmya districts of the western Delta where, according to the Defence Ministry, there were 450 military engagements in which 331 CPB and KNU troops were killed, 457 wounded and over 1,000 surrendered or captured.[29] By the time civilian government returned in 1960, it was claimed (in a highly suspect set of figures) that the total number of insurgents in Burma had fallen from somewhere between 9,000 and 15,000 when Ne Win became prime minister, to just 5,485.[30] White Flag and Red Flag troop numbers were put as low as 700 (down from 3,050) and 209 respectively; against over 1,800 insurgent deaths (including 723 KNU supporters), *Tatmadaw* losses, by contrast, were estimated at just 520.[31]

If the apparent defeat of the country's diverse insurgents suggested by these statistics is an exaggeration (the size and impact of the fast-growing Shan rebellion is certainly played down) the figures do reflect a steady decline in the CPB's military strength, especially when put alongside the mass surrenders of 1957/8. Virtually everyone in the Pyapon and Thayet district White Front units surrendered to add to the swelling ranks of disbanded party cells. As a *Tatmadaw* spokesman admitted, whereas in the ten previous years of civilian government only one important CPB leader, Bo Chit Kaung (*aka* Soe Maung), a graduate of Rangoon University, had been arrested (in 1957), in the first six months of the caretaker administration alone two CC members, Thanmani Maung Maung and the former ABTUC leader, Rajan (*aka* Aung Naing), were captured in their base areas.[32] By the time Ne Win had stepped down two more, Ko Yaw and Bo Nyunt Maung, the ex-PVO commander, had surrendered and Tin Ye, head of the CPB's northern Shan State (No.4) division, had been killed in action near Nawnghkio. Other serious CPB losses included the deaths in battle of PA commanders, Arlawaka, in the CPB's No.3 (Monywa-Shwebo) division, and Saya Kun and U Ba Thein, near Inle in the south-west Shan State. Such experienced men were not easily replaced. On the ethnic nationalist side, by contrast, most of the losses occurred among local district officers; the most important casualty was the Karenni leader, Saw Maw Reh, who had recently stepped down from the Karenni National Progressive Party (KNPP) presidency after being wounded. For a few months he now also briefly surrendered.

The National Democratic United Front and the 1960 Peace Talks
From the CPB's viewpoint the only faint glimmer of light in these difficult years was the gradual, if largely unexpected, *rapprochement* with the KNU. This led in 1959 to the formation of the National Democratic United Front (NDUF), the first really successful insurgent nationalities front in Burma.

It had been a long time in the formation. CPB/KNU relations improved only slowly after the 1952 Zin/Zan agreement. In the Delta, KNU and CPB militia usually cooperated with each other and were careful to avoid territorial disputes. This benefited both sides and allowed troops and party officials to cross safely through each other's territory without having to pass near *Tatmadaw* positions and run the risk of ambush. According to Bruce Humphrey-Taylor, who frequently made the dangerous journey with KNU troops between the KAF's Delta and Eastern Divisions, 'if we saw a red flag flying over a Burman village, we always knew it would be safe to enter'.[33] CPB units were also still active in several districts in the mountains of the south-east, especially around Toungoo and Tavoy-Mergui, though in strategic areas such as Nyaunglebin, PA strength was now decreasing and White Flag officials often had to shelter in KNU villages on their way through. Meanwhile, except in small pockets of the Delta, the Red Flags had very much become a marginal force in Karen-inhabited areas and, during 1957/8, the KNU disarmed the last remnants in the Paan and Thaton districts and forced them to move further south into Amherst district.

At this time most CPB/KNU contacts were still between local district officers; but at the end of 1955, following the CPB CC's adoption of the controversial 'revisionist line', CC member *Yebaw* Mya travelled to KNU headquarters in the Shwegyin hills to explain the CPB's new strategy and to propose a new White Flag/Red Flag/PVO/KNU alliance. But Karen leaders still had plans to form their own ethnic front, the short-lived Democratic Nationalities United Front (DNUF), and wanted any alliance to include the Mons, Paos, Karennis, Inthas, Arakanese and other nationalist forces, so no progress was made (see Chapter 9). But the next year, shortly after the KNU's historic Second National Congress ended, another top-level CPB delegation, including CC members Thakins Zin and Tin Tun, arrived in the Shwegyin hills. This time they agreed to upgrade the Joint Operations Committee of the Zin/Zan agreement into a new Joint Military Committee. With the KNU's adoption of the Karen National United Party's radical Second Phase Programme at the Second Congress and a new military line based on Mao Zedong's 'protracted warfare', it was easy to agree on a joint military strategy: combined operational areas were mapped out. But no agreement was reached on the nationalities question. The KNU's line was still 'self-determination', whereas Tin Tun, a former member of the Constituent Assembly, advocated the right of self-administration, advancing the model of the autonomous regions of China.[34]

If these political difficulties remained, the military potential of the new agreement was swiftly demonstrated on the night of 30 January 1957 when joint CPB/KNU People's Peace Forces overran the towns of Pegu and Pyuntaza on the main Rangoon-Mandalay road, halting all through traffic to Mandalay and Moulmein by blowing up bridges and mining the railway.[35] For the next two years such operations continued, especially in the Sittang valley. For example, in November 1958, following Ne Win's takeover of power, combined CPB/KNU forces launched carefully synchronised strikes against Paungdawthi, the railway stations at Daik-u and Nyaunglebin, and the bridges linking the rail-line to Payagyi. Meanwhile, in 1957 the MPF joined a local Joint Executive Committee of KNUP, MPF and CPB leaders in the Pegu Yomas.

Only in May 1959 with the formation of the NDUF, however, were these joint committees upgraded into a formal military alliance. The reluctance was entirely on the Karen side and for two main reasons. First was the staunch anti-communism of many of the KNU movement's veteran Christian leaders; the 'socialist' KNUP, despite its predominance in many KNU administrative departments, could hardly negotiate without their approval. Second was the KNU's firm stand (supported by KNUP radicals) on the right of Karen (or Karenni or Pao) self-determination. The CPB, like the AFPFL or any other national party, was essentially seen to represent external ethnic Burman interests. This fitted in with the KNU's guiding principle (since the failure of negotiations in 1947/8) to establish a 'liberated' Karen Free State first, before agreeing to discuss territory with any party or government in Rangoon, be it the AFPFL, Socialist Party or CPB.

By 1959 the situation had changed dramatically. While the KNU had been little affected by the 1958 'arms for democracy' movement (unlike the CPB), Karen leaders had felt very isolated by the mass Mon, Pao and Arakanese surrenders that year, which had brought the immediate demise of the ethnic DNUF (see Chart 2). Meanwhile, after the KNUP's First Congress in January 1959, Mahn Ba Zan and the KNUP leaders were able to strengthen their control over the KNU movement; they showed their Marxist-Leninist hand by engaging in constant behind-the-scenes political manoeuvring. As a result Saw Hunter Tha Hmwe, president of the KNU's governing body, the Kawthoolei Revolutionary Council (KRC), was increasingly outwitted on many key decisions (see Chapter 11).

Thus this time, under additional pressure from the military caretaker administration, both CPB and KNU leaders were keen to reach agreement. Again their meetings began at the KNU's headquarters in the Shwegyin hills, but a *Tatmadaw* operation forced delegates to move further east to the KRC's Mewaing camp, which housed the central offices of all the KNU's main administrative departments. Representing the CPB were four CC members, Thakins Zin and Tin Tun, *Yebaw* Htay and Col. Ye Maung; on the KNU side were Mahn Ba Zan, Skaw Ler Taw and Saw Than Aung; and representing the fledgling New Mon State Party (NMSP), formed with KNU help in the aftermath of the 1958 MPF surrender, was Nai Shwe Kyin.

Again there were disagreements over the nationalities question with neither side prepared to compromise. They did, however, agree to put their relationship on a more formal footing by establishing a joint military alliance, the NDUF. To get round their political differences, Skaw Ler Taw remembers, they agreed on one principle: 'to cooperate on the points we agree upon, to work separately on those where we disagree.'[36] NMSP chairman, Nai Shwe Kyin, who married the sister of a senior CPB functionary in Pegu district, concurs: 'The understanding was Mao's dictum "the enemy of my enemy is my friend."'[37] But the key words cementing the alliance were undoubtedly 'national democratic', reflecting the three parties' study of Mao's two-stage theory of the united front (see Chapter 7). Though its communist overtones have gradually been relaxed, the expression lives on in ethnic insurgent politics today.

On 16 May 1959 the NDUF was formally inaugurated; the initial signatories were the CPB, the NMSP and the KNUP, but not the KNU. This reflected both the KNUP's growing independence from Tha Hmwe and the objections of a number of veteran Karen conservatives who, like Tha Hmwe, rejected any formal relationship with the CPB. A month later the names of the Chin National Vanguard Party (CNVP, *Chin Oosi Apwet*) and KNPP were added. (The CNVP was a small insurgent organisation of southern Chin, then only 40 guerrillas strong, closely linked to the CPB and formed in Pakokku and Thayet districts in March 1956.[38]) They then agreed to set up an NDUF presidium and to hold joint meetings at least once a year; the post of NDUF secretary would change by rotation annually, with each party having the power of veto.

Of the five original members, only the CPB and KNUP regularly took part in NDUF meetings and operations. Even more importantly, within four years there was a major split in the KNU, the first of several by different ethnic insurgent fronts over the troublesome question of cooperation with the CPB. But divisive or not, for the CPB and KNUP it was the beginning of a long and often highly effective alliance coordinating military operations across Lower Burma, which endured well into the 1970s. Quite likely, without the NDUF neither the CPB nor KNUP would have survived as long.

The government press in Rangoon at first mocked the new alliance; one report referred to the KNU as the CPB's 'suicide disciples'.[39] But privately many of Burma's new soldier-politicians were worried. During the caretaker administration the *Tatmadaw* had clearly won back the initiative from Burma's different insurgent forces, especially in the Delta. But though a highly optimistic assessment estimated that KNU troop-strength fell from 3,700 to 1,695 in this period (both figures are definitely underestimates), the Defence Ministry noted that Karen forces were now recruiting in the eastern mountains and 'their strength may possibly increase'; indeed by the army's own figures the KNU now controlled Burma's largest insurgent army.[40]

This anxiety led senior army commanders to offer to meet KNU leaders for secret peace talks in Rangoon in early 1960, shortly before they handed back power. It was the first time both sides had met since the battle of Insein a decade earlier. The initiative came from Brig. Aung Gyi, the army Vice Chief-of-Staff, who contacted Bo Kyin Pe (*aka* Ko Doe), the KNUP's Delta president, and Mahn Mya Maung, the KAF's Delta commander, by letter. As a reminder of the threat the KNU still posed, on 10 January a 200-strong KAF guerrilla force ambushed a train north of Moulmein, killing 17 passengers including several police and government officials.[41]

After a brief exchange of messages, in early February Gen. Kaw Htoo and Skaw Ler Taw flew by helicopter from Papun to join Kyin Pe in Rangoon for a series of four meetings spread over ten days. In comparison with the 1963 peace-parley after the 1962 coup, Skaw Ler Taw found the 1960 talks 'very informal'.[42] On the army side were Brigs. Aung Gyi, Aung Shwe and a number of junior officers, including Col. Maung Maung, whom the KNU had briefly held in custody in 1949 and who was now used as the army's main spokesman. Their tone Skaw Ler Taw remembered as 'surprisingly conciliatory. They spoke as military officers about to hand over power. Unlike AFPFL leaders they were willing to use expressions like "ending the civil war."'[43] But for the Karen delegation the implication was clear that by making an agreement now, the KNU's position would be immeasurably strengthened before the politicians took over again in Rangoon. On the specific question of an enlarged Karen State, army leaders gave the impression of being sympathetic to a redrawing and redefinition of territorial borders, but insisted they had no power to discuss constitutional matters. A new Karen State, they said, could only be agreed once the KNU had entered the legal fold. In the meantime, they were quite prepared to accept KAF troops and local KNDO militia, estimated by Skaw Ler Taw at 20,000 men under arms at the time, into a reformed Karen Rifles and a Special Police Reserve. This the Karen delegation rejected because, 'according to Saw Ba U Gyi's Four Principles there was no Karen State and the inference was still one of surrender.'[44] As a compromise the *Tatmadaw* team suggested the token handing over of 'one gun and one pistol' as a symbolic gesture of reconciliation, but this proved no more acceptable and the talks were called off.

It is perhaps an indication of the wide gulf Karen leaders believed still existed between the two sides that, after the delegates returned to their base areas, they did not even consider it worthwhile calling a full KNU meeting to discuss the failure of the talks.

The Return of U Nu

Back in early 1960 the future importance of the NDUF and the KNUP/CPB alliance was completely overshadowed by election fever and the belated return to parliamentary government. By common consent the general election of February 1960 was the fairest of the four conducted since independence and almost twice as many people voted as had in 1956. (The fourth election in 1990, by contrast, was carried out with Aung San Suu Kyi and many leaders of the main opposition parties under arrest and virtually all political campaigning barred.) But given the *Tatmadaw*'s claim to have restored law and order in the country and the fulsome praise heaped upon Ne Win, it was highly symbolic of the country's verdict on military rule that the 'clean' AFPFL of U Nu, who had become the caretaker administration's most outspoken critic, won a decisive victory, gaining 52 per cent of the votes cast and 157 seats in the Chamber of Deputies compared to the 'stable' AFPFL's 30 per cent and just 42 seats.[45]

Meanwhile support for the pro-communist NUF, severely damaged by internal splits and the exigencies of military rule, collapsed badly to just 5 per cent. Some NUF candidates even had to try and run their campaigns from gaol. But most likely, as Josef Silverstein points out, for most voters in the war-ravaged country, U Nu's election pledge to make Buddhism the state religion and to create new states for the ethnic minorities compared favourably with the stable AFPFL of U Kyaw Nyein and U Ba Swe, which merely promised to continue the 'work and style' of the caretaker administration.[46] U Nu himself, to the displeasure of the many military officers supporting the Swe/Nyein faction, described the election as a simple choice between 'fascism and democracy'.[47] There were striking parallels with the 1990 general election where, after a similar period of emergency military rule, the army's attempt to ensure the succession of its own preferred candidate, the National Unity Party, was overwhelmingly rejected by the people. Notably, too, as in 1990, a number of former insurgent leaders, including Thaton Hla Pe, leader of the Union Pao National Organisation (UPNO), and Nai Aung Tun, president of the MPF, won seats in Parliament, thus giving a clear boost to the ethnic nationalist cause.

Yet, despite its popular mandate, U Nu's 'clean' AFPFL or *Pyidaungsu* (Union) government, as it became known, lasted just two years. As with the collapse of the AFPFL government in 1958, various reasons can be put forward, but a major cause was undoubtedly the continued failure of a truly democratic, multi-party system of government to take root. U Nu's landslide victory meant one-party rule still continued with all the attendant personal and factional infighting within a small party leadership that had torn the AFPFL apart before.

This time a feud broke out between the 'Thakins', the old-guard more socialist-oriented veterans from the trade unions, and the 'U-Bos', a more ideologically conservative younger group who favoured individual membership to the party. In earlier days U Nu had thrived on such crises, but now in his 54th year and without the support of his erstwhile allies, U Ba Swe and U Kyaw Nyein, he suddenly appeared a very tired man, quite incapable of mediating between the two sides. With his frequent threats to resign and increasingly public preoccupation with Buddhism (in mid-1961 he even withdrew to a Buddhist retreat for 45 days), he seemed to have lost the will to govern. Many of his decisions were hasty and ill-thought out. Frank Trager called him 'disorganised'.[48] A more charitable view is that his devotion to Buddhism simply became incompatible with the hurly-burly of political life.

However, though the deficiencies in the quality and personnel of the *Pyidaungsu* administration were obvious, in the final analysis, as in 1958, the government's failure to resolve the urgent problems of the day was what caused U Nu's ultimate downfall. The same paralysing economic malaise that had enveloped Burma since independence still existed. Once self-sufficient in petroleum, fuel was now scarce with oil production having barely reached half pre-war levels; during the 1961 monsoon the government was knocked back even further by disastrous floods which left 200,000 homeless and wiped out an estimated 300,000 acres of paddy.[49]

Adding to the military's growing frustration was the continuous internal bickering of Burma's above-ground political parties which, despite grandiose schemes like the 2,000-page KTA (Knappen-Tippets-Abbet Engineering Co.) development blueprint for Burma drawn up in 1953, still seemed unable to come to terms with the country's manifest problems. A coherent economic strategy, whether encouraging the private or state sectors, had yet to be developed. 'We've had 12 years of independence,' Brig. Aung Gyi complained bitterly, 'and what have our politicians given us? We still cannot manufacture even a needle. At this rate our country will go to the dogs sooner or later.'[50]

The Revival of Insurgency
Above all, despite the well-publicised successes of the caretaker administration, there was still the civil war. This time, however, adding fuel to the situation were not only the CPB and KNU insurrections, but the fast-spreading new insurgencies in the Shan and Kachin States. These brought in their tow the explosive constitutional questions of federalism, secession and minority rights which had remained largely undiscussed during the political turmoil of the 1950s.

Paradoxically, the years 1960-2 marked one of the lowest ebbs in the CPB's fortunes in its entire 52-year history. In May 1960 the CPB CC repeated the offer of 'peace through negotiations', but this time Than Tun's 'letter from the jungle' was virtually ignored.[51] Though there were few more major losses for the PA in its remaining 'liberated zones', the CPB leadership suffered a series of rather more damaging psychological blows. In September 1960, Ma Mya Win, Than Tun's younger sister, was killed in a surprise raid on a CPB camp near Oktwin; in November Ma Hla May, wife of Politburo member, Ba Tin, and a key underground women's organiser in Upper Burma, voluntarily turned herself in. (Politburo member Than Myaing's wife, Daw Khin Gyi, had also surrendered earlier in 1960.) Much to the CPB's discomfort, on her surrender she said she 'no more believed in communism'.[52] The same month CC member Thakin Tin Mya was shot and arrested in the heart of Rangoon along with nine other undercover party members as he tried to make contact with MPs; in a coordinated operation two key operatives of the CPB's White Dove cell in Insein, which for many years had been sending secret wireless reports of army troop movements to party headquarters in the jungle, were also picked up.

The following year these setbacks continued when the CPB's veteran ABTUC organiser and candidate CC member, Mukerjee (*aka* Pyu Win), was arrested in a raid near Paungde. Meanwhile in Rangoon a belated attempt by CPB activists to revitalise the fragmented trade union movement by forming a Workers and Services Council (WSC) ended in failure when U Nu promulgated legislation outlawing the first strike organised by the WSC at the State Commercial Bank. Following Ne Win's coup virtually all the WSC leaders, including U Aung Thein, Ko Thein Aye, Ko Aung Gyi and Ko Shwe Ok, were arrested or went underground.

But though the CPB insurgency reached its quietest point since 1948, this hardly reflected the overall military situation in the country at large. During 1960/1 the KMT problem, which had always posed a far more threatening international dimension, flared back into life in the eastern hills; rumours of a plot by 'foreign powers' to 'overthrow U Nu and then draw Burma into SEATO' were not totally ill-founded.[53] There were especially angry scenes in Rangoon after a Burmese airforce fighter was shot down and its pilot, Noel Peters, killed by a nationalist Chinese aircraft near the Shan State border with Thailand. The plane was widely believed to be carrying American supplies and, despite denials from Washington, an ill-disguised American role was confirmed when it was revealed that over five tons of US-made arms and ammunition had been discovered after the capture of the great KMT bastion at Mong Pa Liao near the Laotian border the previous month.[54] Three people were killed and 52 injured in rioting which broke out after the police used tear gas to break up a massive demonstration organised by pro-CPB SUF students in front of the American embassy.[55]

In the face of a possible superpower conflict (thousands of communist Chinese troops were still pursuing KMT remnants along the Yunnan border) few politicians in Burma took the CPB's offer of a joint anti-KMT 'national' alliance seriously; once again the problem was only settled when U Nu turned to the United Nations for help.[56] Eventually, during 1961, 4,200 of the KMT's 10,000 troops still estimated to be operating inside Burma were reported to have been 'repatriated' to Taiwan through Thailand, bringing to a close the last major flare-up in KMT military activity.[57] After this, the KMT remnants of Gen. Tuan Shi-wen's Fifth Army and Gen. Li Wen-huan's Third Army, often referred to collectively as the 93rd division, degenerated into an ever more ineffectual intelligence-gathering force in strongholds along the Thai border, still well-protected by the CIA and Thai army for their anti-communist buffer role, but increasingly financing their activities in the Shan State with opium, jade, arms and other black-market trafficking.

Of equal concern to *Tatmadaw* commanders was the problem of the KMT's one-time ally, the KNU, which, far from being crushed during the caretaker administration, appeared to have emerged more ebullient than ever. It was exactly as Brig. Aung Gyi and the army leaders had feared. Indeed, the early 1960s marked one of the most active periods of the Karen insurrection as the KNU went on a sustained political and military offensive. In the 1960 election KNUP officials in the Delta urged nationalist supporters to vote, where possible, for NUF candidates, but in the Karen State KAF guerrillas disrupted the election by attacking polling booths and destroying ballot-boxes. In late 1960 and early 1961 newspapers carried daily accounts of a bewildering array of KAF attacks hundreds of miles apart: train ambushes in the Delta, naval raids off Mergui, and the sacking of government outposts in the eastern hills.[58] The offensive peaked in the most startling month of all, March 1961, when the provincial town of Penwegon on the main Mandalay-Rangoon rail-line was overrun; in three days both the Mandalay Express and an armoured train *en route* to Ye were ambushed with heavy loss of life.[59] KAF units several hundred strong were reported roving across the eastern hills; in the Delta, after an exodus of civilians into the capital, the head of the *Tatmadaw*'s Rangoon Command was forced to deny rumours that local KNDO militia were about to attack Insein.[60] In an editorial *The Guardian* of Rangoon described the complete change in atmosphere: 'Just over a year ago, the police force vindicated its valour by seeking out the rebels on its own initiative and inflicting losses on them. Since then the reports have been mainly of the police force having to defend themselves from the pressing onslaughts of the rebels.'[61]

At a press conference on 31 March, U Nu denied the situation was 'as bad as' 1949/50 and instead tried, rather unconvincingly, to blame the escalating violence on the *Tatmadaw*'s success in forcing KAF troops out of their eastern strongholds.[62] Even more alarmingly, the following month the Burmese War Office claimed to have captured documentary evidence that Saw Hunter Tha Hmwe, who still headed the KNU's governing KRC on the Thai border, had tried to 'procure arms from Formosa through Bangkok'.[63]

The result was a sustained army offensive against the KAF's Eastern Division, the *Tatmadaw*'s largest since 1955. But, though it achieved a few well-publicised successes, including the death in an ambush of the KAF Chief-of-Staff, Gen. Min Maung, and the capture alive of the KRC Minister of Forests, Mahn Shan Phale, it failed to pin down the KAF's highly mobile brigades. The KRC's headquarters at Mewaing and the large KAF strongholds at Kyeikdon and Leke, west of the Dawna Range, were captured but the local Karen garrisons and villagers, now well versed in hit-and-run warfare tactics, simply retired deeper into the forests.[64]

Refusing to acknowledge the KNU's resilience, U Nu preferred to attribute its growing confidence to the KMT's resurgence along the Thai border. To this there was some truth. KNU leaders today confirm that Dr Tsiang, Gen. Li Mi's veteran political adviser, came to see Saw Hunter Tha Hmwe during this period and the question of arms supplies and a new joint military front, involving other ethnic insurgent forces in eastern Burma, was discussed. KNU leaders freely admit that these talks were partly responsible for encouraging Tha Hmwe to go ahead with the formation of the short-lived Nationalities Liberation Alliance (NLA) of 1960-3 which, in complete contrast to the KNUP-backed NDUF, deliberately excluded the CPB (see Chapter 11). Critically, however, U Nu failed to recognise that the KRC's contact with the KMT and ill-fated NLA was the first concrete sign that Tha Hmwe was becoming disillusioned with Mahn Ba Zan and the KNUP activists who now dominated the KNU movement. Tha Hmwe's willingness to talk with the KMT simply represented the latest stage in his long-running, though unsuccessful, attempts to win aid from SEATO and the West.

It was, in fact, *The Guardian* of Rangoon that pinpointed the rather more obvious reason for the speed and strength of the KNU's revival: 'the joint KNDO-communist command... Now, we regret to say, this separateness is no longer there, and the KNDO and the Communist Party of Burma are under one unified operational command.'[65] Mistakenly, *The Guardian* speculated that the CPB was now taking control of the KNU. In fact it was the KNU, which was now by some way the stronger of the two.

The Outbreak of Rebellion in the Shan and Kachin States
Worrying as the KNUP/CPB and KNU/KMT alignments in southern Burma may have been, the new rebellions in the Shan and Kachin States were now the major cause of anxiety in Rangoon. The Shan nationalist movement had started quietly in the mid-1950s with the formation of a number of cultural associations by young Rangoon and Mandalay university students. With support from prominent Shan personalities they had begun to hold seminars and produce patriotic literature and magazines.[66] But from the foundation on 21 May 1958 of the *Noom Suik Harn* (Young Warriors), a small underground resistance group led by an ethnic Shan from China, Saw Yanda (*aka* Chao Noi), in the years 1959-61 the Shan insurrection spread with remarkable speed. Hundreds of university and high school students flocked to join the cause. Just as the growth of the modern 'Burmese' nationalist movement can be dated back to the reaction against British colonialism and the formation of the Young Men's Buddhist Association at the turn of the century, so the Shan movement can be linked to the KMT invasion and the influx of ethnic Burman troops and officials into the state.

The outbreak of the insurrection is now usually dated to November 1959 when

Tangyan in the northern Shan State was captured by a rag-tag force of about 1,000 men led by a Rangoon University science student, Chao Kyaw Tun, and a mixed race Wa-Shan, Bo Maung.[67] A hero of the anti-KMT resistance, Bo Maung had joined the rebellion along with a large body of fellow mutineers from the UMP, catching Rangoon completely by surprise: 26 government troops and officials were killed and 17 wounded in this first battle of the Shan campaign. But despite a *Tatmadaw* propaganda campaign belittling the new rebel leaders, in the following weeks the insurrection rapidly developed in the same lawless form Eric Hobsbawm describes in his classic study of peasant rebellion, *Bandits* (see Chapter 5). In some areas army spokesmen described their new opponents as warlords or opium smugglers, in others as deserters or self-seeking politicians, while more thoughtful articles in the Rangoon press uneasily noted the number of young students attracted to the nationalist cause.[68]

By 1960 spontaneous uprisings were breaking out right across the state. One young Shan leader from Rangoon University, Khun Kya Nu, who headed north from the Thai border in mid-1960 on a recruitment drive for the largest rebel faction, the Shan State Independence Army, estimates that 40,000 troops could have been enlisted on the spot if only the guns could have been supplied.[69] Though arms were few, hundreds of police, troops and government officials were none the less killed, including Hkun Shwe Htoo, MP for the southern Wa substate, and Dr Karl Herzceg of the Asia Foundation. A particular target was the government-backed All Shan State Peasants Organisation (ASSPO), 92 of whose members had been assassinated by the end of 1960. In response ASSPO leaders instructed their members, many of whom were serving as government defence militia, to lay down their arms and refuse to cooperate with the *Tatmadaw* because it had failed to guarantee their security.[70]

Then on 7 March 1961, in another spectacular attack which took the government completely by surprise, a group of young Kachin nationalists, led by another former Rangoon University student, Zau Tu, raided the treasury in Lashio and carried away 90,000 kyats. Like the Shan insurgent movement, the Kachin movement had begun as a small cell on the Rangoon University campus in the late 1950s; this daring assault, just a few years later, signalled the outbreak of the insurrection by the Kachin Independence Organisation (KIO), founded on 5 February 1961, which within a decade developed into one of the most successful and best organised of all the armed opposition movements in Burma.

In the 1948-50 period it might have been possible to write off these fresh uprisings as part of the general insurgent chaos in the country. But these new movements were quite different. Unlike the Karens, Karenni, Pao, Mon, Rakhine and *Mujahid* who had been in rebellion virtually since independence in 1948, the Kachins and Shans were signatories to and keen supporters of the Panglong Agreement. For ten tumultuous years, while the country had been locked in mortal combat, they had loyally stood by the new Union.

Their new leaders, however, were a different breed. Most had grown up since the end of the Second World War. Several of the KIO's founders were Rangoon University students organised by two brothers, Zau Tu and Zau Dan, whose father had been a Christian pastor in the Kachin-majority Hsenwi district of the northern Shan State. Making contact with their older brother, Zau Seng (a veteran of Naw Seng's Pawng Yawng rebellion of 1949/50 who subsequently joined the KNU), they quickly gathered around them other retired veterans from the *Tatmadaw* and the wartime allied forces, including such experienced commanders as N'Chyaw Tang, a graduate of Saugar Military High School in India. At the same time they quietly won the support of a number of leading Kachin intellectuals headed by Brang Seng, headmaster of Myitkyina Baptist Mission High School, whose uncle, the Lawdan *Duwa* Zau La, had been one of the Kachin delegates at Panglong. In 1958, echoing the move of the Shan leaders, Brang Seng formed a popular youth club, the Kachin Youth Culture Uplift Association; over the next few years the Kachin youth movement played an increasingly important role in galvanising anti-AFPFL and anti-Rangoon protests in the Kachin State.

Amongst the Shan leaders there were even more Rangoon University students and a striking number of former policemen, army recruits and monks, including the charismatic *pongyi*, U Gondara, in Kengtung. Like the Kachins, between 1958 and 1960 they sent a number of student delegates, including Sai Pan and Sai Kyaw Sein (*aka* Hso Ten), into the Kawthoolei mountains to meet KNU leaders. This inspired Tha Hmwe to form the NLA in April 1960, which he hoped would open a new military front in north-east Burma. Perhaps most worrying of all for Rangoon was the number of sons and relatives of the *Sawbwas* and other leading administrators in the Shan State who were now prepared to take up arms. Prominent amongst these were Khun Thawda (*aka* Pi Sai Long), whose mother was a Hsipaw princess and whose stepfather, Dr Ba Nyan, was a leading official in the state government at Taunggyi, and Khun Kya Nu, whose father, U Kya Bu, was a signatory at Panglong.[71]

Their decision to go underground had little to do with the existing insurgencies in the country. Rather, it was part of a growing sense of frustration, expressed by virtually all the minority peoples in Burma, with the progressively more centralised and Burmanised form of government in Rangoon, which they protested was taking little account of their opinions or needs. This was reflected in some heated arguments in Parliament where MPs from the opposition Kachin National Congress, which had been allied with the AFPFL throughout the 1950s, kept up a sustained barrage of protests.[72] By January 1961 even the Kachin State government felt ready to complain about the appalling condition of the state's few roads, which had steadily deteriorated since the departure of the British. On the state's only major road, the 174-mile track linking the state capital, Myitkyina, with the northern Shan State, only 27 miles had been tarred or metalled, making the road virtually impassable in the rainy season.[73] Today the situation is little better.

Though some years in the planning, U Nu's insistent pushing of Buddhism as Burma's official state religion throughout the *Pyidaungsu* government's period of office was also seen by the mainly Christian Kachin peoples as running counter to the voluntary spirit of the Union. In 1961 this undoubtedly served as a rallying cry for the KIO cause. The handing over of three Kachin villages to China the same year only compounded a growing sense of distrust and the KIO's demand for secession became a very popular cause. AFPFL leader U Ba Swe's much publicised description of the KIO as 'only a little spark' must rank as one of the greatest Burmese political understatements of all time.[74]

In legal terms the causes of the uprising in the Shan State are rather more complex and have been dealt with more fully elsewhere.[75] Like the smaller Kayah (Karenni) State, which had been in the throes of revolt since 1948, in theory the Shan State had the legal right of secession after a ten-year trial period. But, in another curious anomaly under the terms of the 1947 Constitution, many of the administrative powers in the state had been left, not to the people or the new parliamentary government, but to the hereditary *Sawbwas* and their families. As Chapter 4 explains, these rights were originally granted as an enticement to persuade the Shan leaders to join the new Union in 1948. It was therefore hardly surprising that, once independence was achieved, the *Sawbwas* came under immediate pressure (not only from the AFPFL but also from many of their own subjects) to renounce these extraordinary political powers which were more akin to the privileges enjoyed by the *Maharajahs* in India.

Nor had the Shan State, a vast highland plateau the size of England and Wales, escaped the civil war unscathed. Not only were PVOs and the CPB entrenched in small pockets (mostly in the south-west around Inle and in the north-west of the state from Lawksawk to Namhsam), but the KMT invasion had caused considerable death and destruction. Indeed, much of the trans-Salween region remained under KMT control throughout the 1950s. In 1949/50 there were also military incursions into the state by the KNU and Naw Seng's mutineers from the First Kachin Rifles (Lashio, Kuktai, Namhkam and even the state capital, Taunggyi, all at one time fell to different rebel forces); in the early 1950s the well-organised Pao insurrection, led by Thaton Hla Pe and Bo Chan Zon, took root in the mountains around Taunggyi. In fact the Pao rebellion began less as an uprising against the AFPFL than as a resistance movement against what Aung Kham Hti, chairman of the PNO, describes as the reimposition of 'feudal *Sawbwa* rule' after the British left.[76]

Consequently, by 1952, with the state under martial law and the *Sawbwa* levies quite unable to cope (despite support from hundreds of government troops moved in to protect them) a number of autonomous rights had already been prorogued. Also at this early stage, recognising the inevitable, the hard-pressed *Sawbwas* voluntarily announced that in principle they were ready to surrender their administrative powers.[77] However, only in 1957/8, as the fateful time-limit on the right of secession approached and the demand for Shan independence began to grow, were the political pressures on the *Sawbwas* intensified. Finally, at a colourful ceremony in April 1959 in Taunggyi attended by Gen. Ne Win during the caretaker administration, the 34 remaining *Sawbwas*, assuaged by the persuasive lure of comfortable pensions for life, formally agreed to sign away their rights in a Renunciation Treaty *The Nation* newspaper in Rangoon eulogistically described as the Shan Magna Carta.[78] (PNO leaders, too, who had laid down their arms one year earlier described it as the successful summation of their ten-year campaign.)

With the Shan *Sawbwas* (the most potent symbol of the historic independence of the Shan states) now officially retired, moves were immediately begun in Rangoon, reportedly instigated by Ne Win, to persuade the new Shan government to surrender altogether the legal right of secession from the Union.[79]

Few of the Shan State's estimated six to seven million people, of whom little more than half are ethnic Shans, would have defended the *Sawbwas'* right to their virtually unfettered political powers in the 1947 Constitution. These were more an outdated legacy from the days of British rule than any genuine expression of local political aspirations. Not all Shan princes were as enlightened as the Yawnghwe *Sawbwa*, Sao Shwe Thaike, who had been chosen as Burma's first president. But the constitutional changes now being rushed through by largely ethnic Burman politicians in Rangoon (which made no concessions to Karen demands during the decade-long KNU insurrection) threatened the delicate balance in the political relationship agreed by Aung San and the Union's founders in 1947 between the Shan State and the central government. In the Shan State, ethnic Shan as well as Pao, Kachin, Palaung, Lahu and Wa leaders from all political sides (not just those preparing to go underground) called for urgent and far deeper discussions on the questions of secession, federalism and the whole future course of the Union.

In the Karen State, even the official state president, Dr Hla Tun, who cooperated with the AFPFL government throughout the 1950s, complained that the powers provided for the Karens under the 1947 Constitution were insufficient, while the pro-NUF All Burma Karen Organisation stepped up its parliamentary campaign for a new census and a complete reinvestigation of the Karen cause.[80]

The same views were voiced by the leaders of ethnic minorities elsewhere in Burma who had been granted very much less in the 1947 Constitution. In December 1960, for example, the Chin Affairs Council, echoing the demand of the underground Chin National Vanguard Party, reiterated a call first made in 1958 to create a separate Chin State, including the fertile Kale-Kabaw valley which had been carved off into Burma Proper. Significantly, the Chin Affairs Council, which voted unanimously against U Nu's state religion proposal, included members of both the stable AFPFL and governing *Pyidaungsu* parties. Their grievances had a familiar ring: a lack of real autonomy and central government neglect of the hills. As they complained, not one high school had been built in the entire Chin Division in all the years since independence. Burma's 'honeymoon period' was over, warned the Chin minister, U Zahre Lian.[81]

The following year U Nu, finally keeping to a promise made as early as the Regional Autonomy Commission of 1948, announced the creation of new Mon and Arakan States, which would be completed by September 1962.[82] But in Arakan dissatisfied Muslim MPs and community leaders continued to push the demand for more Islamic rights and the legal separation of the Mayu Frontier Division from Burma.[83] Though the government was boosted during 1961 by the surrender of some 500 heavily-armed 'Rohingya' *Mujahid* guerrillas commanded by Rauschid Bullah and Mustafiz, who had remained active along the East Pakistan border since independence, many local Buddhist and Muslim inhabitants have told me that, as intra-village raiding continued, there was the very real danger of a religious explosion, the like of which Burma had never seen.[84]

Moreover, despite the surrender of U Seinda's APLP in 1958 and U Nu's promise of an Arakan State, worrying evidence began to surface that all was not well in the majority Buddhist-Rakhine community. In 1961, former Cabinet minister U Aung Zan Wai, who in 1947 had led Arakan into the Union by accepting the AFPFL's terms, warned that the 'people of Arakan had expected the government to be magnanimous' in creating an Arakan State and developing their territory at the same pace as Burma Proper.[85] But 14 years later, he wrote, Arakan was neglected, Arakanese-Burman racial tensions were rising and the people were being forced to press their demands; conflict, he warned, would result if they did not get justice.[86] In June 1960 Maung Sein Nyunt disappeared underground with 30 of U Seinda's former lieutenants to form a new separatist organisation, the Arakan National Liberation Party. Meanwhile local members of the Red Flag CPB, led by Kyaw Zan Rhee, plotted to form an independent Communist Party of Arakan, which finally came into existence on 11 March 1962.[87]

Though most of these new armed movements still posed a potential rather than a real threat, Saw Hunter Tha Hmwe and the KRC quickly seized on the possibility of a rapid expansion of Burma's insurgencies. With the eventual support of Skaw Ler Taw and the KNUP leaders, on 29 April 1960 the NLA was set up under Tha Hmwe's presidency at a meeting attended by the Karenni leader, Saw Maw Reh, and Zau Tu, Zau Mai, Sai Pan and a number of other Kachin and Shan student representatives. By early 1963 the NLA had ended in failure, but its original plan (to coordinate simultaneous Karen, Karenni, Shan, Mon and Kachin uprisings across eastern Burma and to appeal for international support) had been extremely serious in intent; in its short life the KRC was to send three NLA military columns into the Shan State to hold talks with various Shan, Palaung and Kachin rebel leaders and to offer advice and training (see Chapter 11).

The 1962 Military Coup

Such talk was highly alarming to Gen. Ne Win and his fellow army commanders, who watched with unease as ethnic leaders around the country, both above and underground, began to call for a new political dialogue. Many *Tatmadaw* hardliners felt the very basis of the Panglong Agreement was now being called into question by ethnic representatives in Parliament.

The focus of the army's concern was what became known as the Federal Movement, a discussion group begun in the Shan State in early 1960 by Sao Shwe Thaike. It is important to stress that, contrary to what Ne Win and the *Tatmadaw* leaders, the Rangoon establishment and even some Western writers have alleged, this was not a clandestine underground group of insurgent sympathisers intending to take the ethnic minority states out of the Union. Rather, it was the inception of the legally constituted Shan government in conjunction with a number of prominent politicians, MPs and individuals. It may have appeared ill-timed given the growing number of insurgencies in the country; even within the Federal Movement, there were clearly wide differences of opinion over strategy. But it was still a sincere attempt to solve Burma's problems within the constitutional framework of the law and to head off the threat of armed rebellion. According to Shwe Thaike's son, Chao Tzang Yawnghwe, who joined the Shan rebel movement from Rangoon University after the 1962 coup: 'It was a format for further discussion, and was not in any way sinister or seditious'.[88]

The National Religious Minorities Alliance, set up at the beginning of 1961 to oppose U Nu's state religion legislation, was the earliest indication of a growing cooperation between ethnic minority leaders. It included Christian, Muslim, Animist and even Buddhist representatives, mostly from the Shan and Kachin States. But the first real evidence of the support the Federal Movement commanded came in June/July 1961 at a minority people's conference in Taunggyi staged by the Shan leaders, Sao Shwe Thaike and Sao Hkun Hkio, a former AFPFL Foreign Minister. Of the 226 delegates, who included Kachins, Karens and Chins, only three expressed any reservations and this only was to urge greater diplomacy for fear of upsetting the military.[89]

Their solution was ambitious: a looser 'federalised' form of constitution with powers shared equally between the minority states and the Burman-majority areas. These, they proposed, would now have to be reconstituted as one: a single 'Burma' state with powers no different from any of the minority states. This, they argued, would guarantee both greater self-government for each nationality and prevent the monopolisation of all political and economic power by the centre in

Rangoon.[90]

Any such solution was anathema to Ne Win and the *Tatmadaw* leaders who, in over a decade of constant fighting under their slogan 'One Blood, One Voice, One Command', had come to see themselves as the lone protectors of the Union's national integrity and the Federal Movement as merely another guise for the insurgents' separatist demands. None the less U Nu, always a pragmatic politician who saw little harm in talking, agreed to meet the leaders of the Federal Movement and finally, in mid-February 1962, after several delays, a 'federal seminar' began in Rangoon at which the ethnic minority leaders were at last allowed to put their case.

U Nu never gave his reply because, in the early hours of 2 March 1962, on the eve of his scheduled speech, troops surrounded all the key points in the city and Ne Win once again seized power. This time even tanks were used. Unlike 1958 there were no doubts about his motives. It was a coup, pure and simple.

Though some historians and politicians still look for other reasons for the coup (ideological, personal or economic), it is unnecessary to look further than the words of the coup leaders themselves. At 3 a.m. on the morning of the coup Ne Win told the Chin minister, U Zahre Lian, who had been picked up and taken to army headquarters: 'Federalism is impossible; it will destroy the Union.'[91] A few days later Brig. Aung Gyi, the main spokesman for the new Revolutionary Council, was even more explicit: 'We had economic, religious and political crises with the issue of federalism as the most important for the coup.'[92] With one eye still on the country's insurgencies, Burma, he explained, could not afford 'such a luxury as federalism'; the chaos in neighbouring Laos, he claimed, would only be repeated in Burma.[93]

Many, indeed most, observers say Ne Win got it completely wrong. U Nu has since said that in the speech he was preparing to deliver to the federal seminar, he had no intention of giving in to any secessionist demands. But given the scale of the conflagration then enveloping Burma's Indo-Chinese neighbours, the breakup of the Union was undoubtedly a powerful motivating fear, which was borne out by the *Tatmadaw*'s immediate actions. In the aftermath of the coup the predominantly leftist or socialist leaderships of the AFPFL and NUF were at first largely ignored. On the night of the coup only U Nu, his Cabinet ministers and the leaders of the federal seminar were arrested (Sao Sailong, the Kengtung *Sawbwa*, was even seized from his hospital bed) and most, like U Nu, spent the next five years in detention. Sao Wunna, the Kayah (Karenni) State chairman and Burma's longest-serving Cabinet minister, was charged with being part of a 'feudalist conspiracy' to bring about the secession of the minority states from the Union. For weeks photographs of arms and ammunition, allegedly seized from his home, were reprinted in the army-controlled press in a clumsy and unconvincing propaganda campaign. In this the 'feudal' *Sawbwas*, a largely retired and inchoate amalgam of unlikely political personalities, were painted as the real villains of Burma's history:

> Like vampires thriving on the blood of others, the *Saophas* [*Sawbwas*] had no inclination to relinquish their stranglehold of the people. That was the real reason at the back of their demand for federalism which they did under the cover of promoting the interests of the minority nationals and their states. Their conspiracy was ultimately to secede from the Union and establish tiny independent sovereign states.... Thanks to the timely intervention of the Defence Services, the Union of Burma has been saved from

an unthinkable fate.[94]

It should be emphasised that leaders of the insurgent KNPP, which led the nationalist cause and controlled much of the Kayah State, still insist that Sao Wunna had no connection with them.[95] Moreover, Shwe Thaike's son, Mye Thaike, who was shot in the head by a soldier, was not the only immediate fatality in what is usually, but mistakenly, described as a bloodless coup. The Hsipaw *Sawbwa*, Sao Kya Seng, also mysteriously disappeared after being stopped at an army check-point near Taunggyi, where dozens of other Shan leaders were being rounded up.[96]

On the other hand, some claim the charges against the Federal Movement were just a pretext. Certainly Sao Hkun Hkio, who spent five years in solitary confinement without trial, believed this.[97] 'It is most incredible,' claims Chao Tzang Yawnghwe, Mye Thaike's brother, 'that those from the West writing about Burma should, like parrots, repeat the charges made by the coup-makers of 1962 and other Burmese against the Federal Movement'.[98] Having briefly tasted political power once before, so this thesis runs, Ne Win and the army strong men were simply anxious for more.

Historically it is a convincing argument. Their movement may have crept up virtually unnoticed by Burma's politicians of the 1950s, but the military tradition they now espoused was a powerful one, dating back across the centuries from the founder of the modern *Tatmadaw*, Aung San, to the all-conquering Burman monarchs, Alaunghpaya in the 18th century and Anawrahta in the 11th. Ignored by his political rivals in Rangoon, Ne Win had been quietly building up his reputation as an international statesman, visiting the Soviet Union in 1961 after successful trips to China, the USA and Great Britain.

Any doubts about the historic scale of the army's plans were soon dispelled. One month after Ne Win seized power, Brig. Sein Win, another much-decorated BIA veteran from the Second World War, explained the coup was just 'the second half of a revolution' that had begun with the struggle for independence; the *Tatmadaw*'s job would now be 'to transform the society to socialism'.[99] 'We are just Burmese revolutionaries and socialists who are keeping pace with history', claimed the manifesto of Ne Win's new creation, the Burma Socialist Programme Party.[100]

Thus just a decade and a half after Thakin Soe, Than Tun and Burma's 'communist' revolutionaries had taken up arms with the declared object of wresting power from the country's democratically elected government by force, their longtime military opponents but former comrades-in-arms, Ne Win and the leaders of the *Tatmadaw*, had themselves succeeded in seizing power.

They, however, were dressed in the new garb of 'socialist' revolutionaries.

PART THREE
INSURRECTIONS IN THE NE WIN ERA

11

Military Rule and the Peace Parley

One of the many paradoxes of the 1962 military coup is that, far from offering a solution to Burma's political violence, it both poured oil on the flames of the country's ethnic insurgencies and, in effect, restored the CPB to its former position as Burma's leading opposition party. Once again Thakin Than Tun and the CPB's struggling leadership were to enjoy a degree of national credibility that had eluded them ever since the caretaker administration.

At a stroke Burma's political landscape was transformed and, in many ways, simplified. With the AFPFL and all other above-ground opposition parties outlawed, national party politics, as in the turbulent days of 1948-52, once again became characterised by armed struggle, this time developing into a largely three-cornered battle between the *Tatmadaw*, the CPB and the different ethnic armies. In fact, until the democracy uprising of 1988, the only other political force of any significance to enter the national arena was U Nu's short-lived Parliamentary Democracy Party which, with the help of the KNU, tried to overthrow the government in the early 1970s.

The coup undoubtedly took the country by surprise. What was perhaps most remarkable at the time was the confidence of Ne Win and the members of his Revolutionary Council (RC) who had seized power. Like the AFPFL government of 1948, Burma's new rulers were a group of close friends rather than representatives of the country at large. Army commanders still in the field later admitted they were baffled by news of the military crack-down in Rangoon. But, as Josef Silverstein comments: 'From the outset the coup leaders never seemed to doubt the legitimacy of their actions.'[1]

Saw Maung and the Ne Win loyalists who led the bloody coup of 1988 still claim the army is the only force in Burma historically incapable of political bias. But back in 1962, while invoking the legacy of Aung San and the *Tatmadaw*'s role in Burma's wartime resistance, army officers had already turned their backs on one of the key principles of their founder, Aung San. Ne Win ignored the crucial fact that Aung San himself had made the highly symbolic decision in 1945 to resign from the army and lead the independence struggle from the political front benches. Rather than being a continuation of Burma's struggle for freedom, the military coup was thus a political deviation.[2]

The Structure and Character of the BSPP

The extraordinary way in which a mishmash of selected Marxist, Buddhist and nationalist principles were hastily cobbled together in the *Burmese Way to Socialism* has already been described in Chapter 7. But the BSPP's hazy rhetoric never disguised the military foundations of Ne Win's rule. A few writers, historians and political scientists, most notably Robert Taylor, have tried to place the *Burmese Way to Socialism* in a Burmese political and historical context and, as a result, have often been quoted in the army's defence.[3] Certainly Ne Win will leave a mark on Burma's history as large as Alaunghpaya, Bodawpaya or any of the other all-conquering Burman monarchs. Those close to him confirm his keen regard for history.

But Ne Win's reforms eventually resulted in an army-dominated state that owed more to decidedly 20th century forms of political repression than to any uniquely Burmese socialist Arcadia. If there was any 'socialism', it was the national socialism he had gleaned as a *Thirty Comrade* in Imperial Japan. In the face of countrywide rebellion and such obvious ethnic, cultural and political diversity, any notion of Aung San's 'unity in diversity' or 'federal' democracy was abandoned; instead security became the government's major concern. For a quarter century Ne Win followed a very simple, twofold strategy: he concentrated on building up a highly centralised system of administration from the centre in Rangoon while, in areas of rural insurgency, carrying out relentless counter-insurgency programmes in a bid to crush armed opposition once and for all.

In neither task was he particularly successful. At the time of the 1988 coup a third of the country was still affected by the insurgencies and in vast ethnic minority areas central control was negligible. But if the pace of the *Tatmadaw's* 'socialist' revolution appeared surprisingly laconic, this is not to doubt the far-reaching purpose of Ne Win's reforms. It took until 3 January 1974, after a much disputed national referendum, for a new Constitution to be introduced.[4] But Ne Win's chosen vehicle for reform, the BSPP, was announced as early as July 1962 and the *Tatmadaw's* new ideology was contained in two major policy statements published during the first year of military government: the *Burmese Way to Socialism* and *The System of Correlation of Man and his Environment*.[5] At the same time a historical institute was established and a highly partisan study, *The Roots of the Revolution*, published; this highlighted the army's role in Burma's national liberation struggle.[6] The flimsy principles outlined in these thin tomes were never enlarged upon. They were collectively written and no literature ever developed to suggest Ne Win was in any way a Burmese Mao, Tito or Castro.

From the outset, the army ensured its political control of the country by establishing dozens of identical 'security and administrative councils' led by serving or retired military officers. These spread from Rangoon into the minority states and rural countryside and ranged from the state or divisional level to the village tract. As an added safety net, agents of the omnipresent Military Intelligence Service (MIS, *aka* Defence Services Intelligence), from an interconnected web of specialist police, economic and army security departments, were infiltrated into every walk of national life. Then, as the BSPP slowly began to evolve, even the BSPP's administrative districts were set up to run parallel to the divisions of the *Tatmadaw* command. Thus, the local regional commander, whether setting rice quotas or co-opting porters to carry supplies, has always had the last word.

Moreover, while BSPP-led mass worker and peasant organisations were being built up to replace the disbanded trade unions of the 1940s and 1950s, the BSPP itself continued to be dominated by the military. As late as 1972, ten years after the coup, over half the BSPP's 73,369 full members still came from the army or police.[7] In recent years, given the large numbers of veterans from the standing army of 190,000, it is hard to find a more accurate breakdown, but the same military predominance prevails. In fact, rather than implying the overthrow of the BSPP government, the 1988 coup simply reasserted the army's existing control; the country's new military ruler, Gen. Saw Maung, was the BSPP's last Minister of Defence. Indeed, only one civilian of any note, Dr Maung Maung, ever served in the higher ranks of the BSPP. Virtually all other Cabinet, state, divisional and even ambassadorial posts were held by military officers. From the mid-1970s they usually officially 'retired' from the defence services before taking up these positions; this unsubtle sleight of hand was continued by the avowedly 'civilian' National Unity Party led by ex-army officer 'U' Tha Kyaw, which Ne Win loyalists formed in October 1988 after the collapse of the BSPP.

Under the BSPP the military was also able to extend its control over the national economy. Though with its lucrative banking, shipping and commercial interests, the Defence Services Institute was the largest of the nationalised domestic enterprises, the thousands of shops and small or large-scale businesses the state now took over were also supervised by serving or retired military personnel. Hundreds more military officers were appointed to the senior ranks of the now purged Civil Service.

The same totalitarian safeguards were written into the 1974 Constitution. A 'socialist society' was declared the 'goal of the state', but at the same time the principle that Burma become a one-party state was enshrined as the country's main article of faith (Article 11). Though there were clear guarantees for the basic rights of all citizens before the law 'regardless of race, religion, status or sex' (Article 22), the exercise of any such rights must not be 'to the detriment of national solidarity and the socialist social order' (Article 153b). Moreover, though the seven largest minorities were now apparently recognised by states of their own (Chin, Kachin, Karen, Kayah, Mon, Rakhine and Shan), the unitary structure of both the BSPP and government put an end to all discussion of rights of autonomy, secession or independent political representation. Just seven years after he seized power, Ne Win proclaimed his vision of the united, harmonious nation he was creating: 'Our Union is just one homogeneous whole. A Chin, for instance, can go wherever he likes within the Union and stay wherever he likes. So, too, a Burmese. Everyone can take part in any of the affairs, whether political, economic, administrative, or judicial. He can choose his own role.'[8]

These words cannot, however, disguise the enormous changes Ne Win sought to impose on Burma's cultural and political life. It was as if the country had entered a 26-year sleep walk. As Ne Win gave full vent to his latent xenophobia, Burma overnight became one of the most isolated and hermetically sealed countries in the world. Not only was travel abroad prohibited except for a privileged few, largely the military élite, but any international influences were abruptly shut out.

Even horse-racing was banned, though in a curious insight into Ne Win's mentality, he remained an avid racegoer on his frequent trips abroad.

The first international organisations to be singled out and expelled in 1962 were the Ford, Fulbright and Asia Foundations, long suspected (in some cases correctly) of covert CIA or SEATO activities. During the following years all foreign journalists and missionaries were banned and the few tourists admitted each year were restricted to 24-hour (later seven-day) visas. Even the strategic Rangoon-Mandalay highway project being planned with a resumption of US aid was halted. Then, after the 1964 nationalisation of virtually all foreign (largely Indian and Chinese) and domestically-owned companies and businesses, there was a mass exodus from the country of the last remaining foreign businessmen. Significantly, one of the few foreign companies allowed to keep its trading links was the West German manufacturer, Fritz Werner, which for many years remained the *Tatmadaw*'s main source of arms and military technology.

Even teaching English, in one of Asia's most literate countries, was drastically curtailed; in 1966 Rangoon University's English chair was abolished and, with the 1965 nationalisation of schools, full weight given to Ne Win's highly 'Burmanised' view of Burma's diverse cultures and history. Eventually in 1979 Burma left the Non-Aligned Movement as a protest against superpower manipulations (this time Soviet). In this one area, at least, even Ne Win's sternest critics gave him credit, for his determined and skilfully charted neutralism undoubtedly kept Burma, unlike Thailand, Laos and Cambodia, from being dragged into the Vietnam War.

This, however, is only the external face of the land that became known as the 'Albania of Asia'. In the final analysis Ne Win's rule was built on a climate of fear. Internal opposition or dissent, whether from the political left or right, was ruthlessly quashed. At least five officers from the original 17-man RC, Brig. Aung Gyi, Col. Saw Myint, Col. Maung Shwe, Col. Kyi Maung and Col. Chit Myaing, were later arrested. Ne Win has never hesitated to imprison even the closest of his former comrades, the two Gen. Tin Oo's, later Minister of Defence and MIS chief respectively, being the best-known among them. (The former, after his release in 1980, became chairman of the National League for Democracy (NLD) in 1988, but was arrested again the following year and sentenced to three years hard labour; the latter was released from gaol in 1989 in what appeared to be part of an internal power struggle between the new MIS chief, Khin Nyunt, and Ne Win's military old guard.) Fittingly, one of the almost forgotten RC members Ne Win had imprisoned, Col. Kyi Maung, emerged from retirement many years later to lead the NLD to victory in the 1990 general election after Tin Oo, Aung San Suu Kyi and the other senior NLD leaders were arrested. Within four months, however, he was once again arrested.

This stultifying fear of Ne Win still permeates even the top levels of the army leadership. Whether through higher salaries and pensions or access to restricted goods sold at subsidised prices, under the BSPP and its SLORC successor the military has in general represented the only really privileged class in Burma. Insulation from the worst hardships of Ne Win's rule was perhaps one of the main reasons why the 1988 crisis crept up on the *Tatmadaw* commanders so unexpectedly. Several times different army units, including MIS, have been purged without explanation, but only one serious plot against Ne Win has ever been publicly confirmed when in 1976 a number of senior officers were arrested and their leader, Capt. Ohn Kyaw Myint, sentenced to death for planning to assassinate Ne Win and the country's leaders. (Another assassination plot was uncovered the following year, this time organised by Rakhine and Karen nationalists led by Mahn Ngwe Aung, a Rangoon University graduate and former BSPP township chairman, but his scheme did not closely involve the military.[9])

Generally anti-intellectual, the army has thus become a largely self-supporting organisation that stands apart from the rest of society and recruits from the rural peasantry and, to a lesser extent, the urban working class. Army leaders have denied this. 'The *Tatmadaw* does not constitute a separate class. We are of the working people,' claimed Brig. Thaung Dan in 1965.[10] But as many village boys have told me, entry into the army provided their only means of escape, social elevation or simply making a living. Predominantly Burman (especially at the officer level) it still forms the bedrock of Ne Win's support.

As a result it has always been Ne Win's civilian rivals who have aroused the army's deepest suspicions. In the immediate aftermath of the 1962 coup only U Nu's ministers and the representatives of the Federal Seminar were arrested. But in the following months the net was spread ever wider. Ne Win's repression was nothing if not systematic.

Ne Win's Political Crack-down

The first to feel the cold winds of change were the country's student activists who since the 1920s had stood in the forefront of political protest. This time when demonstrations broke out on the Rangoon University campus, the *Tatmadaw* replied with horrific force. On 7 July 1962 troops were sent in after students took control of the university in anti-army protests that had begun over the introduction of new campus regulations. Volleys of gunfire echoed around the campus as troops repeatedly shot from close range into the massed ranks of young demonstrators. In a final contemptuous act early the next morning, troops dynamited the student union building, which had been the focal point of Burma's freedom struggle since the 1930s. The explosion was heard over the entire city. The RC later claimed only 16 protesters were killed and 41 wounded (Ne Win called them 'saboteurs') but many eyewitnesses put the final death toll much higher.[11] Survivors still believe there were as many as 300 casualties and claim a number of students were still inside the union building when it was blown up.[12] In a tragic forerunner of the events of 1988, many of the students of the 1962 generation never met again. When the universities finally reopened later that year, several hundred were missing. The rest were presumed dead, in prison or underground, largely with the CPB or Karen National United Party (KNUP). Over the next two years virtually the entire executive councils of RUSU and ABFSU joined the CPB, along with Khun Thet Lwin (an ethnic Pao), president of the Ethnic Students Federation. Others student leaders, such as present-day KNU members, Mahn Sha La Pan and Thamain Tun, joined rebel Karen forces in the Delta.[13]

As Ne Win alleged, pro-CPB activists led by SUF chairman, Ba Swe Lay, had undoubtedly been involved in the earlier protests, but many of those who took part deny they initially had any interest or involvement in the communist cause. 'The army had to blame the CPB. It was the only justification they could think of,' said Dr Marta, an eyewitness to the killings and a member of the students' Karen association.[14]

In rare displays of disunity over the last few years arguments have broken out between Aung Gyi, Sein Lwin and other army leaders over who actually gave the orders to kill unarmed students. Aung Gyi, who originally took the blame, now accuses two former colleagues, Cols. Than Sein and Kyaw Soe, for using explosives, though it would seem obvious that Ne Win, as head of the RC, should take ultimate responsibility.[15] Certainly since 1962 the army has never hesitated to use live ammunition to put down street protests, while in up-country areas soldiers have always had free use of their guns. The undeniable fact remains that the violence of the army assault on Rangoon University was premeditated and this one act cast a dark shadow over the entire era of BSPP rule which will never be forgotten.[16]

This by no means marked the end of the crack down on students. When protests started again later that year, the universities were again immediately closed and, in another clear anticipation of 1988, were only reopened following a near yearlong interval after a new system 'based on socialist moral values' had, according to Education Minister Col. Hla Han, replaced one that 'was a legacy of the capitalist colonial past'.[17] For the next few years student activists continued to organise secretly on different campuses around the country, especially in Mandalay and Rangoon, though with ever increasing difficulty under the watchful eye of the MIS. But by the mid-1970s, following the disturbances that broke out over the army's handling of the funeral of former UN Secretary-General U Thant, student movements in the country were at a virtual standstill and strictly for the foolhardy or extremely brave. For the CPB and most ethnic insurgent groups a vital source of recruits and support had been cut off.[18]

Since that time education has undeniably been used as a political weapon in Burma; under reforms introduced in the 1970s it has become increasingly difficult (and not only for financial reasons) for students from up-country areas to travel. At the first sign of disturbances schools and universities are immediately closed. As with economic development, ethnic minority students feel they are discriminated against the most. In the war-torn ethnic states, with the later exception of Moulmein College, not only are there no universities (only state colleges) but very few local scientific, educational, cultural or development projects have ever been established. The school system has thus been used as another means of social control and the last quarter century has seen a remarkable decline in educational standards in what was once one of the most literate countries in Asia. This is something the present generation of students deeply resent. Under the BSPP Burma twice won UNESCO prizes for special literacy campaigns; but in 1987, in a typical manipulation of statistics for which the BSPP became notorious, the previously reported literacy rate of 78.6 per cent was startlingly dropped to an appalling 18.7 per cent, largely to comply with the strict conditions for admitting Burma to Least Developed Country status at the UN.[19] The true figure no doubt lies somewhere in between.

Ne Win's next major target was the above-ground opposition. When the BSPP's formation was announced, his original intention appeared to be have been much broader: to create a single party which would bring together the interests of the *Tatmadaw* with those of the three major legal parties: U Nu's *Pyidaungsu*, the Swe-Nyein 'stable' AFPFL and the NUF. Success, however, was limited and it was only from the NUF (and from only a handful of leaders at that) that he found any takers. Their inspiration was Ne Win's radical vision of an all-encompassing *Burmese Way to Socialism*. Former CPB members or communist sympathisers,

Thein Pe Myint, U Chit Hlaing, U Saw Oo (ideology), U Ba Nyein (economics) and former rebel PVO leader Bo Htein Lin, all fluent in Marxist terminology, were persuaded to join *Tatmadaw* commanders, Brig. Tin Pe, Col. Kyaw Soe and Col. Than Sein to develop the language of the BSPP's socialist doctrine.[20] The captured CPB CC member, Thakin Tin Mya, also joined the BSPP and another CC member, former *Thirty Comrade* Bo Ye Htut, who surrendered in 1963, was appointed as an instructor at the BSPP's main training school; the former RF CC member, Daw Saw Mya, who also joined the BSPP, was posted to the Central People's Workers' Council. The result was an unlikely mix of personalities. Even the former rebel PVO chief, Bo Po Kun, was appointed ambassador to Thailand, while his former comrade-in-arms, Bo La Yaung, another *Thirty Comrade*, was given a job at the Trade Ministry. But a former *Tatmadaw* officer (he requests anonymity) whom Ne Win ordered to sit in on these meetings to keep watch on U Ba Nyein, plays down their importance: 'Ne Win was just using them. He was very good at manipulating people to make use of their skills.' They were, however, not chosen at random. These men were all ethnic Burmans, highly patriotic, anti-AFPFL, on the political left and, perhaps most importantly, supportive in the following years of Ne Win's preoccupation with agricultural rather than urban development programmes.

It should be added, then, that these former communist supporters were not the only ones initially taken in by Ne Win. According to the Buddhist monk, the Ven. U Rewata Dhamma, secretary of the International Burmese Buddhist *Sangha* Organisation, who then had close ties with the military:

> Many people supported Ne Win when he first seized power. Many were fed up with U Nu and the way he had played around with issues like the ethnic minority question. They liked the idea of a strong ruler who promised change and who could solve all their problems. It was rather like Hitler in Germany. The trouble with Ne Win is that, whatever his intentions, power (it was never money) corrupted him.[21]

For most neutral citizens the shootings at Rangoon University brought any early optimism to an abrupt end; when other political leaders, alarmed at Ne Win's continued accumulation of power, continued to baulk, the arrests soon started again. In August 1963, when the country was still gripped by excitement over the peace parley then underway in Rangoon, most of the remaining leaders from the stable AFPFL and *Pyidaungsu* parties were detained. They included many of the key figures and friends who had guided the country through the first turbulent years since independence, men such as the socialists, U Ba Swe and U Kyaw Nyein, the former Justice Minister, U Khin Maung Latt, and the ex-PVO Cabinet Minister and *Thirty Comrade*, Bo Min Gaung. Three months later, after the peace talks broke down, Thakin Lwin and the leaders of the BWPP and NUF were also picked up along with three more of the *Thirty Comrades*, Bo Let Ya, Bo Ba La and Bo Htauk Htain. These arrests in Rangoon were followed by the detention of hundreds of NUF leaders and supporters across the country and many spent years in gaol. In a disturbing warning of things to come, no reliable army statistics were ever released. But according to one rough estimate from press clippings, over 4,500 civilians were arrested during 1962/3 under the RC's emergency legislation, most of whom came from the three main 'legal' opposition parties.[22] Finally, on the symbolic anniversary of the outbreak of the CPB insurrection, 28 March 1964, all opposition parties were banned altogether.

Until 1988 Ne Win only once appeared to deviate from his totalitarian course when, in an unexpected move in 1968, he set up the short-lived Internal Unity Advisory Body. Consisting of U Nu and 32 other political and ethnic leaders from the 1950s who had just been released from gaol, their brief was to put forward to the RC their own suggestions for constitutional reform in the cause of national unity. Their recommendations, however, which largely reiterated the call for a return to 'federalism' and the 1947 Constitution, were all summarily rejected.[23] Shortly afterwards U Nu took the opportunity to slip out of the country to begin his own armed insurrection.

Similar pressures were brought to bear on the press which, despite growing political interference during the last days of the *Pyidaungsu* government, until then had remained relatively free from censorship. One by one newspapers were closed down and dozens of writers and journalists, including U Law Yone, the internationally respected editor of *The Nation*, were gaoled. Then in 1964, following the introduction of the government's own news service and the publication of its two official mouthpieces, the *Forward* weekly and *Working People's Daily*, all the remaining independent papers, such as the pro-communist *Kyemon* and pro-Soviet *Botahtaung* of Thein Pe Myint, were closed down and nationalised. From over 30 daily papers at the time of the 1962 coup, by the 1980s only six were left, all printed in Rangoon. Following the 1988 coup the number shrunk even further to just two, the Burmese and English-language editions of the *Working People's Daily*.

The same restrictions were placed on libraries and publishing companies. Publications or press scrutiny boards enforced tough regulations under the 1962 Printers and Publishers Registration Law, which governed not only the text, language and subject of new books and journals but even the number of copies printed. This resulted in a plethora of privately-owned magazines containing only short stories, for these were easier to replace if rejected. All were for entertainment; no news periodicals were permitted. Over the years the same laws were extended to film, music and video companies.

Ethnic minority writers struggling to expand the production of books in their own little-published languages were immediately hit by these draconian measures. Licences to print the country's remaining Chinese and Indian-language papers were discontinued in January 1966. Instead, following the nationalisation of schools, successive BSPP administrations embarked on what ethnic minority leaders allege was a straightforward policy of Burmanisation. Even now minority languages are rarely taught or used beyond the fourth grade in school; ethnic minority publications are restricted to little more than folksy, housewife magazines, such as the Karen *Our Home* and *Go Forward*. The distribution of religious literature, including the Bible, has also been restricted and BSPP officials and censors have complained to Christian pastors about the militant language of the Old Testament which, they claim, is an incitement to rebellion.

Nor did the Buddhist *Sangha* escape Ne Win's reforms. The first restriction was on the number of Buddhist holidays, which many agreed were an impediment to national progress. In 1962 all Buddhist monks were also ordered to join a national register. When large numbers refused, the RC created the All Buddha *Sasana Sangha* Organisation, which, at a conference of 2,000 monks at Hwambi in March 1965, compliantly agreed that the issuing of ordination certificates was not contrary to the teachings of Buddha. This sparked off mass demonstrations in towns across the country. In Mandalay young monks ransacked and destroyed the local BSPP offices; in response the army arrested over 100 monks and closed down several monasteries.[24] After this clamp-down organised protests by the *Sangha* subsided, though monks were again prominent in the street demonstrations surrounding U Thant's funeral in 1974. But it was not until the late 1970s that Brig. Sein Lwin brought the clergy under the control of the Ministry of Home and Religious Affairs as part of a relentless BSPP campaign against endemic corruption in many local monasteries.

In his defence, it can be argued that from the beginning Ne Win had been wary of the resentment caused by U Nu's state religion campaign of 1960/1 and was determined to put Buddhism on a par with the country's other religious faiths. The reaction in the Kachin State, where violent disturbances had broken out, showed that religion was a potentially explosive issue. But whatever his reasons, the result was the same. As the *Tatmadaw* set about building the BSPP and its own mass worker and peasant organisations, the monks, like all other organised sections of the community, were excluded from any political input.

However, the extraordinary restructuring of Burmese society Ne Win embarked on in 1962 must be seen as (indeed often only makes sense as) another corollary to the long war against the country's diverse insurgent armies, which the *Tatmadaw* continued to attack at every opportunity throughout the military crackdown in Rangoon. Similarly, despite the arrests of U Nu and former adversaries in the AFPFL, there was no let-up in attacks on the government by the CPB, KNU or other armed opposition groups.

Within two years Ne Win was to try and mobilise the whole country behind a determined national campaign to crush the insurgencies once and for all. But first in 1963, just as he attempted to engage sympathetic elements on the left in a constructive dialogue, he also appeared ready to talk with rebel leaders.

Despite the continued arrest of hundreds of above-ground opposition leaders, the almost forgotten year of 1963 in fact saw the lowest level of insurgency in any year since independence.

The 1963 Peace Talks

The peace parley of 1963/4 is very much a part of both the armed opposition's and the *Tatmadaw*'s set-piece histories, with each side continuing to repeat its own well-rehearsed version of events. The *Tatmadaw*'s view has been reduced to accusing its opponents of 'insincerity' and 'duplicity', while surviving opposition leaders claim that the talks were only a pretext to buy time and justify the *Tatmadaw*'s escalation of the war.[25] 'The negotiations failed,' claims Mon leader Nai Shwe Kyin, who was part of an NDUF delegation that included the CPB, 'because the *Tatmadaw* only wanted us to surrender. Our troops would have to go and gather in one place. They would surround us and we would have to ask permission to move. We wouldn't even have been allowed to contact our own people.'[26] According to KIO leader Zau Mai: 'They were very good at "Divide and Rule". They were good students since they had learnt it from the British. But whatever they said, all they were interested in was our surrender.'[27]

But certainly back in 1963 Ne Win appeared to think he might be able to win over a number of top insurgent leaders. The talks, the RC explained, were agreed to for two reasons, to 'liberate the working masses' from '15 years of insurrections' and to allow underground organisations that 'professed a belief in socialism to participate sincerely in the building of the socialist society in the Burmese way'.[28]

Ne Win personally wrote to Mahn Ba Zan and the leaders of the socialist KNUP (which included a number of troops from the wartime BIA in the Delta) whom he thought might be sympathetic. Describing the '14-year civil war' as a 'disaster for our country', he warned that the 'real peace which is demanded by the people cannot be established alone... only through mutual cooperation and personal relationships'.[29] 'I've taken hold of the tiger's tail and I can't let go,' he later told Mahn Ba Zan in Rangoon. 'Please help me.'[30] Ironically, after the talks had finished the only group that actually laid down its arms was the smaller Kawthoolei RC faction led by the previously condemned 'rightist' Saw Hunter Tha Hmwe who, in an extraordinary about-turn, became lauded in the state media as a 'true revolutionary' and 'patriot'.[31] The KNUP and CPB, by contrast, both of which denounced Ne Win as a 'fascist', were vilified.

Thus different accounts of the peace parley need to be approached with caution, for there has been a good deal of historical rewriting. The later vitriol of *Tatmadaw* reporting contrasts with the good humour and optimism of the time. In its latest version the *Tatmadaw* even claims that the first peace talk overture came not from the RC at all but the CPB (on 8 May) because of fears that the recent surrender by Bo Ye Htut might lead to a series of mass defections from its ranks.[32] In fact the CPB had previously sent Bo Ye Htut on a secret peace mission into Rangoon before the 1958 split; his surrender this time, as events soon violently demonstrated, reflected a growing divergence in the CPB leadership over political strategy.

Karen leaders take a different view. They argue that what really encouraged Ne Win to agree to peace talks in 1963 was the split in the KNU movement in April that year (at the Third Kawthoolei National Congress near Papun) into KNUP and KRC factions. This, they say, local army commanders immediately urged Ne Win to exploit. It is certainly a convincing argument. Since 1960 the KNU had steadily expanded its territory and, with backing from the NDUF and NLA united fronts, was Burma's largest insurgent organisation, with base areas stretching from the Arakan Yomas in Burma's far west across the Delta into the mountains of the south-east.

Ultimately, it is best to conclude, a combination of unusual circumstances in 1963 led Ne Win to give the peace talks the go-ahead. The first indication of his change of heart was the announcement of a general amnesty on 1 April 1963. Then, after a visit to Rangoon by the Chinese head of state Liu Shao-Chi, several leading officials surrendered, including Bo Ye Maung and Bo Sein Tin, along with Bo Ye Htut from the CPB's central military committee. The substance of Liu Shao-Chi's talks is undocumented and *Tatmadaw* leaders deny that any external pressures were brought to bear, but these two crucial events so shortly after the amnesty call undoubtedly encouraged Ne Win to continue. The news of the split in the KNU, the CPB's main ally, would have put the final card on the table.

The peace talks also brought in groups from different parts of the country, such as the Communist Party of Arakan (CPA), which had no connection with either the KNU or CPB. Leaders of these groups say that as far as they were concerned the real trigger for the peace parley was the RC's surprise announcement on 11 June of its willingness to meet representatives of the armed opposition. Crucially, they noted, there were firm guarantees of a ceasefire and safe passage to and from their jungle bases. This satisfied all their previous demands and there appeared to be no pre-conditions. At the same time, they admit, like leaders of the CPB and

KNU, many of them incorrectly interpreted the RC's offer as a sign of Ne Win's weakness and thought he was desperate for a solution. Now satisfied that there was something to be gained from talks, virtually all (eventually 13 in total) the country's diverse insurgent forces agreed to join the peace parley in the capital. The CPB's main requirement, that its long-distant comrades in China should be allowed to join it for the duration of the talks, was acceded to through an exchange of letters, with the obvious complicity of Beijing.

The first preliminary delegation to arrive in Rangoon was from the Red Flag CPB at the end of June, led by Politburo members Kyaw Win and Daw Ngwe Zan, wife of the Red Flag leader, Thakin Soe. But for most citizens the first hint that anything special was in the offing came with the arrival in Rangoon during July of two CPB delegations by air from China, led by former *Thirty Comrade* Bo Zeya and CC members *Yebaw* Aung Gyi and Thakin Pu. With them they brought radio transmitters and other Chinese aid and equipment, finally quashing any remaining doubts over Chinese support for the CPB. (A third delegation, led by Ba Thein Tin, arrived at the beginning of September bringing the number of 'Beijing returnees' to 29.) Members of these teams were then granted permission to travel on to meet Thakins Than Tun, Zin and Chit at the CPB's central head-quarters in the foothills of the Pegu Yomas near Paukkaung for a historic CC meeting which for the first time in nearly 15 years reunited the CPB leadership. For the party's battle-weary veterans it was a rare, euphoric moment.

While they were still talking the start of the first peace parley was announced to the Burmese people with the news that a 20-strong Red Flag team headed by Thakin Soe had arrived in Rangoon from Arakan on 10 August. For the next few days they were taken on tours of state-run enterprises around the city and visited friends and relatives, including the leader of the now-revived Internal Peace Committee, Thakin Kodaw Hmaing. From the first, however, Thakin Soe cut something of a tragi-comic figure after what *The Guardian* of Rangoon quaintly called his 'hibernation in the jungle'.[33] The Red Flag's main demand was for free elections. But seated behind portraits of Stalin, as he railed against the 'revisionist' Krushchev and 'opportunistic' Chinese, Soe appeared more than a little out of touch. After just three meetings the RC accused the Red Flags of 'amazing effrontery' and abruptly called the talks off. The very next day on 20 August the Red Flag team were dispatched back to Sittwe by air to disappear once again into the deep forests of the Arakan Yomas.

The abrasive failure of these talks set the tone for other negotiations now under way. Some of these talks began with local army commanders in up-country towns such as Lashio and Loilem and continued sporadically over the next few weeks. But all, save the Kawthoolei RC whose Education Minister Saw Ba Tun was already in Rangoon, ended in failure. Ne Win himself met several of the delega-tions but most of the talking was done by other RC members, particularly Colonels Hla Han and Saw Myint, who were then very much in favour.

Continuing Rangoon's ingrained habit of playing down ethnic minority questions, the nationalist delegations received little analysis in the state media at the time. The delegations given least attention were the Shan State Independence Army (SSIA); Shan National United Front (SNUF); *Noom Suik Harn* and Tailand National Army teams headed by Khun Thawda (sometimes meeting with the RC alone, sometimes jointly) which put forward the demand for a federal state system (10 August-27 December); a KIO team in Mandalay under another former

Rangoon University student, Zau Dan, which argued for an independent Kachin State with rights of secession and self-determination (31 August-15 November); and the CPA whose chairman, Kyaw Zan Rhee, demanded a 'Republic of Arakan with the right to secede from Union of Burma' (18 July-18 November).[34]

None of these demands, opposition leaders claim, were treated seriously by the RC. Veterans of these talks, though many have never met, are unanimous that they were given only the option of dissolving their forces and integrating with the BSPP. None admits to being surprised or disheartened by the outcome and leaders of all three parties claim they were only too glad to benefit from some rare, if scant, publicity for their causes which saw the rapid expansion of their forces after the talks broke down. Both the KIO and SSIA recruited large numbers of high school and university students in the following year. From their dismissive attitude at the time, it would appear that *Tatmadaw* commanders underestimated both the popularity of the insurgents' demands and the military potential of armed nationalist movements to continue their extraordinary growth.

In 1963, however, these meetings were overshadowed by the RC's talks with the CPB and its NDUF allies, the KNUP, Karenni National Progressive Party (KNPP), New Mon State Party (NMSP) and Chin National Vanguard Party. The KNU had met briefly with U Nu and Ne Win in 1949 and again with army commanders in 1960. But this time, after sending a preliminary 'tripartite peace mission' team into Rangoon from the Delta under the KNUP's general-secretary, Bo Kyin Pe, representing the KNUP, KNPP and NMSP, the KNUP Politburo decided to meet together with the NDUF as one team. All parties agreed they wanted to present a strong united front.

But first, while their negotiating team was still assembling from different base areas in the country, on 28 August an eight-man CPB delegation headed by CPB general-secretary, *Yebaw* Htay, and including the PA's Chief-of-Staff, Bo Zeya, *Yebaw* Aung Gyi and Thet Tin, arrived in Rangoon to an excited welcome from their families and above-ground supporters. Then, after a press conference by *Yebaw* Htay on Rangoon radio on 2 September in which he refused to be drawn into any political comment on the RC but reiterated the CPB's long-held position that its insurrection had started in self-defence, the talks began in earnest.

Between 2 September and 31 October the RC had eight official meetings with the CPB, and between 8 October and 14 November seven with the NDUF. The CPB team was also augmented by the arrival in Rangoon on 20 September of another CC delegation including Bo Yan Aung, *Yebaw* Mya, *Yebaw* Toke, Bo Myo Myint and headed by Politburo member, Thakin Zin, who was then secretary of the NDUF. But as with the previous talks of 1949 and 1960, these meetings never really got beyond the stage of discussing ceasefire details. This had caused the failure of the previous talks and has jeopardised every meeting since. Recognising this intransigence, the KNUP's record of the peace parley confirms just how low the NDUF felt forced to set its objectives. In its own pre-meetings with the CPB it agreed on a four-point opening strategy: to show we want to establish real peace in the country; to demonstrate we really want a ceasefire; to show we have enough strength to face the enemy; and to create mutual understanding on joint military committees and territory.[35] According to the CPB's present chairman, Ba Thein Tin, it was over this last issue that the talks finally broke down after the RC put forward four conditions the CPB rejected as 'unreasonable and unjust': All CPB troops must be concentrated in designated areas; troops must not leave these areas without permission; all CPB organisational work must stop; and all CPB fund-raising must stop.[36] The KNUP's report, invoking the memory of all those who had 'sacrificed their lives for the revolution', gives the same reasons:

> As the RC keeps on demanding our unconditional surrender we cannot accept it. If we follow the RC's demands to stop all our organisational work it means that we must abolish our Party. If we follow the RC's demand to stop our administration it will mean that we must hand over all our territory to them. And if we follow the demand to gather all our troops in one place then it will mean they can crush us any time.[37]

From Ne Win's viewpoint, however, there was still a fear that an official cease-fire would mean the partition of the country, as the RC's final report specifically warned had happened in Korea and Vietnam.[38] Here ceasefires had meant the acceptance of well-defined base areas where 'insurgents' had been able to consolidate their administration. In 1963 the map of Burma would suddenly have looked very different; vast areas of the country, beginning at Rangoon's doorstep, would have disappeared under a chaotic mosaic of colours.

Thus once it became clear, contrary to Ne Win's expectations, that none of the parties were prepared to join the BSPP, there was nothing left to discuss. This, however, was by no means the end of the peace parley story. All the surviving but scattered veterans of these talks to whom I have spoken confirm that once they arrived in Rangoon they realised the talks were going to be a largely cosmetic affair. They therefore decided to use their time to meet family and friends. Many were immediately struck after their long years in the countryside by the degree of resentment that already existed against the RC. The KNUP's official report, for example, listed a number of reasons why Rangoon residents were predicting a workers' uprising, including shortages of goods, a thriving black market, lack of press freedom, the *Tatmadaw*'s conflicts with students and monks, widespread dislike of the RC's nationalisation programme and the army's growing 'monopolisation' of all walks of life. The CPB and NDUF delegates thus wasted no opportunity to broaden their political contacts.

Certainly no side comes out of the peace process particularly well. In calling the talks off on 14 November, the RC accused the NDUF of 'lacking honesty and sincerity' and of using the ceasefire as an opportunity to continue 'setting up a parallel government' in the country; the NDUF, on its part, discovered the RC was bugging its private conversations.[39] The NDUF also accused the army of carrying out military operations during the ceasefire period, while several troops, including an army major, were killed by the NDUF in Henzada district in what Ba Thein Tin insisted at the 1980/1 peace talks was only a 'counter-attack'.[40]

But from the RC's viewpoint, undoubtedly the most worrying development was the 100-mile Six-District Peace March from Minhla to Rangoon in early November; it was this which precipitated the peace parley's sudden end. According to eyewitnesses, thousands of spectators gathered along the way to chant anti-government slogans. Even more ominously for the army, speakers at the mass rally (estimates of the crowd were as high as 200,000) at the end of the march in front of Rangoon's City Hall publicly supported the NDUF's demand to be allowed to keep its weapons and territory.

Ostensibly these demonstrations were organised by the People's Peace Committee supported by the above-ground NUF, but both NDUF and CPB officials, despite their denials at the time, now admit their involvement. Using the freedom of the city, the CPB delegates had been able to meet many of their underground sympathisers. On his arrival in Rangoon *Yebaw* Htay embarked on a flurry of activities, visiting the leader of the peace movement, Kodaw Hmaing, before going on to the Martyr's Mausoleum to lay a wreath at Aung San's tomb. In the following days he also met ex-Brigadier Kyaw Zaw (now a CPB CC member), the relatives of students who had joined the CPB, the leaders of various ethnic and opposition parties (including the BWPP) and the presidium of the NUF at its headquarters in Lewis Street. Here he was reported as saying the amnesty had no relevance for the CPB: 'It's something only for criminals to take advantage of.'[41] Then, on 10 September after reading a personal letter from Than Tun, the NUF issued a statement (which the *Tatmadaw* now says was actually drafted by the CPB official, *Yebaw* Ba Khet) identifying itself with the CPB's views on the best ways to achieve internal peace.[42] From this point on, while the peace parley continued in secret, the People's Peace Committee held nightly meetings in Rangoon and dozens of other towns up and down the country to encourage the drive for a political solution.

The army since claims to have captured documents proving that, before the talks even began, CPB leaders cynically decided at a Politburo meeting on 18 August to use this 'peace offensive' simply as a tactic in its long-term strategy to seize power.[43] Again this kind of analysis underestimates the genuine hopes for peace in Burma and the spontaneous reaction of peoples around the country once news of the peace parley became known. In fact much of the support for the peace committees came from ethnic minority leaders who are invariably written out of the *Tatmadaw*'s account. KNUP, KRC, KNPP and NMSP delegates were also able to resume underground contacts with Mon and Pao leaders who had surrendered in 1958. Indeed one of the main organisers of the Six-District Peace March was also one of Burma's most experienced politicians, wartime Cabinet Minister and former president of the insurgent Pao National Organisation (PNO), Thaton Hla Pe, who was twice offered the presidency of the KNU in 1950. After 'coming into the light' with the PNO in 1958 and winning a seat in the 1960 general election, Hla Pe had allied with the NUF but remained secretly in contact with his former allies in the KNUP and KRC. Former insurgents from the Mon People's Front (MPF), angered by the arrest and imprisonment with U Nu of their leader, Cabinet Minister Nai Aung Tun, also lent their support and in Moulmein the Peace Committee was especially active where it was headed by another former Mon rebel, Nai Non Lar, who after his release from gaol many years later became chairman of the NMSP.

The Peace Committee's mobilisation on this scale presented the RC with its greatest threat. With the support of veteran national leaders like Kodaw Hmaing and Kyaw Zaw, much of the liaison work was carried out by younger NUF activists, including present NLD member U Tun Tin (who had been imprisoned during the caretaker administration) and former rebel PVO Bo Mya Thwe. Despite the events of 1962, RUSU and ABFSU students, as one might expect, once again played a leading role; they distributed over 100,000 bags of rice donated by various monasteries and well-wishers to the peace marchers on their tired arrival at the university campus in Rangoon. Only at this point, according to former RUSU leaders, did CPB student activists (including Red Flag supporters) try to mingle with the marchers. In fact, reflecting the ground swell of support for peace, this mammoth feeding operation was carried out by a coalition of student fronts from very different political backgrounds, including the Ethnic Students

Federation.[44]

When the Rangoon peace march finished, another mass peace rally was scheduled in Mandalay for the following weekend, at which Thaton Hla Pe was again expected to speak. Few observers were surprised when the army moved in on 14 November before it could take place and the peace talks, including those with the CPA and KIO, were summarily called off. Hla Pe was one of over 900 people, mostly from the BWPP and NUF, who were arrested in the following days; having closely watched the activities of the peace committees, MIS agents knew exactly who they wanted. On 15 November, the day after the talks ended, Nai Non Lar and the MPF leaders in Moulmein were all picked up and many spent years in gaol without trial.[45] Again the *Tatmadaw* released no reliable information on the true numbers arrested, but by the end of the year it was generally accepted that over 2,000 NUF supporters, including dozens of trade union leaders, had been imprisoned. Ironically, many of these were the very people with whom Ne Win originally appeared to believe he could work. To complete this whitewashing of history, in the army's subsequent accounts of the events of this period the popular role of the peace committees and the NUF was virtually expunged.

Tragically, in the ruthlessness with which all political opposition was systematically teased out and ground down and hundreds of political opponents arrested, killed or forced underground, there can be seen clear precedents for the army's actions in the aftermath of the 1988 coup as another new restructuring of Burmese society was begun. Indeed many of the key players (Ne Win, Sein Lwin, Dr Maung Maung and Aung Gyi) were exactly the same men who had engineered the events of 1958-60 and 1962-5.

In 1963, however, the army did not get everything its own way. With the breakdown of the talks fighting immediately resumed. While Ba Thein Tin flew back to China, the NDUF delegates, separating into four teams, left Rangoon on 15 November: the NMSP to Moulmein, the KNUP and KNPP to Toungoo, and the CPB to Taunggyi or Paukkaung. Written in to the terms of the ceasefire agreement was a three-day pause before either side recommenced military actions. But on 17 November 1963 the KNUP and KNPP teams, which had flown into Toungoo with Thakins Zin and Tin Tun of the CPB, were followed and attacked in a combined operation by three army regiments. They only narrowly escaped ambush. Across Lower Burma and into the eastern hills fighting immediately resumed in the same depressingly familiar pattern.

This time, however, for both the *Tatmadaw* and the CPB there was one major difference. In addition to the long-running rebellions of the CPB's NDUF allies in Lower and Central Burma and the splintered insurgencies of the Red Flags and Rakhine communists in Arakan, they now had to contend with increasingly well organised nationalist insurgent movements in the Shan and Kachin States. Indeed in just one decade Burma's forgotten north-east was to become the largest and most important battlefield in the civil war.

Domestic and international press coverage of the rapid escalation of fighting in the north was, however, completely overshadowed by another unexpected crisis, namely Mao Zedong's Great Proletarian Cultural Revolution in neighbouring China. Within two years this was to be bloodily re-enacted on the streets of Rangoon and in the jungles of the Pegu Yomas with dire consequences for the CPB and the entire communist movement in Burma.

The Surrender of the KRC

Before proceeding, in the RC's defence it should be added that there was one eventual success from the peace parley process, i.e. the 'surrender' in 1964 of Saw Hunter Tha Hmwe's KNU Kawthoolei RC faction (though this was so loudly trumpeted at the time it obscured just how few Karen rebels actually came in). The KRC defection, however, sowed the seeds for a complete east-west split in the KNU movement, much to the *Tatmadaw*'s advantage, which has never been properly overcome; for this reason it requires some further explanation.

Even today the KNU movement is still astonished by Tha Hmwe's surrender. Of all the Karen leaders he, the president of the KNU's governing KRC, was regarded as the most fervent nationalist. Even some of his closest ex-colleagues describe him as a 'racialist'; in a famous article he once wrote: 'U Nu is as cunning as Stalin, Ne Win as shrewd as Lenin.' But in what appeared to be a remarkable volte-face at the beginning of the talks, Tha Hmwe called Ne Win the 'Father of Peace'. Mika Rolly, who was a member of the KRC delegation in Rangoon, has a more straightforward explanation. '*Moosso* [Tha Hmwe] was simply tired. He did not think we could win without foreign aid. He had tried everything possible but never succeeded.'[46]

KNU veterans now date the beginning of Tha Hmwe's doubts to the aftermath of the KNU's 1956 Second National Congress, at which he set up an underground Karen 'embassy' in Bangkok. For KNU guerrilla fighters long isolated in the jungles of Burma, the political atmosphere across the border came as a shock. At the time Thailand, under growing US pressure, was ineluctably being drawn into the Indo-China conflict and was in the grips of cold war paranoia. As the headquarters of SEATO, established in 1954, Bangkok was awash with various American, CIA and KMT agents. Here the Karen team was surprised to find that the KNU's recent agreements with the CPB and adoption of the Second Phase Programme were already well known and being treated with some concern. American analysts had the somewhat bizarre idea that the KNU's declaration of a Free State of Kawthoolei fitted into a grand communist strategy, orchestrated by China, to overrun South-East Asia by declaring 'autonomous nationality regions' across the mainland peninsula.[47] Tha Hmwe travelled to Bangkok several times to meet various American, Thai, KMT and SEATO officials to ask for arms. But after one trip he warned the KRC: 'Unless we change our line we will get no help. The quickest way to get help will be to drive out the left leaders.'[48]

His plea, however, fell on deaf ears. His irritation with the KNUP grew by the day as he found himself increasingly outfoxed by its leaders who, in the manner of any other Marxist-Leninist vanguard party, would meet in advance of KRC or KAF conferences to draw up their own plan of campaign. A particularly bitter argument broke out after the First KNUP Congress in January 1959, at which the KNUP drew up a draft Constitution for the KNU with a new order of hierarchy: the KNUP at the top as the 'élite party of the Karen revolution', an elected political and military council representing all KAF military brigade areas to supervise the administration of party policy, the KNU as a 'mass organisation' and, at the bottom, the KRC as a central governing body for handling day-to-day affairs.

The rift between Tha Hmwe and the KNUP then widened with the formation in 1959 of the NDUF, though, in deference to his objections, the KNU's name was kept out of the final treaty of 16 May. If the NDUF accounted for many of the Karen nationalist movement's military and political gains in the early 1960s, the

KNUP's open alliance with the CPB now brought to the surface much of the unease felt by Karen community leaders at the time of the adoption of the Second Phase Programme. While KNUP members were already in control of most of the key military and administrative positions in the KAF's Delta Division, in the Eastern Division (and especially on the governing 25-man KRC) the balance was more delicately poised. With constant transport and communication difficulties and long delays between district meetings, the KRC, the one central KNU body that met with any regularity, had itself in many respects begun to take on the public character of a political party, sometimes taking up positions quite different to the KNUP. This was an experience later repeated by a number of emergency administrative bodies established by other insurgent fronts in Burma, such as the Tailand RC (established by the Shan United Revolutionary Army/Shan United Army) today. Tha Hmwe now began to share much of the more fundamentalist Christian and Buddhist Karen leaders' disillusionment in the Second Phase Programme; ironically he had at first been one of its most enthusiastic supporters. In particular, Tha Hmwe grew increasingly critical of his old comrade, Mahn Ba Zan. In many ways the two men, both devout Christians, cut a striking contrast: the Sgaw Karen, Hunter Tha Hmwe, an impassioned orator and populist leader, who described himself as a 'capitalist' as against the Pwo Karen 'socialist', Ba Zan, a stoic, cautious politician who relied on the importance of party organisation.

But for the sudden outbreak of rebellion in the Shan State during 1958/9, which introduced an unexpected new dimension to the war with Rangoon, this might well have marked the end of Tha Hmwe's protest. However, after a stream of visits to the KRC's headquarters in the east by young Shan leaders allied with Chao Noi's *Noom Suik Harn* and the arrival of Kachin student leaders from Rangoon, Tha Hmwe was encouraged to form the Nationalities Liberation Alliance (NLA) of April 1960 (see Chapter 10). As he explained at its founding meeting, the new front would be quite separate from the CPB-backed NDUF and would not contain a 'Burman' component. The plan he then proposed was remarkable in its breadth, no less than the annexation of the entire east and south-east of Burma by simultaneous ethnic nationalist uprisings. These, he was convinced, would gain outside support.

Though evidence to support this remains circumstantial, Tha Hmwe always inferred he was acting on foreign advice. The KRC's former general-secretary, Skaw Ler Taw, described the NLA as 'more or less a CIA plan'.[49] Certainly after his surrender in 1964, Tha Hmwe spoke enigmatically of the failure of the KRC's efforts to work with both 'leftist' and 'rightist' groups and the 'colossal expenditure' of maintaining representatives in Bangkok.[50] The chosen intermediary was again apparently the KMT, long the CIA's secret arm along the border which during the late 1950s enjoyed a short revival of arms supplies from Formosa; the KNU now freely admits to having had this contact. It would appear, however, that with the second KMT evacuation in 1961 this plan, if indeed it was ever very far advanced, was immediately suspended.

If Tha Hmwe's initial hope was to open the door to Western aid, it is significant that he was also able to get support from KNUP leaders who considered that CPB attempts to organise among ethnic minorities in North East Burma were unlikely to succeed. Tha Hmwe in fact called the NLA's founding meeting without first informing his KNUP colleagues, but the NLA's military programme was drawn up by Gen. Kaw Htoo, head of the KNUP's military bureau, and the political line by KNUP/KRC general-secretary Skaw Ler Taw. Skaw Ler Taw saw no contradiction between the KNUP's support for both the NLA and NDUF: 'In trying to overthrow a common enemy we need the unity of all revolutionary forces. The NLA was based on nationalism, the NDUF on class and we had to recognise many nationalities did not trust the communists.'[51] Thus with Tha Hmwe as president and the Shan student leader, Sai Kyaw Sein (Hso Ten), as secretary, the NLA was formally inaugurated in a small ceremony on 29 April at the KRC's headquarters near Papun; the Karen, Karenni, Shan and Kachin delegates then proceeded to the KAF's 5th brigade headquarters in the Thaton hills for a grand May Day reception (see Chart 2).

Despite this optimism the NLA swiftly proved a failure; certainly its military activities, initially worrying as they were to Ne Win, were completely lost sight of amidst the political turbulence in Rangoon. From the beginning Tha Hmwe appeared to have fatally miscalculated the strength of the *Noom Suik Harn*. Three military columns were sent north. The first was a battalion from Bo Lin Htin's 5th brigade, but after crossing into the Kayah State the column was tied down by just two sections of local Kayah police and, suffering heavy casualties, was forced to withdraw. A few months later a combined 3rd/7th brigade force led by Ba Shine (an ex-Karen Rifles commander) followed and this time, avoiding government outposts, was able to cross into the Shan State. Here it found the fracturing of the Shan nationalist movement, which has continued ever since, already under way; most of Chao Noi's student followers had already left his headquarters at Pieng Luang on the Thai border and headed north to form a new organisation, the SSIA. Instead Ba Shine was able to make contact in the south-west of the state with another new faction (the SNUF) and a number of joint operations were carried out in the Mong Nai/Wan Salong area. But after a year in the north amidst the continuing splits and feuds of the Shan movement, Ba Shine decided to return.

Tha Hmwe had one last try. With the outbreak of the Kachin rebellion in February 1961, the KNDO's veteran underground organiser, Mika Rolly, was sent north to try and make contact with the Kachin leaders. Travelling with 300 troops via Chao Noi's headquarters at Pieng Luang, Rolly proceeded north with a small detachment (holding talks with Palaung and Shan rebel groups along the way) before finally reaching the KIO's forest headquarters in the hills above Lashio.[52] Rolly had no idea what to expect. Originally he had hoped to meet Naw Seng, the KNU's ally in the battles of 1949, but now he found Naw Seng had remained behind in China. Instead he met Zau Seng and Zau Tu, two of the three brothers then leading the KIO. A number of outline agreements were reached but both parties recognised that, with the Kachin rebellion just beginning and several hundred miles separating the two forces, the KIO could be of no real help. Rolly thus returned in early 1963 (at the same time as Ba Shine) to find events now overtaken by the decisive and final split between Tha Hmwe and the KNUP, which for a time threatened to destroy the entire Karen nationalist movement.

This long simmering dispute finally broke into the open at the Third Kawthoolei National Congress in April 1963, at the KRC's Kasawa camp in the hills one day north of Papun. This was to be the first full KNU Congress since the adoption of the Second Phase Programme in 1956. Now, in the aftermath of Ne Win's coup, 1963 was a year with change in the air and Tha Hmwe made no secret of his objectives. As KRC president, he explained, he had called the Congress to repeal the ideological basis of the Second Phase Programme. However, 1963 also marked the high point in the KNUP's leftward swing and while the KNUP/Tha Hmwe faction balance on the 25-man KRC remained uncertain, KNUP domination of KNU organisation in the Delta was by now complete. On the eve of the Congress the KNUP held its own Second Congress and, with the arrival of KNUP delegates from the Delta, Tha Hmwe knew he would be defeated before the Congress had even started. A total of 58 delegates, representing all the KNU districts in the Delta, Pegu Yomas and Eastern Division, were able to attend.

In his opening address Tha Hmwe called for the abandonment of the KNU's 'anti-imperialist line' and urged the Congress to look to the West for friends and aid. The KNUP representatives immediately rejected this, as did most of the other delegates from the east, including the Papun-Paan 7th brigade commander, Bo Mya. An argument then developed over the definition of the 'enemy' of the Karen people. Tha Hmwe wanted 'the Burmans', the KNUP favoured 'Burman chauvinism', a term Tha Hmwe considered synonymous with communist ideology. As the atmosphere deteriorated there was a brief discussion about dividing up areas of influence to prevent a complete breakdown, but on the third day Tha Hmwe and 11 supporters on the KRC walked out and moved camp a few miles to the west (into Lin Htin's 5th brigade area) where they formed a new organising committee. Several attempts were made to persuade them to return and the possibility of forming a third 'neutral' party headed by Skaw Ler Taw from the KNUP and Mika Rolly from the Tha Hmwe faction to heal the rift was briefly discussed. Each time Tha Hmwe adamantly refused to return and eventually, on 24 April 1963, the Congress continued without him.

The withdrawal of Tha Hmwe's supporters left 13 members on the KRC, a majority of just one. All were KNUP CC members. The remaining Congress delegates decided that, by its actions, the Tha Hmwe faction had effectively forfeited its position on the KRC and no longer had any right to use its name.[53] Somewhat confusingly, however, until his surrender the following year, Tha Hmwe did continue to use it and his group became known in the Rangoon press as the 'KRC' party.

Now, without Tha Hmwe's opposition, the Congress quickly ran through a list of motions and reports, which were virtually the same as those presented to the KNUP's Second Congress the previous month; in the Congress minutes the identities of the KNUP, KNU and KRC are virtually indistinguishable. The KNUP had in effect taken complete control of the KNU movement. But in view of the Tha Hmwe defection, in a long analysis of the Karen revolution, it was felt necessary to add a historical explanation as to why the KNUP had been formed:

> In 1947 the Karen National Association, the Buddhist Karen National Association, the Karen Youth Organisation, and the Karen Central Organisation came together as the Karen National Union to forge national unity. But though the KNU was formed, its foundations were still not firm and did not reach all levels of society. To reach the lowest level and to be deeply rooted amongst the Karen people we needed to form an élite party. That is why we decided to form the KNUP.[54]

Revealingly, the KNUP also added what was to be the clearest statement of its adoption of a communist ideology, carefully expressed in terms which neither challenged the role of the CPB as Burma's sole proletarian party nor weakened the KNU's nationalist platform: 'For the progress and development of the Karen people we accept Marxist-Leninism as our guiding principles. But we do not accept the KNUP as a workers' party but as a nationalist party for the progress and development of the Karen people.'

The nationalities question is discussed more fully further on in this account, but it is worth emphasising that, even at this stage, there was never any suggestion of forming a Karen Communist Party. Indeed of all the areas of ethnic insurgency in Burma, only in Arakan, where social and political conditions are closest to those in central and Lower Burma, have such 'nationalist' communist movements really taken root.

Gen. Ne Win moved quickly to take advantage of the KRC split. Even before the final break the RC in Rangoon seemed aware of the deep disagreements within the KRC leadership and, most unusually, no late dry-season military offensives were launched during March and April to try and disrupt the Congress. The split occurred in mid-April 1963; the first peace overtures followed on 11 June. This presented the Karen leadership with a dilemma. To discuss the proposals the KNUP sent a delegation to talk with the KRC leaders still staying with Lin Htin near Thaton. At first Tha Hmwe rejected any possibility of negotiations with the RC. But while the KNUP delegation was still at Lin Htin's camp, a new delegation sent by Ne Win and headed by Maxie Po Thein, a prominent above-ground Karen leader, arrived carrying gifts and supplies (including two elephants) and a personal invitation for Tha Hmwe to go to Rangoon. After talking all night, Tha Hmwe agreed to go but proposed that the KRC and the KNUP go separately. (The KNUP now sent a radio message to the KNUP Delta headquarters saying it believed Tha Hmwe had been bribed. This was intercepted by the *Tatmadaw* and Ne Win angrily denied the allegation when he later met KNUP leaders in Rangoon.)

Thus, in August 1963, two separate Karen delegations arrived in Rangoon. KNU leaders remain convinced that Ne Win's original intention was to try and win over Mahn Ba Zan and the 'socialist' KNUP leadership. In the end he netted Tha Hmwe and the nationalist KRC faction. Discussions with the KNUP and the NDUF finished within three months, but the talks with the KRC continued for over half a year.

None the less, the final peace treaty of 12 March 1964 appeared to make a significant number of concessions to the Karen cause; as it turned out it was the only 'political' settlement ever agreed between the Ne Win regime and any of Burma's insurgent organisations. Under this short-lived accord, the KRC agreed to drop any demands for the right of secession and, in return, the RC agreed to re-title the Karen State by the nationalist name 'Kawthoolei' and to introduce machinery whereby the controversial proposal to enlarge Kawthoolei to include Karen-majority areas of the Irrawaddy and Tenasserim Divisions could be considered.[55] Furthermore, to safeguard the interests of Karens living outside these areas, KRC officials would now be appointed to sit on the RC's security and administrative committees in each district and the KRC would be allowed to take part in writing Burma's new Constitution.

Tha Hmwe, at least, appeared satisfied. Speaking in Sgaw Karen on the Burma Broadcasting Service on 22 March he made a stirring call to the Karen people. Criticising the 'rightist and leftist deviations' which had divided the KNU in the past, he alluded to the Bible as the only way to peace. Since 1960, he claimed, the KRC had been following 'God's Path'; the Old Testament had shown the way to 'the Karen national revolution', while the New Testament now showed the 'way to live our life', a flattering allusion he compared to Aung San who had led the

Burmese national revolution and Ne Win who was now carrying out the 'social revolution'.[56] A few weeks later Tha Hmwe went even further and declared his complete faith in the *Burmese Way to Socialism*: 'This programme is not something new to us. We Karens have practised this kind of programme since the days of our ancestors.'[57]

Yet, despite a number of government-staged mass rallies, these exhortations met with little response from the Karen community. Of the KNU's senior leaders only a handful came in, including KRC ministers Saw Ba Tun and Phado Wari Kyaw and military commanders *Bogyoke* Ohn Pe, Bo Lin Htin and Bo Truman. Moreover, very few Karen troops followed them in laying down their arms. Of the KAF's military divisions only Lin Htin's 5th brigade in Thaton district, the 3rd battalion of Bo Truman's No.3 Nyaunglebin brigade and a few soldiers from the KRC's headquarters in Papun district surrendered (probably less than 10 per cent of all Karen forces at the time). Virtually all were from the Eastern Division; very few Karens surrendered in the Pegu Yomas or Delta Division.

But Tha Hmwe's reputation had probably already suffered irreparable damage. In February 1964, shortly before the Peace Treaty was signed, without provocation KRC troops attacked a KNUP base at Kaypu village north of Papun, in a raid apparently coordinated with the *Tatmadaw*. The 17 KNUP supporters who were killed included a veteran KNDO organiser from Thaton, CC member Ohn Pe Nyunt, who was first brutally tortured. Though Lin Htin led the raid, documentary evidence later surfaced to confirm Tha Hmwe's suspected role. The attack was designed, Tha Hmwe's opponents allege, as a demonstration by Lin Htin to *Tatmadaw* commanders that they still had not learnt how to fight the KNU. In retaliation KNUP/KAF troops led by Bo Mya attacked and burnt down a number of villages under Lin Htin's control near Thaton.

Viewed from the 'liberated zones', Tha Hmwe's defection and the 1964 peace accord never emerged from the shadow of these deaths; within months KRC supporters had begun to slip away from the towns back into their old base areas. Moreover, KRC veterans allege, no progress was ever made on the constitutional changes promised by Ne Win. According to Mika Rolly, Tha Hmwe realised his mistake within a year.[58] Tha Hmwe himself remained under virtual house arrest until his death several years later, but already in 1965 he had secretly sent Rolly back to resume contact with the KNU, the SSIA, the KIO and his other former insurgent allies.

Emerging from Rangoon, Rolly swiftly headed across the countryside to the north-east towards the Kachin hills. Much to his amazement, far from finding the insurgencies now in abate after three years' military rule, he discovered the country was besieged by a scale of local insurrections that even he, veteran guerrilla fighter that he was, had never expected to see again.

But above all, he was surprised to find that for the first time the civil war in Burma was attracting serious attention abroad. Some of this interest was coming from the USA, now deeply embroiled in the Indo-China conflict.

The first country, however, to signal its concern was Burma's great neighbour, China, which was now in the throes of the Cultural Revolution.

12

Cultural Revolution

Burma in the mid-1960s was a land in nationwide revolt. 'A Country Goes Underground', the headlines once again rang out as departing journalists filed their last
copy.[1] From Rangoon to Burma's far-flung borders a new tidal wave of insurgencies swept across the country. But this time, unlike 1948-50 or 1960/1, much of
the damage to the central government's authority was self-inflicted. As the
Revolutionary Council (RC), ever more repressive by the day, pushed through its
ill-conceived nationalisation policies, the lives of millions of citizens across the
country were badly disrupted. The years 1963-7 saw the flight of some 300,000
'Indians' and 100,000 'Chinese' from the country, few of whom were vastly
wealthy but most of whom had played the vital middle-man role in Burma's
teetering subsistence economy of the 1950s. Not only were the major export-
import businesses, such as rice, timber and oil, taken over but all department
stores, wholesalers and shops. Vital goods like medicine and petrol were now in
urgently short supply.

The Spread of a New Wave of Insurrections
Caught in the middle of these upheavals were the long-suffering Muslims of
Arakan. Many had difficulty proving any entitlement to Burmese citizenship and
feared for their right even to stay in the country. On 26 March 1963 yet another
former Rangoon University student, Muhammad Jafar Habib, reformed the
Mujahid movement under a new name, the Rohingya Independence (later Patriotic) Front, while Zafar Sani was reorganising guerrilla units amongst the Muslim
community along the Naaf River in the far north. At first working in alliance with
the Rakhine 'nationalist' insurgent fronts, the Communist Party of Arakan (CPA)
and the Arakan National Liberation Party (ANLP), but later fuelled by abundant
arms supplies during the Bangladesh liberation war, Sani's Muslim National
Liberation Party had by the early 1970s become the second largest insurgent force
in the state after the CPB.[2] And here in Arakan another underground nationalist
front, the Arakan National United Organisation (no connection to the earlier
parliamentary ANUO), was also begun in 1963 by another former insurgent war-
hero, Bo Kra Hla Aung, ex-commander of the wartime Arakan Defence Army,
who had surrendered with the PVOs in 1958.[3]
    Then, in May 1964, following the first extraordinary 'demonetisation' of the
Burmese currency which saw thousands of citizens across the country losing their
hard-earned savings, a new generation of ethnic insurgent movements rose up
overnight. Amongst those which later became better known were the Kayan New
Land Party (KNLP) in the south-west Shan State, where in early June 300 Kayan
villagers attacked the *Tatmadaw* outpost at Pekon, sparking a vicious bloodbath,

the Shan United Army (SUA) of Khun Sa in Loimaw district further north, and the Zomi National Front (ZNF), an ethnic Chin organisation, which was formed with the help of the Karen National United Party (KNUP).[4]

In the same period the insurrection of the Kachin Independence Organisation (KIO) in north-east Burma spread with astonishing speed. From small bridge-heads established in the mountains around Lashio, Kuktai and Bhamo during 1961/2, the KIO grew from a small guerrilla band of less than 100 to a highly organised army with new mobile battalions growing at a rate of more than one a year (by 1989 the KIO had 21).[5] By 1966 these had penetrated as far as Myitkyina, the Hukawng valley, the Naga hills and the strategic Kamaing jade region. Here in the Kachin hills some of the heaviest fighting in Burma occurred as the *Tatmadaw*, in an early rehearsal of its *Four Cuts* strategy, embarked on a drastic scorched earth policy. Thousands died unreported in the world outside.[6]

Further south in the Shan State the situation for the *Tatmadaw* was even more alarming. Ne Win's coup and the arrest of the Federal Seminar leaders had meant the collapse of the elected Shan administration and left the state under virtual military occupation. The death in gaol shortly afterwards of Sao Shwe Thaike only added to the growing political anger. Thousands more young Shans resolved to take up arms and on 22 April 1964 representatives of the three largest rebel Shan organisations, the Shan State Independence Army (SSIA), the Shan National United Front (SNUF) and the newly formed Kokang Resistance Force of the former MP, Jimmy Yang, agreed to join forces in the present-day Shan State Army (SSA) at the SSIA's headquarters, hidden in the mountains close to the Thai border.[7] The following month, at a secret meeting across the border in Chieng Mai, the SSA in turn formed the Shan State War Council. Headed by Shwe Thaike's wife, the former MP and *Mahadevi* (queen), Sao Nang Hearn Kham, the War Council embarked on a strategy similar to the KIO by trying to expand its forces into a state-wide organisation incorporating other rebel forces, such as Khun Sa's SUA in Loimaw, the Tailand National Army around Kengtung and the remnants of the *Noom Suik Harn* in the south.

Ultimately the SSA had less success than the KIO. There were not only local CPB and refugee KMT forces to contend with (and this was before the CPB 'invasion' of the Shan State from China in 1968) but also ethnic minority armies, such as the KIO and KNLP. The state was on the brink of an alarming political and ethnic explosion which, in its complexity, had parallels only with Lebanon. For example, in 1966 two battalions of the ethnic Palaung National Force (formed on 12 January 1963 and led by Captain Kham Thaung) serving under the SSA's 1st brigade in the northern Namhsan-Namkham districts, broke away to set up their own nationalist front. In 1968/9 these two battalions then split, the 6th under Kham Thaung and Kyaw Hla allying with the KIO, and the 5th under the three sons of the Tawnpeng *Sawbwa*, Khun Li, Khun Aye and Chao Nor Far, allying with the KMT and SSA. In 1970, however, their stronghold at Wang Mai was overrun by their PNF/KIO rivals and both Khun Li and Khun Aye were killed shortly afterwards, while Nor Far and the 5th battalion remnants were forced to join yet another force, the Shan United Revolutionary Army (SURA), in exile on the Thai border. Meanwhile, in 1976, Kham Thaung's PNF became the present-day Palaung State Liberation Organisation/Party.[8]

Local Wa, Pao and Lahu militia also began forming along predominantly racial lines and, like Khun Sa's SUA and the breakaway SURA of Gon Jerng (*aka* Mo

Heing) in the Laikha region, rejected the idea of incorporation with the SSA. In 1969 a former CPB member, Gon Jerng, allied SURA, now with several hundred troops, with the KMT remnants of Gen. Li Wen-huan's Third Army; the KMT, in turn, wore SURA uniforms on their frequent undercover missions inside the Shan State! Viewed from outside, the situation was an unholy mess.

For the RC in Rangoon, the prospect of 8,000 guerrilla fighters backed by thousands of potential new underground supporters in the towns, joining together in one powerful united force was a terrifying prospect which, in 1967, Ne Win desperately tried to defuse by allowing any insurgent or simply 'bandit' group to reform as a local *Ka Kwe Ye* (KKY) government defence militia. Free to continue policing and trading in their own areas as they saw fit, the KKY system seriously undermined the SSA's plans and several local units defected, including the SSA's 2nd and 6th brigades in Mong Leun and Monghsu districts, Khun Sa's SUA and a number of Kokangese and Wa militia. By August 1968 the RC claimed that over 1,500 Shan insurgents had laid down their arms; the following year another 863 predominantly Wa troops from 'Prince' Maha San's Ving Ngun Force followed suit.[9] Eventually over 20 KKY units were formed, but they brought hardly any decrease in the overall levels of lawlessness. Since many KKY were already financing their struggles from opium trafficking and the thriving Vietnam War arms black market, there was a huge explosion in weaponry and narcotics trading, this time by government-protected groups.

Meanwhile, many of those who had surrendered in previous amnesties began to go underground. The first were troops from the Karen National Union's (KNU's) former 5th brigade (Eastern Division) in Thaton district, who had surrendered under the 1964 KRC peace agreement. On 30 September 1965, in one of the most extraordinary moments in the history of the insurgencies, their ebullient and well-read commander, Bo Lin Htin, was lured into an ambush and assassinated by government troops. Lin Htin had been feared by military officers on both sides for his dangerous unpredictability. On one notorious occasion in 1960 he had attacked the Thai border town of Mae Sot after a dispute with local officials. In Rangoon he had grabbed the headlines by marrying a former Miss Burma who had once been romantically linked with Ne Win. The exact circumstances of his death remain shrouded in mystery, but it was little secret that before his departure Lin Htin had tried to use his SEATO, CIA and KMT contacts from his Bangkok days to approach several embassies in Rangoon, including the American and Australian ones, to try and win support for a planned anti-Ne Win coup. He had also held secret talks with a number of dissident *Tatmadaw* officers in an attempt to persuade them to join him. In 1965 the short-lived National Liberation Council (NLC) was formed in Rangoon by ex-BNA Karen officer, Hanson Kyadoe, and former *Thirty Comrade*, Bo Yan Naing, before they, too, disappeared into the Kawthoolei mountains to talk with KNU leaders and then travel on to Bangkok. If anything was agreed, Lin Htin took the details to his grave, but his plan was well known to KNU leaders, namely to establish a new base area in the remote Tavoy-Mergui districts of southern Tenasserim which, unlike the mountains along the Thai border, could easily be supplied by land and sea. Following his death, rumours swept Rangoon and Moulmein of unmarked submarines surfacing in the Gulf of Martaban and, though there is no evidence that Lin Htin ever received any official encouragement, few Karen leaders today believe it is entirely coincidental that within four years this very plan resurfaced with the NLC's successor, U Nu's

CIA-backed Parliamentary Democracy Party (see Chapter 14).

Many of Lin Htin's soldiers were ethnic Paos from the small Pao community around Thaton who, since the earliest days of the insurrections, had thrown in their lot with the KNU cause. But in the Shan State in November 1966, 84 former rebel Pao troops led by Bo San Thein (until 1958 commander of the Pao National Organisation's 'Diamond' Division in the Maikaung Range south of Taunggyi) also returned underground and began reforming their old units in protest at the RC's refusal to release Thaton Hla Pe and the other Pao leaders arrested during the 1962/3 military crack-down. This time, influenced by local CPB cadres and sensitive to the complex ethnic tensions in the state (Bo San Thein himself was assassinated by SURA in 1968), Pao villagers and farmers, undoubtedly one of the most prosperous groups in the state, joined together under a new name, the Shan State Nationalities Liberation Organisation (SSNLO). Hla Pe and his deputy, U Kyaw Sein, were not released until 1970 and did not finally reach the SSNLO's extensive 'liberated zones' until 1972. This, in turn, precipitated the bloody split in the Pao movement in 1973 into the present-day factions, the nationalist PNO which supported Hla Pe and the pro-CPB SSNLO.[10]

In the same period veterans of the Mon People's Front, most of whose leaders had been imprisoned, also began to go underground to join Nai Shwe Kyin's New Mon State Party (NMSP) in the countryside around Moulmein, many immediately on their release from gaol. From just 100 armed supporters in 1963, by 1971 the NMSP had reached its 1958 troop levels again with over 1,000 men and women in small mobile columns and guerrilla units, roving up and down the seashore.[11]

In the whole of Burma at this critical juncture only one group seemed to have any doubts about continuing the armed struggle: Thakin Soe's fast-diminishing Red Flags. On returning to party headquarters in the hills near Akyab after the peace parley, the party held a CC meeting at which it was decided to send a five-strong peace mission, known as the First Prophet of Peace, back to Rangoon. The team included Soe's wife, Daw Ngwe Zan, daughter, Ni Ni, and Gen. Kyaw Win. But they were all promptly arrested and thrown into gaol. For the next few years small Red Flag units remained quietly active in their last rural strongholds around Pyapon and Twante in the Delta, the Chin hills, Yaw township and Arakan. Eventually in 1970 the First Prophet of Peace team was released and this set the scene for Thakin Soe's own Second Prophet of Peace mission and the effective collapse of the entire Red Flag movement.

Not surprisingly, though played down in the state media, the bewildering scale of these new insurrections changed the whole pattern of the civil war and had the important effect of reducing pressure on all the insurgent forces in Lower Burma, particularly the CPB, the KNUP and a new Karen faction under the formidable hill Karen commander, Bo Mya. In January 1966, after talks with the NLC, he ordered all KNUP officers and cadres to leave his territory and, as head of the KAF's Eastern Division, seized control of the Dawna Range and much of the Thai border region (see Chapter 14). Here he began to reform the 'nationalist' KNU, rapidly building up a 10,000-strong army which was later surpassed in strength only by the CPB.

At the same time, behind the armed opposition's growing confidence and determination was the belief that Ne Win's coup and the failure of the peace parley had brought to an end the last traces of any central government legitimacy in Rangoon. There is no evidence that the military coup and the formation of the

BSPP did anything other than fuel the country's insurgencies. This is not idle speculation. In early 1966 Ne Win was forced to admit that the situation was worse than when he had seized power in 1962.[12] In October 1967, following repeated CPB or joint KNUP/CPB attacks in Lower Burma, editorials in the *Working People's Daily* warned that communist guerrilla activity had again reached its 1950 level. The next month, in an incomplete account, Beijing Radio reported a remarkable array of CPB attacks around the country. As a rare overall picture of CPB operations over a four-month period in the late 1960s, they are worth mentioning in full. Compared to today they are breathtaking in their variety: the capture of Kyauktaw town in Arakan; the death of 20 policemen in an ambush at Palaw (Mergui district) and the capture of another 12 officers near Bassein in the Delta; 'victories' by the People's Army (PA) in battles with the police and *Tatmadaw* in Minbu, Pyu and Tharrawady districts; 'guerrilla' attacks in Zigon and Minhla towns; the execution of 'reactionary' headmen and policemen in government-controlled areas around the country; and, finally, attacks on trains, bridges, roads and railway installations in regions as scattered as Yamethin, Henzada, Pyuntaza, Gyobingauk, Ye and Tavoy.[13] Moreover the reports did not mention the massive new front along the Chinese border in north-east Burma which the CPB, with Chinese backing, was now about to open up.

As in 1948-52, the question must be why was the CPB, unlike its neighbours in China and Indo-China, so unable to exploit conditions of such outright opposition to the central government? Though, like the KNU, the Shan and Kachin nationalist movements initially looked to the West for their models (in its founding statement the SSA issued a specifically anti-communist warning), few disagreed with the CPB's denunciation of Ne Win's RC as a 'fascist' regime, a definition the CPB shared with its NDUF allies. As the CPB was now the only surviving opposition force with roots in the Burman-majority population, many looked expectantly to the PA to carry the war back into the Burman heartlands.

In the final analysis the answer can ultimately be adjudged to have been a combination of three major factors. Undoubtedly one reason was the increasing effectiveness of the *Tatmadaw*'s counter-insurgency measures, particularly after 1969 when Ne Win's totalitarian reforms really began to bite. A second answer must again be the extraordinary complexity of modern Burma. Indeed within a few years the picture was made a good deal more complicated by U Nu's arrival in the countryside to build up his own CIA-backed National United Liberation Front in competition with the CPB in a bid to bring together the different insurgent armies in a broad anti-Ne Win alliance. For a few years U Nu's followers, who included many senior political leaders from the 1940s and 1950s, were able to win away several of the CPB's potential allies, including the NMSP, with the promise of arms and democracy.

Undoubtedly, too, this time many of the CPB's wounds, like those of the RC, were self inflicted. Following the rejected Browderist line of compromise in 1945 and the revisionist 'peace and unity' line of 1955, the CPB had once again misjudged the political mood of the country and was now about to make its third and, without doubt, most appalling political mistake, only this time by taking a drastic step to the extreme political left.

The Deterioration in Burma-China Relations and the 1967 Anti-Chinese Riots

CPB leaders contend that the outside world has misunderstood its so-called Cultural Revolution of 1967/8. Since 1975 its Politburo has tried to bring this bloody chapter to an official close and its worst excesses have been increasingly condemned by its leaders, though for many Burmese citizens this was still a good few years too late. However, the CPB's Cultural Revolution was not simply a blind imitation of the political witch-hunts in neighbouring China. Nor was it, as is commonly believed, instigated by the CCP after violent anti-Chinese riots broke out in Burma in 1967.

From the breakdown of the peace parley in 1963 (which China appeared not to have expected) came the first signs of the CCP's distancing itself from Ne Win's RC. Chinese leaders privately treated the RC, as a military government, with some suspicion. These doubts were not helped by the worsening Soviet-Chinese split. Not only did the Rangoon press and Thein Pe Myint's *Botahtaung* take an openly pro-Moscow line, but the Soviet Union, whilst not yet completely turning its back on the CPB, welcomed the Ne Win coup and the *Burmese Way to Socialism*. Because of Chinese influence, Moscow Radio claimed, the CPB had been unable 'to come out of the forest' and join with the 'revolutionary democrats' to 'take part in the building of a non-capitalist Burma'.[14]

Moreover Chinese fears of superpower destabilisation after Ne Win seized power were not helped by the CIA-backed KMT remnants' defiant new lease of life along the Shan State/Thailand border, especially since they had all supposedly been evacuated by airlift to Taiwan after the last United Nations intervention in 1961. Having divided their forces into two main commands (Gen. Li Wen-huan's 1,400-strong Third Army based at Tam Ngop on the Thai border and Gen. Tuan Shi-wen's 1,800-strong Fifth Army at Mae Salong), these aging anti-communist veterans plunged back headlong into the maelstrom of Shan politics. Gen. Li's troops infiltrated the heart of the Shan State on the west bank of the Salween River, while Gen. Tuan took the Chinese border to the east. But, as US military involvement in Vietnam increased by the day, the most worrying new force for Mao Zedong and the communist leaders was the 400-strong First Independent Unit under Gen. Ma Ching-kuo, which Chiang Kai-shek's own son, Chiang Ching-kuo, controlled directly from Taiwan. Quickly recruiting local Wa and Shan villagers, Gen. Ma embarked on a short-lived campaign of cross-border Intelligence gathering and sabotage which merely inflamed the political temper.[15]

Squeezed between what they regarded as Soviet 'revisionism' along China's vast northern borders and American 'imperialism' in Indo-China, Korea, Taiwan and now Burma, Chinese leaders were clearly frustrated by Ne Win's studied silence over which side the RC was going to support. Neutrality alone was not going to be enough in the face of what Chinese communist analysts described as 'superpower hegemonism'.

None the less in line with its policy of 'friendship' between the peoples of all nations, China continued to honour its aid projects in Burma (initiated after the signing of the 1960 border treaty) until the final break with Rangoon in 1967. These included the construction of several bridges and power stations and an interest-free £30m loan. Chinese officials even made light of the nationalisation in 1963 of Beijing-controlled bank assets. In 1964 Zhou En-lai and in 1963 and 1966 Liu Shao-chi both visited Rangoon; in between Ne Win visited China and, at these meetings, both sides upheld the 'five principles of peaceful co-existence'. And despite Beijing's unhappiness over a new border agreement between Burma and India in early 1967, when the anti-Chinese riots broke out in June that year, there were still 400 Chinese 'technical assistants' in the country.

To understand the real reasons behind Mao Zedong's Great Proletarian Cultural Revolution of 1966/7, China analysts have long agreed that it is necessary to look to internal Chinese factors rather than at any international or diplomatic considerations. Mao's original intention appeared to have been a ruthless purge of the party hierarchy (or indeed anybody considered lacking in revolutionary zeal) simply to put the communist movement in China back on the rails after a succession of disastrous economic and political failures, notably the Great Leap Forward. Yet, as Mao let loose his youthful Red Guards, the extraordinary events of the summer of 1967 had repercussions far beyond China's borders. Not only in Rangoon but at Chinese embassies around the world local Chinese staff, sporting their distinctive Chairman Mao badges, began distributing thousands of copies of Mao's *Little Red Book*. In London, for example, one axe-wielding diplomat caused great consternation as he took to the streets before the cameras of the world's press. But whereas in the West the local citizenry were generally bemused by such displays, in Rangoon, where a staunchly pro-Maoist group under the chargé d'affaires, Hsiao Ming, had taken control of the embassy, events took a much more sinister turn and ultimately got completely out of hand.

Two additional factors have to be borne in mind when trying to explain the extraordinary violence of the reaction in Burma. The first was the 1967 rice crisis. During late 1966 and early 1967 rice shortages, famine and growing numbers of anti-government demonstrations were reported in towns and villages across Burma. Official rice allocations were proving woefully short. Many observers felt the confrontation with China was to provide a useful distraction. Perhaps the worst incident occurred in Sittwe in Arakan where, on 13 August, troops from the *Tatmadaw*'s Twentieth Battalion opened fire on demonstrators and, according to eyewitnesses, killed or wounded 270 people.[16]

The second was the increasingly xenophobic atmosphere that enveloped the country after Ne Win's seizure of power. Once again, as in the 1930s, the 'Burma for the Burmans' call was frequently heard and, though never officially admitted, was an important rallying cry for the BSPP cause. Yet, when compared to the ethnic Indian population, Burma's estimated half million Chinese were relatively well integrated into the local community, Ne Win himself being of mixed-blood descent. However, as in most 'overseas' Chinese communities of the time, there was a political division between those who supported the 'nationalist' KMT of Taiwan and the mainland communists. One survey in 1962, for example, calculated that of the 39,000 students in the 259 Chinese schools in Burma, 22,000 attended pro-Beijing schools.[17] Following the final nationalisation of schools in 1966, Chinese embassy staff retained close contact with this exile community (particularly school pupils) and, when the Cultural Revolution started, stepped up their activities by handing out Maoist badges and literature and, in some cases, holding Maoist training classes.

When in mid-1967 these young students began coming to classes in red badges and arm bands, it was publicly taken by the RC as a provocation. A series of official and stern articles in the national press warned Chinese parents that their children must obey the laws of the land. The warnings were ignored and Chinese students, perhaps foolishly, took to the streets in protest.

No one anticipated the astonishing backlash they appeared to promote from the Burman population. This invoked memories of the worst communal clashes of the 1930s and 1940s. On 22 June Chinese buildings and property in Rangoon were looted or destroyed; over the next few days dozens, possibly hundreds, of ethnic Chinese and a number of ethnic Karens, apparently mistaken for Chinese, were killed or injured. 'I never thought I would see Chinatown take such a hammering,' said one former RC officer who witnessed the riots. Requesting anonymity, this same officer has cast doubt on how spontaneous these riots really were. He told me that at the height of the rioting he was present in a room in which journalists and army officers were spreading the news by telephone to other towns in Burma; he understood this as a deliberate attempt to spark off the other anti-Chinese riots that followed.[18] The evidence is stark; a number of Chinese community leaders accused of fomenting the disturbances were later given seven-year gaol sentences, while Khin Maung, a Burman accused of stabbing to death Liu Yi, a Chinese Embassy official, was merely convicted of 'criminal trespass' and given a three-month sentence.[19]

The violence continued for the best part of a week. On 26 June a 2,000-strong mob tore the official seal from the Chinese Embassy in Rangoon. The next day the Chinese Teachers' Federation building was burnt down; on 28 June, in another mob attack on the Embassy, Liu Yi was murdered and another official wounded. This signalled the final break in diplomatic relations between the two countries (though surprisingly Chinese aid projects were not officially terminated until October). Yu Ming-sheng, the local *New China News Agency* representative, was expelled for his alleged role in leading the students. For a few months Burmese officials continued to insist that plans for the Chinese 'revolt' had been 'drawn up in Beijing'.[20]

These killings provoked mass anti-RC rallies in dozens of cities across China. A million people reportedly attended a demonstration in front of the Burmese Embassy in Beijing, where an effigy of Ne Win was publicly burnt. In the following weeks the battle moved onto the airwaves with Beijing Radio repeatedly denouncing Ne Win as a 'Burmese Chiang Kai-shek' and accusing the RC of 'fascism', 'sham socialism', 'looting' and 'massacres'.[21]

Even more ominously, on 15 August, the CPB's founding anniversary, Beijing Radio broadcast a message of 'proletarian internationalist' support for the CPB's armed struggle. There was, the CCP announced, a 'profound friendship' between the two parties:

> It is our firm conviction that the CPB headed by Comrade Thakin Than Tun, which persists in the revolutionary line of 'to win the war and seize political power', will assuredly further unite the whole party and the people of all nationalities in Burma, overthrow the reactionary Ne Win government, and win complete victory in the revolutionary war in Burma.[22]

For the first time, the CPB's China-based leaders regularly began to appear in public at official government functions. At a memorial rally for Liu Yi on 5 July, Ba Thein Tin himself gave the keynote address.[23] The Chinese media began to praise the CPB's Maoist political line and military victories and, for the first time, gave open access to CPB spokesmen. In one report in August 1967, for example, Ba Thein Tin claimed that, with PA base areas and guerrilla zones now established in two-thirds of the country, the CPB's military offensive was about to escalate to 'final victory'. 'Extensive guerrilla warfare has besieged the country,' he declared.[24]

In fact at that very moment PLA commanders and Red Guards in south-west China were helping CPB cadres prepare Naw Seng's North-East Command (NEC), soon to launch its dramatic invasion of the Shan State from China on 1 January 1968. Godowns were hurriedly being built along the border to hold arms and other military supplies and a KIO delegation then in China (the SSA had declined to join them) was being pressured daily by CCP officials to join forces with the CPB. Zhou Enlai, who was responsible for political affairs and Lin Piao, military, both personally met KIO representatives Zau Tu and Brang Seng in their unsuccessful efforts to persuade them.

Nor was the RC totally insensitive to the forces it had unleashed. Burma, *The Guardian* of Rangoon warned, was on 'the edge of a volcano. It were all well if Maoists kept Maoism and their "God" to themselves. But, they seem to think that their "God" must be the one and only God for all mankind.'[25]

Reformation of the CPB, 'Mao Zedong Thought' and the CC's 1964 Line

In virtually all accounts of the CPB's own disastrous Cultural Revolution, the high drama of fanatical Red Guard units in China and a new CCP-backed proletarian upsurge coming to the support of communist parties in Vietnam, Thailand and South-East Asia, tends to overshadow any serious analysis of the CPB's own decisions and actions. The ruthless purges then underway in the Pegu Yomas of central Burma, though obviously influenced by events in China, began quite independently and, CPB cadres say, were certainly under consideration some time before the Red Guard movement in China. Though some contingency plans to bring the CPB closer to China had been set in motion a few years earlier and Ba Thein Tin had set up a 'coordinating committee' in Beijing with Khin Maung Gyi on his return from Moscow, enormous logistical problems hampered direct contact between China and CPB forces in Burma (except by wireless transmitter). A plan in the mid-1960s to open up a better supply route through new base areas in the western Shan State under CC member Thakin Tin Tun, who moved to the Indaw region to establish a new district headquarters, was a failure. Under attack from the *Tatmadaw* in the west, PA units found themselves hemmed in by the KMT, SSA and other ethnic nationalist forces in the east.

Thus to understand the real significance of the CPB's Cultural Revolution, CPB leaders say it is necessary to look, not to 1967, but back to 1963 and the train of events set in motion by the breakdown of the peace parley. *Yebaw* Htay's team returned to the CPB's forest headquarters in the Pegu Yomas near Paukkaung in a reflective mood: discussions revealed three major strands of thought. Bo Ye Htut's surrender earlier that year expressed a widely held view that few had previously dared state, namely, had the CPB been right to take up arms in the first place? This had been the main source of the CPB's disagreement with the BWPP and NUF in the 1950s. While not renouncing armed struggle, the 1955 line had clearly been an attempt to bridge this gap. Since 1952, many cadres argued, the CPB had been in non-stop retreat and forced to rely on opportune moments like the 1958 split.

The increasing repression of the RC and the failure of the peace parley had disabused other waverers who placed more emphasis on the struggle above ground and might have once harboured notions of helping former comrades to develop the *Burmese Way to Socialism*. This group formed a second faction (headed by Ba Tin, *Yebaw* Htay and Bo Yan Aung) which thought that the CPB should have made better use of the Rangoon talks to broaden the peace movement and work with different political groupings in the cities, rather than simply stepping up its own underground activities as an adjunct to the armed struggle. Indeed CPB defectors later claimed Ba Tin submitted his own report to a Politburo meeting on 25 December 1963 which suggested that the CPB should take some of the blame for the failure of the talks. This publicly contradicted Than Tun who put the entire blame on the RC's use of 'blackmail'. 'With these words Goshal [Ba Tin] had practically dug his own grave,' wrote *Yebaw* Thit Maung.[26]

A third group headed by Thakins Than Tun, Zin, Chit and Bo Zeya now became the dominant faction. Joining forces with the 'Beijing returnees', who had been well drilled at Chinese political academies in the intricacies of 'Marxist-Leninist-Mao Zedong (M-L-M) Thought', they undertook a detailed analysis of the CPB's faltering history. The outcome, the CPB's '1964 line', was adopted at a CC meeting held at the CPB's forest headquarters (which had been moved further south in the Pegu Yomas near Nattalin town) from 9 September to 14 October 1964.

Of the CC's 20 members, 11 were able to attend; the main absentees were the representatives from Arakan, the North, North-West, Tenasserim and China.[27] At this historic conference they unanimously agreed to keep the controversial definitions of Burma's 'pseudo-independence' and 'semi-colonial' status and the primacy of the armed struggle was reaffirmed against what was now termed 'the armed counter-revolution' of 'Ne Win's military junta'. Than Tun himself defined the new line in the best known of his later speeches: 'To win the war and seize political power, it is necessary to use force as the central means; it is necessary to establish the union of all nationalities with the peasantry as the basis and broaden the united front; and the work of party building is the key.'[28] The 1964 line marked the third major turning point in the CPB's political strategy since the end of the Second World War and has, in effect, remained the basic strategy of the CPB ever since. Amidst the many changes introduced, two decisions were to be of historic significance.

The first can be tied directly to international developments. With the Soviet-China split now out in the open, the CPB squarely lined itself up behind Mao Zedong's China and immediately discarded the 1955 'revisionist' line. This, it now decided, was the work of the reviled Krushchev and of the 'Brezhnev renegade clique' who had 'inherited his mantle'. Worse still, on the 50th anniversary of the Soviet October Revolution, the CPB CC declared that the Communist Party of the Soviet Union was now supporting Ne Win's 'pseudo-socialism': 'These traitors are denying the universal truth of Marxist-Leninism that the bourgeois state cannot be superseded by the proletarian state through the process of "withering away", but, as a general rule, only through a violent revolution; they are trying to substitute in its stead parliamentary means.'[29]

The CPB now became the CCP's most loyal ally in the region, overshadowing even the Communist Parties of Thailand (CPT), Malaya (CPM) and Indonesia, which were then becoming increasingly militarily and politically active. The extent of this loyalty does much to explain the later antipathy with Vietnam and how in the late 1970s CPB units came to exchange gun-fire with Vietnamese and Laotian troops across the Mekong River. For a time, too, the CPB, much to the alarm of the US and Thai governments, was expected to act as a major conduit for Chinese arms supplies to the CPT and CPM. That they never really succeeded (only jungle communication lines were established) owes much to the activities of a hotchpotch of other insurgent forces: the KNU under Bo Mya, the KMT remnants of generals Li and Tuan and, to a lesser extent, the SSA, SUA and other armed rebel factions in the Shan State, all of whom, independently of one another, prevented any real build-up of CPB forces along the Thai border.

The second important decision was the CPB's enthusiastic adoption of 'Mao Zedong thought'. No CPB propaganda would be replete without reference to the wisdom of Chairman Mao's teachings. The CPB had been loosely following the principles of Mao's protracted warfare since the early 1950s, but then so had the Vietnamese communists, Ho Chi Minh and Gen. Giap and Fidel Castro and the Cuban communists. This was as far as the similarities went. In the CPB's case, underlying the adoption of 'Maoism' and the 1964 line, CPB cadres explain, was the conviction that since 1948 the CPB's strategy of the 'armed seizure of power' had been poorly thought out and generally half-hearted. The belief now, inspired by the zeal of Aung Gyi and the Beijing returnees, was that by escalating the war and simply adopting the right Maoist principles, victory would be quickly won. When compared with the odds that Mao had faced in China, Aung Gyi argued, the situation in Burma, where there was already countrywide rebellion, a restive peasantry and a widely disliked government, could not have been better for a genuine 'M-L-M' Communist Party.

The irony is that while in Rangoon Ne Win and the *Tatmadaw* colonels were trying to adapt Marxist principles to their own uniquely 'Burmese' form of socialism, the CPB, which for many citizens had always been the real voice of socialism in Burma, was now to try and fit Burma into an entirely 'Maoist' Chinese mould. Coming at a time when the CPB's reputation was at its highest point in years, this proved a disastrous error and, within a few years, led to the near destruction of the communist movement in Burma. For the next decade, at the height of the Maoist upsurge in China, CPB and CCP rhetoric were virtually indistinguishable.

Adopting the 1964 line meant completely reorienting CPB priorities. Recognising the main social characteristics of Chinese society, Mao Zedong's successful strategy of people's or protracted warfare had ultimately hinged on four important tactics: relying on the peasantry rather than the urban working class; creating rural base areas; totally mobilising the community behind the Communist Party and its armed forces; and encircling the cities from the countryside.[30] As Ba Thein Tin explained: 'In colonial and semi-colonial countries the armed struggle led by the Communist Party is essentially a peasant's war led by the proletariat.'[31]

This was an important departure from Lenin, who had always believed a successful communist insurrection would depend largely on the political mobilisation of the working class or urban proletariat who, through the Communist Party, would come to lead a united front of other progressive forces or classes. In Russia, in particular, since many peasants were also landowners, communist theoreticians believed the *kulak* class could not always be counted on as a political force. Mao also set great store by the strategy of the united front, but in predominantly rural countries like Burma or China, where for the most part a 'peasant war' was being fought, its applications were, he believed, often necessarily limited.

It should be stressed that the CPB's turn to Maoism and enthusiastic support for Mao's Great Proletarian Cultural Revolution did not mean that it was slavishly looking for aid from its powerful neighbour, as has often been claimed in Rangoon. In fact quite the reverse. Mao's principles of protracted warfare were based entirely on self-reliance and a clever tactical strategy to defeat a far stronger enemy. Self-reliance and the ability to fight on independently in any circumstances are imperative, wrote Lin Piao, Mao's deputy and Defence Minister, in 1965, before he fell from grace:

> If one does not operate by one's own efforts, does not independently ponder and solve the problems of the revolution in one's own country and does not rely on the strength of the masses, but leans wholly on foreign aid (even though this be aid from socialist countries which persist in revolution) no victory can be won or be consolidated even if it is won.[32]

These words made a deep impact on the CPB leadership back in the green forests of central Burma. Throughout the 1960s the CPB had continued to boast that the 'red flags of the revolutionary armed struggle' were flying over the Pegu Yomas, parts of the Delta, Tenasserim seaboard and the 'national minority areas' of Arakan and the Shan State; meanwhile guerrilla forces were still constantly on the move between Minbu, Mandalay and the Dry Zone further north.[33] In all these areas PA commanders had, on their own initiative, gone on the offensive following the breakdown of the peace parley in a steady stream of attacks, which at that time were still often reported in the Rangoon press. But following the announcement of the 1964 line, the CPB CC embarked on a far more centralised system of military planning and the textbook adoption of protracted warfare tactics to build up what they described as new Red Power liberated territories. Run strictly on Maoist principles, it was planned that with these Red Power strongholds the CPB would gradually encircle government towns and positions till final victory. There was a new gospel, still preached by CPB cadres today: 'A Communist Party armed with Marxist-Leninism-Mao Zedong thought can carry out a long war so long as it uses the countryside as the base area and relies on the peasant masses.'[34]

To carry out this strategy the CPB CC redivided the country into three types of regions. The first, the 'base areas', such as the Pegu Yomas, Arakan Yomas and central 'Three M' (Mandalay-Meiktila-Myingyan) triangle, were entirely under CPB control. The whole population would be mobilised, either in new youth, women, worker or peasant unions, or as soldiers in the PA or local defence militia. The PA would defend these areas in conventional warfare if necessary, but their main purpose would be to serve as secure, rearguard bases where front-line troops and cadres could recuperate or be trained.

The second, the guerrilla zones, such as the Delta or along the coastal plain of Tenasserim (especially Tavoy-Mergui), were partly under CPB control and partly still being contested with government forces. The main objective here would be to upgrade operational zones into base areas; the main tactic would be mobile guerrilla warfare. PA troops and political commissars would have to keep constantly on the move to avoid detection and to take advantage of the changing front line in the war.

The last, mainly the cities, were totally under government control. The main objective here would be for small teams of cadres and guerrillas to penetrate and harass the army's communication lines, gather intelligence and spread anti-government propaganda, while at the same time building up party support among workers and peasants.

The two keys to the whole strategy were mobility and party building. Given the broad spread of its forces, even the CPB's leaders are uncertain of the true number of party members in this period (figures of between 5,000 and 10,000 are usually mentioned), but a vast increase in the party's size was planned. It was envisaged that within a few years each village in the country would have at least one party member.

Details of the 1964 line were sent by courier to district party officials around the country. To introduce the new strategy, rather than summon local or provincial cadres to central headquarters, it was decided to build up a model Red Power base area first. This would serve as a central 'hard-core' region from which communist forces could expand and link up with other liberated territories, including those controlled by the KNUP and the CPB's NDUF allies.

The region chosen was the Pegu Yoma highlands where the CPB committees for Tharrawaddy, Prome, Thayetmyo, Toungoo and Pegu had for some years kept their district headquarters. With its thinly populated range of forested hills, hidden valleys and low mountains, some 250 miles long but in places just 40 miles wide, running through the heart of Burma, the Pegu Yomas was ideal for guerrilla warfare with small underground forces, as had already been demonstrated in both the Saya San rebellion of 1930-2 and the Second World War. The inhabitants were a scattered mix of Burmans, Karens and Chins who eked out a precarious living working the forests. The KNUP defended the southern end of range, but much of the rest was under CPB control; it was the strategic base area from which PA units had for many years operated with virtual impunity, moving to the east into the Sittang River valley, west to the Irrawaddy, north to Meiktila or Minbu, or south towards the Delta. Save for timber, the mountains were of little economic significance, but on all sides of the range, from Taikkyi to Magwe and from Pegu to Yamethin, lay thousands of villages in one of the most fertile regions of the country. Many of these were already under loose CPB control and provided an important source of revenue and recruits.

After the 1964 CC meeting CPB leaders began moving up and down through the range giving training classes to local party officials and recruiting new party members. Fatefully, overall charge of this task was entrusted to one of the leading Beijing returnees, *Yebaw* Aung Gyi, a former Rangoon University student leader and one of the party's most travelled ideologues, who chose as his helpers other members of this select group including Bo Tun Shein, who had also previously studied in Moscow and Prague, Bo Tun Nyein, a BIA veteran, and Soe Win, a leader of the 1949 civil servants' strike. Contrary to popular belief, they were not young men. Most were experienced political veterans, already in their forties.

They decided to locate the epicentre of their Red Power movement in Paukkaung township, a rice-growing region of some 70,000 inhabitants, where the CPB's Prome district committee had several years earlier set up its forest headquarters. It was ideal guerrilla terrain. From here CPB units could safely infiltrate towards Paungde in the south and Thayetmyo in the north, or retreat deeper into the Pegu Yomas if attacked, or even escape into the Sittang valley to the east. The position was secured by cutting the Prome-Toungoo jungle road, thus preventing any sudden movement of government forces across the mountains; meanwhile the Central Marxism-Leninism School was established at a scattered forest settlement renamed the Golden City of Peking, which embraced the three village tracts of Kaungsi, Theegon and Kadinma. Party cadres were called in from the surrounding countryside and the Delta to begin new political science classes. These concentrated on four main subjects: philosophy, economics, party construction and the people's army. Seventeen people, including one CC member, two divisional and five district committee members (the rest were from central headquarters), attended the first course given by the Beijing returnees, which began on 25 March 1965. Though *Yebaw* Htay was the course principal, real authority lay with Aung Gyi; details of the classes were later revealed in the Rangoon press after a number of cadres defected.[35]

Shortly afterwards, towards the end of 1965, came the first real warnings of the approaching problems. Ba Tin and *Yebaw* Htay, both experienced trade union organisers who had always fostered close contacts with the NUF and other political movements in the cities, had never been convinced of the Red Power strategy in the first place. The CPB, they believed, was turning its back on its natural political base and, along with another former trade union leader, Bo Yan Aung, and a number of second-line leaders, including *Yebaw* Ba Khet, they became increasingly critical of the Beijing returnees' sloganeering and predictions of imminent victory. According to defectors, when in December 1965 Than Tun presented another programme for Victory Within Four Years, Ba Tin satirised it as a 'Boe Boe Aung' project (Boe Boe Aung was a legendary mystic).[36] For the first time a real rift was developing in the CPB Politburo with Thakins Than Tun, Zin and Chit, apparently impressed by the energy and commitment of the Beijing returnees, believing the Red Power plan offered the only real solution to all the party's past failures.[37]

With the arguments continuing, on 16 August 1966 Thakins Than Tun and Chit met four of the Beijing returnees, Aung Gyi, Thakin Pu, Tun Shein and Myo Tint at Saw Village, Zigon township, to discuss how to counter the growing dissension within the party. They resolved to borrow directly from China (where Red Guards had started to purge the party apparatus) and form the CPB's own vanguard movement of youth training teams. Aung Gyi had already formed some Red Guard youth teams at CPB central headquarters during 1965. These, it was agreed, should consist of model 'hard core' communists who would support the party line; in the main the training teams selected university and high school students who had fled to the jungles since the military coup and were, as a result, regarded as being especially full of Maoist fervour. Prominent amongst these were Soe Win, son of U Hla, former editor of the *Ludu* newspaper, and Aung Thein Naing, nephew of Bo Yan Aung.

The Line of 'Purge, Dismiss and Eliminate' and the Death of Than Tun
As in China, however, when they moved into the villages with their provocative 'dismiss the 55 deviationists' slogan, the Red Guards swiftly slipped away from party control. Daily classes were held on the Cultural Revolution in China at which Aung Gyi and other returnees preached the importance of class-consciousness and the need for cadres to be 'merciless, to kill even their own parents if necessary'.[38] Local party units were purged and young Red Guards replaced experienced cadres. Violence lay not far behind. By the end of 1966 rumours of the first executions of 'reactionary' party officials and villagers had started to reach Rangoon. A number of veterans were reportedly killed in grisly ritual killings during which, eyewitnesses claim, Red Guards such as Than Gyaung and

Zelat, the sons of Thakin Chit and Bo Yan Aung, dipped their shirts in their victims' blood.[39] Though not yet officially approved by the CPB Politburo, they had embarked on what became known as the 'intra-party revolutionary line' or the 'line of purge, dismiss and eliminate'.

On 27 April 1967 Ba Tin and *Yebaw* Htay were both suspended from the Politburo and several prominent officials, including *Yebaw* Ba Khet, quickly sensed the dangers and ran away. Others were not so lucky. The final explosion appeared to be triggered by the Chinese Red Guard movement in Rangoon with which the Burmese Red Guards were in complete sympathy. It would be wrong to try and tie events too literally, but in various parts of the country the CPB now had contact with Chinese officials and aid workers and the party's youthful Red Guards were closely following the Maoist upsurge in both Beijing and Rangoon.

Finally, in June 1967, as the confrontation with the Chinese Embassy in Rangoon moved towards its climax, an orgy of internecine violence took heavy toll of the CPB leadership in the Burmese jungles. Conducted in the humiliating manner of the Moscow trials, these ruthless killings have been well described elsewhere, but for once the state media did not need to exaggerate.[40] On 18 June Ba Tin, one of the CPB's six founder members and for over two decades its leading ideologue, was executed after a summary trial. Next was party secretary, *Yebaw* Htay, whose execution squad included his own son, Pho Htoo, who was even photographed leading the chants for his own father's death. These two stalwarts of the communist movement were derisively decried as 'Burma's Deng Xiaoping' and 'Liu Shao-chi' respectively. These words soon came to haunt the CPB.

The bloodbath did not end here. For the next two years 'dismissed' in CPB terminology became synonymous with 'liquidated'. A reign of terror was unleashed across the Pegu Yomas from the Red Guard Prome district head-quarters. The cadres were allegedly fuelled in their militancy by the arrival of young Chinese students after the riots and killings in the cities. To their eternal discredit, Than Tun and the party leaders did not try to stop them. At a meeting on 15 December 1967, Than Tun and the remaining Politburo members passed a resolution announcing the adoption of the 'intra-party revolutionary line' and ordered party units around the country to conduct their own purges. Eleven days later, on 26 December 1967, Bo Yan Aung, one of the great heroes of Burma's national liberation movement, was taken out of custody and executed. It was over a quarter of a century since he had made the historic journey with Aung San to Amoy to begin Burma's freedom struggle, Though long in ill-health, he had vainly tried to prevent the excesses of the summer.

As the purges continued government troops were rushed into the mountains in strength to try and take advantage of the CPB's confusion. On 16 April 1968 the *Tatmadaw* scored a rare propaganda coup when Bo Zeya, the PA's China-trained Chief-of-Staff and another of the most respected of the *Thirty Comrades*, was killed in action on the Prome-Tharrawaddy border. Further north a strike force of 1,000 men overran the CPB's headquarters in the 'Three-M' triangle and killed the CPB's Meiktila district chairman, Hla Thein. Later the same year government troops in the Pegu Yomas near Pyu killed another of the CPB's founder members, the Bengali, Dr Nath. Several other senior party officials were captured or killed in follow-up raids. In the same period another of the Beijing returnees, CC member and former ABPO leader, Thakin Pu, died from disease; the ex-Politburo member, Thakin Than Myaing, was expelled from the party (in China); and yet another CC member, *Yebaw* Mya, who soon became one of the *Tatmadaw*'s most damaging sources of anti-CPB propaganda, made secret preparations to surrender.

Only belatedly did Than Tun appear to wake up to the enormity of what was taking place around him and try to bring the Red Guard leaders to heel. In early August 1968 Bo Tun Nyein, who had led the executions of Ba Tin, Htay and Yan Aung, was himself arrested and executed after being charged with 'counter-revolution' and 'trying to set up a rival party headquarters'. Over the following month Tun Shein, Soe Win and several other former RUSU student cadres, including Kyaw Khin, Thein Tun and Aung Thein Naing, met the same fate. But this came too late to save Than Tun. On 19 September the *Tatmadaw*'s 77th light infantry division successfully stormed the CPB's central headquarters on the Myayabin Ridge, 13 miles west of Kywebwe, seized Than Tun's personal diaries for the years 1966-8 and uncovered the dead students' graves. Following routine practice, PA troops separated into different directions and most of the CPB central headquarter's force managed to escape, Than Tun along with a small party of trusted comrades. But at 5.30 in the afternoon of 24 September, exhausted after five days' non-stop flight, Than Tun was shot dead without warning by one of his bodyguards, Maung Mya. His assassin was allegedly a government agent who had been carefully planted to wait for just such an opportunity. The next morning Maung Mya, who claimed to be an army 'deserter' when he joined the CPB in 1966, gave himself up to the *Tatmadaw*.[41]

None the less, even after Than Tun's death, another CPB CC member, Soe Than, a former ABPO leader and party secretary of the Delta Division, was purged and executed. The cycle of violence involving the Beijing returnees only reached an apparently poetic conclusion with the death in action of *Yebaw* Aung Gyi in a four-hour battle in the Ngabyema grasslands, west of Pyuntaza, on the afternoon of 3 April 1969 as his force desperately fought to break out of an army encirclement operation. From then on the occasional execution of party members for the alleged 'crime' of 'revisionism' did occur, but on a much reduced scale.

The death of Thakin Than Tun, perhaps the only nationalist hero of the 1930s and 1940s whose reputation as a political leader came close to matching that of his brother-in-law, Aung San, was a crushing blow to party morale and was greeted with genuine sorrow by many of even his most determined opponents. The son of a timber merchant, he was born in 1911 in Pyinmana and graduated from a teacher training college in Rangoon; it was as a schoolteacher with a talent for writing powerful speeches in both Burmese and English that he first met Aung San, U Nu and other young leaders of the student movement of the 1930s. His imprint shone bright on every stage of the national liberation struggle. He was a key member of the *Dobama Asiayone*, co-founder of the *Nagani* Book Club and in 1940, before being interned by the British, travelled to India with Aung San to meet Nehru, Gandhi and leaders of the Indian National Congress. He became Minister of Land and Agriculture in Dr Ba Maw's wartime Cabinet and was the AFPFL's first general-secretary. As even the Rangoon press commented, his skills as a political organiser were probably without equal among his contemporaries.[42] Unlike many communist leaders in Burma, he was never a mere ideologue, but was a man of extraordinary achievement and energy; in later years he came to be looked on as somewhat of a fallen idol in the country at large.

In China, Chairman Mao sent Zhou Enlai and Kang Sheng to deliver his sympathies in person to Ba Thein Tin and Pe Tint; the CCP's CC published a message of 'profound condolences' and expressed its 'shock' at his death in the battle against the 'reactionary rule of imperialism and its running dogs in Burma'.[43] But however much the country or the international communist movement grieved his death, it was nothing compared to the damage that the bloody purges of the CPB's Cultural Revolution had done to the party's name. Government predictions during 1968 of the CPB's imminent demise were, however, premature: continuing PA actions in Arakan, the Delta, Tenasserim and throughout the Irrawaddy and Sittang valleys showed that local CPB units were far from dead. The RC, too, was painfully slow to wake up to the scale of the CPB 'invasion' in north-east Burma where, with full military backing from China, the CPB had already opened up a major new front along the 2,100 km border.

The conclusion of this desperate chapter made the CPB increasingly less attractive to Burma's disaffected youth and, from 1968, there was a drastic decline in the number of young intellectuals and students joining the party. This can partly be explained by the much tighter security noose that Ne Win had now managed to impose around the cities. But unlike in the 1940s and 1950s, in the great political crises of the 1970s (the 1974 workers' strike, U Thant's funeral, the 1975/6 student demonstrations, the 1976 assassination plot), though underground CPB activists were still in the cities, they rarely dared show their hand. The ultimate proof of this came in 1988 when, in the midst of the democracy uprising, virtually all the CPB's troops and cadres were stranded in their mountain strongholds far from any real influence or contact. It was a far cry from the crises of 1948, 1958 or even 1963, when communist supporters could be openly seen in any street. From this point on, for most Burmese intellectuals and city-dwellers, the CPB was very much an estranged party of 'jungle dwellers'.

The scale of this damage has since been admitted by CPB leaders themselves. In 1975, following the deaths of Thakins Zin and Chit, the new CPB chairman, Ba Thein Tin, issued an appeal on the CPB's radio station heard by CPB cadres across the country, who correctly interpreted it as a veiled instruction finally to end the intra-party line:

> Please do not brand everything revisionism and fight it.... While fighting revisionism as the main target politically, left-dogmatism must also be dealt with.... A comrade who has political and ideological differences must not be punished physically. Look at our policy towards prisoners of war. We fight furiously in battle, but we do not physically torture those who surrender or are taken prisoner. If we can even treat our enemy prisoners in this way, would it be right to punish our own comrades because of political or ideological differences?[44]

This contrasts startlingly with Ba Thein Tin's earlier (and later) words. In 1967 at the height of the killings he simply characterised the purges as a 'fierce struggle' in which the 'Marxist-Leninism of Mao Zedong's thought triumphed'.[45] A year later, invoking the evidence of the Cultural Revolution in China, he was even more forthright: 'The revolution in Burma has improved rapidly because of our great faith in the guidance of Mao Zedong thought.... It is the most basic assurance for the victory of our revolution in Burma.'[46] The CCP, too, claiming the 'road of revolution has never been a smooth one', publicly praised the CPB for purging its 'revisionist' clique who followed Krushchev and the 'renegade, traitor and scab', Liu Shao-chi, in mistakenly believing 'there was no need for armed struggle'.[47]

But at the CPB's Third Party Congress in 1985 a very different picture emerged. The CPB's 'duplication' of the Cultural Revolution in China and the adoption of the 'intra-party revolutionary line' of 'purge, dismiss and eliminate' were 'wrong', Ba Thein Tin said, in virtually every respect:

> It was a line which a Communist Party should never have carried out. The revisionist label was tagged on everything in sight, and violent attacks, purges, dismissals and killings were carried out under this line. The errors committed under that line [sectarianism, abolition of inner-party democracy and destruction of the principles of democratic centralisation] had very far-reaching negative effects and ideologically, politically, organisationally, the party and the revolution suffered severe setbacks both in the style of work and other areas. Revolutionary base areas in the Lower Burma Division, the Delta Division and the Upper River Areas Division were all destroyed. There were serious repercussions within the party masses, the party work forces and the people. The party became a great source of fear; no one dared speak out, offer suggestions or deal with the party. Darkness hung over the whole party and no one dared to do party work properly.[48]

In short, the intra-party line was a self-admitted disaster. However, what many analysts failed to notice amidst the countrywide condemnation of the killings was that the CPB had itself completely changed in character since the introduction of the 1964 line. China's generous financial and military backing, which began in late 1967, undoubtedly threw the party an unexpected new lifeline, but Burma's political problems were still very much more complex than that. The deaths of Than Tun, Ba Tin, Htay, Bo Zeya, Yan Aung, Aung Gyi, Dr Nath and other senior party leaders had in themselves done nothing to improve the national popularity of either the RC or the BSPP. Nor had they solved the underlying causes of the countrywide insurrections. Burma was still a land in rural revolt. Moreover, confounding virtually all expectations, as events now dramatically showed, the CPB was itself by no means finished.

The Political Character of the Maoist CPB
With perhaps the sole exception of the quixotic Thakin Soe, the communist movement in Burma never threw up such individual thinkers and leaders as Tito in Yugoslavia, Castro in Cuba, Ho Chi Minh in Vietnam or Mao in China. The White Flag movement always followed the more orthodox international trends. Even after adopting the 1964 'M-L-M' line, the CPB never became like the Khmer Rouge under Pol Pot in Cambodia or *Sendero Luminoso* (Shining Path) in Peru, though it did become one of the most dogmatically Maoist communist parties in the world. From 1964 onwards only the 'genuine' Marxist-Leninist communist parties in China, Albania, Thailand, Indonesia, Malaysia, Cambodia and Australia met with the CPB's whole-hearted approval.[49]

Rhetoric aside, it can be argued that the greatest impact of the CPB's 1964 line was felt not in the political arena but on the battlefield. The CPB's survival over the next two decades was further illuminating evidence, if any was still needed, of the genius of Mao's original conception of 'people's war' as well as of its inherent weaknesses. Over the same period a number of ethnic nationalist liberation movements in Burma successfully incorporated many of the principles of Mao's protracted warfare into their military training. Well into the 1980s Burma was clearly ripe for the kind of 'politicised' rural or peasant warfare he had envisaged. To understand the CPB's continued appeal it is important to turn away from the excesses of the Pegu Yomas and look elsewhere, to compare the experiences of other CPB units in the country. Most welcomed the 1964 line; only the 1967 intra-party line caused objections. Purges in the CPB's Delta Division had already started at the time of Than Tun's death and a number of leaders, including Soe Than who was executed in January 1969, had already been summoned to the Pegu Yomas. The Tenasserim Division committee under Tun Shein (not the Beijing returnee) was luckier and escaped any executions, though the Red Guards had reportedly earmarked it as next for purging. Otherwise most of the other CPB state, divisional or district units were small or still being formed, including those in the Shan and Kachin States which, with Chinese aid, were now rapidly growing in size.

This then left the CPB strongholds in the 'North-West Division' and Arakan 'Province', as the CPB, following China's example, prefers to call the ethnic minority states. Linked to one another by base areas in the vastness of the Arakan Yoma mountain range, their experiences were interestingly different, but both proved to be models in Maoist organisation.

The North-West Division under CC member Thet Tun, a senior officer in the Burma Rifles at the time of the 1948 mutinies, openly rejected the 1967 line but adopted many of the 1964 Red Power principles. Undoubtedly one of the PA's most able commanders, Thet Tun was often regarded as a 'renegade' within the CPB movement, but remained untouchable. He built up around himself a loyal band of dedicated followers; as he patrolled the central Arakan Yomas, constantly criss-crossing Taungup, Kyaukpyu, Minbu and Thayet districts while trying to expand CPB territory, he became something of a folk hero among local Chin, Rakhine and Burman villagers. Though one of the poorest regions in the country and cut off from any external support, the number of men under arms rose steadily, reaching an estimated 500 regulars and 800 village militia in the mid-1970s. Most of these were ethnic Maya and Zainbow Chins, but they also included southern Chins and former members of the CPB's small NDUF ally, the Chin National Vanguard Party, which the CPB absorbed shortly after the 1963 peace parley. Interestingly, despite a number of attempts, a broad-based Chin insurgent movement has never been established.[50]

Thet Tun managed to establish a major new base area around the Pokaung mountain and to build up supplies of arms and ammunition through carefully planned raids on government patrols and outposts. According to local veterans, head-on clashes with stronger *Tatmadaw* forces were always avoided. The strategic Minbu-Ngape road, for example, was repeatedly cut and by 1972 PA troops were able to repenetrate the plains in the east (in Sidoktaya and Thayet townships) to resume guerrilla activities, while the coastal towns of Ma-I, An and Letpan to the west were all attacked, Letpan for the third and last time in 1976 when, it was claimed, 60 government troops were captured with their weapons. A brilliant organiser and tactician, Thet Tun always remained one step ahead of his opponents until, hopelessly outnumbered by one of the largest *Four Cuts* operations ever mounted, he surrendered in 1980 after four years of near constant retreat.

The Example of Arakan
The CPB's Arakan Province committee, located in Arakan's pivotal Sittwe (Akyab) district further north, is perhaps the best example of the effectiveness of

the 1964 line. Being the one CPB region I was able to visit and a model of CPB organisation, it will be commented on at some length.[51] Here the intra-party line was implemented by the Sittwe district secretary, Kyaw Mya. During 1967/8 three lower rank officials were executed for 'revisionism' (i.e. according to cadres they were prepared to consider 'exchanging arms for democracy') and, to show that not all Beijing returnees spoke with one voice, one of the last to be executed for this crime was another of the returnees, Aung Mya (*aka* Ba Pru), who had been sent to Arakan from the Pegu Yomas in 1965. A member of the CPB's 'provisional' committee (one rank below CC) he had always disagreed with Kyaw Mya over the 1967 line and, despite frequent arguments with his colleagues, never changed his stand. Finally, in 1973, according to another provisional committee member, Kyaw Maung, he 'had to be killed'. The words, then, of Kyaw Maung are revealing:

> I can't say the Cultural Revolution was wrong. It was more the 1964 line or, at least, the way it was implemented. It should have been done differently. Until 1967 there was great ideological confusion in our party so we can blame the inner-party struggle on our own weaknesses. Before this we had drifted, sometimes to the right and sometimes to the left. But after 1967 the party had a much clearer line and made a lot more progress. Our party structure wasn't changed much, but the number of party training classes was increased and there was a much greater emphasis on Mao Zedong thought.[52]

Like most party cadres, he explains the significance of the 1964 line as the re-affirmation of the primacy of 'armed struggle' against the people's three main enemies, 'imperialism, feudal-landlordism and bureaucratic capitalism and their agents' (i.e. the AFPFL or BSPP). Since 1964, Mao's dictum, 'political power grows out of the barrel of the gun', has been a much favoured CPB quotation.

The Arakan CPB now became very much a party of the rural proletariat. Like many party officials promoted at this time, Kyaw Maung, who joined the CPB in the midst of the 1958 surrenders, is from a peasant background. As a result, students and intellectuals from the cities felt discriminated against, though they claim their attitudes changed after repeated sessions of 'self-criticism'. According to Tun Win, a Rangoon University graduate: 'There was an anti-educated ideology. It wasn't a party decision, just some leaders. They said a revolutionary doesn't need to be educated. They believe a worker or farmer can perform all the same tasks.'[53] Reading or writing English, or even listening to English on the radio, one of the few sources of outside information, were discouraged. Like the BSPP, though for different reasons, the CPB was trying to exorcise all traces of the colonial ghost.

This marked a drastic change from the 1940s and 1950s, when the party was dominated by university-educated intellectuals like Aung San, Ba Tin, Thein Pe Myint, Than Tun, Aung Gyi and Bo Zeya, who were as fluent in English as in their own Burmese language. Like Thet Tun in the North-West Division, the Arakan party was heavily influenced by one man, present-day Politburo member, Kyaw Mya, BA. An ethnic Rakhine, a founder member of the Arakan (White Flag) CPB unit at Athuthema village, Myohaung in 1947, and a government district officer in Paletwa during the British and Japanese administrations, like many local CPB officials in Arakan in the 1950s, he had an educated background. But the mass surrenders of 1957/8, which nearly wiped out the Arakan Province CPB and its allies (the PVOs and APLP), led to a marked hardening of attitudes.

Until then, veterans claim, 'economically and militarily' the CPB controlled much of the mountain and coastal region between Rathedaung, Sittwe, Myohaung and Pauktaw in the north, while to the south smaller armed units were scattered down through the PVO/APLP-dominated districts of An, Sandoway and Gwa, where they linked up with other CPB units in Lower Burma.

The surrender of 700 CPB followers under U Maung Hla Sein in 1958 badly set back CPB influence in the division. It meant the Sittwe District Party virtually had to start from scratch again; just three platoons of troops were left. In 1959 a new forest headquarters was established in Ponnagyun, one of Sittwe's nine townships and, sending out small guerrilla teams, CPB cadres again began to fan out through the surrounding villages and forests. Sometimes the party's 'fighters' would go first, then the political commissars would follow. But mostly the party units were small, often tiny cells of two or three people. By 1960 these teams had re-entered the Kyaukpyu district, 75 miles to the south. From 1963, with the breakdown of the peace parley, the party once again rapidly increased in size.

Significantly, in the light of its difficulties with the ethnic question elsewhere in Burma, during these years the CPB had few problems recruiting among the local Rakhine and 'hill-tribe' populations and quickly overtook rival insurgent forces in the region, with whom PA guerrillas often fought if they crossed paths. Though little reported, the insurgent situation in Arakan was highly complex and needs some clarification to understand the CPB's success. Arakan's estimated 2.5 to 3 million inhabitants have always been, as events in 1988 again demonstrated, among the most intensely political people in Burma. There have always been and still are at least five (sometimes more) insurgent forces operating inside Arakan and the adjoining Chin hill tracts. In historical order the best known are the CPB Red Flags, the *Mujahids*, the (Marxist) ANLP, the CPA and, representing a new generation of less left-orientated nationalist radicals who came to the fore in the aftermath of Ne Win's coup, the Arakan Independence Organisation (AIO) and the Arakan Liberation Party (ALP).

In the 1960s, constant CPB pressure forced Thakin Soe's Red Flag remnants (along with the small Chin National Liberation Party established in the early 1960s by Chin Ba Maung and later commanded by Win Maung in the northern tri-border region) to retreat further into the interior into their last strongholds in Taywechaung, Minbya township and the Chin hills. Meanwhile, the former followers of U Seinda, who in 1960 joined Maung Sein Nyunt's ANLP, eventually decided to concentrate their efforts in the far north around Rathedaung, Maungdaw and the Naaf River, where in the mid-1970s they reached a maximum armed strength of 120 armed guerrillas.[54]

Then in 1972, the first units of the AIO, formed on 20 May 1970 by another group of Rangoon University students and trained by the KIO, arrived in the Rachaung area of Kyauktaw township after a remarkable 'long march' from the Kachin State. Here, under their president Tun Shwe Maung, they established a small rural base with an armed force of 80 troops. The AIO's founders had originally been inspired by the teachings of the revered Arakanese historian, the 'Rakhine-Myanmar Pandit', U Oo Tha Tun. But when in 1977 a second detachment of AIO troops, led by two more Rangoon University graduates, Kyaw Hlaing and Maung's brother, San Kyaw Tun, tried to repeat the perilous journey from the Kachin border, they were ambushed on the way by both the *Tatmadaw* and Indian Army (which apparently mistook them for Mizo guerrillas). Of the 58 soldiers who set out, 15 were killed, including San Kyaw Tun, and only six, led by Kyaw Hlaing, reached Arakan. The rest disappeared *en route* or were captured.[55]

The same year a heavily armed advance column of over 100 men from the ALP (formed 1972), who had been trained by the KNU in south-east Burma, attempted an even longer 2,000-mile journey around Burma's borders. But this ill-fated advance force was also intercepted by the *Tatmadaw* after losing its way in the vast Chin hills, the one area in which there was no insurgent force to guide it. It was decimated: 51 troops (including the leader, Khaing Mo Lin, formerly of the Burma Navy, and William, an ethnic Saline Chin who commanded a small Chin section which hoped to establish its own nationalist force in the Chin State) were killed and 50 captured. In fact, though its main armed wing remained with the KNU, until the late 1980s the ALP's presence in Arakan was largely as a secret underground cell.[56] Leaders of both the AIO and the ALP (the KIO tried to persuade them to join forces while they were passing through its territory) now concede that their failure to work together, for largely factional reasons, was a mistake of historic proportions.

The CPB's greatest conflict was always with the AIO's ally, the CPA. After its first congress on Phado Island in 1964, the CPA rapidly increased in size, its reputation enhanced by its participation in the 1963 peace parley. Many of its founders and early supporters were former Red Flags, but in these years it also recruited a number of defectors from the White Flags and police, such as Aung Hla, an ethnic Mro who mutinied with his 20-man unit and their weapons.[57] In 1972/3 progress was interrupted by a damaging split of the movement into two factions, headed by the two key Red Flag defectors, Kyaw Zan Rhee and Maung Han, who had formed the CPA in 1962. As its own 'policy statement' admits, the CPA was formed 'in the womb of the Red Flag CPB' and, until the 1973 split, most of the CPA's rules and regulations were copied, word for word, from the Red Flags. Kyaw Zan Rhee, who was criticised for continuing to hold Red Flag views, now drifted away through the mountains to the north with a small force of 50 loyal followers; he eventually surrendered in 1980. (In 1988, after taking a prominent part in the democracy uprising in Sittwe with other former insurgent leaders, including Bo Kra Hla Aung of the PVOs, the Red Flag, *Bonbauk* Tha Kyaw, and U Maung Hla Sein, ex-White Flag CPB, he co-founded the now legal Arakan People's United Organisation; but it was the Arakan League for Democracy, headed by Dr Saw Mra Aung and the 82 year-old U Oo Tha Tun, who was imprisoned by MIS on the eve of the polls, which made the best showing in the state.)

The larger 'nationalist' grouping, led by the party's present chairman, Maung Han, thus took over the CPA's main operational areas. Throughout the 1960s and 1970s small units from the CPA's 300-strong army moved throughout Arakan, but mostly in the north around Kyauktaw and down along the coast through Pauktaw and the offshore islands from their main base area in the Myebon-Minbya hills. In each area the CPA was able to build up a small underground presence (guerrilla units and cadres sometimes pushing as far south as Ramree Island and Sandoway) and it established contact with a number of prominent lawyers, teachers, doctors and even local BSPP officials.

But there was little communist solidarity. Maung Han and the leaders of the CPA (that rarity in Burma, a separatist communist party) still describe the CPB as 'unstable' on account of its past swings in political direction.[58] While, like the Red Flag CPB, the CPA adopted a generally pro-Soviet political outlook (a Soviet-style independent People's Republic being its main goal), it was anxious not to tie itself to international communist trends and was more concerned with the problems of communism in small nations, such as the struggle for liberation in Ireland. The CPA has also enjoyed better relations with other 'ethnic' parties in Burma, especially the NMSP in South East Burma which, via the long sea route, has over the years been an important conduit for arms.[59] Thus, after acrimonious talks soon after the CPA's founding, CPA and CPB units began to exchange gunfire on sight. As late as 1977 Aung Kyaw Tha, the CPA's Paletwa township chairman, was killed by the CPB, while two years later four CPB troops were killed by the CPA near Minbya.

In fact, though continually affirming its belief in the 'united front', the CPB only managed to reach a *modus vivendi* with the *Mujahids* of the far north and this, too, only after a number of skirmishes in the 1960s. A pact with the Rohingya Patriotic Front was eventually agreed in 1973, but despite the fact that the *Mujahid* factions could, with open Bangladeshi sympathy, arm several hundred local Muslim villagers along the upper reaches of the Naaf River, in military terms the agreement had little significance. Life in the Muslim community was shattered when, amidst widespread allegations of army brutality, rape and murder, over 200,000 local villagers fled across the border in 1978 in the wake of the *Tatmadaw*'s heavy-handed *Nagamin* census operation. Later, after an international outcry, most of these Muslims were allowed to return under tight security as bona fide Burmese citizens, but local community leaders have never forgotten that at the time the army, in complete contradiction of the truth, blamed all the trouble on 'armed bands of Bengalis', 'rampaging Bengali mobs' and 'wild Muslim extremists' ransacking indigenous Buddhist villages.[60] Thousands more Muslims have since continued to go into exile in countries as far apart as Pakistan, Egypt and across the Arab world where they have often been dubbed Asia's 'new Palestinians'.

Rakhine groups, such as the AIO, have over the years given public support to the Muslim cause, but Muslim-Buddhist relations are still extremely tense; apart from the various *Mujahid* fronts, no insurgent group has made much progress in the Muslim community. Historically the situation is complex, with small ethnic sub-groups such as the Muslim Kamans still living on offshore islands, but community leaders on both sides persist in the 'ethnic' characterisation of their respective religions as either Buddhist-'Rakhine' or Muslim-'Rohingya', both terms in fact being derived from the same ancient word for Arakan. Derogatorily, they refer to each other as Buddhist-*Magh* (bandit) or Muslim-*Kala* (foreigner) and no accurate ethnic or religious population census has ever been taken to try and resolve the situation.

In the face of such state-wide opposition, the CPB concentrated on establishing base areas in two main regions: Ponnagyun close to Sittwe, and along the Limyu River east of Myohaung. Militarily, CPB commanders agreed, the war in Arakan would be won or lost in the battle for control of the large marshy, but fertile, plain behind the port of Sittwe. From these sanctuaries CPB guerrillas could penetrate all the townships of north and central Arakan and travel freely along the Kaladan River into the Chin hills. Then, in 1971, in one of the most spectacular raids of all the insurrections, the CPB joined forces with 800 heavily armed troops from the ethnic Mizo National Front (MNF), led by Laldenga from north-east India; they occupied Rathedaung town and seized a vast quantity of goods, gold and cash from the treasury. Like the Nagas further east, these battle-tested ethnic Mizos enjoyed the support of China; they had originally taken sanctuary in East Pakistan in the late 1960s after a push by the Indian Army on their homes across the Mizoram border. In June 1966, the MNF had already launched one offensive into the Chin hills in an attempt to stir up their restive Chin relatives when they attacked Falam and captured over 150 rifles and weapons. Displaced once again by the Bangladesh liberation war, they at first proved a formidable ally for the CPB, which helped MNF forces disperse among local villages in hidden valleys throughout north Arakan. During 1972 and 1973 local CPB units, often with Mizo support, claimed to have seized 100 weapons in guerrilla attacks on government positions and to have inflicted heavy casualties in the process. For its part the *Tatmadaw* claimed in a nine-month period in 1973 to have killed 122 'insurgents' in north Arakan, mainly CPB, Mizos and *Mujahids*, and to have captured or caused the surrender of 450 others.[61] But in general, as these figures reveal, into the mid-1970s both sides fought a low-intensity guerrilla war, with government forces for the most part concentrating on defending towns on the plains.

Local party officials now concede that these were halcyon days for the CPB; with the money confiscated in these raids and donations flowing in from many local villagers (usually 10 per cent of the annual crop, plus an average five kyats and one basket of rice per family), CPB troops spread east into the Paletwa and Labawa districts, west to the Mayu Range and south through the Arakan Yomas to link up with Bo Thet Tun's men in the North-West Division. After the Delta Division, the Arakan CPB was probably the most self-sufficient of all the district parties, supplying up to two *lakh* kyat annually to CPB central headquarters in the Pegu Yomas. Eventually in 1973 relations with the MNF suddenly and, according to CPB leaders, inexplicably turned sour; the Mizos killed 21 CPB cadres on their retreat north to build up new base areas in the Bangladesh Chittagong Hill Tracts, this time with the approval of the Bangladesh government which had now fallen out with India. In retaliation, the Indian government armed and supported the insurgent Chakma *Shanti Bahini* group inside Bangladesh, which meant that the entire tri-border region was taken over by a complex array of competing ethnic armies, including Mizos, Chakmas, *Mujahids* and Rakhine nationalists. (Other Rakhine forces, like the AIO, which met the MNF in this period, say the real reason for the MNF's turn on the CPB was the Mizos' dream of a 'Greater Mizoram', which one day would include their Chin brothers in Burma. Groups like the CPB, which were also organising in the Chin community, were seen as their natural competitors.[62])

During these peak years, in addition to local militia the Arakan CPB formed a 1,000-strong hard-core military force, of which half were full-time 'fighters' and half also political organisers. All recruits to the party were expected to undergo military training and 'military and political training schools' were established in each township. Basic courses usually lasted three months and consisted of two main subjects: 'military', which concentrated on weapons' training and positional or guerrilla warfare; and 'politics', which consisted of four main classes: party constitution, Marxist philosophy, economics, and the ideology of people's war. Course books included *The Selected Works of Mao Zedong* (especially *On Protracted War*) and selections from *Das Kapital*. But the main teaching was centred on the CPB's own *Political Notes*, 12 volumes of between 80 and 200 pages each, which were collectively written by the CPB's Central Education Committee in the Pegu Yomas during 1965 and which included extracts from Mao, Marx, Lenin, Stalin and Than Tun. Until the mid-1960s the Arakan CPB also received copies of the party's popular journal, *People's Power*, published in the Pegu Yomas, but from the 1970s had to rely on producing its own texts and publications by Gestetner.

Hundreds of villagers and urban recruits passed through these classes, but party membership was more difficult and usually took three years to complete. To be accepted, candidates had to prove two qualities: their ability to work hard and 'their class consciousness and loyalty to the party's ideology'.[63] This could be done only by constant study, public speaking and reading. Intellectuals who joined from the towns, even if experienced underground operatives, were usually put to work with farmers in the fields for a few weeks before being allowed to go on to training classes. Once accepted, following Mao's famous precepts, members were expected to obey the Red Army's 'Three Demands and Eight Points for Attention' and were forbidden to drink alcohol, marry or play cards. (Marriage regulations were only usually relaxed for veteran cadres.) Non-party member recruits to the CPB's PA (estimated in Arakan at two-thirds of the total force) were usually allowed to sign up and leave when they wanted, but at all levels political control by the party was absolute; as in China, from district and township levels down to the rural villages, there were constant mass party meetings of villagers, cadres and troops. Each platoon of 30 soldiers, the CPB's usual operational size in Arakan, had a political commissar; after each battle and at least once a month the group would hold a public 'self-criticism' session.

Administratively the party organisation was highly centralised along Maoist lines. As a full CC member, Kyaw Mya should in theory have been the party's representative at CC meetings in the Pegu Yomas. Instead, because of the many travel difficulties, he received instructions by wireless or courier, though later, as Politburo member, he did attend meetings at Panghsang. The supreme political body in Arakan itself was, and still is, the Arakan Provisional Committee; it has seven members elected at the full Arakan Congress, usually held every five years (the last was in 1983). With a military and political staff of about 100 people, the Provisional Committee mostly stayed in the cool air of the mountains above Buthidaung, where, as a precautionary security measure, it relocated its forest headquarters by a few miles every six months. The CPB's Sittwe district committee, with a staff of 70, also had its administrative headquarters in the mountains nearby. It was a secure position and many families joined the party cadres there. With only rolling hills and virgin forest running the 100 miles north to the Bangladesh-India-Burma triangle border region, the CPB's Rathedaung Party unit to the south could easily block or give warning of any sudden *Tatmadaw* advance from the plains.

Coming under the Provisional Committee were the CPB's main administrative departments (political, military, economic, education, culture and judicial), each of which had representatives or set up local committees at the township and village levels where the CPB controlled base areas. For example, in Buthidaung-Rathedaung the CPB ran four middle schools, while each CPB-controlled village usually had a primary school, an agricultural cooperative, a peasant union and a home guard militia. Entertainment was provided by 'singing and dancing' teams of farmers, soldiers and youth cadres who toured the villages. Justice in CPB courts was, however, severe and the death penalty was automatically enforced for murder or rape. For lesser crimes, imprisonment was usually the penalty.

The overall result of this CPB *Yenan* in north Arakan was an administration and party which was strongly proletarian in flavour. Like other party units, it was also predominantly male, with only one platoon of women soldiers at general headquarters. As in other areas of Burma, CPB cadres admit that explaining conceptual political questions or even different styles of government to subsistence farmers untouched by any outside influence (be it British, AFPFL, BSPP, CPB or ethnic nationalist) presented many problems. But in general, after the military coup at least, the basic distinction in agricultural policy between the CPB and BSPP was better understood and the CPB had few problems recruiting local farmers. The CPB's policy since 1948 had always been 'land to the tiller'. This meant the farmer was the real owner of the land. By contrast, under the BSPP land was owned by the state and the farmer was, in effect, a tenant required to produce fixed quotas which had to be sold at pre-set (usually low) prices back to the state. As a result many farmers traded illegally on the black market to avoid these restrictions and in the hills, at least, were generally able to remain self-sufficient, with their lives as little affected by the 20th century as they could help.

Significantly, dislike of the BSPP was often most intense in areas close to towns, where farmers had little choice but to obey government regulations and were frequently conscripted to serve as porters in *Tatmadaw* operations. In these situations the CPB could usually make quick political gains; in most rural areas its main appeal was the 1964 Maoist agricultural line of 'rely on the poor peasants and farm labourers, unite firmly with the middle peasants, neutralise the rich peasants and concentrate attacks on the landlords'.[64] On this basis land was redistributed, with each farmer receiving the same allocation. According to one cadre, 'If there are just 10,000 acres and 10,000 people, each in theory gets one acre.'

Another important factor in motivating support for the CPB was the complete economic neglect of Arakan since independence. Under the British, Arakan was one of the most prosperous regions in Burma and had one of the highest levels of education; the pre-war prime minister, Sir Paw Tun, for example, was an ethnic Rakhine. Rakhine civil servants, like the Karens, reached the top levels of the colonial service and after independence, one such officer, U Kyaw Min, successfully led a vociferous right-wing nationalist movement, the Independent Arakanese Parliamentary Group (IAPG), against the AFPFL government in Parliament (most of the left-wing nationalists had gone underground). 'AFPFL carpet-baggers were more blatantly overbearing in Arakan than anywhere else,' wrote British historian, Hugh Tinker. Kyaw Min, former editor of *The Nation*, virtually whitewashed the AFPFL candidate for Sittwe in the 1950 by-election, while in the 1951 election the AFPFL took only three seats to the IAPG's 17.[65] As parliamentary politics became ever more complex, the IAPG allied itself with the left-wing NUF; during the 1958 AFPFL split, Kyaw Min even became one of U Nu's ministers as he exhausted every possible parliamentary method to push the demand for an Arakan State.

Despite these pressures on central government from both the above-ground and underground opposition, over the last 40 years there has been absolutely no tangible development in Arakan at all: only a steady regression in the quality of roads, transport, housing, education, employment and life in general. In their concern for security matters in central Burma, the largely Burman leaders of the *Tatmadaw* have taken no interest (except in the counter-insurgency field) in either Arakan or their close Rakhine cousins. Only one car road, the mountain road from Taungup to Prome, links Arakan with the rest of Burma. Insurgent leaders are unanimous that this apparently deliberate neglect of Arakan is the main source of political discontent. According to the CPA's former general-secretary, Thein Pe, 'The country is kept backward by Burmese colonialism. There is no modern industry except cottage farms and a few essential works like rice mills and small timber mills.'[66]

Leading on from this, perhaps the most important aspect of the CPB's relative popularity in Arakan and the North-West Division was that, like the CPB's NEC on the China border, it was able to build up an army of ethnic minority recruits, despite the rival attractions of other insurgent forces operating in the same area. This was something the CPB never achieved in Karen, Kachin or Mon-majority regions. Whereas in other areas of Burma and even the NEC, both the party and PA were nearly always Burman-led, in Arakan the CPB consisted more or less entirely of ethnic minority volunteers. The Arakan CPB was largely ethnic Rakhine (including most of its top leaders) with a number of 'tribals', mostly Chins, Kamui and Mro, in the mountains to the east. Through the 1960s and 1970s it doggedly opposed (and indeed was ready to fight with) the CPA, ANLP and AIO which, even today, it regards as narrowly nationalist. Only in the early 1980s, in much reduced base areas in the mountains along the India-Bangladesh borders, were ceasefires arranged: 200 years ago, a group of Rakhine CPB cadres conceded one night around the forest campfire, it might have been possible to think of an independent Arakan nation, but not in the modern world.[67] As a proletarian party, they explained, the CPB is rather a party of class and does not recognise 'nationalism' as a distinguishing class characteristic. Its one apparent concession to the minority cause was a Nationalities Organisation led by Sein Nyunt Tha, an ethnic Chin, who was also a CPB district committee member.

Significantly, then, in 1985, even before the great ethnic mutinies in north-east Burma in 1989, Sein Nyunt Tha broke away from the CPB with two dozen followers to set up his own ethnic nationalities organisation. After his own ousting in 1987, it became the present-day Tribal National Party led by another former CPB township officer, Pa Di Phru. In 1988 the Tribal National Party became a founder member of the NUF of Arakan, which finally brought together the CPA, AIO, ANLP and ALP in one nationalist alliance (only the CPB and Muslim fronts did not join); today this coalition rivals the CPB's fast diminishing insurgent influence in the state.

In Arakan there is other evidence that the CPB's dogmatic reliance on Mao Zedong thought, while successful in helping the party set up and organise many of its base areas, left it dangerously weak in other key fields. Though CPB teams had penetrated Sittwe, Myohaung, Kyauktaw and the other main towns of Arakan, they had to operate in conditions of much greater secrecy than smaller nationalist organisations like the CPA and AIO which, while fewer in troop numbers, enjoyed rather more urban support, especially from teachers, lawyers and civil servants. This appeared not to concern CPB leaders who believed implicitly in Mao's patient strategy of the encirclement of the towns by the party's rural base areas:

The backbone of the revolution are the working people and the alliance of workers and peasants. Burma is really a peasant country and it is mostly peasants who join our party after they become more politicised. Of course, we have some contact with workers but they are very few in Burma. Industrial workers live in the cities which is the stronghold of the Ne Win regime. It is not true it is our ideology to organise only in the hills, and we do move into the towns according to circumstances. But our main line is armed revolution. This means we are an above-ground movement. We have declared ourselves. Organisation in the towns is underground work, and this must always combine with our main above-ground movement and our main task, armed revolution.[68]

This strategy, however, did not develop simply as a pragmatic reaction to circumstances. Back in August 1967, at the height of the CPB's bloody purges, Ba Thein Tin revealed that the split within the party developed partly over an argument about the wisdom of waging a Maoist 'peasant war led by the proletariat' based on protracted warfare principles: 'It conflicted with the bourgeois idea of launching an insurrection through general strikes in factories, schools and ships and of first capturing political power in cities and then spreading to the countryside.'[69] In 1979 Ba Thein Tin repeated these arguments, once again alleging that the purged Politburo member, Ba Tin, author of the 1947 thesis, *On the Present Political Situation in Burma and Our Tasks*, had as early as 1958 urged the CPB to give up the 'violent revolution' of armed struggle in favour of an urban 'general strike and uprising'.[70] The CPB's movement into the countryside in the 1960s was clearly a highly conscious decision, based on a strict ideological premise, which was to have far-reaching historical consequences. Ba Tin, whose pragmatic suggestion was reviled, was instead executed for his 'revisionist' ideas.

Thus, even here in the CPB's relatively successful backwater of Arakan, there were early warnings of two crucial issues, the nationalities question and the leadership's concentration on rural warfare, which continually dogged the party over the next two decades and ultimately led to its virtual downfall in 1989. The CPB rarely tried to compete with the *Tatmadaw* in the towns where feeling against the BSPP was often at its most extreme.

First, however, came the dramatic intervention of the CPB's China-backed NEC, which for a moment threatened a military division of Burma as damaging as in Vietnam, Laos and Cambodia, where in the late 1960s communist forces had enjoyed the same degree of Chinese support.

For the first time since the early 1950s, conventional warfare, not guerrilla warfare, was just beginning.

13

The North-East Command and the Four Cuts

Since the bloody purges of 1967/8 and the death of Thakin Than Tun, the history of the CPB has been very much a story of two halves. While the new CPB chairman, Thakin Zin, and the reconstituted party leadership continued their desperate battle with the *Tatmadaw* in the Pegu Yomas, the Delta and the heartlands of central Burma, in Burma's remote north-east the China-backed North-East Command (NEC), headed by party vice-chairman, Thakin Ba Thein Tin, grew rapidly in size to become the single largest insurgent force in Burma since independence, with as many as 20,000 troops and village militia under arms. Within just five years the NEC had seized control of thousands of square miles of the country's most rugged mountain terrain with remarkable ease. Had the NEC been able to link up with PA forces in central Burma (the main object of the Chinese 'invasion' plan) the political picture in the region would have looked very different today; Burma may well have gone the way of its neighbours, Vietnam, Laos and Cambodia, where equally determined communist forces, also backed by China, eventually won victory in the mid-1970s after nearly three decades of 'protracted warfare'.

CPB hardliners now claim not to have been disheartened by the setbacks of 1967/8. In a stirring oration at Than Tun's funeral Thakin Zin exhorted CPB supporters to be ready to 'follow the path stained with the blood of our late chairman'. A new 23-man CC was chosen, with Thakin Zin as chairman, Ba Thein Tin (in Beijing) as his deputy and Thakin Chit as secretary, with nine new military commanders appointed to coordinate operations around the country. Certainly Zin's demand for sacrifice was to be fulfilled, but much sooner than many expected; by 1975 over half had met with violent ends.[1]

None the less, with the certainty of new military aid from China, CPB leaders still had reason to feel optimistic. As Ne Win set about paving the way for the 1973 constitutional referendum and consolidating BSPP rule, the years 1968-75 were undoubtedly the most complicated in military terms in Burma since 1948-50. The CPB's rapid decline in central Burma was to be more than matched by the speed of the build-up of the People's Army (PA) in the NEC.

In addition to the fast-spreading ethnic insurgencies, in 1970 a new threat to Ne Win emerged in south-east Burma in the form of U Nu's CIA-backed Parliamentary Democracy Party (PDP) which, with a peak armed strength of 4,000 men, began to send guerrilla units on sabotage missions into Rangoon and other towns in Lower Burma. With popular leaders, international credibility, a jungle radio station and even its own coins and currency, the PDP at first looked likely to make rapid territorial gains. From the beginning the CPB ruled out any possibility of working with U Nu and the PDP's 'reactionary' and 'capitalist' leaders and there continued to be a remarkable lack of unity between Burma's different insurgent fronts. It was hardly surprising that at times Ne Win and his Revolutionary Council (RC) officers felt surrounded by hostile neighbours and battlefield foes on every side. Burma's continued political isolation was just one inevitable result.

In the midst of so many conflicting events it is impossible to maintain any sense of narrative, so each campaign in each part of the country is dealt with separately (for the PDP see Chapter 14). But while various protagonists argue that many of the party's setbacks in the 1970s (following the violent excesses of the CPB's Cultural Revolution) were self-inflicted, two crucial factors need to be singled out. First, the determination and ruthlessness with which the officers of the *Tatmadaw*, now well-practised in the art of counter-insurgency, fought their own dogged campaign; and second, the equally determined opposition from Burma's ethnic nationalist armies, several of which, most notably the Kachin Independence Organisation (KIO), resisted the CPB with equal fire. Hundreds more lives were lost in these bitter but little-reported wars and, like the PDP and BSPP, the CPB's continued failure to find a solution to the ethnic question at even this turbulent moment, once again highlighted the dilemma which has faced all national parties in Burma since independence.

The full scale of the CPB's failure did not, however, become apparent until 1989. For many years it was disguised from the outside world by the CPB's most stunning success in all the hard years since 1948 — the build-up, somewhat contradictorily, of an almost entirely ethnic minority army: Naw Seng's NEC.

China and the NEC: 1967-73

CPB leaders today concede that the NEC would never have materialised had it not been for the massive infusion of Chinese aid to the CPB which began in 1967. The true scale of this aid, whether advisory, financial, logistical or military, can never be fully gauged; over the last two decades in South-East Asia, it has been surpassed only by the CCP's support for Pol Pot and the Khmer Rouge in Cambodia. Various figures have been reported; CPB leaders have privately told other insurgent leaders that in 1967 a ten-year aid programme consisting of contributions to the CPB's annual budget was agreed to build up the NEC. This, Ba Thein Tin told a visiting Shan State Army (SSA) delegation in 1977, he estimated at 56 million kyats (approximately £5.5m) per annum.[2] And it was this time-limit, CPB leaders claim, rather than the rapid changes in China following Mao Zedong's death, which accounted for the downturn in aid after 1977.

But such figures give little account of the extraordinary impact of Chinese aid in one of the world's most neglected backwaters among such little-known peoples as the 'wild' Wa, who still reputedly practised head-hunting. Only in 1978 did the CPB claim to have eliminated the custom.[3] In addition to abundant supplies of tractors, trucks, radios, communication equipment, ammunition and modern weaponry (including AK 47s, mortars and miscellaneous anti-aircraft and field guns), hundreds of cadres and troops were trained along the border of China's Yunnan Province where they were given food, clothes and daily stipends. Roads and bridges were built by Chinese workers and a number of local hydro-electricity projects completed. Senior party leaders and dozens of junior cadres were granted free access to China; war casualties were routinely evacuated across the border to hospitals in Wanting, Meng Lian, Paoshan and Kunming. Compared to the hardships CPB units faced in the Delta, the NEC troops wanted for nothing.

Despite all this aid, Beijing's public support for the CPB was relatively short-lived and, from 1971, 'government to government' relations with Ne Win and the RC were once again gradually resumed. In a clever trick of political illusion, the aid was for the most part channelled to the CPB through the CCP's Yunnan Province Committee, which was responsible for relations with other communist parties in South-East Asia, including the CPT and CPM. In 1971 Beijing made a similar gesture towards the US-backed Thanom government in Thailand, with diplomatic relations quietly restored despite obvious Chinese support for the CPT. In 1974 formal relations with Malaysia were also resumed with a visit to Beijing by Tun Abdul Rahman.

But in Burma's case it was an act of extraordinary hypocrisy on both sides. Both, for their own reasons, preferred to maintain the international fiction that the CPB's build-up in Burma was simply an internal affair. For Ne Win, at least, there were some extenuating circumstances; in diplomatic circles the well-known saying, 'When China spits, Burma swims', was again much in vogue. Sensibly following the precedent of U Nu's successful policy of appeasement in the 1950s, *Tatmadaw* commanders were careful not to upset their counterparts across the border. 'There is much difficulty in fighting these insurgents,' Ne Win warned in March 1968. 'We have to be very careful lest our bullets go into the other country.'[4] By contrast the Soviet Union felt no such inhibitions. 'Beijing is frankly meddling in the domestic affairs of a sovereign neighbour,' claimed Moscow radio. 'Servicemen of the People's Liberation Army of China regularly infiltrate northern Burma from Yunnan Province. They act as instructors in the rebel detachments.'[5]

China's position was less excusable. Presumably Mao Zedong and the CCP leaders were anxious not to spoil their reputation as the voice of Third World neutrality between the superpower manipulations of Soviet revisionism and American imperialism. Blatant military interference in the affairs of an avowedly socialist non-aligned Asian neighbour hardly squared with this role. But the CCP's suppression of news of its involvement was quite deliberate. While for the next few years the Chinese media frequently carried battle news from central Burma of its 'fraternal' ally, the CPB, no mention was made of the NEC or the CCP's military help. But there can be no doubt that for a few brief years a common strategy between the CCP, the CPB and Ba Thein Tin was secretly evolved. To the continued embarrassment of Rangoon, Ba Thein Tin was at first accorded preference over (and later equality with) BSPP representatives in Beijing. As late as 1976 CPB leaders were featured prominently in official press coverage of the mourning ceremonies after Mao Zedong's death. Ba Thein Tin, for example, was filmed embracing Mao's successor, Hua Kuo-feng, and bowing in front of Mao's coffin; two months later Ba Thein Tin and Pe Tint were officially received by Hua who hosted a banquet for them.[6]

Whatever the later state of China-Burma relations, a series of articles in the Beijing press in late 1967 on the eve of the CPB invasion gave clear warning of China's support for the coming offensive. In an official statement on 31 October, the Chinese government 'solemnly' warned the Ne Win regime not to persist in its 'perverse course' by 'wantonly opposing China': 'No force can break the traditional friendships between the Chinese and Burmese peoples. The Chinese people will continue to give resolute support to the Burmese people's revolutionary struggle till final victory.'[7] Two weeks later an eulogistic article by Ba Thein Tin was published:

Comrade Mao-Tse Tung is not only the great leader of the glorious Chinese Communist Party and the heroic 700 million Chinese people, but also the great leader of the proletarians and revolutionary peoples of the whole world.... The Great Proletarian Cultural Revolution initiated and led by Chairman Mao [has] made China the powerful vanguard and base of world revolution which no force on earth can destroy.[8]

Four days later the official *New China News Agency* finally set the scene: 'Chairman Mao is like the sun spreading light wherever his thought shines. The brilliant light of Mao Tse-Tung thought shines over the tempestuous Irrawaddy River and the route of the Burmese people's revolution. It is advancing full of courage and will reach the shore with final victory.'[9]

In essence the NEC strategy was simple. To receive Chinese aid it was planned to build up a succession of individual base areas along the Shan and Kachin State borders, which PA units could use as stepping stones to link up with the CPB central headquarters under Thakins Than Tun, Zin and Chit in central Burma. Since any ethnic Burman presence in the region was minimal, this necessarily entailed winning the support of local villagers from an array of different ethnic backgrounds: predominantly, in numerical order, Shan, Kachin (mostly Jinghpaw-Maru-Lashi-Lisu), Wa, Lahu, Akha and Chinese. But this was more difficult than it first appeared. In the midst of the violent ethnic conflicts in north-east Burma in 1967, there was no compelling reason, other than arms, why the hill peoples, many of whom were illiterate and suspicious of outsiders, should support a group of ethnic Burman communists arriving from China. Many communities had only just recovered from the traumas of the Second World War.

As a result, it has often been claimed that the CPB's first invasion force was made up largely of 'Chinese' volunteers from China. In fact it was more complicated than that. Families of different nationalities, including Chinese, live on both sides of the border. In Yunnan Province, for example, there are large Kachin, Lahu and Shan (Tai) autonomous regions and many minorities on both sides of the border speak Chinese as a second, if not first, language. A KIO column from the Shan State I once travelled with carried a number of Chinese-language videos (in the absence of any in their own Jinghpaw language) about Kachin life in Yunnan, which they watched at every opportunity.

Thus eventually, with help from local Chinese Army commanders and instructors, the CPB's China-based leaders, Ba Thein Tin, Pe Tint, Khin Maung Gyi, San Thu, Tin Yi (*aka* Ne Win) and Than Shwe, were able to cobble together a force that enlisted villagers from both sides of the border. Adding to the NEC's Chinese appearance were several young Chinese who had gone underground in the aftermath of the anti-Chinese riots in Rangoon. A number of Red Guards from China were also recruited. 'It was a natural progression,' a former Red Guard once told me. 'It was not enough to go into the countryside and work with the farmers. To fight imperialism and revisionism, we all agreed, a real Red Guard joined the CPB.' One consequence of this pervasive Chinese influence, much to the consternation of *Tatmadaw* officers and rival insurgent forces trying to listen in, was that CPB commanders and wireless operators frequently used Chinese codes to transmit battlefield instructions. Ironically, one of these Chinese volunteers from 1968, Li Ziru, who rose to the CC in 1985, became one of the main leaders of the CPB mutinies in 1989. Other Chinese volunteers who rose to high rank included the future commander of the 815 region, Lin Ming Xian, born in Panghsai on the Burmese side of the border, and Zhang Zhi Ming, a former Red Guard and

Chinese citizen.

As Ba Thein Tin and his team embarked on the difficult task of building up the NEC, they enjoyed a remarkable stroke of good fortune. Long forgotten in China's Gweichou Province were some 300 remnants of Naw Seng's First Kachin Rifles who had led the unsuccessful Pawng Yawng rebellion of 1949-50 before taking sanctuary in China. Now mostly married and employed in mundane factory jobs and other civilian occupations, most were only too glad of the chance to join a new PA of ethnic minority troops to carry the war back to Burma. Naw Seng, once much criticised for the ferocity of the *Tatmadaw* operations he had conducted against the CPB in 1948 before he mutinied, was persuaded to take military charge of the NEC, while a number of other veterans from the Kachin Rifles and British Army took up important positions. Best known among these were Hpalang Gam Dee, Zau Mai and an ethnic Karen, Tun Tin, all three of whom later became full CC members of the CPB. Other volunteers had invaluable skills as wireless operators and medics; by recruiting them the CPB's fledgling army gained a degree of battlefield experience and professionalism, on familiar home terrain, which gave it a decisive military advantage. But perhaps most important, Naw Seng's appointment as commander-in-chief gave the NEC a figurehead of local respect in a remote mountain region virtually untouched by the 20th century, which it is unlikely any local communist (and certainly no ethnic Burman) could have achieved. A winner of the British Burma Gallantry Medal, Naw Seng's exploits were legendary among the local hill peoples. For nearly two decades his 'return' had been eagerly awaited.

Buoyed by the support of the Pawng Yawng rebels and the assurance of Chinese military aid, the CPB sought to win over the diverse 'national revolutionary minorities' in the region which, according to Maoist theory, should be enlisted in the communist cause. In north-east Burma in the late 1960s the CPB was almost spoilt for choice. In the Shan State in virtually every valley and on every mountain top a different ethnic army, KKY militia or local warlord force was fighting to gain control. But in 1967 the CPB's main target was the powerful KIO, which had already overrun most of the Chinese border region in the Kachin State and controlled much of the Kuktai region in the northern Shan State. In the second half of 1967 a KIO delegation, led by its vice-president, Zau Tu, made the trip to Beijing. Here they were regaled by both CPB and CCP officials, including Zhou En-lai, on the wisdom of joining forces with the CPB. Full military support was offered and, according to KIO veterans, warehouses were already being constructed along the border in anticipation of their agreement. There was only one condition; aid would have to pass through the CPB.[10]

For the KIO leaders, long isolated from the outside world and largely dependent on captured weapons, it was a highly tempting offer; in these early years the KIO's dealings with the CPB, like those of most other nationalist groups, were extraordinarily naive. KIO leaders freely admit this today. Kachin leaders were initially extremely cautious about the communist victory in China; and their doubts were fuelled by the steady wave of migrants and refugees, including ethnic Kachins, fleeing across the border into Burma after the failures of the Great Leap Forward and the Cultural Revolution. Indeed at the time of the CPB's approach, Zau Tu's older brother, KIO president Zau Seng, was on the Thai border negotiating with Gen. Li and the Third KMT Army at Tam Ngop. In fact in the early 1970s the KMT, rather than the CPB, became the KIO's main source of arms supplies. By 1966 KIO columns had already started making the arduous trip back and forth to the Thai border ferrying jade to sell in exchange for weapons.

None the less, on 15 January 1968, apparently unaware (KIO leaders say) of fighting with the CPB which had already broken out inside Burma, Zau Tu and Ba Thein Tin signed a joint agreement (written in both Burmese and Jinghpaw) to set up a military and political 'united front' to fight the 'Ne Win revisionist government'. The KIO received several hundred badly needed weapons. Revealingly, this was the last time an agreement between the CPB and KIO paraphrased communist language so exactly. For a brief moment, giving way after months of argument, the KIO's predominantly Christian leaders accepted that the war would be waged under 'the guidance of Mao's thoughts' against 'imperialists, feudal-landlords and capitalist-bureaucrats'.[11] Within four months the agreement was in shreds after clashes between rival troops over territory in the Mong Ko area. The CPB's error was then compounded when it persuaded two local KIO leaders, Ting Ying and Zalum, in the Kambaiti-Hpimaw region on the Chinese border to defect and join the party. It was the beginning of an expensive and inconclusive eight-year war with the KIO which soon cost the CPB any chance of making inroads into the highly vulnerable Sagaing Division to join up with CPB forces in the west. Of all the CPB's military errors, it was a tactical blunder without parallel.

Also visiting China during 1967/8 were leaders of the Naga National Council (NNC) from north-east India, led by Thuingaleng Muivah, whose insurrection had spread across the Burma border into the Naga hills. The CCP agreed without hesitation to arm and train this Naga force and for several years the NNC was often singled out for praise in the official Chinese media, along with the insurgent Mizo National Front (MNF) of Laldenga, whose troops did not reach China until the 1970s.[12] Notably, in the case of the Nagas, Mizos and later several other ethnic rebel movements to arrive from north-east India, no pre-conditions were set on their accepting the leadership of a communist or 'proletarian' party, which was the CCP's position on the KIO and insurgent nationalists from Burma. Support for the NNC thus appeared to have been motivated simply by China's border conflict with Delhi.

The CPB and the communist parties of Thailand and Malaya were the CCP's model parties in the region. These three allies were seen as the main bulwarks against KMT and American 'imperialism' in peninsula South-East Asia.[13] Ironically, the NNC's acceptance of this Chinese aid in 1967 produced an ideological split in the Naga movement which, many years later, led to the formation of the present National Socialist Council of Nagaland faction of Muivah (which remains closer to China) and the nationalist Federal Government of Nagaland group of the late A.Z. Phizo.

For the moment, however, the main thrust of the CPB's advance was not to the north into the troubled China-India borderlands, but southwards into the Shan State. War zones were designated for each new base area in the NEC. The first to move was '303' on the Chinese border in the far north. In the early hours of New Year's Day 1968 a 300-strong assault force, led by Naw Seng, Khin Maung Gyi and Than Shwe, attacked the sleepy border village of Mong Ko. The fighting was over in 30 minutes.[14] Four days later CPB troops entered the 404 war zone in the Kokang substate to the east. Here, amongst the local 'Kokangese' population (predominantly Chinese intermixed with Shans, Palaungs and other hill peoples), the CPB enlisted the support of a local nationalist warlord, Pheung Kya-Shin, who, by the end of the year, had delivered virtually the entire substate and its inhabitants to the CPB. It was an important victory. In the same period the *Tatmadaw* also tried to build up a rival Kokangese KKY force under another nationalist warlord, Lo Hsing-han, while the SSA (and later U Nu) supported the Kokang Resistance Force led by former Kokang MP Jimmy Yang. Symbolically, it was Pheung Kya-shin, who had never actually joined the CPB in the long years since, who started the mutiny in 1989 that led to the NEC's final disintegration.

But back in 1968, from these two bridgeheads the CPB rapidly spread its influence. Troops were quickly infiltrated along the banks of the Shweli River, west of Namhkam, into what became known as 'war zone 202'. Further north CPB persuasion in the Kachin hills finally paid off in April 1968 when Ting Ying and Zalum broke away to set up the 101 war zone in the Chepwi-Laukhaung region, east of the Kachin State capital, Myitkyina. Here most of the KIO recruits were from the Maru and Lashi sub-groups, two of the six Kachin ethnic families, while Zau Seng and most of the other senior KIO leaders at the time were from the majority Jinghpaw. The CPB was not alone in trying to use divide and rule tactics to split the KIO. In the same period the *Tatmadaw* set up the Nung-Rawang levies around Putao in the far north of the Kachin State to try and stop KIO expansion towards the Indian border. Meanwhile fighting had already broken out between the KIO and Naga villagers organised by the *Tatmadaw* in the far west of its territory in the Sagaing Division.

If establishing the 101 war zone virtually ended the CPB's progress north, further south the NEC was unstoppable. On 28 March 1970, the anniversary of the CPB insurrection, the key border town of Panghsai (Kyukok), astride the Burma-China road, fell in fierce fighting, opening the door to the CPB's advance. Fanning out southwards and westwards CPB troops poured through in regular battlefield formations, with Mong Mau in the northern Wa hills falling on 1 May.

Two events determined the next line of Naw Seng's attack. Skirmishes with the KIO's 4th brigade in the Kuktai region of the northern Shan State made it clear it would not be easy to win the hearts and minds of local villagers. The main reason Naw Seng had abandoned the Pawng Yawng rebellion in 1950 was because it pitched his own Kachin force against Kachin troops in the Burma Army, making no difference at all to the balance of power in Rangoon.[15] Moreover, in early 1969 an overture to the SSA headquarters in the adjoining Hsipaw region had been rejected. Delivered by a young CPB cadre, Sai Aung Win, an ethnic Shan and former activist at Rangoon University who personally knew several of the SSA leaders, it invited the SSA leadership to Beijing to discuss the formation of a united 'Nationalities Movement' against the Ne Win regime. In return, a contemporary SSA report claims, the SSA was offered the choice of an independent or federal state after the government was defeated.[16] This the SSA angrily interpreted as simply a ploy by China 'to make Burma her puppet' by using the national minorities 'led by the CPB' to overthrow Ne Win by force.[17] Thus, with both the KIO and SSA publicly making their objections clear, the NEC had to consider whether it was worth risking opening up a second front against other insurgent armies by pushing in massed formations down the old Burma Road, its most natural line of advance. Eventually, it was decided, it would be wiser to send smaller guerrilla units instead to try and probe their way through.

The NEC's second concern was the *Tatmadaw*'s tactical reply. Heavily outnumbered by the CPB, most government positions and local KKY forces quickly crumbled. But in October 1970 four *Tatmadaw* brigades, backed by aerial support, were rushed to the fertile Mongsi valley, the main rice-producing area in the Kuktai region west of the Salween River, where a 1,500-strong CPB strike-force had captured several outposts. Here, after several days of heavy fighting, the CPB was forced to retreat. Late the following year, an even larger battle was fought at the small town of Kunlong on the only major crossing point on the Salween River leading to the China border. Here, after 42 days of bitter fighting and hundreds of casualties on both sides, CPB commanders were forced to give up their attempt to capture and hold the town. Against the CPB's human tidal-wave tactics learned from China, the *Tatmadaw* used overwhelming aerial support. If the *Tatmadaw* was prepared to use such heavy firepower to defend selected towns and positions in the middle of such a vast mountain landscape, CPB leaders reasoned it would be better to concede control and simply filter troops through along the many hidden trails in the forest.

The cost to both sides in these battles was immense. In a 10-month period in north-east Burma in 1972, the CPB claimed to have fought 157 battles with Ne Win's 'mercenary army' in which 1,105 'enemy troops' were 'annihilated' and one air force jet shot down.[18] Against this, the RC claimed to have killed 500 communists in the Mongsi battle alone.[19]

With the failed attempt on Kunlong, the NEC stopped for a brief period of consolidation. On the anniversary of the CPB uprising in March 1971 a communist radio station, the Voice of the People of Burma (VOPB), somewhat confusingly began to broadcast from China at the very moment normal diplomatic relations between China and Burma were being resumed. Indeed in August 1971 Ne Win visited Beijing where he was received by Mao.[20] The VOPB's purpose, however, was simply to find a convenient way of getting round the ambiguity in China's relations with Burma. Its first announcer was clearly recognisable as a former announcer on Beijing radio's Burmese Service. The VOPB also allowed the CPB to publicise its growing military successes in the NEC without drawing attention to China's involvement. Broadcasting daily from the Yunnan border (the station only moved across the border in the late 1970s) in Burmese, Shan, Jinghpaw and Chinese, the VOPB was for many years the CPB's official mouthpiece with its oft-repeated diet of battle reports padded out with pro-Chinese, anti-BSPP, anti-American and anti-Soviet propaganda. Heard right across the country, it provided an important outlet for party news. In one of its earliest reports, on the anniversary of the CPB's founding in August 1971, the five key policies for the CPB's armed 'seizure of power', laid down by Than Tun, were enumerated and broadcast to the country. These have been repeated countless times since:

Concentrate on military affairs
Concentrate on the peasant base
Form alliances with nationalities
Expand the united front
Party construction is the key factor.[21]

Previously neither Beijing nor Rangoon had acknowledged the scale of the war in the NEC. Now the whole world was aware of its existence.

Following this breather, while small PA units continued to infiltrate westwards across the northern Shan State, during 1972/3 the main NEC force, now estimated at 4,000, rushed southwards along the China border through the virtually undefended Wa substates. Here a number of local militia were co-opted into the

PA while others were put to flight. During 1973 the entire Wa region east of the Salween River, except for the small towns of Panglong and Hopang, fell to the NEC and the CPB leaders followed south to set up a new headquarters at the sleepy border village of Panghsang. In the process, much to the delight of its Chinese backers, the CPB crushed the last KMT units still gathering intelligence on the China border. In November 1973, for example, the PA claimed to have killed 17 KMT soldiers and to have captured another three from a 'spy force' hiding in the hills near Mong Mau.[22]

More or less simultaneously the CPB annexed a vast base area running down to the Laotian border in the south. This became known as the 815 military region (named after the CPB's founding anniversary, 15 August) and was inhabited by predominantly Akha, Shan, Lwe and Lahu farmers. At the same time the CPB won over a key ally when the Shan insurgent leader, Khun Myint, head of the 1,000-strong Shan State Army East (the former Tailand National Army) in the Kengtung area, agreed to join forces with the CPB. Briefly operating as the Shan Peoples Liberation Army, Khun Myint's force was later integrated into the NEC as the PA's '768 brigade'.

In a fierce battle in late 1973 the *Tatmadaw* regained the remote town of Mong Yang situated in one of the few large plains in the trans-Salween region. This the CPB decided to abandon after the *Tatmadaw* continued to bomb its positions from the air, but a rare eyewitness report by a Burmese journalist shortly afterwards revealed for the first time the desperate nature of the fighting.[23] The CPB allegedly used Wa boys, some as young as 13 or 14 and armed only with hand grenades, in human tidal-wave attacks, while the town's Buddhist pagoda, where the CPB's 'Chinese' artillery had taken up position, was wrecked by the *Tatmadaw*'s aerial bombardment. Moreover, more disturbing evidence was uncovered of high-level Chinese involvement and the graves of four apparently senior Chinese officers were discovered after the town was captured and Chinese slogans, praising Mao Zedong, the CPB and 'people's democracy', were seen chalked up on walls about the town.[24]

The recapture of the isolated outpost at Mong Yang, however, could not disguise the success of the NEC offensive. From Panghsai in the north to the Laotian border and the Mekong River in the south, the CPB now controlled virtually the entire Shan State border with China, a distance of some 550 miles. Only a narrow enclave around Namhkam and Muse in the far north, which the army managed to hold onto after repulsing a major CPB assault in March 1973, remained in government hands.

It was a remarkable six-year campaign which, while hardly mentioned in the Rangoon press, saw one CPB victory after another. Ne Win and the BSPP contrived to make the NEC build-up look like a succession of defeats for the CPB, but many families in Burma today, who had sons caught up on both sides of the battle lines, know only too well the heavy cost of this bitter war in the cold mountains. Though both the CPB and *Tatmadaw* were prone to exaggeration, publicising victories and rarely acknowledging defeats, the CPB's final summary of the battle for the north-east is generally regarded as a revealing picture of the fighting. Between January 1968 and December 1973, the VOPB claimed, there were 1,783 battles in which fighters under the CPB's leadership 'put out of action' (i.e. killed or wounded) 11,400 government troops, of which 1,136 were captured; of this grand total, 2,420 were lost in 502 battles during 1973.[25] (Unlike several

other insurgent armies in Burma the CPB, like the KIO, always had a good reputation for releasing prisoners after 'political re-education'.) The CPB has never
admitted its own losses (which were generally lower) as it steam-rollered its way
through the mountains overrunning remote government outposts. But in the great
battles at Mongsi, Kunglong and Mong Yang, its casualties may well have been
much higher. Between June 1971 and March 1973 the *Tatmadaw* claimed to have
killed over 3,000 insurgents in north-east Burma, but these figures include the
KIO, SSA, Wa and even KMT remnants.[26] In reality, the army was often hard
pressed to distinguish one force from another.

At the same time, the VOPB claimed, 500,000 ethnic minority villagers in the
north-east region had been 'liberated' and organised by the CPB.[27] In the process
500 peasants unions with over 40,000 members and 550 women's unions with
over 10,000 members had been established, while thousands of villagers had been
trained as local people's militia. In the northern Wa region alone, where 200,000
villagers were mobilised to work on road construction projects, 2,000 militia had
been armed. Here a census in early 1973 revealed 170,000 villagers, predominantly Was, Kachins and Chinese, from 1,000 villages had come under CPB
rule.[28] No one now doubted the military correctness of Mao's tactics. 'Winning
victory after victory', the CPB was now constructing self-sufficient Red Power
base areas, encircling the cities, from which the revolution would soon spread;
'the enemy is bound to be crushed,' claimed the VOPB.[29]

Little noticed at the time amidst this heady stream of victories was one setback
which did not augur well for the future, namely the mysterious death of the NEC's
remarkable commander, Naw Seng. Various accounts of his death have circulated
for years. According to the CPB, he was killed in the Wa hills in 1972 in an
unfortunate accident when he slipped over a cliff while out hunting deer with his
batman. Others believe he was assassinated. The *Tatmadaw*, for example, claims
he was beaten to death with a stick after falling victim to another purge of
'revisionists', allegedly for his lack of conviction in dealing with the KIO.[30]
Perhaps the real truth will never be known. KIO leaders have been reluctant to be
drawn into the controversy, but those who travelled to China to meet Naw Seng
during this period never found any reason to doubt his loyalty to the CPB.
According to Zau Mai, the KIO's present-day Chief-of-Staff, who met him three
times: 'He told us if we really wanted to help the Kachin people, it was up to us.
He couldn't do anything. But if you want to know the real truth about his death
you will have to find his batman.'[31] Thamain Tun, a KNUP leader from Lower
Burma who made the long journey to China, also believed the official version of
the time; this suggested Naw Seng had been drinking heavily after being called
back to face criticism after the CPB's defeat at the Kunlong ferry.[32] But accidental
or not, as many insurgent leaders have pointed out, the years 1968-72 under Naw
Seng's military direction marked the CPB's greatest ever period of military expansion. With his death (and certainly from 1975) the great set-piece victories and
'liberation' of new territories declined drastically.

The Tatmadaw's Response

For the moment, however, the NEC's advance into north Burma was
overshadowed by events in Lower Burma. During the same period CPB forces in
the Delta and Pegu Yoma Divisions, led by Thakin Zin, were virtually wiped out.
Critically, Ne Win and the *Tatmadaw* generals never lost their nerve or sense of

purpose. Indeed the CPB's build-up in the NEC simply appeared to hasten the introduction of a plan they had already been working on for some years. Faced with the prospect of a military invasion from China, army field commanders set about preparing new defence lines. Though never officially admitted, contingency plans were set in motion for a partition of Burma along the lines of Vietnam and Laos, where communist armies supplied from across the Yunnan border had also seized control of vast stretches of the mountains and rural countryside. Similar discussions were taking place among senior army officers and political leaders in Thailand and Malaysia, where for a short time communist aid succeeded in getting through to the CPT and CPM.[33]

In Burma's case, Ne Win had long realised that the war would be lost or won in central Burma and the Burman heartlands (geographically, economically and politically the key to control of the country). Moreover, in the Shan State, in 1973, the *Tatmadaw* was forced to abandon its controversial KKY militia plan after increasing international criticism of the open drug-trafficking activities of several of the KKY's best-known commanders. A number (led by Lo Hsing-han who had taken part in the Kunlong battle) immediately went underground with hundreds of armed followers and allied themselves with the SSA, the KIO and other nationalist rebels, while the Wa KKY leader, Maha San, after a few years in the political wilderness, went on to form the present Wa National Organisation. In the south of the Shan State, too, the *Tatmadaw* was effectively hamstrung in early 1973 by the unexpected outbreak of the Lahu uprising, led by Pu Kyaung Long, the Lahu's spiritual man-god. Though the army responded fiercely in reprisals against Lahu villages in the Mong Hsat region, the revolt still festered on and today his son, Paya Kya Oo, heads the Lahu National Organisation, the latest in a line of Lahu rebel fronts.

Faced with revolt on this scale, the *Tatmadaw* made ready to abandon territory. Defence lines were established in the north-east along the west banks of the Salween and Irrawaddy rivers, which throughout history have proven a natural obstacle to invading armies. Should the situation deteriorate any further, second defence lines were pencilled in along the western edge of the Shan plateau and along the eastern edge of the Arakan Yomas. This thinking partly explains the absence of economic investment or road building in the hills, despite boundless opportunities for cheap timber, mining and hydro-electric projects. In the ethnic minority states, only a heavily defended power station at Lawpita in the Kayah State has ever been built; any other developments could have fallen into CPB or nationalist hands. Even the Lawpita power station was subject to frequent guerrilla attack and was put out of action as recently as 1988 in a rocket attack by the Karenni National Progressive Party (KNPP) after the Saw Maung coup. Industrial development (largely for munitions and the military) was instead concentrated around Prome and the middle reaches of the Irrawaddy River, where the government could be safely evacuated and regroup.

Just as the *Tatmadaw* had long since given up trying to take the Thai border region from the Karen National Union (KNU), KNPP, NMSP, KMT, SSA and various Shan rebel factions whose military bases and jungle encampments dotted the frontier (or the Bangladesh border from the CPB, Mizos and *Mujahids*), it now simply abandoned the China border to the CPB and KIO. Since this time it has frequently acted more like a guerrilla army in rebel-controlled areas. Composed as it is of mainly ethnic Burman troops, the *Tatmadaw* (rather than the

CPB) has more often appeared the 'invader'.

Only in the CPB's pivotal 108 region in the Lawksawk-Kyawkku districts, north of Taunggyi, did the *Tatmadaw* go on an all-out offensive. *Tatmadaw* commanders were quick to read the signals. In 1969 CPB guerrillas from the NEC's Shweli River 202 war zone under present-day Politburo member, Kyin Maung, made contact with CPB remnants in the Mogok region, while other troops pushed on through to the Nawngkhio area and linked up with units of the CPB's Shan State central headquarters. This was the point at which the NEC planned to break through into central Burma and join up with Thakin Zin. But sustained army pressure during 1968/9 saw the death in action in September 1969 of the PA's Shan State central bureau commander, Bo Soe Maung, a Rangoon University graduate and Burma Rifles veteran, while the following year the CPB's CC representative for the Shan State, Thakin Tin Tun, and his wife, Daw Myint, were captured and killed in an army ambush 24 miles east of Lawksawk. After these losses, leading CPB organisers and CC members (such as Myo Myint who was sent up from the Pegu Yomas in 1971, and Taik Aung, a Beijing returnee who had led many of the bloody purges in the Pegu Yomas before travelling up to the NEC) tried to build up the 108 region among the Shan, Palaung, Danu and Pao villagers in the area. But constant army operations throughout the early 1970s ensured CPB guerrillas were kept on the move, along with other local rebel forces such as the Shan United Revolutionary Army of Gon Jerng, and quickly reduced the hills to a devastated backwater where no insurgent force has ever gained a really firm foothold.

However, though these local counter-insurgency operations were effective, they served only as a distraction to prevent the CPB establishing a secure route by which to bring troops and supplies from the NEC into central Burma. Indeed, for a few years Ne Win seemed ready to let the NEC continue its build-up along the China border uninterrupted.

For now as fighting still raged in the remote mountains of north-east Burma, the entire focus of the *Tatmadaw's* campaign was turned against the oldest and best organised of the CPB's base regions in the Pegu Yomas and the Delta. Here in 1968 the army had quietly unveiled a new strategy which, within just four years was to change the entire face of the war in Burma and more than made up for the setbacks suffered in the NEC.

Today the strategy is well known to the world: the notorious *Four Cuts* campaign.

The Four Cuts Campaign and the Battle for Central Burma

From the earliest days of the insurrections the *Tatmadaw* periodically embarked on scorched earth campaigns, rarely in ethnic Burman areas and most notably against the KNU in the Delta in the early 1950s and the KIO in north-east Burma in the mid-1960s. Ethnic nationalists claim there was an undeniably racial element in planning and carrying out these attacks. But while effective in denying guerrillas food and territory, such operations usually did little more than push insurgent forces deeper into Burma's great mountains and forests. Rebel commanders and their followers invariably escaped, emerging again later to fight another day.

But in the mid-1960s, after the failure of the peace parley while Ne Win sought to establish a security cordon around the cities, a new strategy was drawn up.

Known as the *Pya Ley Pya* (*Four Cuts*), it was a counter-insurgency programme designed to cut the four main links (food, funds, intelligence and recruits) between insurgents, their families and local villagers. (Opposition leaders often claimed the fourth cut was the heads of the rebels themselves.) In recent years, in the face of increasing international criticism, *Tatmadaw* spokesmen have denied its existence, but over the years its use has been well documented and, indeed, frequently praised in public speeches by such leading army officers as Ne Win's long-time deputy, Brig. San Yu, and Gen. Tin Oo, ex-Minister of Defence and present-day NLD leader.[34] The strategy, which is hardly unique to Burma, owes much to the 'new village' tactics developed by British forces under Sir Robert Thompson in defeating the CPM insurgency in Malaysia; it was also similar in concept to the 'strategic hamlet' programme the United States employed, with Thompson's advice, in Indo-China. Both were criticised for their gross abuses of human rights.[35]

The first obvious sign of any change in tactics was in the new language the *Tatmadaw* used to describe the armed opposition. With the breakdown of the 1963 peace parley, insurgents were no longer accorded any political status. They simply became saboteurs, bandits, smugglers, racists and, occasionally, leftist or rightist extremists, united only in their desire to destroy the socialist economic system and bring about the disintegration of the Union. The state media has unswervingly kept to these designations ever since.[36] Now that the army embodied the people's aspirations and the BSPP was the only vehicle for political change, all the people, so the RC argued, had to support it. The *Tatmadaw*, explained Cmdr. Thaung Tin in 1967, had just three main tasks: 'To liquidate the insurgents, to organise the people and to study the party's Programme and Policy.'[37]

The map of Burma was divided into a vast chessboard under the *Tatmadaw*'s six (later nine) regional military commands and shaded in three colours: black for entirely insurgent-controlled areas; brown for areas both sides still disputed; and white was 'free'. The idea was that each insurgent-coloured area would be cleared, one by one, until the whole map of Burma was white. For the black 'hard-core' areas and brown 'guerrilla' zones a standard set of tactics was developed which, after a little refinement, has remained little changed till today. In theory it was an attempt to win the hearts and minds of rural villagers; army commanders called it their own version of people's war.[38] But its application in Burma has been mainly military, with the same basic objective as the 'strategic hamlet' programme in Vietnam and Laos where millions of peasants, rural villagers and hill peoples were forcibly relocated. As an American official in Laos explained in a famous paraphrase of Mao: 'If the people are the sea, then let's hurry the tide south.'[39]

To begin with, selected rebel areas, just 40 to 50 miles square, were cordoned off for concentrated military operations. Army units then visited villagers in the outlying fields and forests and ordered them to move to new 'strategic villages' (*byu hla jaywa*) under military control on the plains or near the major garrison towns in the hills. Any villager who remained, they were warned, would be treated as an insurgent and ran the risk of being shot on sight. After the first visit, troops returned periodically to confiscate food, destroy crops and paddy and, villagers often alleged, shoot anyone suspected of supporting the insurgents. It was, they claim, a calculated policy of terror to force them to move.

Villagers' reports of such attacks, though rarely recorded in the world outside, are legion from all corners of Burma since the *Four Cuts* began.[40] One bedraggled party of 220 Karen refugees I saw arriving at the Thai border with their meagre belongings in 1987 gave eyewitness details of how government soldiers had killed 31 of their relatives, apparently at random, since the *Four Cuts* campaign was officially introduced amid much fanfare in the vicinity of their homes in the Shwegyin hills in 1975. 'Each year three, four or five villagers have to die,' said Pah La Hai, a 43 year-old farmer. 'The Burmese soldiers shoot them without reason. They will kill all the villagers. No one must stay there any more.'[41]

Even more graphically, with a television crew from Britain's Channel Four, in December 1989 I secretly filmed a Burmese Army unit systematically looting a civilian Karen village at Sitkaya, which it had entered, with guns blazing, the day before. At least seven villagers were killed, 20 were captured and over 200 escaped, including several wounded women and children, by swimming across the Moei River into Thailand.[42] Those arrested were promptly press-ganged into front line porter service carrying supplies for their army captors. Local Karen leaders insist that such scenes are identical to those they experienced 20 years earlier in the Delta. For the *Tatmadaw* in the *Four Cuts* campaign there is no such thing as an innocent or neutral villager. Every community must fight, flee or join the *Tatmadaw*.

Meanwhile, farmers and families who do travel to the new strategic villages are mobilised to fight on the government's side. The villages are fenced in, usually with the army's blockhouses or barracks located in the centre of the compound to prevent shelling or guerrilla attack. The villagers themselves are trained to act night and day as village look-outs and guards. Even primary schoolchildren are made to take part in the drilling. Guns and ammunition are strictly controlled. Insurgent commanders admit that these 'people's militia', of which thousands have been formed in the last 25 years, have proven one of the most effective components of the *Four Cuts* plan. Across Burma they have divided communities in rebel-controlled areas, making it virtually impossible for families to remain neutral on both sides of the battle lines. A night-time (and sometimes even daytime) curfew is enforced and all food confiscated. This is then rationed back on a daily basis to ensure that all villagers keep close to home and that no stock-piles are hidden in the forest for relatives or rebel forces. All movements in and out of the village have to be reported and visitors or guests registered with the army garrison. Anybody suspected of contact with the rebels, whether as an underground agent or by providing food or intelligence, faces arrest and the possibility of summary execution. Theoretically, all army actions are subject to legal restrictions, but in practise the entire area has been placed under martial law and any military action can thus be justified as a counter-insurgency measure. Only once this framework is in place does the *Tatmadaw* go on an all-out offensive.

To spearhead these first operations in the mid-1960s, special new strike forces, Light Infantry Divisions (LIDs), were created. The first was the 77th in mid-1966; another two, the 88th and 99th, were formed in 1967 and 1968 (today there are nine). Significantly, overall command of these new divisions was given not to the regional military commands but to the Office of the Chief-of-Staff in Rangoon. The intention was deliberate. As counter-insurgency 'shock-troops', they have few qualms about local sensibilities.

On the plains of the Delta dozens of watch-towers were erected along the roads and rivers, or at points where insurgent forces were likely to break cover. Mobile columns then moved out from the towns, constantly criss-crossing back and forth in every direction, to try and flush out rebel units hiding in the *maquis*. The whole district was, in effect, declared a free-fire zone and it became very difficult for insurgents to hide their weapons, or pass themselves off as local villagers, as they had done countless times before. At first rebel forces simply disappeared down well-trodden escape routes to camps hidden deep in the hills and forests. But over the weeks, as the offensive continued, the physical and psychological demands were punishing. Under constant attack and deprived of food, logistical support, and all contact with family and friends, they soon found they were faced with only three choices: a fight to the death, surrender or retreat into the next military zone.

Though a very simple tactic, the *Four Cuts* has proven devastatingly effective. Once a base area is lost, it is virtually impossible for guerrilla forces to infiltrate back into their old stomping-grounds. Most of these counter-insurgency pressures have with time been relaxed, but the new military infrastructures have been kept intact and as a result vast areas of rural Burma, especially in the Pegu and Arakan Yomas and the mountainous ethnic minority states, have not been repopulated since the rebels were forced out. Indeed it was only when the *Four Cuts* operations ran against the borders of Burma's neighbours (Bangladesh, India, China and Thailand) that for the first time any serious military weaknesses in the strategy were revealed. In these remote and sensitive border regions it is militarily impossible to tie down guerrilla forces who have a back-door escape and supply line. According to Col. Aye Myint, a former head of the *Tatmadaw*'s NEC, who had employed these tactics against the CPB, KNU, KIO and SSA, in these mountainous borderlands the financial and logistical costs are too immense for the *Tatmadaw* to bear. Even for the smallest operation, for the campaign to succeed thousands of troops and porters need to be mobilised in advance and brought in to swamp the area.[43]

The army had tinkered with these tactics in the Sagaing Division, Kachin State and south-west Burma during 1965-7, but it was in the Lower Delta that the campaign was first fully unveiled. Meanwhile, as a diversion, the *Tatmadaw* kept the CPB's central military command busy around the edges of the Pegu Yomas with the campaign of constant military harassment which saw the deaths of such leading party officials as Bo Zeya, Aung Gyi and Dr Nath. The timing was to prove crucial. Despite the purges and blood-letting during the CPB's Cultural Revolution, in late 1967 all the evidence suggested that the CPB (and not only in the NEC) was preparing to go on the military offensive. In the Myaungmya district of the Delta alone the CPB claimed to have 'wiped out' well over 200 government troops during 1966/7.[44] With the exception of Vietnam, the CPB's military prospects compared very favourably with those of any other communist party in South-East Asia.

To break out of their Red Power strongholds in the Pegu Yomas and link up with other party base areas in the Delta, Tenasserim, Arakan and the NEC, seven new mobile battalions, the *Tike Taing Aung* (Ever Victorious), were formed. The deaths of Bo Soe Maung and Thakin Tin Tun in 1969/70 cut short the plan to build up the strategic 108 region in the Shan State, but in the coming years several of these new units, especially the No.4 battalion in the Toungoo district and the No.7 battalion under Thet Tun in the North-West Division, proved quite effective at carrying out raids on government outposts on the plains and at linking up with the party's central headquarters. Government officials, headmen and cooperatives were particular targets and in March 1968, for example, 200 CPB troops overran the town of An in Arakan. Bridges and rail lines were repeatedly sabotaged and by mid-1968 the total night-time curfew on all railways in the country had to be re-imposed. At the same time military operations with the CPB's NDUF ally, the KNUP, were stepped up. In May 1967 an NDUF force attacked Gyobingauk, north of Tharrawaddy, in what was reputedly the largest insurgent operation since Ne Win seized power in 1962, while in early 1968 joint KNUP-CPB forces carried out a number of successful attacks, including the capture of Kyauktaga, near Pegu, and Bogale in the Lower Delta where guerrilla units had penetrated the town in advance. Large stockpiles of weapons and supplies were carted away before the guerrillas melted back safely into the countryside.[45]

The KNUP and the Last Days of Thakin Zin

Gen. Ne Win, however, refused to be distracted. Though from the air the vast riverine plain of the Irrawaddy Delta looks accessible enough, for the modern traveller much of the Delta Frontier is an impenetrable region of great mangrove swamps, forest reserves, muddy rivers and hidden creeks, where government forces have always had to move slowly. There are remarkably few roads. The KNUP, headed by Mahn Ba Zan and, from 1968, by Gen. Kaw Htoo, had always been the most powerful force in this region. The KNU's final split at this stage into two movements (see Chapter 14), in the east under Bo Mya and Mahn Ba Zan and in the Delta under Kaw Htoo, was a damaging blow to Karen morale, but KNUP forces remained largely intact and after the 1962 coup were fuelled by a flood of new recruits from the towns. In the 1950s eight military brigade districts had been set up under the KNUP's military wing, the Kawthoolei People's Liberation Army (KPLA), which stretched from the Arakan Yomas to the Kyaukkyi hills in the east (see Chapter 8). The KNUP's main demand was for a Federal Union of Nationality States of Burma (the Karen State would be socialist) with autonomous regions for Karen-majority districts in the Delta. But with a five-man Politburo elected from a 15-man CC, the KNUP and KPLA appeared to be a carbon-copy of Maoist political organisation and were to prove a formidable CPB ally, though, notably, there is no evidence, even after Mahn Ba Zan's defection, that the Cultural Revolution held any appeal for the KNUP die-hards.[46]

Only in the foothills of the Arakan and Pegu Yomas had the KNUP established really permanent camps, but across much of the Delta KPLA units could move with relative freedom through KNUP- and CPB-controlled villages and base areas. Linking these base areas was an elaborate network of forests, swamps and foothills, known in Karen as *Way-la-phan* (gold and silver highways), through which troops and supplies could be moved. Close to the towns KPLA units had to move with caution, but into the late 1960s villagers around such major towns as Henzada and Bassein remember roving KPLA columns, of up to 300 troops, arriving in the dead of night to pick up supplies and news.

With KNUP support, throughout the 1950s and 1960s both White Flag and small Red Flag CPB units moved confidently back and forth across the Delta, heading north into the Arakan Yomas or skirting around Twante and Rangoon as they crossed towards the Pegu Yomas and the Sittang River. Ethnic Burman villages in the Delta generally lie along rivers and roads, whereas Karen villages tend to be in the forests and interior. Under the CPB's veteran Delta Division secretary, Soe Than, five district committees were established with party cells and supporters in most of the Delta's townships; in the countryside small guerrilla units and mobile columns moved freely under the cover of night. Tipped off by villagers well beforehand, they always slipped away easily before any *Tatmadaw* advance.

If transport difficulties hindered army operations, the Delta's military significance was not lost on Ne Win, San Yu, Aye Ko, Tin Oo and the *Tatmadaw* strategists. It was a perfect guerrilla haven in the middle of the economic hub of Burma. The Irrawaddy Delta, an army spokesman explained, 'could be compared to the womb of the insurrection. From it continually flow funds to breed insurrection raging in so many parts of the entire country.'[47] Taxes on villagers, fish farms, timber mills, rubber and forestry plantations had long provided the bulk of funds for both the KNUP and CPB. Documents captured from the CPB in 1969 revealed that 200,000 kyats in contributions and 'loans' had been collected by its Myaungmya district committee the previous year alone, while the Kawthoolei RC estimated that in the 1950s the Delta Division's No.2 and No.7 brigades in the Myaungmya-Bassein districts had raised a third of the four million kyat annual income supporters sent to the KNU's general headquarters in the eastern mountains.[48]

It was therefore in this region that the *Tatmadaw* first unleashed the full force of its new tactics. Probing hit-and-run attacks during 1966/7 had tested KNUP and CPB defences along the plains and the southern edge of the Arakan Yomas. Then on New Year's Day 1968, just as Naw Seng was beginning the CPB offensive in the NEC, the 88th LID launched the first stage of the *Four Cuts* campaign. Codenamed Operation *Moe Hein*, it was swiftly followed by Operations *Shwelinyone* and *Shwelawin* in the South-West Command. Bit by bit, small areas of the Delta were cordoned off, villagers ordered to move to the new strategy villages, and all road and river transport suspended. Then, with the district apparently cleared of 'innocent' civilians, *Tatmadaw* columns and gunboat patrols began to seek out CPB and KNUP forces in what Beijing mockingly called the 'frantic counterrevolutionary encirclement and suppression campaigns' of the 'Ne Win clique'.[49]

At first most CPB and KNUP forces escaped; they even launched several counter-attacks in the Bassein-Myaungmya area in which a number of boats and army vehicles were destroyed. But when a party of senior KNUP leaders, headed by Delta secretary, U Soe Aung, tried to move from the Arakan Yomas across the Delta towards Maubin to give speeches and raise morale, they found government troops everywhere.[50] Around Myaungmya they discovered a vast trap had been set. Look-out towers stretched as far as the eye could see. The first victims were KNDO village militia and party officials who had little choice but to run or face arrest. But now the KPLA's regular battalions also found their way blocked as they tried to retreat into rear base areas and the number of arrests and casualties began to climb steadily. An emergency meeting of district officers and brigade commanders was held near Pyapon in the KPLA's 5th brigade area; U Soe Aung's party then travelled on by boat and foot northwards into the Pegu Yomas to the KNUP's mobile headquarters (on a small tributary of the Pegu River) for a full CC meeting called by KNUP general-secretary, Bo Kyin Pe, to discuss the *Four Cuts* offensive and the damaging KNU split. No solutions were reached but the seriousness of the deteriorating situation was brought home at the end of the meeting when several CC members found the routes back to their Delta base areas were blocked. Indeed several, including Kyin Pe, never returned.

Into 1969, as more and more insurgent camps were uncovered, the *Four Cuts* campaign began to build up a momentum of its own and the CPB now also started to feel the squeeze. Caught on the hop and confused by the new tactics, veteran party leaders, long safe in their own communities, were slow to react. In March 1969, 52 year-old Thakin Bo U, a senior member of the CPB's Delta Division committee, only narrowly escaped capture when his headquarters was attacked. In their flight his staff left behind radios, typewriters, tape recorders, Mao Zedong literature and virtually the entire administrative machinery of the CPB's Myaungmya district branch. Whereas in the past senior party organisers invariably slipped away, this time they found their escape blocked. After two months constant pursuit in an ever-tightening snare, on 23 May Bo U's dead body was captured (his family had been taken alive two days earlier) when the 27th Burma Regiment, backed by a 1,000-strong people's militia, finally ran his party to ground in the forests south of Labutta. A former president of the Myaungmya District *Dobama Asiayone*, a veteran of the anti-Japanese resistance and post-war ABPO leader, he was one of many local peasant leaders who had gone underground with the CPB in 1948 and typified exactly the kind of cadre and respected community figure the CPB had relied on heavily through the long years since. Amidst the more spectacular battles and clashes in the Pegu Yomas and NEC, such little-publicised deaths of local district and township CPB officers were hardly noticed at the time. But it was precisely the loss of such experienced organisers as these which, the *Tatmadaw* recognised only too well, was gradually sapping the CPB's strength and destroying its battle-tested infrastructure.[51] On 15 August 1969, the thirtieth anniversary of the CPB's founding, PA units yet again staged a headline-grabbing attack by sabotaging a Rangoon to Mandalay goods train, but for once this annual gesture could not deflect attention from the CPB's rapidly worsening plight in Lower Burma.

The KNUP fought the main rearguard action, but the hot-pursuit tactics were instantly effective and within four years, as successive phases of the *Four Cuts* operation rolled slowly northwards, thousands of CPB and KNUP supporters were isolated and their village networks destroyed. Only small bands of stragglers remained, some secretly returning to their villages. Hundreds more surrendered or were killed or wounded as the death toll rose inexorably higher. In five weeks in early 1971, in the ninth phase of the *Shwelinyone* operation in Ngaputaw township, 262 insurgents were reportedly killed, captured or forced to surrender, while in a four-week period in the tenth phase in the Henzada district further north, another 192 insurgents were 'put out of action'.[52] Newspaper photographs showed how well prepared the insurgents had been; in one operation alone 250 firearms, 2,000 rounds of ammunition and 22 elephants were confiscated.[53]

The obvious success of these operations strongly suggests that in many areas there were villagers, tired after so many years of rural insurgency, who were only too glad to help the *Tatmadaw* if their cooperation offered the prospect of peace. Though the KNUP was particularly well organised in the Delta's large Karen community (and the *Tatmadaw* is still highly nervous of KNU activists getting back into the Delta), the bloody purges of the CPB's Cultural Revolution had clearly done great harm to the party's reputation. In early 1971 virtually the entire Henzada district committee of the CPB surrendered. Led by Ko Soe Kyi, brother-in-law of the former Delta secretary, Soe Than, who was purged in 1969, they were clearly still embittered over the execution of so many veteran CPB supporters on such obviously spurious charges. 'The accusations were mere fabrications,' Soe Kyi claimed. 'This exposed the lack of inner party democracy in the CPB.'[54]

By 1971 the *Tike Taing Aung* battalions in the Delta had been smashed and remnants forced to scatter north to try and regroup in the Pegu Yomas. Only a few die-hards stayed with the KNUP's last Delta strongholds in base areas along the southern edge of the Arakan Yomas. During 1972 KPLA units of 200-300 men still carried out raids in Gwa, Lemyethna and Ngathainngyaung townships with varying degrees of success; but events this year were overshadowed by the death in April of KNUP chairman, Kaw Htoo, from heart disease. His place was taken at a hurriedly called CC meeting by Mahn Mya Maung after his chosen successor, Kyin Pe, was killed in action. But even here in these remote foothills and deep forest reserves, as the *Four Cuts* continued its remorseless path, there was no end to the insurgents' heavy losses. On 6 September 1973 Soe Than's successor as Delta secretary of the CPB, Bo Aung Pe, was killed in a forest reserve west of Lemyethna, while the same month Bo Aung Htin, the CPB's divisional commander, was one of several prominent party officials in Bassein and Ngaputaw districts who were killed or captured. Between September and December 1973, the *Tatmadaw*'s South-West Command claimed that over 600 insurgents and their dependents had surrendered during Operation *Tainglongaung*, while another 300 had been killed.[55] Two KNUP CC members, Saw Tun Aye and Saw Mya Yin (whose wife was killed), were also captured, but the most bitter blow was the death in an ambush near Ngaputaw of the former naval officer, Saw Jack, who had mutinied with his vessel at the beginning of the insurrection to lead the KNDO attack on Bassein. Later a staunch leftist and successful guerrilla commander, Saw Jack had long been one of the heroes of the Karen revolution.

The KNUP remnants eventually evacuated to the safe sanctuary of the eastern mountains, where several veteran leaders still remain. Had it not been for the NEC, the CPB's collapse would probably have been even more abrupt. Certainly in central Burma, within eight years of the start of the *Four Cuts* campaign, the CPB had virtually disintegrated as a military force. Only in the North-West Division under Thet Tun, whose 250-strong No.7 *Tike Taing Aung* battalion frequently struck down along the plains, was the PA actually able to increase in size in this period.

But both sides recognised the final battle for central Burma would be fought in the party's Red Power strongholds of the Pegu Yomas. Here, from 1968, CPB and KNUP leaders continued to arrive from the Delta with alarming news of the *Four Cuts* campaign and tried to work out ways of resisting the coming offensive. During this period a number of historically important meetings between the two parties took place in which Kaw Htoo, Skaw Ler Taw and the KNUP leaders made their objections to the CPB's 'nationality' policies very clear. But by this stage the other NDUF members had left. The Chin National Vanguard Party had been absorbed by the CPB, while the KNPP and the NMSP had both broken away, the latter to join Bo Mya and Mahn Ba Zan in U Nu's National United Liberation Front.

The KNUP further antagonised the CPB by setting up two ethnic fronts of its own, the short-lived United Nationalities Front (UNF) and, in 1967, the rather more successful Nationalities United Front (NUF), which deliberately excluded the CPB (see Chart 2). The UNF was established in the Papun hills during the 1965 rainy season, shortly before Bo Mya's defection; it included the KNPP, the Zomi National Front (ZNF, an ethnic Chin group set up with KNUP help the same year), the newly formed Shan State War Council (SSWC) and Kayan New Land Party (KNLP, set up on KNUP advice the previous year), as well as representatives of the armed Pao nationalist movement which was then being reformed. A joint military and political programme was agreed, but the UNF fell apart shortly afterwards when the SSWC president, the *Mahadevi* Sao Nang Hearn Kham, a firm 'royalist', rejected the front's 'socialist ideology'.[56]

The KNUP had rather more luck at its second attempt. The NUF was set up in December 1967 at a meeting of KNUP, KNPP, ZNF, KNLP and Pao representatives in KNPP territory on the Toungoo-Karenni borders. (The NMSP was also represented by KNUP CC member, Than Aung, who attended under the Mon name, Nai San Meit, shortly before his defection to join Bo Mya.) Again a joint programme was drawn up, but this time it was agreed to take it one stage further and form a mixed-race NUF battalion 'to try', according to Skaw Ler Taw, 'to forge the bonds of better racial understanding', the first time a united front in Burma had employed this tactic.[57] Composed of detachments of KNUP, KNPP and KNLP troops, in early 1968 this joint NUF force, under Bo San Lin (political commissar) and Bo Man Maung (commander), moved into the south-west Shan State and operated for several years as far north as Honam-Laikha in support of the Kayan and Pao movements, suffering considerable hardships in the many battles to come. Of the original 60 KNUP troops who travelled north, by 1972 only 44 were still in active service. Ironically, despite the NUF's avowedly 'nationalist' ideals, this KNUP force is locally best remembered for its support for the pro-CPB faction of Tha Kalei in the 1973 split which has since divided the Pao movement into two rival parties.

However, despite the formation of the NUF, with the defection of Mahn Ba Zan to the east, 1967 marked the political watershed in the rise of the KNUP movement. From 1968 onwards the KNUP was fighting for its very life, but despite its disagreements with the CPB, the KNUP-CPB alliance in Lower Burma did endure to the very end. It was very much, KNUP veterans insist, an alliance of equals and in this period the KNUP sent no less than four 'study missions' to China to try, unsuccessfully, to establish formal relations and win CCP aid (see Chapter 16). Though fighting did break out in the Pegu Yomas with one virulently anti-CPB KNUP commander, Bo Nyaung Ye, and a number of CPB officials were killed, for the most part KNUP leaders say they were unaffected by (indeed largely unaware of) the bloody purges of the CPB's Cultural Revolution. The CPB's base areas in the Pegu Yomas were always further north.

To meet the *Tatmadaw*'s challenge, in 1970 the two sides decided to form a joint *Aung Naing* (Victorious Victory) brigade, commanded by Bo Pone Kyaw (CPB) and Bo Toe Kyi of the KNUP. From sanctuaries in the southern Pegu Yomas it carried out a number of successful operations, sweeping down onto the plains between Rangoon and Prome and attacking army convoys and positions, especially in Tharrawaddy and Letpadan. At the same time, both parties stepped up guerrilla activities to try and prevent the growing concentration of army forces around the Pegu Yomas range. Occasionally the VOPB reported battles. In March

1973, a *Tike Taing Aung* unit reportedly overran a *Tatmadaw* outpost in a village on the Sittang River, Toungoo district, killing 32 government troops and taking 19 prisoner.[58] On 3 November later that year, the *Aung Naing* brigade attacked an army camp on the upper reaches of the Pegu River, killing four soldiers and capturing another 13.[59]

At this desperate moment neither the KNUP nor CPB were helped by the arrival of two rival insurgent forces (a KNU force under Bo Tha Sein, sent by Bo Mya, from the east and an allied 150-strong PDP battalion under Bo Tet Tun) which both reached the Pegu Yomas in 1972 in a forlorn attempt to establish their own 'liberated zones'. Fighting immediately broke out and both forces were eventually repelled. But it was almost as if Thakin Zin, Kaw Htoo and the NDUF leaders had already decided to fight to the last. Even at this late hour, few tried to surrender or escape. At the beginning of 1974, as the last KNUP and CPB remnants from the Delta arrived in the Pegu Yomas, the VOPB broadcast details of the situation in the Delta and the NDUF CC's desperate appeal to its supporters 'to maintain the tradition of the revolutionary Karen and Burmese people in replacing those who had fallen.'[60]

Now it was the turn of the Pegu Yomas to feel the onslaught. In a six-month dry-season offensive running into early 1974, the army's 77th LID suffered heavy casualties as it tried to capture the mobile forest headquarters of the CPB, KNUP and NDUF. Shortly afterwards CPB wireless operators in the Pegu Yomas sent warnings to Ba Thein Tin and the NEC that army units had begun forcibly 'uprooting' villages and 'looting and destroying paddy'.[61] Their tone was increasingly desperate. In one of his last recorded speeches Thakin Zin accused government soldiers of starving out and attacking innocent villagers and called Ne Win and the *Tatmadaw* leaders 'ten times more ruthless than their US or Japanese masters'.[62] By the end of the year the Pegu Yomas had been cleared of virtually all human habitation.

The success of the army's last major offensive in central Burma, Operation *Aung Soe Moe*, is graphically described by CPB defectors in *The Last Days of Thakins Zin and Chit*.[63] It was a bitter battle to the death in which quarter was neither asked nor given. During April 1975 a number of KNUP units under CC members Mahn Mya Maung and U Soe Aung, who were my main informants and in the last party to leave, escaped across the Sittang River to the east (one soldier and five women recruits drowned in the attempt), where they eventually rejoined the KNU under Bo Mya. From 600 men under arms at the beginning of the final offensive (400 from the local Pegu Yomas brigade and just 200 remnants from the once proud Delta Division), KNUP leaders estimate just over 100 KPLA soldiers made this final journey into the Nyaunglebin hills to be reunited with another 150 KNUP troops and officers, including Bo San Lin and Skaw Ler Taw, then on duty in the east. Here in the Dawna Range a number of KNUP survivors are still active in the KNU leadership. By contrast, CPB forces in central Burma were decimated.

For the last six months of 1974 units from the CPB's central headquarters, separating into ever smaller teams, continued to duck and weave across the mountains as they desperately tried to wriggle out of the army's tightening noose. But by this stage the *Tatmadaw*'s front line commandos were well versed in the art of 'going bush' in hostile terrain for weeks on end, short of food, water and shelter. As the chase continued, the number of casualties, women, children and deserters, left behind on the forest trails began to rise steadily.

By the beginning of 1975 Thakins Zin and Chit and the leaders of the party's central headquarters were cornered in the forests along the Yenwe Chaung. A three-pronged assault force from the 107 Light Infantry Regiment was sent in to track them down. On 26 February CC member *Yebaw* Toke was killed in an army ambush and eventually, on 15 March, government troops caught up with the rest of the party leadership near the confluence of the Phutkya and Pein streams. According to Col. Aung Htay, director of MIS, the army had resolved to capture them both alive out of respect for their role in Burma's 'freedom struggle'.[64] They were now both in their mid-sixties. But when troops moved in to demand their surrender, Thakin Chit defiantly opened up with an M79 grenade launcher, while Thakin Zin blazed away with his pistol. Both were instantly cut down in a hail of bullets. 'The curtain falls,' claimed an army spokesman, 'on the last of the CPB men in the Yoma.'[65]

The CPB's losses were catastrophic. Not only had Thakin Zin, a wartime CPB organiser and former vice-chairman of ABPO, been a widely respected voice of authority in Burma's liberation struggle and an important figurehead for the communist cause in succession to Than Tun, but Thakin Chit, a former teacher, joint-founder of the Socialist Party and ABTUC leader, was without doubt one of the most skilful behind the scenes organisers in mobilising workers and peasants in Burma since the earliest days of the Thakin movement. It was Chit, one-time secretary to U Nu, who colleagues today attribute with sending to Japan many of the *Thirty Comrades* for military training. Their names were now added to the growing death toll of the CPB's most able leaders. Than Tun, Ba Tin, *Yebaw* Htay, Bo Zeya, Aung Gyi, Dr Nath, Tin Tun and Aung Pe were all dead, their party units and cells in tatters, their military defeat total. No casualty figures exist for the CPB's central military command, which once boasted about 1,000 full-time soldiers under arms, but under Operation *Aung Soe Moe* the *Tatmadaw*, which itself admitted that 135 of its troops had been killed and 143 wounded, claimed to have killed 172 CPB troops, captured 149 and accepted the surrender of 500 more.[66] Only a handful filtered away. At first army spokesmen claimed that only 18 cadres had escaped, but in October reported that Bo Pone Kyaw, the NDUF brigade commander, and Soe Kyi, an alternate CC member, had been ambushed and killed in the forest near Daik-U. They were leading what was probably the last of the CPB's scattered armed units still militarily active. It was a conclusive victory and after nearly three decades of constant warfare, which saw the deaths of thousands of government soldiers, Ne Win and his generals undoubtedly felt they had good reason to celebrate. Only their much-publicised final analysis, 'the CPB has totally disintegrated', was wrong.[67]

U Thant's Funeral and the 1974-6 Street Protests
Perhaps the most telling evidence of the CPB's decline, despite the build-up of the NEC, was not on the battlefield but in the towns and cities. Despite the twin threats of the CPB and U Nu's PDP in south-east Burma, intense MIS counter-intelligence operations in the early 1970s generally kept the political situation quiet in the main conurbations while the RC pushed ahead with the 1973 constitutional referendum. Thousands more political activists were arrested and not until 1973 were many of the political prisoners held without trial as far back as 1962 released.[68]

In mid-1974, shortly after the BSPP announced a surprise political amnesty following the success of the referendum, towns across the country were twice convulsed by massive anti-government demonstrations. First came workers' strikes, which broke out in May in Rangoon, Mandalay, Chauk, Meiktila and Yenangyaung against a backdrop of rising inflation and growing food shortages. Government corruption and the corrosive effects of the black market, from which many military officers so clearly prospered, were particular sources of anger.[69] After 12 years of military mismanagement the economy was a complete shambles. Ne Win preferred to put all the blame on agriculture. 'Rice is the root cause of this problem,' he claimed.[70]

But Burma's problems ran deeper than this. Across the country food was being hoarded, prices offered to farmers by the state were far too low and the country's infrastructure was virtually non-existent. In early June a number of workers were arrested for organising a strike at the Insein railway-yard. This triggered a series of high-spirited rather than violent protests, which erupted at other factories and workshops nearby. Several BSPP officials were foolishly taken 'hostage' to demand the workers' release. No one, however, was prepared for the brutality of the army's response. On 6 June troops opened fire to disperse strikers at the Thamaing textile mill and Sinmaleik dockyard; military spokesmen officially admitted killing 22 'workers and onlookers' and injuring 60 more.[71] Other reports put the death toll at more than 300 civilians and allege, in what may well have been a precursor to the events of 1988, that ethnic Chin and Kachin troops were especially brought in from the battlefront to carry out Ne Win's orders.[72]

Once again, as in 1962, heavy repression clearly worked and brought the protests to an abrupt end. Few observers took seriously the army's claims that the CPB had engineered the protests. Undoubtedly this would have been so in the 1940s and 1950s, when it was inconceivable to imagine a street protest without the CPB's involvement, but this was no longer the case. Over the next days the army announced it had arrested two CPB agents at the Okkyin gunny factory and uncovered CPB cells in Yenangyaung and Magwe, but an appeal to 'comrade workers' on the VOPB on 9 June to continue their 'uprising of the people' clearly had a very distant and second-hand ring, which fooled nobody.[73]

CPB activists also had little to do with the demonstrations at the end of the year over the funeral arrangements for former UN secretary-general, U Thant. Of all the protests against Ne Win since 1962 this was the most potent. When Ne Win, apparently out of personal jealousy, sought to deny Burma's most respected international statesman full funeral honours and bury him quietly in an out of the way plot, Buddhist monks and students seized his coffin and, after a highly emotional service of their own, buried his remains on the site of the former Students Union building the army had blown up in 1962. In response, troops were immediately sent in to take control of the campus and to rebury his coffin at a cemetery near the Shwedagon Pagoda. This in turn provoked rioting across the city, with students reportedly cheered on by citizens in the streets as they attacked soldiers and police.[74] Martial law was declared, the universities were closed and 16 people were officially reported killed, hundreds more injured and over 4,500 arrested before the army restored control.[75]

This time Ne Win could hardly blame the CPB. Most of the demonstrations were clearly spontaneous, though this did not stop the state media trying to inflame racial tensions, with now characteristic disregard for the truth, by blaming the growing social upheavals on, amongst other things, 'greater delinquency among Anglo-Indians'.[76] In fact many of the student activists whose first experiences of political action were in the street protests of 1974, such as Tun Aung Kyaw, later chairman of the All Burma Students Democratic Front, resurfaced over a decade later to lead many of the strike centres which sprang up across the country during the short-lived democracy summer of 1988. Today they put the 1974 death toll much higher as once again Burma witnessed the sad spectacle of the disappearance of hundreds of youngsters from another generation of students: some killed, some to gaol and some into the rebel underground. Since many have never met again, nobody knows the true figures.[77]

The army's response to these mass protests was to throw the security blanket even further around the country. Amongst the hundreds arrested, a number of well-hidden communist activists were uncovered, including Dr Nyun Chit, a CPB sympathiser in Mandalay, and Thakin Lay Maung, whom student leaders say had for years been running secret training classes in organisation and agitation.

This, however, was not the end of the protests; anti-BSPP feelings ran high for many months. In mid-1975 over 200 students and workers were given four to nine year gaol sentences for their part in demonstrations (ostensibly over the high cost of living) at which they vociferously demanded the release of prisoners gaoled in the U Thant disturbances.[78] Again the universities were closed and the army returned to its habit of blaming the CPB, this time after a series of VOPB broadcasts supported the protesters. The discovery of a few leaflets, allegedly distributed by CPB sympathisers, appeared to lend some weight to these charges. But significantly, when a number of student leaders, named by the army as 'communist' organisers, escaped underground, it was to the south-east and the remnants of U Nu's 'rightist' PDP on the Thai border and its ally, the reformed KNU under Bo Mya, that they fled and not the CPB.[79] Indeed throughout 1974-6 the PDP, now led by U Thwin and the three *Thirty Comrades*, Bo Let Ya, Bo Hmu Aung and Bo Yan Naing, was now grabbing most of the world headlines. In March 1974, in the largest battle in the Dawna Range since the Second World War, a joint PDP-KNU force of 1,500 attacked the sleepy border town of Myawaddy in a bloody five-day battle before the army called in three of its aging jet fighters and they were forced to retire.[80] Small PDP guerrilla units were constantly on the move, setting off explosions in terrorist attacks on public buildings in Rangoon and other towns in Lower Burma. These attacks resulted in a number of fatalities and several PDP supporters were later sentenced to death and executed for their alleged involvement (see Chapter 14).

The last major demonstrations in this short cycle of protest broke out in March 1976 on the 100th anniversary of the birth of the late Thakin Kodaw Hmaing, the much revered leader of Burma's peace movement. This time MIS was better prepared; it moved quickly to close down the hostels as student activists at Rangoon University began to prepare a new wave of demonstrations to mark his birthday. Dozens of students were arrested, including biology student Tin Maung Oo, an ethnic Chin from Arakan. His colleagues say he organised many of the 1974 and 1975 protests, but then went underground to contact PDP leaders, Bo Let Ya and U Thwin, in the jungle before returning to Rangoon. Less than two weeks after his arrest he was sentenced to death for high treason and secretly hanged a few months afterwards. Today he is regarded as a martyr by many students in Burma, but unlike most of the student leaders who preceded him (and despite the BSPP's attempts to label him an 'extreme leftist'), he no longer looked to the CPB for guidance or inspiration.[81] Many of his friends believe the severity of the army's response was coloured by the discovery that same year of Capt. Ohn Kyaw Myint's plot to assassinate Ne Win. Even Gen. Tin Oo, the Minister of Defence, was sent to gaol for seven years for not reporting details of the plot. Clearly Ne Win was determined to crush all opposition, be it from the CPB, ethnic nationalists, workers, students or the army.

The Demise of the Red Flags

Almost lost sight of amidst the struggles of these years was the final collapse of the Red Flag CPB, the last remnants of which were forced out of the Delta in the early stages of the *Moe Hein* and *Shweliyone* operations. Thakin Soe himself remained in the Red Flag's last major base area in the mountains between Pakokku and Myohaung in the north Arakan Yomas where several hundred followers tried to keep the cause alive. The army still maintains the fiction that he was 'captured' in November 1970. His arrest, as the story is told, came after 11,000 villagers in the North-West Command were mobilised in Seikphyu township to hunt him down under the *Tatmadaw's* 'people's militia' programme.[82] According to this version, he was arrested and handed over to the army by local villagers, along with his wife, Daw Khin Su, their child and another CC member, Aung Kha. But this story is flatly contradicted by the Red Flag survivors who stayed with him till the end. According to their account, apparently believing he could now achieve political change by face-to-face negotiations with Ne Win, following the release from gaol in September 1970 of his former wife, Daw Ngwe Zan, and Gen. Kyaw Win from the Red Flag's 'first prophet of peace' mission, Thakin Soe decided to lead his own 'second prophet of peace' mission to Rangoon. Confirmation of this came at his extraordinary trial at Insein gaol in 1973 where, defended by the former Red Flag student supporter, U Ko Yu, he applied for membership to the BSPP and his former colleagues, Kyaw Win and Myint Aung, testified against him. Eventually the 68 year-old Soe received the death sentence (though the 1974 amnesty may well have been timed to give him a reprieve) and he spent the last years of his life as a familiar, if somewhat eccentric, figure on the Rangoon political scene, living just long enough to form an unsuccessful new 'democracy' party in the aftermath of the 1988 uprising.

It is not widely known that before he gave himself up, he also instructed the rest of his followers to remain behind while he went in 'to organise the BSPP' so it could not be said that 'the Red Flags had surrendered'; he reportedly said he would summon them later once peace had been achieved.[83] Even after receiving the death sentence he still managed to send one enigmatic message to the jungle: 'I am not like Castro or Dimitrov. I have found a new way.'[84] This his supporters understood as meaning he was now working inside the BSPP. In the following years most of the remaining Red Flag leaders in the Chin hills were killed or captured (three CC members, including Thakin Ba Kun, surrendered in 1973); the last major military operation against the Red Flags was launched as long ago as 1975 in Seikphyu township. But in 1987 I was surprised to discover the last Red Flag unit, just 20 cadres strong, in the company of remnants of the Chin National Liberation Party on the Bangladesh-Arakan border. Having been disarmed by the MNF some years earlier, it was sheltering under the protection of two other insurgent groups, the AIO and CPA. Headed by veteran CC member Thaw Da, its members were still watching developments in Rangoon and awaiting what their insurgent hosts jokingly called the 'third prophet of peace' mission.[85]

The CPB, however, with strongholds in Arakan, the North-West Division and the NEC, had not yet come to such a sorry pass. Despite the disastrous losses in the Pegu Yomas, 1975 was a strangely uncertain year in South-East Asia. With the great communist victories in Indo-China, many countries (and certainly Thailand and Malaysia) were preparing for what they believed would be the next wave of communist insurgencies to sweep down through the region.

Burma, where 10,000 CPB troops with the full backing of China had already seized control of much of the China/Lao/Thai border region, appeared to have a head start. Many counter-insurgency analysts, still unaware of the growing rift between China and Vietnam, expected this to be where the communists made their next move.

Since the early 1950s, to stave off this perceived communist challenge in South-East Asia, the United States government had backed a succession of fragile democracies, monarchs, dictators and military regimes across the region. Most of these ventures were unsuccessful. And yet in Burma, despite widespread dislike in Washington for the socialist colours of the AFPFL and BSPP and open US support for SEATO and the covert transportation of arms (via Taiwan and Thailand) to the KMT, the lone US-backed attempt to destabilise the government in Rangoon had not come until the late 1960s with U Nu's PDP.

Ironically, it was only at this moment, when the CIA and US State Department were very much calling on their friends abroad, that the full scale of the PDP's failure became clear. In the international press and diplomatic dispatches of 1974/5 the *Tatmadaw*'s great victories in central Burma hardly received a mention. Counter-insurgency, domino theories, rural violence and the escalating student and worker protests in both Burma and Thailand were the burning issues of the day and these led directly to the bloody military coup in Thailand in 1976 and to an ultimately successful attempt to change the political leadership of the KNU.

It is thus necessary to backtrack for a moment and examine the fate of U Nu's PDP which, though its military successes were few, was to contribute to a complete change in the complexion and balance of the civil war in south-east Burma with long-term implications not only for the *Tatmadaw* and CPB but for all the country's restive national minorities.

14

The Failure of U Nu's Parliamentary Democracy Party, Karen Unity and Emergence of the National Democratic Front

'If Castro could make it with thirty men, so can I.'[1]

With these bold words, in 1969 U Nu headed for the hills. Government officials in Rangoon have usually insisted that Burma's insurgent fronts have consisted of only an odd assortment of communists, black marketeers and ethnic separatists. In fact, nothing could be further from the truth. Since Ne Win seized power in 1962, a succession of very different 'Burmese' nationalist groups have continued to take up arms against the central government. Disappearing into the countryside, they, like the CPB, have soon found themselves compelled to come to terms with ethnic rebel forces already controlling large areas of the country and, over the years, a number of new Burman ethnic-minority united fronts have been formed.

Until the Democratic Alliance of Burma (DAB) in 1988, by far the best known was the National United Liberation Front (NULF), headed by U Nu and formed in 1970 through an alliance of U Nu's insurgent Parliamentary Democracy Party (PDP), the Karen National Union (KNU) and New Mon State Party (NMSP). Into the mid-1970s the NULF counterbalanced the challenge posed by the CPB before ethnic-minority leaders broke away in disillusionment in 1976 to set up the present-day National Democratic Front (NDF). Though there are reasons to believe that the events of 1988 have taken these political relationships into a new era, it is important to compare the experiences of these past fronts with those of the CPB and BSPP. 'Hopeless,' was the one-word verdict of Bo Mya, the KNU's veteran president, on the entire NULF experience.[2]

The Rise of the PDP and the CIA: 1965-70
Insurgent leaders have always claimed that the birth of a new generation of armed resistance movements was an inevitable and entirely justifiable reaction to Ne Win's military coup. The Shan State Army (SSA) and new ethnic parties initially caught most of the world headlines, but this time a new 'Burmese' force was emerging which, for the first time since the PVOs and army mutineers of 1948-50, was going to lay challenge to the countrywide might of the *Tatmadaw* and CPB.

The mass arrests of 1962/3 and Ne Win's imprisonment of hundreds of eminent politicians from the 1950s, including U Nu, U Ba Swe and Sao Shwe Thaike, had decimated the leadership of what may loosely be described as the 'democratic' opposition, i.e. those who believed in a multi-party or parliamentary system of government. Many of their supporters now claimed they had no alternative but to take up arms. Both the CPB and BSPP have characterised these new groups as 'rightists', but they in fact represented a broad spectrum of political belief. Over the next few years a succession of underground parties and cells were formed (most quite independently of each other) and these eventually resulted at the end of the decade in the formation of the PDP and NULF.

Those now plotting rebellion against Ne Win at first faced serious difficulties. Without arms and ammunition, they appeared to have only two real choices, to join the CPB, which for most ex-AFPFL supporters was out of the question, or to make their way through ethnic rebel-held territory to Thailand to try and win support from the West.

A number of underground factions emerged spontaneously. One of the first was led by student activist, Tin Maung Win. He was the son of U Win, former AFPFL ambassador to the USA and member of the All Burma Secret Students Organisation, which had close connections with Brig. Aung Gyi and Col. Kyi Maung, both of whom had resigned from the Revolutionary Council (RC) in 1963 as a protest at Ne Win's increasingly dictatorial behaviour. In March 1965 Win travelled into the Dawna Range to ask Bo Mya and the leaders of the KNU in the east for territory where he could bring students for armed training. But, according to Win, these contacts, which indirectly implicated Aung Gyi and Kyi Maung, were discovered in May after his return to Rangoon and the three men were arrested.[3] Both Aung Gyi and Kyi Maung deny ever plotting armed insurrection, and with fitting irony it was Kyi Maung who many years later led the NLD to victory in the 1990 election.

That same month a group of senior above-ground Karen politicians who had escaped imprisonment by Ne Win secretly formed a National Liberation Council (NLC) in Rangoon.[4] In September the group was joined by several prominent Burman leaders planning to go underground. Sandhurst-educated ex-brigadier Hanson Kyadoe, a Pwo Karen from the Delta who had served as a battalion commander in the wartime BNA, was appointed chairman and the *Thirty Comrade*, Bo Yan Naing, his deputy. A former general-secretary of Rangoon University Students Union and hero of the Shwedaung battle in 1942, Yan Naing had covered himself with the greatest battlefield glory of perhaps all the BIA veterans. The NLC was ultimately to form the nucleus of U Nu's PDP, but in 1965 it sent men underground to the Thai border to make contact with Karen leaders such as Saw Tha Din and Bo Mya, who were regarded as being on the political right. Secretly travelling on to Bangkok shortly afterwards, Kyadoe, Yan Naing and his brother-in-law Zali Maw, the son of wartime prime minister Dr Ba Maw, were joined shortly afterwards by another of the *Thirty Comrades*, Bo Setkya, a former leader of the Socialist Party.

The only avowedly right-wing cell in Burma at the time, remnants of the small Burma Democratic Party founded by Thakin Ba Sein in 1947, was another vocal group then trying to open a door to the West. In 1965 one of its leaders, Saw Aye Dwe, an ethnic Karen and vice-chairman of the Burma chapter of the Asian Peoples Anti-Communist League, also held talks with Bo Mya before going on into Thailand to make contact with the US-based World Anti-Communist League.

Over the next few years in Bangkok these political exiles attracted considerable attention in Western military circles. They met representatives of the South-East

Asia Treaty Organisation (SEATO), which had been carefully monitoring the movements of the KNU and KMT in eastern Burma since the early 1950s. But it was only when U Nu decided to take up arms that the PDP movement really gathered momentum.

Imprisoned without trial in March 1962, even after his release from detention in October 1966 he had continued to claim in private that he was still the lawfully elected prime minister of Burma. Then after a disastrous cyclone in Arakan in May 1968, he took the opportunity to move again amongst his countrymen and to use the Buddhist lecturer guise he has since frequently adopted. Refusing to accept donations of more than one kyat per person, U Nu quickly raised 400,000 kyats for the disaster victims at public rallies — which showed he had lost none of his popularity with the people.[5]

U Nu was clearly upset by the growing poverty and suffering he saw. Even at this early stage he reportedly discussed with close confidants, such as U Law Yone, former editor of *The Nation*, plans to escape the country and raise an army abroad.[6] For a moment, however, he hesitated, deceived, he later said, by what at first appeared to be signs of a growing political liberalisation of the RC. During 1968 hundreds of political detainees, many held without trial since 1962-4, were released from gaol. U Nu, in particular, placed great store by his appointment at the end of the year to the 33-man Internal Unity Advisory Board (see Chapter 11), where he and many of his former parliamentary colleagues were invited to put forward suggestions for political reform.

With Ne Win's rejection of their proposals, however, Nu's disillusionment was complete.[7] Sensing the outcome even before Ne Win had formally replied, U Nu left the country in April 1969 with his wife and several members of his family under the pretext of a religious pilgrimage to India for urgently needed medical treatment. But in the months before his departure he had carefully tested the political waters during a countrywide lecture tour on Buddhism, attracting ever larger crowds as he went. The state-controlled media angrily responded with veiled references to black marketeers and 'old politicians' who had sold the country out to Chinese and Indian capitalists.[8]

In private U Nu was not nearly so circumspect. Swearing his supporters to secrecy, he formed an inner circle with three influential advisers. Their political credentials were impeccable: Bo Let Ya, a *Dobama* veteran, joint-founder of the CPB, *Thirty Comrade*, former Minister of Defence and deputy prime minister; U Thwin, ex-BIA and former Minister of Trade; and Aung Gyi, Ne Win's long-time deputy and architect of both the 1958 and 1962 military administrations. According to Aung Gyi, at their very first meeting U Nu revealed his plan when he told him:

> I am going to revolt. I would very much like you to participate. There is no need to give me an answer now. I have obtained approval from the government to go to India. After a month of my departure I will declare, from a country abroad, a revolution. Should you agree to that matter, come out to any foreign country using your own methods within one month of my departure. We can discuss details when we are outside.[9]

As the man closest to Ne Win, Aung Gyi refused to take up arms and advised U Nu that the *Tatmadaw* 'would retain its loyalty to the *Bogyoke*' (Ne Win). But Thwin and Let Ya, Aung Gyi remembers, were convinced the whole country, including the army, 'would rise up and follow him'.[10] Ironically, Nu failed to win support from two of his closest political allies from the 1950s, the 'feudalist conspirators', Sao Hkun Hkio and Sao Wunna, on whom Ne Win had initially placed the entire blame for the 1962 coup (see Chapter 10). 'Since it is not possible to challenge the *Tatmadaw* in warfare,' warned Sao Wunna, 'a political leader should not even consider armed rebellion.'[11]

Bo Let Ya and the advocates of armed struggle were, however, heartened by the rapturous crowds which flocked to hear U Nu at his last public appearances on the eve of his departure for India. At crowded meetings in Mandalay, Pakokku and Moulmein, Nu cleverly continued to feign illness in order to convince the authorities they should allow him to leave. By contrast, there was no problem getting the Indian government to agree to receive him. Still a highly respected statesman in the international community, Nu had always been close to the late Indian prime minister, Jawaharlal Nehru, and this relationship had continued with his daughter, Indira Gandhi.[12]

Once out of the country, U Nu swiftly put his plan into operation. In India he met up with Law Yone and Let Ya, who had also contrived to leave the country for medical treatment. In August the three men travelled on to Thailand where, in safe houses off Bangkok's Sukhumvit Road, they discussed their strategy for an armed rebellion launched from Thai soil with Bo Yan Naing and the other NLC exiles. For Yan Naing and Let Ya there was a strong sense of *déjà vu*. It was nearly three decades since they had passed that way with Aung San and the Japanese. (The other *Thirty Comrade*, Bo Setkya, died shortly before U Nu's arrival.)

Having reached agreement, Nu and Law Yone immediately flew to London for their historic press conference of 29 August 1969, organised by the respected Anglo-Burman journalist, Max McGrath.[13] Announcing the formation of the PDP, Nu expressed the hope that his campaign would force Ne Win to relinquish power peacefully, but left no doubt of his willingness to use force. Ne Win's actions, he declared, left 'the elected leaders of Burma with no option but to call on the people to oppose his regime with all means at their disposal'.[14]

Continuing on their whirlwind tour, U Nu then headed for the USA where, in a series of ever more militant interviews, he denounced Ne Win as 'more terrible than Ivan the Terrible'.[15] By the end of the year, he claimed, the PDP would have men fighting inside Burma. This, he predicted, would set off a popular uprising which would lead to the overthrow of Ne Win 'within a year'.[16]

U Nu's unexpected appearance as an insurgent leader on the world scene presented Washington with a political dilemma. While in the United States Nu called on the Nixon administration to suspend arms' sales to Rangoon, which had quietly been resumed after a visit to America by Ne Win in 1967. In 1962, in the general exodus of foreigners from the country, Ne Win had expelled a number of suspected CIA agents or informants working for the Ford and Asia Foundations. But despite distrusting Ne Win and his Burmese brand of socialism, after the fiasco of the KMT invasion in the 1950s successive administrations had (until Nu's arrival) kept to a safe policy of trying to maintain Burma's neutrality as an anti-communist buffer in an increasingly volatile region. The *Tatmadaw* was after all fighting the CPB insurrection.

The picture here becomes murky. Whatever America's future role in the PDP (and it was completely concealed), the natural focus of the exile movement was not the US but Burma's neighbour, Thailand, which was then firmly under

Washington's military umbrella. Not only was virtually the entire border under the control of various Karen, Karenni, Mon and Shan insurgents, but Thailand itself was fast becoming a major arena for the war in South-East Asia. The country was flooded with American officials and troops: US agents were directing Thai security forces against the fast-spreading insurgency of the Communist Party of Thailand (CPT) which, at its Third Congress in 1961, had resolved to begin 'armed struggle'; and Bangkok itself was the capital of the region's burgeoning black market arms trade. In this stormy sea, for American strategists the PDP (like the KMT, KNU or Vang Pao's ethnic Hmong army in Laos) was just another lifeboat.

The first problem U Nu faced was one that confronts soldiers the world over: money. This is the most confusing chapter in the whole PDP episode and the one that should have given Nu the clearest warning of the debacles to come. Law Yone, Nu's chief fund raiser, carried to his grave the PDP's closest financial secrets which included donations from a variety of different Western companies and businessmen, but he did tell Josef Silverstein in 1972 that $1m was paid up-front to the PDP by the Canadian Asmara oil company, with the promise of a further $2m when PDP troops entered Burma and $10m more when they reached Rangoon.[17] In exchange, Law Yone said, Asmara would receive lucrative oil concessions from U Nu's future civilian government.

Other PDP and NULF leaders confirm that the initial $1m payment was made, but the exact source of the money remains a mystery. In the early 1970s the American Embassy in Bangkok was the nerve centre for dozens of counter-insurgency operations in the region involving the Thai Army and police, the KMT and thousands of Thai and ethnic-minority villagers. But while clearly sympathetic to Burma's anti-communist rebels, US officials took care to build up an elaborate screen around their activities, carefully distancing themselves from U Nu, the PDP and Burma's insurgent armies. By contrast, they showed no such hesitation in Laos or Cambodia, where in 1970 the Sihanouk government was overthrown and replaced by the CIA-backed regime of Prince Lon Nol. America's object was to ring Thailand with a wall of neutral buffer states or sympathetic rebel armies, a task which at least until the mid-1970s was successfully accomplished. So veteran insurgent leaders scoff at the notion that US officials were never involved with the PDP. First, CIA-trained Thai Intelligence officers and border patrol police, who reported daily to their US masters, acted as liaison officers with the different insurgent groups along the Burma border: the Thai Army openly enlisted the KMT, KNU, NMSP and Khun Sa's Shan United Army (SUA) as anti-communist allies in the late 1960s and early 1970s.[18] Secondly, officially 'retired' CIA officers such as William Young and a number of other American sympathisers openly consorted with U Nu and the PDP leaders and helped act as fund raisers.[19] One face that became extremely familiar was the journalist Sterling Seagrave, son of the famed 'Burma surgeon' missionary, Dr Seagrave, whose hospital at Namhkam in the Shan State was abruptly taken over by the *Tatmadaw* in 1965. Husband to one of Law Yone's daughters, Seagrave had travelled to Thailand in advance to help pave the way for the arrival of U Nu and his father-in-law in 1969.

There is no doubt then that from the beginning both US and SEATO officials were aware of U Nu's plans in what for them, when set alongside the Indo-China conflict, was a very low-risk insurgency operation. In the 1960s the CIA endorsed virtually any mission in South-East Asia that stopped the spread of communism. And in the late 1960s information about Red Chinese aid to Ho Chi Minh, the Pathet Lao and now the CPB flooded in from KMT and CIA agents along the Yunnan border. But this still does not explain the involvement of a Canadian oil company. Because of the 'oil' label, several former PDP leaders still think the money might have come from Howard Hughes. Others, such as Tin Maung Win, believe it came from a Californian oil company. But one veteran US Intelligence officer, who was present on several occasions when money was handed over, has no doubt who was behind the payment, whatever sympathetic source may have put up the cash: 'Of course it was the CIA. It was simply a question of finding a decent cover. Somebody said, "You can't say this is CIA money." So somebody else said, "What shall we call it? Oil money? OK, that will do." So wherever it appeared to come from, it was still the CIA.'[20]

With this important financial hurdle safely negotiated, U Nu's next problems were more urgently political. While the announcement of the formation of the PDP (reported by the BBC and begrudgingly acknowledged by the RC in Rangoon) had not yet provoked the expected popular uprising, it had caused considerable excitement in the cities and produced a steady stream of political dissidents to the border. One of the first to arrive was U Thwin who reached Bangkok in October 1969; here he joined forces with Nu, Law Yone, Yan Naing, Kyadoe, Zali Maw and the NLC leaders active along the border since 1965. At the end of the year, another group of young democracy activists arrived who had been secretly distributing pro-Nu literature in towns in Lower Burma. Led by Tin Maung Win, whose father died in the jungle *en route*, they comprised a new kind of middle-class political activist typified by Ye Kyaw Thu, a bank manager from Rangoon.[21]

Comfortably settling in Bangkok, the PDP leaders were able to form a viable leadership which, on paper at least, looked impressive: U Nu (president), Bo Let Ya (vice-president), U Law Yone (general-secretary), U Thwin (joint secretary), Tommy Clift, a former chief of the Burma Air Force (foreign and financial affairs), Hanson Kyadoe (Chief-of-Staff), Bo Yan Naing (deputy Chief-of-Staff), Zali Maw (legal affairs). With these influential names, for a brief moment the PDP achieved a unity of sorts among the diverse non-communist Burmese nationalist groups along the border. Nu was particularly keen to recruit a remarkable student force, set up by a former Rangoon student from Pyinmana, David Zaw Tun, who had gone underground with a few followers near his home town in 1968. Here they formed a 50-strong army, the Internal Unity and Peace Organisation and, persuading a number of local Burman, Kayan, Pao and Shan villagers to join them, began to ambush *Tatmadaw* patrols. Zaw Tun was eventually persuaded to come down to Bangkok to join U Nu and, as one of the few young PDP officers with actual guerrilla experience, was appointed commander of the PDP's Special Division.[22] (Ironically, after his departure, Zaw Tun's force was disarmed by another insurgent army, Shwe Aye's Kayan New Land Party (KNLP), and its weapons confiscated.)

Ultimately U Nu was able to win over volunteers from all the main Burmese opposition groups, the single exception being the CPB which, by contrast, had denounced the PDP from the very beginning. Indeed, the handful of small CPB units still active in Tenasserim melted into the forests as soon as the first PDP clashes broke out both here in Tavoy-Mergui and in the Pegu Yomas.

Though recruitment was easy, PDP leaders always realised the key to the success of their movement would depend on reaching an agreement with the diverse ethnic rebel forces along the Thai border. For a group of predominantly ethnic Burman politicians who had spent much of the first 15 years of Burma's independence fighting these very same ethnic armies, it was always likely to prove a difficult task. Several parties, though agreeing to allow PDP troops to pass through their territory, refused outright any alliance with U Nu. The Christian-led Kachin Independence Organisation (KIO), for example, which had taken up arms in 1961 during U Nu's *Pyidaungsu* government, had never forgiven him for provoking the Buddhist state religion issue that year. The Karenni National Progressive Party (KNPP), on the other hand, which was then allied in the Nationalities United Front with the pro-CPB Karen National United Party (KNUP), was now more intent on activating its legal right, under the 1947 Constitution, for total secession from the Union of Burma. It was U Nu, they claimed, who had first sent government troops into the Karenni State in 1948 and ordered the murder of their leader, U Bee Tu Re.[23]

Meanwhile, in the war-torn Shan State the PDP appeared uncertain over which insurgent force to try to work with. Units of the SSA, undoubtedly the most powerful and best organised of the several Shan nationalist forces, generally operated in the mountains deeper in the interior, while the Shan-Thai border was under the control of a motley array of insurgent forces, including the KMT, SUA, the Shan United Revolutionary Army of Gon Jerng and the Shan State Nationalities Liberation Organisation (SSNLO). Faced with this confusion, U Nu decided to appoint the former Kokang MP and SSA veteran, Jimmy Yang, now in retirement in Thailand, as his special adviser on Shan affairs; Yang considerably improved his credentials by first soliciting a friendly $10,000 donation from the KMT's Gen. Li Wen-huan as a gift for U Nu.[24]

Looking beyond the Shan State, U Nu took a calculated gamble and decided to ignore the existing Zomi National Front (ZNF), which was allied with the KNUP, and subsidise the formation of the Chin Democracy Party, led by former Chin minister, Mang Da Laing. PDP leaders calculated that the Chins, until then the most loyal ethnic minority to the Union, could play a key role in swinging the balance of the civil war away from Rangoon. U Nu also secretly tried to recruit U Lun Pum, another former Chin minister and member of the 1968 Internal Unity Advisory Board. Pum, however, turned informer and supplied MIS with damaging inside information on the PDP's plans.[25]

The PDP took another risk in overlooking the powerful Pao-majority SSNLO under Tha Kalei, which then controlled much of the south-west Shan State and, like the KNPP, KNLP and ZNF, was close to the KNUP. Instead U Nu recruited, initially as a bodyguard, a promising Pao student, Khun Ye Naung, who was one of several young men originally sent to the border from Rangoon by Thaton Hla Pe to join the SSNLO. Ye Naung was soon given 70 troops and sent into the Thaton district to try and build up a PDP force among the 50,000 local Pao inhabitants. But the plan failed badly and in 1975 Ye Naung, a highly opportunistic political operator, rejoined the Pao nationalist movement before surrendering two years later. Few observers were surprised when he resurfaced in Rangoon during the 1988 democracy uprising, initially as one of U Nu's political advisers, before joining the breakaway Democracy Party.

By contrast the PDP had little trouble enlisting the support of the NMSP, which in 1970 abruptly broke off all contact with the CPB and the NDUF and NUF alliances. The main intermediary was U Thwin, former MP for Kyaikmaraw in Mon territory, who offered Nai Shwe Kyin and the NMSP commanders generous financial inducements. From this time on, of all the ethnic insurgent parties, the NMSP appeared the most comfortable with the PDP's Burman leaders. In fact local Mon/Burman relations along the Tenasserim plain have never been marked by as much racial antipathy as those, for example, between the hill Sgaw Karens and Burmans.

The KNU was undoubtedly the most important element in the PDP plan. With well over 15,000 armed supporters in the field, at this time it probably still outnumbered in military strength even the CPB. But despite widespread suspicion of U Nu among veteran Karen leaders, in approaching the KNU the PDP was helped by a largely unexpected event. This was the second major schism in the Karen movement which in 1966 saw the emergence of a staunchly nationalist, pro-Western faction under the Eastern Division's military commander, Bo Mya, who broke away from the CPB-allied KNUP in Lower Burma.

Little noticed at the time, despite an initial lack of political sophistication this breakaway faction rapidly came to dominate the KNU movement, increased dramatically in military size and, with the later possible exception of the KIO, posed the most serious challenge to the *Tatmadaw* of all Burma's ethnic minority armies. By the mid-1970s this reconstituted KNU movement under Bo Mya and Mahn Ba Zan had abandoned the NULF, welcomed back the KNUP remnants from the Delta and led the formation of the NDF which for the first time brought together a dozen ethnic minority armies from around the country. Within a decade the NDF had grown to rival the CPB as a political force in the country; indeed it was to the KNU and NDF 'liberated zones' that most democracy activists fled from the cities in 1988.

Since most armed resistance to the *Tatmadaw* is still being coordinated from NDF territory and since most Western observers view the war in Burma from the perspective of the KNU-NDF bases along the Thai border, the split in and eventual reformation of the KNU movement needs to be examined in more detail.

Bo Mya, Political Changes in the East and Second KNU Split

Just as in the mid-1960s the CPB's armed struggle became divided between two major arenas of conflict in central and north-east Burma, so in the decade 1965-75 the Karen revolution became a story of two halves as the rift between Karen leaders east and west, which had begun under Saw Hunter Tha Hmwe, became increasingly pronounced. Most observers spoke of this split in terms of pro- and anti-communist factions and, indeed, this was part of the truth. But beneath the surface was a fundamental difference in ethno-political outlook which had surfaced in the 1950s but generally been suppressed. In the Delta, ever since the Karen Rifles failed to seize power in the set-piece battles of 1949-50, local KNU leaders had always tried to accommodate other insurgent groups in the region, whether Burman, Mon, Chin, or Rakhine. This was not simply a matter of convenience. In the Delta the Karen population is entirely ethnic Pwo or Sgaw and, though both groups still frequently live in separate villages, they also share many of the customs and life-styles of their Burman neighbours. Over 80 per cent are Buddhists and many communities, especially in the Henzada and Twante districts, have become entirely Burmese-speaking.

In the east, where the KNU is still active in much of the border region, the situation was very different. These remote mountains along a 500-mile stretch of the Thai border had hardly been brought under British (much less Burman) rule and were the last areas to be politically organised by the KNU government. If there is an ethnic Burman population here at all, it is very much in the minority. Along the Tenasserim plain there are many Pwo Karen, Mon and even Shan villages, but in the hills the population is predominantly Sgaw and other hill Karens: a mixture of Animists, Buddhist-Animists and Christians who have converted to Christianity only within the last 80 years. Even today social conditions in the mountains are obviously less developed than in the Delta. Shifting slash and burn agriculture is still widely practised and amongst the many distinctively dressed 'tribal' Karens of the Toungoo and Papun hills it is still possible to find many villages untouched by the 20th century.[26]

At the beginning of the insurrections, under the KNDO's Eastern Division the KNU had appointed a number of prominent Karen elders and dignitaries, largely mission educated and English speaking, to take charge of local administration. But as the KNU struggled through the 1950s to set up a centralised civilian infrastructure, the eastern military command became increasingly dominated by local hill Karen recruits. Two young officers stood out: Shwe Hser, commander of what became the KNU's 6th brigade in the Dooplaya district in the countryside south of Kawkareik, and Bo Mya, commander of the 7th brigade in the Paan-Papun districts to the north. They had much in common. Both were Animist Sgaw Karens born within a few miles of each other in the Papun hills; both had been young when the Karen rebellion broke out; and both, it was said, owed their early promotions to KNUP organisers who thought they could manipulate them more easily. In fact over the past 30 years it has been these two men who have had a decisive influence on the political direction of the KNU.

Their critics, both in Rangoon and in the KNU, have accused them of building up personal fiefdoms in the manner of warlords.[27] Shwe Hser is widely regarded as one of the shrewdest of the KNU's veteran commanders. He has developed his own highly adept system of mobile guerrilla warfare in the southern Dawna Range and, to all intents and purposes, the 6th brigade command still leads a life of its own. But it is above all Bo Mya's shadow which looms large over the Karen nationalist movement; in Burmese society today he enjoys an almost mythological reputation which, depending on one's perspective, lies somewhere between a modern-day Robin Hood, Billy the Kid, Che Guevara or Abu Nidal.

Among the KNU's largely university-educated leadership, Bo Mya (his real name) is an enigma. Born in Hti Moo Khi village, Papun, in 1926 (the exact date is unknown) the young Mya attended a local Burmese vernacular school in Papun to just the fourth grade.[28] To account for his meteoric rise in the KNU movement, local villagers tell the story that he is a descendant of Saw Koo, the last independent Karen *Sawke* in the Salween district, but there is no evidence to support this. His upbringing was probably little different from that of any other hill Karen in the 'excluded areas' in the last days of British rule. Along with many others of his generation, Bo Mya attributes the major turning point in his life to the catastrophic events of the Second World War when, barely into his teens, he witnessed BIA atrocities in the Papun hills. As a result, he volunteered to serve as a policeman under the Japanese administration, which many hill Karens saw as offering some protection against the BIA's worst excesses. But when on the night of 23 February 1945 a Force 136 unit under Col. Peacock parachuted into the Papun hills, Mya was in the first party to reach his jungle encampment the next morning. Within a week 600 local Karen recruits had been armed and Mya was attached to the staff of Peacock's deputy, Saw Butler, a former schoolteacher and holder of the Military Cross who had swiftly risen during the war to become one of the highest ranking Karen officers in the British Army.[29] If any experience marked Bo Mya out from his contemporaries, it was this. After the war Butler kept Mya, who for a time had worked as a mess orderly in a canteen, on as a personal aide cum servant, though, according to some colleagues, he became more of an adopted son, staying with Butler in Rangoon and travelling with him on government service around the country.

Saw Butler was one of the most prominent Karen leaders to refuse to join the KNU and, in the mid-1950s, he became secretary to the Karen State Ministry. Bo Mya, by contrast, returned to the east at the outbreak of the insurrection and joined the KNU's Highlander battalion as a company commander. In the early 1950s there was a hiccup in his career when the battalion was disbanded after the fall of Hlaingbwe and its commander, Nah Moo, surrendered.[30] Mya also went down to Paan (he is adamant he did not surrender) and he and his men were allowed to keep their arms in a short-lived *Pyu Saw Hti* militia before returning to the KNU side. On his return Bo Mya continued his rapid rise through the ranks and in the early 1960s was promoted to the rank of colonel to take command of the Eastern Division's 7th brigade. Bo Mya was undoubtedly one of the most successful KNU commanders of his generation. His more daring military exploits became legendary in the eastern hills and his name often surfaced in the Rangoon press as a particularly ruthless commander.[31] Even some of his closest colleagues say he was 'wild and unruly' in those years.

But none of these events gave any indication of the impact he was now to have on the civil war. In private he had already expressed doubts about the KNUP's increasingly pro-communist line, but at the time of the Tha Hmwe split, though never a KNUP member, he had sided with Mahn Ba Zan and the KNUP. In fact his critics point out he owed his precipitate promotion to Eastern Division commander in April 1963 to the defection of his predecessor, *Bogyoke* Ohn Pe, along with Tha Hmwe and Lin Htin. But within a year, as he tightened his grip on the Eastern Command, he underwent a dramatic change of heart.

Bo Mya always maintained he was acting in the name of the 'Karen revolution'; his oldest associates prefer to date the change to his marriage that year to a Seventh Day Adventist Karen and his conversion to Christianity. Certainly from this time on, of all the KNU's predominantly Christian leaders, Bo Mya's political statements were the most deeply imbued with references to Christianity and the Bible. In the course of many discussions he once told me: 'We, as a nation that believe in God, consider communism as Satan's tool.'[32]

The religious conversion of one man, however, can hardly account for the important changes he was now able to effect on the political direction of the Karen movement. In the aftermath of Ne Win's coup, there were two other major, if largely coincidental, developments, which completely altered the face of the insurgencies in Burma. The first and most important was that when Ne Win began to introduce the *Burmese Way to Socialism* in 1963/4, there were disastrous consequences for the Burmese economy. Many key sectors of the economy collapsed (see Chapter 5) and the hitherto backward and neglected hill tracts along the Thai border assumed an unexpected geographic and economic importance.

Since 1947 the KNU movement had had to be entirely self-supporting. Revenue was gathered from a variety of sources, mostly local household taxes in KNU-controlled areas and levies on the handful of industries (such as timber mills and rubber plantations) still in operation. More spectacularly, these funds were augmented by occasional bank robberies or train and bus hold-ups; in one famed incident a plane carrying Treasury funds to Sittwe was hijacked and forced to put down on the beach near Bassein.[33] In the early 1950s customs gates had been opened at a number of KNU posts along the Thai border, but there was little local traffic. As a result there were few surplus funds for distribution to local KNU forces and most units had to raise their own income and find their own weapons. During the 1950s the KNU's entire Eastern Division only gave between 200,000 and 300,000 kyat a year towards the Kawthoolei RC's four million kyat annual budget; most of the rest came from the Delta where there were numerous fish farms and forestry plantations.[34]

However, from 1963, the dramatic rise in the new black market trade with Thailand disturbed the Eastern Division's sleepy isolation forever. A flat 5 per cent levy on the value of the flood of goods now crossing the Thai border provided local commanders with an ever expanding source of income. With swift access to Moulmein and the Delta, the KNU rather than any other rebel force became the main beneficiary; and with the *Tatmadaw* tied down by the war with the CPB in central and north-east Burma, the KNU's Eastern Division suffered relatively few disruptions. The first new Karen customs gate was opened by Shwe Hser at Phalu, south of Myawaddy, in the 6th brigade area in 1964. The following year Bo Mya opened another gate at Kawmoorah (Wangkha) in the 7th brigade area to the north. As trade escalated, new check-posts were opened up from the Mawdaung Pass in the south to Sawta on the Kayah State border, 400 miles to the north. Indeed Myawaddy remained the only BSPP-controlled town on the entire Karen-Karenni border, while Tachilek was the only government-held town on the Shan State border to the east. One important trading post was at Three Pagodas Pass (jointly controlled with the NMSP) on the old Japanese Siam-Burma railroad, which quickly grew into a frontier settlement of 5,000 Karen, Mon and Indian inhabitants with a cinema hall, temples, churches and even a mosque.

The effect on several towns in neighbouring Thailand was equally dramatic. The sleepy outpost of Mae Sot, the pivotal centre of much of this new trade, rapidly turned into a bustling new market town. By the 1970s Bo Mya's main base at Kawmoorah was sometimes producing as much as one *lakh* kyat in a single day's trading when up to 1,000 cattle would splash across the Moei River into Thailand at the end of the long journey across the Dawna Range from central Burma. Transported in the other direction were radios, watches, high-quality sarongs and other manufactured goods now unavailable in Burma. Added to this income was revenue from timber mills and tin and antimony mines run jointly with local Thai businessmen. Vast profits were generated though opium, which was an important source of income for insurgent groups in the Shan State, has always been strictly prohibited.[35] In the peak year of 1983 KNU Finance Minister, Pu Ler Wah, estimated incomes at 500 million kyat (£50m at the official exchange rate), an astonishing figure for an otherwise impoverished backwater.

The political changes Bo Mya was now able to introduce have to be seen against the background of this dynamic new trade. This abundant source of finance effectively changed the entire locus of power in the Karen revolution. The 6th and 7th brigades, once amongst the weakest and most poorly equipped of all the KNU divisions east or west, rapidly expanded during the 1960s (fuelled by 'Vietnam-surplus' weapons bought on the Thai and Laotian black markets) to become the KNU's strongest.[36]

These traders, or 'economic saboteurs' as the BSPP described them, were not the only new visitors to KNU bases in the east. With the continuing clamp-down in Rangoon, through 1965 a steady stream of political dissidents also began to arrive at Bo Mya's general headquarters, then at U Moo Tha on the northern Moei River. These included student leader Tin Maung Win and Saw Aye Dwe, who made no secret of his right-wing views. But the group from the NLC were the most closely listened to. Kyadoe, the NLC's Pwo Karen chairman, had always argued against the KNU's separatist views. He once told KNU leaders: 'You must work with the Burmans; they are like your shadow.' Now in secret talks with Bo Mya and the KNU's eastern leaders, Kyadoe and Yan Naing, who were as opposed to the CPB as the BSPP, he urged the KNU to sever all connections with the communists.

A combination of these factors now jelled in Bo Mya's mind and gave him the opportunity he later said he had been waiting for. During 1964 he had already begun his own military reorganisation of the Eastern Division, appointing to senior positions a number of hill Karens, including Col. Taw Hla and Saw Gladstone, who had served with him in the 1950s. Many complained of a lack of help from KNUP leaders in the Delta during a *Tatmadaw* offensive in the east after the 1963 peace talks broke down; several voiced fears that the KNUP leaders might yet be won over by Ne Win's 'socialist' rhetoric. Thus in April 1965, after a meeting of Eastern Division commanders from which KNUP officials were excluded, Bo Mya met KNUP chairman, Mahn Ba Zan, in the hills north of Papun and urged him to call a national congress to review the KNU's 'socialist' political line. Ba Zan agreed to do this, but events now moved too quickly and the meeting was never held.

Bo Mya later accused KNUP leaders of using delaying tactics. On 4 January 1966, without any prior warning, he issued a unilateral order that all KNUP troops and officials based in the Eastern Division leave immediately and join the main body of KNUP forces in the Delta and Pegu Yomas. In personal letters to Mahn Ba Zan and Skaw Ler Taw, the two KNUP leaders to whom he had been closest, Mya requested they leave peacefully. Despite Tha Hmwe's failure to elicit Western support before his surrender, he intended to try and get arms supplies from 'foreigners' and had been warned that he would never get any while he remained with the KNUP.[37] He added he wanted two years to try this plan and if he did not succeed he would then reconsider the situation.

Faced with this stark ultimatum, KNUP leaders had little choice but to comply. While KNUP domination of the nationalist movement in the Delta had long since been complete, in the Eastern Division the KNUP was still only organised in any real strength in the strategic No.2 (Toungoo) brigade district linking central and south-east Burma where Mahn Ba Zan and the KNUP's senior leaders usually stayed. Here in the hills above Kyaukkyi a mobile KNUP force was to remain for the next decade, but its general headquarters was now moved to the foothills of the southern Pegu Yomas. A 10-year hiatus followed before the rift was healed (and under very different circumstances).

By his action Bo Mya had effectively staged a *coup d'état* and the entire Eastern Division fell under his control. For the moment the abrupt departure of the KNUP leaders left a large vacuum in the political administration of the eastern hills which needed to be filled. As a first step Mya announced the formation of a new governing body, the Karen National Liberation Council (KNLC), the name clearly echoing the influence of Kyadoe and the NLC. No records exist today of the KNLC and no elections were ever held. Senior administrative posts were mostly nominated by Bo Mya and filled by staunchly anti-communist hill Karens with two former policemen, Saw Po Han and Benny Htoo, taking the positions of Ministers of Justice and Defence. KNLC veterans support the assertion that behind this new front was the calculation that foreign support would now be forthcoming. According to Htoo: 'At the time we were hoping to get help from abroad but nothing came. We were swindled so often... the whole revolution.'³⁸

Modelled on the Kawthoolei Governing Body and the Karen RC of the 1950s, the KNLC was essentially another emergency military administration in a pattern repeated many times since by other rebel fronts in Burma. Usually without some form of political initiative, they have been of short duration or have degenerated into what are usually described as 'warlord' organisations and the KNLC might well have proved no exception. Indeed the only lasting legacy of the KNLC today was the adoption of a new name for the KNU's military wing, the Karen National Liberation Army (KNLA).

With trade now flourishing along the Thailand-Burma border, in mid-1967 Bo Mya got another important boost: KNUP chairman Mahn Ba Zan, followed by a party of four other senior KNUP officials, Ba Thin, Than Aung, Tha Byit and Maung Maung, crossed over to join him. This was less unexpected than it first seemed. At the time of their expulsion opinion had been divided amongst KNUP leaders. Some, such as the party's leading ideologue, Bo Kyin Pe, had loudly denounced Bo Mya as a 'stooge of imperialism'. With the Lower Delta still regarded by most Karen leaders as the key battleground, the temporary loss of the east was not expected to make much difference in the overall war with Rangoon. Others, however, such as Mahn Ba Zan, who had stayed in the eastern hills, had looked for a compromise from the very beginning.

There has since been considerable speculation, heightened by government propaganda, that behind their defection was a growing disillusionment with the CPB brought on by the excesses of its Cultural Revolution of 1966-8. Undoubtedly it was a contributory factor, but hardly decisive. The KNUP 'returnees' in fact brought back to the east much of their KNUP ideology. That Mahn Ba Zan did not at the time try to win over the rest of the KNUP movement is an indication of the strongly pro-communist line still held by the majority of KNUP leaders. At the July 1967 KNUP CC meeting he did not even raise the issue. Instead he sent a letter saying he was in poor health and asking Kaw Htoo to chair the meeting in his place. Two weeks later Ba Zan, who had now moved into the Papun hills close to Bo Mya's general headquarters, sent another letter announcing his resignation by declaring he was on his way to try and get 'national unity' with the KNLC.

Mahn Ba Zan quite likely believed he could win Bo Mya over, but instead there was a long battle of wills between the two men which Bo Mya eventually won in 1976 when he replaced Ba Zan as president of the KNU. The first result of their discussions was the Karen National United Front (also known as the KNU Front),

formed in September 1968 at To-Do-Plaw on the northern Moei River, with Mahn
Ba Zan as chairman and Bo Mya as KNLA Chief-of-Staff. In many respects the
KNUF was a halfway house on the road to the reformation of the KNU. According to Col. Marvel who represented the KNLC: 'Our idea was to reconcile our
differences into a temporary front until a future path could be agreed.'[39] But a
number of important decisions were made at the To-Do-Plaw meeting which had
an immediate impact on the direction of the Karen movement. Of these, by far the
most striking was the agreement to return to a political platform based on Saw Ba
U Gyi's 'four principles of the Karen revolution' (see Chapter 8). According to
Saw Ba Lone of the KNU's education department, this was a direct consequence
of the KNU's revolutionary experience:

> After 20 years we found we had to use the simplest system to approach our people. If
> the political discussion was too complex, our people could not always understand.
> Especially we found the CPB-KNUP discussions had not worked. The traditions and
> culture of the Karen people are very simple. Saw Ba U Gyi recognised this. His four
> principles are based upon the concept of national unity.[40]

It is significant that at this stage the KNUF still contained much of the KNUP's
ideology. The KNUF's military line, introduced by Bo Maung Maung, was virtually identical to the military programme the KNUP adopted at the July 1967 CC
meeting; the KNUF's economic policy was still to nationalise all the timber and
mineral resources of the Karen people. But perhaps the most far-reaching (though
at the time most misunderstood) change was to adopt the goal of 'national democracy' as opposed to the KNUP and CPB's 'people's democracy', which ethnic
minority leaders had begun to identify simply with a communist system of
government. Though it was not immediately obvious, Mahn Ba Zan, Bo Mya and
the KNUF leaders were coining a new and very different usage for the Maoist
term, 'national democracy', which marked the beginning of an ideological polarisation between the CPB and most of Burma's other insurgent ethnic parties.
Rather than being the first step in Mao's two-stage theory of revolution (see
Chapter 7), 'national democracy' became an objective in itself. (The debate over
exactly what it means is still being waged.) In 1976, while Bo Mya swung the
KNU further to the political right, he and Mahn Ba Zan fell out over this issue.
But, in general, since the KNUF's formation in 1968, the term 'national democracy' has been increasingly used by virtually all Burma's ethnic insurgent groups
to describe what might best be summarised as a 'federal' parliamentary system of
government that allows national minorities political, economic and cultural rights
as distinctive as those enjoyed by the French or Italians in the cantons of
Switzerland or the Lahu and Kachins in the autonomous regions of China.

This, however, did not immediately satisfy all Bo Mya's conservative supporters
and doubts over both 'national democracy', which many recognised as a communist term, and Mahn Ba Zan and the KNUP returnees continued. The KNUF's
decision to maintain the KNUP's 'anti-imperialist/anti-feudalist line' further
amplified these ambiguities; several KNLC leaders, including Defence Minister
Benny Htoo, refused to join the KNUF in protest.

Despite these dissenting voices, the return of five of the KNUP's most able
organisers undoubtedly injected a new sense of urgency into Bo Mya's expanding
political organisation in the east. Though the military remained firmly under
Mya's control, the KNUP returnees took up important administrative positions in
the KNUF and immediately began work on the reformation of the KNU. From

1970, the name KNU replaced KNUF on most policy documents and it is largely from the KNUF reforms of 1968-70 that the KNU administration of the east is still recognisable. Seven administrative districts were set up (Thaton, Toungoo, Nyaunglebin, Tavoy-Mergui, Dooplaya, Paan and Papun) with economic, agricultural, forestry, mineral, health and education departments in each. These, in theory, were centralised with each reporting to the KNU's general headquarters on the northern Moei River; but in practice, especially in finance, each had to learn to be self-sufficient.

The KNLA, too, was reorganised with the five main brigade areas redefined; No.1 Thaton, No.2 Toungoo, No.3 Nyaunglebin, No.6 Dooplaya and No.7 Paan, with regular KNLA units and KNDO village militia in each. In addition a number of special battalions under Bo Mya's personal control were set up; No.20 in Papun district, No.101 at the important trading-post of Kawmoorah, and No.10 in Tavoy-Mergui which had previously been an area of dispute between the 6th brigade, the KNUP and various other local Karen militia.[41] Here in 1970 Padoh Ba Thin was sent down to set up a KNUF administration at Mawta on the Tenasserim River, a task he successfully accomplished.

With an army that grew rapidly to over 10,000 well-armed combatants, including KNDO village militia, the new KNU movement in the east made a decisive entrance into insurgent politics in the country. Indeed, in a display of longevity only matched by the Kachin Independence Organisation in Burma's far north, the KNLA survived virtually intact until the fierce battles of the late 1980s when a number of strongholds on the Thai border were abandoned.

The NULF: 1970-4

The new KNUF movement, with its great military strongholds along the Thai border, was therefore the main focus of U Nu's concern as he set about building his own resistance army. But gaining an agreement between these bitter battlefield foes did not prove easy. For the PDP the advantages of an alliance with the KNUF were self-evident. The KNU provided both a territorial launching pad for operations deep into Burma and a secure liaison post for contact with the PDP's backers in Thailand. For the KNUF, the advantages were less obvious. Nu himself made it clear that without Mahn Ba Zan's agreement he did not expect the NULF to get off the ground and he was always careful to cultivate the latter's support. He did eventually manage to win him round, but only after strained and protracted negotiations with Ba Zan and Bo Mya in Bangkok during 1969 and early 1970, after he had slipped away from Rangoon. From this alliance the KNUF won some short-term gains, including a sizeable slice of U Nu's war chest and the promise of arms supplies to follow. But perhaps most gratifying of all to Karen leaders was the first hint, after 20 years' harsh warfare, of real international recognition for their largely forgotten struggle. They were invited to open a liaison office in Bangkok and during the years 1970-3 a KNUF team, headed by Col. Marvel, worked quite openly in the city.

On 25 May 1970 the new NULF was signed into existence in Bangkok by U Nu for the PDP, Mahn Ba Zan for the KNU and Nai Shwe Kyin for the NMSP. Strikingly, in this historic declaration, U Nu, seated across the table from his former enemies, made a greater acknowledgement of the justice of the ethnic minority cause than he had done in all his years as prime minister. The NULF's first goal promised a complete change in central government policy and specifically reintroduced the word 'federal', omitted from the 1947 Constitution: 'To overthrow the advocate of the "Great Burma Policy" and the military dictator Bo Ne Win's "sovereign government", and to form a just, democratic, progressive, developed and peaceful Federal Union Republic.'[42] Both the NULF and Federal Republic would be based on the principles of equality and justice and would include all nationalities in the Union. This would mean that national boundaries between the different races, including the Burmans, would have to be re-examined and new Mon, Arakan and Chin states created with full powers of local autonomy. As a result, this would bring the total number of states in Burma to eight: Arakan, Chin, Kachin, Karen, Karenni, Mon, Shan and, for the first time, Burman. Inside Burma the NULF's main tactic would be 'armed struggle', but in the international arena it would remain strictly 'non-aligned'.[43]

Though the exact amounts were never revealed, KNU leaders say they received a down payment of four million Thai baht from the PDP, while the NMSP gained two million baht. This money was supposed to be spent on arms and ammunition, but in the NMSP's case, there was a huge row over how it was actually used; eventually, in 1981, this led to a damaging six-year split of the NMSP movement into two rival factions under Nai Shwe Kyin and Nai Non Lar.[44]

None the less from this springboard the PDP's armed wing, the Patriotic Liberation Army (PLA), got underway with promising speed. Crucial was the support of the Thai authorities who did nothing to stop the build-up of an exile Burmese Army from their territory. Three commands were established: the Northern under Jimmy Yang, the Central under U Thwin, and the Southern under Bo Yan Naing, who was given responsibility for underground contact with schools and universities in the Delta. With arms cheaply available on the Thai black market and PLA forces able to train in camps on both sides of the border, PDP officers swiftly recruited and trained an army of local village boys and dissidents from the cities, reaching a peak strength of 4,000 regular soldiers, their uniforms brightly emblazoned with the dragon symbol of the 'Saturday-born' U Nu. Unarmed recruits swelled PDP ranks by another 6,000 camp followers.

Of the three armies, Jimmy Yang's Northern Command in the Shan State was the most ineffectual. Faced with the CPB 'invasion' from China and hoping to avoid the entanglement in the opium trade which had badly sabotaged the activities of most other Shan armies, Yang reportedly secured $200,000 from the NULF and set about forming an élite 100-man commando force, armed with M16 rifles and M79 grenade launchers.[45] Putting the clock back 15 years, his plan was to travel around the Shan State negotiating with the different rebel armies and BSPP-backed KKY militias with the intention of restoring the traditional *Sawbwas* to power. Once installed in government, they in turn would appeal to their former subjects to come down from the hills and lay down their arms.[46] But by September 1971, the date Yang had set for his army to jump off from Tam Ngop into the state, his predominantly Shan soldiers, disillusioned with their Kokangese commanders, had begun deserting in droves.

Another extraordinary project, orchestrated by the ex-CIA agent William Young whose family of Christian missionaries still had divine status in parts of the Shan hills, was to raise ethnic Wa and Lahu armies in support of U Nu. This, however, came to nothing; PDP plans in north-east Burma were not helped by Young's advice to local chieftains not to work with Jimmy Yang.[47] In 1972 PDP hopes in the Shan State were briefly raised when troops from the SSA's new political wing, the Shan State Progress Party (SSPP), commanded by Khun Kya Nu and Chao Tzang Yawnghwe, made their way down to the Thai border and began building up a new base area in the Mawkmai-Mong Mai region. But Yawnghwe, who travelled on into Thailand to meet U Nu, was not impressed; the PDP already appeared to be running out of money and could only offer the SSA 40 HK33 assault rifles.[48] At the same time, hard-pressed SSPP leaders in the north recognised that an alliance with U Nu would draw immediate fire from both the CPB and *Tatmadaw*. Eventually, in December 1972 the SSPP merely agreed to issue a joint statement with the PDP's youth wing, the Patriotic Youth Front; and instead it decided to concentrate on working with other ethnic forces along the Thai border, later becoming an influential voice in the formation of the NDF in 1976.[49]

Further south in Tenasserim and the Karen and Mon States the PDP had considerably more success. Operating from the safe sanctuary of KNU and NMSP bases, Bo Let Ya, U Thwin, Hanson Kyadoe and Bo Yan Naing launched a series of imaginative campaigns. A rebel NULF radio station with an alternate youth channel, the Patriotic Youth Front Radio, came on the air in May 1970 with an avalanche of anti-Ne Win propaganda. 'Countrymen,' U Nu began in his first broadcast, 'time was when I could talk to you frequently on the radio. But it has been eight years since General Ne Win and his group seized power and I could not even say goodbye.... Now that I am able to greet you once again, let me tell you why we are fighting the Ne Win clique.'[50]

Not surprisingly, the broadcasts caused great excitement inside the country and happened to coincide with an outbreak of student demonstrations in Rangoon following brief disturbances at the South-East Asia Peninsular games the previous year. The military quickly quelled the protests, but only after a number of buses, cars and state-owned shops had been damaged. In another act of political bravado in 1971, the PDP minted hundreds of gold coins stamped with U Nu's name on one side and an eight-pointed star representing the eight federal states on the other, which they claimed were being used as the accepted currency in Burma's 'liberated zones'. These were distributed to foreign embassies and press agencies abroad and, invoking what he called the 'Ethiopian principle', U Nu called on the international community to recognise the legitimacy of the NULF cause.[51] (Italy's attempt to gain recognition in 1938 for its occupation of Ethiopia was internationally rebuffed since the legal government still occupied part of the country.) Other political stunts followed, including leafleting several towns inside Burma from the air.

As a combative military force, however, the PLA was slow to get off the ground; when compared to the do or die battles then underway against the KNUP and CPB elsewhere in the country, its campaign pales into insignificance. Crucially the hoped for defections from the *Tatmadaw* never materialised. At the beginning of 1971 the first PLA units, having completed six months' training courses, started penetrating through ethnic rebel areas into the Tavoy, Moulmein, Thaton and Toungoo districts and began to attack *Tatmadaw* outposts. In the first two and a half years of the PDP's life, PLA commanders claim (though their figures should be treated with caution) to have killed 925 government troops and wounded over 1,000 against losses of only 88 dead and 92 wounded; 30 battles were reported in 1971, 80 in 1972 and 47 in the first half of 1973, reflecting the steady escalation of the war.[52] Many of these battles were in joint operations with KNU and NMSP forces, which guided PLA units across the mountains. Joint

NMSP-PLA forces, for example, repeatedly sabotaged the Moulmein-Ye railway line, while KNU-PLA units operated from the jungles of Mergui to the mountains of Toungoo, over 400 miles to the north, where they blew up the vital Lawpita hydro-electric plant's power lines, which caused regular blackouts in Rangoon.[53]

This was about as far as PLA-NULF forces went, for the alliance never lived down U Nu's abrupt departure from the PDP in January 1972. For close observers there had always been something uneasy about the NULF alliance, not least U Nu's participation in it. Despite his cynical nickname of 'Karen Nu' in the Rangoon press, KNU leaders always regarded Nu as one of their most implacable opponents; Karen veterans still hold hin responsible for the way the AFPFL outmanoeuvred the KNU in the political battles of 1947-9. The prospect of U Nu, the self-styled Buddhist man of peace, sharing the hardships of jungle life in rebel territory with such veteran KNU leaders as Marshall Shwin, Bo Mya and Mahn Ba Zan always had an uncomfortable irony. U Nu in fact rarely left Bangkok.

There were a number of unresolved issues. To start with, many KNU commanders in the east were reluctant to allow hundreds of ethnic Burman troops into their territory. Certainly they did not relish the prospect of giving up hard-won frontline positions to the PLA and this led to a number of arguments. The strongest protests were from KNU 1st brigade officers in Thaton district who had refused to obey Bo Mya's order to work with the PDP. Reformed after Lin Htin's surrender in 1964, the new 1st brigade continued Lin Htin's aggressive tradition of carrying the war back to Rangoon, but its reputation for ill-discipline and warlordism lingered. Particularly notorious was one battalion commander, Bo Din Gha, whose men had once attacked a KNUP column in which Mahn Ba Zan had been travelling. Ba Zan never forgot this. Matters finally came to a head with the NULF in late 1970 when the brigade commander, Kyaw Hoe, came to tell Bo Mya of his difficulty getting his officers to obey orders. Mya responded by inviting eight company commanders to his general headquarters for talks. When they arrived on 22 February 1971, all eight were arrested and summarily executed, with Mya reputedly finishing some of the victims off himself.[54]

After this inauspicious start the NULF made little progress. U Nu's main argument with the ethnic nationalist leaders was over the initial 1970 NULF treaty agreeing to the goal of a 'federal union republic'. The treaty's main architect was the KNU's veteran strategist, the Christian and avowed socialist, Mahn Ba Zan. Following the united front principles he had developed with the CPB, Ba Zan always maintained that his intention was to find wording acceptable to all parties, but which left the key details to be decided until after Ne Win had been overthrown. However, once the treaty had been circulated back in the 'liberated zones', on closer inspection, many KNU officers protested that in agreeing to join a federal union, the KNU appeared to have given up its long-held demand for the right to self-determination, which, since the KNU's foundation in 1947, they had always identified with the right of secession granted to the Karenni and Shan States in the independence Constitution. Bo Let Ya and most of the other PDP leaders had few objections to this. But when, under KNU and NMSP pressure, this right was restored in April 1972, Nu immediately resigned.[55] Chastened by official attitudes he had encountered in Bangkok, where covetous eyes are still cast on parts of Tenasserim and the Shan State, in his resignation speech Nu maintained that the right of secession would encourage foreign interference in Burma's internal affairs. Rather than being a guarantee of self-determination, he argued that this extraordinary right borrowed in haste from the Constitution of the Soviet Union could well lead to the eventual integration of Burma's territory with its neighbours.

In 1973 U Nu went into a seven-year period of retirement and Buddhist contemplation in India before returning to Rangoon under the 1980 amnesty. Despite his departure, PDP fortunes at first appeared to be bolstered by the arrival at the border of another of the *Thirty Comrades*, Bo Hmu Aung, Nu's former Defence Minister, who since his release from gaol in 1967 had acted as trustee of the Shwe Dagon Pagoda. Other PDP leaders were less certain. According to Tin Maung Win: 'I knew it was all over then, but we didn't want to let everything collapse. So each PLA commander just grabbed what he could, just to survive and try to control the situation.'[56] Ethnic minority leaders watching the PDP's disintegration were far more scathing. According to Khun Okker of the Pao National Organisation:

> When they first arrived in our areas, we were very impressed. Many men, like Tin Maung Win and David Zaw Tun, had already risked their lives and suffered considerable hardships. But then they went down to Bangkok. When they came back six months later they were flush with money. They all had cars and stayed in air-conditioned hotels. Of course their men in the jungle got disillusioned when they heard their leaders were behaving like that.[57]

Certainly with U Nu's departure, the glue holding the party together became badly unstuck and the PDP leadership was riven by internal arguments and personality conflicts that only he might have prevented. Three regional PLA commands continued to function, though increasingly independently of one another: under Bo Hmu Aung in the northern Papun-Toungoo districts, U Thwin in the central Kawkareik-Moulmein-Paan region, and Bo Yan Naing in the south between Three Pagodas Pass and Mergui. During 1972 Bo Mya and U Thwin both dispatched their own KNLA (13th battalion) and PLA columns, under Bo Tha Sein and Thwin's brother-in-law, Bo Tet Tun, into the Pegu Yomas at the height of the *Tatmadaw*'s *Four Cuts* operation. Here they clashed with both the CPB and KNUP before being forced to return. Then, in a disastrous operation at the end of the year, a heavily armed detachment from Yan Naing's Southern Command was ambushed shortly after being smuggled ashore near Bogale in the Lower Delta. Of the 110 men who set out from Ranong (in Thailand) on their perilous voyage across the Gulf of Martaban, Bo Aung Din, deputy-commander of the operation, believes only 11 survived.[58] Of these ten were captured and just one escaped to tell his comrades the tale.

For a moment these failures were disguised from the outside world. In March 1974, in what ironically proved to be the NULF's largest operation, a predominantly Karen NULF force of 1,500 troops unsuccessfully attacked the border town of Myawaddy in a pincer movement from the KNU's strongholds at Phalu and Kawmoorah in a battle for once reported in the world press.[59] Unlike the CPB, the NULF was never to hold a major government town for any length of time. Shortly afterwards at the Ninth KNU Congress, Karen leaders resolved to quit the NULF alliance. Later that year, in a bid to boost morale, the PDP's name was changed to People's Patriotic Party (PPP). But by 1975, despite a violent upsurge in anti-government protests in Rangoon, PLA troop strength had dwindled dramatically and many PDP leaders began to drift into exile. Some, like Myaungmya Ba Swe, even returned to Rangoon.

As with the KNUP-CPB alliance in Lower Burma, many close individual friendships between Burman and ethnic minority troops were forged as units from both sides shared the dangers of battle together. But the political problems persisted as the PDP remnants broke into several ever smaller factions. In July 1975 Bo Yan Naing was expelled from the PPP in the PLA's Southern Command for attacking Karen troops in a dispute over taxation. Tin Maung Win meanwhile established the Union Solidarity Party in the Tenasserim jungle, while Bo Hmu Aung responded by organising his own short-lived Anti-Fascist People's Unity Party on the Karen/Kayah State border. Only PPP forces on the central front, led by Bo Let Ya and U Thwin, remained at all militarily active.

U Thwin, in particular, was accused by the *Tatmadaw* of masterminding a sustained terrorist bombing campaign in the cities of the kind the CPB had generally refrained from making. Between 1972 and 1977 hundreds of civilians were wounded and dozens killed in intermittent and highly unpredictable attacks by PLA sabotage teams on supposedly 'government' targets in towns in southern Burma. In Rangoon, several police stations, government buildings and shops were bombed; also hit were the central railway station, *Bogyoke* Aung San market (both several times), the West German Embassy, the Rangoon general hospital and the Waziya cinema. Such attacks did nothing to improve the PLA's image (a favoured method was a hand-grenade lobbed without warning into a building); the climate of fear I witnessed on the streets of the capital was still tangible a few days after one such attack in 1977. Though they have produced no evidence to support this, PDP veterans claim these attacks on civilians were carried out by MIS *provocateurs*, but a number of PLA members were caught red-handed with explosives and several, such as Nyunt Tin who was accused of exploding a hand-grenade in *Bogyoke* market in March 1975, were executed.

The BSPP responded by launching a series of draconian counter-intelligence operations, keeping constant watch on the movements of U Nu's former colleagues; and a number of prominent AFPFL supporters, including former MP for Waw township, U Toe, were imprisoned on treason charges. The security forces may have been over zealous, but they were certainly effective. Crucially the PDP-PPP diehards were in no position to push their advantage during the mass anti-government protests of 1974-6. A number of student leaders did make contact with U Thwin and Bo Let Ya; one of them, Tin Maung Oo, was later executed by the BSPP (see Chapter 13). A few dozen more, led by Ye Myint Soe, a Rangoon University law student, fled to the Thai border to join Let Ya. But though they continued publishing anti-BSPP propaganda, they found that the PDP remnants along the Thai border were already a largely spent force.[60]

In late 1978 Karen soldiers moved to quash what was left of the PDP movement; its activities were becoming an increasing embarrassment to the KNU's attempts to police the Thai border. By this stage the PDP remnants had split into just three armed groups, each several dozen strong, in the jungles of Tavoy-Mergui under Bo Yan Naing, Bo Let Ya and Dr Mahn Myint Saing, an ethnic Karen and relative of the KYO leader, Mahn Ba Khaing, who had been assassinated with Aung San in 1947. Fighting started between these groups in the vicinity of the Mawdaung Pass after the assassination of Aung Let Ya, Bo Let Ya's son, allegedly by the Myint Saing faction. (One of Bo Yan Naing's sons had earlier died from malaria and another been murdered in Thailand after a late-night argument.) This time the KNU decided to intervene and, in the final battle of 29

November 1978, Karen loyalties were uppermost as Col. Marvel, on Bo Mya's orders, led a KNU assault on the Na Shi Naung camp of the two *Thirty Comrades*, Bo Yan Naing and Bo Let Ya. NULF veterans from all parties agree that Yan Naing caused most of the original trouble, but the most famous casualty of the battle was Let Ya, unintentionally hit by a stray bullet. Ironically, of all the PDP leaders, it was Let Ya whom Karen leaders, including Col. Marvel and Bo Mya, say they had most trusted and respected.[61] Thus died in the most futile and tragic circumstances yet another of the great heroes of Burma's freedom struggle.

Let Ya's death was the final nail in the PDP's coffin; by the time of the 1980 amnesty the NULF dream was completely dead. PDP leading lights such as U Nu, Bo Hmu Aung and Bo Yan Naing returned to Rangoon in a blaze of publicity; they were personally received by Ne Win and photographed with other former insurgent leaders, including the Red Flag veteran, Thakin Soe. Much to the amusement of the Burmese public, in pictures published in the Rangoon press, Ne Win's chair was raised so that he sat a head taller than his battlefield adversaries.

Their surrenders were followed by a stream of other PLA soldiers and officers back to Rangoon, including Mahn Myint Saing and U Thu Wai. Others had already gone into political exile: Tin Maung Win and Ye Kyaw Thu to the USA, Bo Aung Din to Britain, while Zali Maw and several others remained in Bangkok. David Zaw Tun became a tour guide in north Thailand where he brought Western travellers on exotic package tours to the border to take pictures of his former Karen comrades in their jungle camps. Only U Thwin, who remained a marked man in Rangoon for his role in the PLA bombing campaign, stayed in close contact with the KNU and kept alive a small PPP cadre force which intermittently published his *Arthit* journal. And while U Nu and many of the PDP veterans who had surrendered re-emerged in Rangoon in 1988 in the vanguard of the new democracy parties, U Thwin and the expatriate exiles rejoined in the jungles the KNU and the students from the cities in the present-day Democratic Alliance of Burma.

Reformation of the KNU, Thai Security and the NDF: 1973-6
However, long before the final break-up of the PDP, Karen leaders had begun to look in new directions and the KNU movement went through a number of changes which once again transformed the insurgent map of Burma. At first most of these changes were the result of chance or informal meetings. In the early 1970s, with much of mainland South-East Asia plunged into warfare, the KNU's strongholds along the Thai border became important meeting points for many of the region's arms dealers and traders. The bases at Kawmoorah, Phalu, Maw Po Kay and Three Pagodas Pass assumed the status of small towns with clusters of villages scattered in the forests around the KNLA defence lines. Leaders from other powerful insurgent groups in the region became frequent visitors, including two from north-east Burma, the KIO and SSPP, which, while rather more preoccupied with the CPB and the war in the north, had now established military bases on the Shan State-Thailand border.

Both groups easily outnumbered in military strength the KNU's allies in the NULF and were generally scathing of the PDP. Of the NULF armies, the 1,000-strong NMSP had long been under the KNU's wing and, while effective as a guerrilla force in Mon communities on the plains, depended on the KNU for secure military base areas in the mountains along the Thai border. The other NULF forces had been a great disappointment to Karen commanders. U Nu's plan to build Pao, Kokang, Shan, Wa and Lahu armies, loyal to the PDP, came to nought, while Mang Da Laing's small Chin Democracy Party, with just 100 soldiers based on the Karen-Karenni borders, failed despite several attempts to set up underground cells in the Chin hills. In fact it was the even smaller ZNF, which in 1972 set up its headquarters in KNPP-controlled territory nearby on the Pai River, which was more popular with most of the other ethnic armies.

Thus with the decline of the PDP and disillusionment setting in over the prospects of ever working with any ethnic Burman party, thoughts inevitably turned to setting up a new nationalities front which this time would exclude any Burman group. For several years meetings continued with different permutations of Burma's then myriad ethnic organisations and several new fronts were created. These talks were given new urgency by the 1973 referendum and the moves towards the 1974 Constitution which formally instituted a one-party state and BSPP rule. The best known front, the Revolutionary Nationalities Alliance (RNA), was formed at Kawmoorah in May 1973 by the KNU, SSPP, KNLP and KNPP, which had drifted away from the NDUF alliance with the CPB several years earlier; the Communist Party of Arakan was also represented at the meeting but did not apply to join. (See Chart 2) The RNA's aim after the overthrow of the Ne Win regime was to establish 'a genuine federal union of independent national states based on the principle of equality and national self-determination'.[62] At the same time, the KNU gave training to a number of other armed opposition groups, including the Arakan Liberation Party (ALP), formed in July 1972, whose troops were also quartered at Kawmoorah. In May 1975 the RNA was then superseded by the Federal National Democratic Front (FNDF) at another meeting of KNU, SSPP, KNPP, NMSP and ALP leaders. Reflecting many nationalist parties' deep distrust of the BSPP, CPB and PDP, the aims of the FNDF (a 'federal union' based on the principles of 'national independence, equality and progress of all nationalities') expressly ruled out a one-party state and, quite deliberately, no 'Burman parties' were invited to join.[63]

These fronts, which largely only existed on paper, became the forerunners of the NDF, which was finally inaugurated on 10 May 1976 at the KNU's new general headquarters at Mannerplaw (Victory Field) on the northern Moei River at one of the largest meetings of insurgent leaders ever held in Burma. Thirteen insurgent groups were represented at the founding meeting, though only nine initially joined and membership has since fluctuated to stand at eleven in 1991 (see Chart 2).[64] The NDF later became the only ethnic minority front to have had a really significant impact on the course of the civil war in Burma. But initially deep differences over issues as diverse as territory, federalism, the right of secession, narcotics and the CPB needed to be ironed out and these took several years to resolve. (They are looked at later.)

For the moment Karen leaders were occupied with the final preparation of the KNU movement for the 'third phase' of the Karen revolution. This had been mooted ever since the KNUF's establishment in 1968, but had taken a back seat during the troubled life of the NULF. A study group, including Mahn Ba Zan, Maung Maung and Than Aung from the KNUP returnees and Bo Mya and Pu Ler Wah from the KNLC, was formed to draw up a new KNU Constitution. But despite the 1970 decision to reuse the name KNU, the KNUF reforms were only officially sanctioned in September 1974, when the 'Ninth KNU Congress' met at

Bee Hee Lu on the Moei River.

This, the last of the KNU Congresses, laid the basis for a substantial shift in
KNU policy towards the political right which has endured into the 1990s. At a
stroke much of the history of the Karen revolution was rewritten. One senior
KNU CC member described the Congress report to me as 'deeply flawed. Many of
the facts and details are just guess-work'. The 1953 and 1956 Congresses, where
KNUP influence had been uppermost, simply disappeared from the records.
Instead, in the first of a new list of 'ten articles of the aims and objectives of the
KNU', the need for a Karen 'vanguard party' (the KNUP) was dropped: 'The KNU
is the sole organ for the development of the Karen national cause, the élite of the
Karen national revolution. The KNU is the highest organ for all Karen people and
represents all Karen people.'[65] The aim of the KNU was reaffirmed, somewhat
confusingly, as 'national democratic revolution', but on the vexed question of
class analysis, which the KNUP had also promoted, the KNU had a new answer:
'There is no division in class amongst the Karen peoples. Every farmer, worker,
intellectual, petty and national bourgeois are the strength of the KNU. We will
have a good relationship with every class and organisation from the outside world
(Article 3). Patriotism is our sole ideology. We will never accept dogmatism
(Article 4).' In recognition of the difficulties of the past, the need for 'self-
criticism' was accepted as were warnings against 'warlordism' or 'leftist and
rightist divisions or adventurism and opportunism' (Articles 6-8). Significantly,
too, the KNU decided to leave the NULF alliance, though with the PDP's rapid
break-up the news was never formally announced.

The Congress also approved many of the administrative reforms already introduced by the KNUF. The National Congress would be the KNU's supreme
legislative body and would elect the KNU chairman/president, the general-secretary, their deputies and a ruling 25-person central committee. Four administrative
wings were set up: 'party organisation' under the KNU president, which would
also be responsible for propaganda and external affairs; 'justice'; 'military'; and,
for day-to-day administration, a 16-member 'Central Executive Committee'
chosen from the CC, from which the heads of the various KNU ministries (like
Health, Education, Agriculture, Finance, Mining, Forests) would be selected.

The process of reform continued in rather more unexpected circumstances the
following year when the last KNUP strongholds fell in the Pegu Yomas. Mahn Ba
Zan and Bo Mya had no hesitation in allowing Mahn Mya Maung, U Soe Aung
and the bedraggled KPLA remnants to cross into KNLA territory in the east. Here
they were reunited with Bo San Lin, still moving with KNUP forces in the
Kyaukkyi hills and south-west Shan State, and Skaw Ler Taw, who had just
returned from the marathon three and half year journey of the KNUP's Dawna
team to Panghsang and China. The news he brought was one of disappointment
with Ba Thein Tin and the CPB's North-East Command (NEC) and the rejection
by China of any direct aid to the KNUP or any other ethnic nationalist party in
Burma (see Chapter 16).

All that was left was the KNUP's final re-amalgamation with the KNU. Realistically there was no other option. Permission was given for the KNUP survivors to
hold a congress at the KNLA's 20th battalion base at Sawta on the Salween River.
Beginning in September 1975, the Congress continued for two and a half months.
But in a long review of KNUP history, which included a full report of the Dawna
team's expedition to China, discussion eventually came to centre on just two

resolutions of the KNU's 1974 Congress. The first was the decision to sever formal relations with the PDP, a movement the KNUP had always regarded as completely unacceptable. But secondly and more importantly, KNUP leaders decided the KNU's adoption of a political programme based upon 'national democratic principles' meant the KNU still implicitly accepted the KNUP's 'anti-imperialist/anti-feudalist line'.[66] Both parties, the KNUP leaders convinced themselves, were still in a stage of 'national democratic' revolution. In fact within a year Bo Mya was to move to change this, but at the time KNUP leaders pronounced themselves satisfied and at the end of the Congress voted for the KNUP's dissolution and incorporation with the KNU.

This was not quite the end of the KNUP. The unease of both KNUP and KNUF veterans when discussing this final reunion remains obvious even today. Though the rift healed with time, their political differences were never discussed by a full KNU Congress. The remaining KNUP fighters were formed into a new '14th battalion' posted in the mountains north of Papun. To accommodate the KNUP's experienced party leaders, the KNU CC was increased to 33 members. Several KNUP veterans went on to take up leading positions in the KNU (Mya Maung as Mining Minister, Soe Aung as Agriculture Minister, Skaw Ler Taw as propaganda chief and San Lin as vice-president). Here they rejoined Mahn Ba Zan and other KNUP veterans, including Than Aung, today KNU joint vice-president and Padoh Ba Thin, KNU general-secretary, who had joined Bo Mya in 1967.

This perhaps accounts for the enigma that has puzzled many Western observers over the last decade. Despite the KNU's obvious move to the right under Bo Mya's anti-communist leadership, KNU statements and policy documents are still often couched in what can only be described as 'leftist' language. The BSPP government has often tried to make capital out of this obvious contradiction, but this tension surfaced only once, in 1978, when a platoon of ex-KNUP soldiers from the 14th battalion, led by Saw Paul, defected from the KNLA to join the CPB and were allowed to pass through territory controlled by a left-wing faction of the KNPP on its way north. This angered Bo Mya so much that he ordered the immediate disbanding of the rest of the battalion and sent KNLA troops into the Kayah State to help the KNPP leadership crush this pro-CPB movement, which today survives as the Karenni State Nationalities Liberation Front.

By this stage Bo Mya's domination of the KNU was already complete. In August 1976, for the second time he had quietly seized control of the KNU movement, replacing Mahn Ba Zan who was forced to stand down as president.

As on the occasion of Bo Mya's previous 'coup' in 1966, a look at the background circumstances is revealing. With the final communist victory in Indo-China in 1975, many diplomatic observers thought a communist takeover in Thailand through the fast-spreading CPT insurgency was now a real possibility and a communist victory in Burma, despite the CPB's losses in the Pegu Yomas the previous year, could hardly be ruled out. Already there was evidence of CPT guerrillas being supplied across the Laotian and Cambodian borders. One important new area of CPT expansion, Western analysts reported with alarm, was in the remote Karen-majority areas of north-west Thailand. An attempt by the CPB and CPT to link up was widely predicted as during 1975/6 the CPB continued to make inroads into the Shan State towards the Thai border. From the mid-1970s (and even occasionally now) there were reports that CPT cadres were passing through the hills on the opposite bank of the Moei River from KNU territory and that armed CPT units were openly patrolling many remote forest roads. In February 1976 one estimate put the total rural population in Thailand already under CPT control at just over one million and CPT military strength at somewhere between 7,000 and 10,000 and still rising.[67]

In early 1976 Thanin Kraivichien and the Thai generals again prepared to seize power (the short-lived civilian government of 1973-6 was finally overthrown in October 1976), but the writing was already on the wall. Thailand's entire security situation was under review. The most immediate beneficiaries of these new perceptions were the remnants of the KMT's 3rd and 5th armies under the aging Chinese generals, Li Wen-huan and Tuan Shi-wen, whose role as an anti-communist task force along the Shan border was being reinforced through a reaffirmation of the border 'buffer' strategy also extended to their long-time rival in the opium trade, Khun Sa's SUA. Until the early 1980s, from their bases on Thai territory they both performed the highly valued functions of virulently anti-communist border militia in one of the few areas of north Thailand where the CPT was unable to make much impression. Indeed units of both armies were hired to act as guards in road construction projects in areas of CPT insurgency as far south as Nan and Tak.[68]

The same adjustments were made to Thai Army policy along Thailand's other borders. In February 1976, a banning order from Thailand on seven rebel leaders from Burma was announced. Six were former PDP leaders, including Bo Let Ya, Bo Hmu Aung and Bo Yan Naing, but also on the list was KNU president, Mahn Ba Zan, picked out in Thai and US military circles as the KNU's most important left-wing sympathiser. The official reason given at the time was the Thai government's desire to improve relations with its BSPP neighbour and this was partly true; the activities of these PDP remnants, many of whom were scratching a living as forest labourers across the Thai border, had become a major irritant. But Tin Maung Win, one of those banned and subsequently forced into exile was told that the expulsions were because of the PDP's involvement with the student movement in Burma.[69] In the eyes of Thai officers, their very presence on Thai soil could be construed as an encouragement to Thailand's own highly active student movement which had mobilised the street protests that led to the fall of the Thanom regime in 1973. Clearly some very long-term geo-political planning was taking place.

Examination of one of the first series of interviews ever given by Karen leaders to Western journalists a few months later reveals the depth of the gulf that was developing. While Mahn Ba Zan still continued to talk of the KNU's 'national programme in the interests of the four major classes, the workers, peasants, petit-bourgeoisie and patriotic national bourgeoisie', Bo Mya was much more blunt.[70] In an analogy he has since repeated many times, Mya compared the KNU to a '"Foreign Legion" for Thailand, guarding their borders and preventing links between the Burmese communists and the Thai communists. If the West would help us with money and recognition, they would not regret it.'[71] And it was on this very issue of 'Western' aid that Mahn Ba Zan was now forced to resign.

Though the evidence is circumstantial, several veteran Karen leaders have told me that they believe the CIA engineered Mahn Ba Zan's dismissal. Alleged one KNU CC member, 'It did not need any action. Just a quiet word or threat by the Thai Army to close the border would have been enough.' Certainly in mid-1976, immediately after the NDF had been formed, the long-awaited power struggle between Bo Mya and Ba Zan finally broke out.

To the outside world it might have appeared a surprisingly complicated argument over semantics, but in the context of Burma's long-running insurgencies it at last brought to the surface the whole question of the KNU's ambiguous political alignment, which had existed since the Second Phase Programme was adopted in 1956. Till the end, though never a communist, Mahn Ba Zan defended the KNU's original Maoist intention of a 'national democratic' line, i.e. at the present 'national liberation' (united front) stage of the Karen revolution the KNU would ally with any sympathetic, progressive revolutionary force, whether the peasantry, socialists, communists or patriotic bourgeoisie.[72] Indeed the goal, 'national democratic', had been kept in both the KNU's 1974 'ten articles of aims and objectives' and the new FNDF and NDF alliances.

Mahn Ba Zan's concept of 'national democracy' was in many ways a political hybrid, a theory borrowed largely from Mao Zedong in the difficult days of the 1950s to impose an ideological discipline on the Karen revolution and the diverse social, military, political and ethnic forces with which it came into conflict. By the early 1970s he had clearly dropped any intention of moving on to Mao's second stage of 'people's democracy', but he still maintained his socialist ideals. Two months before he was ousted he spelled these out in terms that sent a shiver of alarm across the Thai border. While criticising the 'social imperialism' of the CPB and denouncing the Soviet Union as 'the most dangerous imperialist power and ally of Ne Win', Ba Zan publicly praised the Chinese government's 'high priority support for minority rights' and expressed the hope that Burma's minorities might win Chinese 'political support in the future as well'.[73] In what he saw as an emerging triangular conflict between the CPB, the Rangoon government and the national minorities, the KNU would, he warned, ally with whichever side accepted the 'essentials' of the KNU-NDF's programme.[74]

This was the final trigger for Bo Mya to act. Contradicting this interpretation, he now insisted that a clause in the KNU's 1974 'Interim Period Policy' document, which asserted 'any country' could give aid to the KNU, be amended to specify that the KNU would accept aid only from 'capitalist' nations. Through 10 August 1976 a day-long argument continued at an emergency CC meeting called at Bo Mya's house on the riverside near Mannerplaw. It finally ended with Bo Mya getting his way. Mahn Ba Zan resigned to become 'honorary adviser' to the KNU and was replaced by Bo Mya as president. With Bo Mya now assuming the posts of Ministers of Foreign Affairs and Defence in addition to his position as KNLA Chief-of-Staff, the stage was set for a substantial change in KNU policy and organisation. One of the most important was to cleanse the KNU's 'national democracy' objectives of any class or Marxist implications. Declared the KNU in 1986: 'The national liberation movement of the KNU is a "National Democratic Revolution", whereas the CPB is mainly engaged in the "People's Democracy Revolution" for the liberation of classes. The two policies are, therefore, absolutely different.'[75] This caused one of the KNU's founder leaders, Mika Rolly, to remark: 'National Democracy? People's Democracy? They're all communist words. Nobody knows what they're talking about.'[76]

If Rolly's frustration at the ideological split, which cost the KNU movement two decades, is obvious, the benefits to the Thai government of Bo Mya's return to power were immediate. But as long as the CPT insurgency continues, albeit on a near non-existent scale, KNU leaders are reluctant to discuss their possible role in dampening down the CPT movement. Until the late 1980s CPT cadres were still active in several remote areas along the Kawthoolei border from Prachuap Khiri Khan in the south to Tak and Mae Sariang Provinces in the north. Indeed on one occasion I met armed CPTs (acting as guards to local Thai businessmen) travelling through KNU territory with the knowledge of local KNU commanders; of necessity there has to be a lot of 'live and let live' in the daily life of the liberated zones.[77]

But under Bo Mya's staunchly nationalist leadership, the KNU has undoubtedly given the Thai government invaluable help in blocking the spread of communist insurgency in the region and (like the KMT and SUA) has frustrated the CPB's attempts to link up with the CPT. A tenuous line of communication still exists through Tavoy-Mergui and the remote mountain forests around Mae Sariang, but it is no exaggeration to say that, but for the KNU's determined opposition, a solid line of sympathetic 'liberated zones' straddling both sides of the border might have linked the communist parties of China, Burma, Thailand and Malaya. The CPT was for some years able to establish supply lines through Laos, Cambodia and Vietnam, but the CPB, CPT and CPM were always ideologically closest to the CCP.

The outcome of the CPT insurgency, in particular, might have been very different. Indeed so successfully did the KNU perform this role that until the late 1980s the entire Kawthoolei border was left virtually unguarded, leaving the Thai Supreme Command free to concentrate troops against the CPT and the wars raging along the Laotian and Cambodian borders in the east. And the KNU's help was not confined to the Kawthoolei side of the border. Its leaders have privately admitted to me that on several occasions, in response to requests from Thai officers, they crossed into Thailand to disarm Karen villagers who had been organised by the CPT. The mass surrenders in Tak Province during 1982/3 of over 6,000 communist sympathisers and their dependants along with over 700 heavily armed CPT guerrillas, most of whom were ethnic Karens or Mons, showed that the CPT's presence on Thailand's western border was once no idle threat.[78]

The Thai Army owes a debt of deep gratitude to the KNU and NDF alliance, which might explain why senior Thai Army officers are reluctant to turn their backs on the KNU, despite the closening of Rangoon-Bangkok ties in the late 1980s. Apart from the sleepy 'Asia highway' Mae Sot-Myawaddy river crossing which had to be forded, the KNU was the *de facto* government along most of Thailand's western border. Because of its support, no serious restrictions have ever been placed on the lucrative cross-border trade out of which it and several other NDF members have financed their struggles. KNU (and KNPP, NMSP and KIO) leaders have remained on close personal terms with senior Thai intelligence, police and army (especially Third Army) officers. Karen casualties have been treated in Thai hospitals and KNLA commanders have been allowed untroubled access to Thailand and the region's thriving arms black market. KNLA arms purchases have always reflected the region's other wars. Into the late 1970s most of the KNLA's arms were described as 'Vietnam surplus' (sometimes 'Laotian' or 'Thai'); today most are Chinese-made 'Khmer surplus'. The result has been that, though lacking in field-guns and larger conventional weapons, KNLA units have frequently been as well, if not better, armed and equipped than their *Tatmadaw* counterparts. Certainly in radios and battlefield communications, the KNLA has for many years stood some way in advance.

The consequences of Bo Mya's rise to power and the political consolidation of the NDF are considered in Chapters 16 and 19. Not all NDF members supported the KNU's anti-communist line, but it did mean that in the mid-1970s when the CPB's NEC launched its most serious military offensives, westwards towards the heartlands of central Burma and south towards the Thai border, a line of generally pro-Western armies stood in its way. Ultimately most of these were to prove equally successful at resisting *Tatmadaw* encroachments into their territory.

For the moment, however, it was still towards China and the CPB threat from the far north that military analysts in both Rangoon and Bangkok were anxiously looking.

15

The War in the North, Opium and the 1980/1 Peace Parley

Disastrous as the deaths of Thakin Zin and Chit may have been, events soon showed that all was not lost for Burma's communists with the collapse of the CPB's Central Command. A stream of VOPB broadcasts cut through the airwaves, denouncing the *Tatmadaw*'s bragging claims of victory and sending a clear reminder that the CPB was still far from finished. Even more ominously, breaking a self-imposed silence since the VOPB opened in 1971, on 20 May 1975 a message of 'deep condolences' from the CCP's CC was broadcast on Beijing radio, expressing sorrow at the loss of the CPB leaders who had died 'heroically in action' and the conviction that the CPB, drawing on its 'glorious tradition of revolutionary struggle', would one day overcome its difficulties and 'win thorough and complete victory'.[1]

In the following weeks, in a rare display of international solidarity, other condolences were sent by the Albanian Workers' Party and the communist parties of Malaya, Thailand, the Philippines, Indonesia, Poland, North Kalimantan and Italy (M-L).[2] At the same time the official Chinese media, including Beijing radio's Burmese-language service, again began to carry CPB propaganda statements. In May 1975 the *Peking Review* published a bitter denunciation of the 'Ne Win-San Yu military regime' by the CPB's CC, which derided Ne Win's boasts to be 'building socialism' and warned of the recent urban riots and build-up of CPB Red Power base areas elsewhere in the country.[3] The revolutionary situation in Burma and South-East Asia, the CPB claimed, was 'excellent'; turning 'grief into strength' over the heroic deaths of Zin, Chit and the country's other 'proletarian martyrs', the CPB's People's Army (PA) would 'continue to march ahead wave upon wave along the path crimson with their blood'. The Communist Party was still sure to win as long as it continued the armed struggle and the correct Marxist-Leninist-Mao Zedong principles: 'The difficulties we face at present, including the difficulties in our base areas in the Pegu Yomas mountain area, are entirely different in nature from those besetting the enemy. They do not stem from insoluble, fundamental class contradictions, but are temporary difficulties which revolutionaries constantly encounter in the course of their advance.'[4]

The Position of China
Such publicity in the Chinese press once again underscored the degree of the CCP's military and political commitment to the CPB. The CCP's long-term support for the CPB, whether for ideological, geo-political or even more simply personal reasons, still remains a matter of some speculation. Certainly it is a

subject on which both CCP and CPB officials have consistently refused to answer any questions. As will be seen, aid to the CPB was gradually reduced from the late 1970s. But it is worth emphasising that military supplies to the CPB were continued long after aid to its ideological partners, the Communist Party of Thailand (CPT) and Communist Party of Malaya (CPM), was ended. Indeed technical, financial and humanitarian assistance continued right up until the 1989 ethnic mutinies which brought about the collapse of the North-East Command (NEC). Moreover the CCP's abrupt cut-off of all aid to these breakaway factions pushed most of the mutineers into immediate negotiations with the Rangoon government, raising the question of how far China had been sustaining the CPB insurrection in north-east Burma all along.

Until the 1989 collapse, the CPB had maintained large warehouses, filled to the rafters with Chinese arms and ammunition, in base areas dotted along the Yunnan border. Wide-eyed visitors were amazed to see that many of the boxes had never been opened; in fact these stockpiles were so great that the CPB itself became a major arms broker to other ethnic insurgent forces in north-east Burma well into the 1980s.

The CPB played an important ideological role for the CCP, which is much undervalued by Western commentators. As a communist party in a neighbouring country, the CPB supported and publicised the changing ideological 'correctness' of the CCP through over three decades of war and conflict in the region. This the CCP could show off to its own peoples, its neighbours and the Third World. For example, having in June 1976 applauded the CCP on the defeat of Liu Shao-chi's 'revisionist clique' and the 'rightist chieftain Deng Xiaoping', the following year (after Mao's death) the CPB CC was quick to support the CCP's 'smashing of the Gang of Four' and Deng's restoration to power in another congratulatory message prominently featured in the Chinese press.[5] The CPB's tone towards China has always been eulogistic.[6]

There is no question, however, that the CPB steadily lost favour after Deng Xiaoping came to power and then paid the penalty for its slavish support of Mao's Cultural Revolution and its own personal attacks on Deng. There have been rumours, too, the substance of which must remain unproven, that Chinese generals, having supported the NEC's build-up with a motley assortment of adventurers and cadres from China, then became concerned about the possibility of their colluding with the KMT once they entered Burma; these fears continued to grow with the disgrace of Mao's heir apparent, Lin Piao, who was killed when his plane was shot down on a flight to the Soviet Union. As China's Defence Minister, Lin Piao had been closely involved in the initial planning of the NEC. In 1972/3, so it was said, 100 volunteers suspected of being loyal to him were abruptly called back to China in circumstances that have never been properly explained.

But leaving aside the now indisputable fact of history that for a brief period in the late 1960s the CCP clearly backed Than Tun and Burma's communists to seize power, China has always shown a marked ambivalence towards Burma and the CPB and this attitude continues to the present day. (Privately CPB officials have admitted to me that Chinese officials have told them, whatever their day to day actions, the long-term goal of Chinese policy has always been to prevent the establishment of hostile regimes in Rangoon.) Questions over this curious relationship were again raised by a surprise visit to Beijing by Ne Win in

November 1975, shortly after the Chinese press had publicly and provocatively grieved the death of Thakin Zin. In his talks with Chinese officials, Ne Win delicately expressed the hope that the 'differences' between the two governments could be solved by 'patience, mutual understanding and accommodation'.[7] No such restraint, however, was felt by the Soviet Union which accused China of supporting the CPB insurgency by sending armed, mixed-nationality units across the border to 'create chaos' in the country.[8] China's oft-claimed friendship with Burma, claimed *Pravda*, was mere 'lip-service'.

Two years later, as further evidence of Beijing's indifference to BSPP sensibilities, the official *New China News Agency* carried near simultaneous reports of a meeting between Ne Win and the Chinese ambassador in Rangoon and the new CPB chairman, Ba Thein Tin, paying his respects to the remains of Chairman Mao in Beijing. At the end of the month, just ten days after Ne Win had made another short stop-over visit to China, Ba Thein Tin was mentioned second only to Cambodia's leader, Pol Pot, 'amongst the distinguished guests at the main table' at China's National Day reception.[9] Perhaps shrewdly, Ne Win was quick to exploit this apparent contradiction; in December 1977, in a surprise move from such a rarely seen world leader, he became the first foreign head of state to visit Phnom Penh since the Khmer Rouge had seized power in 1975: a trip some analysts have put down to Chinese moves to try and break Pol Pot's international isolation and counter growing Vietnamese influence in the region.[10] According to this theory, Beijing's order to Ba Thein Tin to move the CPB's central offices and clandestine radio station, the VOPB, across to the Burmese side of the border shortly afterwards was simply a pay-off for Ne Win's cooperation. From 1977 Chinese technical and economic assistance to Burma, on the basis of the existing *pauk phaw* (kinsmen) relationship between the two countries, also began to increase steadily.

But perhaps the most extraordinary evidence of the CCP's support for the CPB was still to come: a two-hour film, *The Inextinguishable Flame*, which a Chinese film crew travelling through CPB base areas made in 1978 and which was shown in cinemas across the country.[11] The film is pure, stage-managed Maoist propaganda; frame after frame shows the vast ranks of the CPB's PA, thousands-strong and in heavily armed formations, marching into battle on different fronts in northeast Burma and winning victory after victory. Between times, CPB cadres dressed in Chinese uniforms are seen healing the sick, giving lectures or being enthusiastically welcomed by farmers, students, ethnic minority villagers and other 'revolutionary' forces, such as the Kachin Independence Organisation (KIO). Ba Thein Tin, hidden in a large Chinese greatcoat and Maoist cap adorned with a red star, is virtually indistinguishable from Mao. If the film had ever been shown abroad, it would have completely changed international perceptions about the scale of Beijing's commitment to the CPB.

Only belatedly, after the deaths of Thakin Zin and Chit, did the world wake up to the strength of the CPB's NEC. From 1978, at the end of what its leaders say was an original ten-year plan, Chinese aid to the CPB was gradually reduced and most of the remaining CCP advisers were ordered home. But it most certainly, as *The Inextinguishable Flame* then froze in time, still had considerable military potential. Ultimately the CPB and the *Tatmadaw* were to fight each other to a standstill in the cold of Burma's great mountains and the sticky heat of its malaria-ridden forests, in a war unseen by the world outside. No side ever won complete military victory.

The Reorganisation of the CPB: 1975/6

Assured of continued Chinese backing, for the second time in less than a decade the CPB began an urgent reorganisation of its leadership. At an expanded meeting of its CC in May 1975, a new Politburo and 32-man CC, including 14 'candidate' members, were hurriedly chosen. The CPB did not want for experienced cadres. Thakin Ba Thein Tin, a veteran of the *Dobama* movement, the anti-Japanese resistance and a Politburo member since 1946, was chosen as chairman; Thakin Pe Tint, another *Dobama* and party veteran from Pyinmana was elected as his deputy; while the Moscow-trained Khin Maung Gyi, ten years their junior, became second-deputy. Unlike the 1968 CC chosen in the Pegu Yomas, several had considerable international experience. Ba Thein Tin, for example, had visited Britain and India in 1947/8 and, following his arrival in China in 1953, had continued to travel extensively, making trips to the Soviet Union and Vietnam. Others of the CPB's China-based leaders, including Thein Aung and San Thu, had also studied in the Soviet Union. The new line-up, however, reflected the CPB's dependence on China and the NEC. Of the seven-man Politburo only one (in Arakan), Kyaw Mya, was actually based outside the Shan State or China.[12]

For the next few years the armed struggle remained the cornerstone in the CPB's militant strategy to seize power and the set-piece battles in the NEC continued. But with the adoption of the new CC, a number of changes appeared in the CPB's style and methodology. The most obvious was the political predominance of Ba Thein Tin and the CPB's other China-based leaders, some of whom had now spent the best part of two decades in China where they had lived through the Great Leap Forward and the Cultural Revolution. Even before Mao's death they appeared to be abreast of the coming changes in China. In his first broadcast to the country as chairman, Ba Thein Tin signalled a major change in philosophy when he ordered party units to stop punishing members for ideological differences. 'Left-dogmatism', he warned, should be watched out for as much as 'revisionism'.[13] Stressing the importance of collective leadership, he urged veteran officials in the party's remaining base areas to take extra responsibility for training new cadres (especially young people and women) and to continue the key task of building the party.

Ba Thein Tin then ran through a brief outline of the CPB's tactical strategy which, while it echoed the speeches of Thakin Zin, showed a number of refinements. Though he repeated that 'nothing but armed struggle can bring us victory', he emphasised that in present circumstances this would largely need to be guerrilla or mobile warfare and had to be tied in with other forms of struggle; the only exception he singled out was the rejected revisionist or legal approach, which was still forbidden. Practising the principles of self-reliance, the CPB had to win the support of the peasantry, who made up the bulk of the population, to fight what he described as essentially a peasant war in a semi-colonial country. The CPB would also have to forge a broad 'worker-peasant alliance' and 'united front', which would include 'the urban petty bourgeois, national capitalists, progressive democrats and all the nationalities'. The key, Ba Thein Tin explained, 'is to strengthen the CPB and its leadership role', lending fuel to the allegations of MIS officers in Rangoon who have since seen CPB instigators as being behind every anti-government protest.[14]

From this time the CPB became one of the most academic and staunchly Maoist of all the communist parties in South-East Asia, its radio station and journals putting out a regular stream of commentaries and articles, often penned by Ba Thein Tin himself, on a wide array of international and domestic concerns. There were frequent, fashionable references to 'objectivism', 'subjectivism' and other favoured Maoist themes. In intellectual volume the CPM's clandestine Voice of the Malayan Revolution and the CPT's Voice of the People of Thailand, with which the VOPB was usually compared, were soon left far behind. Frequently returned to subjects were agriculture, the economy, students and workers, the 'mercenary' *Tatmadaw*, BSPP corruption, the glowing example of the People's Republic of China and homilies on the lessons of Mao Zedong thought.[15] A particular tactic was to home in on a specific issue, often in response to a statement by Ne Win or another government official, with a detailed rebuttal of the BSPP and a lecture on the CPB's position. To a foreigner tuning in on BBC or CIA listening stations, such broadcasts often gave the impression of important 'insider' knowledge in the corridors of power in Rangoon and contrasted sharply with other insurgent forces, especially the PDP remnants of U Thwin. But for most citizens in Rangoon, Mandalay and other government-controlled areas, it did not disguise the CPB's increasingly distant-sounding voice.

The CPB did, however, score one rare propaganda victory. In July 1976 former *Thirty Comrade*, Brig. Kyaw Zaw, a much lauded battlefield hero of the *Tatmadaw*'s campaigns against the KNU and KMT in the 1950s and supporter of the now-defunct NUF, defected with his family to the CPB's general headquarters at Panghsang, where he was appointed to the party's Central Military Commission. Kyaw Zaw had also been a member of the CPB at the end of the Second World War but, while he remained secretly in contact, had not gone underground with Bo Zeya, Bo Yan Aung and his other wartime comrades. Now, wrongly suspected of involvement in the army plot against Ne Win, but clearly appalled by the deteriorating state of the economy and the brutality of the army's clamp-down in the cities (his son, Kyaw Zaw Oo, had also been closely involved in the March student demonstrations), in an impassioned talk on the VOPB shortly after his arrival, he denounced Ne Win as 'morally depraved'.[16]

Curiously, Brig. San Yu and the *Tatmadaw* high command made no apparent attempt to stop Kyaw Zaw's flight to the jungle, leading to speculation by other insurgent parties, such as the KIO, with whom San Yu had refused to deal as equals during secret peace talks in 1972, that senior BSPP officials regarded the CPB as a useful military counterbalance to nationalist influence. They would not have allowed Kyaw Zaw to slip away so easily, so their argument runs, if he had tried to escape to the KNU like Bo Let Ya, Bo Hmu Aung and the PDP supporters of U Nu.

But coming from one of that select band of comrades of which Ne Win was also a proud member, Kyaw Zaw's detailed criticisms were highly damaging. For the first time he publicly revealed what had long been common knowledge: Aung San and the other heroes of the independence struggle had once seriously considered removing Ne Win from military office because his behaviour under the Japanese had led them to believe he had 'fascist' tendencies. The 'double-faced' Ne Win had not been sacked, he explained, only because of his 'cunning'. Now urging citizens of all nationalities to join the 'people's democratic revolution led by the CPB', Kyaw Zaw censured troops: 'Your life is the life of an assassin and a murderer serving the power-mad and evil king, Ne Win'.[17]

Such personal attacks on Ne Win and the sermonising of the CPB leaders, daily beamed into Burma from secret transmitters on the Yunnan-Burma border, must be seen only as an adjunct to the CPB's determination to seize power by force. As Ba Thein Tin reminded the country in his inauguration speech, despite the loss of the party's Delta and Pegu Yomas strongholds, the PA still controlled large 'liberated' base areas in Arakan, the North-West Division, Tenasserim and the Shan and Kachin States.[18]

The main objective was to find a way of infiltrating cadres back through the existing base areas into the Burman heartlands where they could start the slow process of building up new 'liberated zones' around the towns. In the mid-1970s the CPB appeared to have several options.

The least likely was Tenasserim (Tavoy-Mergui). Here CPB forces under PA commander Bo Soe Lwin, a former army officer, and U Saw Han, the division secretary, were very much a shadow of their former selves. Though they had 400 men under arms and moved with relative freedom up and down the coast and off-shore islands between Tenasserim town and Tavoy, over the previous few years they had been squeezed out by the KNU and PDP in the mountains to the east and the New Mon State Party (NMSP) and *Tatmadaw* on the plains to the north. Since the late 1960s all four parties had made considerable efforts to take control of the area for themselves and, as a result, relations between rival soldiers were tense.

Cross-border contact and a number of joint jungle camps had also been established with the CPT, which had now built up large base areas of its own along the Burmese frontier stretching down through southern Thailand to the Malaysian border. For many years the CPT was able to help supply the CPB's Tenasserim Division with medicine and arms, including M16 rifles, RPGs and M79 grenade-launchers. But by now the main CPB troop force was too isolated in the remote rain forests of Tavoy-Mergui to act as a major conduit for CPB infiltration back into Lower Burma. In an unusually frank announcement in 1979, while claiming to have set up guerrilla or base areas over 8,500 square kilometres of Tenasserim, the CPB Politburo revealed the local party's full weaknesses: there were only 115 full party and 25 youth members in the entire division; peasant and fishermen's unions had been set up in just 33 out of the 240 villages the party claimed to control; and fighting was mainly confined to small guerrilla ambushes.[19] Moreover, the Politburo admitted, contact with the party centre had been lost for many years.

Eventually, with help from the CPT and NMSP, contact was restored through northern Thailand and the Politburo in Panghsang sent financial assistance through CPB-CPT couriers who secretly travelled back and forth. But in 1983 the staff of the CPB's Tenasserim Division general headquarters, who had complacently set up a permanent camp in the Thayetchaung area close to Tavoy, were surrounded by the *Tatmadaw* and attacked; 20 cadres and a number of women and children were killed and the divisional leadership was forced to take temporary sanctuary in KNU territory in the hills to the east. The other party units retreated into the forests along the Thai border. Die-hard communists, but an interesting mixture of Burmans, Tavoyans, Karens and Mons, shortly afterwards they told one local KNU officer that their only objective was 'survival until the mission from the north is completed'.[20]

The weakness of the Tenasserim party unit effectively left the CPB leadership with a choice between PA forces in the NEC and the combined party units in the North-West Division, headed by Thet Tun, and in Arakan, led by Politburo member, Kyaw Mya. The NEC, with the prospect of China's continued military backing, represented the most obvious solution to the CPB's dilemma. While radio instructions were sent to Thet Tun's men to push back into the Irrawaddy valley from the west, the CPB's Central Military Commission, chaired by Ba Thein Tin, drew up in October 1975 what became known as the '7510 plan' for a fresh military offensive from the Chinese border to link up with guerrilla base areas along the western edge of the Shan plateau. From these sanctuaries, it was planned, they could secretly slip back into the Pegu Yomas and down onto the plains of central Burma. Indeed, in heavy fighting in early 1975, the PA claimed to have already made considerable advances in the northern and eastern Shan State. Over 500 government troops, including Nyunt Tin, deputy-commander of the 99th Light Infantry Division (LID), were reportedly killed and another 60 taken prisoner.[21] Both sides then lost hundreds more lives during June after the PA launched its first major offensive on the west bank of the Salween River in an attempt to establish a new base area in the Tangyan region of the northern Shan State. Repeated aerial strikes and 17 close range bayonet battles were reported before the CPB was forced to retreat.[22]

Ne Win's Reply: The Four Cuts in Arakan and the North-West Division

Ne Win refused to panic. If the *Tatmadaw* had rushed up troops into the remote mountain valleys of the north-east to try and destroy the CPB's PA (not to mention the KIO, Shan State Progress Party (SSPP) and other elusive insurgent forces in the hills), it is quite likely they would have simply disappeared, crippled by malaria, over-extended supply lines and guerrilla ambushes. This was what befell the British Chindits and the Chinese and Japanese armies in the Second World War. Certainly it would have played into insurgent hands and been exactly what rebel commanders wanted. 'We welcomed *Tatmadaw* attacks,' explained Major Zaw Bawn, then commander of the KIO's 4th brigade in the northern Shan State. 'If they came up in strength, we would simply retreat and try to draw them further into the mountains. Then we would slip round the back to ambush their supply lines. At one time it was our best way of getting new weapons.'[23]

This did not stop *Tatmadaw* columns, even today, being lured into well-prepared traps on unfamiliar territory. But in the mid-1970s Ne Win once again took careful stock of the situation. Despite the success of the *Four Cuts* campaigns in the Delta and Pegu Yomas, he recognised the battles ahead would be different; they would be fought against local hill peoples in difficult mountain terrain and in dense virgin forests. In the north-east several insurgent forces, notably the CPB, KIO and SSPP, were well armed and trained and capable of out-fighting the *Tatmadaw* in conventional and guerrilla warfare. Each army, whether through jade, opium or other black market taxation, had its own source of finance. And each could put several hundred troops into battle, if the occasion demanded, before retreating back into safe mountain strongholds.

The sheer diversity and scale of the armed opposition (compounded by the PDP, KNU and other ethnic nationalist forces in south-east Burma) caused Ne Win to rely initially on the already established 'inner' and 'outer' ring of defence lines and to continue his clever policy of containment, namely fighting the war on several fronts in seesaw fashion according to the relative strengths and merits of the different rebel forces. Thus in 1975 the *Four Cuts* campaign was introduced against the KNU in the Shwegyin hills for the first time. In 1977 and 1980 further operations were launched at KNU strongholds in the northern Dawna Range and around Three Pagodas Pass. In between times, major offensives were launched against the KIO and CPB in the NEC in response to KIO-CPB attacks. If any serious strategic mistake was made, it was the army's reliance on mule trains and human porters to carry supplies across the mountains, rather than helicopters which would have caused guerrilla forces far greater problems. Financial constraints were now uppermost under the creaking *Burmese Way to Socialism*; the *Tatmadaw*'s ageing air fleet was becoming very decrepit. Leaving aside the shameful enforced enslavement of tens of thousands of ethnic minority villagers to carry supplies into the firing-line, it was an oddly inefficient way of fighting a modern war.

However, though these battles along Burma's eastern borders gained what little there was of world attention, in another masterstroke of *Tatmadaw* planning, the real step by step *Four Cuts* operation was switched against CPB forces to the west in the Arakan Yomas. The Rangoon generals correctly recognised that, without access to outside arms and support, this was likely to be the CPB's weakest link. For six hard years, until they reached the safe sanctuary of the India-Bangladesh tri-border region, it was to be the CPB and other insurgent forces in the north-west who felt the full heat of the *Four Cuts* campaign.

In 1973/4, while fighting continued in the Pegu Yomas, the *Tatmadaw* had already carried out a number of probing operations against Thet Tun's forces in the Thayetmyo-Mindon districts on the eastern flank of the Arakan Yomas. With the deaths of Thakin Zin and Chit and the collapse of the CPB's Central Command, full attention was turned to the north-west. Two tactical divisions were set up: No.1 under the Western Military Command in Arakan; and No.2 under the *Tatmadaw*'s 66th LID, which was assigned the difficult task of following Thet Tun and his divisional headquarters whichever way they turned. In 1975, sustained military pressure was put on CPB strongholds in Arakan and the North-West Division for the first time, though this was reduced in 1976/7 by tactical division No.1, CPB cadres believe, because of heavy fighting elsewhere in Burma. Further south, however, the pressure on Thet Tun's jungle headquarters was relentless. Trailed constantly by up to eight mobile battalions, his party was forced back deeper across the Arakan Yomas into An township, fighting repeated guerrilla battles all the way. In the one report it managed to send out, it accused the *Tatmadaw* of the wholesale destruction of villages and paddy, as during 1976/7 it ruthlessly cleared the mountains of all human habitation.[24] The well-publicised surrender early in 1978 of 138 Chin families in Mindon township, who had been supporting the CPB for many years, was grim testimony to the effectiveness of the army's tactics.[25] The Arakan party secretary, Kyaw Mya, discussed the deteriorating situation in March of that year with an advance party sent by Thet Tun, before travelling on (via Bangladesh and China) to the CPB's general headquarters at Panghsang, where he had now been summoned.

There was, however, no respite. In 1978, along with the other insurgent parties in Arakan (CPA, AIO, ANLP and *Mujahids*), Kyaw Mya's own local force was badly hit by Operation *Ye The Ha* against rebel strongholds in the mountains around the Sittwe plain, while Operation *Nagamin*, directed at the Muslim population of the far north, caused over 200,000 villagers to flee in terror over the

Bangladesh border. Road-blocks, ID checks and tight restrictions on travel were enforced across the state and there were frequent, documented reports of rape, army harassment and the indiscriminate shooting of civilians (see Chapter 12).

Deprived of all food and support, insurgent leaders soon realised that to have any chance of survival they would have to move. The first group to withdraw was the AIO, which in 1979 retreated from its Kyauktaw base area to the Bangladesh border. Other rebel forces prepared to follow suit. On 16 April 1980 Maung Han and the CPA leaders left their last permanent general headquarters in the Myebon hills to join the exodus to the north, leaving just a few small guerrilla squads behind.

Meanwhile, CPB forces marshalled by Kyaw Mya's successor, Saw Tun Oo, began congregating in their last major base area in the mountains above Buthidaung to await the arrival of Thet Tun and his party who, accompanied by several families with children, were now hurrying their way north. They were to come desperately close. According to survivors, his predominantly Chin force got as far as Myohaung township where it found its way blocked by the Kaladan River. Unable to cross since all boats along the river had been seized or destroyed, they were eventually run to ground in July 1980 and forced to surrender. Of the estimated 1,000 troops once under his command, only 64 were left for the final surrender. Photographs in the government press were of an emaciated group of survivors, virtually unrecognisable after years of subsistence living in the forest.[26] Then, in an extraordinary gesture emphasising the forgotten but personal nature of the war, Ne Win promptly invited Thet Tun, his old comrade-in-arms, to lunch.

The collapse of the North-West Division was largely overshadowed by the growing number of surrenders that year under a new amnesty (announced 28 May) which saw the return to Burma of U Nu, Bo Hmu Aung, Bo Yan Naing and hundreds of other political activists from the crumbling PDP resistance. But it was still a shattering blow to the CPB's attempts to re-enter the inner ring of defence lines around the central plains. In Arakan, Kyaw Zan Rhee, leader of a breakaway faction from the CPA, surrendered with 52 troops along with the AIO founder and chairman, Tun Shwe Maung, adding to the illustrious list of veteran insurgents 'entering the light'.[27] Meanwhile, the remaining CPB forces withdrew from Buthidaung in August 1980, leaving a small rear-guard troop under Kyaw Maung to cover their retreat. Eventually some 900 CPB troops, cadres and camp-followers arrived on the Sengu River in the Bangladesh Hill Tracts in late 1980 where they took temporary shelter before separating into several new base camps astride the Bangladesh-India-Burma border. Here they resumed contact with their estranged allies, the Mizo National Front, which controlled much of the area, and ceasefires were agreed with their insurgent opponents, the CPA, AIO, ANLP and *Mujahids*. For once political differences were forgotten as they all concentrated their energies on trying to penetrate back into their old base areas.

Arakan has never been reclassified as a completely 'white' area, but with the CPB, CPA and other insurgent remnants largely confined to remote forests in one of the world's least accessible mountain regions, there is no real threat to government control. Guerrilla operations are met with immediate military reprisals against insurgent base camps and suspected sympathisers and there have been frequent allegations of army atrocities.[28] Consequently, while still the largest single force in the region, the CPB has gradually dwindled to less than half its previous strength with many cadres forced to return to farming simply to support their families. Indeed the only military operation to hit the headlines came not from the CPB but the CPA, which in a daring raid in May 1986 infiltrated a heavily armed guerrilla force, led by Maj. Twan Aung Cho, into Minbya and seized control of the town after a gun-fight in which two policemen and two civilians died. At dawn the following morning they escaped by boat with 33 weapons after releasing all the prisoners from gaol and holding a large public rally in the town square. But the raid backfired badly. In the following months 25 CPA soldiers and underground sympathisers, including the prominent lawyer and CC member, Khaing Soe, were picked up in a draconian army security operation in which troops painstakingly checked on the movements of virtually every inhabitant in the north of the state. Instead of retreating back into the hills, the CPA guerrillas had mistakenly tried to go undercover in monasteries and houses in the towns.[29]

Though the *Tatmadaw's Four Cuts* campaign in Arakan provided striking evidence of the effectiveness of the army's counter-insurgency tactics, it did little to resolve the underlying problems of the *Burmese Way to Socialism*. In two journeys along the border in the late 1980s, I found ample evidence of BSPP misrule (conditions which in other parts of Burma the government blamed on 'economic' or 'racial' saboteurs): a stagnant economy, BSPP corruption, a largely rural rice-growing population, a lively black market, ethnic discontent and insurgents in the mountains. In short, despite the success of the *Tatmadaw's Four Cuts* campaign, Arakan was a microcosm of Ne Win's Burma.

The PA Offensive in North-East Burma: 1975-80
Long before the party's final 'retreat to the border' in Arakan, it was already clear that the real battle on which the CPB's success was likely to hinge would be fought in the rugged borderlands with China and Thailand. Despite continued support from China, time was not on the CPB's side. As the army continued to tighten its grip on the cities, the CPB's leadership wrestled with two major tasks: launching the reinvasion of central Burma and trying to establish its own administration in the Shan and Kachin States.

As a vast mountain wilderness the size of Great Britain, with few roads and even less industry, the region hosts a greater variety of insurgent and ethnic armies than perhaps any other place on earth. In sheer complexity, the insurgent politics of north-east Burma is matched only by that of Afghanistan and Lebanon, where each ethnic and political faction has had similarly frequent recourse to arms. For many local inhabitants plunged into the middle of this chaos, the CPB was simply another 'colonial' army of occupation to be resisted as bitterly as any Burman, Chinese, Japanese or British army of the recent past.

What the CPB did have, however, was arms in abundance. By the late 1970s, through a series of uneasy alliances with other ethnic armies, the CPB was (at least on paper) the strongest partner in the 30,000-strong insurgent force confronting the *Tatmadaw* in the north-east. Though all figures must remain approximate, these totals can be broken down as follows: PA 10-12,000, CPB village militia 8,000, KIO 6,000, SSPP 5,000, SSNLO and other ethnic allies 2,000. As a result, in many areas the *Tatmadaw* was hopelessly outnumbered.

Yet, despite these formidable numbers and the apparent cooperation of these different ethnic allies, the CPB at first persisted in trying to launch the 'reinvasion' of central Burma on its own. From 1975 until the 1989 collapse, it constantly changed the names and numbers of its military regions and units to confuse the *Tatmadaw* and to give the impression of a steady build-up of forces. But to all intents and purposes, with a peak armed strength of between 20,000 and 25,000 men under arms, the only really secure CPB base areas remained enclaves backed up against the Chinese border.

Hemmed in by the KIO in the far north, PA units led by Ting Ying and Zalum in the 101 war zone of the Kachin State found it difficult to make any inroads. With about 1,000 troops and village militia, their position in the remote mountains between the Hpimaw and Kambaiti passes was impregnable; guerrilla units and small mobile columns frequently struck at army camps along the roadside between Sadom, Chipwe and Laukhaung. For example, PA units in the 101 region claimed they killed 154 government troops in 1977 and 283 in 1978, and took over 400 prisoner.[30] The same year, in one of the most famous battles of the 101 war zone, PA troops overran the forward headquarters of the *Tatmadaw's* 15th Light Infantry Regiment at Htawgaw, capturing 47 troops and a great horde of supplies and ammunition.[31] A decade later similar battles, on only a slightly reduced scale, were still being reported.[32]

However, the main thrust of the CPB's offensive was always westwards across the Shan State. To feed the line of the PA's advance, two new military regions were established, the 'north-east', encompassing the five districts of Namhkam, Kuktai, Kokang, Northern and Southern Wa from the old 202, 303 and 404 war zones, and the 815 region in eastern Kengtung. In late 1975 the 815 commanders launched another major offensive against the 88th LID in the Mong Yawng area to the south, consolidating their control of the mountains running down to the Laotian border. In August the following year the predominantly ethnic Shan 768 brigade, which consisted largely of troops from the Shan State Army East dissolved two years earlier, was established in the mountains east of the fertile Mong Yang valley with its headquarters at Hsaleu. Led by Khun Myint, a veteran Shan nationalist, and Sai Noom Pan, a former Rangoon University student wounded in 1962 during the army assault on the university campus, the 768 brigade began to build up a large base area of its own squeezed between the 'north-east' and '815 regions'.

The same year another column of 200 CPB troops tried to break out from the former 202 war zone along the Shweli River into the Shwebo area to try and link up with existing guerrilla base areas in the west. But the CPB's main line of attack was spearheaded by the PA's 683 brigade into the heart of the Shan State to try and link up with CPB remnants in the 108 region in the Kyawkku-Lawksawk area in the mountains above Mandalay. Here, from the mid-1970s, increasing numbers of Chinese-made weapons at last began to get through.

The fighting was frequently desperate, often rivalling in intensity the earlier campaigns of Naw Seng's NEC and the great battles of 1948/9. Already in mid-1975 the *Tatmadaw* had prevented the CPB's first attempt to cross the Salween River into the Tangyan area, where rival troops from Khun Sa's Shan United Army (SUA), the SSPP's 1st brigade and the KIO's 4th brigade had established footholds. Then in heavy fighting during 1976 the *Tatmadaw* succeeded in holding the outposts of Kunlong, Hopang and Mong Yang and the outer ring of defence lines. Instead the PA had to settle for strengthening its base areas along the eastern bank of the Salween River which now reached as far west as Pangyang in the central Shan State. But in early 1977, following a new series of alliances with the KIO, SSPP and SSNLO, which all stood in the way of the CPB's attempt to hurdle the mountains to the west, the 683 brigade again crossed the Salween River. For the next two years multi-battalion operations were launched by both sides in continuous waves of attacks and counter-attacks, with both sides claiming decisive victories. Day after day the Shan valleys echoed to the sound of artillery and machine-gun fire.

Making sense of these conflicting battle reports is difficult, but veterans of these bitter campaigns, which saw frequent hand-to-hand combat, confirm the heavy loss of life. Probably the largest single battle was a 29-day engagement at Pangkaw-Chu Shwe near Hopang in October 1977, where the VOPB (mocking BSPP claims of victory) reported hundreds of government 'mercenaries' had 'died ignominiously at the hands of the people'.[33] In its final battle report for 1977, in north-east Burma alone the CPB claimed to have killed 1,735 government troops, wounded or captured another 2,500, seized 550 weapons and 200,000 rounds of ammunition, and shot down two planes.[34] In the first nine months of 1978, the CPB claimed a further 930 government troops lost their lives.[35] Only rarely were CPB losses admitted, but later its Politburo admitted a casualty ratio of one to four in the PA's favour, which it described as 'not bad'.[36]

The cumulative weight of these repeated CPB offensives gradually began to produce results; for the first time battles and ambushes began to be reported from Mogok, Mong Hsu, Kehsi Mansam, Kunhing, Laikha and Loilem, as well as the familiar battlegrounds of Kokang, Kengtung and Mong Yang, confirming the progress of PA units through to the west of the state. Meanwhile the VOPB also began to carry regular battle reports of the CPB's allies, building up a gradual picture of the remarkable scale of the forces confronting the *Tatmadaw* in north-east Burma: the SSPP in the southern Shan State and Kyaukme, Namhsam and Hsipaw districts further north, the SSNLO around Taunggyi in the south-west, and the KIO from the northern Shan State through the Kachin State to the Sagaing Division and the Indian border.

For its part, in an unusually frank report in early 1978, the *Tatmadaw* admitted to over 250 troops killed or missing and 229 wounded during Operation *Ye Min Aung* of February and March that year; at the same time it claimed to have captured the bodies of over 300 CPB troops and put out of action as many as 500 more, figures hotly disputed by the CPB.[37] Even allowing for exaggeration by both sides, such figures confirm the appalling loss of life, which must then be put alongside the thousands of unrecorded civilian casualties, the devastation of hundreds of remote hill farms and communities, and the perpetual drain of casualties from malaria, malnutrition and other unseen hazards. But if obsessive secrecy was one of the hallmarks of BSPP administration, the worrying scale of the *Tatmadaw*'s losses was confirmed in bizarre circumstances in May 1978 when the chief of the army's North-East Military Command, Col. Min Naung, was abruptly called back from the front and downgraded to head of the country's fire service department. It was an embarrassing demotion clearly calculated to send a warning to other senior officers.[38]

These heavy casualties were not, however, totally in vain; though for the next decade CPB columns continued to filter across the Shan State to the west, the CPB never succeeded in building up a really firm bridgehead in the mountains on the west bank of the Salween River through which the PA could funnel arms and ammunition. Once across the Salween River and away from secure base areas along the Chinese border, the PA's supply lines, like the *Tatmadaw*'s, were severely stretched. The logistical problems involved were immense. Though the CPB had convoys of Chinese trucks at its disposal, the PA's best roads in the main ran from the north to the south, linking base areas and towns along the China border well away from the fighting.

Recognising the let-up in the CPB's momentum, in November 1979 the *Tatmadaw* counter-attacked for the first time in force on the east bank of the Salween River, launching Operation *King Conqueror* in the Mawhpa region. It successfully pushed forward to the Loi Hsia-Kao mountain, which had commanding views across the region to the CPB general headquarters at Panghsang 30 kilometres away. In 1980 the CPB did launch two major operations: it briefly overran the border town of Muse, seizing $100,000 in Burmese kyat and a large arsenal of weapons, and later Mong Yawng, 250 miles to the south, in a display of military strength that would have convinced Ne Win of the CPB's continued fighting potential. But in many ways these bloody counter-punches acted as a prelude to the 1980/1 peace talks. A rare western journalist visiting the headquarters of the *Tatmadaw*'s Eastern Military Command in Taunggyi in August 1980, found the hospital overflowing with casualties and estimates of the army's losses running as high as 5,000 killed or wounded since Operation *King Conqueror* began. 'They failed to make more than a dent in communist defences,' one informant told him. 'The effect has been very sobering. The army is trying to hold what it has but is paying a heavy price for it.'[39]

The PA felt the same heavy losses and from this point on the CPB's military and political tactics underwent a significant change. Most observers date this change to the cut-back in Chinese aid which began in 1978 and about which Ba Thein Tin had been warning his ethnic allies (see Chapter 13). Western analysts saw it as further evidence of Deng Xiaoping's growing influence. But whatever the exact reason, the decline in arms' supplies and financial assistance from China forced CPB leaders to be more cautious in their use of resources and to look for other ways of diversifying their sources of income.

With control of the expanding cross-border black market trade in the region, the CPB could make good some of these losses with a straight 4 per cent tax on all goods passing through its territory. Everything from bicycles, crockery, tooth-paste and medicine (from China) to animal skins and timber (from Burma) daily passed through the dozens of CPB check-points along the border. At the time of the aid cut-back, the CPB Politburo estimated that in the north-east military region 68 per cent of its income already came from trading, while 25 per cent came from the 'centre', presumably funds passed from China.[40] Over the next few years border settlements, such as Panghsai and Mongla, grew, like the KNU bases on the Thai border, into thriving market towns with video halls, beauty salons and a constant flow of hill peoples, businessmen and international traders, including Indians and overseas Chinese, making the dangerous trek through the mountains.

Local taxes, usually set at 100 kyats per family and/or 10 per cent of the annual crop, were also collected. In the early 1980s the CPB also began to take a growing interest in the lucrative jade trade, most of which was under KIO control. In the main, it was heavily defended KIO convoys which would transport the freshly hewn rocks from the important Hpakan mining region in the west of the Kachin State to the Thai and Chinese borders.

The Narcotics Trade
But the most radical sign of the CPB's economic liberalisation was its growing toleration of poppy cultivation by local hill farmers. With the PA's entrance into north-east Burma, many of the country's most prized poppy fields in the otherwise impoverished Wa and Kokang substates fell under CPB control. Little of the wealth associated with the international narcotics trade has ever reached the farmers of Burma. The real profits are made elsewhere: in the West, by Chinese *Chiu Chau* syndicates and, to a far lesser extent, by the various insurgent armies in the Shan State, notably Khun Sa's Shan United Army. (In the 1980s, by Khun Sa's own admission, the SUA took control of two-thirds of the cross-border narcotics trade with Thailand.[41]) A *joi* (1.6 kilos) of raw opium, which in the 1980s sold for as little as US$20 (the farmer's price) in the Shan State, could fetch as much as $200,000 on the streets of New York after refining into pure heroin.

First encouraged by the British, it was the CIA-backed Kuomintang Chinese who in the 1950s promoted the trade to its international dimensions. The importance of this trade was not lost sight of by young Shan nationalists during the rapid spread of the Shan rebellion in the early 1960s. Many were still smarting from the devastation caused by the KMT invasion. 'To fight you must have an army, and an army must have guns, and to buy guns you must have money,' Gen. Tuan Shi-wen of the KMT Fifth Army once explained; 'In these mountains the only money is opium.'[42] But for most hill farmers in the Shan and Kachin States, beset by poor soil, water shortages, a non-existent economic infrastructure and the constant dislocation caused by the war, there was absolutely no alternative cash crop. With an estimated annual harvest of between 500 and 1,500 tons (there are no reliable figures) Burma and Pakistan quickly became the world's largest producers of illicit opium.

All long-term observers agree that the twin problems of insurgency and narcotics are inseparable. Over the years governments in neighbouring Thailand and Laos, the main conduits for Burma's opium trade, have also had great difficulty scaling down local production. As a result, they have been given considerable international aid. In the 1980s the US briefly supported the ill-fated and internationally condemned 2,4-D (a compound used in the production of Agent Orange) crop-spraying programme in Burma, which led to the Burmese Airforce dumping this toxic defoliant on 60,000 acres of mountain forest and dozens of ethnic minority villages in the Shan State. However, the *Tatmadaw*'s use of 2,4-D in the choice of areas hit appeared to be motivated more by counter-insurgency considerations than poppy eradication and during the spraying period local production actually went up! For their part, various nationalist groups, coordinated by the SSPP, several times offered the entire opium harvest to the US for a pre-emptive purchase price at a fraction of market value ($20m for 400 tons was the commonly mentioned figure). Such offers have never been accepted, partly because of a farcical experience with the KMT in 1972 when, after the US government had contributed $1m for the public destruction of the KMT's opium stockpile of 26 tons, an 'extra' 27th ton suddenly became available at the last minute in return for more cash. Significantly, then, despite various international initiatives, the only time production has fallen and prices have soared (as in 1979 and 1980) there was a more straightforward explanation: two successive years of drought.[43]

The CPB in north-east Burma was thus simply the latest inheritor of the opium problem. Certainly the *Tatmadaw* has had no compunctions in dealing with organisations and individuals involved in the narcotics trade, especially with the KKY defence militia of the 1960s and early 1970s. For years army officers and prominent traffickers, especially former KKY commander Khun Sa, have had a close understanding. In the 1980s *Tatmadaw* attacks on Khun Sa's bases were exceedingly rare. I myself have met both Thai and Burmese officers at military bases of the SUA's successor, the Tailand Revolutionary Council. The clearest example of Ne Win's ambivalence has been the case of former Kokang KKY commander and insurgent leader Lo Hsing-han, who, having been extradited from Thailand in a blaze of publicity in 1973 as the 'Mr Big' of narcotics trafficking and condemned to death, was released from gaol in 1980 (see Ch.16). Close to Gen. Aye Ko, a key BSPP leader and former head of the North-East Command, Lo returned to Lashio to begin rebuilding another local *Pyi Thu Sit* homeguard militia. In 1989 few observers of the Shan State's tangled politics were surprised, then, when he resurfaced with another former Kokangese rebel leader, Pheung Kya-shin, to again play a prominent role on the *Tatmadaw's* side in fuelling the CPB defections. Opium and this time heroin production once again soared.

It would be fair to say that all these parties, including Khun Sa and the *Tatmadaw*, started out with varying degrees of political sincerity, but have inevitably become tainted by the endemic corruption of the international narcotics trade. In the absence of any real anti-narcotics programmes in the hills, it is easier for the US Drug Enforcement Agency, the UN and the governments of Thailand and Burma to blame 'kingpins' and 'bandits' rather than seriously investigate a trade that comes dangerously close to the upper echelons of power. Unlike South America, drugs money in South-East Asia has always been laundered without trace.

By contrast, in the early 1970s the CPB (like the CCP) took strong measures against warlordism and the opium trade through enforced crop-substitution programmes. For this they won several plaudits.[44] But from the mid-1970s, in response to a series of setbacks (plagues of rats in the Wa hills, the reduction in Chinese aid, continued military instability) and in deference to local sensibilities, these restrictions were gradually relaxed. The evidence was striking. Visitors to the party's general headquarters at Panghsang in 1973, shortly after the PA took control of the area, were impressed at the scale of the CPB's eradication programmes; a few years later they found poppy fields lining the route.

District CPB leaders began collecting an estimated 20 per cent of the local crop, which they sold to merchants from the main trading centres of Lashio and Tangyan and, like other insurgent armies (and some local *Tatmadaw* units), took a tax on opium caravans passing through their territory.[45] Western accusations of large-scale heroin refining taking place in CPB territory with acetic anhydride smuggled in from China were inaccurate, but the obvious problems associated with the trade became a growing political embarrassment to the CPB's Maoist principles. Eventually, at the party's Third Congress in 1985, a number of regulations were introduced against the opium trade, including the prohibiting of party members from any individual involvement and the death penalty for large-scale heroin traffickers.

Ironically, CPB leaders claim, it was the implementation of these anti-narcotics measures that sparked off the 1989 mutinies.

Ba Thein Tin's 1978 'Political Report': The CPB's New Agenda
Ignoring the narcotics issue and the problems caused by the cut-back in Chinese
aid, CPB chairman, Thakin Ba Thein Tin, prefers to date the crucial changes in
the party's tactics at the turn of the decade to a historic meeting of the CPB
Politburo at Panghsang in November 1978 attended by Thakin Pe Tint, Khin
Maung Gyi, Myo Myint, Kyin Maung and Tin Yi (only Kyaw Mya was absent).
Ba Thein Tin presented a complex 'political report' which he claims established
the CPB's agenda for the next decade.[46]

Foreign analysts of Burma's insurgencies have often been struck by the slow
rate of evolution of new ideologies or strategies by the country's diverse political
parties (whether the AFPFL, BSPP, CPB, KNU or KIO) when compared to
national liberation movements in other parts of the world. But on the insurgent
side, at least, with front line units isolated from the outside world and deployed
across thousands of square miles of some of the world's most inhospitable terrain,
years have often passed between meetings of key commanders and political leaders to discuss new tactics. The result has been the fostering of die-hard attitudes
by those who have led the war from the front. These difficulties were once
graphically described by U Khine Maung, a Rangoon University graduate and
dedicated communist cadre in Arakan: 'Everything we have — every gun, every
inch of territory, every piece of clothing — was bought with blood, the blood of
our people. There can be no surrender.'[47]

None the less according to Ba Thein Tin, it was this one 'political report' which
rang the changes for the CPB and, with a few refinements, was unanimously
approved at a meeting with another 13 members of the CPB CC at Panghsang in
early 1979.[48] It was then broadcast as a Politburo report on the VOPB between
November 1979 and March 1980 after additions by different working groups from
the full CC.[49] This Politburo report, he claims, formed the basis of the resolutions
passed several years later at the CPB's Third Congress in September 1985
(remarkably, the first since the insurrections began) when just 170 of the party's
estimated 5,000 members made the trek to Panghsang for the 24-day conference.

While it was only in the 1985 Congress report that the full scale of the CPB's
past ideological errors (including the 1955 'revisionist line' and the 1967 'inter-
party line') was admitted, the 1979 Politburo report set in motion the political
changes of the 1980s and formed the basis of most Western observers' political
understanding of the CPB. Firmly lining the CPB up behind the primacy of armed
struggle, Marxist-Leninist-Mao Zedong thought and the example of China, it
expounded the CPB's views on the Ne Win regime (which represented
'imperialism, feudal-landlordism and bureaucratic-capitalism') as well as on the
domestic and international situations. Now Soviet 'socialism-imperialism' and
Vietnamese 'hegemonism' were to be resisted as much as old-fashioned 'US
imperialism'. The CPB conjured up an image of 90 million people, led by the
'genuine Marxist-Leninist' parties in Kampuchea, Thailand, Malaya and Burma,
coming together to halt Vietnamese expansion into the region. There were also a
number of rare insights into the CPB's secretive workings with the publication of
the party's Constitution in full, and detailed descriptions of life in its main base
areas. One of the most interesting revelations, suggesting an unsuspected degree
of CPB influence in the communist world, was the news that the CPB Politburo
had written to both the Khmer Rouge (which it supported) and the Communist
Party of Vietnam, urging a ceasefire and a peaceful resolution to the bitter border

war which had led to the Vietnamese invasion.

Ba Thein Tin himself considers that the importance of the decisions of the 1979 CC meeting/Politburo report (and thus the 1985 Congress) can be divided into three main areas. First, the drawing up and ratification of the party's general programme in the light of 'the experiences of the last 30 years of the armed struggle'.[50] Notable here, he says, were the warnings against 'sectarianism' and 'leftist' and 'rightist deviationism'. Second, the revision of the party's Constitution to 'suit the changing conditions' of the world. And third, the adoption of new 'party-building', 'military' and 'agricultural' lines.

CPB leaders have since been mainly preoccupied with the latter three, largely overlapping, areas. All three new lines reflected the CPB's determination to continue its long-term strategy of building up Red Power base areas amongst the rural peasantry, the 'backbone of the revolution', to encircle the towns. But also apparent was an increasing pragmatism and openness in discussing political problems. Despite the rapid build-up of the PA and its control of vast rural areas, CPB leaders privately concede that in this period active party membership in the whole of Burma was probably at a maximum of 5,000 cadres, a third of whom were also soldiers. But, as the Politburo now revealed in its 1979 report, in the 3,033 villages of the CPB's main base area, the north-east region, there were only 1,259 members, falling well short of the CC's 1964 directive to recruit at least one party member from each village. This, the Politburo warned, had to be urgently rectified: it was the absence of a 'vanguard party' of the proletariat which had caused the failure of peasant and patriotic rebellions against the British in the colonial age; now the CPB alone (the only 'great, brilliant and correct Marxist-Leninist party in Burma') could defeat imperialism in the prevailing era of 'imperialism, socialist revolution and revisionism'.[51]

The party's difficulties in building up membership in the poverty-stricken backwaters of the minority states are commented on in the next chapter. But it was clear that the new 'military line' for the first time hinted at a scaling down in militancy. While vowing the PA would go on the offensive whenever the situation allowed, the Politburo report, describing the present reality as 'when we are weak and the enemy is strong', announced the CPB's new military line would be 'strategic defence'; this it defined as 'mobile defensive warfare which is active'.[52] In essence this meant a greater concentration on guerrilla operations and the abandonment of the costly human tidal wave tactics of the past. At the same time, tailoring this strategy to the present conditions in Burma (a 'backward, semi-colonial, semi-feudal, agrarian country with uneven political and economic development') the Politburo once again confirmed its belief that a 'people's war' in Burma could only be fought as part of the ongoing 'agrarian revolution' being waged under its leadership. Indeed, ignoring the recent worker and student protests in the cities, the CPB Politburo specifically turned its back on calling a 'general strike and uprising' by 'copying the October revolution of Russia'.[53] That, it explained, would be to misunderstand the social conditions of Burma. Protracted war, agrarian revolution, party-building and self-sufficiency were the tools which, they claimed, would lead the party to victory; Cambodia, where Pol Pot estimated 80 per cent of the Khmer Rouge's weaponry had been seized from the 'enemy', was cited as a particularly good example for the party to follow.[54] The CPB's estrangement from the cities was thus destined to continue.

The results of these political refinements took a few years to filter through into front line areas under battle-hardened PA commanders. But the CPB's political rivals were quick to detect a liberalisation in official party attitudes. Some attributed this to Deng Xiaoping's economic reforms in China, where CPB leaders still frequently travelled, others to the arrival of Kyaw Mya from Arakan and Kyaw Zaw from Rangoon, neither of whom had lived through the upheavals of the Cultural Revolution. There were frequent arguments with political hard-liners like the deputy-commander of the NEC, Taik Aung, formerly a front line commissar with the 683 brigade and, next to Ba Thein Tin, the most influential of the Beijing returnees. Kyaw Zaw, however, despite his illustrious war record, was generally regarded as out of date by the party's China-trained cadres. A more poignant, though largely ignored influence, was the growing number of ethnic minority cadres in the middle-ranks of the leadership, men such as the Kachin CC members, Zau Mai and Hpalang Gam Di; murmurs of dissatisfaction were reported throughout all levels of the party organisation.

The Peace Talks and their Aftermath
Perhaps the clearest evidence of the CPB's growing pragmatism came with the 1980/1 peace parley. The CPB's initial response to the 1980 amnesty had been to launch the attack on Mong Yawng. Then, on 23 September, in an unexpected gesture after the amnesty period had ended, it sent a letter proposing talks to Ne Win. (It waited, according to Ba Thein Tin, to show it was not simply kowtowing to BSPP demands.) Though CPB leaders have refused to admit that Chinese pressure lay behind this apparent change of heart, subsequent events revealed the extent to which Beijing was aware of all developments. Diplomatic observers later dated this seeming reversal to a visit by China's Foreign Minister, Huang Hua, to Rangoon in November 1979, just seven weeks after Ne Win had withdrawn Burma from the Non-Aligned Movement in protest at pro-Soviet/pro-Vietnamese manipulations at its controversial Sixth Summit conference in Cuba. (Burma had backed China, vocally supporting the right of Pol Pot and the banned Khmer Rouge to attend.) Press communiqués made no mention of the details of their discussions, but after Huang Hua had thanked Burma at a public banquet for its 'just stand' at the Havana conference, the CPB was rumoured to have featured high on the agenda, with the BSPP pressing for China to cut off support.

Compared with the negotiations in the same period of its ally, the KIO, the CPB's talks with the BSPP did not get very far. The KIO meetings, by contrast, which came as the result of lobbying by Baptist and Catholic Church leaders, whom neither side wanted to be seen to refuse, continued on and off for nearly ten months between August 1980 and May 1981. But while KIO troops came down from the hills to be reunited with their families and play football with government troops (the KIO leader Brang Seng astonished one congregation in Rangoon by turning up in church unannounced), there was little let-up in hostilities between the CPB and Ne Win.

After the activities of the people's peace committees in 1963, army leaders were understandably anxious to keep news of the CPB talks quiet. Even the manner in which details of these negotiations belatedly emerged showed the depths of this distrust. Both sides initially agreed to keep the talks secret, CPB leaders say, in deference to a request from Ne Win. But once he addressed the BSPP on the subject after the talks had broken down, both sides talked at some length.

Their versions largely corroborated each other. Two meetings were held, the first in October 1980 when delegations headed by Ba Thein Tin and Ne Win met in person in China during another surprise visit to Beijing by Ne Win.[55] Indeed without explanation Ne Win had abruptly left the meetings with Brang Seng and the KIO leaders, which had just started in Rangoon, to make this unscheduled trip, leaving Brig. San Yu and the MIS chief, Gen. Tin Oo, to continue the talks alone.[56] In China Ne Win also met Deng Xiaoping and Hua Kuo-feng, but both parties tactfully refrained from public comment.

The second meeting took place in Lashio the following May when a CPB team consisting of vice-chairman, Thakin Pe Tint, and CC members, Ye Tun and Hpalang Gam Di, were helicoptered in from the hills to meet BSPP EC member, Maj.-Gen. Aye Ko, BSPP secretary, U Than Hlaing, and head of the North-East Military Command, Col. Myint Lwin.

As in 1963, both sides failed to come out of the peace parley with much distinction, each accusing the other of using the talks simply to try and gain a temporary advantage. From the beginning CPB leaders were aggrieved that though Ne Win had agreed to an unannounced ceasefire with the KIO, he would not accept one with the CPB. This Ba Thein Tin interpreted as a Machiavellian attempt to divide the CPB from its allies and the party from its armed forces.[57] The CPB also accused *Tatmadaw* commanders of trying to increase this uncertainty by spreading rumours of a massive offensive to smash the CPB once and for all following the inevitable breakdown of negotiations.[58] Allegations of other dirty tricks then followed with the VOPB accusing MIS officers of deliberately separating the CPB delegates on the flight to Lashio so they could be interrogated individually before the meetings began.[59]

But after the bloody battles of the past 15 years, there was always an air of unreality about the idea of an easy, peaceful settlement to the war; and the second conference, in contrast to the drawn-out discussions with the KIO, lasted just one day. Both sides appeared to be merely going through the motions. In his private meeting with Ne Win, Ba Thein Tin took a surprising tack by trying to persuade his old comrade-in-arms of the need for peace by invoking the dangers of the international situation, particularly the conflicts in Afghanistan and Cambodia, which he claimed were a threat to the stability of small countries like Burma. Harking back 40 years, he reminded Ne Win that the victories against Imperial Japan had only been possible because of the unity which then existed between the CPB, the *Tatmadaw*, the People's Revolutionary Party and other 'patriotic' forces.[60] But given the scale of China's aid to the CPB in the past decade, any invocation of the dangers of outside interference doubtless appeared ironic.

However, as with the KIO, the major stumbling block this time was the 1974 Constitution. According to Ba Thein Tin, the talks broke down before the CPB had even finished representing its position when Aye Ko suddenly demanded three new conditions: '(1) The abolition of the CPB. (2) The abolition of the PA under the command of the CPB. (3) The abolition of all our liberated areas. Everybody can see from this that the military regime was demanding complete surrender.'[61]

On 14 May Ne Win unilaterally announced that the talks had been terminated. This appeared to hasten the end of the KIO talks, which had now moved to the Kachin State capital, Myitkyina. On 31 May Ne Win allowed the last ceasefire deadline to pass without replying to the KIO's latest position. This surprised many observers, both at home and abroad, since during the course of the negotiations the KIO, invoking the memory of Panglong and Aung San, had dropped its long-held separatist demands, even proposing it would accept the one-party rule of the BSPP in exchange for Kachin 'autonomy' and greater control over local administration, security, economic and social affairs.[62] In reply, Ne Win argued that since the 1974 Constitution had been adopted by referendum, the BSPP had no right to accede to demands which had not been accepted by the vote of the people. In the CPB's case, there was also the added obstacle of Article 11 of the Constitution which had established Burma as a one-party state. There was no place in Burma's political framework, Ne Win argued, for a second political party.[63]

Both KIO and CPB leaders insist these were simply the arguments of convenience of an army old guard reluctant to give up any inch of political power. But the discussions did have an important side benefit in that they pushed the slow political debate in Burma one small step forward. The issue of multi-party democracy, which the CPB (like the communist parties of China and the Soviet Union) accepted in principle rather than practice, was picked up in subsequent CPB propaganda as part of the party's growing awareness of the ethnic minority issue and of the complex social conditions in Burma. Indeed, by the mid-1980s it had become a standard political demand. The BSPP's ultimatum to the CPB to 'surrender, dismantle and join the BSPP' was disparagingly dismissed by the VOPB: 'A stately white elephant will not pass through a gate meant for dogs.'[64] But over the following years the CPB was also to broadcast frequent appeals for new peace talks under the three banners of 'ending the civil war, developing democracy and building national unity' in a new multi-party system of government.

This time the termination of the talks did not see a major escalation of the war. With the CPB still deploying 15,000 troops in north-east Burma, the heavy losses of the 1970s had taught the *Tatmadaw* that it would only be at enormous cost that the CPB's strongholds could be taken. Equally troubling to the *Tatmadaw* were the ethnic insurgencies which, through the increasing cohesion of the National Democratic Front (NDF), were becoming an urgent matter of countrywide concern. This negated any euphoria over the final collapse of U Nu's PDP remnants in the 1980 surrenders and was reflected in the focus of *Tatmadaw* military operations. With the CPB relying more and more on guerrilla warfare, an 18-month lull followed. Only at the end of 1982 did the army resume the short-lived second and third phases of Operation *King Conqueror* in the mountains east of Kengtung, in the Man Manghseng region of Southern Wa, and the Loi Pang Lom range, north-west of Tangyan. Eventually the army retreated after suffering several hundred casualties in CPB counter-attacks. But there were many serious accusations of army atrocities against local villagers, including rape, murder, the destruction of houses and property, and the maltreatment of porters forced to carry supplies to the front.[65] Sadly, such allegations were to have an all too familiar refrain in the 1980s. Several defenceless villages were completely destroyed in air raids.

From here on the army's main preoccupation was with the ethnic forces of the NDF. With its general headquarters at the KNU's Mannerplaw stronghold in south-east Burma, the NDF had been revitalised in 1983 by the return of the KIO, whose leaders admitted they were hurried into greater cooperation with their allies by the failure of the peace parley. In potential troop numbers and operational areas they far surpassed the CPB. In response, in 1984 a major *Four Cuts* campaign was launched against the KNU in the northern Dawna Range and in 1987 against the KIO in Burma's far north. Meanwhile local *Tatmadaw* units moved out of their barracks to launch similar well-publicised operations against the KNPP in the Kayah State, the SSPP in the Maymyo-Hsipaw-Mong Kung triangle and the PNO and SSNLO in the south-west Shan State. Even the remote base areas of the National Socialist Council of Nagaland, whose main conflict was with the Indian Army across the border, came under attack. Indeed the only parties to escape this sustained offensive were the 'warlord' SUA and SURA forces of Khun Sa and Gon Jerng who, after Gon Jerng broke off his alliance with Gen. Li Wen-huan's KMT remnants in 1984, unexpectedly joined forces the following year. They then swiftly expanded their territory along the Thai border by attacking other insurgent forces, such as the SSPP and PNO, whose main forces were then tied down fighting the *Tatmadaw* deeper in the interior.

Suddenly, after over 30 years' relentless armed struggle, it was the ethnic insurgents, long derided as 'racialists', 'saboteurs', and 'separatists', who were winning the domestic and international headlines. The CPB now shared this preoccupation and, in 1986, this led to a joint agreement between the NDF and CPB which, for the first time since the insurrections began, brought the CPB into equal alliance with virtually all the ethnic nationalist parties in Burma.

It was, however, to come a good few years too late. For, as the 1988 democracy uprising approached, the CPB was itself about to be riven by ethnic dissension.

16

The Nationalities Question

Since the earliest days of the insurrections, communist propaganda had repeatedly stressed the importance of the 'united front' and the need for the CPB to win the support of Burma's ethnic minority peoples. The National Democratic United Front (NDUF), formed in 1959 with the support of the Karen National United Party (KNUP), was to be the jewel in the CPB's ethnic crown. Political rhetoric, however, failed to disguise the many flaws in the CPB's position. Certainly its record of success over the past 40 years was no better than that of the BSPP or AFPFL. No Burman-led party has ever gained countrywide ethnic minority support and the CPB was never to win the whole-hearted backing of Burma's diverse ethnic armies.

Of all Burma's ethnic insurgent forces, the KNUP undoubtedly reached the most effective political and military understanding with the CPB. But even KNUP veterans, who themselves once followed an avowedly 'Maoist' military line, have made the same accusations of 'blinkered vision' against the CPB.[1] Not only was the CPB for the most part in military competition with the different ethnic forces, but nationalist leaders have persistently alleged that whilst accepting that indigenous races should be granted the same political and cultural rights enjoyed by the many minorities in 'autonomous regions' in neighbouring China, the CPB has completely failed to understand the causes or grievances of the ethnic nationalist movement. This is a failing, they say, they share with other international communist parties as well as the AFPFL, BSPP and U Nu's PDP.

The CPB's strict class analysis of the situation in Burma allowed no distinct 'political' role for the minorities. In CPB terminology, the nationalities question was covered by the 'class' discussion of peasant or agricultural problems. But indigenous peoples like the Karens, who have been fighting for the right of self-determination since the end of the Second World War, have never accepted simple political platitudes. The CPB's errors were probably at their worst during the 'racial war' of 1949-52, but with the formation of the NDUF in 1959, its leaders appeared to think that no more work was needed. To ethnic minority leaders this was just another example of Burman chauvinism. There was no political reason why they should support the CPB any more than the BSPP, AFPFL, National League for Democracy, National Unity Party or the other new democracy parties of 1988. It took the CPB many years to wake up to its complacency, but by then many opportunities had been wasted and great damage done. In two remarkable months in 1989, when the whole world was still shocked at the speed at which the BSPP had collapsed, the CPB, long the BSPP's most dogged opponent, was itself brought to the edge of extinction by ethnic revolt.

A CPB broadcast from Beijing in 1969 summed up the standard communist position on the nationalities question. Conceding that the 'correct handling of this issue' was 'the key to seizing victory of the revolution', the CPB praised itself for the formation of the NDUF and its 'correct national policy' on the common political basis of the 'national democratic revolution'. The CPB would also continue trying to work with the 'progressive armed forces' of other nationalities. The statement then went on to make a controversial definition: 'The CPB stresses that the national question in Burma is in essence a question of the peasantry. The armed struggle of the nationalities is an armed struggle of the peasants against feudal oppression. The correct settlement of the national question is the realisation of the worker-peasant alliance under the leadership of the working class.'[2]

In a country with few urban workers of any nationality, such dogma has always rested uneasily with the minorities. In the CPB's political lexicon, the term 'worker', which in Marxist-Leninist analysis is more usually identified with the urban or industrial working class, has been broadly stretched to include forestry workers, carpenters, blacksmiths, potters and other artisans who are really part of the rural proletariat, quite indistinguishable in most agricultural communities from local farmers and peasants. Amongst the many semi-nomadic sub-groups of the Karens, Kachins and Akha, such an analysis is mind-bogglingly inapt. Over the years the CPB had considerable success in eliminating the familiar communist targets (corrupt landlords, headmen, government officials and army officers) while pushing ahead with farming cooperatives, trade unions, literacy programmes, hospitals and schools. But beyond the remote confines of the CPB's mountain base areas, the concept of a revolution 'led by the working class' has hardly proven a powerful rallying cry of national political identity, especially when put alongside the conflicting calls of the many different ethnic liberation organisations.

I, for example, frequently witnessed the political indifference of many villagers in the Tenasserim Division (who from one valley to another may vary from Karens to Mons, Tavoyans, Burmans, Shans and even Salum Sea-Gypsies) to the political enticements of the BSPP, CPB, KNU, NMSP or PDP remnants. A prosperous, undisturbed life is their daily priority. Across Burma many armed groups, especially in the Shan State, have justifiably started off in the midst of war as village or community self-defence organisations and it was in this context that many nationalist movements first took up arms. It is striking that the CPB's most obvious success with mass organisation amongst the national minorities was in the Indian community in the Rangoon factories and dockyards of the 1940s and, to a lesser extent, among the Karen and Mon populations on the plains of Lower Burma in the 1950s and the Rakhine population of Arakan. These four groups generally live in urban or rural conditions most similar to the Burman majority.

Two very different viewpoints expressed to me by Rakhine insurgent leaders in 1987 seemed to sum up the dilemma in applying any modern ideology, whether Western, Asian or home-grown, to suit the complex social and political conditions of post-colonial Burma. The more positive view was expressed by Kyaw Maung of the CPB's Arakan Province provisional committee. A veteran military and political commissar from a peasant background, he totally accepts the CPB's 'classless' position on the nationalities: 'A communist has no chauvinism. I am a Burmese citizen, yet at the same time I am a communist. I am also an ethnic Rakhine, but I will not oppress other races. That is to be a communist.'[3] This view was strongly contradicted by U Kyaw Hlaing, a Rangoon University history graduate and chairman of the Arakan Independence Organisation (AIO) which, like many other nationalist groups, has always won more support from the intellectual community: 'People always underestimate chauvinism. Burmese communists and socialists think a one-party system is the way to restore the Fourth Burmese Empire. At independence many Burmans thought Marxism was an ideology which would restore their lost empire.'[4]

To me, at least, this critical statement encapsulates the one central reason why successive governments and parties in Burma since independence, be they AFPFL, CPB, NUF, BSPP or the more recent State Law and Order Restoration Committee (SLORC), have failed to resolve the country's very deep problems of political representation, equality and justice. Like so many post-colonial countries in Africa and Asia (Ethiopia and Indonesia are two good examples) central governments, usually of one dominant or majority race, have 'inherited' territories and peoples of often stunning ethnic diversity and very different stages of economic development from their colonial rulers. Border or territorial wars are only the most obvious symptom of this phenomenon. Most in their struggle to hold on to power have searched for simple 20th century formulas (usually Marxism, quasi-Marxism or Western-style parliamentary democracy) to legitimise their control on political power. The centralised, Stalinist models of China and the Soviet Union have proven a particular inspiration. In many countries, amidst the paraphernalia of anthems, patriotism and national liberation days, history has frequently had to be rewritten. But the end, a united country, has always justified the means.

What is most remarkable about Burma is the total absence of political dialogue and failure even to acknowledge the scale of the problem. One searches the archives of the AFPFL, CPB and BSPP in vain for any serious debate on the political, economic, social and cultural consequences. In the four decades since independence virtually no reliable economic or political data have been gathered on the ethnic minority issue by any party at all. Of all the BSPP's many flawed institutions, none has been more ineffectual than the Academy for the Development of National Groups, founded in 1965 as the centrepiece of BSPP policy towards the minorities. Located near Sagaing in the heartland of Burman culture, like other BSPP organisations, it was largely staffed by the relatives of army personnel.

No indigenous institutions reflecting the aspirations and goals of the peoples themselves have ever been allowed to evolve. As in many other countries in the region (Malaysia, Laos, Vietnam, Thailand, Indonesia and the Philippines) most governments (including the US) see the ethnic minority question first and foremost in terms of national security. The models of India, Pakistan, Sri Lanka and Bangladesh, to which Burma was tied until 1937, may well make a more relevant comparison, though one few Burman nationalists would accept. It is significant that all four countries, as they approach the end of the 20th century, are still beset by ethnic and religious conflicts on a similar scale. Only the form is different. They have, however, produced a far greater literature. Sadly, in Burma's case, all the evidence suggests that, as SLORC (after the smashing of the democracy movement in 1988) now imposes its own vision of the 'Burmese Way to Democracy' on the country, the ethnic question is once again being dealt with in the same historically piece-meal fashion.

Certainly despite the collapse of the NDUF in the early 1970s and the attempt to build up the North-East Command in the Shan and Kachin States, the CPB made remarkably little effort to build bridges with other nationalist forces in Burma. 'Narrow nationalism' was branded a proletarian crime akin to 'revisionism'; and CPB leaders, in their defence, would point to their own mixed ethnic ancestries. Ba Thein Tin describes himself as a 'Tavoyan', while Than Tun and Soe, like many Burmese in Lower Burma, both claimed Mon descent. Even Than Tun's successor Thakin Zin was part Pao. But this can only explain a small part of the CPB's confusion. One Shan leader who spent long periods in the CPB's multiracial NEC in the 1970s claimed it, too, was divided along ethnic lines: 'The political leaders are Burmans, the military commanders are Chinese, the administrative staff are Kachins, and the soldiers are Was, Shans, Palaungs, Akhas and Lahus.'[5]

The KNUP's Dawna Team Expedition
In particular, the CPB's close ally, the KNUP, has produced much evidence of inconsistencies in the CPB position. Following the breakdown of the peace parley there were frequent disagreements between the two sides, interrupted only by the purges of the CPB's bloody Cultural Revolution. But in October 1969 as the dust began to settle, delegations headed by Thakin Zin and Bo Kyin Pe, secretary-general of the KNUP, met in the Pegu Yomas to try and settle these differences. While praising the Red Flags as a true 'revolutionary' force, the KNUP accused the CPB of being 'lax in its attention' to building the NDUF and described its claim to be representing all Burma's nationalities as divorced 'from realities'.[6] The KNUP specifically warned the CPB that while it agreed that the revolution in Burma should be waged under 'the leadership of the proletariat', this by no means meant that the KNUP, the NDUF, the Karens or any other minority peoples would accept the leadership of the CPB.[7]

This argument eventually seemed to be accepted; even today KNUP veterans keep a copy of a document of a new CPB line towards the ethnic nationalities, first discussed, they say, with Than Tun shortly before his death in 1968 and again brought up at NDUF meetings with Thakin Zin in 1969 and 1970. CPB leaders passed this new line in the Pegu Yomas on 21 January 1971. In it Thakin Zin declared a new Union would be formed on the basis of 'equality' after the 'national democratic' revolution had been completed and the people's 'common enemy', the Ne Win regime, had been overthrown.[8] Noting that China had chosen the form of 'autonomous regions' and Russia the 'Union of Independent Republics' for their indigenous nationalities, the new 'Union Republic of Burma', Zin declared, would have to create its own form of government to fit the particular social conditions of Burma. The exact details of the system would have to be worked out after victory, but in principle the CPB agreed: '(1) The Burmans shall have a separate state like the Kachin, Karen, Kayah, Chin, Shan and others; (2) The New Union of the Socialist Republic of Burma shall be voluntarily established from the states of the nationalities; (3) There shall be the state governments and the central federal government.'[9] Remarkably, when former KNUP general-secretary, Skaw Ler Taw, reached Panghsang *en route* to China in 1973, Ba Thein Tin and the leaders of the CPB's NEC denied any knowledge of this treaty. Indeed they described Thakin Zin, their own chairman, as 'out of touch'.[10] Even the CPB's official propaganda of the late 1960s briefly used this wording. In March 1968, for example, a statement from the CPB's CC published in the *Peking Review* also described the goal of the CPB as a 'people's democratic federal front'.[11]

The political arguments between the KNUP, KNU and CPB and the contentious issues of communism's 'people's democracy' versus the minorities' 'national democracy', which have remained at centre stage in ethnic insurgent politics in Burma, are described earlier in this account (see Chapters 7 and 14). But it is worth recording here that by the time of the KNUP's 1975 collapse and the reformation of the Karen National Union (KNU), many Karen nationalists, including those holding left-wing views, were already completely disillusioned with the CPB. The KNU had always seen itself as an independent movement, a potential ally on equal terms with the CPB and certainly under nobody's political umbrella.

Only with the report of Skaw Ler Taw's Dawna team, on his return from China in 1975, were the worst fears of most KNUP die-hards realised. But as early as 1968/9, in response to many leaders' growing doubts about the CPB, the KNUP had already sent three secret delegations to China to investigate the tumultuous developments in the communist world from across the border. This, they say, was entirely in keeping with the KNU's demand for self-determination and was a move echoed by several other minority fronts in the region, including the Mizo National Front and Naga Federal Government in India. KNUP veterans claim these visits were the logical conclusion to their own study of Marxist-Leninist-Mao Zedong ideology. The main purpose of these preliminary teams, however, was to prepare the way for the KNUP delegation led by Politburo member Skaw Ler Taw; and their talks with Chinese officials and CPB leaders, including their former Kachin ally, Naw Seng, produced little.[12]

The three and a half year journey, of the 37-strong Dawna team provides a bewildering account of the insurgent chaos inside Burma at the time. It set out from the Toungoo hills in December 1971 and returned in mid-1975 to find the KNUP/CPB strongholds of central Burma in ruins. On its way it had to pass through a complex mosaic of territory controlled by rival forces: the KNU under Bo Mya (who gave it supplies), the Karenni National Progressive Party (KNPP), the Shan State Nationalities Liberation Organisation (SSNLO), the Shan State Progress Party (SSPP), the Kachin Independence Organisation (KIO), the Palaung State Liberation Organisation (PSLO) and the CPB. It in fact took two attempts to reach China, but only after a number of joint battles with other rebel forces against government troops in which several KNUP members were killed. Indeed at one stage, after reaching the SSPP's main base area near Mongtung in the northern Shan State, the team had to return all the way south to the Thai border to try and find an alternative route to China through Laos.

Had it not been for the dramatic change in the military situation in the eastern Shan State during the 1972/3 dry season, the team's journey might well have ended here. But, in a concerted offensive in the NEC, CPB forces pushed down through the Wa substates and captured Pangyang close to the Salween River. Radio contact had been maintained throughout and now CPB vice-chairman Ba Thein Tin sent a message inviting the Dawna team to the NEC's new headquarters at Panghsang on the Chinese border. Thus, with the road finally open, the Dawna team arrived in October 1973 nearly two years after setting out, accompanied by a 96-strong armed escort from the SSPP which, after some initial reluctance, had decided to send along its own delegation headed by CC member Hso Ten.

First impressions were not good. From the beginning the Dawna team felt CPB officials were trying to delay its progress. In preliminary talks with Politburo member, Khin Maung Gyi, and Tin Yee and Zau Mai, the commanders of the 303 region, they were told that the Chinese Communist Party was already aware of their mission and had asked the CPB to arrange training classes for them in Panghsang. Political lectures the KNUP and SSPP teams both rejected, but military and medical classes from the CPB's China-trained cadres were accepted. These, however, turned out to be a disappointment and the KNUP officers agreed that, when compared to CPB forces in Lower Burma, the People's Army (PA) in the NEC lacked military discipline. In some areas, such as signals and communications, it lagged far behind. Thus to fill in time, the SSPP and KNUP soldiers helped with various construction projects, including a military parade-ground, which is still used by Wa forces today.

Only in the second week of December did permission come through for the two parties to cross into China to travel to Sumao, where Ba Thein Tin and the China-based section of the CPB leadership were then staying. Here Skaw Ler Taw explained that since they had come all this way to China, they wanted to meet CCP officials first.[13] This was accepted, but rather than meeting Mao Zedong and members of the CCP CC as they had expected, a conference was set up with the seven-man Sumao Province Committee headed by Col. Kwan, a veteran of the Long March.

Though the talks proceeded at a leisurely pace, they immediately revealed the depth of the CCP's ideological and material support for the CPB. For the first six days the KNUP and SSPP presented papers on the history of their struggles, the nationalities question and the purpose of their missions. CCP officials then took several days to reply and, according to Skaw Ler Taw, carefully avoided any embarrassing situations: 'They were very wise. They introduced their experience by saying not to copy but to compare. If it was of any help, we could use it. But they always made it clear they thought our situation was quite different.'[14]

The first day was taken up with a review of the hardships of the Chinese revolution and the military and political problems the CCP had faced. On the second day attention was turned to the more difficult question of the 'national revolution' in Burma. They left no doubts over their position:

> They stressed the importance of the leadership of the workers' party and the dictatorship of the proletariat. But in Burma they said the CPB was the only true workers' party so it would not be advisable to have two revolutionary workers' parties. One of them said, 'You can have a progressive party and study Marxism, but two workers parties would only be counter-productive. They would work like parallel organisations.' As a matter of principle, they said, the CCP supported all national democratic revolutionary movements, like the KNUP and SSPP, and was opposed to the military government of Gen. Ne Win. Elsewhere in the world, the CCP was already supporting other anti-imperialist movements fighting military regimes and was always ready to help. But in Burma's case the CCP recognised the CPB as the only legal workers' party and was already giving them military support. Any aid or help we wanted must be requested from them.[15]

It was a position they were not to change in several days of talks. The KNUP-SSPP delegations were then taken on a long tour of Yunnan Province. Compared to Burma, most of the delegates were impressed by what they saw. Many of the villages they visited were inhabited by ethnic Shans and there was a great deal of interest in the Shan autonomous region of Sipsong Panna and the Nationalities

College in Kunming. Others were struck by the stability of prices for essential goods, such as rice and salt, wherever they travelled and by the theatre and cultural groups which had come from Beijing to give performances in even the most remote border areas. Such concern by the central government for ethnic minority states in Burma, delegates agreed, was inconceivable.

Only after this journey was completed did the party return to Sumao to meet Ba Thein Tin and the rest of the CPB's NEC leaders for the talks that finally brought into the open the obvious differences of opinion between the KNUP and the CPB leaders north and south. From the outset Ba Thein Tin urged them not to think of only the Karens and Shans, but of all Burma. But on the national question he was quite clear. The CPB model would be based on the Chinese unitary system. This would mean autonomous regions for the minorities. There could be no question of a federal union and he rejected news of the KNUP's discussions with Thakin Zin in the Pegu Yomas. Thakins Zin and Chit, he believed, were now 'isolated' and their knowledge and outlook limited.[16] For the immediate future, CPB strategy was to maintain its existing base areas in central, western and southern Burma while building up new base areas in the north-east with aid and supplies from across the Chinese border; these could then be filtered through to the hard-pressed base areas of Lower Burma. Turning to the KNUP, he objected to it forming the Nationalities United Front in the south-west Shan State, which he complained rivalled the NDUF; and there was a discussion over why, if the KNUP, like the CPB, accepted the 'leadership of the workers', the KNUP would not accept the leadership of the CPB as Burma's sole proletarian party. This, however, the KNUP was still not prepared to do.

On this inconclusive note the talks ended, though both parties were offered a generous gift of arms and equipment. The Dawna team, because of the long journey ahead, took only some AK47s and rifles and had to decline the offer of bazookas and other heavy weapons. But the SSPP, which could reach base areas only one week away, accepted 30,000 rounds of ammunition and a large quantity of explosives for mine warfare.

Looking back many years later Skaw Ler Taw's personal feeling was that it was not Thakin Zin but Ba Thein Tin and the CPB's China-based leaders who were 'out of touch'. Their mission, he sadly concluded, was 'more or less a failure': 'We had learnt a lot about China, communism and the CPB, and we had also seen a lot of the other nationalities in Burma. But we had agreed before we even started out that we were not prepared to accept the leadership of the CPB. It was a long way to go just to repeat this message.'[17] For the CPB, however, the visit was not a total disappointment. In May the following year, Hso Ten and another party of SSPP leaders returned to Panghsang for a stay of one year; this led to a substantial shift in SSPP policy to the political left and, within a few years, to a split in the SSPP movement into pro and anti-CPB factions.

The Dawna team was now left with the long journey home. Setting out in April 1974 the return leg took just over a year to complete after a detour through the northern Shan State. But when the party finally arrived in May 1975 at the general headquarters of the Pao leader, Thaton Hla Pe, in the hills overlooking Inle Lake, it was in for a shock. Here its members got the first inkling of the KNUP's complete military collapse in the Pegu Yomas. Hurrying on into Karenni territory, they found a message awaiting them from their chairman, Mahn Mya Maung, to proceed on to Bo Mya's general headquarters at Mannerplaw for reconciliation talks with the KNU. The reformation of the KNU movement is now history.

In most respects the KNU's long experience of relations with the CPB came to an end in 1975 and Bo Mya, despite a number of contacts in the 1980s, never really relented on his anti-communist line. It is noteworthy that, despite these long years of contact, very few Karens actually joined the CPB and in very few Karen communities has the CPB ever been able to establish base areas: in recent years only in Tenasserim where the Karen population is scattered. On the CPB's 1989 CC there were just two Karens, Saw Tun Tin, a veteran of Naw Seng's long march north into China in 1950, and Saw Ba Moe, who defected from the Dawna team in 1974. KNUP veterans say that through their own study of Mao Zedong they had long become wise to CPB tactics. According to Skaw Ler Taw:

> The CPB had a standing order to split nationalist parties. Mao said that in any organi- sation there are three groups: the progressives, the neutrals or moderates, and the conservatives. Like Mao, the CPB's policy was to join with the progressives, win over the neutrals and expel the die-hards. We soon realised that this was what the CPB had been trying on us ever since our first meetings in 1952.[18]

If this had been the limit of the CPB's arguments with ethnic nationalist forces in Burma, it is possible that the party's reputation might have been salvaged. In fact, as far as Ba Thein Tin's NEC was concerned, the war in Burma was just beginning. As Karen leaders now retired from the central political stage to concentrate on consolidating the KNU movement and building up the National Democratic Front (NDF), a host of very different insurgent armies were now coming into increasing conflict with CPB forces from the NEC.

Certainly the history of CPB/ethnic minority relations in north-east Burma was never a happy one and contrasts badly with the efforts of Than Tun, Thakin Zin and the party's former leaders in Lower Burma. Though the NEC was more or less entirely dependent on ethnic minority recruits (the CPB's leadership in the NEC was initially 80-90 per cent ethnic Burman while the PA was over 90 per cent ethnic minority), the CPB succeeded in regularly upsetting its potential allies.

At issue has always been the same insistence that the 'revolutionary national minorities' accept the leadership of the CPB as Burma's 'sole proletarian party'. But, explained Abel Tweed, a leader of the KNPP, who in 1977 took charge of an ill-fated KNPP expedition to meet the CPB in the northern Shan State: 'The CPB seemed to want to practise the same chauvinism as the BSPP government.'[19] Indeed many ethnic leaders have accused Ba Thein Tin and the NEC of following a 'fight or join' policy towards their forces while arms supplies from China were plentiful, only changing course when they had no other choice but to compromise. Ultimately it was a policy which was to prove the CPB's undoing. When the 1989 mutinies began, the party found it had precious few friends amongst the armed nationalist opposition.

The Kachin Independence Organisation

The first group to fall foul of the CPB was the predominantly Christian KIO which, despite signing an agreement with Ba Thein Tin in China on the eve of the NEC invasion, claims it was subsequently forced into a wasteful eight-year war with the CPB. The war was partly caused by arguments over territory and the CPB's unsubtle attempts to win away KIO defectors; but equally, KIO leaders claim, it was caused by the dismissive attitude of CPB commissars and Red

Guards, still hyped up on the euphoria of the Cultural Revolution in China, to the legitimacy of the Kachin struggle. 'There were constant arguments,' explained Zau Mai, the present-day KIA Chief-of-Staff. 'If we refused to accept their leadership they immediately called us the "running dogs of imperialism" or "bourgeois-minded".'[20]

The consequences of this bloody war in the rugged mountains of the north-east were extremely grave and, much to the detriment of both parties, pitched Kachin against Kachin, only playing into the hands of the *Tatmadaw*. Fighting broke out in the Kachin substate area of the northern Shan State in 1968 and rapidly spread. A number of truces were agreed by local commanders but these were just as quickly broken. In June 1972, at the height of the CPB's offensive, there was even a three and a half month ceasefire agreed between the KIO and the *Tatmadaw*'s NEC, led by Col. Aye Ko, during which the army tried to persuade the KIO to join forces against the CPB. In return the KIO requested supplies from the government. This Brig. San Yu turned down and following the army's ambush of a KIO party in the northern Shan State, fighting between all three sides swiftly resumed.[21]

The same year the KIO's late chairman, Zau Seng, who in 1966 had opened a KIO liaison office near the KMT stronghold at Tam Ngop on the Thai border, officially joined the KIO to the World Anti-Communist League (WACL) and, in 1973, travelled on to attend a WACL conference in Taipei, Taiwan. As the fighting continued, on 1 March 1975 his brother Zau Dan, the third of the three brothers who had founded the KIO in 1961, was killed in a CPB ambush. This resulted in the KIO's most determined push yet against the CPB; over 1,000 troops were brought into the northern Shan State, including units from the KIO's allies, the AIO and the PSLO, for Operation Black Cat Storm, devised by Zau Dan's successor, Zau Mai. KIA commanders estimate in this one operation alone 400 PA troops were killed or wounded; only after both sides had fought each other to a standstill was a truce called.

Reconciliation was now helped by a quite unrelated event, which had an unexpected impact on the political direction of the KIO movement. In August 1975 Zau Seng, his brother and KIO vice-chairman, Zau Tu, and KIO secretary, Pungshwe Zau Seng, were assassinated near their Tam Ngop base by a group of young KIA soldiers led by Lt. Seng Tu. The reason Seng Tu gave when he transmitted the news to the KIO general headquarters over 200 miles to the north, was intense dissatisfaction by junior KIA officers with the corruption and life-style of their leaders whom, he claimed, were spending more and more time in Thailand away from their men and the armed struggle.[22] They were by no means the first or last insurgent leaders ensnared in the complex world of black market arms dealing in Thailand to have faced such accusations. Since 1966 Zau Seng had kept several hundred troops on the border, constantly rotating them every few months, to secure an outlet for Kachin jade (and also, reputedly, opium) to exchange for arms and ammunition. Shortly afterwards Seng Tu was himself executed in a counter-coup by KIO officers loyal to Zau Seng, who alleged he was an MIS agent long infiltrated into KIA ranks, like Maung Mya, the CPB soldier who had assassinated Than Tun.

This is the official KIO story, but a number of ex-KIA soldiers who lived through these turbulent months have confirmed the growing antipathy in the ranks to their fallen leader. Certainly KIO leaders back in the northern hills at first appeared to accept Seng Tu's explanation. But whatever his real purpose, the sudden deaths within just two years of four of the key men from the KIO's original founding leadership saw the rise to power of a new generation of leaders headed by two more Rangoon University graduates of the 1950s, Brang Seng, ex-headmaster of Myitkyina Baptist High School, and Zau Mai, a former government civil servant. While hardly pro-communist, both were generally more sympathetic to China. 'Of course we don't think China is perfect,' explained Brang Seng, 'but if we compare the cultural and political rights the Kachin people in China have been granted with the situation in Burma, I don't think there would have been the Kachin uprising.'[23] Significantly, both men attribute the KIO's simultaneous involvement with both the Chinese KMT and the CCP to its isolation from the outside world. According to Brang Seng, Asia's two million Kachin peoples scattered across the India-China-Burma tri-border region were 'landlocked', vastly outnumbered by Burmans, Indians and Chinese, and without any external support.

As evidence of the continued influence of China, in early 1976 Brang Seng and Zau Mai travelled to Kunming in Yunnan Province where for three months they held meetings with Ba Thein Tin, Khin Maung Gyi and the new CPB Politburo. Despite continuous pressure on the KIO to accept the CPB's leadership and warnings that the KIO was the only 'nationalist' force to be resisting this demand, on 6 July 1976 a joint military agreement was signed, based on the important 'principle of equality'.[24] Both sides pledged themselves ready to join together in the struggle against the Ne Win regime and the 'three evil "isms"' it represented, 'imperialism, feudal-landlordism and bureaucratic-capitalism'. They also agreed to stand on China's side in the global battle against the Soviet and American super-powers. But notably, unlike the 1968 joint treaty that had been encouraged by Lin Piao (see Chapter 13), this time there was no mention of Mao Zedong thought or the CPB's political leadership.

For both sides it was an important compromise and the first evidence of a growing political pragmatism. Had it come a few years earlier, the outcome of the war in north-east Burma would undoubtedly have been very different. Under this new agreement CPB troops were allowed for the first time to move through KIO territory in the Kachin and northern Shan States to penetrate deeper west into Burma. With the new Chinese weapons the KIO was now given (through the CPB), between 1977 and 1979 the KIA quickly overran dozens of *Tatmadaw* outposts along the strategic Myitkyina-Bhamo road, including the military stronghold at Namsam Yang. Government losses were stunning. In this period the KIA claims to have killed, wounded or captured over 3,000 government troops and seized hundreds of weapons. With 8,000 men and women under arms, the KIO was able to consolidate its control in four brigade areas stretching from the Naga hills and Sagaing Division in the west, the Indian border in the Himalayan foothills to the north, and down along the Chinese border into the northern Shan State.[25] As a result, for nearly a decade government forces rarely left the towns in Burma's far north.

When compared with other ethnic insurgent forces in the region, the KIO's militant resistance to the CPB can be seen to have had historically important consequences in ensuring the continued rise of the Kachin nationalist movement. Following the defection in 1968 of the Maru-Lashi leaders, Ting Ying and Zalum, in the 101 region, the KIO was largely able to avoid any further splits over the question of working with the CPB. As a result, the present-day KIO is made up of supporters from all the ethnic Kachin sub-groups (the Jinghpaw, Maru, Lashi, Atsi, Lisu and, to a lesser extent, the Nung-Rawang) as well as local Shans and Chinese. This is despite considerable political violence, first in the Naga hills in 1963, then in the Nung-Rawang area of Putao in 1964/5, in which as many as 200 lives were lost. Much of the trouble, Kachin nationalists say, was caused by *Tatmadaw* officers who championed local Nung-Rawang villagers against the KIO, which they tried to depict as simply an ethnic Jinghpaw movement.

KIO leaders claim to have learned a bitter lesson from their mistakes in over-reacting at that time. The evidence appears to bear them out. Bound together by a unique but intensely loyal clan system which has survived the dislocation of war and the impact of the modern world, KIO agents today can be found wherever Kachin people live, whether in Rangoon, the *Tatmadaw*, Kunming, Bangkok, Hong Kong or even the United States. A staunchly nationalist rather than ideologically dogmatic movement, the KIO is different from other ethnic nationalist parties in Burma. Ironically, in its early years the KIO was widely regarded as a radical leftist movement and, in 1964, soon after the Kachin uprising began, was responsible for banning the traditional *Gumsa* or *Duwa* 'feudal' system of village organisation in the hills in favour of the *Gumlao* or 'democratic' system, which has so excited western anthropologists.[26] In the upheavals which followed a number of traditional headmen were killed.

Like the KNU in the south, the KIO became an important safe haven for other smaller insurgent groups; armed training was given to a number of nationalist armies, including the short-lived Chin Independence Army of the 1960s and the present-day AIO and PSLO. Rebel groups from north-east India, such as the MNF, also regularly passed through KIO territory on their way through to China and, by the early 1980s, the KIO's headquarters at Pajao on the Chinese border had become as important a liaison post for insurgent forces in the region as the KNU's general headquarters at Mannerplaw. Banned from Mannerplaw, at Pajao CPB delegates had to take their place on equal terms with representatives from rebel forces as varied as the SSPP, PSLO, National Socialist Council of Nagaland (NSCN), Federal Government of Nagaland, United Liberation Front of Assam and People's Liberation Army of Manipur.

KIO leaders, like Brang Seng, attribute their successful resistance to the BSPP and CPB to two additional factors, Christianity, which the majority of Kachins today practise, and a Kachin belief in their prior existence as a 'nation'. It is inter-esting to note that while the KIO has expanded into the Shan State and Sagaing Division, where large Kachin communities live, the same is not true of the SSPP or other Shan insurgent movements, even though in both the Kachin State and Sagaing Division there are many Shan-majority districts.

Despite the KIO's opposition, the CPB did have some initial success in 1968 in winning over the local KIA officers Ting Ying, a Lashi, and Zalum, a Maru, in the Chepwi-Laukhaung region (see Chapter 13). Their names can be added to those of other ethnic leaders like Khun Myint (Shan) and Pheung Kya-shin (Kokangese) who integrated their forces with the PA. These, however, were very much the exception. Throughout the 1970s the CPB's activities triggered an extraordinary series of divisions amongst other ethnic groups in north-east Burma, echoing the earlier split of the KNU into the KNUP and KRC factions. For this many nationalists have never forgiven the CPB. Nowhere are these feelings today more deeply felt than in the Shan State.

A State of Strife: The Shan State

Though KIO columns frequently came down to the Thai border, KIA military activities outside its strongholds in the Kachin State were largely confined to the Kachin-inhabited mountains around Hsenwi-Kuktai in the northern Shan State where the KIA's 1,000-strong 4th brigade held sway. Always the most powerful ethnic force in the Shan State, despite a perennial shortage of arms and ammunition, was the Shan State Army (SSA). Throughout the 1970s the SSA could call on in excess of 9,000 trained volunteers (mostly Shans), but could usually arm only half at any one time. Since its formation in 1964 the SSA has continued to enjoy widespread intellectual and rural support, especially in the north of the state, the Shan political and economic heartland. Though squeezed between the *Tatmadaw*, KKY, CPB, KIO, PSLO and other smaller ethnic insurgent forces, the SSA was eventually able to build up four large interconnecting base areas, running north to south, on the west bank of the Salween River:

   No.3 brigade in the Kyaukme, Namhsan, Namtu districts;
   No.1 or 'central' brigade in Hsipaw, Lashio, Mong Hsu, Kehsi Mansam;
   No.7 brigade in Kunhing, Takaw;
   No.2 brigade in Langhko, Mongpai and Mawkmai down to Mong Mai on the
   Thai border.[27]

The strength of these forces was always likely to bring the SSA into conflict with the CPB. Privately CPB leaders had always been dismissive of the 'aristocratic' pedigree of several of the SSA's founders, but in April 1966 Than Tun wrote to the *Mahadevi* Sao Nang Hearn Kham, chairman of the Shan State War Council (SSWC) and wife of Burma's late president, Sao Shwe Thaike, in surprisingly modest terms. Claiming to be fighting for the 'liberation of the Shan peoples', he urged 'the fighting unity of all nationalities'.[28]

Since the beginning of the insurrections CPB forces had been operating in many valleys in the west of the Shan State. With the advent of thousands of fresh CPB troops from China under Naw Seng's NEC, the SSA's predominantly intellectual leaders, who had taken up a strongly anti-communist and pro-Western position at their foundation in 1964, became even more suspicious (see Chapter 12). Historically many Shans have felt in danger of being swamped by China. Indeed one SSA communiqué in June 1968 warned of 'Mao's master plan... to enslave other nations and peoples around the periphery of mainland China' and correctly predicted the coming conflict between the CPB, China and Ne Win's Revolutionary Council (RC).[29] Not only had SSA commanders lost hundreds of troops as deserters to the government's KKY units during 1967/8, but they now feared losing even more to the CPB as they came under intense military pressure from the NEC's 202 and 303 war zones in the east.

One result of this military squeeze was the long overdue formation of the SSA's political wing, the SSPP, under the chairmanship of another former Rangoon University student, Khun Kya Nu (*aka* Hseng Suk), at Khum Pang village, Kehsi Mansam township, in August 1971. The move was hastened, SSPP leaders concede, by the political challenge posed by the CPB. But these were difficult years for the SSPP. In heavy fighting during a six-month period in late 1970 the SSA's 1st brigade, commanded by the *Mahadevi*'s son, Chao Tzang Yawnghwe (*aka* Khun Loumpha), and Sai Zam Muang, claimed to have put out of action over 600 government troops from the army's crack 77th, 88th and 99th Light Infantry Divisions in the northern Lashio-Hsenwi districts alone.[30] Then in 1971/2 the

SSA fought a brief territorial war with its former ally, the KIO, in the Hsenwi-Kutkai area after which, outgunned and outfought, it quickly drew back, prompting the *Mahadevi*, shortly before her exile to the West, to list the SSA's enemies as 'the KIO, CPB and Ne Win regime', in that order.[31] Indeed in this period one SSA unit near Namhsan fought almost 30 battles with three different enemy forces in just one month, the *Tatmadaw*, the KIA and the KMT remnants.[32]

But it was the CPB invasion that alarmed Shan leaders the most and in 1973, worried by the speed of the NEC's advance, the SSPP asked the Thai government to approach Gen. Ne Win to try and organise immediate peace talks 'to prevent the country from falling into the hand of the CPB'.[33] Then in September 1974 Khun Kya Nu finally agreed to a tri-military pact in the pivotal Hsipaw area with Zau Dan, KIA Vice Chief-of-Staff, and Kham Thaung, president of the KIO's close ally, the PSLO, which had broken away from the SSA's 1st brigade in 1966. Kham Thaung himself was badly wounded in a battle with the *Tatmadaw* in 1979 and later died from his injuries; sole leadership of the PSLO then fell to another co-founder of the nationalist movement, Kyaw Hla. But now enjoying good relations with both the SSPP and KIO, the PSLO developed into a highly effective guerrilla army, with two battalions and 1,000 troops, in the Palaung-majority mountains north of Namhsam and in the fertile tea-growing hills of the former Tawngpeng substate.[34]

Of the other Shan forces, the Shan United Revolutionary Army (SURA) led by Gon Jerng (*aka* Mo Heing) was always under the wing of the KMT's 93rd Division/Third Army remnants of Gen. Li Wen-huan. A former CPB member, Gon Jerng had broken with the CPB to form the short-lived Shan State Communist Party of 1956-8 when the party rejected demands for a separate Shan committee. Initially impressed by the CPB's anti-AFPFL propaganda, as a devout Buddhist he had become increasingly disturbed by the land redistribution programme it introduced in the western Shan State in 1954. He described it as a 'premature undertaking', given the abundant land still available and the obvious poverty, by Burmese standards, of most landowning Shan and ethnic minority hill farmers the CPB now classified as 'rich':

> These policies wrecked the cohesion of the Shan peoples fighting for freedom. The CPB insisted it was not a question of Shan freedom but rather liberating workers and peasants from the yoke of feudalism and imperialism. In most communities in the Shan State these terms were hardly relevant. Instead it seemed to me that the CPB was forcing the Shans to submit to communism by Burmanisation.[35]

Having surrendered at Hsipaw with 400 other Shan communists (under the 'arms for democracy movement' of 1958), later that year Gon Jerng joined the *Noom Suik Harn* and, after losing an arm fighting with the *Tatmadaw* near the Thai border, returned to the Laikha region a year later to form the Shan National United Front with Khun Kya Nu. A founder member of the SSWC and SSA in 1964, Gon Jerng quickly grew irritated with the youthful intellectualism of the SSA's student leaders and, like the KIO, found himself increasingly drawn to Gen. Li Wen-huan's CIA-backed KMT forces which, at that time, still operated in much of the southern and central Shan State. Formally established in January 1969 after breaking away from the SSA the previous year, SURA's main 1,000-strong force usually remained entrenched in the mountains around Gon Jerng's headquarters at Pieng Luang on the Thai border. Here for the next two decades Gon Jerng maintained a staunchly anti-communist and pro-Buddhist stance.[36]

After a brief but bloody war with the SSA in 1972, only one under strength 300-troop battalion led by Kam Jate, a popular guerrilla commander, remained permanently in Gon Jerng's former stronghold in the hills above Laikha.

Also based around the thriving black market town of Pieng Luang and at Tam Ngop nearby, Gen. Li's troops operated mainly on the Thai side of the border as an officially sanctioned anti-communist border police force. Here they frequently clashed with the Communist Party of Thailand (CPT) in the 1970s, but when they entered the Shan State it was often in the uniforms of SURA troops. For SURA, the KMT and the Thai Army it was an extraordinary but unpublicised marriage of convenience, which lasted nearly two decades and in which their open drug trafficking activities went virtually ignored.[37] But it backfired badly on the nationalist movements in the Shan State, especially the SSPP, which was continually trying to win Western understanding for its cause and the attendant problems created by the opium trade. Gen. Tuan Shi-wen's Fifth Army at Mae Salong further to the east was generally regarded as the more effective of the Taiwanese and CIA KMT intelligence-gathering units operating along the China border, but was equally implicated in the opium trade. Heroin refineries operated freely at Mae Salong and in most other KMT bases. Not surprisingly, in their reports KMT operatives, like the *Tatmadaw*, continued to blame the ethnic rebels and later the CPB, giving the nationalist movements a bad reputation in the West and in the corridors of power in Washington, which it has taken many years to shake off.[38]

With the dissolution of the other Shan forces during the 1960s, either to the KKY or CPB, there remained the highly anti-communist Shan United Army (SUA) of Khun Sa, which fought the notorious Opium War with the KMT in 1967 for control of the cross-border opium trade.[39] Originally known as the Anti-Socialist United Army, the SUA has always been something of a maverick 'trader's army', built on a fierce personal loyalty to Khun Sa in his Loimaw home district and in the Doi Larng mountain region along the Thai border. Here ethnic Shan or Thai identity is virtually indistinguishable. All parties, including the *Tatmadaw* and, for many years, the Thai Army, found it more expedient to trade with Khun Sa's heavily armed militia of 1,500 troops than to fight it. Khun Sa himself has twice been officially employed as a KKY commander. Indeed, after the CPB set up its general headquarters at Panghsang in 1973, one of the first forces to arrive to do business was a convoy of the SUA's quasi-militia merchants.[40]

Khun Sa has always been nothing if not the great survivor of Shan politics. Having been imprisoned by the *Tatmadaw* in 1970 when he was suspected of preparing to go underground again with his KKY force, in 1973 his jungle comrades kidnapped two Russian doctors to secure his release. Their go-between was the Thai general, Kriangsak Chommanand, who had been stationed in the southern Shan State during the Second World War. Khun Sa remained in Rangoon for a while, acting as middleman for *Tatmadaw* officers returning with jade, rubies and other precious stones from the north-east front, before absconding in 1976 to join his men once again to rebuild his SUA movement.

The Pao Nationalist Movement

In the early 1970s another powerful force emerged in the south-west of the Shan State, which for a time appeared likely to bring together the diverse ethnic races in the mountain ranges around Taunggyi into one united anti-BSPP front. The SSNLO had been formed in 1966 by veterans of the (Union) Pao National Organisation (PNO) who, like their then ally, Gon Jerng, had laid down their arms during U Nu's 'arms for democracy' amnesty of 1958. This time their initial demand was for the release of the former MP and wartime cabinet minister, Thaton Hla Pe, and for other prominent Pao leaders imprisoned by the RC during 1962-4 (see Chapters 11-12). When Ne Win refused, they promptly went underground again and the Pao movement rapidly spread back into all the PNO's former base areas. With solid support amongst the Shan State's fast-growing Pao population (then already estimated in excess of 300,000 inhabitants) living along the strategic gateway to the eastern mountains, they posed a considerable threat to the RC's attempt to establish BSPP control in the ethnic minority states.

During 1968 the SSNLO fought a brief war with the CPB in the Inle Lake region. In October that year it suffered another setback after fighting broke out with local SURA forces and its leader, Bo San Thein, was assassinated by Gon Jerng's men when he went to attend peace talks. Shortly afterwards the SURA commander responsible, Major Hla Khin, was killed in retaliatory action. Following this debacle, the Pao leadership was briefly taken over by Hla Maung, a former CPB defector, then U Maung He, chairman, and Tha Kalei, Chief-of-Staff, an ethnic Sgaw Karen who was one of a number of Karens sent up by the KNU in 1949 to help organise the resistance of their Pao cousins. Quickly building up a guerrilla force of about 2,000 troops, in the late 1960s and early 1970s the SSNLO went on a sustained offensive which saw a remarkable series of daylight attacks on government-held towns and heavily armed *Tatmadaw* convoys in the mountains. Hundreds of weapons were captured. Under this new leadership the SSNLO built up good relations with other ethnic forces in the region, especially the SSA (SURA and SUA, by contrast, were both suspected of supporting a return to the old *Sawbwa* system) and recruited troops from several different racial backgrounds, including Shans, Karens and Danus.

But in the prevailing political climate of the early 1970s, Tha Kalei and his commanders soon came under the influence of both the CPB and KNUP, which sent present-day KNU vice-president, Bo San Lin, to work with them as an adviser. Much to the CPB's displeasure, in 1967 the KNUP had set up its own Nationalities United Front (NUF) which deliberately excluded the CPB and, with the support of the KNPP and Kayan New Land Party (KNLP), a mixed-race NUF battalion was deployed along the Shan-Kayah State borders. According to Tha Kalei, SSNLO troops never actually joined this joint-NUF battalion, though NUF troops did move into one of the SSNLO's main base areas in the Maikung range and, in the early 1970s, frequently joined the SSNLO and KNLP in battle.[41]

However, the dominant political influence on the SSNLO was not the KNUP but CPB cadres from the Kyawkku-Lawksawk 108 region to the north. These were led by political commissar U Tun Myint (*aka* U Moe *aka* Mya Min), and CC member Myo Myint, whom Thakin Zin had sent up from the Pegu Yomas in 1971 to liaise with Ba Thein Tin and the NEC. Both men spent long periods of time with Tha Kalei and the SSNLO leaders in their forest camps. If not to the Pao leaders, it was clear to all outside observers that the SSNLO figured large in the

CPB's plan to build the ethnic minority 108 region into a major military base area to link up with the NEC.

Disagreements soon started over the release from gaol of Thaton Hla Pe and the other Pao leaders. At first they were unable to leave Rangoon, but in July 1972 Hla Pe and Kyaw Sein finally escaped to SSNLO territory, one month after a CC meeting had appointed Tha Kalei as the party's new chairman. Eyewitnesses to the turbulent events that followed are adamant that much of the trouble was stirred up by CPB cadres, especially Myo Myint, who conspired against Hla Pe night after night around the forest campfires. They were afraid of the apparent influence this veteran nationalist might bring to bear on impressionable hill villagers, despite his leading role in the 1963 'peace committee' movement. For many nationalists nothing exemplified more clearly the differences between the CPB of the 1950s and the ideologically hidebound Maoist party it had become after the Cultural Revolution than the persecution of Hla Pe.

CPB leaders have since tried to play down their involvement; indeed, at that time the *Tatmadaw* was also employing all kinds of tricks to try and divide the Pao movement. But the degree of the CPB's interference was revealed in an extraordinary broadcast on the VOPB in late 1973 which accused the 'reactionaries and traitors', Hla Pe and Kyaw Sein, of being sent by Rangoon to oppose the 'ideologically correct' struggle of the SSNLO, which had already accepted 'the leadership of the working class', i.e. the CPB.[42] Tha Kalei himself claims he was merely trying to prevent the SSNLO from slipping back into the 'narrow nationalist' movement it had been in the 1950s and was keen to attract supporters from all social and ethnic backgrounds: 'The nationalist movement finished in 1958,' he explained. 'We believed if we could develop an ideological movement, we would win. In the Shan State there are many races. We have to work together if we want to overthrow the government.'[43]

Fighting between the two sides, however, had already broken out in November 1973 following an SSNLO CC meeting at Hpasam village, Honam township, when several Pao commanders, including Aung Kham Hti, Gee Daung (a Karen) and a young Rangoon University law graduate from Thaton, Khun Okker, opposed Tha Kalei's proposal, allegedly egged on by Myo Myint, to 'take action' against Hla Pe and Kyaw Sein.[44] In reply, Tha Kalei claims Hla Pe accused the SSNLO of being taken over by the CPB and of abandoning the Pao cause, and demanded the arrest of Myo Myint who was at the meeting.[45] By night, 22 nationalist leaders protected by a small armed escort escaped through the jungle, taking Hla Pe and Kyaw Sein with them. In the reprisals that followed, three of Hla Pe's supporters, including one of his sons, were killed.

For the next year intense arguments continued in the Pao community over which side to follow. These resulted in the deep split which completely divided the Pao movement into two much reduced factions. In March 1974 the SSNLO loyalists of Tha Kalei made a joint military pact with the SSPP and in July held formal discussions with the CPB. (The CPB claims the SSNLO joined the NDUF; Tha Kalei denies this.) Meanwhile Hla Pe returned with a small force under the new name, the Shan Nationalities Liberation Front, into the Maikung Range while his principal lieutenant, Aung Kham Hti, moved further north into the Taunggyi region, skirmishing with SSNLO troops and recruiting villagers on his way. According to Aung Kham Hti, they did not use their Pao name at first to avoid CPB accusations that they were anti-Shan nationalists. Eventually, in a combined manoeuvre in December 1974, Hla Pe's forces simultaneously overran SSNLO positions on the Salween River near Mae Aw on the Thai border and in the Maikung mountains further to the west, forcing Tha Kalei, his political staff and several families to take temporary shelter at the KNPP's general headquarters on the Pai River nearby. Squeezed between Hla Pe's troops, SURA, the KMT and the *Tatmadaw*, shortly afterwards Tha Kalei went up to Panghsang to ask the CPB for arms and training, a request that was immediately granted. After six months training, Tha Kalei returned with his men and four platoons of CPB soldiers to help him reorganise the SSNLO's former base areas.

Until the 1989 CPB mutinies the split continued and rebel Pao territory remained divided between these two rival factions. Weary after over three decades of constant toil and hardship, Hla Pe died from ill health at the age of 66 in the jungle in 1975 shortly after the Pao split became permanent. But the two groups still continued to promote very different versions of the Pao liberation movement: the SSNLO headed by Tha Kalei and backed by the CPB, and the 'nationalist' wing led by Kyaw Sein and Hla Pe's eventual successor, Aung Kham Hti, who helped reform the PNO at the Londa Congress at the village of that name in the Maikung Range in December 1976. The two leaders could not have been more different: Tha Kalei, a rustic Sgaw Karen interloper, undoubtedly popular with his troops, who is still regarded as one of the most effective guerrilla commanders in Burma past and present, and Aung Kham Hti, a charismatic ex-*pongyi*, who won the backing of many educated Paos. Today these continue to support the revival of a Pao cultural movement which might, indeed, one day shed light on many neglected aspects of Burma's political history.[46]

In 1977 the PNO had to overcome a further setback when Khun Ye Naung, former Pao representative to U Nu's PDP, who had been given the important job of liaison officer with Thailand, surrendered to the *Tatmadaw* with 66 soldiers and what was left of the estimated 8 million baht (£200,000) he was alleged to have accumulated. Then, after Kyaw Sein had resigned to take the blame, Aung Kham Hti took over the presidency full time and began rebuilding the PNO to a peak strength of 800 troops, mostly ethnic Pao village militia. The SSNLO, by contrast, claimed to have 300 regulars and 200 village militia, half of whom were Paos, the rest Karens and Shans. Guerrilla fighting between the two sides continued into the 1980s with the SSNLO usually backed up by the CPB, which sent troops from the PA's 4045 and 4046 battalions, led by a Chinese commander, Taut Pong, into Pao territory. While the SSNLO remained one of the CPB's most loyal allies and kept representatives at the CPB's Panghsang general headquarters, the PNO joined the ethnic minority NDF and sent delegates to Mannerplaw.[47] (The BSPP shrewdly responded by appointing an ethnic Pao and former *Tatmadaw* major, Tun Yin Law, head of the Shan State, thus keeping ethnic politics in the Shan State neatly on the boil.)

The personal antipathies continued even after the CPB and NDF forged a joint military alliance in 1986. According to Khun Zani Zet (a PNO officer badly wounded in a clash with the SSNLO-CPB), battles with the SSNLO or CPB out-numbered those with the *Tatmadaw* by three or four to one throughout this period.[48] As late as November 1987 Bo Nay Myo, a former PNO delegate to the NDF and nephew of Major Thura, commander of the PNO's Northern Division in the Taunggyi-Laikha region, was allegedly assassinated by the CPB when he unwisely paid a return visit to his home village unarmed. On 21 February a ceasefire was agreed between Tha Kalei and Aung Kham Hti at Naung Hai village, Yawnghwe, after the intercession of local Buddhist monks, but only one year later in February 1989 after the democracy uprising did the two parties begin talks on political reconciliation at Pongcho village, Honam. With the 1989 CPB collapse, the peace process accelerated and by the end of the year the SSNLO had sent representatives to the Mannerplaw general headquarters of the NDF. Finally, in July 1990, I met Tha Kalei at Mannerplaw negotiating with Khun Okker of the PNO about reintegrating their two forces.[49] However, 15 bloody years had already been lost and matters became only more complicated in March 1991 by the surprise, bilateral ceasefire with the *Tatmadaw* by Aung Kham Hti and the PNO's general headquarters' troops in the Taunggyi region, causing yet another split in the Pao movement.

The Shan State Progress Party and Tailand Revolutionary Council
The second local force to split over the question of working with the CPB was the SSPP. For many years SSA commanders resisted all blandishments from the CPB to join forces; in 1972, alarmed by the CPB's continued build-up, SSPP leaders, Khun Kya Nu and Chao Tzang Yawnghwe, even sent a small force south to establish a new base area in the Mong Mai-Mawkmai area on the Thai border. This was intended to serve as both a military fall-back point away from the CPB advance and a liaison post from which to try and win support from U Nu's PDP, Thailand and the West. The following year, however, the KNUP finally persuaded the SSPP in the north to send along a delegation, headed by CC member Hso Ten, with an armed escort to accompany the Dawna team expedition to China.

Ironically, the KNUP delegates were to return to Lower Burma in some disillusionment, but Hso Ten, Khwan Mong and the SSPP delegates were much more impressed. With one eye on developments in Indo-China, many said on their return they were convinced a communist victory was now imminent throughout South-East Asia and were stunned by the ease with which the NEC had brushed aside the *Tatmadaw* garrisons at Panghsang, Pangyang, Mengseng, Mong Ma and Mong Yang during 1972/3.[50] Hundreds of casualties had been inflicted in the process and the CPB now controlled the entire northern and central trans-Salween regions. After meeting local CCP leaders and touring the Tai (Shan) autonomous regions of Yunnan, they returned to their central headquarters in the mountains near Mong Tung with a large quantity of ammunition and explosives passed to them via the CPB.

The following year Hso Ten returned with another team for a stay of one year and in 1975 a mutual defence pact was agreed, despite reservations expressed by Khun Kya Nu at a stormy meeting near Panghung. Indeed at that very moment 300 miles to the south, the party general-secretary, Tzang Yawnghwe, was leading another SSPP delegation to the KNU's headquarters in the northern Dawna Range where, in May that year, the Federal National Democratic Front (FNDF), the forerunner of the NDF, was formed. Rather like the KIO, which at the same time was developing relations with both the KMT and CCP, the SSPP leaders felt they had little choice but to work on two fronts at once.

But back in the mountains of the north, as the CPB continued its remorseless path into the Shan State, the situation soon looked very different. The initial attraction for most Shan commanders, headed by the SSA's Chief-of-Staff, Sai Zam Muang, had been arms; but for others, such as Hso Ten, who eventually applied to join the CPB, it was ideology. According to Khun Kya Nu, even Zam Muang, who later turned against the CPB, proposed at one CC meeting that the SSPP should accept the 'line of "people's democracy" and the "four-class" struggle'.[51] Not only was there the beckoning model of China, but in the mid-1970s Panghsang itself offered the fleeting vision of a racially mixed society, free from ethnic prejudice. Following Naw Seng's death, another Kachin, Zau Mai, was made the CPB's new Chief-of-Staff, while other minority leaders, such as Pheung Kya-shin (Kokangese) and Sai Aung Win (Shan), were given important positions in the military and administrative hierarchy. Former SSPP leaders like Khwan Mong openly admit they were at first highly impressed by the CPB's apparent ability to organise in a hitherto impenetrable mountain region of such economic backwardness and ethnic diversity.[52] Virtually the entire PA now confronting SSA positions consisted of ethnic minority recruits. In 1976 the CPB won an important new ally when Khun Myint, commander of the SSPP's affiliate, the Shan State Army East (SSAE) in the Kengtung area, agreed to merge his 1,000-strong force with the PA.

There was also the question of security as SSA units continued to fight battles on several fronts at once. Though the SSA's main strongholds, deep in the mountains of the northern and central Shan State, had generally proven resilient to *Tatmadaw* attack, the CPB base areas to the east offered security for the wives and children of SSPP leaders in the sort of safe 'family lines' other insurgent forces had long since built up around Burma's borders. Following the 1975 treaty with the CPB, the CPB's 'liberated zones' for several years provided a safe sanctuary for SSPP supporters, while SSA units at the front remained constantly on the move. The SSPP's administrative general headquarters in the mountains of the Hsipaw-Mongyai-Kehsi Mansam triangle was rarely able to stay in any location for more than one week, sometimes moving out on operations with up to 1,000 troops and sometimes retiring back into the forests with as few as 100. Certainly for most Shan soldiers, the alternative headquarters that Khun Kya Nu had established in the beautiful valley of Mong Mai on the Thai border, 200 miles to the south, appeared very remote indeed.

But it was above all the prospect of unlimited supplies of arms and ammunition that veteran SSA commanders say was decisive. One of the rare pictures reaching Western journalists in the 1970s of 'CPB' troops, decked out in Chinese uniforms and bristling with Chinese weaponry, was in fact of SSA troops returning from the Yunnan border. On just one trip shortly after the 1975 defence pact was signed, Sai Zam Muang returned with 1,000 weapons, including mortars and recoilless rifles.

The CPB's offer of arms supplies for the KIO, SSNLO and SSPP at this moment was timely. In the early days of the insurrections KIA troops sometimes went into battle with only two bullets each, while after each skirmish SSA troops would be expected to account for every bullet they had used. Moreover, an extraordinary attempt by the SSPP in the early 1970s to seize control of the opium trade in the Shan State had ended in abject failure. Ostensibly the SSPP had wanted to offer the annual opium harvest for sale to the US at a pre-emptive purchase price, but more realistically it was a determined effort to take financial charge of the lucrative black market trade out of which its KKY/KMT/SURA/SUA rivals were financing their struggles.[53] A bitter reminder of this failure came in 1975 when the SSA had to beat off an attempt to seize control of its southern base areas by the Kokang KKY remnants of erstwhile ally, Lo Hsing-han, who was then imprisoned in Rangoon.[54]

Amidst growing financial difficulties, Khun Kya Nu was ousted as SSPP president at an emergency conference at Wan Kyaung Nar Mai, Langkhor township, in March 1976, and Tzang Yawnghwe was invited to retire for medical treatment. Significantly, the SSPP rank-and-file regarded both men as 'pro-Western'. Tzang Yawnghwe and Khun Kya Nu themselves blame their defeat on (amongst other things) communist 'intrigues'.[55]

The result was the damaging regional split in the SSPP movement, north and south, which has continued to the present. The SSPP's northern group led by Sai Myint Aung (*aka* Khun Obon), Sai Zam Muang and Hso Ten, who kept permanent representatives at Panghsang, resolved to approach the CPB Politburo to ask for more arms. The only price Ba Thein Tin demanded was ideology. Unlike the KIO, which since 1968 had staunchly resisted all CPB and CCP pressure to accept the CPB's 'guiding' leadership, the SSPP's northern leaders eventually gave way. While in the south the SSPP's new acting president, Sai Pan, issued a strident statement denouncing the CPB as a 'racist party guilty of aggression and oppression against the people of the Shan State', the northern leadership, headed by Sai Zam Muang, was forging a completely contradictory alliance with the CPB.[56] On 30 January 1977 the VOPB broadcast a shock communiqué announcing the formation of a united front between the CPB and SSPP. Defining itself as a 'progressive and revolutionary national party which has accepted Marxism-Leninism-Mao Zedong thought as its basic and guiding ideology', the SSPP vowed to 'march together with the CPB towards a communist world'.[57] But the true degree of the SSPP's submission was revealed in the subtext. Accepting that the CPB was the 'sole proletarian party in Burma' and that the 'people's democratic revolution' could only be led by a proletarian party, the SSPP stated that all the oppressed nationalities and their revolutionary forces 'must unite under the leadership of the CPB'.[58]

The extremes of these two statements, issued just eight months apart, reflected the depth of the split in the SSPP leadership and came close to destroying the entire movement. Other factors (personal, military, geographic and financial) were undoubtedly involved; and many SSPP leaders still deny they ever accepted the CPB agreement. But the consequences were far-reaching and caused deep political uncertainty, which still pervades all levels of SSPP organisation. While the southern SSPP led by Sai Pan and Seng Harn (*aka* Sai Nyan Win) worked with the PNO and the NDF, the SSPP's other acting president, Sai Myint Aung, stayed with his men in the SSA's northern base areas.

Dissension soon set in. Sai Myint Aung, a veteran Rangoon University student who, like Sai Pan, had joined the *Noom Suik Harn* in 1958, was killed in action in December 1978 in a clash with the *Tatmadaw* 30 miles west of Hsipaw, while a third Rangoon University veteran, Hso Ten, was stripped of all posts and for several years wisely stayed in exile with the CPB. That same year Sai Zam Muang, the SSA's highly popular Chief-of-Staff, and his deputy, Bo Pan Aung, both of whom initially supported the CPB agreement, travelled to the Thai border with a 700-strong task force with the apparent intention of building up a major new base area along the Thai border, in cooperation with the southern SSPP, to open a new door to the West. Warning that CPB leaders were urging them to join the PA, they made little attempt to hide their alarm at the turn CPB/SSPP relations had taken and said they feared being swallowed up like the SSAE.

Both mysteriously disappeared shortly afterwards on a secret mission near Mae Sai in Thailand. Exact details are uncertain, but it is generally accepted that after crossing the border at the invitation of a local Thai intelligence officer, they were lured to their deaths by agents of Khun Sa's SUA, whose headquarters was then located on the Thai side of the border at Ban Hin Taek nearby. Their bodies have never been found but their presumed deaths were a shattering blow to SSA morale. Across the state large numbers of troops immediately put down their arms and went back to their villages refusing to continue the fight; for three years many local commanders were left to struggle on alone without orders or any coherent sense of purpose. Only in 1981, at the SSPP's two-month Second Congress at the southern headquarters at Mong Mai near the Thai border, did SSPP leaders from across the state finally gather again to try and resolve their difficulties. The outcome was the restoration of the SSPP's 'national democracy' line and a decision to work more closely with the NDF, the rejection of the 1975 defence pact with the CPB, and the election of a new 27-man CC under Sao Hso Lane, virtually the last of the Rangoon University veterans from 1958 still active in the field. Indeed of the original 1971 CC, only 11 now remained.

However, after the meeting, most of the SSPP's northern leaders (led by Naw Merng, Sai Lek and the new SSA Chief-of-Staff, Sao Hso Noom, an ethnic Wa and son of the Mong Loen *Sawbwa*) headed back north and immediately resumed contact with the CPB, in clear defiance of the congress resolutions. 'Arms not ideology' was their motivation.[59] Since as many as 80 per cent of their weapons were Chinese-made, they depended on the CPB for ammunition. The result was a second disastrous split in the SSPP movement in less than a decade. On 4 March 1983 the VOPB broadcast a joint SSPP/CPB statement in which the SSPP Politburo accepted the struggle in Burma had to be a 'people's democratic revolution' waged under the leadership of the proletariat. Moreover, to the anger of many Shan nationalists, the wording showed a subtle rephrasing, reinforcing the CPB's authority over the SSPP. While the CPB was defined as the 'sole party of the proletariat', the SSPP was now simply a 'revolutionary and progressive national party'.[60]

Historically, the agreement could not have been worse timed. The SSPP's enemies were quick to strike. In March 1983 heavily armed units from Khun Sa's SUA, which the Thai Army had ousted from its stronghold at Ban Hin Taek the previous year, overran the SSPP's southern headquarters in the Mong Mai valley, beginning a sweep of positions held by the SSPP's Pao, Wa and Lahu NDF allies along the Thai border and prompting the surrender to the BSPP in June that year of the party's disillusioned president, Sao Hso Lane. Indeed, Hso Lane, who ordered his troops to attack the Thai border patrol police before retreating into the interior, appeared to panic and was stripped of all positions prior to his surrender. SUA gunmen then went on an assassination spree, killing a number of veteran SSPP leaders displaced along the border, including Sai Pan and Seng Haan, a former NDF secretary. With the loss of Mong Mai, the SSA's 2nd brigade simply disintegrated. Some units joined the SSA's 7th brigade to the north; the rest, under their military commander, Zam Mai, and CC member, Khwan Mong, joined Gon Jerng's SURA.

These bloody events, which saw Shan killing Shan, now coincided with one of the periodic twists in the regional opium trade which makes Shan politics so hard to follow. In early 1984, with the CPT insurgency firmly on the decline, the Thai government, having two years earlier turned on Khun Sa's SUA, finally decided to move against the embarrassing political anachronism of the KMT, which was equally heavily implicated in narcotics trafficking. All KMT troops, now officially known as 'Chinese irregular forces', were ordered to disband and their families to integrate into the local Thai community. Some 15,000 KMT dependants in 13 Chinese settlements along the border were affected; the announcement was later followed by a frightening and unexplained massacre of 30 KMT villagers at Pieng Luang by local Thai rangers.[61]

Quickly sensing the winds of change, on 1 April 1984 Gon Jerng broke off his 15-year alliance with the KMT and, issuing an appeal for Shan unity, formally dissolved his 1,000-strong army to lead the SSPP defectors in forming the new Tailand Revolutionary Council (TRC). (Though this has never been admitted, the previous month Thai intelligence also alleged Khun Sa met the head of the *Tatmadaw*'s Eastern Command, Brig.-Gen. Aye San, in Mong Ton where he was given the green light by Rangoon to sweep the border.) This drastic reorganisation in Shan politics was completed in April 1985 when Gon Jerng and Zam Mai, under intense military pressure from Khun Sa whose troops had by now overrun all the valleys surrounding the TRC's Pieng Luang headquarters, agreed to merge forces with the SUA. Virtually the entire Shan-Thai border region between Tachilek in the east and Mong Mai in the west, a distance of 150 miles, had come under Khun Sa's control. Together they boasted a new force of between 3,000 and 4,000 soldiers, including militia deeper inside the Shan State around Laikha, under Kam Jate, and Mong Yai, where Khun Sa's stepfather had been a local *Myosa*. Known as the Mong Tai Army, they were nearly equal in strength to the SSA. Though Gon Jerng was nominally still president of the TRC, real power lay with Khun Sa who, by his own admission, controlled the transport and distribution of two-thirds of the Shan State opium crop. This in 1987 he put at a remarkable 1,000 tons per annum, ensuring the rapid build-up by the TRC of a vast arsenal of modern arms and supplies, reputedly including SAM missiles, bought on the Thai black market.[62]

Long derided as 'opium warlords', both Khun Sa and Gon Jerng, then 54 and 61 years old respectively, were to bask in some rare publicity in the international press and represented a formidable challenge to the SSPP.[63] Both Gon Jerng and Khun Sa were openly contemptuous of the SSPP leaders, whom they described as 'communists'.[64] In a belated search for legitimacy Khun Sa even proposed his force should be called the 'real' SSA, with which the SUA had once been briefly allied. Indeed, sitting beneath portraits of the King and Queen of Thailand, Khun Sa, a master of political brinkmanship, suggested to me that if the TRC could not succeed in achieving military secession from Burma, the 'eight million Shan peoples' should consider joining their ethnic 'brothers' in Thailand.[65]

None the less, the TRC's colourful but conservative brand of fervent nationalism was not without its local appeal. Life at TRC camps involves much flag waving, hill tribe dancing and Khun Sa's highly public patronage of Shan/Buddhist culture. Eventually, by a mixture of coercion and persuasion, Khun Sa, himself a mixed race Shan-Chinese, was able to put together a surprisingly broad leadership which included some famous names from the world of Shan insurgent politics: Zam Mai and Khwan Mong from the SSPP; Kam Jate, Khern Sai, an ethnic Chinese intellectual, and Chao Nor Far, son of the Palaung *Sawbwa* of

Tawngpeng, from SURA; the veteran 1958 student leaders, Sai Tun Aye and Khun Maha, both of whom came out of retirement; various Kokangese and Kachin commanders; and last, but not least, from his own SUA the military hard-liners, Khun Seng (his uncle), and the Manchurian, Chang Tse-chuang, who had arranged the 1973 kidnapping of the two Russian doctors.

At the same time hundreds of Lahu, Wa, Akha and other hill tribe boys, some as young as nine years old, were conscripted for basic military training, adding to the TRC's multi-ethnic flavour. Indeed, of all the 'Shan' nationalist armies, the SUA and later the TRC were always the most ethnically mixed. For example, though throughout the 1980s the grumbling narcotics war along the Thai border with Khun Sa's long-time 'Chinese' KMT rivals continued, I was surprised to find in meetings with Khun Sa and the TRC leaders that Chinese is a frequently used language of communication, especially in commerce.[66] In ethnic diversity the TRC thus came to rival the CPB, though, notably, without any Burman influence. But unlike the predominantly Shan SSPP, the TRC demanded that all other ethnic forces in the Shan State join its army.

The scale of this debacle finally brought some sense of proportion to the SSPP movement, which throughout this turbulent period was the only ethnic Shan force actually fighting the *Tatmadaw*. After the premature death from ill health in 1984 at the young age of 37 of the northern SSPP leader, Hso Noom, leadership passed to Sai Lek (a former 3rd brigade commander) and a group of veteran nationalist leaders who had survived the many hardships of the past 20 years together. Less dogmatic than many of their fallen or departed comrades, they readmitted Hso Ten to the party leadership and set about consolidating their position in the more populous north of the state through a prudent combination of joint military operations with both the CPB and their NDF allies, the KIO and PSLO. In 50 small-scale engagements in 1985 alone the SSA claimed to have killed 223 government troops and to have wounded 340 others.[67] Whereas the TRC largely relied on military strength, the SSPP, like the KIO in the Kutkai region to the north, continued to administer an effective system of village, youth, women and parent-teacher organisations in its 'liberated territories'. Into the late 1980s SSPP base areas still ringed Lashio, Hsipaw, Kyaukme and most other towns in the central and north-west Shan State.

It was thus the SSPP, along with the KIO and PNO, rather than the TRC or CPB, that gained a flood of new student recruits during the 1988 democracy uprising; by the time of the 1989 CPB collapse, the joint SSPP-PSLO-KIO forces in the northern Shan State were by some way the NDF's largest. Ironically, at this point Hso Ten, who had remained close to the CPB throughout, once again sided with his former CPB colleagues who had declared a ceasefire with the *Tatmadaw* and, breaking with Sai Lek, began the third major split in the SSPP movement.

The Karenni National Progressive Party

The Pao and Shan movements were by no means the only nationalist parties to be badly divided by the activities of the CPB's NEC in this period. Two more NDF members suffered the same divisions due, they allege, to CPB manipulations as the communist Politburo sought to expand the party's influence west.

The next was the KNPP. Though a founder NDUF member in 1959, the KNPP withdrew from the NDUF in the late 1960s after joining the NUF. This, according to KNPP chairman, Saw Maw Reh, a former bombardier in the British Army,

allowed the KNPP to concentrate on re-establishing the historic right of independence once legally enjoyed by the Karenni (Kayah) State.[68] Taking control of the
fast growing cattle and black market trade with Thailand, which passed through
KNPP check-points along the east bank of the Salween River, the KNPP built up
its military wing, reaching a peak strength of 1,000 troops under arms, including
guerrilla units which roved far and wide across the mountains into the adjoining
Shan and Karen States.

The arrival of Tha Kalei and soldiers from the SSNLO during the 1973/4 Pao
split changed this situation. Equipped with copies of Mao's *Little Red Book* and
often in the company of U Tun Myint and other CPB cadres from the 108 region,
together they tried to convince younger KNPP officers to change the KNPP's
'nationalist' line and allow CPB troops to pass through their territory to the south
and west. Initially the KNPP leaders agreed to allow an advance force of 140 CPB
troops (mostly ethnic Was) to stay at the KNPP's northern base at the Tatamaw
ferry on the Salween River. According to Abel Tweed, then a junior KNPP
officer, he was told by Tun Myint, one of only two ethnic Burmans in the CPB
team that came down: 'You are only speaking about the national question. That is
very narrow. You cannot succeed. But join the party and together we can defeat
Rangoon and establish communism.'[69]

Like many other nationalist leaders in Burma, Saw Maw Reh, Aung Than Lay
and the KNPP's British-trained old-guard were worried by the rapid changes in
South-East Asia brought about by the communist victory in Indo-China in 1975.
In the 1970s there was also growing CPT influence along the Karennis' eastern
border. After years of isolation, many felt distinctly uneasy about the nagging
CPT/CPB presence on their doorstep. Wary of fighting the CPB, they also
worried that younger KNPP members might be secretly sympathetic to the
communists' aims and objectives. Thus, having refused to join the National
United Liberation Front with U Nu in 1970, the KNPP joined the KNU and
southern SSPP leaders in a succession of meetings in the mid-1970s to form a
new non-Burman nationalities front to stand up to both the BSPP and CPB. As a
result, the KNPP was a founder member of both the 1975 FNDF and the NDF of
May 1976.[70]

This, however, did not defuse the situation. In 1977 the Karennis' close cousins
and allies in the hills to the north-west, the Kayan New Land Party (KNLP),
resigned from the NDF to join Tha Kalei and the SSNLO in allying with the CPB.
An estimated one-third of KNPP leaders, such as Abel Tweed and Ramond Htoo,
are also ethnic Kayans and, in principle, both parties supported the eventual
integration of Kayan and Karenni territory. Shwe Aye and the KNLP leaders
immediately travelled up to Panghsang to try and organise a regular supply of
arms and ammunition from the NEC. Several younger Karenni leaders,
encouraged by SSNLO and CPB cadres, felt the KNPP should now do likewise.[71]

The KNPP was in a state of growing confusion. Eventually 200 KNPP delegates
from across the Kayah State gathered for the party's Fourth Congress at its general
headquarters at Huai Plong on the Pai River in September/October 1977 to try and
resolve these issues and to clarify the KNPP's relations with Thailand, where
incorrect rumours had already reached intelligence officers that it had joined the
CPB. Though no final decisions were taken, Saw Maw Reh agreed to stand down
temporarily from the leadership, which passed to the 39 year-old son of one of the
five Karenni *Sawbwas*, Hte Buphe. A Rangoon University history graduate and

former director of culture in the BSPP's Kayah State government, Buphe was a popular choice amongst Karenni youth. Meanwhile, following in the footsteps of the KNUP's Dawna team, the congress decided to send a KNPP study mission to the north to hold talks with the CPB, SSPP, KIO and PSLO to investigate the true situation in the NEC for themselves.

It turned out to be a nightmare trip. On 16 April 1978, shortly after setting out, the KNPP Chief-of-Staff, Saw Mun Na, was killed in an ambush by government soldiers when he entered a village market in the southern Shan State. Struggling on without a leader, the 140-troop column eventually reached the SSPP's headquarters in the mountains near Lashio only to find that the SSPP was also deeply divided over the question of working with the CPB. The KNPP team then promptly split into two groups. According to Abel Tweed (who led the larger faction which returned home), on their arrival the SSA commanders, Sai Zam Muang and Bo Pan Aung, who had just returned from Panghsang, told them of their disillusionment with the CPB and strongly urged them to turn back immediately.[72] The SSPP's acting president, Sai Myint Aung, however, quietly took aside a smaller group of 13 soldiers, led by a former schoolteacher Than Nyunt, and, giving them food and supplies, encouraged them to go on to the CPB alone.

Meanwhile, back in the Kayah State, fighting broke out between the two KNPP factions. Angered by the recent defection of a few ex-KNUP troops to the CPB, the KNU president, Bo Mya, sent troops to help out his NDF allies, Hte Buphe and Saw Maw Reh. Arguments still continue over what actually caused the bloodshed to start. Matters were not helped by CPB commissar, Tun Myint, choosing this moment to send 80 PA troops through KNPP territory to Mae Senam in the south, ostensibly to make contact with the CPT, but in reality, Saw Maw Reh alleges, to support KNPP defectors who were planning to join them. This, however, is a charge the mutineers deny.[73] Sixty KNPP troops broke away, led by the KNPP's young general-secretary, Sai Thiha, an ethnic Shan, who was killed in an ambush by Saw Maw Reh loyalists near Me Se on 17 October. In the following weeks more deaths followed.

Though the KNPP had long enjoyed widespread support throughout the Karenni region, the split in such a small nationalist movement proved disastrous and the KNPP has never regained its former strength. A neglected and sparsely populated mountain backwater, the Kayah State rivals only the Chin, Wa and Naga hills in its chronic underdevelopment. Indeed the KNPP was briefly forced to turn to the KMT for financial help and, as further proof of the broad spread of the KMT empire, several thousand rounds of ammunition were allegedly donated by the president of China Airlines, who had met a KNPP delegation in Bangkok.[74]

For the KNPP worse was still to follow. At the end of 1978 the Karenni defectors formed a rival force, the Karenni State Nationalities Liberation Front (KSNLF) and sent 38 members, led by a former student leader, Nya Maung Me, to Panghsang to join Than Nyunt and undergo training with the CPB. By 1981 they were ready to return. Separating into small cells of 10 to 30 troops (and with the help of the SSNLO, KNLP and CPB 4045 and 4046 battalions), they began infiltrating through the mountains into the north, west and south of the state to open up a direct line of contact with CPT cadres in the Mae Hong Son Province across the Thai border.

Saw Maw Reh and the KNPP leaders were outraged. The same year CPB forces under Politburo members, Khin Maung Gyi and Pe Tint, accompanied by a number of CPT cadres returning from China, again began pushing down into the south-west Shan State in strength. Tun Myint and Tha Kalei increased the pressure by asking the KNPP for normal relations to be restored and requested they be allowed to send their troops through KNPP territory to the south. The KNPP, however, refused any discussion until all the guns the KSNLF faction had 'stolen' at the time of the split were returned.[75]

Fighting immediately broke out between the two Karenni factions and, in April 1982, the KNPP killed Than Nyunt during a *Tatmadaw* offensive, after he had entered a front-line KNPP camp near Pasawng for talks. His death did not discourage his comrades. With the KSNLF leadership now taken up by Nya Maung Me, a cousin of Abel Tweed, the KNPP's new Chief-of-Staff, they continued trying to organise political cells in the towns and villages by preaching the virtues of 'people's democracy', though they objected to being tagged 'Karenni communists' by the KNPP. 'We are not communists,' explained Nya Maung Me. 'We are fighting for democracy. The KNPP stands only for Karennis and an independent Karenni State. We want to represent all the races of Karenni, including the Shan minority, in a federal union of Burma.'[76] With only 150 men under arms by 1988, against the KNPP's 500, they were protected by their CPT allies on the Thai border to the south and by the SSNLO and KNLP to the north; but they were to become as well known as the KNPP and KNLP for their underground movement in the state capital, Loikaw. Concentrating on the more populous area west of the Salween River, in the 1988 democracy uprising Loikaw was one of the only towns in the whole of Burma where the *Tatmadaw* claimed to have found first-hand evidence of CPB activity inside the city; for their part, KNLP and KSNLF leaders freely admit sending arms and cadres into the towns during the protests and in the aftermath of the Saw Maung coup, along with the KNPP, they gained dozens of new recruits.[77]

Like the SSNLO, they were left high and dry by the 1989 CPB mutinies and immediately resumed contact with their former KNPP comrades. But unlike the SSNLO, which began talks on reunification with its PNO rivals, serious differences remained with the KNPP which, while supporting the idea of a federal union of Burma, still insisted that the independence of Karenni and the right of self-determination be established first. Only then, according to Saw Maw Reh, could the Karenni people freely decide exactly what political rights they wanted.[78]

The Lahu Nationalist Movement
The Lahu National United Party (LNUP) was the second NDF member to split over the question of working with the CPB. Still headed by Pu Kyaung Lon, the aged Lahu chieftain, 'man-god' and former KKY commander, who had begun the Lahu uprising in late 1972 (see Chapter 5), the LNUP had always been a loosely organised militia. With control of the dominating mountain stronghold at Doi Larng on the Thai border and able to call on an estimated 1,000 villagers under arms, the LNUP was the most powerful force in the mountains of the Mong Hsat region. A member of the majority Lahu Nyi (Red Lahu) sub-group, Pu Kyaung Lon's following, while winning over a number of Christian recruits, was strongest amongst the traditional Animist Lahus who still practise slash and burn hill farming; he claimed 200,000 supporters scattered in small communities in the densely forested mountains lying between the Thai and Chinese borders in the south-east Shan State.[79] (Kyaung Lon also recruited a number of Lahu soldiers

living on the Thai side of the border.) The LNUP joined the NDF shortly after its founding in 1976 and occasionally worked with both the KMT and SSPP, but always maintained a reputation for independence and extreme bravery, even fool-hardiness, in battle. Most rivals, including the *Tatmadaw*, gave LNUP soldiers a wide berth.

The LNUP's problems really began with the old man's death in 1979 at the reputed age of 112. Leadership passed to his 'Buddhist' son, Paya Kya Oo, who with the help of local Chinese traders quickly built up Doi Larng into a notorious casino town, replete with gambling dens and heroin refineries run by the infamous trafficker, Lao Su, who had escaped from a Thai gaol in 1977. This boom time was shattered in 1981 when the town was raided and burnt down in a surprise *Tatmadaw* attack. Meanwhile, little noticed, a young LNUP lieutenant, Abi, whom Kyaung Lon had sent to Panghsang with 70 troops in 1977 on another ethnic minority 'study mission', returned at the end of 1981 with several CPB cadres and, instead of reuniting with Paya Kya Oo, set up his own camp nearby. (In 1970 Kyaung Lon himself reputedly visited China, where over 300,000 Lahus live as a guest of the CCP.) As more CPB troops came down to join him, Kya Oo was quickly squeezed out. This split, LNUP supporters allege, left the door open to Khun Sa, who in January 1982 had been ousted by the Thai Army from his general headquarters at Ban Hin Taek across the Thai border nearby.[80] Five of Abi's heavily outnumbered troops were killed and seven wounded as a 700-strong SUA strike force overran Lahu positions on the Doi Larng mountain, while Kya Oo and 200 LNUP remnants retired to the village of Mong Na nearby. First, however, they killed Lao Su, who had unwisely thrown in his lot with Abi.

Eventually, in January 1984, a dispirited Kya Oo and 130 followers surrendered to the nearest Burmese Army garrison in Mong Ton. Here they were reformed by the *Tatmadaw* into a local *Pyi Thu Sit* defence militia and, less than a year later, disappeared back underground with their weapons to form the present-day Lahu National Organisation (LNO). In late 1985 the LNO, a much weaker force than the old LNUP, was readmitted to the NDF and given military training by the KNPP and PNO under the NDF Central Command.

Meanwhile, Abi's force, with full military backing from the CPB's 6th brigade, continued to organise in Lahu villages in the south-east Shan State. In retaliation, the Burmese Army razed dozens of Lahu villages lying between Mong Hsat and CPB base areas around Kengtung to prevent the CPB gaining a firm foothold in the region and causing thousands more Lahu refugees to flee into the mountains and forests. As an illustration of the haphazard nature of survival on this wild frontier, Abi was assassinated in 1985 at Na Ban Kaw village near Loi Kham, a murder variously attributed to both MIS and SUA agents. Following his death his small Lahu force, now led by Thein Myint, a mixed race Indian-Shan from Loilem, was largely taken over by the CPB, which at the time of the 1989 mutinies had sent down several hundred Wa and Lahu troops and pushed right up to Khun Sa's SUA/TRC positions around the base of the Doi Larng mountain. To the anger of Kya Oo, Khun Pang and the LNO leaders, CPB cadres were now clearly trying to establish their own base area in former LNUP strongholds on the Thai border among the Lahu villagers they themselves were initially responsible for dividing.[81]

Such accusations form a common pattern among nationalist groups the CPB has contacted in the NEC. They appear to substantiate the view of Skaw Ler Taw and the KNUP leaders that such divisions were the deliberate result of tactics the CPB learnt from Mao Zedong: to work with 'progressives', win over 'neutrals', and isolate 'conservatives'; communism on the Chinese model, they argued, would provide the answer to all Burma's problems.

The evidence for these charges is compelling. Starting with the KNU in 1963, numerous nationalist movements have split at one time or another over the question of working with the CPB: the KIO, SSNLO-PNO, SSPP, KNPP and LNUP. Some groups have survived; others, such as the SSAE, were absorbed. From Than Nyunt of the KNPP to Hso Ten of the SSPP, from Tha Kalei of the SSNLO to Abi of the LNUP, there has been a succession of talented nationalist leaders, picked out by the CPB as being particularly progressive or open minded, who have been secretly persuaded to defect to the CPB or turn against their 'reactionary' leaders. Despite the frequent promise of arms, few parties have ever gained in military and political strength. The harsh verdict of Khun Okker, an influential leader of both the PNO and NDF, who made frequent undercover journeys throughout eastern and north-east Burma in the 1970s and 1980s, is telling: 'There is no party which has been stronger because of CPB protection and support.'[82]

And this list is incomplete. The names of the Kokang Resistance Force of the 1960s, or of the Naga National Council (which split, partly through CCP influence, into the present-day Federal Government of Nagaland and NSCN factions on the Indian border today) also could be added. But perhaps the most poignant group is one that was completely crushed by the CPB's invasion of the eastern Shan State in the early 1970s, the ethnic Wa movement.

The Wa Nationalist Movement

It was in fact an ethnic Wa, Bo Maung, a mutineer from the Union Military Police, still much revered by Wa nationalists, who had kicked off the Shan uprising with the 1959 attack on Tangyan. Asia's estimated two million Was (including Palaung-Was), divided between China, Thailand and the eastern Shan State, live in what is undoubtedly one of the last great mountain wildernesses in the modern world. No reliable population statistics exist; the Chinese authorities put the present Wa population of Yunnan at just over 300,000, while the Lawa population in Thailand is numbered in the hundreds. As a result the Wa, along with their Lahu and Akha neighbours, have become one of the most marginalised of all the minority peoples in South-East Asia.

British rule scarcely reached into the Wa heartlands in the Trans-Salween region. Colonial records pejoratively recognised only two kinds of Wa subgroups, the 'wild' and the 'tame'. Virtually the only Wa custom to have been closely recorded was a predilection for taking human heads which, displayed on posts on the approach to each village, were believed to ward off evil spirits and ensure good crops. Indeed, as late as 1939 a Sikh doctor, resplendent with turban and beard, accompanying a British route-march into the Wa substates, had to be rushed out under military escort when Wa head-hunters came looking for this near mythical catch.[83]

In reality, traditional Wa society, like that of the hill Kachins and Karens, consisted of hundreds of clannish and often feuding village communities in an ever-changing amalgam of alliances and confederations rather than the political 'states' that British administration had implied. None the less Maha San, son of the last *Sawbwa* of Ving Ngun, claims it was Wa 'nationalism' that kept the colonial government at bay: 'When we were united, even the British could not control our land.'[84] Like the Kokang substate controlled by the Yang *Sawbwa* family to the north, in the 1950s the northern and southern Wa substates under the three educated *Sawbwa* families of Mong Loen, Nawi and Ving Ngun continued to be run on almost feudal lines. The picture changed dramatically with the bush-fire spread of the Shan uprising in the early 1960s and Ne Win's military coup. A number of Was, such as Sao Noom, the son of the Mong Loen *Sawbwa*, joined with the SSA. The *Tatmadaw* responded by disarming the Was of Nawi and Mong Loen, but the remote Was of Ving Ngun, led by Maha San and his older brother Maha Khoung, put up a spirited resistance and pushed the army back.

The *Tatmadaw*, however, soon found itself battling with an even more formidable foe. Throughout the 1950s the AFPFL government had for the most part turned a blind eye to the war between the KMT remnants of Gen. Li Mi and the Chinese Red Army on the Yunnan border (see Chapter 9). But in the early 1960s, after the second cosmetic 'evacuation' of KMT forces to Taiwan, Gen. Tuan Shi-wen's Fifth Army and several hundred intelligence operatives from the First Independent Unit of Gen. Ma Ching-kuo reactivated their listening stations along the Yunnan border with a fresh infusion of Taiwanese funds. After recruiting several hundred local Wa, Lahu and Shan soldiers, the KMT teams once again began their cross-border sabotage missions.[85]

In the 1950s China had countered with the Red Army, but this time Lin Piao replied by sending CCP cadres to organise amongst Wa villagers on the Burma side of the border. According to Maha San, at some point during 1965 they stopped using the name 'CCP' and instead called themselves 'CPB'. And with some communities already divided by the KMT's unwelcome presence, they had some early success. This softly-softly approach, however, soon changed and from 1967/8, with the formation of the NEC, it was made clear to Wa leaders that the 'CPB' was prepared to use force. The tougher strategy also had its rewards, and the promise of arms swiftly won over two local Wa chieftains, Kyauk Ni Lai and Pauk Yo Chang.

The Wa movement was now to be split even further by a third political manoeuvre from outside, this time by the Burmese Army. Faced with the twin challenges of the SSA and CPB, the *Tatmadaw* invited the Ving Ngun force to join the KKY programme and, in February 1969, over 850 heavily armed Wa rebels, commanded by Maha San and his relatives, marched into Tangyan to pledge their loyalty to the union.[86] Next to the Kokang KKY of Lo Hsing-han and the Loimaw force of Khun Sa, they were to make up the third largest KKY militia in the Shan State. For Maha San and the Wa leaders, already under pressure from the KMT, SSA, *Tatmadaw* and Khun Sa's KKY, the *Tatmadaw*'s KKY programme seemed the best way of stemming the CPB advance. In fact it was to fracture the Wa movement even further and several ever smaller local Wa factions immediately sprang up as the KKY organisation spiralled out of control. This meant that by the time of the CPB NEC's main advance into the Wa substates during 1972/3, what was left of the Wa nationalist movement was already hopelessly divided.

The CPB's victory in the Wa region, east of the Salween, was total. CPB cadres told Wa villagers that if they joined the PA they would be fighting for the liberation of an autonomous Wa province, like those in China, and would form the vanguard force to liberate the rest of Burma. Once achieved, they would be free to go back home. The results of this party line were impressive. No exact figures are available, but Wa leaders estimate at least one member of each Wa family has at some stage served in the PA. With up to 12,000 ethnic Was, including village militia, serving in the PA at any one time, the Was have for the last two decades formed the largest ethnic group under rebel arms, along with the Karens in Lower Burma. Undoubtedly in such a poverty-stricken backwater, the offer of a uniform, food and modern weaponry has proven a powerful enticement to a sturdy mountain people fighting for what they believed was their independence. Wa soldiers have been much admired (and feared) for their outstanding bravery and, over the years, have been keenly recruited by the KMT, SUA and *Tatmadaw*. Their casualty rates, however, have been appalling; Wa leaders calculate over 30,000 young Wa men have died in the PA alone.[87] Moreover, Wa leaders were slow to graduate through the political ranks of the administration and it took until 1985 for the two Wa leaders, Kyauk Ni Lai and Pauk Yo Chang, to be appointed to the CPB CC. Significantly, both were to play a leading role in the 1989 mutinies.

But back in 1973 the 'traditionalist' movement of the Wa *Sawbwas* and chieftains was effectively destroyed by the twin intrusions of the CPB and *Tatmadaw*. Already pushed out of the Wa substates by the CPB invasion, Ne Win's decision to disband the KKY in 1972/3 saw Maha San and the Wa leaders go underground along with Lo Hsing-han's Kokang force and Khun Sa's SUA to ally with the SSPP. Coming down with a few hundred troops and their families to the Thai border, Maha San settled in the SSPP's southern base area near Mong Mai and in July 1976 established the Wa National Army (WNA). Working closely with the SSPP and NDF, his commanders slowly began forming a new military force to try and regain their homelands.

In 1978 the fledgling WNA was caught in another unexpected twist of fate. In a meeting with the SSPP's Chief-of-Staff, Sai Zam Muang, shortly before his disappearance, Maha San was told that since the SSPP was now allied with the CPB and was receiving arms from China, it could no longer help the WNA.[88] Moreover, though he did not disguise his own doubts over the CPB, Zam Muang claimed that the CPB Politburo had promised him that the SSPP would eventually be allowed, as a 'revolutionary' ally, to take over the administration of the Wa 'liberated' territories once the situation had stabilised. Therefore the WNA soldiers, if they wanted to return north to their homes, would have to join forces with the SSPP.

This ultimatum by their hosts caused the WNA to break into several small factions with two officers, Maha Sai and Ngyi Aung, defecting with their men to the SSPP before surrendering under the 1980 amnesty with the remnants of Lo Hsing-han's Kokang KKY. Maha San himself moved to Pieng Luang to stay with Gon Jerng's SURA where he tried to resurrect the WNA. Two other nationalist groups, one led by Ai Hsiao-hsu, son of the Yawngbre *Sawbwa*, and his wife Mrs Li Yi Seng (*aka* Daw Yok Swe), Maha San's sister-in-law, and the other by Bo Kan Seur, built up their own forces with KMT backing around the military base at Pang Taw further east on the Thai border. Nearby another 100-strong Wa force led by Ta Ma, which was completely under KMT control, also set up camp, reputedly as a front for narcotics trafficking; opium addiction has remained an endemic problem amongst Wa soldiers along the Thai border. None the less, all four forces were able to enlist a steady supply of recruits in the early 1980s from the Kengtung area and the estimated 10,000 Wa refugee families who had fled westwards in the wake of the CPB invasion. Eventually, in March 1982, Mrs Li Yi Seng, Kan Seur, Maha San and his long-time colleague, Khun Lu Maha, a Rangoon University graduate and son of the Nawi *Sawbwa*, agreed to merge their 500 troops into a new WNA.

No sooner was this unity achieved than the Wa movement became embroiled in the bloody border war that broke out in 1982/3 after the KMT's main rival, Khun Sa's SUA, was driven out of Thailand. Hundreds of Wa soldiers and their families were dislocated by the fighting, which saw the SUA quickly overrun the SSPP, PNO and LNUP strongholds around Doi Larng and Mong Mai, and Khun Sa eventually join forces with Gon Jerng's TRC. Once again the Was, who had shown a marked gullibility in previous political horse-trading, fell victim to the upheavals. Exploiting differences in the WNA leadership, Gen. Li Wen-huan's KMT remnants, by now little more than an armed merchant militia, used their wealth to build up the Wa National Council (WNC) faction of Ai Hsiao-hsu and Kan Seur on the Doi Ang Kham mountain to try and recapture Doi Larng from the TRC for what were presumed to be their own business purposes. Meanwhile in the west, with financial help from other local KMT veterans, the NDF armed and encouraged the Wa National Organisation faction of Maha San and Khun Lu Maha to seize back the strategic Mae Aw-Mong Mai gateway to the Shan State for its own NDF forces. In both mountain locations hundreds of Was were killed or wounded over the next few years in hand to hand fighting and sporadic artillery bombardments, which continued right through the 1988 democracy uprising. With thousands of Wa troops also serving in the CPB PA, *Tatmadaw* and TRC (Maha San's brother, Maha Ja, even defected from the government in Tangyan to join the TRC in 1986), it meant that at the time of the 1989 CPB mutinies, ethnic Was were serving in no less than five proxy armies in the Shan State: those of the CPB, *Tatmadaw*, KMT, TRC and NDF. 'Everyone is using Wa soldiers and everyone is trying to ally with the Wa,' said Maha San. 'But it is the Wa who are dying and it is the Wa who always get the blame for the opium trade.'[89]

During 1987, following the 1986 joint military pact between the NDF and CPB, a *rapprochement* was achieved between the NDF and the different Wa leaders; Maha San himself went for talks with Khun Sa and met his brother. The WNC faction of Ai Hsiao-hsu, in particular, rapidly grew in size with the help of SSPP and KIO troops who had dug in around the Doi Ang Kham mountain; this position was reinforced by the arrival of several hundred Wa troops from the CPB's 6th brigade (now their NDF allies), who had come down to the Thai border to begin their own attacks on the *Tatmadaw* and TRC. For once enjoying a breathing space, the WNC was able to send back several armed columns to the north to test the political waters and bring back new recruits. Some NDF leaders training the WNC even claimed they were secretly working on CPB defections and said they were encouraged by the disillusionment with the CPB, which many of the Wa troops in the PA privately expressed.[90]

But when the CPB mutinies occurred, the WNA forces on the Thai border were still very much bystanders in what was a largely internal CPB affair. Maha San and the WNA delegation, which travelled up to the CPB's former general head-quarters at Panghsang in the wake of the 1989 coup, were at first treated with distrust and excluded from any political input. Meanwhile, the main breakaway

Wa force led by Kyauk Ni Lai, still showing the influence of years of CPB propaganda, went ahead with ceasefire talks with the *Tatmadaw* under the deliberately 'anti-racial' and non-Wa name, Burma Democracy Solidarity Army.[91] Only later in 1989 did they join forces with Ai Hsiao-hsu's WNC and reform under the new nationalist name, the United Wa State Army.

The result of all these intrigues has been that the 'rebel' ethnic Wa movement, like those of the Pao, Karenni, Lahu and Shan, has become deeply divided by the maelstrom in insurgent politics brought about by the CPB's activities in eastern Burma over the last 20 years; its future, despite the high optimism of 1989, remains impossible to predict.

The Kayan New Land Party

Perhaps the only party the CPB won over by argument alone and which still retained its identity intact, was the Kayan New Land Party (KNLP). Formed on 8 August 1964, the KNLP has been led for over two decades by another Rangoon University student of the early 1960s, Shwe Aye (*aka* Nyaint Lu Tha), who took over the leadership from the veteran nationalist leader and wartime resistance hero, Bo Pyan, after he surrendered at the end of 1964 (see Chapter 5).

The Mongpai (Mobye) substate home of the Kayan minority on the border between the Karen and Shan peoples of Burma has throughout history been a particularly complex and volatile region of the country. Personal disagreements between the predominantly Catholic Kayans, like Bo Pyan, and Baptist Karennis, like Saw Maw Reh, were largely responsible for the continued separation of Mongpai and its estimated 30,000 inhabitants from their close Karenni cousins in 1948. With the spread of the Kayan insurrection in the 1960s, the *Tatmadaw* tried to exploit these religious differences by promoting the Buddhist community and minority Shans. The BSPP appointed to government office another wartime hero, Bo Hein Zar, a Kayan Buddhist who had originally been appointed by the Shan princes to take care of their interests after the Kayan uprising of 1936-8 which ended *Sawbwa* rule. These differences persisted and eventually in the democracy uprising of 1988 Bo Pyan and his son rejoined the KNLP, while Bo Hein Zar's grandson, Kyaw Zan, still allegedly trying to revive the Buddhist-Christian issue, opposed them as chairman of the BSPP's Mongpai township council.

In the countryside, by contrast, Shwe Aye and the KNLP's underground organisers had some success overcoming these religious and ethnic differences. The party grew steadily in size, recruiting Buddhists and Christians, it claimed, in equal numbers. Territorial demarcation has, however, always been a problem for the KNLP and, like the more numerous Paos, the Kayans very much see themselves as a 'Karen' minority on the Shan State borderlands.[92] Kayan nationalists have always wanted to represent all Burma's estimated 100,000 Kayan-Yinbaw peoples, including those elsewhere in the Shan State and in the Pyinmana hills; in the early years this led to political disagreements with the KNPP, which also includes many Kayans. In fact, though relations with the KNPP have generally remained close, it was on the advice of Than Aung and leaders of the KNUP in the nearby Toungoo hills in June 1964 that Kayan activists finally decided to turn the KNLP into a distinctive non-Karen, non-Karenni movement.[93]

Always sympathetic to the socialist philosophies of the KNUP, which Shwe Aye initially joined from university, to avoid encirclement and *Tatmadaw* attack, the KNLP's hard-core force of between 200 and 250 armed volunteers had to keep on the constant move, usually in the more traditionalist villages of the 'long-necked' Kayan in the forests and mountains along the Shan-Kayah State borders. (From the beginning the KNLP discouraged the curious custom of Kayan women to elongate their necks with heavy brass rings; it now estimates that fewer than 100 women still continue the tradition.) Despite their low troop numbers, with this loyal backing KNLP cadres have survived several major *Four Cuts* campaigns.

Arms and ammunition, however, have always been a serious problem. In the early 1970s Shwe Aye (a member of the KNUP's Nationalities United Front) attended several conferences at KNU bases along the Thai border in search of Western aid to help his land-locked force. At this time the KNLP was virtually dependent for its weapons and supplies on military seizures and in 1976 it became a founder member of the NDF. One year later, disappointed with the low levels of military aid the NDF could offer and unhappy about its anti-CPB stance, the KNLP turned to Tun Myint and the CPB leaders in the nearby 108 region. Travelling north to Panghsang and China, Shwe Aye spent one year studying communism with the CPB and CCP before returning in 1979 with over 100 AK47s and a number of mortars and RPG rocket launchers.[94] Again the CCP refused to aid a nationalities party direct. In Kunming, Shwe Aye says he was bluntly told by one CCP official: 'Communists give only to communists: governments to governments, so we cannot give anything to you.'[95] None the less, under such die-hard officers as Ikaphyu (killed in action in 1982), the KNLP became a close ally of the CPB and the SSNLO and KSNLF; it was often bolstered in military operations by up to two battalions of CPB troops, which travelled down from the 108 region or the Chinese border to join it. In textbook Maoist fashion, the KNLP, SSNLO, KSNLF and CPB shared a common strategy of concentrating their efforts on working with the rural farmers and peasantry.

With these powerful allies, the KNLP, never as ideologically dogmatic as the SSNLO or CPB, was able to build up a highly effective guerrilla base area in the strategic range of mountains along the Paunglaung River above Pyinmana, and this finally gave front-line CPB troops a tantalising view over the Sittang Valley to the beckoning hills of their former Pegu Yomas strongholds beyond.

For a moment it appeared as if years of careful planning by the CPB's military strategists had come to fruition. This, however, was as far as they were going to get.

PART FOUR
THE 1980s — A DECADE OF
UPHEAVAL

17

The Democracy Uprising and the CPB

With the abrasive breakdown of the 1980/1 peace talks, CPB military and political planning underwent a marked change of direction. Continuing to consolidate their strongholds along the Chinese border as part of the Politburo's 1979 'defensive warfare' strategy, CPB leaders agreed to embark on an all-out political offensive to broaden the united front by approaching all other opposition forces, 'without discriminating right or left', across the country.[1] According to Kyin Maung, Politburo member in charge of underground organisation, the key plank in the CPB's programme was the CC's declaration, made after the breakdown of the talks, that 'in order to change the present state of affairs, the one-party military dictatorship should be replaced by a multi-party system'.[2] But largely isolated in the remote mountains of the north-east, it was clear that the success of this new line would hinge on the CPB's ability to forge new alliances with the country's diverse ethnic nationalist forces. These, it was intended, would be used as 'stepping stones' on the PA's march back into the Burman heartlands.

A final reorganisation of CPB operational areas in north-east Burma was begun which, with a few alterations in 1988, was to be the party's last. Four main military regions were established:

- The 'Northern Region' (or Bureau), headquartered at Mong Ko, which was comprised of three regular PA brigades, the 1st (Mogok-Mong Mit), 2nd (Mong Ko) and 3rd (Shweli Valley), as well as troops from the '101 war zone' in the Kachin State.
- The 'North-Eastern Region', comprising six brigades, which though based along the Chinese border frequently moved to the south and west; the 6th (Northern Kengtung-Mong Hsat-Thai border), 7th (Southern Wa), 12th (Northern Wa), 768 (Mong Yang district), 851 (Central Security-Panghsang), and 859 (Northern Kengtung).
- The 'Mekong River Division' (formerly '815 war zone'), which had two full brigades, the 9th based at Keng Khan and the 11th at Mong La, and three mobile battalions, the 1st, 3rd and 14th which operated in the mountains down

355

to the Mekong River-Laotian border.
* And finally, the key 'Central Region' (the former '108 region') in the western Shan State which consisted of four mobile battalions, the 4045 (West Mong Nai), 4046 (East Langkho), 4047 (Loi Tsang) and 502 (Laikha), which often combined with the SSNLO, KNLP and KSNLF.[3]

The NEC's Last Offensive: 1981-7

With 10,000 regular troops, 5,000 local township guards and an indeterminate number of local militia units, the PA was still a force to be reckoned with and probably equalled the armed forces of the CPB's main rival, the National Democratic Front (NDF). In addition, there were also small party units active in Arakan and Tenasserim, which could each call on another 200-300 troops, as well as a number of highly secret underground cells led by Task Force 4828, which mainly operated in Mandalay, Rangoon and Lower Burma.

To support this change in tactics, from mid-1981 high-ranking CPB officials, including Politburo members, Thakin Pe Tint, Khin Maung Gyi and Myo Myint, began moving through the Shan State to the west in heavily-armed columns up to 1,000 troops strong, holding talks with different ethnic forces on their way. According to one Karenni National Progressive Party (KNPP) leader approached, Johnny Soe, who was later executed by the KNPP for, amongst other things, his alleged pro-CPB sympathies, arms were offered without strings, only the proviso that they not be used in any way 'against the CPB or their allies'.[4]

At first the political offensive met with some success. It was immediately obvious to ethnic leaders, hard-bitten after years of inconclusive arguments with communist cadres, that much of the doctrinaire Maoism of previous years had been dropped. In July 1981 the alliance with the powerful Kachin Independence Organisation (KIO) was strengthened after Ba Thein Tin and the KIO leader, Brang Seng, met to compare notes on the failure of the peace talks. In a joint communiqué both sides agreed Ne Win's intransigence had shown the Burmese peoples that it was the BSPP, not they, who had been responsible for the 'destruction of national unity'.[5] Therefore, to force a settlement to the war, they would need to 'make more efforts to forge stronger unity with all other armed forces' fighting the 'common enemy'.[6]

One year later, reflecting the CPB's softening tone, the CPB, KIO, Shan State Nationalities Liberation Organisation (SSNLO) and Karenni State Nationalities Liberation Front (KSNLF) issued a joint declaration urging the whole country to rise up *en masse* to support their call to end the civil war. Even if the BSPP ignored their demands, they vowed to fight on to 'establish a new Burma which is united, prosperous, democratic, where all nationals enjoy genuine equality'.[7] A new united front was formed and it was agreed to open a joint KIO-CPB military and political training school on the Loi Lem mountain between the Shweli and Salween Rivers where students from all nationalities, including cadres from the KIO's close ally, the Palaung State Liberation Organisation (PSLO), could study. Shortly afterwards the KIO, which had called back all its forces during the 1980/1 negotiations, again began sending troop columns down to the Thai border, headed by Chief-of-Staff Zau Mai, and CC member, Col. Zau Seng, and in 1983 rejoined the NDF.

The CPB's Maoist path, however, had not been abandoned altogether. Cross-border contact had also been established with the Communist Party of Thailand

(CPT) and a number of its cadres travelled to Panghsang in the early 1980s. The CPB publicly applauded the decision at its Fourth National Congress in 1982 to continue the armed struggle along Maoist principles; indeed in 1984, after Deng Xiaoping requested that the Thai communists leave China, it was through CPB-KSNLF territory that they returned home.[8] Even more controversially, the CPB did not hesitate to take advantage of the north-south split in the Shan State Progress Party (SSPP) after its Second Congress in 1981 and the alliance with the northern SSPP leadership, headed by Hso Noom, which had caused the original 1976 Shan split, was resumed. Once again the SSPP agreed to accept Marxist-Leninist-Mao Zedong thought, people's democracy and the CPB as Burma's sole proletarian party.

The advantages to the CPB of these new agreements were immediately obvious. PA troops were allowed to move freely through the territories of their allies to support the hard-pressed Central Bureau under U Tun Myint. At the same time CPB troops, predominantly ethnic Was, were allowed in to strengthen the weaker ethnic forces of the SSNLO, KNLP and KSNLF in the south-west. The strategic gains were impressive. By 1983 regular PA units were able to penetrate back to the hills above their former stronghold of Pyinmana and to begin patrolling up and down the western edge of the Shan plateau. Battles were reported in the townships around Mong Mit, Mogok, Mong Hsu, Laikha, Taunggyi, Hopong and, for the first time, Hsiheng, Pekon, Loikaw, Paunglaung and Pyinmana, emphasising the front line spread of the war. In a typical guerrilla attack in early 1985, for example, a joint PA-SSNLO force ambushed an army column near Hopong, destroying one truck, killing ten soldiers and seizing a quantity of arms and ammunition.[9]

At the same time the CPB deliberately changed its style of reporting the war. Heavy fighting was usually only mentioned when announcing government offensives against CPB base areas. Instead, increased publicity was given to KIO, PSLO, SSNLO, KNLP and SSPP battle claims. For example, when in one of the most spectacular insurgent raids in recent years the KIO captured the town of Singaling Khamti in the Sagaing Division in February 1984, killing 30 troops from the 52nd Infantry Division, taking 50 prisoner, and seizing over 60 weapons and one million kyat in cash, this was prominently featured on the VOPB.[10] Added to these allied attacks, in its own battle reports for 1985, the PA claimed to have killed 398 government troops and wounded another 448 in north-east Burma, but these casualties, it said, were inflicted largely in 'self-defence'.[11]

The undoubted high point in the CPB's united front offensive came in March 1986 when a nine-party delegation from the NDF, headed by U Soe Aung of the Karen National Union (KNU), made the long journey to the CPB's general head-quarters at Panghsang and agreed a joint military alliance with the CPB against the BSPP, based on the primacy of armed struggle. The uncertainties surrounding this controversial agreement are dealt with in Chapter 19 (the KNU withdrew from the pact shortly afterwards), but it did mean that for the first time in nearly 40 years of insurgency all the main armed opposition groups and well over 30,000 rebel troops were allied against the 190,000-strong *Tatmadaw*. By any reckoning it was a highly favourable ratio for fighting a guerrilla war. Undoubted shivers of alarm were felt in Rangoon, which broke a silence of many years to explain these complex developments in insurgent politics in the countryside. The government's tone was scornful, but it did reflect the growing military pressures and the steady loss of lives.[12]

The CPB was also quick to take advantage of the split in the Lahu movement. It completely absorbed the Abi faction after his assassination in 1985 and several hundred Wa and Lahu troops from the PA's 6th brigade moved down into the Mong Hsat-Doi Larng region on the Thai border. In sporadic fighting with both the *Tatmadaw* and Khun Sa's Tailand Revolutionary Council, they set up forward positions near SSPP, KIO and NDF camps on the Doi Angkham mountain.

But this was the limit of the PA's advance. All other military ventures ended in failure. In 1981 Force 180, headed by party veteran Bo Kyaw Moe, frustrated by years of confinement in the east, crossed into the Pinlebu area of the Sagaing Division to try and establish a new base area, but the party was ambushed and Kyaw Moe killed. Two years later Force 102 was guided down from the 101 war zone by the KIO and moved into Katha district in the west. But here too they were attacked and, after two years' constant hardship, were forced to retreat to the Chinese border.

The CPB's most disastrous setback came in early 1987. Encouraged by the new NDF alliance, in November 1986 the PA launched its first major offensive since 1980. With KIO, PSLO and SSPP guerrillas cutting roads across the northern Shan State in support, the CPB attacked and captured the strategically located Hsi-Hsinwan mountain north-east of Namhpakka, close to the China border.[13] Casualties on both sides ran into the hundreds, causing the *Tatmadaw* to interrupt a determined *Four Cuts* offensive against the KNU in south-east Burma. Thousands of reinforcements were rushed north and the government's aging air fleet was once again brought out of moth-balls to bomb CPB positions. One aircraft was shot down, but under this sustained aerial and artillery bombardment, in early December PA units began to retreat from the mountain with government forces in hot pursuit. Sensing they had, quite unexpectedly, seized the initiative, *Tatmadaw* commanders continued to push on through CPB-controlled territory and, in early January, to widespread surprise, seized the key border town of Panghsai, which had been in CPB hands since 1970. With a population of 7,000, it was the largest settlement under PA control and was by some way the most important commercial and trading centre in the CPB administration.

CPB units immediately counter-attacked from the rear and shelled the nearby BSPP-controlled town of Muse, inflicting heavy casualties; the *Tatmadaw*'s 77th Light Infantry Division responded by opening a second front over 100 miles to the south by crossing the Salween River to attack Pangyang, west of the CPB's general headquarters at Panghsang. This time the PA was unable to force the *Tatmadaw* front line back and government units dug into the mountains, east of the Salween, clearly preparing for a long stay. Back in the north, CPB forces re-gathered in the party's Northern Bureau headquarters at Mong Ko and began channelling cross-border trade through new roads. But the loss of Panghsai, after nearly two decades of military and political progress in the north-east, was a damaging psychological and financial blow. The storm clouds were clearly gathering.

Political Obstacles: National Minorities and the Changing Attitude of China
To understand the speed of the CPB collapse which followed, two important factors have to be borne in mind. The first is the role of the NDF and the ethnic nationalists. Critics in Rangoon have always maintained that the CPB secretly directed and manipulated the movements of all its ethnic allies. This, however, is very much a point of contention. The build-up and structure of the NDF is dealt with in Chapter 19, but it is important to emphasise here that NDF members like the Pao National Organisation (PNO) and KNPP, both of which clashed frequently with the CPB in the early 1980s, still viewed the PA's advance with alarm. Seen from their side, the 1986 pact with the CPB was simply a matter of convenience, a means of neutralising the perennial challenge of the CPB's far stronger army.

The NDF parties, especially the KIO, took full advantage. While the KIO, SSPP and PSLO in the north began to work openly with the CPB in timing and launching joint military campaigns, their delegates in KNU and KNPP territory in the south were instrumental in forging much closer military and political ties between NDF members. As a result, in 1985/6 joint NDF battalions and commands were established on three fronts: the Northern Command (KIO, PSLO, SSPP); the Central (KNPP, PNO, WNO, LNO); and Southern (KNU, NMSP, ALP). Though, after getting permission, PA units had the right to travel through these war zones, the new NDF commands quickly came to form another important wedge between CPB strongholds along the China border and front line forces in the Central Bureau in the west.

It was also the KIO leaders, Zau Mai and Zau Seng, who finally convinced fellow NDF members like the KNU and NMSP, weary of the unending war in south-east Burma, to make the historic trip north in 1985/6 to see the scale of the war in the north with their own eyes and investigate the true state of relations between the CPB, KIO and SSPP. Until then this had been a source of much suspicion between NDF members; groups such as the KNU and KNPP were convinced the CPB, KIO and SSPP were simply doing China's bidding. After much argument and soul-searching, the 1985/6 NDF trip through KNPP, SSPP, PSLO, KIO and CPB territory to China finally dispelled all such notions.

The increasing military and political effectiveness of the NDF in the mid-1980s had many important consequences. It helped stave off the CPB's military advance and, for the first time, attracted international attention to Burma's forgotten wars. Equally, the change of CPB thinking on the nationalities question, away from the ill-conceived 'fight or join' policy of the 1960s and 1970s towards a belated acknowledgement of the ethnic nationalist cause, was not lost on the PA's predominantly ethnic minority soldiers who had sacrificed so many lives and years fighting 'racialists' in the CPB's name. For example, with the CPB's recognition of Aung Kham Hti and the PNO in 1986, the communists' Pao ally, the SSNLO, was left very isolated after over ten years' internecine bloodshed. For the next three years various Wa, Pao, Lahu, Shan, Kachin and Palaung troops from both the NDF and CPB armies spent increasing amounts of time together in their forest camps, exchanging political ideas away from the CPB's aging Burman leaders.

The second important point to remember in following the CPB collapse was the reaction of China. Though CPB leaders still had access to China and enjoyed a continued modicum of aid, by the mid-1980s this could in no way be compared with the high levels of a decade earlier.

Nationalist leaders in the Shan and Kachin States, who also made frequent visits to China in the 1970s and 1980s, have long since claimed that despite frequent pledges to international proletarianism, Beijing's main priority has always been the security of its vast borders. Yunnan Province, scene of a bloody border war with Vietnam in the late 1970s, has always been regarded as a particularly dangerous flashpoint on the soft underbelly of the country. Even today CCP officials in Yunnan Province, who have the task of dealing with other political parties in South-East Asia, continue to assert there is no contradiction between longstanding 'party to party' relations and any 'government to government' decisions that are made in Beijing.

If the Chinese government had appeared ambivalent about Burma in the past, in the mid-1980s there were increasing signs that this was beginning to change. A joint border survey was undertaken and visits between Burmese and Chinese leaders stepped up. These culminated in Ne Win's visit to Beijing in May 1985, the first in his capacity as chairman of the BSPP. Deng Xiaoping greeted him as an 'old friend' and Ne Win announced there were no special problems between the two countries.[14] For Ne Win, once reviled in Beijing as the 'Burmese Chiang Kai-shek', the visit represented a considerable diplomatic triumph.

These strengthening ties were unaffected by the dramatic events of both 1988 in Burma and 1989 in China, though no doubt both governments felt that in their crushings of student-led 'democracy' uprisings they had something in common. The basis of their improving relationship, however, was not politics but trade.

Though after Mao's death the CPB was increasingly left to fend for itself, Deng Xiaoping and the new Chinese leadership appeared to be in no great hurry to change their policy towards Burma. Though never officially announced, a crucial decision appeared to have been taken in the early 1980s to target Burma as part of a major trade offensive to revitalise the struggling economies of outlying Provinces (like Yunnan) and to expand China's influence in the region. This some analysts have linked to the reluctant acceptance by Chinese leaders of their inability to control events in Cambodia, which had previously been the main focus of Beijing's concern.

Negotiations continued surreptitiously for two years. In March 1987 the Burmese Minister for Trade visited Kunming and Beijing; in early 1988 the governor of Yunnan Province visited Rangoon. On these visits notes were exchanged agreeing to regularise trade between the two countries. In 1988 official trading began with the exchange of a consignment of 1,500 tons of maize from Burma's Myanmar Export-Import Corporation in return for Chinese milk-powder, soap and toothpaste. A number of new hotels, banks and godowns were also constructed along the border.

It was noticeable that, in opening up this new trade, Chinese officials appeared not to distinguish between 'legal' trade through Burmese army check-points (such as Muse) and Burma's thriving black market trade, much of which passed through KIO or CPB territory. Chinese officials were reportedly not unhappy to see the *Tatmadaw* capture Panghsai, which reopened the old Burma Road (government troops were even reported to have crossed into China to attack CPB positions from the rear). But at the time the Chinese trade offensive was orchestrated the *Tatmadaw* only controlled a 60km stretch of the 2,100km border. One immediate beneficiary of the new trade policy was the KIO, which in 1986 began exporting jade through China to Hong Kong rather than relying on the hazardous mule-train route through the mountains to the Thai border for trans-shipment. Even now (1991) a busy trade through territory held by different armed ethnic groups is still being reported, despite the breakup of the CPB's North-East Command (NEC) and improving relations between Beijing and Rangoon.

Chinese planning was nothing if not thorough. In 1987 the Frontier Trade Division of the Yunnan Province Export Corporation drew up a list of 2,000 items for trade: mainly agricultural, mineral and forestry produce such as rice, jade and timber from Burma, and manufactured consumer goods such as bicycles, medicine and household items from China. To help boost the new trade, Chinese officials were reported to have secretly set up a highly effective economic intelligence gathering system in Burma, with agents in Lashio, Rangoon and Mandalay.

The result of these preparations was, from 1986, a sudden influx of Chinese goods into Burma. In 1987 the Yunnan governor put the value of this cross-border trade at 1,000 million dollars. In 1988 it was estimated to have reached $1,500m and in 1989 was expected to have been close to $2,000m.[15] In markets across the country Chinese-made products, such as cigarettes, crockery and rice-cookers, quickly began to predominate and, by careful price manipulation, undercut the price of locally made goods. An unofficial World Bank report in 1988 warned, as yet another symptom of the disastrous collapse of the Burmese economy under Ne Win's *Burmese Way to Socialism*, that 'Chinese products are driving out many Burmese products'.[16] By agreeing to trade on such disadvantageous terms, one official commented: 'The Burmese military elité are sacrificing Burma's long-term interests for short-term survival.'[17]

The rapid build-up of this trade, much of which previously passed through Thailand, had major geo-political consequences and was one of the main reasons for the Thai government's swift recognition of the Saw Maung regime after the 1988 coup. The *Tatmadaw*'s sustained *Four Cuts* campaign against the KNU in the 1980s in south-east Burma took a heavy toll on the local black market trade (in 1988 KNU officials privately admitted a drop of over 50 per cent in revenues since 1984) and the evidence was painfully visible in the increasing poverty in hundreds of rural Thai villages along the border. The lucrative fishing and timber deals struck with the Saw Maung regime through the personal intervention of the Thai Army Chief-of-Staff Gen. Chaovalit, immediately following the military take-over in Rangoon, were interpreted by many observers as simply an opportunistic attempt to compensate for the ecological devastation of Thailand's own environment and to win back the economic initiative from China. With heavy fighting still continuing between the Burmese Army and the KNU, NMSP, KNPP and other insurgent fronts along the Thai border, the general cross-border trade was still far below the levels of the early 1980s.

Long-term indications are that, despite the apparent changes in Burma since 1988 and the decline of the CPB, trade relations with China will continue to prosper. In October 1989 the most high-powered *Tatmadaw* delegation ever to visit China, including army Chief-of-Staff Lt-Gen. Than Shwe, head of MIS Brig.-Gen. Khin Nyunt, head of the Northern Command Brig.-Gen. Kyaw Ba, and Minister of Trade Col. Abel, travelled to Beijing for convivial talks with Prime Minister Li Peng and their Chinese hosts.[18] Chinese officials at first refused to be drawn into what they described as Burma's 'civil war' and rejected an initial request to sell military supplies to the *Tatmadaw* across the border. But both sides pledged to work for improved trade and military relations and the *Tatmadaw* publicly thanked China for its 'correct stand' on Burma's democracy uprising. Within a year, as the scale of the CPB collapse became clear, the façade of China's neutrality came down and arms sales (including twelve F-6 or F-7 jet fighters and four gunboats) to the value of 1,000 million dollars were allegedly agreed.

If a common thread in China's policy towards Burma over the past decade has been the promotion of trade, various theories have been advanced for the political abandonment of the CPB and the about-turn in attitudes towards the *Tatmadaw*. Indeed, given the convulsions of the last 50 years, there is no reason to believe this will be the final twist. The Burma-China border is likely to remain a turbulent frontier region for many years to come. The engineer of these changes, of course, was Deng Xiaoping and, as he embarked on his economic liberalisation reforms, the CPB's hard-line support for the Cultural Revolution was never forgotten.

None the less, aid to the CPB was continued for some time after it had been cut off to the CPM and CPT. Diplomats have speculated that the Vietnamese invasion of Cambodia caused the first major shift in Chinese policy. According to this argument, it was feared that continued support for the CPB could push Burma, which had left the Non-Aligned Movement in 1979 in protest at Soviet behaviour (see Chapter 15), back into the Soviet camp. In particular, before the seismic changes in both Burma and Eastern Europe it was speculated that potential successors to Ne Win, such as Brig. San Yu, were likely to be far more pro-Soviet.

But there was another important reason. The CCP's willingness to deal with the KIO so openly in the mid-1980s was an indication of the attention the CCP had begun to pay to the struggle of Burma's ethnic minority forces. In early 1989, shortly before the tumultuous events of China's democracy uprising and the bloodshed of Tiananmen Square, KIO leaders were advised the whole border would shortly be thrown open to free trade. Though since the late 1960s insurgent chiefs, such as Brang Seng, had been frequent visitors to Kunming and Beijing, until then the official Chinese position (that any aid from the CCP must be distributed through the CPB) had never been changed. But in the early 1980s, following the breakdown of the 1980/1 peace talks, several insurgent leaders reported that Chinese officials had for the first time begun to take serious notice of their criticisms of both the CPB and BSPP. Minorities such as the Shans, Kachins, Akhas, Lahus and Was also live in large numbers on the Yunnan side of the border where autonomous regions have been established and few of the racial problems in Burma have been experienced. In particular, ethnic minority troops served with distinction in the border war with Vietnam and CCP officials privately contrasted the perennial inability of the CPB to make better use of the huge amounts of aid they had diverted to the NEC to their own successes on the other side of the border. This apparent acceptance that the CPB was never going to achieve victory may account for the CCP's offer, first made in 1981, of pensions and retirement homes in China for any CPB elders who wanted them.

The CCP's acknowledgement of ethnic nationalist grievances consisted for the most part only of humanitarian aid, such as places for KIO cadres at medical training schools in Yunnan, but CCP officials did listen with interest to requests from the KIO and NDF for Chinese officials to act as intermediaries in their disputes with both the CPB and BSPP. The CPB's role in China's strategic planning for Burma was gradually being eclipsed. When the CPB's ethnic mutinies occurred, the CCP, other than finding sanctuary for Ba Thein Tin and the CPB leaders, did nothing.

The more cynical would argue that Chinese policy over the last few decades has been open to any eventuality and was intended to allow Beijing to influence all cross-border parties. There was never any danger, despite constant rumours to the contrary, that the CPB would turn to Vietnam or Laos, with whom contact could easily have been established through the 815 war zone across the Mekong River. Indeed, right up until the 1989 collapse, the CPB Politburo (under Chinese pressure) secretly allowed 'rightist' guerrillas from Gen. Vang Pao's CIA-backed ethnic Hmong resistance and the United Lao National Liberation Front to travel through CPB territory to China. Here they underwent training and discussed plans to coordinate anti-Vietnamese resistance in Laos, Cambodia and amongst ethnic minority villagers in the highlands of Vietnam.

The communist parties of both Thailand and Malaya declined dramatically when Chinese aid was withdrawn. In December 1989, in the midst of the CPB collapse, the CPM's 41-year armed struggle also poignantly came to a formal close; its veteran chairman, Chin Peng, returned by air from China to sign a peace accord with Thai and Malaysian government officials and agreed to the disbanding of the last 1,500 CPM soldiers. It could be argued that, but for substantial Chinese support following the Vietnamese invasion, the Khmer Rouge might well have gone the same way.

None the less throughout the 1980s the CPB appeared likely to be able to hold its own, whatever the vagaries of Chinese policy, the PA's battlefield setbacks or the political changes in Rangoon. The PA still possessed a vast stockpile of arms and ammunition. Appearances, however, were to prove deceptive.

The unresolved ethnic problems of the north-east were what ultimately caused the disintegration of the CPB's military command. Nationalist leaders had long been optimistically predicting such an event. Even so, the speed with which the CPB breakup occurred took its leadership by surprise. On the eve of the 1989 mutinies, considering the tumultuous developments of the past year, the CPB's 75 year-old chairman, Ba Thein Tin, wrote to me in highly confident terms about the CPB's 'correct' policy towards the minorities:

> Ethnic nationalities in Burma have been subjected and exploited by great Burmese chauvinism for thousands of years and in addition to the divide-and-rule policy of British imperialists. Naturally, it is quite justified for the ethnic nationalities to take up arms and fight for their legitimate rights. Since it is a just struggle, our party fully endorsed their struggles. In 1986 CPB and NDF agreed to fight against the military regime as the main common enemy and to solve the problems existing among ourselves through discussion and consultation. Our present policy towards the ethnic nationalities is this: we are fully opposed and are fighting against the great Burmese chauvinism as the main danger while at the same time we are opposed to narrow bourgeois nationalism.[19]

He then outlined the CPB's armed strategy for the military overthrow of the 'Ne Win-Saw Maung' regime. This, he argued, should be followed by the formation of a 'provisional government' of all opposition forces which would supervise 'free and fair' elections to a Constituent Assembly whose prime duty, as in 1947, would be to draw up a new constitution. He then concluded: 'We therefore consider that what Burma needs today is not a one-party dictatorship, but a multi-party system which will ultimately guarantee and set up a democratic, peaceful, united and prosperous new Burma.'[20]

When contrasted with the militant language of the past four decades, Ba Thein Tin's words, devoid of all references to Marxist-Leninist-Mao Zedong thought, marked a very moderate point of view. Listeners to the last VOPB broadcasts of 1988/9 found it hard to believe that this was the Maoist party of class-hating zealots, Red Guards and Beijing returnees of yesteryear.

Despite Ba Thein Tin's confidence, after two decades of one-party CPB rule in the mountain remoteness of the north-east, resentments were dangerously close to the surface. As the first 'government' ever to try and establish a uniform military, political and educational administration in this isolated backwater, the CPB had always faced a formidable task. In a self-congratulatory VOPB broadcast in 1980, its Politburo reported that in the North-East Region alone the CPB had established a 'liberated zone' of 28,000 square kilometres (including a 7,000-square kilometre guerrilla zone) with over 3,000 villages and a population of 436,000.[21] Nearly 900 peasant unions, which formed the political basis of the CPB administration, had been set up with 87,000 members, as well as 1,000 women's unions with another 33,000 members. In addition, 183 day-schools, 299 night-schools and 30 medical centres had been opened.[22] In the '815 military region' to the south, which consisted of another 5,000 square kilometres of intermixed CPB guerrilla and base areas, a further 38,000 villagers lived.[23]

But the day to day problems of administration in the midst of war and the abject poverty of local villagers were vast. As the Politburo explained, there were more than 15 different nationalities living in the region: Wa, Shan, Chinese (including Kokangese and Yunnanese Muslims), Kachins (Jinghpaw-Maru-Lashi-Lisu), Akha, Palaung, Lahu, Pao, Burman, Lu, Danu, Karen and Indian, as well as various unidentified tribes, mainly Akha or Lahu offshoots. Several still had no written scripts of their own. Though the CPB claimed to have improved the quality of its organisation, as in the 1950s and 1960s, party-building and the training of cadres remained a perennial problem. Bertil Lintner, the only Western journalist to have reached Panghsang, compared the quality of CPB administration very poorly with that of the predominantly Christian KIO to the north.[24]

For many young communists, the party's aging Burman-dominated leadership, built around the austere personalities of Politburo members Ba Thein Tin, Pe Tint, Tin Yi, Khin Maung Gyi, Myo Myint, Kyin Maung and Kyaw Mya, all in their 60s or 70s, appeared to be increasingly out of step with the political realities of modern-day Burma. Critics privately reflected the same could be said of San Yu, Aye Ko and the aging *Tatmadaw* veterans surrounding Ne Win in Rangoon. Both sides were still fighting the war they had begun in different circumstances at a very different time and place 40 years before. Certainly for illiterate ethnic minority villagers and hill farmers living in remote mountain communities, esoteric communist discussions of the CPB's favourite pet themes (pseudo-independence, imperialism and bureaucratic-capitalism) meant very little, especially for those who lived alongside the 'liberated zones' of the KIO, SSPP and PSLP. Indeed most of the country's population had now been born since the disastrous events of 1948, the fateful year of Burma's independence.

Some of these criticisms were taken on board at the CPB's Third Congress at Panghsang during September/October 1985 (see Chapter 15), when a number of veteran cadres were retired and five younger ethnic minority leaders appointed to the 29-person CC. These included the ethnic Karen, Saw Ba Moe, who now took charge of the Central Bureau, and Kyauk Ni Lai and Pauk Yo Chang, two ethnic Was who had joined the CPB in 1968. Though Ba Thein Tin and the orthodox China-trained old guard kept their positions on the Politburo, ethnic minority members now made up one third of the CC.[25] These belated appointments, however, did little to stop the growing racial disaffection within the party.

The Alleged Role of Communists in the 1988 Democracy Uprising

The CPB had now enjoyed two decades of Chinese support as it strove to build up a communist bastion in north-east Burma; if the PA had been able to use these bases as a springboard to get back into central Burma, the picture in Burma today would undoubtedly have been very different. But even before the ethnic mutinies of 1989, the great demonstrations in the towns and cities across the country during the democracy uprising of 1988 had already exposed many gaping weaknesses in the CPB's position.

In the year following the Saw Maung coup, the military officers of the new State Law and Order Restoration Council (SLORC) in Rangoon claimed that the whole democracy uprising from beginning to end had been inspired and organised by the CPB. Coming on the golden jubilee of the patriotic anti-British '1300 revolution' of 1938 and the 40th anniversary of the outbreak of the CPB insurrection, SLORC charged that since the 1985 Congress the CPB had quietly been preparing a new offensive by activating old contacts in the cities to commemorate the beginning of its long armed struggle on 28 March 1948. The main instrument of this plan, it claimed, was the CPB's cleverly named 4828 underground cell. As army officials pointed out, the first major student demonstrations began on schedule in March after the apparently spontaneous 'town and gown brawl' at the Sanda Win tea-shop in Rangoon.

In the days immediately following the coup the state media widely reported the discovery of CPB propaganda in Rangoon and Loikaw and army officers tried to persuade Western diplomats that the CPB had 'revealed its hand' when it persuaded demonstrators to seize the Ministry of Trade building in Rangoon (see Chapter 1). The *Tatmadaw* had no choice, they argued, but to take action.

Nobody who lived through these turbulent months seriously believes this version of events, though to justify the coup it has since remained the staple diet of *Tatmadaw* propaganda.[26] The most remarkable attempt to sustain this communist conspiracy theory was a six-hour press conference by MIS chief, Brig. Khin Nyunt, in August 1989, details of which were circulated to foreign governments under the title, 'EXPOSED: With Documentary Evidence, WIDESPREAD CONSPIRACY BY BURMA COMMUNIST PARTY ABOVE AND UNDERGROUND ELEMENTS TO DESTABILISE & TAKE OVER STATE POWER', which outlined with photographs and complex diagrams the purported activities of underground CPB organisers throughout 1985-9. Riddled with inconsistencies and half truths, it was clear that Khin Nyunt's brief was to find details, however bizarre, of communist infiltration to justify in one historic sweep the military coup, the bloodshed and the subsequent arrest of thousands of democracy activists.

Few diplomats took Khin Nyunt's claims seriously. Such allegations, they suggested, were clear evidence of a dangerously paranoid mind. These murmurings multiplied when, in another press conference the following month, without apparent embarrassment Khin Nyunt accused rightist 'treasonous minions within and traitorous cohorts abroad', including the BBC and Voice of America, of conspiring together to destabilise the situation in Burma.[27] Several opposition leaders, including student activist, Moe Thee Zun, and veteran army hero, Thakin Bo Khin Maung, were even attributed a starring role in both conspiracy plots!

It would have been surprising if there had been no CPB involvement in the events of the summer. But SLORC's attempt to tie the vast countrywide protests to the CPB (amidst two demonetisations and a complete economic collapse) was far fetched in the extreme. The man SLORC accused was Politburo member, Kyin Maung, who at the 1985 CPB Congress had been ordered to step up underground activities in central Burma.[28] CPB propaganda made it clear that party leaders were aware of the deepening economic and political crisis in the country and had long predicted the coming disturbances, though hardly on the subsequent scale. 'There can be no doubt that this period, this turning point in history, will be a very dangerous test for the military clique,' ran one VOPB broadcast in late 1987. 'If not this year, then victory will come next year. The future belongs only to the people.'[29]

The CPB was not alone in such portentous predictions. To suggest that in three years it could have created such extraordinary nationwide underground organisation without MIS or anyone else apparently noticing is to distort the truth. Amongst other allegations, MIS officials claimed that the CPB underground, led by Dr Zaw Min and Thet Khaing, son-in-law of CC member, Kyaw Zaw, had organised the Rangoon and Mandalay General Strike Committees, infiltrated student unions across the country and set up a variety of pro-CPB fronts in towns such as Monywa, Sagaing and Prome, all of which became major centres of the democracy movement. Their intention, MIS believed, turning the party's back on its Maoist rural warfare strategy, had been to prepare the ground for a general strike to bring the BSPP government down. Indeed many of the disturbances, Khin Nyunt alleged, were simply 'urban guerrilla warfare' by the CPB: 'The *Tatmadaw* took over power just in time on 18 September 1988 and so the CPB's plan to grab power was foiled.'[30] 'I saved the country from an abyss', claimed the SLORC chairman, Gen. Saw Maung.[31]

Tatmadaw accusations against the CPB did not end with Saw Maung's seizure of power. Having dismissed the events of 1988 as a CPB plot, Ne Win loyalists immediately developed a second line of attack. They began to denigrate as 'CPB fronts' many of the newly legalised political parties that had sprung up in the aftermath of the military coup. SLORC's main target was Aung San Suu Kyi's National League for Democracy (NLD), undoubtedly the most popular of the 234 parties formed. During July 1989 as many as 6,000 of its supporters and democracy activists were taken into custody. With the country already under martial law even tougher new military regulations were introduced and the NLD's two main leaders, Aung San Suu Kyi and Tin Oo, were both placed under arrest.[32] Eventually both were banned from contesting the 1990 general election altogether.

SLORC did find some public support for MIS claims of CPB 'infiltration' of the NLD from former Brig. Aung Gyi, initially an NLD supporter, who resigned in protest at the alleged influence of communist sympathisers surrounding Aung San Suu Kyi.[33] NLD members responded by accusing Aung Gyi of doing the bidding of his master, Ne Win, all along. But MIS chief Khin Nyunt took these accusations further by alleging that the CPB had first tried to promote Suu Kyi's mother, Daw Khin Kyi, as a new 'national leader' to take over the government from the BSPP during the democracy uprising. He claimed that both Ba Thein Tin and Kyaw Zaw had secretly written to her and that only when she died in December 1988 did they turn their attention to her charismatic daughter whom, they believed, carried the magic of her father's name. Taking advantage of the Burmese people's 'tendency to hero-worship', Khin Nyunt explained, the CPB had exploited Suu Kyi's popularity and infiltrated the party. Secret communist agents, he went on, had made the NLD 'unwittingly tread the CPB path of defying all authority' by organising anti-SLORC protests in the cities to coincide with CPB military offensives in the countryside.[34] With SLORC now reproducing Sein Win's controversial 1959 book, *The Split Story*, many of these accusations were highly reminiscent of the *Tatmadaw*'s charge that there had been a close collusion between the CPB and above-ground opposition parties during the short-lived parliamentary era of the 1950s.

These highly complex allegations are obviously tendentious. One reliable CPB source describes Khin Nyunt's accusations on CPB underground movements in Upper Burma as at best 'half-correct' and in Lower Burma as 'completely incorrect'. There are two far simpler explanations.

First, as Politburo member Kyin Maung admits, there were a number of CPB cadres active in the cities, but the *Tatmadaw* has greatly exaggerated their role, particularly in Rangoon.[35] One student connected with the party's Task Force 4828 in Lower Burma described their numbers as a 'handful of people', mostly operating around Rangoon University and Rangoon Institute of Technology, who had to 'move very secretly' since MIS had already infiltrated virtually every other political group on campus.[36] Their activities, he said, consisted largely of reproducing articles from the CPB's general headquarters at Panghsang and forming discussion groups 'to spread their net'. Veteran cadres had also secretly hidden a radio transmitter which in the past had sent messages 'to the jungles'. This small group does claim, quite unbeknownst to virtually all other student activists, to have been involved in the Rangoon Institute of Technology demonstrations in March which began after the first student martyr, Maung Phone Maw, was killed. But this, the 4828 informant said, was the virtual limit of their influence as, fuelled by a variety of economic and political grievances, the demonstrations escalated beyond all expectations.[37]

In the upheavals that followed, trailed everywhere by MIS agents, leaders of the democracy uprising frequently addressed meetings at which CPB supporters were secretly present. But there is no evidence that these small CPB cells were able to impose their will. Student leader and Rangoon University physics graduate, Moe Thee Zun, whom Khin Nyunt accused by name of being 'recruited' by the CPB, while clearly on the political left, was scathing in his denial: 'The army has two tactics to deal with political opponents. First they accuse you of being a communist. If this does not work, they call you a secessionist. They have nothing else to say. It was always quite clear from our objectives that we are not communists.'[38] Instead, like other strike leaders, he accused the *Tatmadaw* of deliberately misreporting the great democracy demonstrations in an attempt to show evidence of the CPB's role. For many citizens one of the most glaring examples of this was the publicity SLORC gave to touched-up photographs of young protesters marching with 'hammer and sickle' emblems and red banners adorned with the 'fighting peacock' crest of the Students Union. The hammer and sickle, set against a red, green and yellow background, was, as every Burmese schoolchild knows, one of the emblems of the *Dobama* movement of the 1930s, which many students rushed on to the streets to emulate during the heady days of 1988.

This leads to the second and more serious explanation of why the *Tatmadaw* claimed that the CPB had had an 'organising' role. Given that Marxism had been at the forefront of Burma's political evolution since the 1930s, there are undoubtedly tens of thousands of Burmese citizens who were once involved in CPB or communist-related activities, but who are now playing an active role in very different walks of modern-day life. It is to this section of society that army leaders were for the most part referring and, indeed, it was from this group that many of the older leaders of the democracy movement emerged.

A careful distinction, however, needs to be made between the minority who were still directly supporting the CPB and those who had long since moved on in new political directions. The evidence is overwhelming that the great majority of these political veterans were trying to build new democracy parties. But the net of accusations that MIS officers now cast revealed how deep rooted *Tatmadaw* fears of the CPB were and the highly compressed time-scale in which Ne Win loyalists had come to operate after 40 years of civil war.

The anachronistic People's Volunteer Organisation (PVO) of the 1940s and 1950s, which was legally allowed to reform as a new political party after the 1988 coup, was once again routinely described as a pro-CPB front. The names SLORC dramatically 'revealed' as evidence of present-day CPB activities in the cities involved an extraordinary trip down memory lane into the CPB's past. Immediately after the coup, former CPB CC members, Thakin Tin Mya and Bo Ye Htut, who had left the party to work with the BSPP in the early 1960s, were taken into custody. Indeed Tin Mya was singled out as one of the 'veteran politicians' responsible for encouraging Aung San Suu Kyi to enter politics.[39] Other names included U Soe Win, younger brother of the CPB's fallen Chief-of-Staff, Bo Zeya; Kyaw Zaw's daughter, Daw San Kyaw Zaw; Thakin Zin's wife, Daw Kyi Kyi; and former Burma Workers and Peasants Party (BWPP) leaders, Thakin Lwin and U Aung Than (Aung San's brother), both of whom, though they had never joined the CPB, had been imprisoned by the army in the past. 'A leftist force' was active in Rangoon, warned Khin Nyunt, comprising 'families' from the CPB's old Pegu Yomas strongholds, former CPB 'prisoners' who had been released and 'Coco Island returnees' from the 1950s and 1960s.[40] What Khin Nyunt never directly said but clearly implied by these detailed family lineages, was that Aung San Suu Kyi, who had unexpectedly reappeared from the West to claim back her father's mantle from Ne Win, was also the niece of Thakin Than Tun, the CPB's inspirational leader who had led the party underground so many years before.

But far from proving an omnipotent CPB conspiracy led by veteran party cadres in the cities, the extraordinary and uncontrolled explosion of new political forces in Burma during 1988/9 was the most conclusive reminder yet of the factional and often intensely personal nature of Burmese politics. 'Family feuding' was what one inside observer called it after U Nu, Aung San Suu Kyi, Tin Oo and Aung Gyi had failed to agree on a unified set of tactics on the eve of the Saw Maung coup.

What 'communist' or CPB influence there was could be divided into two categories, largely from the middle-aged and older generations who supported the democracy movement in two rather different ways. The first group were those who had flirted with the CPB or Marxist ideologies in the 1950s or worked with the above-ground National United Front (NUF). Many of these joined the National League for Democracy (NLD) which, with an estimated three million registered members at the time of the second military crackdown in July 1989, had clearly far surpassed all other parties in becoming the main vehicle for the aspirations of the democracy movement. Eight members of the NLD's 33-strong CC were picked out by both MIS and Brig. Aung Gyi as alleged 'communists', but their careers hardly supported Khin Nyunt's charge that 'the thinking of the NLD is dominated by CPB thinking'.[41] U Ko Yu, for example, was a Red Flag sympathiser at Rangoon University in the 1950s who subsequently earned a high reputation for himself as a lawyer in Rangoon defending, amongst others, the former Red Flag leader, Thakin Soe. Three other equally respected members of the Rangoon Bar Council were also named, all of whom had connections with the Marxist Study Group at Rangoon University in the 1950s: U Tun Tin, a prominent member of Kodaw Hmaing's Internal Peace Committee and the NUF, who had twice been gaoled by the army; U Tin Shwe, who had reputedly briefly joined the White Flags after university; and Daw Myint Myint Khin, a leading women's organiser of her generation.[42] But any contact with the CPB was now extremely distant. As with the NLD's two senior leaders, Aung San Suu Kyi and the former army Chief-of-Staff, Gen. Tin Oo, the CPB charge could hardly be made to stick and they were all eventually imprisoned or disbarred from the 1990 election on a variety of quite separate but equally trumped-up charges. Tin Oo was sentenced to three years hard labour for 'contacting, writing and sending false anti-government reports to foreign organisations and leaders', including the International Labour Organisation, while Aung San Suu Kyi was kept under house arrest for having an alleged 'unlawful association' with a quite different 'insurgent organisation', the NDF.

The second much smaller category of former communist sympathisers active in the democracy movement pursued a political course that more closely followed the CPB, though this was often hard to prove. This loose grouping consisted of former CPB activists who had quietly surfaced to agitate or lead many of the local anti-BSPP movements around the country; it was to these CPB veterans, with their long experience of underground political organisation, that many students often turned for guidance. After nearly three decades of military rule, there was virtually no one else. Indeed the entire democracy movement was frequently characterised by the same extraordinary naivety later echoed by similar democracy uprisings in China and Eastern Europe. 'We knew we needed "isms" if our movement was to develop,' said one pro-CPB student.[43]

Typical of these communist supporters were U Hla Shwe and U Nyo Win, both former EC members of Rangoon University Students Union who went underground with the CPB following the breakdown of the 1963 peace parley, joined the PA in the Pyapon district of the Delta and were captured a few years later. Even after his release from gaol, Hla Shwe was imprisoned twice more during the 1980s for allegedly continuing his underground CPB work. These veterans, like opposition activists from other political backgrounds (especially U Nu supporters), were quick to seize the many opportunities that 1988 afforded and frequently popped up at meetings and demonstrations in Rangoon, Mandalay and other towns around the country to give their advice and suggest ways of broadening the struggle by using their old contacts. Hla Shwe, for example, who had only been released from gaol in July, gave talks on political agitation at the first meeting of the All Burma Federation of Students Unions in Rangoon on 28 August 1988, where his son, Aung Khaing, who openly disagrees with his father's 'communist' views, was a prominent student leader.[44]

Following the Saw Maung coup most of these old-timers stayed in the towns to form political cells and organisations reminiscent of the many fractured left-wing parties of the 1950s. With all public meetings of more than five people strictly banned, many of these groupings, they admitted, were an attempt to get round the tough martial law restrictions. The National Politics Front, made up of members of the Rangoon and Mandalay General Strike Committees, pulled in a broad array of patrons and supporters such as the NLD's U Win Tin, former editor of the *Hanthawaddy* newspaper, and Daw Myint Myint Khin. The most ambitious front was the League of Democratic Allies, formed in February 1989, which consisted of 11 left-wing parties, including the resurrected AFPFL, the PVOs, the student-backed Democratic Party for New Society (DPNS) of Moe Thee Zun, the People's Democratic Party led by ex-BWPP leaders, U Aung Than and Thakin Lwin, the National Politics Front, and the People's Progressive Party, headed by Hla Shwe, Nyo Win and Khin Maung Myint, who had spent much of the last three decades in gaol for his pro-CPB sympathies.[45]

The latter two parties were banned altogether in September 1989, along with the Evergreen Young Men's Association (which had been active in Monywa district), for allegedly forming part of an 'overt organisation' of the CPB; many of their leaders were sent to join the thousands of NLD supporters and other democracy activists already in gaol. Hard-pressed MIS agents still had other political ghosts from the past to worry about in the form of Thakin Soe's Unity and Development Party, and former BWPP leader Thakin Chit Maung's Democratic Front for National Reconstruction. There was even the 'Main' AFPFL of Cho Cho, daughter of the late socialist leader, Kyaw Nyein, who was also harassed and arrested.

In fact, despite this concentration on the CPB, the next major round of arrests in December 1989 did not come from the left but from the League for Democracy and Peace of ex-prime minister U Nu and former *Thirty Comrade* Bo Hmu Aung, both of whom had returned to Rangoon under amnesty in 1980 after their failed insurrection. The detention of these elderly gentlemen smacked of increasing desperation. It had long since become apparent that Saw Maung, Khin Nyunt and Ne Win's loyalist old guard were wanting to clear the way for their own party, the National Unity Party (NUP), headed by former army colonel, U Tha Kyaw, to win the 1990 general election. Everybody immediately recognised that the NUP was simply a reconstituted BSPP in new clothes. The country remained in a state of deep crisis, all universities were closed and martial law restrictions were still rigidly enforced. To counter this grim image, SLORC tried to convince the outside world that the situation had returned to normal. All government salaries were doubled, the country was renamed 'Myanmar' and unbridled business opportunities were offered to foreign entrepreneurs willing to take part in Burma's new 'open door' trade bonanza.

Few observers were deceived, but as Burma moved towards its first general election in 30 years, SLORC's repressive tactics were clearly paying off: no one was publicly talking politics. Certainly, in view of the upheavals to come, nobody dared mention the long suppressed ethnic question, other than to say a settlement would be a good thing. Though it was underground operatives of ethnic organisations like the KNU, NMSP, KIO and KNLP that most openly penetrated the towns during the upheavals of 1988/9, even during the collapse of the NEC in the first half of 1989 the army continued to pin much of the blame for the disturbances on the CPB.

While such black propaganda may have served as a useful distraction at the time for the Ne Win loyalists, the danger for the political analyst who tries to unravel these accusations too closely is that ultimately they fly in the face of all reality and ignore the turbulent direction of Burma's history. The millions of workers, *pongyis*, students and other young people who took part in the great demonstrations of the summer represented a new generation, bitter over the political failings of their elders. Clearly uppermost in the street campaigning, posters and speeches was a deep resentment of Ne Win, MIS and the BSPP. The army was generally absolved of all criticism since many people believed the soldiers would support them, but it was also obvious that the people were calling for a complete break with the past. Whatever changes come to Burma, it is likely that the language of Marxism, as in Western and Eastern Europe, or at least some form of 'Burmese socialism', will continue to play its part in the political vocabulary of the country; it is impossible to turn anywhere in Burma today and not find echoes of the CPB-AFPFL-BSPP past. But in 1988, in the towns and communities of Burma the CPB's presence was minimal and undoubtedly at its lowest ebb since 1948.

During the course of interviewing hundreds of political activists who had led the summer demonstrations from the front, I found only a handful who had had any involvement with the CPB movement at all. The evidence is compelling. In the aftermath of the army crackdown over 10,000 students and civilian activists fled underground into the insurgent-controlled mountains. Of these an estimated 5,000 went to the KNU, 2,000 to the KIO and 1,300 to the NMSP, but only a few hundred to the CPB, either to Panghsang in the North-East Region, to Mong Ko in the Northern Bureau or into the jungles of Tenasserim. In fact most of these did not even join the CPB, but its allies the KNLP and SSNLO in the south-west Shan State, before being sent on to the Chinese border for arms and training. These formed the nucleus of the small Democratic Patriotic Army which was briefly active in the Shan State during 1989/90.[46]

Since the army's bloody clamp-down, dozens of local political cells and parties have remained active in Burma. It is impossible to generalise about them, for there are so many scattered groups of young people dreaming up ways of forming the next band of *Thirty Comrades* to change the political course of their country. But the unanimity of Burma's young people in their verdict in 1988 on both the CPB and BSPP was startling. After 40 years of political infighting by their parents, most seemed indifferent to dogma or ideology and remarkably willing to accept the right of all political parties to exist, including the CPB and BSPP, as long as they were prepared to stand by the results of any freely held election. 'Our politics are national politics, not party politics,' explained Moe Thee Zun who fled underground after his own organisation, the DPNS, was crippled by arrests. 'But we could not solve our problems by political means. That's why we have resorted to armed struggle. We did not plan things this way, but we were pushed by the military.'[47]

A common sentiment was expressed by the Revd. Ashin Kimazara, chairman of the All Burma Young Monks Union, which in November 1988 joined hands with the NDF in the insurgent Democratic Alliance of Burma: 'Ne Win's *Burmese Way to Socialism* has not materialised in Burma so how can we realise communist ideology? Communism is even stronger than socialism.'[48]

The View of the CPB

Perhaps the last word should be left to Kyin Maung, CPB Politburo member in charge of Task Force 4828, whom MIS Chief Khin Nyunt personally accused of stirring up and coordinating the countrywide civil disobedience in 1988 as a cover for the CPB's bid to seize power. His version of events tallies closely with what actually happened. Pointing out that Task Force 4828 had existed for several years before the 1985 Congress at which these plans were allegedly hatched, he freely admits that the CPB cadres, Thet Khaing and Tin Aung, both of whom featured prominently in SLORC accusations of CPB agitation, were members of the 4828's 'leading cell'.[49] Both attended the 1985 Congress and subsequently returned underground in central Burma, travelling extensively between Rangoon and Mandalay over the next four years. Then in his late 30s, Thet Khaing was an important party official who served for over 15 years on the battlefield and in the political above-ground. On his dangerous undercover assignments in between times, he had posed as a food merchant. His luck finally ran out in July 1989 when he was arrested in Tamwe. The fate of Tin Aung is not known. A former student leader and Coco Island detainee of the 1960s, like many CPB activists of his generation he received his political education in gaol where he was held with such prominent communist sympathisers as CPB CC member, Aung Naing (*aka* Rajan), ex-CPB commander, Ohn Maung, and author, Bhamo Tin Aung.

Kyin Maung also admitted that, following the CPB CC's adoption of the 1981 'multi-party democracy line', the party had embarked on a policy of communicating this view to 'personages from all walks of life as food for thought for what we should do'.[50] However, he believed that because 'the conditions, both objective and subjective, were not ripe yet for the masses to come forward with this slogan, it could only play a propagandising role at that time'. Playing down any influence that Task Force 4828 might have brought to bear, Kyin Maung claimed that the next stage in the CPB's political campaign came only on 28 March 1988, when its CC 'raised the slogan demanding a provisional government composed of various parties, forces and personages. It was a sequel to the 1981 idea, being more specific and practical'.[51] The CC's 28 March statement, confirming Kyin Maung's chronology, was subsequently broadcast on the VOPB, but not until several weeks later, in fact on May Day, as the democracy movement gathered momentum.

This time the CPB's proposals received a far more positive response but not, he says, due to any particular activity on its part:

> The people of Burma have decided enough is enough. Through successive demonstrations (one should say tests of strength) prior to the 1988 upheavals, they had learnt to unite and stage demonstrations on a broader scale. The slogans of our party reached them at this crucial period and, through their own experience, they came to see that these slogans coincided with their wishes. Thus the demand for democracy, multi-party system (or the abolition of the one-party dictatorship), peace, national economic development etc., came to the fore during the upheavals.

A BIA veteran and staunch communist to the end, Kyin Maung then finished with a modest and surprisingly frank appraisal of the CPB's role, which contrasts starkly with the loud rhetoric of its Maoist and Marxist-Leninist past. Indeed it stands as a highly fitting epitaph to the communist movement in Burma and is a memorial to the lessons learned in Burma's long struggle for democracy: 'We had never said that we initiated the upheavals. Nor did we say that our cadres comprised the leading core. On the contrary, we firmly believe that the upheavals had so much impact only because all the forces for democracy took part. Marxism holds that it is the people who make history.'[52]

18

The 1989 CPB Mutinies: The End of the Road?

There can be little doubt that if the great democracy uprising of 1988 had occurred at virtually any stage in the first 30 years of Burma's independence, the CPB would have been ready to strike. But this time, despite its considerable military strength in the Shan State, it was immediately obvious that the CPB was no longer in any position to affect political events in the cities. And though the CPB, like the National Democratic Front (NDF), took the considered decision not to inflame the situation by trying to take military advantage of the *Tatmadaw's* difficulties, its prestige clearly took a damaging blow. Indeed the first public attempt by the CPB CC, isolated as it was in the remote mountains of the north-east, to put its full support behind student demands which so closely echoed its own (the formation of an interim civilian government to oversee multi-party elections) came as late as 4 September 1988, just two weeks before the Saw Maung coup.[1]

A belated reminder of the CPB's military potential, however, did come immediately following the coup when on 24 September a 1,500-strong force, including units from the 5th, 7th and 768th brigades of the People's Army (PA), overran Mong Yang in the CPB's first major assault on a government-controlled town since 1980. The attack, Ba Thein Tin explained, was in support of the students.[2] But it backfired disastrously. Not only did it concentrate *Tatmadaw* resolve back on the one thing it was good at, namely fighting insurgents (and dozens more troops were killed shortly afterwards when the KNU overran the army garrison at Mae Tah Waw on the Thai border), but both sides suffered very heavy casualties. It was a drastic setback to the morale of the CPB's ethnic minority fighters. In the early stages of the offensive the CPB claimed to have killed 127 government troops, including the commander of the 11th Light Infantry Battalion, and wounded another 184.[3] But in retaliatory attacks after the CPB captured the town, the *Tatmadaw* was accused of the indiscriminate aerial bombing and shelling of Mong Yang and several surrounding villages. According to the State Law and Order Restoration Council (SLORC), the bodies of over 200 CPB soldiers were discovered when the town was retaken, but Politburo member Kyaw Mya claimed many of these were in fact civilians caught in the firing-line by army shelling.[4] In the following days the CPB also accused the *Tatmadaw* of unleashing a wave of terror on local villagers suspected of helping the CPB attack; the 72-year-old chief headman of Mong Yang, Shan Lan Pang, was allegedly tortured to death. Hundreds more civilians were forced into front-line porter duty for the Burmese Army.

For many local ethnic minority leaders, this indiscriminate killing and brutality was yet another example of the minorities suffering for the political problems of Burma. Whatever the violence of the short-lived democracy summer, nothing compared to the ferocity of the Mong Yang battle.

After the retreat from Mong Yang the CPB continued to step up military operations and was invited to attend the inaugural meeting of the Democratic Alliance of Burma (DAB) at the general headquarters of the KNU-NDF at Mannerplaw on 14 November. Here it was agreed to expand the NDF to include the newly formed All Burma Students Democratic Front (ABSDF), the General Strike Committee from Rangoon and a dozen other fledgling political fronts from across the country. Receiving the invitation too late to make the 300-mile journey across the mountains to attend, Ba Thein Tin instead sent a message pledging to support all efforts to overthrow the Saw Maung regime and establish 'a multi-party democracy system', promising the CPB would increase military cooperation with the NDF.[5] One month later on 13 December, in one of the most savage blood-baths in the CPB's 40-year insurrection, PA units, supported by the KIO, wiped out an entire column from the *Tatmadaw*'s 3rd infantry battalion near Kongsa, 20 miles east of Kuktai. According to the CPB's account backed up by photographs, 106 government troops were killed, 17 wounded and 15 captured including the column commander. All their weapons and nearly 200,000 rounds of ammunition were seized.[6]

For CPB commanders the Kongsa battle was a welcome victory after the Mong Yang setback, but clearly it was not seen this way by the PA's rank and file. Thousands were now preparing to defect. There was a genuine war weariness and deep dissatisfaction with Ba Thein Tin and the CPB's ageing leadership over any number of issues — ethnic, military, economic, personal and political. But undoubtedly the overriding feeling, soon to be loudly voiced, was that the minorities were being used merely as cannon-fodder in the CPB's unending war with Rangoon. In early 1989 Shwe Aye, Tha Kalei and Nya Maung Me of the KNLP, SSNLO and KSNLF, three of the CPB's closest allies, travelled up to Panghsang to 'clarify the CPB's leadership theory of the revolution' and tell Ba Thein Tin, in the light of the democracy uprising, that 'the CPB's leadership was not working'. Here they also heard rumours that on 20 February 1989 Ba Thein Tin had convened a crisis meeting, details of which were apparently leaked, after Chinese officials had approached CPB leaders and, this time, tried to persuade them to retire into China.[7]

The defections began virtually without warning on 12 March 1989 when ethnic Kokangese units, led by Pheung Kya-shin, the 'warlord' Kokang leader who had joined the North-East Command back in 1968, defied the party leadership and, with the support of local Wa troops, seized control of the CPB's Northern region headquarters at Mong Ko. Here they established a new insurgent group, initially known as the Kokang Democracy Party. KIO officials later admitted that Pheung Kya-shin and the Kokang nationalists had mentioned this idea to them as early as 1980 when they advised them against it as they thought it 'too early' to break away from the CPB.[8]

At first the CPB Politburo tried to play down the mutiny, describing it simply as the 'Kokang affair', and pledged to settle the dispute peacefully. Ruling out any broader political implications because 'it has nothing to do with other areas or nationalities', they accused the Kokang leaders of breaking away in protest at measures introduced by the party the previous year to restrict the opium trade.[9] Indeed they alleged the Pheung family leading the mutiny had bribed several local Wa commanders with opium to join them. The Pheungs, they pointed out, had never been members of the CPB, while Li Zhong Qiang, another prominent

Kokangese dissident, had been expelled from the party for polygamy. Equally seriously, they accused the breakaway group of being in contact with two of the most notorious figures in Burma's narcotics trade, the former KKY commanders, Lo Hsing-han, who was also an ethnic Kokangese, and Khun Sa, commander of the Tailand Revolutionary Council (TRC), who had troops operating in the nearby mountains around Tangyan.

Confirmation for their involvement and the first hint of any *Tatmadaw* role soon came when Lo Hsing-han, still a powerful influence in the region despite his apparent retirement from politics after his 1980 release from prison (see Chapter 15), travelled up to Kokang on 20 March for talks. In the 1960s and 1970s the Lo family and the Pheungs had been sworn battlefield enemies. But as yet it still appeared CPB leaders were unaware of the seriousness of the split. Kyaw Mya, himself an ethnic Rakhine, claimed other ethnic units in the CPB's PA, including Kachins, Was, Lahus and Shans, had all sent wireless messages to Panghsang, pledging their loyalty to the party.[10]

The NDF was equally unsure how to handle the situation. It was little secret that for several years it had helped the Wa National Organisation (WNO) of Maha San as a counterbalance to CPB and TRC influence in the Shan State. Some NDF leaders even dreamt of undermining the CPB's apparently firm foothold amongst the Wa living along the Chinese border. In 1987, for example, the KNU had helped train over 500 Wa troops at Doi Angkham in preparation for a secret mission to the north. But the NDF's Military Command immediately realised it was to nobody's advantage, with the *Tatmadaw* stepping up pressure on the KNU in south-east Burma and the KIO in the north, for units of the PA, the Burmese Army's strongest opponent, to collapse or (worse still) begin fighting one another. Thus, at the end of March the NDF made an attempt to mediate between the Pheung family and the CPB, but this quickly ended in failure.

The next defections were even more dramatic. On 12 April, just one week after the KNLP-SSNLO-KSNLF delegations had arrived to begin talks with Ba Thein Tin, PA units under the CPB's Wa CC members, Kyauk Ni Lai and Pauk Yo Chang and the ethnic Chinese Li Ziru, mutinied and seized control of Khun Ma township in northern Wa. Four days later they stormed the CPB's general head-quarters at Panghsang, 50 miles to the south, where they captured the VOPB radio station and the PA's great arms' warehouses and, in an orgy of destruction of communist literature and materials, began smashing portraits of Marx, Engels, Lenin, Stalin and Mao. 'Your ideology is divorced from reality and the path you have chosen is also divorced from the people,' warned the rebels' new Burma Nationalities Broadcasting Station three days later. 'The people no longer accept your narrow racial policy and the leadership provided by a small clique of people.'[11] Until 1979, the mutineers conceded, the CPB had been correctly analysing the political and economic conditions in the Wa region to lead the nationalities' struggle properly. But now, pledging they would continue the fight 'for the cause of national democracy' and the 'equality of nationalities', they announced they had broken away to set up a new Wa region Nationalities Provisional Committee to administer their territory.[12]

Meanwhile, elsewhere along the Chinese border the mutinies continued to spread rapidly. While Wa troops seized control of the North-East region, within days they were joined by the predominantly Shan 768 brigade under Khun Myint and Sai Noom Pan, who had borne the brunt of the Mong Yang battle, and the mixed Akha, Lahu and Shan troops under Lin Ming Xian in the 815 Mekong region to the south. This meant that in just over two months virtually all the CPB's permanent base areas in the Shan State had collapsed.

Only a few hundred troops in the 202 region in the Shweli River valley, a few in the 101 region of the Kachin State, in the Tenasserim Division, in Arakan State and in a few out of contact pockets in the central region in the western Shan State, perhaps just 1,500 troops in all, had remained loyal to the party leadership. The list of defectors was astounding. The PA mutineers, with over 10,000 troops behind them, had seized control of virtually all the CPB's bases and armouries and no less than five CC members had joined them, namely the Kachin, Zau Mai, the Karen, Tun Tin, the Chinese volunteer, Li Ziru, and the two Was, Pauk Yo Chang and Kyauk Ni Lai (a sixth, the Shan, Sai Aung Win, who initially agreed to join, surrendered in July 1990). Of the remaining CC members in north-east Burma two, Soe Thein, political commissar of the North-East region, and Mya Thaung, political commissar of northern Wa, were arrested. The rest were allowed to flee hurriedly across the border into China with their families and several hundred loyalists. Only the Karen, Saw Ba Moe, remained behind in the south-west Shan State with his SSNLO-KNLP allies.

Equally telling was the muted response of the Chinese authorities across the border. While in most areas CCP officials were immediately reported to have terminated food supplies to the defectors, they made no attempt at all to interfere with the rapid spread of the mutiny. At first several of the CPB leaders were kept under virtual house arrest in Meng Lian, but others were allowed to travel in China while they planned their next move. Eventually a compromise was reached and in July the remaining CC members, including Ba Thein Tin, Pe Tint, Khin Maung Gyi, Tin Yi, Kyaw Mya, Kyaw Zaw and their followers and families, were allowed to move to Panwa on the Chinese border in the 101 region of the Kachin State where an agreement had been reached between the KIO and local CPB forces, led by Ting Ying and Zalum.

Even at this desperate stage CPB veterans still believed they could retrieve the situation. 'We are not demoralised,' wrote Kyaw Mya. 'Our party is not yet eliminated. We will strive our best to organise the whole people, raising high our banner, for the freedom of the oppressed people.'13 For the first time admitting shortcomings by the CPB leaders, he revealed the party had now embarked on a new strategy. Troop units which were still loyal would step up guerrilla activities, while CPB cadres would travel around the country to re-establish contact with their many stranded party units and supporters. The CPB, he explained, had also asked for help from the NDF and pledged to work to 'unite all the forces who are fighting against the common enemy'.14 Indeed on 1 November 1989 a joint 101 region/KIO force attacked the *Tatmadaw* near the confluence of the Mali Hka and Me Hka rivers, inflicting over a dozen casualties and seizing a number of weapons. Next to the small party units in Arakan, Tenasserim and under Saw Ba Moe in the south-west Shan State, this was probably the CPB's last military blow. For even this strategy was soon overtaken by events.

The mutinous CPB factions, though divided, still represented a formidable fighting force. Both the Kokang and Wa forces made contact with local KIO-SSPP-PSLO units of the NDF with whom they had been sharing the dangers of the battlefield for several years now. But it soon became clear, repeating the highly fractious nature of Shan State politics in the past, that the new breakaway parties had already begun to develop along racial and regional lines under a number of powerful local leaders. Kyaw Mya described them as 'feudal lords exploiting the people with narrow nationalist views'; their real goal, he alleged, was to win control of the opium trade.[15] Five main factions quickly emerged:

- The Myanmar National Democratic Alliance Army (formerly Kokang Democracy Party) under Pheung Kya-shin, with an estimated 2,000 troops, including several hundred ethnic Was previously stationed by the CPB in the area.
- The Burma Democracy Solidarity Party (also Burma National United Party), renamed in late 1989 as the United Wa State Army, under Kyauk Ni Lai, Pauk Yo Chang, Zau Mai and Li Ziru, with some 12,000 soldiers and village militia.
- The breakaway 768 brigade Shan faction under Sai Noom Pan and Khun Myint, who briefly resurrected the original Shan nationalist name from 1958, the *Noom Suik Harn*, with approximately 1,000 troops.
- The 1,200-strong National Democratic Army in the former Mekong River Division under Lin Ming Xian, a former Chinese volunteer, who is also son-in-law of Pheung Kya-shin.
- And finally the 101 region, still working with the CPB refugees, with some 700 troops commanded by Ting Ying and Zalum.

But just as had happened so often in the past, politics in the Shan State had now gone into another of its quite unpredictable spins. Tension was reported not only between the five breakaway factions, but also with the NDF and CPB forces operating further in the interior with the SSNLO and KNLP of Shwe Aye. The former 768 brigade commanders in the Kengtung district, Sai Noom Pan and his deputy, the Welsh Shan, Michael Davies, both died in assassination attempts (according to one report Noom Pan took his own life after being wounded), while most of the Wa troops under Saw Ba Moe in the Central Bureau continued to desert and go back home. But with the CPB's centralised supply and communications infrastructure in tatters, there was no one party which was completely able to stand by itself. All had large stockpiles of arms and ammunition, but food (and especially rice) was soon in desperately short supply.

Not surprisingly, the main beneficiary of this unexpected turn of events was the SLORC in Rangoon which, while still continuing to publicise the CPB threat in the army-controlled press, was now pressing ahead with full-scale military offensives against the armies of the NDF and their thousands of student supporters from the cities who had joined them in the DAB. The campaigns during 1989-90 against the KNU, KNPP and NMSP in south-east Burma, where most of the students had fled, were the *Tatmadaw*'s most sustained and successful in years. Yet at even this moment, MIS chief Khin Nyunt still sought to justify the arrest in central Burma of Aung San Suu Kyi, Tin Oo and hundreds of NLD supporters as a timely move to foil another CPB plot which, he claimed, was determined to turn Burma into 'another Lebanon'.[16]

In fierce competition for several months, both the NDF and *Tatmadaw* tried to court the breakaway CPB factions. On 20 April 1989 the Kokang leaders met in Lashio with Lo Hsing-han and former Brig. Aung Gyi who, having done much to instigate the 1988 uprising, in 1989 once again began to toe the *Tatmadaw* line. Two days later MIS chief Khin Nyunt travelled with a military delegation to the nearby town of Kunlong where he reportedly met Pheung Kya-shin's younger brother, Kya-fu.[17] A ceasefire was arranged and the *Tatmadaw* agreed to supply the mutineers with a reputed 500,000 kyat, two cars and fresh food supplies. For both sides it was simply an alliance of convenience. Privately, the Kokang leaders told their former NDF colleagues that they had agreed to the ceasefire to give themselves a breathing space and claimed that Khin Nyunt, angered by the Bush administration's abrupt cutoff of the controversial 2,4-D crop-spraying programme in protest at the 1988 killings, had encouraged them to step up opium production to compensate for their financial difficulties.[18] Indeed in one message he sent to the Wa mutineers at Panghsang, Pheung Kya-shin explained he 'understood well Burmese treachery', did not 'believe in Saw Maung', and would 'never believe in the Burman'.[19]

The same ambiguities emanated from the breakaway Wa rebels. An NDF delegation travelled up from the Thai border in June, headed by Shwe Ya Hae of the KNU, and found that though in principle they were ready to join the NDF, the Wa leaders were waiting for the best offer of food and supplies. Clearly, they still had some hope of help from China. 'We are not against communist nations,' the Wa spokesman, Pi Sai Tang, told the NDF team, 'only the CPB. CPB policy is not tolerable to the Wa people.'[20] But compared to the *Tatmadaw*, which now had windfall profits from the sale of lucrative timber, fishery and oil concessions abroad, the amounts the NDF could offer were paltry. A second NDF delegation, headed by Maha San, which reached Panghsang in September, transmitted an urgent message to the NDF general headquarters at Mannerplaw that though there had been 'no change in attitude towards enemy', any 'delay' by the NDF would be 'dangerous'.[21]

It was into this vacuum that Khin Nyunt immediately plunged. As a result of a succession of highly secret talks between April 1989 and January 1990, to which SLORC has never fully admitted, the Kokang, Wa, 768, 815 and eventually 101 regions (the latter being the last to declare a ceasefire on 5 December 1989) formed a Peace and Democracy Front and a military truce with SLORC was agreed until after the May 1990 election. At these first meetings there was little discussion of politics. Kyauk Ni Lai, Ting Ying and the breakaway leaders revealed to other ethnic forces that SLORC proposed their armies be disbanded and reformed as people's militia similar to the discredited home guards of the 1970s. This they rejected and the Wa leaders replied by demanding an autonomous Wa State east of the Salween River. But it was widely understood that by agreeing to a ceasefire and to supplying the mutineers with food and fuel, the *Tatmadaw*, with its many troubles in the cities, was desperate for a break in hostilities.

SLORC had another unexpected bonus in November 1989 when a faction of the SSPP, led by the quixotic Hso Ten who had remained close to the CPB, broke away from SSPP general-secretary, Sai Lek, and joined the ceasefire with 1,500 armed followers, leaving Sai Lek with just 300 loyalists in the mountains around Lashio in KIO territory to the north. Following him was a local faction of the Palaung State Liberation Party, headed by Kyaw Yin, but further defections from the PSLP for the moment failed to materialise.

It was early days yet and in December 1989 the *Tatmadaw* began a major offensive against the KIO in the Kutkai region of the northern Shan State and along the Chinese border in the Kachin State, in which hundreds of casualties were reported. In April 1990 Pheung Kya-shin's Kokang mutineers joined in the fighting on the *Tatmadaw* side, but after suffering a number of casualties and the defection of several dozen Wa troops to the KIO, a ceasefire was called in July and a Kokang delegation travelled to the KIO general headquarters at Pajao. Here they tried to persuade the KIO not to interfere with the new timber, distillery and opium businesses which they said Lo Hsing-han, his brother Lo Hsing-min, and the Pheung family had been allowed to open by Khin Nyunt to develop the Kokang region.[22] Confusing matters even further, there were also reports of armed clashes between Kokang forces led by the Pheung family and those still loyal to the old *Sawbwa* family of the Yangs.

Despite the continued fighting, SLORC officials in Rangoon began describing the war-torn north-east to diplomats and UN officials as a 'white area' and even talked confidently of receiving international development aid. Breaking Burma's isolation, this message was carried by army officials to a series of international narcotics seminars in China, Pakistan and the US; in April 1990, it was repeated by SLORC Home and Religious Affairs Minister, Lt.-Gen. Phone Myint, at the World Ministerial Drugs Summit in London where, in a frank exchange of words, British officials repeated growing international allegations of Burmese military involvement in the narcotics trade. Without any means of independently checking *Tatmadaw* claims, the British Home Office Minister, David Mellor, queried why SLORC denials should be believed; according to US-UK intelligence reports, since the 1988 coup Burma's opium output had doubled to over 2,000 tons per annum.[23]

These doubts were added to when the breakaway Wa forces of Kyauk Ni Lai and some of their non-NDF brothers in the WNC, headed by Ai Hsiao-hsu, chose this moment to launch a full-scale territorial war with Khun Sa's TRC for control of the strategic Doi Larng mountain on the Thai border. Khun Sa, too, had long enjoyed the *Tatmadaw*'s tacit support, but with casualties running as high as 1,000 killed or wounded in fighting with the United Wa State Army (UWSA), which continued well into the 1990 monsoon season, many observers attributed the outbreak of fighting to a skilful piece of 'Divide and rule' by Khin Nyunt and his MIS officials, who were now working overtime in the Shan State.

Meanwhile, further north the remaining CPB leaders in the Kachin State had been squeezed out even further in December 1989 when the predominantly Kachin troops in the 101 region changed their name from 'People's Army' to 'New Democratic Army' after joining the Peace and Democracy Front. After their first talks with *Tatmadaw* officers, Ting Ying and Zalum returned to encourage the CPB CC to contact SLORC since they believed it would recognise the CPB as a political party if it relinquished the armed struggle. This Kyaw Mya described as 'wishful thinking'. In a statement the Communist Party might have made 40 years before, he explained: 'If there is no armed oppression and if there is genuine democracy there is no need for the people to take up arms.'[24]

None the less, though they expected SLORC to 'flatly refuse' (which it did), the CPB remnants sent a letter to Gen. Saw Maung offering to attend talks anywhere in Burma. Meanwhile even some of these veteran leaders appeared to lose heart. Ba Thein Tin tactfully retired for medical treatment in China where his deputy, Pe Tint, died shortly afterwards from throat cancer. Myo Myint, the former Northern Bureau commander, meanwhile moved to Sichuan Province, while the rest, including Kyaw Mya, had little choice but to work with the mutineers in the 101 region. Kyaw Mya himself, an insurgent organiser for over 40 years, was given responsibility for 'alliance affairs'. But just to show the *Tatmadaw* was not getting everything its own way, the UWSA refused to join in the war with the KIO and tried to mediate between the KIO and Pheung Kya-shin. Then in July 1990 the 101 region leader, Ting Ying, was demoted by his own men and replaced by Salang Muk Ying for allegedly giving too many concessions to Brig. Khin Nyunt, who in early April had helicoptered up to Lauhkaung in the 101's base area for talks near the Chinese border. The 101 group thus appeared divided between those still loyal to the CPB, those who favoured rejoining the KIO, and those who wanted to build a new party altogether.

Like all Burma's insurgent parties, the breakaway rebels had been excluded from the 1990 general election and for the *Tatmadaw* the burning question still remained: just how could these temporary ceasefires be transformed into a lasting peace?

The Outlook for the CPB
Though relatively little blood had been shed, quite how the CPB's ageing leadership could hope to resurrect the party and its former authority in the country was now far from certain. An unknown number of CPB hard-liners had already been killed in the early mutinies, though the only two casualties the Wa mutineers sustained in their attack on Panghsang were inflicted by KNLP soldiers who, unaware of what was going on, opened fire.[25] Fittingly, the subsequent actions of their Kayan, Pao and Karenni allies were to provide the CPB Politburo with one of its few glimmers of hope. After apologising to Kyauk Ni Lai and the Wa leaders, the KNLP and its SSNLO and KSNLF allies sent representatives south to improve relations with the PNO, KNPP and NDF, with whom they had been feuding throughout the 1980s; in July 1990, after a 13-year interval, their leaders Shwe Aye, Tha Kalei and Nya Maung Me travelled to the NDF's general headquarters at Mannerplaw to apply to join the DAB. They rejected overtures from both the *Tatmadaw* and Khun Sa's TRC and showed their left-wing ideals were not totally dead by forming a five-party united front, the All Nationalities Peoples' Democratic Front, comprising the SSNLO, KNLP, KSNLF, the CPB-trained Democratic Patriotic Army and the remnants of the CPB's Central Bureau. Because unity talks between the Pao and Karenni movements were already underway, the DAB rejected their application, which technically included the CPB, whose representative, Saw Jacob, had quietly followed them. But with Tha Kalei as president and the CPB's Saw Ba Moe (an ethnic Karen) as joint-secretary, they remained confident they could build up a progressive pro-democracy force in the western Shan State. According to Shwe Aye, 'The CPB is not totally extinct. When compared to us, the CPB is far better organised in underground tasks. They can operate in the whole country.'[26]

As a military setback, however, the CPB's territorial losses in north-east Burma in 1989 were far more devastating than the fall of its last strongholds in the Pegu Yomas of central Burma in 1975 or the Delta in 1970. This time there were no major base areas to fall back on and in the present climate, despite China's continued support for the Khmer Rouge and the old-guard communist revival after Tiananmen Square, there appears to be no likelihood of China (or any other party or country such as Vietnam) beginning aid. In a decade that has also seen the virtual collapse of the CPB's two closest allies, the CPM and CPT, old-style Maoist communism would appear to have no further appeal in the region.

Ironically, the 1989 mutinies came at a time when for the first time in a decade, following the army's brutal suppression of the democracy uprising, CPB forces in several parts of the country had begun reporting faster political progress. This was especially true of Tenasserim and Arakan, both of which, unlike the eastern Shan State, had been major centres of the democracy uprising. Here their cadres and units had been welcomed by local villagers and townspeople. Underground CPB cadres had also reported growing success in Mandalay, Monywa and several other towns in the north. But the CPB's hope that it will one day again be able to wage armed struggle on anything like its previous scale must remain a pipe-dream. A change of political line and an appeal to its many ageing supporters in the cities might produce one last great rallying-cry charge of emotion, but in the rapidly evolving world of the late 20th century, in view of the enormous changes in the Soviet Union, Eastern Europe, Vietnam, Cambodia and even China, the tide of history is clearly no longer on the CPB's side. If nothing else, the experience of Burma provides a further illuminating example of the historical legacy of communism: just as Marxism was one of the main ideological instruments for the political emancipation of the working class in the industrialised countries of the West in the 19th and 20th centuries, so Maoism proved one of the most popular, if largely unsuccessful, weapons for peasant-based rebellions in the post-colonial world.

The consequences of the 1990 general election are looked at in Chapter 20; in most respects the CPB was now completely overtaken by the new democracy parties in the towns and the armed ethnic opposition and DAB in the 'liberated zones'. Yet, despite the apparent control by Ne Win loyalists and the *Tatmadaw* of the political process in the cities, overall the picture remained one of turmoil. Nowhere was the confusion more apparent than in north-east Burma where, with the collapse of the CPB, the 1990s began with the topography of the Shan and Kachin States once again resembling the complex map of the late 1960s when the region was coloured in with an extraordinary array of ethnic nationalist, communist, warlord, *Tatmadaw* and KKY military forces. This time the armed forces of the student ABSDF, who fled underground in 1988, must be added.

It was from this morass that the CPB was now seeking to emerge. By mid-1990 tenuous contacts had been re-established between most of the party's remaining regional cells, but activities consisted of little more than letter writing and intra-party discussion. Officially the party continued to promote the same four-point platform it had advocated since the upheavals of 1988 (a countrywide ceasefire, a provisional civilian government of national reconciliation, elections to a Constituent Assembly, and a new constitution) arguing that any election held by the military would be rigged. But once the scale of the NLD's victory became clear, the CPB threw its support behind an immediate transfer of power to Aung San Suu Kyi. 'We are trying our best to consolidate the NLD and form a broad united front of all the anti-SLORC forces and individuals,' wrote Kyaw Mya. 'The oppressed people of all nationalities are now in angry mood and they are waiting their time.'[27]

Once again the CPB veterans returned to the example of the key moments in Burma's national liberation struggle. Accusing the military of 'nasty tricks' and deliberately delaying the hand over of power to the NLD, on the 51st anniversary of the party's founding, 15 August 1990, a new policy statement was issued, calling for a 'National Conference' open to 'every force or democratic personage who looks forward to the progress of the country'. The idea closely followed a similar suggestion put forward by SLORC in Rangoon (see Chapter 20), but it was clearly intended that the CPB-proposed National Conference, by contrast to SLORC's army-dominated meeting, would echo the great mass rallies at the Naythuyein Hall and Shwedagon Pagoda in 1945 'after the victory over the Japanese fascists'.[28] Only such a meeting, the CPB claimed, could solve the 'internal' war and the ethnic, economic and social problems which had divided the country since independence.

Despite its many difficulties, the party's tone was still strongly upbeat: 'As for a nation, the present situation in Burma is an excellent opportunity rarely found in one's history.'[29] But as Thakin Pe Tint, the party's vice-chairman, proudly explained in the 1981 peace talks, 'A Communist Party never surrenders.'[30] For all its many weaknesses the CPB remains Burma's oldest political party and its footsteps have dogged every important political event in the country since its inception in 1939, and this includes the 1988 democracy uprising. In its 52-year history, more than 45 of which have been taken up in armed struggle, the CPB has survived many crises and shown an extraordinary ability to survive and return. Amongst the older generation in Burma it is hard to find a family that has not been touched in some way, for better or worse, by the CPB insurgency.

Whether the present young generation, as it now struggles to take charge of Burma's destiny, will show the same enthusiasm for the CPB cause, however, now appears out of the question. Some students have talked mysteriously of the 'new' or 'real' Communist Party now reorganising amongst workers and students in the cities, which they say should have been the CPB's real political base all along. When SLORC led a crackdown on monasteries and young monk organisations, leading a boycott of soldiers' families, in October 1990, it claimed to have found piles of communist literature. It is also clear that discussions of Marxism, socialism and communism are likely to remain common currency in political arguments in Burma until the country's doors are really opened to the outside world. All the main parties contesting the 1990 election in one sense or another had a 'socialist' past: the National Unity Party (BSPP), U Nu's League for Democracy and Peace (AFPFL) and the National League for Democracy (BSPP-AFPFL-NUF). The three years since the coup have only increased the country's isolation and Burma's young people, few of whom speak English or any other foreign language, are deprived of contact with any other modern literature or materials. The only exceptions are the increasing numbers driven into exile, where they are deliberately kept by the military out of harm's way.

None the less, most young people speak of both the CPB and BSPP as the baggage of a failed and warring past that has brought the country to the brink of ruin. Yet little has happened since the coup, despite the excitement caused by the 1990 election, which suggests that the military old guard have really changed their ways. The same underlying problems remain; a new generation of young people has already gone underground since 1988 to begin a new wave of insurgencies.

This time, however, they have not gone to the CPB but to the ethnic nationalists in the mountains, long depicted as 'bandits', 'renegades' and anti-Burman 'separatists' in the Rangoon press.

Burma's future is impossible to predict. But for the CPB, at least, one thing is certain. After over four decades of protracted warfare, the coming decade will be the hardest of all.

The War Goes On: The NDF and the KNU

If the national minorities had become increasingly peripheral to the mainstream course of political events in Burma in the years since independence in 1948, the situation was to change dramatically with the democracy uprising and the turbulent events of the years, 1988-90. Not only was it to the ethnic minority armies in the mountains that thousands of young students and civilian activists fled from the cities following the Saw Maung coup, but the 1990 general election delivered dozens of ethnic minority candidates from no less than 19 national minority parties to the new People's Assembly. This in turn set off a scramble for ethnic minority support, similar to the political wheeling and dealing of the 1940s and 1950s, as the victorious National League for Democracy (NLD), under constant pressure from SLORC, vainly tried to set about the task of drawing up Burma's new constitution.

A new era had undoubtedly dawned. Just as Ne Win's 1962 military coup had changed the face of Burmese politics by outlawing all parties except his own Burma Socialist Programme Party (BSPP), so the 1990 election had brought into legal existence a complex array of new and largely unknown political organisations, leaving the political picture in Burma more uncertain than ever. There were now, in effect, three main political forces in the country; SLORC and the *Tatmadaw* which, claiming descent from Ne Win and Aung San, continued to sweep aside all dissenting voices and reserve for itself the role as the ultimate arbiter of Burma's political fate; the 27 new 'legal' political parties, spearheaded by the NLD, which won an overwhelming 392 of the 485 seats to the new People's Assembly; and the armed opposition which, though most parties were allied in the new Democratic Alliance of Burma (DAB), was still represented by over 20 insurgent forces including the breakaway CPB defectors.

As the peace talks between SLORC and the breakaway CPB rebels during 1989-90 had shown, the political relationships between all three movements were unclear; this had been emphasised when a young student from the underground All Burma Students Democratic Front, Soe Myat Thu, was found in Aung San Suu Kyi's house when she was arrested in July 1989. Indeed, though no real evidence was ever produced, the NLD's alleged contacts with 'insurgent organisations' was one of the main reasons SLORC gave for her continued detention. At the same time, while SLORC and the Ne Win old guard deliberately slowed down any rapid transfer of power and continued to speak aggressively of the *Tatmadaw*'s determination to 'crush' all insurgent opposition, in his epoch-making speech of January 1990, SLORC chairman, Gen. Saw Maung, appeared to turn his back on Ne Win's hard-line approach when he surprisingly described the insurgencies as 'political' questions which could only be decided by negotiations with a future civilian government (see Chapter 1).

As a political signpost to the future, the 1990 election brought the relationships between all three groups into clearer focus (this is examined in the final chapter). But it is with the near forgotten ethnic rebels in the mountains that the political narrative must first be resumed.

Life in the 'Liberated Zones': The NDF

When in the second half of 1988 a generation of Burma's most talented young people made the decision to go underground, it was a very alien world that they were entering. Arriving in small bedraggled groups at dozens of rebel camps across the country, many were shocked to find schools, hospitals and the machinery of well-run governments and armies functioning around most of the ethnic borderlands. Many students, brought up on a strict diet of BSPP propaganda, said they were completely unaware of the scale of the wars raging inside their own country. Initially most said they had come for sanctuary after witnessing the arrests, shootings or deaths of their friends; many expressed the naive hope that arms and ammunition would be awaiting them from Thailand, India, the US, the UK and sympathetic governments abroad. On every count they were disappointed. Some students quickly went on into exile, some returned to their homes, while still others, impatient for results, made no secret of the limitations, as they saw it, of the ethnic forces they encountered. But many stayed and enthusiastically took on board the cause of the ethnic minorities, which they described in propaganda statements as the major impediment to the country's development. After their own brutal treatment by the security forces and the wanton destruction of ethnic minority villages they witnessed on their way, many said they now understood for the first time the die-hard attitudes of veteran insurgent leaders like Bo Mya, Brang Seng, Saw Maw Reh and Nai Shwe Kyin.

These extraordinary meetings in the 'liberated zones' of political dissidents from the cities and insurgent leaders from the countryside in the second half of 1988 resulted in the Democratic Alliance of Burma (DAB) of November 1988 (see Chapter 1). This was not simply political opportunism by Burma's ethnic rebels, as a stream of commentaries in the state media alleged, but the logical result of a lengthy process of strategic planning by nationalist forces.[1]

The military nucleus of the DAB was the 11-party National Democratic Front (NDF), which is today the best known of all Burma's insurgent united fronts. But the NDF is by no means Burma's first nationalities alliance. Starting with the Democratic Nationalities United Front of 1956, there has been a long succession of nationality alliances dominated by ethnic minority forces (see Chart 2). The National Democratic United Front (1959-75) with the CPB, and the National United Liberation Front (1970-4) with U Nu's Parliamentary Democracy Party, were the only two that really brought together ethnic minority and Burman majority forces. With their demise in the mid-1970s most nationality parties, recognising their armies posed little threat to the balance of power in Rangoon, settled for the less provocative policy of protecting their own territories and cultures and working with other ethnic forces in the region.

The NDF finally broke this mould. Formed at the general headquarters of the Karen National Union (KNU) at Mannerplaw in May 1976 shortly before Mahn Ba Zan was ousted (see Chapter 14), like most of its predecessors, in its early years it rarely proved effective; only with the return of the Kachin Independence

Organisation (KIO) in 1983 was it for the first time really galvanised into action. To the disquiet of other NDF members, the KIO had abruptly withdrawn its representatives from the Thai border in 1980 and unilaterally taken part in the abortive peace talks with the BSPP. The KIO's public alliance with the CPB worried Bo Mya and the NDF leaders even more.

Their experience in Rangoon, KIO chairman Brang Seng freely admitted, finally convinced the KIO it was hopeless to expect ever to achieve anything by fighting on alone (see Chapter 15). This view was shared by most other NDF parties and the return of 8,000 battle-hardened Kachin troops (including many women recruits) in Burma's north-east made the NDF a far more formidable proposition. This, in turn, was an important factor behind the *Tatmadaw*'s decision during 1983/4 to change the focus of its military operations away from the CPB. NDF leaders claimed to be able to call on over 20,000 volunteers under arms from the Himalayan foothills on the India-China border to the dense rain forests of Tenasserim.

The most critical decisions reflecting these rapid changes in the NDF's political organisation were taken at its Third Plenary Central Presidium. This meeting at Mannerplaw in October 1984 was attended by representatives from nine NDF parties, including KIO Chief-of-Staff, Zau Mai, who, a quarter of a century after having slipped into the jungle from Rangoon University to make contact with the Karen underground, was reunited with the KNU's veteran leaders. Over the years most NDF members had redefined their political goals, generally watering down any 'separatist' language, but here for the first time the demand for the right of secession by all NDF members, including the KNU, was explicitly dropped and the political goals of the NDF were rewritten in terms designed to win support from the Burman majority:

> The NDF does not want racial hatred. It is struggling for liberty, equality and social progress of all indigenous races of Burma, because Burma is a multi-national state inhabited and owned by all. In the so called Burma of today, the National Democratic Front intends to establish a unified Federal Union with all the ethnic races including the Burmese.[2]

Veteran Kachin, Karen, Karenni, Mon and Shan leaders may still dream in their hearts of independent nations.[3] But, despite a few wobbles, all NDF members have stuck by this 'federalist' line through the hard years since. Certainly from the day a common, though admittedly vague, political platform was agreed, the NDF has appeared a far more potent force, both at home and abroad.

This, of course, by no means signified that the NDF had overcome all its political difficulties. Karen leaders, in particular, remained sensitive to charges that the KNU was to blame for the NDF's earlier lethargy, pointing out that it was the KNU alone which had been giving arms, finance and training to weaker NDF members, such as the Pao National Organisation (PNO) and Arakan Liberation Party. (The KIO, for its part, had frequently bailed out the Palaung State Liberation Party, especially after the death in battle of its founder leader, Kham Thaung, in 1979, but had also looked in other directions, giving training to various non-NDF Chin, Arakanese, Naga and even ethnic resistance groups from India.) Serious contradictions still existed within the NDF. The most obvious was the absence of any group representing the Burman majority and deep disagreements still continued over relations with the CPB. The KIO and Shan State Progress Party (SSPP), for example, had joint treaties with the CPB, while the

PNO and Karenni National Progressive Party (KNPP) frequently clashed with CPB guerrillas. Beneath the surface, too, were territorial disputes between NDF members, including the KNU and New Mon State Party (NMSP), KIO and SSPP. There remained very different policies on the narcotics question. While the KIO, SSPP and Wa National Organisation admit to their involvement in the opium trade (they claim they are powerless to stop it passing through their territories), others, especially the KNU, are strongly opposed to opium and enforce the death penalty for convicted traffickers.

There have been several important insurgent groups active elsewhere in Burma that are not members of the NDF, notably the Tailand Revolutionary Council (TRC) in the Shan State and the National Socialist Council of Nagaland (NSCN) in Burma's far north. While the NDF talks of self-determination for all Burma's ethnic races and the creation of new nationality states (including a 'Burman' state) and a complex system of local autonomous regions for minorities within each state, the TRC advocates a simple system of 'national' states for what it describes as the five major 'nations' of Burma: the Burman, Kachin, Karen, Karenni and Shan. In the one-party days of the BSPP, finding a compromise between such differing philosophies (let alone common ground with the CPB's unitary model of multi-party democracy) was an impossible task.

Given the scale of these difficulties, it was important just how much progress the NDF was able to make. Behind these reforms was a growing war weariness which few NDF leaders tried to conceal; long before the democracy uprising most had been openly expressing their desire to find a way out of Burma's disastrous cycle of insurgency. One of the NDF's most ambitious moves was to set up three military fronts to cover the whole of Burma (see Chapter 17). By 1987 joint NDF battalions had been trained and battle tested in each region. While their effectiveness on the hard-pressed southern front has been limited, there can be little doubt that the activities of NDF members elsewhere in Burma, especially by the KIO-SSPP-PSLP in the north-east, had some success in diverting attention away from Kawthoolei. In 1987 the BSPP government was forced to launch a massive, largely unsuccessful offensive it could ill afford in the Kachin State.

The NDF has also succeeded in attracting increasing international attention to Burma's forgotten wars. In 1987 two NDF delegations, one headed by Major Hsar Ta Nor of the KNU and one by Brang Seng of the KIO, for the first time travelled extensively abroad, visiting several countries in Europe and Asia, including the UK, West Germany, Switzerland and Japan. Their call, much to the BSPP's anger, was for international efforts to help end Burma's civil war; in reply, the *Working People's Daily* called Brang Seng the 'devil incarnate'.[4] History finally came full cycle in London where, 41 years after the Karen Goodwill Mission of 1946, Hsar Ta Nor addressed the Foreign Affairs Committee of the House of Commons and, in the House of Lords, Brang Seng met Lord Listowel, the last British Secretary of State for Burma, and Lord Bottomley, the British representative at Panglong.[5] Indeed Brang Seng's uncle, Zau La, was one of the Kachin delegates at that historic conference which did so much to shape the future course of Burma. I myself witnessed this extraordinary meeting in November 1987 as the two wizened old men, clearly shocked by what they heard, squirmed uncomfortably as Brang Seng tearfully told them of the hundreds of thousands of deaths which followed their hasty departure from Burma. For all parties concerned, it was a highly symbolic moment.

Considerable efforts were also expended on trying to forge greater unity amongst insurgent fronts inside Burma. One notable success was the healing in December 1987 of the split in the NMSP which for six years had divided the Mon nationalist movement into two factions headed by the veteran nationalist leaders, Nai Shwe Kyin and Nai Non Lar.[6] Ironically, one side-effect of the NMSP's reunion was an immediate increase in Mon military strength, which led to an upsurge in tension with its old ally, the KNU. For several years arguments over taxation and territory had been escalating between front-line KNU and NMSP troops (especially from the Nai Shwe Kyin faction) in the Thanbyuzayat-Mezali area and a number of clashes had occurred. In July 1988 the dispute finally erupted into a major battle at Three Pagodas Pass, in which most of the town was destroyed, over 100 lives lost and the NDF paralysed at the height of the democracy uprising. Regardless of who was to blame, it was a political error as great as any in the history of the insurgencies and saw friend shooting friend from buildings on either side of the pass. When an NDF mediation team led by the KIO and SSPP moved into the area, the dispute was quietly settled, but the whole bloody episode served as an important reminder that racial tensions in Burma are not simply an ethnic minority/Burman majority issue.

Despite this setback, over the years the NDF has had some success in getting different insurgent groups in Arakan round the same table. In 1985 a National Unity Front of Arakan was established, which in 1988 was expanded to bring together the main Rakhine nationalist parties, though, significantly, not the Islamic *Mujahids* (see Chapter 12). So far, attempts to mediate between Khun Sa's TRC and NDF members in the Shan State have met with little success. There have been frequent battles; in March 1985, for example, Bo Mya despatched a KNU mortar team north to help the NDF's Wa and Pao allies in a pitched battle with the TRC at Mae Aw. Since then tension has been gradually defused, but despite a controversial visit by Bo Mya to meet Khun Sa in December 1987, distrust remains high.[7]

However, the most controversial move was the attempt to reach some kind of political accommodation with the CPB in the mid-1980s. Indeed for a time it threatened to destroy the NDF's new-found unity. At the KIO's instigation, in March 1985 a joint NDF team, led by KNU CC member U Soe Aung, set out with a heavily armed escort on a goodwill tour through rebel-held territory across Burma to try and resolve the NDF's many internal differences. Eight months later, after several battles with government troops along the way, the party arrived on 19 November 1985 at the KIO's headquarters at Pajao, 600 miles to the north, amidst scenes of wild rejoicing, ensuring a full NDF presence north and south for the first time. For the NDF it was an important political boost; here its team was able to hold talks with several other insurgent groups in the region, including the CPB, the NSCN and various rebel Manipuri and Assamese groups from north-east India.

But when, accompanied by Brang Seng, it returned south into the Shan State to meet Ba Thein Tin and the CPB leaders at Panghsang, the signing of a joint military accord threw the NDF into temporary disarray (see Chapter 17). In August 1986, KNU president Bo Mya rejected the treaty outright and delivered a forthright denunciation of the CPB, in which he accused it of drugs-trafficking, 'chauvinism towards the indigenous peoples' and 'marching towards a communist state in accordance with the doctrine of Marxism-Leninism'.[8] On his return Mahn

Sha La Pan, the column's military commander and a KNUP veteran of the trips to China, was demoted to the rank of private and sent to the front. U Soe Aung waited some months longer, only returning in February 1988 when the political temperature had cooled.[9]

Bo Mya's irritation with the NDF still continued after its Second Congress of May-July 1987. This was attended by Brang Seng and SSPP general-secretary Sai Lek, who had both made the dangerous journey down to the Thai border to try and placate Bo Mya. At the congress the other nine NDF members, most of whom had fought with the CPB at different times in the past, insisted that the CPB alliance was purely a matter of military convenience and that they would stick by the terms of the agreement. The advantages of the treaty became immediately obvious, especially in the Shan State where troops and cadres from both organisations were for the first time able to move freely through each other's territory, allowing guerrilla forces far greater mobility than in the past.

Such arguments, however, failed to win Bo Mya over and KNU and NDF leaders eventually had to agree to disagree on the subject. With his maximum two terms of office now up, Bo Mya, who had been NDF president virtually since its inception in 1976, was replaced by the Karenni president, Saw Maw Reh. On the eve of the democracy uprising this saw a growing estrangement between the KNU and the NDF and, in March 1988, despite the heavy fighting with the *Tatmadaw* echoing in the hills nearby, Bo Mya openly told me of his disillusionment with the NDF and the possibility of the KNU leaving if the NDF did not take greater account of his views. His main grievance was what he termed the KIO's 'unilateral style'; he was concerned that, since the failure of the 1980/1 peace talks, the KIO had been acting on the secret instructions of the CPB and China, a charge Brang Seng absolutely rejects.[10] However, at an ensuing KNU CC meeting that same day, few voices spoke up in Bo Mya's support and, with the democracy uprising and the near simultaneous collapse of the CPB, these differences quickly receded into the past.

Kawthoolei in the 1980s
As these events clearly demonstrated, in recent years the KNU and KIO have come to dominate the NDF movement. The SSPP, the only comparable organisation in military strength, has all too frequently been divided by infighting and political splits. Groups such as the NMSP, KNPP, PSLP and PNO have all controlled their own liberated territories, but these areas are minute compared with the vast areas controlled by the KIO, KNU, or CPB. Without the fierce resistance of these more powerful forces, many of the weaker NDF members would have found it virtually impossible to have survived in their present form any sustained military pressure from the *Tatmadaw*.

Life in the 'liberated zones' of the KIO in north-east Burma has been vividly described by a Swedish journalist, Bertil Lintner, and his wife Hseng Noung, who is an ex-SSPP veteran.[11] But it was in KNU territory in the south that most of the key military and political developments in the 1980s took place; it was here that most foreign observers first came to learn of the war in Burma after the failure of the democracy uprising in 1988.

In many ways the two movements were characterised by their respective leaders, ex-headmaster Maran Brang Seng (born 1931), unusually for an insurgent leader in Burma an intellectual without a military background, and Karen military strong man Gen. Bo Mya, a ruthless guerrilla fighter since the days of the Second World War. In recent years Brang Seng has featured more frequently in the international headlines. A regular visitor to China and, more recently, to Thailand and the West, he has often appeared to be two or three steps ahead of his contemporaries, both in Rangoon and in the *maquis*. Indeed Brang Seng, a devout Baptist, has often been mentioned as somebody who, in a more peaceful world, would have made an able and perceptive leader of the country. But Bo Mya is more typical of the military hard men who have come to the top and survived the civil war.

Bo Mya's slow rise to power, which is analysed earlier in this account, owed much to the complex geo-politics of South-East Asia in the Vietnam era of the 1960s and 1970s. But if the KNU's abrupt shift to the right under Bo Mya largely relieved Thai fears about its undefended western border, his tough leadership had equally serious implications for the Karen nationalist movement inside Burma. Little public dissension has been permitted and no KNU congresses have been held since 1974. Political decisions have been made either at meetings of the 33-man CC or, more usually, by a five-man standing committee of Bo Mya's closest advisers. In part, this can be attributed to the difficulties of transport and communication, with KNU base areas today strung out along a mountainous 500-mile stretch of the Burma-Thailand frontier. Radio contact has been maintained with front-line units of the KNU's military wing, the Karen National Liberation Army (KNLA), but KNU officers operating in military brigade districts such as Nyaunglebin and Toungoo further to the west have rarely come back to Bo Mya's general headquarters at Mannerplaw near the junction of the Moei and Salween Rivers. But partly, too, this clear lack of democratic centralisation, common to other insurgent groups in Burma, has been due to Bo Mya's authoritarian style of leadership; key statements and policy changes have sometimes been issued, much to the consternation of KNU veterans, without any prior discussion at all.

Against these failings must be set the powerful unifying role Bo Mya has played in keeping the Karen nationalist movement together. Like the SSPP or the KIO, it is easy for outside observers to forget the scale of the difficulties the KNU has faced, divided as it is by territory, language, religion and politics. Bo Mya's major achievement has been in generating a coherent sense of identity amongst such ethnic diversity and poverty in the eastern hills. Even his sternest critics concede that his bulldog brand of nationalism exerts a powerful pull. Though it is a comparison he does not relish, the two insurgent leaders who have come closest to emulating his uncomplicated nationalist appeal, are the veteran 'opium warlords', Gon Jerng and Khun Sa, in the Shan State to the north. It was not until 1985 and 1987 respectively that their paths finally crossed and, though there were deep disagreements over narcotics and the nationalities question, they did indeed find they had much in common.[12]

One major weakness, however, which many critics have laid at Bo Mya's door, has been the KNU's failure to penetrate back into its old strongholds in the Delta, despite a continuing flow of Karens from towns and villages across Lower Burma to join the KNLA in the east. With much of Lower Burma under a watchful military guard since the great *Four Cuts* campaigns of the 1960s and 1970s, it was always going to be a difficult task and certainly the CPB fared little better. But it is here the majority of Karens live and, if ever the Karen revolution is to succeed by armed struggle alone, KNLA commanders agree it is an essential task. In 1978 the BSPP warned of insurgent attempts to 're-establish a foothold' amongst Karen villagers along the Letpadan-Nattalin plain, where many communities had been forcibly relocated at the height of the 1974/5 Pegu Yomas campaign.[13] But this referred to the last dying attempts by KNUP remnants to reorganise in the area and to this day few Karen villagers have been allowed to return to their homes in the hills. Only two real attempts have been made by the KNU to carry the war back into Lower Burma and both ended in failure. In September 1982 an underground KNU cell in Rangoon was smashed after a bungled attack on the government radio station, in which two policemen and two guerrillas were killed.[14] And in February 1983 a heavily armed column of 200 KNLA troops attempting to infiltrate westwards into the Pegu Yomas was intercepted near Nyaunglebin soon after crossing the Rangoon-Mandalay railway line and crushed.[15]

As befits a true Sgaw Karen of the Papun hills, Bo Mya has always rather concentrated on maintaining KNU rule in the rugged hills in the east, over which he has presided since 1963. It is here, in the 'liberated' mini-state of Kawthoolei, a country unmarked on any map, that the flame of the Karen rebellion has been kept alive; it is here, at the start of the 1990s, that travellers could see an alternative vision of Karen society, very different from that under the BSPP-SLORC governments in the Delta, where all public expressions of Karen language and culture have been disappearing fast. From the Mawdaung Pass to the Toungoo hills an impressive network was established of KNU government departments, hospitals and clinics and hundreds of village schools, serving the seven main KNU administrative districts. These included five high schools, of which three have since been forced to move to refugee camps in Thailand. Given the lack of resources, standards remain surprisingly high. Indeed, most of the teachers are university graduates, including a number who are the children of KNU veterans, secretly brought up by relatives in the towns. The main medium of education is Sgaw, but in the ethnic Pwo villages, which lie mostly in the valleys to the west, Pwo is still used. Burmese, too, is taught but is categorised (and only half in jest) alongside English and Thai as a 'foreign language'.

In most respects, reflecting the weakness of central control, each administrative district is self-supporting and responsible for its own day-to-day affairs. This is both a weakness and a strength: it means that KNLA units cannot always count on support from neighbouring brigades, but it makes it difficult for the *Tatmadaw* to tie down and destroy a central command structure. The KNU's organisational system, largely developed by the now-defunct KNUP, is copied by many other ethnic insurgent fronts in Burma and is therefore worth describing in detail. Each district puts up six representatives to the full KNU congress which, in theory, is held every four years. From this group a minimum of two delegates are then elected by congress to the KNU CC. Since no KNU congress has been held since 1974, however, new CC members are usually appointed by KNU general head-quarters if and when the need arises. These two representatives are usually the senior KNLA commander and political 'governor' in each district, which ensures a broad geographic representation, along with a nominal number of veterans from the Delta, at the annual CC meetings at Mannerplaw. In addition, in recognition of the growing age of the KNU leadership (the average age of CC members is well over 60), in 1984 17 younger KNU officials were appointed as 'candidate' CC members to be trained as the next generation of KNU administrators. From this full CC Bo Mya then selects a central standing committee and a Cabinet of 'ministers' who run their departments from Mannerplaw. But, given the distances involved and difficulties of communication, much of their work tends to be advisory or supervisory.[16] (Similarly, the KIO has held no full congresses since the 1960s and relies on its CC as its decision-making government; the SSPP, likewise, has held only two congresses since its formation in 1971 and the KNPP just five since 1957.)

Other than this, the districts are left largely to their own devices. Only the mining and, more recently, forestry departments have been placed under the direct control of general headquarters and, though not unknown, transfers of personnel between the different brigade areas are comparatively rare. This is the most striking difference between the KIO and KNU. It has often been said that since Zau Seng and the KIO's founders first trained with the KNU in the 1950s, they learnt not to copy the KNU's worst mistakes. As a result, obvious differences in political and military philosophy have evolved. The 6th brigade under Col. Shwe Hser, for example, stands some way to the left of the 7th brigade under Col. Htay Maung. But a standard system of administration has been introduced and each district follows the *Policy of Rules and Regulations of the Karen National Union* laid down by the 1974 congress. At the village level in most base areas, KNU councils and health, agricultural and education boards have been set up which elect representatives to the KNU township committees. These, in turn, elect the members of each district committee. This full district committee is then the supreme administrative body for each district and liaises closely with the governor and the regional KNLA command, which also maintains a presence in the villages through the local KNDOs who are usually farmers, young boys or retired soldiers.

In many ways the KNLA operates as a parallel administration inside Kawthoolei. In fact, in several areas, it is the real administration, relaying messages and taking quick day-to-day decisions depending on the state of the fighting. The KNLA bases are thus the main hub of KNU administration in the districts. In front-line areas KNLA units keep constantly on the move and KNU organisers have to carry out their duties in villages or temporary jungle camps. But in the secure rear base areas, a string of permanent KNLA strongholds were built in strategic military positions, usually close to the jungle trade roads leading towards the Thai border. The traders themselves, amongst whom MIS agents often travel in disguise, are kept at a safe distance, but the offices of all the main KNU departments are kept in scattered civilian settlements around the defence perimeters and each weekday (Saturdays and Sundays are religiously observed) these come alive with the busy clatter of typewriters and the hum of radio transmitters. Like insurgent bases on the Thai and Chinese borders, most camps have generators and their own supplies of electricity and, despite the endemic malaria throughout Kawthoolei, enjoy a surprising air of affluence in their remote, but often idyllic, jungle settings. Punctuating life at the bases is a full litany of nationalist festivals and holidays, Revolution Day (31 January), KNU Day (5 February), Martyr's Day (12 August), when the camps come alive with military parades, traditional 'Don' dancing, and theatre performances in Karen national costumes.

Noticeable, too, at all KNU bases is the number of churches and the strong influence of Christianity amongst the senior KNU leadership. Virtually everyone on the KNU CC today is a practising Baptist. Of the others, most are Seventh Day Adventists, including Bo Mya and his assistant, Dr Marta. Even so-called Buddhists, like Vice-President San Lin, take full part in the regular Christian festivals and celebrations. In 1988 Saw Htila, the one Buddhist *pongyi* in the senior KNU administration, announced his intention to become a Christian. This predominance of Christian leaders is also reflected in many of the district administrations, though not at the village or township level where most officials are Buddhists or Animists. This contrast is at its most striking in the military, where Buddhist recruits are in the majority. Indeed, many KNLA units in the Thaton and Papun districts are entirely Buddhist or Buddhist-Animist. On one trip I met a KNU 'song and dance' troupe from Thaton, whose performances, despite many references to Saw Ba U Gyi and the Christian heroes of the Karen revolution, were entirely in Burmese and deeply imbued with Buddhist imagery.[17] Having observed a similar scale of political organisation and cultural vitality at Mon, Pao and Shan insurgent camps, all of which are staunchly Buddhist, I would caution against reading too much into Christianity as a cause of insurgency, as Burman leaders have all too frequently alleged. But so synonymous has the KNU become with Christianity that many Western journalists on fleeting visits to Kawthoolei have routinely, but erroneously, described it as simply a Christian movement.

Over the last decade many of Bo Mya's pronouncements have become increasingly interwoven with Christian sentiment and the KNU judicial system now reflects a distinctly Old Testament view of Christian morality. There are strict prohibitions against alcohol and pre-marital sex. In theory, the death penalty for adultery still exists, though this is not a modern imposition. Unlike the Akhas and other hill peoples in the region, most Karen sub-groups and Animists have traditionally kept strict intra-village sexual mores. Freedom of religion is, however, one of the most important articles of KNU faith and there are Buddhist temples or shrines in many villages in KNU-controlled territory. There are even a number of Muslim mosques, though noticeably few of either have been built at KNU bases. Despite this obvious contradiction, there have been few incidents of religious rivalry, other than in refugee camps where Western missionaries have sometimes upset religious sensibilities. Many Karen leaders accredit this religious tolerance to Bo Mya himself, who has become something of a fabled father figure amongst the hill Karens in the east. Many have been the recipients of his generosity in building village schools or wells and, unlike the university educated KNU leaders from the Delta, he is definitely regarded as 'one of us'. The Christian churches for the most part also operate independently of the KNU and, despite obvious difficulties, strive to work on both sides of the battle lines, sending Karen missionaries trained at Bible schools in Kawthoolei into rural communities throughout south-east Burma.

But the key to Karen resistance has always been the KNU's armed wing, the KNLA. Still run along British lines, with British ranks and formations, the KNLA high command today reflects the violent course of Burma's nationalist struggles over the past 50 years. Virtually the entire leadership are veterans of the Second World War. Since 1949 these officers have been duplicating many of the battles and skirmishes of that time, over the same terrain and with much the same tactics and equipment. Where they have been unable to get hold of more sophisticated weaponry through seizures or black market purchases, they have shown considerable ingenuity by manufacturing their own at minimal cost.

KNU leaders have always been reticent about discussing KNLA troop strength, but at its peak in the early 1980s senior commanders agree that 5,000 regulars and 5,000 KNDO village militia was probably the maximum figure. Deployed against three *Tatmadaw* divisions, or 30,000 combat troops, this still represented a sizeable force. Each family in KNU base areas is usually expected to nominate one son, if required, to join the KNLA; service is usually for an initial period of seven years. During this time marriage is not permitted. Because of the deteriorating military situation since 1984, a new regulation prohibiting marriage before the age of 35 has been introduced for those who stay on in KNLA service. The same conditions apply for women who join (generally as nurses); but as in other insurgent organisations, it is rare for women to achieve higher rank in either the party or army. The KNLA provides food and uniforms, but other than a daily cheroot allowance, recruits receive no pay. Most soldiers have to get by on pocket-money from their families to buy luxuries like biscuits and soap. It is, by necessity, a flexible system, but it has meant that the KNLA can at short notice call up or demobilise large numbers of troops according to the state of the war. In one form or another, all the KNLA brigades have so far survived the KNU's military setbacks of the late 1980s.

Conditions for serving soldiers are frequently harsh. After undergoing basic training, troops are sent on long tours of duty to the front. Most battalions rotate their troops, i.e. while two companies are on active duty one is kept in reserve. But this can still mean months on front-line patrol. Like the Wa recruits to the CPB's People's Army or the Chins in the *Tatmadaw*, KNLA troops have displayed remarkable endurance and bravery; there can be little doubt that for many hill Karens service in the KNLA has for many years been an entirely respectable vocation. My impression is that in the war zones villagers have little choice but to become either pro-KNU or pro-government: captured officials or soldiers can expect little mercy from either side.

A visitor to the KNU's various brigade areas is perhaps most struck by the very different levels of prosperity. In theory KNLA organisation and finance are centralised, but in practise each brigade is largely responsible for raising its own funds and arming its own troops. This has meant that its strongest brigades, the 6th and 7th, with their once lucrative trading bases along the Thai border, have continued to prosper, while the smaller ones, such as No.2 (Toungoo) and No.3 (Nyaunglebin), have had to rely on their own dwindling resources. The extremes at one stage were vast. This meant that while the hazardous guerrilla war for front-line units deep inside Burma continued, in the early 1980s Kawmoorah and several of the major KNLA trading posts along the Thai frontier began to resemble the jungle outreaches of some vast 19th century commercial empire. Individual commanders built up personal fortunes and a number invested their money in businesses in Thailand. Those I interviewed have insisted all profits are used for the benefit of the KNU, but other party veterans privately question the validity of these claims. Accusations of 'warlordism' have not been made by the *Tatmadaw* alone. In 1981, in a caustic warning shortly before his death, Mahn Ba Zan told one young Rangoon University recruit: 'The Karens can survive poverty, but I am not so sure they will be able to withstand prosperity.'

As a result, at a time when many observers believed the KNU should have been expanding the war, a dangerous complacency was developing. In 1977 a

Tatmadaw advance on the 101 Special Battalion headquarters at Kawmoorah was easily halted and in 1980 a major offensive directed at the 6th brigade's trading post at Three Pagodas Pass had been pushed back, leaving life in the 'liberated zones' largely untouched and KNLA commanders confident of their ability to resist any *Tatmadaw* attack. In 1983 the KNU staged a rare propaganda coup after the kidnapping of a young French engineer and his wife engaged on a French government-aided cement plant construction project near Myaingale when the couple were released on the Thai border several weeks later to generally favourable plaudits from the world press.[18] But, confided one younger CC member: 'The best thing the Thais could do is close the border. Then we'd be really forced to go down into Burma and fight.'

These warnings were starkly brought home in January 1984, when the *Tatmadaw* for the first time launched a major *Four Cuts* offensive against the KNU's main strongholds in the northern Dawna Range. This time the target was the KNLA's strongest brigade, the 7th, in the pivotal Paan-Hlaingbwe districts north-east of Moulmein. The army's first move, largely lost sight of in an unusual rainy-season assault on Maw Po Kay, was the capture by army commandos of the Nawtaya mountain peak which, at over 6,000 feet, has commanding views along the range. This heavily fortified outpost proved a vital forward base for coordinating *Tatmadaw* operations and for bringing troops and supplies in by helicopter out of the range of KNLA guns. (Elsewhere, after the KNLA shot down in mid-1983 three Bell helicopters donated by the US under an anti-narcotics programme, the *Tatmadaw* refrained from using its fragile control of the air and the war has largely been fought on the ground.)

For weeks beforehand hundreds of porters, press-ganged into service, struggled through the mountains carrying supplies to the front. But expecting another dry season hit-and-run offensive, KNLA commanders were slow to react. In the first strike the KNLA's strategic base at Mae Tah Waw on the northern Moei River was overrun by a 2,000-strong assault force from the *Tatmadaw*'s 44th Light Infantry Division, effectively cutting KNLA lines north to south. Finally waking up to the danger, KNLA troops, abandoning every rule of guerrilla warfare, began digging into fixed positions around their strongholds at Klerday, Maw Po Kay, Mae La and Kawmoorah further south to defend their prosperous trading posts. These the army failed to capture in a series of costly frontal assaults, but, despite steadily rising casualties, the *Tatmadaw* did not now withdraw.[19]

Instead, having achieved a foothold in the heart of KNU territory and with hundreds of the 7th brigade's best trained and equipped troops pegged down on the border, concentration was focused on the other main objectives of the *Four Cuts* strategy, namely severing the KNLA's financial lifeline, cutting military supply lines and cutting rebel links with the civilian population.

In the first of these, success was limited. Border trade, KNU leaders admit, was drastically curtailed but by no means eliminated. In March 1988 officers at the KNU's finance and revenue department estimated that income was down by 60 per cent, but by a combination of measures, including opening new trade gates away from the fighting, increased timber extraction and better financial central-isation, the KNU was able to make good some of these losses. In what rapidly became a grim war of attrition, KNLA units on the border remained surprisingly well turned out and equipped. Right up until the democracy uprising, the deep failures of the *Burmese Way to Socialism* were still all too obvious, as thousands of traders continued to run the gauntlet of *Tatmadaw* patrols carrying black market goods to and from the border. Even the summary execution of 42 suspected smugglers by the *Tatmadaw* near Phalu in June 1985 did little to discourage this flow. 'It's incredible. Sometimes they pop out of the forest just minutes after the firing stops,' said the local KNLA commander.[20]

Tatmadaw commanders were probably always aware of the scale of the problems they faced. The drastic decline of the Burmese economy in the 1980s was inextricably bound up with the civil war. As Burma slid towards Least Developed Country status in 1987, Ne Win's two desperate demonetisations of the Burmese currency in a vain bid to bankrupt the insurgent economy were immediately followed by the most serious outbreak of riots and demonstrations in towns across Burma for over a decade. Indeed the two demonetisations, more than any other event, precipitated the eventual upsurge of revolt in 1988.

Equally pressing, *Tatmadaw* commanders have always had to take into account the risk of upsetting their Thai neighbours. Until 1989, when faced with heavy KNLA (or KNPP, NMSP) resistance, they have generally taken care not to move the front line too quickly, too close to the Thai border. When fighting has spilled across the border (and in several little-reported clashes between *Tatmadaw* and Thai troops there have been casualties on both sides), the Thai government has been swift to complain. No real border demarcation has ever taken place between the two countries and there remain a number of potential flashpoints, especially around Three Pagodas Pass, which have still to be resolved.

As with China, Ne Win appeared to settle for a long-term policy of appeasement to try and improve relations with Bangkok and cut off KNU supply lines from the rear. In comparison with the frosty relations of the past, the years 1985-8, even before the democracy uprising, saw a sharp increase in the exchange of diplomatic missions between the two countries, culminating in the visit of Ne Win to Thailand in November 1987 and a reciprocal visit in April 1988 by a 150-strong delegation headed by Gen. Chaovalit Yongchaiyudh, the Thai army commander-in-chief. Among the projects they discussed were an increase in the official trade in teak and, to the alarm of Karen villagers, the construction of hydro-electric dams along the Moei and Salween Rivers in the heart of Kawthoolei to supply electricity to both countries.[21]

A few months later Chaovalit emerged as the *Tatmadaw*'s first international friend after the crushing of the democracy uprising. But at this stage nobody foresaw the coming political upheavals or the corruption and chaos ignited in 1989/90 by the upsurge in the cross-border timber trade (see Chapter 20). The logging initiative was very much the brain-child of Gen. Chaovalit, backed by powerful business interests, following the ecological destruction of Thailand's own forest reserves. Similar approaches were made in the same period to Thailand's other uneasy neighbours, Laos and Cambodia.

Thus, despite the importance of this new economic tie, while Burma's political uncertainties continue, most diplomatic observers agree that any *rapprochement* between the two countries is likely to be slow. The contrast between the xenophobic, austere, military-dominated government of Rangoon and the headlong capitalism of modern Thailand could not be more extreme. While, with the rapid decline of the CPT in the mid-1980s, the KNU no longer represents the same anti-communist bulwark defending Thailand's frontiers, the desire to improve relations with Rangoon has to be carefully counterbalanced against existing local trading interests. As long as the KNU, NMSP, KNPP or TRC remain a potent force, local Thai governors have to acknowledge the presence of Burma's ethnic rebels along their borders. Local Thai-Karen, Mon or Shan relations have always been extremely cordial. Indeed many Thai officers greet the arrival of any Burman soldiers on their borders with apprehension and say the great wars of the 18th century and the sacking of the Siamese capital at Ayut'ia by the Burman king, Hsinbyushin, have never been forgotten or forgiven.[22]

But if the *Tatmadaw* found it difficult to cut insurgent supply lines, it showed no such restraint in attacking the civilian population. The *Four Cuts* campaign in south-east Burma in the years 1984-90 was without doubt one of the most brutal military operations since independence. From 1982 onwards I made frequent trips through KNU-controlled territory and everywhere the evidence gathered in hundreds of interviews points to very much the same conclusion: in the great majority of areas the *Tatmadaw* behaved like a marauding, conquering army. Unlike the *Four Cuts* campaign in central Burma, these attacks have been strongly racial in character and been carried out by predominantly Burman troops against Karen, Karenni and Mon villagers. Alleged Amnesty International in May 1988: 'So numerous and so similar are the accounts of human rights violations given by the refugees that in Amnesty International's view they show a consistent pattern of gross violations of human rights.'[23]

The Amnesty report documented the extra-judicial executions of 60 Karen villagers and 200 other cases of ill-treatment, rape and torture, but this was just the tip of the iceberg. In the same period, similar but largely undocumented allegations were made by other NDF members in the Kachin, Kayah and Shan States, but only the evidence in the Paan-Hlaingbwe districts of the Karen State was graphically seen. By 1988, after five years' constant military harassment, the scene along a 70-mile stretch of the Dawna Range was one of devastation. Dozens of villages had been burnt down, crops confiscated and fields destroyed. Several thousand villagers had moved into new 'strategic villages' on the plains to the west, while over 20,000 Karen refugees had crossed into Thailand. In a concerted offensive, Karen leaders estimated that as many as another 100,000 Karens and Mons could follow, a prospect the Thai government, already beset by considerable refugee problems on its Laotian and Cambodian borders, viewed with understandable alarm.

Brutal the *Tatmadaw*'s tactics may have been, but, as in the 1970s, it achieved many of its objectives. At the time of the democracy uprising, much of the KNU's organisation in its once impregnable northern strongholds was cracking. During 1984 and 1985 most of the villages on the plains in the Paan and Hlaingbwe districts were being placed under *Tatmadaw* control. With the KNLA 7th brigade largely pegged back in the mountains, in 1986 and 1987 the *Tatmadaw*'s focus was changed to the weaker No.1 and No.3 brigade areas to the north-west around Thaton, Shwegyin and Nyaunglebin. In late 1987 and 1988, it moved on to Toungoo and the Kayah State, where troops from the KNLA 2nd brigade had linked up with KNPP units across the border. From all these districts there was a constant flow of villagers towards the Thai border, bringing the same grim accounts of summary executions and *Tatmadaw* atrocities.

At the time it was perhaps hard from the relatively peaceful perspective of Rangoon or Mandalay to understand the enormity of the atrocities that were taking place. Certainly those who know the Burmese people well found such reports difficult to believe. In 1988, in a rare public reply to reports of human rights' abuses in the Karen and Kachin States, the BSPP government claimed: 'The alleged malpractices are effectively prohibited by law as well as by traditions and customs in present-day Burma, whose tolerance and compassion are the hallmark of its culture.'[24] Within weeks, however, such protestations had evaporated in a cloud of smoke as troops brought back from the front line opened fire on unarmed civilians in towns across the country. Television audiences around the world were horrified.

Contradicting Burma's international image as a peaceful Buddhist land, it clearly was a very brutal war. Outnumbered and outgunned KNLA units at the front, played a largely cat and mouse game with the *Tatmadaw*. Only in the 20th battalion Papun district in the north, and the 6th brigade Dooplaya and 10th battalion Tavoy-Mergui districts to the south, did KNU life continue with any degree of normality. The *Tatmadaw* strategy was clear: systematically to destroy, one at a time, each rebel-held district. But even some of these southern base areas were coming under increasing pressure. In 1986 the trading post at Phalu was encircled and, in March 1987, the timber mills at Wale were burnt down. Further south the joint KNU/NMSP base at Three Pagodas Pass was the target of several probing attacks launched from deep inside Burma, resulting in the disruption of work at the antimony mines nearby.

Given the intensity of attacks, it was remarkable how well the KNLA units held on in even the hardest hit areas. Despite the government's far superior manpower and resources (the KNLA has only 81mm mortars and homemade cannons and rockets to counter *Tatmadaw* 105 howitzers, 120mm mortars and Carl Gustaf 84mm rockets), by the time of the democracy uprising Mae Tah Waw was the only important KNLA base to have fallen in five years of non-stop fighting. At the beginning of the campaign, Ne Win was widely reported to have given an 18-month deadline for a decisive victory over the KNU, which he wanted to announce at the Fifth BSPP Congress in August 1985. But the BSPP, like the AFPFL governments of the 1950s, consistently underestimated the KNU's strength and resolve.

Perhaps the most desperate battle was fought at the KNLA base at Maw Po Kay, hidden in a deep bend in the Moei River. From 1984 until 1989, in scenes reminiscent of the First World War, government and KNLA troops remained dug in as close as 100 yards from each other exchanging artillery and sniper fire. Hundreds of lives were lost. Militarily the post had little importance, but it was well known to listeners in Burma as the site of the KNU's broadcasting station (shut down in 1983) and it achieved a symbolic significance for both sides way beyond any strategic value.

Eventually this relentless pressure forced even the most conservative of the KNU commanders to abandon their set-piece tactics. Guerrilla operations, at which Karen troops have always excelled, were once again stepped up and long-range penetration strikes begun on 'military' positions well inside Burma. In 1985 the KNU admitted attacking two trains on the Rangoon-Moulmein line, though Bo Mya has continued to deny KNLA responsibility for a mine which derailed a train near Toungoo in July 1985 killing 67 passengers, and for a bomb which exploded on a train nearing Rangoon in January 1988, killing another eight. Privately many KNLA officers warned that if the *Four Cuts* continued, attacks on 'soft' targets would be an inevitable result. A KNLA grenade attack on Paan in

May 1988, in which eleven people were wounded and two killed, including the principal of the local college, gave an indication of the potential style of future operations. Warned one of the KNLA's more militant young commanders, Capt. Say Do, shortly before he himself was assassinated by a *Tatmadaw* hit squad which crossed into Thailand: 'The Christian faith tells us to love our neighbours, but how can we do this when the Burmese Army is burning down our villages and killing our people? If they burn down our villages, we can burn down theirs. Nothing could be easier.'[25]

Equally controversially, the KNLA also began a number of training classes with Western military instructors who slipped across the border from Thailand. This has led to accusations in Rangoon that the KNLA is employing 'mercenaries'; in October 1985 one French adventurer was killed and his body displayed on national television after a battle near Kawmoorah in which an Australian was also fatally wounded.[26] But rather than being the result of any particular group trying to take control of the KNU, these 'instructors' have come from a variety of bizarrely different backgrounds, including the French and Australian armies and the US-based Soldier of Fortune organisation. This is perhaps less surprising than at first appears. With Thailand the bustling centre of South-East Asia's thriving tourist industry and tens of thousands of young Westerners heading north each year to take part in well-publicised 'hill tribe' treks along the border, the war on the other side has begun to attract increasing attention. As the trekking agencies advertise: 'Adventure is just the price of a bus ticket away.' Some enterprising firms have even offered trips to the 'battlefront', usually Wa and Karenni camps further north near Mae Hong Son, and have found no shortage of takers prepared to pay for the experience.

The result for the KNU has been some very embarrassing international publicity. KNU leaders have always denied handing over money other than a few hundred Thai baht for 'rest and recreation'. Given the furore their appearance has created, opinion over the value of using foreigners has been divided. Senior commanders have privately admitted that courses on handling modern explosives proved particularly useful and led to a series of successful KNLA assaults on well-fortified positions. In one such raid at Kadaingti in February 1987, ten government troops were killed when a forward supply base of the army's No.84 light infantry battalion was overrun and 30 weapons and 150,000 rounds of ammunition captured. But it is my impression, based on the rather curious mixture of instructor-adventurers I have met, that the main value of these foreigners to the KNU has been a psychological one. Feeling the total neglect of the outside world for their forgotten cause, KNLA commanders have simply been grasping at straws.

The most obvious and effective way the KNLA has relieved pressure on its territory has been through the NDF, but before the democracy uprising it also tried other imaginative measures to slow down the *Tatmadaw* build-up along the Thai border. Since 1984, both the Karen Women's Organisation and the Karen Youth Organisation have been reformed to revive grassroots organisation in the villages and to whip up support for the war effort. But perhaps the most striking move (and one which for a time caused considerable concern in Rangoon) has been the attempt to link up with dissident Muslim groups in the region. Unlike the rural Karens, the Muslim community can be found in towns and cities right across the country and has always been regarded with deep suspicion by governments in

Rangoon. Various Muslim insurgencies have persisted in Burma since independence, mostly in Arakan, but there has always been the threat they could spread. In August 1983, after an outbreak of anti-Muslim riots in Martaban, Moulmein and several other towns in Lower Burma, the Kawthoolei Muslim Liberation Front (KMLF) led by 'Brother' Zaid, a former employee of the Union of Burma Airways, was formed from amongst several hundred Muslim refugees who had fled into KNU-held territory. Some 200 KMLF guerrillas were trained in the KNLA 6th and 7th brigade areas, but by March 1987 it had begun to fall apart amidst disagreements between Sunni and Shiite leaders.[27] Ultimately, together with Gyaw Hla's Arakan Liberation Organisation, the KMLF formed the nucleus of the present-day Muslim Liberation Organisation, but non-aligned Muslim platoons and companies still exist in the KNLA.

The great democracy uprising of 1988 gave the KNU and its NMSP, KNPP and PNO allies in south-east Burma a temporary reprieve, for thousands of government troops were withdrawn from the front. Indeed, against all expectations the KNLA was able to recapture Mae Tah Waw in October 1988. But there was some evidence on the eve of the protests that *Tatmadaw* commanders were beginning to feel that they were at last getting on top of the Karen insurgency. In a rare moment of openness in November 1987, a party of foreign military attachés were taken for the first time on a lightning three-day tour of the war-torn Karen State. Here, in Paan, Col. Khin Nyunt, the then little-known head of MIS, predicted the army would 'smash' the KNU 'within two years'.[28]

Meanwhile, in north-east Burma, following the recapture of Panghsai from the CPB in January 1987, the *Tatmadaw* launched its largest operation in years against the KIO, crossing the main Myitkyina-Bhamo car road, which had been under KIO control since the late 1970s, to push up to the KIO's general headquarters at Pajao. With over half the 39,900 square-mile Kachin State under KIO administration and another 25 per cent a guerrilla no-man's land, KIO commanders sensibly evacuated several positions along the China border before going on a sustained counter-offensive across the state. Hundreds of casualties were reported and for once their impact was felt in Rangoon. After a year of such heavy fighting, no less than 126 of the 154 prized *Tatmadaw* gallantry medals announced on Independence Day (January 1988) were awarded posthumously.[29]

This did not prevent Khin Nyunt leading another party of military attachés on a second propaganda tour the very same month. On a two-day round trip to the Kachin State capital, Myitkyina, he boasted the KIO would soon be 'annihilated' and, responding to growing international interest in the NDF's call for a negotiated settlement to the war, publicly ruled out the possibility of any talks with the KIO.[30] This theme was again taken up in April by the army Chief-of-Staff, Gen. Saw Maung, in his talks with Gen. Chaovalit. Then in May, as the democracy movement gathered pace, the Rangoon press scathingly warned that the NDF and KNU were only interested in negotiations because they were 'being defeated militarily time and time again'.[31]

Yet, for all the *Tatmadaw*'s advances against the KNU in south-east Burma over the past few years, when the anti-BSPP demonstrations finally exploded in Rangoon in July, insurgent forces were still in loose control of vast areas of the country and, with the exception of the Chins, underground rebel cadres operated throughout virtually all the ethnic minority states.

This, then, was the picture Burma's young students discovered when they arrived in the jungles in late 1988. While Aung San Suu Kyi and U Nu led the campaign in the cities for the new democracy parties, in the 'liberated zones' there began the most significant reorientation in insurgent politics, fuelled by the CPB defections in the embattled north-east, since the 1960s and the Ne Win coup.

A New Cycle of Conflict? The 1990 General Election and the DAB

All key protagonists are agreed that, whatever the underlying causes, the 1988 democracy uprising was a genuinely spontaneous outbreak of protest. But just as a number of veteran communists from the 1950s and 1960s now re-emerged, so did a familiar cast of characters from U Nu's long-defunct Parliamentary Democracy Party (PDP). Though as with the CPB, the events of that epoch-making summer should not be tied too closely to the activities of any individual member, their provocative and analytical role should not be devalued. Their first move, mocked in Rangoon but historically farsighted, was the formation in exile on the anniversary of Burma's independence, 4 January 1987, of the Committee for the Restoration of Democracy in Burma (CRDB) by such PDP veterans as Tin Maung Win (US), Bo Aung Din (UK) and Zaw Lwin (West Germany). Noisily demonstrating outside Burmese embassies abroad, they called for national reconciliation between the BSPP, NDF and CPB and played an important role in attracting rare international attention to the country's rapidly worsening plight.

The Role of U Nu
In 1987 U Nu, the old man of Burmese politics, embarked on a world tour, once again adopting his respected guise as a Buddhist preacher. On his travels he met several of his former comrades-in-arms in America and Europe, though, now in his 80th year, he claimed he had retired from politics. None the less, on his return to Rangoon, repeating his campaigns of 1968/9, he began quietly travelling the country, delivering lectures on Buddhism and attracting large crowds wherever he spoke.

With Burma's application for Least Developed Country (LDC) status at the UN that year and the BSPP's second demonetisation in two years, U Nu and the PDP leaders, like Ba Thein Tin and the CPB leaders, quickly recognised that the political temperature was rising. But by the time the democracy uprising started in March 1988, these ageing PDP veterans were by no means a united force. A gulf already existed between Tin Maung Win and the CRDB, which was keen to enlist the support of the National Democratic Front (NDF), and those closer to U Nu, who regarded ethnic demands with rather more caution. The CRDB exiles could enter Burma only at the risk of imprisonment or death. As the crisis mounted, several returned to the jungles via Thailand and held talks with Bo Mya, Nai Shwe Kyin, U Thwin and their former NULF allies. Until the democracy uprising was truly underway, however, the NDF kept these PDP veterans at arm's length. Karen leaders, in particular, had not forgotten their past experiences with U Nu, and a request by the CRDB to join the NDF as a Burman component was rejected. The KNU's veteran strategist, Skaw Ler Taw, accepted in principle that the NDF should look for a Burman partner, but added: 'If we choose a Burman group, we have to make sure it is the right one. Who should it be? The CPB? The CRDB? A lot hinges on our making the right choice.'[1]

Meanwhile, inside the cities, as the protests mounted U Nu played an increasingly provocative hand. The 78 year-old Bo Hmu Aung and the former PDP leaders lent their support as advisers to the student-led democracy movement. Abroad, too, CRDB leaders received considerable press attention, especially in Bangkok where, as the great demonstrations of August and September ebbed and flowed, Tin Maung Win kept threatening to jump on board the next plane to Rangoon.

But in Burma's cities the influence of these PDP veterans on student activists and other emerging political leaders was minimal. U Nu's main support came from an older generation who venerated him as a senior citizen (an important distinction in Burmese society) for his religious proselytising and could still recall the parliamentary days of the 1950s. As the democracy demonstrators finally captured the streets in August, a clear rift was developing between the burgeoning National League for Democracy (NLD) movement of Aung San Suu Kyi, which tried to find a new path between the political left, right and army, and U Nu's followers who harked back to the distant era of constitutionalism in the 1950s. Many historians immediately recognised a mirror image of the factional and personal rivalries that had divided the AFPFL, BWPP and CPB in the 1950s. Though U Nu and Aung San Suu Kyi themselves were not held responsible, close observers reported intense competition between members of their families.

Politically astute but always too impulsive for his own good, U Nu made the first move on 28 August 1988 when he formed Burma's first new political party, the League for Democracy and Peace (LDP). This included such notable PDP returnees as Bo Hmu Aung and U Thu Wai, as well as a number of AFPFL stalwarts from the 1950s, including the former Union president, Mahn Win Maung, former Minister of Industry, Thakin Bo Khin Maung, the ethnic Chin, Dr Vum Ko Hau, and the *Tatmadaw* dissidents, Aung Shwe and Saw Myint. Less than two weeks later, U Nu, who had never ceased to regard himself as the legal prime minister of Burma, declared the formation of a rival government, with the promise of elections scheduled for 9 October. It was, he insisted, a morally justified step to regain control of an increasingly anarchic situation.[2] None the less, he received only a lukewarm response from Aung San Suu Kyi and the other democracy activists. And he got even less from the students in the streets who were spearheading the anti-BSPP protests; this was despite initial encouragement from young radicals in Rangoon (see Chapter 1). Critically, too, he lost the support of the influential Patriotic Old Comrades League, headed by Aung Shwe and former Defence Minister U Tin Oo, which later crossed over to Aung San Suu Kyi and the NLD. Nine days later, on 18 September, when the *Tatmadaw* once again seized control, U Nu's government had become a near irrelevance.

Though MIS chief Brig. Khin Nyunt has since tried to convince the world of the existence of a coordinated 'right-wing' plot to rival the CPB's 'communist' conspiracy during the democracy summer, his evidence is unconvincing. The main fall guy in the army's accusations was 52 year-old U Ye Htoon, son of U Chan Htoon, one of the authors of Burma's 1947 Constitution and son-in-law of wartime prime minister Dr Ba Maw. Arrested in November 1988, Htoon was accused of providing funds and foreign contacts for the student movement and of sending students to the border for armed training.[3] Inside Rangoon, Htoon was even charged with setting up his own underground group, the National Freedom Fighters of Burma, with money obtained from 'foreign embassies'.[4] But while student activists from Min Zeya's short-lived All Burma Students Democratic Association and from the better known All Burma Federation of Students Unions (ABFSU), led by Min Ko Naing and Moe Thee Zun, had contacts with Ye Htoon (as they did with CPB sympathisers), they reject the idea that he was in any way their 'rightist fund raiser'. All the democracy activists, they say, were forced to take various subterfuges simply to survive.[5]

This applied equally to the followers of U Nu with whom Ye Htoon and Min Zeya were both secretly connected. After the coup, Bo Hmu Aung and the ailing Mahn Win Maung and Bo Yan Naing, both of whom died shortly afterwards, stayed behind in the cities with U Nu to build up the LDP to become the largest party after the NLD and pro-army National Unity Party (NUP, the former BSPP), while U Thu Wai split for claimed 'tactical reasons' to form his own Democracy Party.[6] Still popular with the people, U Nu kept up the pretence to foreign journalists that he was satisfied with the army's rate of reform.[7] But privately he made it clear he was playing a dangerous game of brinkmanship as he tried, like Aung San Suu Kyi and Tin Oo, to chivy the army along the road to holding multi-party elections and fully abandoning the *Burmese Way to Socialism*. After his own experiences in the jungle, he said that this strategy, and not armed struggle, held the key to successful political evolution in Burma. Once elected, he promised, his first move would be to call for peace talks with all the country's insurgents.[8]

He was only half-way successful. In December 1989, having already moved against Aung San Suu Kyi and the NLD earlier in the year, the *Tatmadaw* generals decided it was time to put their other rivals out of the political running. They called on U Nu to renounce the provisional government he had declared back in September 1988, but he refused. The LDP leaders were then immediately placed under house arrest and disbarred from standing in the 1990 general election unless they signed a pledge disassociating themselves from U Nu's position.

Seven agreed, but five others, including the old *Thirty Comrade* Bo Hmu Aung, stood by U Nu who melodramatically announced he was ready to die. In his final letter of reply, he put the blame for Burma's political tragedy squarely on Ne Win and the *Tatmadaw*, which had now seized power three times from his 'lawful' government: in 1958, 1962 and 1988. Defiantly he explained he could renounce his government only if Ne Win did the same, in writing. If not, then Ne Win and 'his associates' were welcome to 'cut me up, kill me, send me to gaol for life. I will be unperturbed.'[9] Nu's only request was that his body be given to his wife to be put into a sack and thrown into the sea 'as food for the fishes'. But typically, in a farewell note to his followers, he advised that 'revenge is never sweet' and instead urged them to strive for liberation through the *Brahmacariyavada* (practice of noble and lofty thought).[10]

Despite these pacifist words, appearances proved very deceptive. Elsewhere many U Nu loyalists appeared to be playing a very different game. One curious development was across the border in India where U Nu's daughter, Than Than, and her husband, U Aung Nyein, were working for the All India Radio (AIR).

Following the coup, AIR broadcasts were stridently critical of Ne Win and the Saw Maung regime. They frequently publicised statements by students and the LDP and invited listeners to write in with news. Indeed, for a time AIR was reputed to have overtaken the BBC in the national popularity stakes. U Nu had long been a good friend of the Gandhi family and many observers looked expectantly to India, with its democratic parliamentary traditions, to take the lead in fronting the international protest movement, especially since China and Thailand, virtually alone among world governments, appeared so conciliatory to the Saw Maung regime. All these events were at the height of India's military involvement in another former limb of the British India Empire, Sri Lanka.

An important intermediary between the opposition movement and Delhi was the former PDP leader, Dr Mahn Myint Saing, who had led the democracy uprising in Henzada before fleeing to the Indian border with hundreds of other democracy activists. MIS later published extracts of a letter, reputedly written by Bo Hmu Aung and passed via Dr Saing to the Indian prime minister Rajiv Gandhi, in which the LDP asked for Indian support in commemoration of their joint struggles against British colonialism at independence.[11] But while the Indian government allowed 800 students to take sanctuary along the Manipur and Mizoram borders, no military support was provided. Following Gandhi's 1989 election defeat, the new government of Vishwanath Singh, spurred on by worsening tensions in Kashmir and Punjab, moved quickly to extricate itself from any fresh 'Greater India' expansionism in the region. None the less, during 1988-90, in an abrupt change of policy, agents of the Indian secret service, RAW, secretly met the Kachin Independence Organisation (KIO). These meetings, however, had more to do with the war with Naga insurgents in north-east India, who frequently passed through KIO territory, than with Burma's internal politics. It had been no secret that for many years the Indian government had wanted to carry out joint border operations with the Burmese Army (something Rangoon had always rejected) and these inconclusive meetings proved little more than a tentative stab at intelligence gathering. Similarly conflicting signals emerged from Mizoram where, with the formation on the border of the insurgent Chin (Zomi) National Front in 1987 and its acceptance to the NDF in March 1989, the dream of a Greater Mizoram was once again revived amongst many Mizo-Chin intellectuals.

The most intriguing plot involving U Nu's followers occurred not in India, but hundreds of miles away on the Thailand border, where a very different crowd of ex-AFPFL and PDP supporters had gathered after the coup. Out of retirement in Bangkok, where he was practising as a lawyer, came Zali Maw, who was joined by other PDP veterans, including former Chin Democracy Party leader Mang Da Laing and Dr Myint Swe. In October 1988 they were joined from abroad by U Nu's son, U Aung, and, even more surprisingly, by Thakin Bo Khin Maung who had been a member of the provisional government declared by U Nu in September. Their arrival together at the border made a dramatic change in the conspiratorial picture, especially the presence of the 66 year-old war hero, Thakin Bo Khin Maung, who had trained in Imperial Japan.

With financial help from a number of local and foreign backers, including the retired KMT general, Francis Yap, on 19 January 1989 they established the Alliance for Democratic Solidarity Union of Burma (ADSUB) and, with permission from the NMSP, set up a small training camp in Mon territory near

Three Pagodas Pass. Here they went through the motions of forming a new insurgent force which kept in step with the movements of their mentor, U Nu, in Rangoon. Unlike Tin Maung Win's CRDB or the remnants of U Thwin's People's Patriotic Party (PPP), their main demand was for a return to the 1947 Constitution and they appeared hostile to ethnic nationalist demands, though they did provide funds for a small guerrilla group, the Tavoyan Liberation Front, on the Andaman shoreline.

In the following months they attracted a number of prominent army dissidents to join them, including a former chief of the *Tatmadaw*'s Strategic Command, Col. Sein Mya. Subsequently BSPP Minister for Home and Religious Affairs, MIS accused Mya of being involved in a plot during the democracy uprising with other ex-army officers, including Lt.-Col. San Tha, ex-commander of the crack 99th Light Infantry Division, and Major Hla Win of the Burma Air Force, to drop bombs on Rangoon.[12] Both men were arrested in early 1989 before they could escape to the border.

Well organised as they appeared, the activities of U Nu's followers in the ADSUB served only as a distraction to the real democracy movement led by the students. It had remarkably little success at winning over new recruits. Less than 100 students, from the more than 6,000 civilian activists who arrived at the Thai border in the aftermath of the coup, actually joined forces with the ADSUB and, by early 1990, it had begun to break up. Indeed many of its political rivals felt that the establishment of the ADSUB had merely been a cynical ploy by U Nu's supporters to prepare for any eventuality. Just in case rebellion should sweep Rangoon, or *Tatmadaw* units should mutiny, U Nu's followers too would need their own insurgent credentials.

The Student Movement, Logging and the DAB
Such sectarianism cut little ice with most student leaders. Instead, turning their backs on the political squabbles of their elders, they set about creating a patriotic front that would build bridges with all other anti-Ne Win forces. The situation had striking parallels with the late 1930s, the era they sought to emulate, when a group of dedicated student leaders had seized control of the national liberation movement in the face of the factionalism of their elders in the parliamentary and *Dobama* oppositions (see Chapter 3). Whether in the late 1980s such a talented group of young politicians was emerging remains to be seen. Countless student cells proliferated around the country, though nationally many of the key ideas came from a Rangoon student study group, secretly set up in 1984 by a group of neighbourhood friends. Min Ko Naing, Moe Thee Zun and Thet Tun had attended the same primary school in Thingangyunn ward; Winn Moe, Ko Ko Gyi and Maung Maung Kyaw all lived nearby. They had a keen regard for history. Moe Thee Zun's father, a *Tatmadaw* veteran, had even been a bodyguard at Aung San's funeral.

Thus, as the Saw Maung coup approached, the ABFSU's youthful leaders developed a three-pronged strategy (student above-ground, armed underground and party organisation) similar to that pioneered by Aung San in the anti-colonial resistance. It was a deliberate tactic, they claimed, to confront the impending military clamp-down.[13] Well aware that student activists and not Burma's veteran politicians would bear the brunt of any army retaliation, it was decided that Min Ko Naing, the figurehead of the student movement, would remain behind in the cities to act as the main rallying point for the ABFSU, while in early September the armed faction, led by Winn Moe and Aung Naing, began sending members from Rangoon to make contact with the NDF on the Thai border. Meanwhile, it was agreed, their colleague, Moe Thee Zun, would also stay behind in the cities and try to form an opposition party above ground to test the political waters and keep the democracy ideals alive.[14]

This student-backed party, the Democratic Party for New Society (DPNS), was legally registered on 13 October 1988. Loosely allied with the NLD, Moe Thee Zun travelled to Moulmein with Aung San Suu Kyi on one of her few political campaign tours before her arrest. This later led to arguments, for one wing of the DPNS, headed by Moe Thee Zun, criticised what it saw as the NLD's increasing willingness to compromise with the military. Despite the growing number of arrests, the DPNS, its young NLD allies and Min Ko Naing's ABFSU supporters continued to mobilise peaceful demonstrations against the military. These climaxed in March 1989 with a series of successful street protests in Rangoon commemorating the first anniversary of Maung Phone Maw's death and the beginning of the democracy uprising. Eventually, as Armed Forces Day (27 March) approached and the students began to organise a new wave of protests, their movement was effectively crushed with the arrest, torture and subsequent sentencing to 20 years' imprisonment of Min Ko Naing and the flight to the Thai border of Moe Thee Zun and several of the DPNS leaders. Most of the remaining ABFSU, DPNS and NLD youth leaders were picked up in June and July, along with Aung San Suu Kyi and Tin Oo, in the second major wave of *Tatmadaw* arrests. After a year of upheavals, the *Tatmadaw's* control over the streets of the capital was once again absolute. It was virtually impossible for anti-government activists to operate beyond the parameters of the army's strict martial law conditions.

The third (armed) wing of the student movement had rather more success and, contrary to most expectations, managed to survive. The students who fled the cities found sanctuary in the ethnic 'liberated zones', where they had time and space to reorganise. Amidst the hardships of malaria, jungle life and *Tatmadaw* attacks, students claimed they felt more at liberty in their new home in the hills than they had ever done in Rangoon and the towns.[15] The All Burma Students Democratic Front (ABSDF), which vowed to work with the NDF, was formed on 5 November 1988 at the KNU base of Kawmoorah. For the first year it was chaired by Tun Aung Gyaw, a leader of the 1974-6 student movement who had spent several years in gaol. Indeed, in the first few months of the ABSDF's life, the 1974-6 generation of student activists acted as the ABSDF's main advisers; one of the many extraordinary events of that year was the coming together of young people in the jungle with leaders of the 1974 student generation, the 1962 generation and even the 1948 generation.

Then, in the largest gathering of insurgent leaders ever held in Burma, 22 parties, including the ABSDF and CRDB, met from 14-18 November 1988 at the KNU stronghold of Klerday to form the Democratic Alliance of Burma (DAB) (see Chart 2). Rejecting the legality of the Saw Maung regime and the fairness of any elections the *Tatmadaw* might hold, in its first proclamation the DAB called on all democratic opposition forces to join it.[16] Privately, the young students from the cities expressed disappointment at what they saw as the opportunism of many of their political elders now emerging from the political wilderness. These insur-

veterans, rather than the students, were given the senior roles in the DAB. Though some disquiet was expressed, few publicly quibbled with the selection of the KNU's Bo Mya as chairman and the KIO's Brang Seng and NMSP's Nai Shwe Kyin as his deputies, since it was in their territory and under their protection that they were now sheltering. In fact it was widely believed that had Bo Mya not been elected chairman, he would not have cooperated with the DAB. But many democracy activists, who had braved the army's bullets during the street protests of the summer, were upset by the appointment of U Thwin (Bo Mya's third deputy) from the near defunct PPP and Tin Maung Win of the CRDB, both of whom they hardly knew, as the most senior Burman representatives on the DAB Central Executive Committee.

However, for most students, still shocked by the violent behaviour of the army, simple survival and adjusting to the rigours of jungle life were for the moment their main priorities. Unknown numbers of young people succumbed to malaria and disease in their first year in the hills. By January 1989, for example, ABSDF medics at Three Pagodas Pass estimated 80 per cent of the 1,000 students in camps in the area had already come down with malaria and over a dozen had died. On any given day, up to a quarter were too ill to train. Moreover, despite the students' expectation of arms and foreign support, they found that not only had they been virtually forgotten by the West, but that NDF members themselves had precious little to spare.[17]

Compounding their difficulties at this moment was the sudden and unexpected twist in Thai policy in late 1988. Orchestrated by the Thai Army commander-in-chief, Gen. Chaovalit, it saw the Thai government break the international boycott and recognise the Saw Maung regime in return for lucrative logging concessions along the Thai border and generous fishing rights in the Andaman Sea. In January 1989 the Thai Army even began a repatriation scheme, sending students who had crossed into Thailand back to Burma via a 'reception camp' in Tak. This scheme was quickly shelved in the face of international pressure after a number of students who 'voluntarily' returned disappeared. Several were reportedly killed. It was all part of the students' lesson in the fickleness of international diplomacy. Many Thais, in fact, privately supported the democracy cause, and emergency relief was allowed to flow in from Burmese exiles and sympathetic friends abroad, but only enough to keep the students at subsistence level.

In 1989 the students came under even greater pressure when, responding to the threat of the DAB and to clear the way for the cross-border logging trade, the *Tatmadaw* launched its most massive offensive ever against KNU, KNPP and NMSP strongholds along the border. In a complete break with the past, this time a number of deals were struck with Thai businessmen and their powerful military partners in advance, and in a succession of night-time manoeuvres, Burmese troops crossed over into Thailand to attack Karen bases from the rear. Positions that had been impregnable throughout the *Four Cuts* campaign of the 1980s were suddenly very vulnerable and several major bases, including Klerday and Maw Po Kay (in 1989) and Phalu and Three Pagodas Pass (in early 1990), were overrun with the tacit support of the Thai Army's new Task Force 34, which had been set up by Gen. Chaovalit.

In 18 months of heavy fighting the number of refugees in Thailand went up rapidly to over 40,000. Objections were raised only after several failed cross-border attacks on Kawmoorah and the destruction by the *Tatmadaw* of the Thai market town of Wangkha across the Moei River. The Thai inhabitants demanded 20 million baht in compensation.[18] The border situation is likely to remain unstable for many years to come. With the apparent ousting in mid-1990 of Gen. Chaovalit, then deputy-prime minister and the main architect of the Burma-Thailand logging trade, the Thai Army professed to have returned to its former policy of neutrality. Local Thai and Bangkok security and business interests were clearly in conflict and this was further emphasised by the unexpected military coup in Thailand in February 1991. Indeed the coup leader, Gen. Sunthorn Kongsompong, had only returned from a visit to Rangoon the day before. Whether by Sunthorn or his successors, Chaovalit's dream to make Thailand the dynamo of the region's economic prosperity is likely to gather pace in the last decade of the 20th century.

Relations had also turned sour with many of the Thai logging companies which, freed of any environmental restraint, had begun clear-felling on an unprecedented scale in one of the last remaining forest wildernesses in South-East Asia (see Chapter 1). 'Partners in Plunder', read a headline in the *Far East Economic Review*.[19] Embarrassed SLORC officials promised in July 1990 that the two- to three-year logging contracts, sold to over 30 Thai companies up and down the border, would not be renewed and a number of Thai loggers were arrested or killed by the *Tatmadaw*. But it was also clear that these initial payments from Thailand, estimated at $112 million a year, had already bailed out SLORC in its hour of need. The environmental destruction by armed gangs of Thai loggers of broad swathes of virgin forest in Kawthoolei and in parts of the Kayah and Shan States brought the cynical added bonus of an anti-insurgency tactic. As part of their contracts the Thai companies were required to build roads.

The scale of destruction had to be seen to be believed. It far outweighed the existing illegal trade with the KNU (in one forest reserve I visited near Wale well over 100,000 trees were cut down in 1989 alone) and raised furious objections from the NLD and DAB. These protests were picked up abroad and eventually led to a total ban by the United States on all timber imports of Burmese origin. But KNU leaders said they were caught over a barrel; they had been specifically warned by senior Thai Army officers, who threatened at one stage to close the border to rebel arms supplies, not to interrupt the trade. As compensation, in the many areas where the KNU was still in control, they were given 5,000 baht a ton for teak by Thai contractors as compared to SLORC's 20,000 baht.[20] The real profits, of course, were made in Thailand. No single event demonstrated more graphically the desperation of Burma's political and economic collapse to LDC status in the 1980s. (In the same period an undocumented but large-scale logging trade also developed with China, much of which was cut in areas controlled by the CPB defectors and SLORC's insurgent allies.)

It was into the midst of this complex war, which soon rivalled the drugs trade in its scale of corruption, that the students were plunged; many soon realized they were not cut out for guerrilla life. Despite the risk of arrest, over the months a continuing stream disappeared into exile in Thailand. At any one time during 1990, as many as 2,000 young Burmese refugees were estimated to be hiding in Bangkok alone. The ABSDF also sent warnings to try and prevent more students from coming to join them from inside Burma, unless they had no choice but to flee. Hundreds more were sent back to their homes if they were felt to be in no real danger. ABSDF leaders were clearly anxious to avoid being trapped as a political force, like the PDP, in the mountains.

Despite these comings and goings, hundreds of students undertook armed training along the border (often organised by army deserters) and many soon returned to the front. By January 1990, though they had so far collected only 1,000 weapons, ABSDF leaders estimated 5,000 members had completed basic military training and over 30 had died in battle. Most of these casualties were sustained in what ABSDF commanders claimed was 'self-defence'. In December 1989 I met 60 ABSDF troops, including a number of wounded casualties, in front-line bunkers at Phalu, who had volunteered to serve alongside Karen soldiers defending their camp. Indeed two Rangoon University students amongst them, one a former NLD member and one from the DPNS, had only fled to the jungles after the second military clamp-down that July.[21]

Eventually 18 student battalions were formed, ten (numbers 201 to 211) in KNU territory, numbers 101 and 102 with the NMSP, 303 with the KNPP, 601 with the PNO, 701 and 702 with the KIO in north-east Burma, 801 with the SSNLO and 901 with NUFA in north-west Burma. To gain battlefield experience small groups were sent out on patrol with NDF forces, while others trained to be village teachers or barefoot doctors at newly established jungle universities and schools. In their ranks was considerable expertise: doctors, lawyers, teachers and science students predominated in the leaderships of most camp administrations. Still others were sent back into the towns and cities on dangerous underground missions to make contact with their colleagues, including Soe Myat Thu, who was arrested at the house of Aung San Suu Kyi in July 1989.

Amidst these difficulties 70 student leaders, some from as far away as the Indian and Chinese borders, assembled in November 1989 at the KNU's Minthamee camp for the ABSDF's Second Annual Conference. Here, a new leadership was elected, headed by the charismatic Moe Thee Zun, former chairman of the DPNS, and Thaung Htun, a young doctor from Kyaunggon. While outwardly militant, ABSDF leaders were keen to avoid being labelled 'terrorists' and bitterly resented being banned by SLORC as an 'insurgent organisation'. 'We are not the perpetrators of violence,' said Dr Thaung Htun. 'When the *Tatmadaw* attacked us we had no choice but to defend ourselves.'[22] The conference then unanimously agreed on a platform, similar to that of the NDF and CPB, which, it claimed, would set the political agenda in Burma for the following decade. 'For there to be a free and fair general election in Burma,' said Moe Thee Zun, 'we first need internal peace and an end to the civil war, then an interim civilian government which can supervise elections to a Constituent Assembly, and then finally a new constitution.'[23]

The ABSDF's efforts, by necessity, were mainly concentrated in NDF territory. Elsewhere in the country a number of other student forces continued to operate. The ethnic nationalists, in particular, gained a flood of new recruits. The NMSP, for example, claimed to have trained 1,300 ethnic Mon students, mostly from Moulmein, in the immediate aftermath of the Saw Maung coup and many of these later took part in the surprise attack by 300 NMSP troops on Ye town in March 1990. Another small force, the Democratic Patriotic Army, was formed by 250 students staying with the Kayan New Land Party and its CPB allies in the Shan State. Other students, from Mandalay, Lashio and towns in the north, joined the SSPP and KIO, later taking part alongside NDF troops in fierce battles with the *Tatmadaw* near the China border in 1990. Some were students who had been imprisoned in Rangoon and Mandalay after the 1988 coup. Later forced to work as army porters on what they alleged were 'death marches' to the front, only on the battlefield did a number finally escape and join the ABSDF.[24]

Meanwhile, though the universities remained closed, in the towns dozens of political cells were at work. Their activities were dramatically brought to world attention in October 1989 with the hijacking to Thailand of an internal Burma Airlines flight between Mergui and Rangoon. The passengers were released by the two young hijackers soon after landing, once their demand for the release of all political prisoners in Burma had been announced.[25]

The result of the student endeavours was that many NDF and DAB leaders, suspicious at first of their real motives, began to place greater trust in the ABSDF. The road was a rocky one and relations varied considerably from one camp to another. The KNU summarily executed a number of army defectors and civilians suspected of spying for MIS. Karen, Karenni and Mon villagers, in particular, were aware that, by sheltering young Burman refugees from the cities, they had drawn on themselves some of the most intense *Tatmadaw* firepower in years. But their presence at least had one side benefit. Stunned by the contrast between the brutality of the army in the cities and the unexpected generosity of the 'bandit' rebels in the hills, many young students, including those who had relatives in the army, pledged themselves determined to work for the betterment of life in the war-torn ethnic minority regions of the country. ABSDF teams, which included medics and teachers, made constant study trips to talk to ethnic villagers in the hills. They were deeply angered by the poverty, illness and abundant evidence of army ill-treatment they saw. A young doctor from Rangoon, Min Thein, died following interrogation after being captured by the *Tatmadaw* in April 1990 near Bilin, where he had volunteered to work in the Karen community. 'These villages must be the foundation for the new democratic system in Burma,' concluded *Dawn*, the ABSDF's official journal.[26]

Sentiments like these encouraged many ethnic leaders to believe that the student movement now offered the best hope of political change in Burma. The KNU's Saw Ba Lone, himself a Rangoon University student leader from the 1970s, spoke for many when he warned: 'The people see the students as a potent force to over-throw the government. The majority of people keep on waiting, thinking when will these students start again? If they start, then they will follow. But the important thing is that they should step the right path. If they make a wrong move, another generation will have gone.'[27] As they suffered the continued harassment and arrest of their leaders, few democracy activists in the cities disagreed with this assessment. But it was also clear that most Burmese citizens, depressed and downtrodden by the events of the previous two years, overwhelmingly supported Aung San Suu Kyi's call for peaceful political change.

All hopes were pinned on the result of the promised 1990 general election. Most expected a fix comparable to the 1973 referendum. But against all expectations, the final count produced a result as sensational and decisive as the 1988 uprising, proving once and for all Burma's fledgling democracy movement was far from politically dead.

Aung San Suu Kyi and the 1990 Election
As so often in the past, the activities of Burma's insurgent armies went largely unnoticed in the run-up to the 1990 poll. By any standards the 1990 general election, the country's first multi-party vote in three decades, was extraordinary. Not only did it go ahead without any relaxation in SLORC's tough martial law conditions, but Aung San Suu Kyi, U Nu and many of the NLD and LDP's most senior leaders were kept under arrest. Right up until election day (27 May), hundreds of different party activists were still being imprisoned. For example, the respected Rakhine historian and candidate for the Arakan League for Democracy in the Kyauktaw constituency, 82 year-old U Oo Tha Tun, was arrested on 7 May and later reportedly sentenced to three years in gaol.

Nominally, the elections were supervised by a five-person civilian election commission headed by U Ba Htay and Hanson Kyadoe, a PDP veteran, but privately they admitted they had little choice but to obey SLORC orders. The regime employed a number of emergency legal devices, both new and old, to restrict freedom of speech and assembly. These included the 1950 Emergency Measures Act, the 1962 Printers and Publishers Registration Law and the 1975 State Protection Law, under which Aung San Suu Kyi and U Nu were detained; where these could not be made to fit, new martial laws were decreed. All party publications were censored and subject to martial law regulations; each of the 93 parties, representing 2,311 candidates, was restricted to one pre-approved ten-minute statement on state television and fifteen minutes on state radio. All references to Ne Win, the *Tatmadaw*, SLORC and the economy were carefully excised and, with all political gatherings and speeches equally strictly controlled, it was often hard to distinguish one party from another. All existing party emblems were banned (religious symbols, astrological signs and pictures of animals, people and weapons were all specifically prohibited) and parties were forced to choose their insignia from a proscribed list of new items. These included beach balls, combs, tennis rackets and umbrellas. (The NLD cleverly chose the *kamauk* or peasant's hat, which in silent protest became a popular fashion accessory in urban crowds all over the country.) Moreover, on actual polling day, tens of thousands of rural villagers had no chance to vote at all; in many constituencies in the war zones polling figures were very low. In the Shataw seat in the Kayah State, for example, just 871 votes were registered compared to over 160,000 for the two seats in Henzada in the Irrawaddy Division.[28]

The election presented the insurgents with a difficult dilemma. Officially, only in seven constituencies were the polls closed altogether because of the fighting, but this underestimated the real impact of the war. Though the CPB defectors had agreed to a tenuous ceasefire with the *Tatmadaw* until after the election was over, this did not stop the United Wa State Army launching a bloody war against Khun Sa's TRC, nor the Kokang mutineers, at SLORC's instigation, joining in fighting against the KIO in the northern Shan State.

Faced with the loss of Three Pagodas Pass and several key bases on the Thai border, the DAB formed a number of joint columns in south-east Burma to counter-attack in the *Tatmadaw*'s rear. In March a joint NMSP-ABSDF force attacked the key town of Ye, close to the seashore, causing the Burma Air Force to bomb a number of local Mon villages in retaliation, while between March and May joint KNU-ABSDF commando units, up to 400 troops strong, attacked the towns of Papun, Yebyu, Bilin, Mokpalin and Kyaikto, 65 miles east of Rangoon, where they overran the headquarters of the army's 9th Light Infantry Regiment. With *Tatmadaw* forces pushed far closer to the Thai border than in previous years, government supply lines were dangerously exposed and KNU troops went on a sustained rainy-season offensive. Hundreds of small- and large-scale guerrilla operations were launched across Kawthoolei and, in April, the Air Force again had to be brought in to relieve government ground troops cut off by the KNLA's 20th battalion near Dagwin in the Papun hills. Defiantly, Major Walter, who had led the attack on Kyaikto town, claimed it was the kind of guerrilla war they could wage 'indefinitely'.[29]

Similar guerrilla actions were reported by the PSLP and KNPP, whose general headquarters on the Pai River had been overrun by the *Tatmadaw* during 1989. But once again perhaps the most spectacular fighting took place in the Kachin State, unwitnessed by the outside world, where in the first half of 1990 the KIO ambushed three large army convoys: in the Hpakan jade mine area, on the Danai-Ledo road and the Myitkyina-Sumprabum road. The *Tatmadaw* responded by attacking KIO positions in strength and hundreds of casualties were reported in the Hpakan, Myitkyina, Bhamo, and Sadon areas of the Kachin State.[30]

Despite this militancy, both the NDF and DAB, though clearly expecting the election to be rigged, were anxious to show the watching world that they supported the objectives of a multi-party democracy. Indeed they claimed that this is what they had been fighting for all along. Through Gen. Chaovalit the offer of peace talks was made to Gen. Saw Maung, which after a confused exchange of messages was turned down in Rangoon.[31] Bo Mya, like the CPB, then sent a personal letter to Gen. Saw Maung, ending a break in communications of 26 years, to 'show the sincere goodwill and disposition of the KNU'.[32] Claiming that the thousands of young Burmans who had taken sanctuary in Kawthoolei since 1988 had been welcomed like their own 'kith and kin', the KNU denied it was fighting a 'racial war'. 'The experiences of 40 years of civil war,' Bo Mya wrote, 'have proven beyond doubt that the civil war, which is basically a political problem, cannot be solved by military means.'[33] These words were taken up by Saw Maung in his January 1990 address to army commanders, but despite SLORC ceasefires with the CPB defectors, he again ruled out the possibility of any talks on 'political issues' by the *Tatmadaw*.[34]

More convinced than ever that the election result would be manipulated, on the eve of the polls the DAB drew up a 'Provisional Government of Burma', headed by Bo Mya, to be announced once the election fraud became clear. Modelled on the tripartite Khmer coalition, which had UN recognition, it hoped to join with the defeated parties in the towns and provide a new focus for international support.

This raised the confusing question of political relations between the insurgents and the new democracy parties. Throughout the election campaign *Tatmadaw* officers frequently warned of insurgent organisations hiding behind prominent personalities and parties, and in some cases this was true. Thus, according to Brang Seng, though a number of members called for a boycott of the election, on the grounds that the people had the chance to 'vote for democracy', the DAB made no attempt to disrupt the polls.[35]

This, then, was the tense and complicated backdrop to the polls. Under martial law conditions and with NLD and LDP leaders imprisoned, it was a far more contradictory situation than had existed during the parliamentary elections of the 1940s, 1950s and 1960s. The restrictions applied equally to foreigners; all international observers and tourists were banned from the country in the run-up to the polls. At the last minute a handful of selected Western journalists was allowed into Rangoon, but virtually all foreign diplomats felt that so great was the intimidation that a victory by the army-backed NUP was a foregone conclusion. At best they thought the vote would be split, allowing a number of opposition voices to be heard.[36] Under the slogan 'Prevent the Re-enslavement of Myanmar', a propaganda campaign in the state media tacitly backed the NUP, which proudly admitted its BSPP past; SLORC officials continued to conjure up the image of all sorts of communist, rightist and foreign demons waiting in the wings to seize power if any other party should win.[37]

They did not, however, take into account the strength of the Burmese people's desire for change. The result was a stunning victory for Aung San Suu Kyi and the NLD and a crushing defeat for the NUP which, despite inheriting the buildings and machinery of the old BSPP, won only ten seats in the entire country. Against all expectations, thousands of soldiers and ex-BSPP members and their families voted for the NLD, which won 392 of the 425 seats it contested. Voting tactically, most citizens clearly regarded the election as a referendum: a straight choice between 'democracy' as represented by the NLD of Aung San Suu Kyi, whose reputation had soared during her months in confinement, and a continuation of Ne Win's army-dominated rule. Equally significantly, other parties that were expected to do well, including U Nu's LDP and Aung Gyi's Union Nationals Democracy Party (UNDP), which many saw as a pro-NUP stalking-horse, did even more disastrously, winning no seats out of 325 and one seat out of 270 respectively. Both parties had something in common; like the NUP, they relied heavily on elderly leaders and suggested a return to the feuding party politics of the past. By contrast the NLD, according to CC member Nyo Aung Myint, with its blend of civilian and ex-army leaders, was far more a 'mass movement for democracy' than a political party.[38] Myint himself was forced to seek sanctuary in Thailand after he narrowly escaped arrest. It should be emphasised, then, that whatever the scale of the intimidation leading up to the polls, the actual balloting on election day itself was, unlike the 1973 referendum, generally agreed to be fair.

Having set the polls in motion, SLORC officials had all along been prepared for a token multi-party result, but then having done everything to rig the polls in the NUP's favour, were clearly shocked by the scale of the NLD's victory. For a few heady days street celebrations continued across the country in defiance of martial law. There were repeated demands for SLORC to abandon plans for a drawn-out Constituent Assembly, to release Aung San Suu Kyi and all other political prisoners immediately and to hand over power to the NLD. With a popular mandate of such astonishing magnitude, these calls were taken up by a stream of governments abroad, including the US, Australia, the UK and the countries of the EC. The Chinese ambassador in Rangoon also personally congratulated the NLD on its victory and called for the release of Suu Kyi, saying his government wished to see 'national reconciliation in Burma'.[39]

The NLD's acting leader, ex-Col. Kyi Maung, a former member of Ne Win's Revolutionary Council (RC) in 1962, maintained the momentum. In a series of carefully measured interviews he claimed that the NLD could have a new constitution, a revised version of the 1947 one, ready within two months. Then, at a mass meeting of the victorious candidates at the Gandhi Hall in Rangoon on 28-

29 July at the peak of the campaign, in a toughly worded statement known as the 'Gandhi declaration', the NLD attacked the army's delay in handing over political power as 'shameful' and rejected all SLORC's plans for a Constituent Assembly and various consultative pre-meetings as irrelevant: 'It is against political nature that the League, which has overwhelmingly won enough seats in the parliament to form a government, has been prohibited from minimum democratic rights.'[40]

Hopes of a rapid transfer of power were soon dispelled. Instead of Aung San Suu Kyi being released on the first anniversary of her detention, it became increasingly clear that the army hard-liners were digging in. Few doubted that Ne Win was still pulling all the strings from behind the scenes; diplomats in Rangoon reported his was still the first car to take to the streets each night after the 10 p.m. curfew was enforced. In early August, another 500 people were arrested and two monks allegedly killed in protests in Mandalay marking the historic anniversary of the '8-8-88' uprising. As the security forces moved quickly to suppress any sign of opposition, the overall climate was once again one of fear.

Perhaps the most frightened now were the military leaders themselves. As one doyen of Rangoon's diplomatic scene claimed: 'The army leaders are paralysed by fear — fear of the revenge of the people. It's the Nuremburg syndrome which held up political reform in Argentina and Chile for so long.' Col. Aye Myint, ex-head of the *Tatmadaw*'s North-East Command, who defected to join the DAB and his former insurgent foes at Mannerplaw, was even more blunt in his assessment of the growing paranoia of government. For the moment he ruled out any coup from within the army: 'Burmese soldiers are loyal. They are simply obeying orders.' But echoing Aung San Suu Kyi, he insisted the principal motivating political force in the country was now fear:

> People are terrified. The problem is that the Defence Services have become the instrument of just one man. It was the same with Marcos in the Philippines and Ceaucescu in Romania. Everything that happens is down to Ne Win and no more than 100 officers. Get rid of them and our problems will be solved. But if they try to hang on for ever, then the army will begin to split and that will be the biggest disaster for our country.[41]

However, as the weeks went by the continued detention of Tin Oo, Aung Lwin and other senior NLD leaders was becoming an increasing handicap to Kyi Maung and the surviving NLD leadership as they struggled to stand up to the SLORC generals and to force them to honour the election result. MIS chief, Khin Nyunt, openly master-minded SLORC's delaying tactics. While continuing to stress the importance of 'law and order', it was obvious SLORC was making up the rules as it went along. First it took six weeks to announce all the election results; then a two-month moratorium was declared during which defeated candidates could lodge their appeals. SLORC officials continued to promise that a new constitution would be introduced, but there was no clear indication of when and how it would be delivered. To add to the confusion, in late July SLORC announced a new tier of political obstacles. The *Tatmadaw*, it was insisted, would in future only intervene in Burma's political life in defence of what Saw Maung called its 'three main tasks', national unity, national security and national sovereignty. But a new SLORC declaration, No. 1/90, issued through the Defence Ministry on the eve of the Gandhi Hall meeting, tersely decreed a previously unannounced 'National Convention' would first have to be established to draw up the 'guide-lines' for the new constitution.[42] Only after this Convention had met, could the elected People's Assembly begin work on its own 'draft', which would then have to be returned to the military authorities for approval and to the people for a further referendum, setting the political reform process off once again into the distant future.

It was at this point that for the first time in years the ethnic question was seriously raised in Rangoon. The composition of the National Convention was still unclear, but in private discussions SLORC officials intimated that they regarded many of the smaller ethnic parties that had won seats in the election as potential anti-NLD allies of the NUP. According to one scenario a SLORC official outlined to me, the National Convention would consist of one representative from each of the 27 victorious parties (he did not include the six independents) who, with the 'help' of military officers, would draw up the new constitutional 'principles'. Other SLORC members suggested two delegates from each party. But whatever the numbers, it still meant that the NUP and Aung Gyi's UNDP, despite their crushing defeats, would be represented on equal terms with the NLD round a political table at which ethnic minority parties might well be in the majority.

As in the 1950s, it looked as if the political forces of Rangoon would try to use ethnic minority parties to counterbalance each other's influence. Having already renamed Burma Myanmar, more cosmetic reforms of its political map appeared to be under consideration by the military, including the possible creation of a Wa state. A careful explanation of the regime's view was given by the same SLORC official who, typically, spoke only on condition he remained anonymous:

> Burma has 135 ethnic races and 27 parties won seats in the election. Burma has now had three independence constitutions: in 1943 under the Japanese, in 1947 and in 1974. Look at the problems after the caretaker administration of 1958-60. Things did not work out then and the army had to take power again in 1962. This time we do not want a repeat of any of those mistakes. The NLD can't just rush through any constitution they like. The views of all the peoples and parties must be taken into account, and this could mean the creation of new ethnic states and divisions.[43]

Subsequently this statement was repeated, virtually word for word, by Saw Maung and Khin Nyunt, reflecting the tight decision-making process of SLORC officials.

Given Burma's turbulent past, such an explanation, if it had come from any other quarter, might appear reasonable. The imbalanced, landslide victories of the AFPFL in the parliamentary era of the 1950s had already suggested the unsuitability of a simple 'first past the post' electoral system for Burma. Indeed, leaving the ethnic question aside, the NUP's ten seats were poor showing for 25 per cent of the poll against the NLD's 392 for 59.87 per cent. So, as a result of these intrigues, the election results came under closer scrutiny. In a country as racially diverse and divided by insurgencies as Burma, it was always likely that any multi-party election would produce a complex result and the final poll figures certainly bore this out. While the NLD, which itself included many ethnic minority candidates, swept the board in most parts of the country, no less than 19 ethnic minority parties, including the Muslim National Democratic Party for Human Rights in Arakan, also won seats to the People's Assembly. Most of these nationality parties represented Burma's major ethnic groups, the Karen, Shan, Mon, Rakhine, Kachin and Chin; but a number also represented such small sub-groups as the Pao, Kayan, Naga, Mro (Khami) and Ta-ang (Palaung).

Despite their small size, the polling of several parties was impressive. For example, the Shan Nationalities League for Democracy, which now formed the largest single party in the Shan State, won 23 seats out of the 57 it contested, while the Arakan League for Democracy, headed by Dr Saw Mra Aung, the former head of Rangoon's Gandhi Hospital, now represented the largest party in the Rakhine State with 11 seats out of a possible 26.

Compared to the NLD's 392 seats in the 485-seat Assembly, the combined vote of these ethnic parties initially appeared small. But on the basis of 'one party one vote' in the consultative process, they might indeed have an influential say in the drafting of Burma's new constitution. However, despite SLORC's sudden concern for the ethnic minority cause, it was by no means certain that any of the new nationality parties would choose to work with either SLORC or the NUP. As ethnic leaders immediately pointed out, not only did the NLD win approximately half the seats in the ethnic minority states, but most nationality parties were in complete sympathy with its goals. There was little chance, they asserted, of ethnic parties joining up with the NUP and UNDP in committee rooms to out-vote the NLD. This was confirmed when the United Nationalities League for Democracy (UNLD), a 65-seat alliance of ethnic minority representatives, immediately agreed to a joint political pact with the NLD; at the end of August this was followed up when the UNLD supported an NLD deadline for the release of Aung San Suu Kyi and a transfer of power by the middle of September. Initially the NLD considered forming ten new non-racial states of Burma (like Salween or Malihka), but tentatively accepted the UNLD's proposal for eight racially based 'federal' states, including a new Burman state. Either proposal would dissect the powers of the army and sounded remarkably similar to the ideas of the DAB.

This raised the ambiguous issue of where the new ethnic parties would stand on the insurgency question. SLORC officials were anxious to project the elected representatives as the legitimate face of minority aspirations. But yet again they appeared not to have done their homework. With the continuing crisis and repression in Burma, under present circumstances it is obviously impossible to break confidences and reveal any contacts between insurgent forces and the legal political parties, but I have been shown convincing evidence that in some cases they have been working hand in hand. Suffice to say, with many parties being publicly backed by former insurgent leaders and respected community figures, the DAB, CPB and some of the breakaway CPB allies made no attempt to hide their euphoria over the election results. 'We are ready to accept that under the rules by which the election was conducted that the views of the people were freely expressed,' said Brang Seng, though he cautioned that there were 'hundreds of thousands of ethnic minority peoples' who had no chance to vote.[44]

SLORC's idea of a National Convention was then taken up by both the DAB and CPB, though the more cynical might argue that, like the army, it conveniently gave organisations outside the legal framework the chance to have an unelected say in the political process. This, perhaps, was no bad thing. Any reforms at such a portentous moment in Burma's history that did not take account of all shades of political opinion (witness Panglong where the KNU took no part) would leave the door open to future disaster. But above all a national conference would allow all parties an early chance to end the civil war; DAB leaders were insistent that if they were allowed this input, they would happily respect the NLD-dominated assembly as Burma's constituent government. With fierce fighting continuing around the country's borders, few expected Saw Maung to agree to any dealings with insurgent forces except to continue the 'divide and rule' policy of individual peace talks which had successfully broken up the CPB defectors and SSPP. Khin Nyunt sent a series of sympathetic messages to KIO leaders, who replied they could talk only as representatives of the DAB. None the less, in confident expectation of political change in Burma, the DAB set up a 'federal university' at Mannerplaw and continued to work on a detailed version of its own 'federal constitution', which was secretly transmitted to political parties in Rangoon.

As the NLD's deadline for the transfer of power approached, the barnstorming period of political ideas sustained by the euphoria of the election result was abruptly ended on the night of 6 September 1990 when ex-Col. Kyi Maung and his deputy, ex-Col. Chit Khaing, were arrested in Rangoon and subsequently sentenced to ten years' imprisonment on treason charges. In the hotbed city of Mandalay four more senior NLD officials were imprisoned, accused of inciting unrest. That Ne Win's old comrades, Kyi Maung, Chit Khaing and other ex-army leaders were left at liberty for so long was interpreted by NLD supporters as a crude attempt to divide the NLD along army-civilian lines. After such a clear-cut election result, the continued detention of Aung San Suu Kyi and the original NLD leadership and now the arrest of Kyi Maung and the second-line NLD leadership, indicated that the Ne Win old-guard was once again putting down the shutters. Three days later, Brig.-Gen. Myo Nyunt, head of the Rangoon Command, accused the NLD of 'plotting to destabilise the country'.[45] To rub the point in, SLORC officials in Rangoon told foreign diplomats that Aung San Suu Kyi would be freed, but only if she agreed to abandon politics and leave the country forever. Of the NLD's original 22-person Central Executive Committee, 18 had now been detained, while in the following weeks over 40 MPs were imprisoned (two of whom quickly died in gaol amidst torture allegations), allegedly for refusing to sign the 1/90 declaration renouncing any rights to form a government.

As so often in Burma's history, it now fell on the Buddhist monks to take up the political mantle. A last wave of protests and a boycott of religious rites for the families of soldiers was begun until SLORC recognised the result of the polls and freed all political prisoners. Organised by young monks in Mandalay, Sagaing and the towns of the north, it spread rapidly across the country, causing increasing disquiet amongst the army rank and file. But even the clergy were not free from the military's grasp. In late October, the army once again cracked down. It raided over 350 monasteries, took dozens of monks prisoner and ordered all monks to re-register in a new *Sangha* organisation. In a series of derogatory articles in the state press, SLORC officials claimed to have discovered in the monasteries gold, jade, rubies, weapons and 'subversive' literature from the CPB, which they accused of master-minding the boycott.[46]

It was a charge nobody seriously believed. Nothing more aptly demonstrated the chaos and confusion that had descended on Burma than an extraordinary speech on Rangoon radio on 18 October by SLORC chairman, Gen. Saw Maung. In a rambling defence of his own Buddhism and Burman ancestry, he looked back over 900 years to the country's first Buddhist ruler at Pagan who had embarked on an era of military conquest to impose his own religious solution on the people: 'Some have asked me: when are you going to transfer power? I cannot say when. I cannot see into the future. I have to handle the situation as it comes. I cannot tell whether I will drown tomorrow. Human beings are subject to the law of impermanence.... As for the present situation, it resembles the period of King

Anawrahta.'[47]

A desperate warning of the complexity of the country's unfolding political chaos came on 18 December 1990 when, after a perilous trip through the mountains, eight MPs, headed by Dr Sein Win, cousin of Aung San Suu Kyi and MP for Paukkaung, arrived at the DAB general headquarters at Mannerplaw to make their own declaration of a 'national coalition government'. Like Suu Kyi, Western-educated Sein Win carried the magic of the Aung San name; his father, Ba Win, had been assassinated with his uncle, Aung San, in July 1947. The MPs' first act was to declare a ceasefire with the DAB. Claiming a mandate from over 250 fellow MPs, they said that attempts to form the government in October (first at a monastery in Mandalay, then at a foreign embassy in Rangoon) had been foiled and that one of their colleagues, NLD CC member, U Maung Ko, had been tortured to death by the MIS. They were careful, however, to draw a legal distinction between the new coalition government, which consisted only of elected MPs, and the DAB with which the coalition government was now allied in a new 'Democratic Front of Burma', headed by Bo Mya. Once again the cycle of insurgency in Burma had thrown up an unexpected new alignment of political forces. While Ne Win's *Tatmadaw*, allied with the CPB defectors, remained firmly ensconced in the cities, the ethnic forces of the DAB had joined hands with the elected representatives of the people.

In a fast moving game of political chess, SLORC immediately strove to break up the new political alliance by stepping up its offers of a ceasefire to selected NDF members, guaranteeing for the first time their right to hold weapons and control territory. SLORC's strategy met with immediate success when, running desperately short of ammunition since the CPB collapse, leaders of the KIO 4th brigade in January 1991, the PNO in March and PSLP in April, took unilateral advantage of the offer to give their troops a respite. Rumours even circulated that these long-time, battlefield foes of the *Tatmadaw* would be allowed, like the CPB defectors, to attend SLORC's National Convention, while Aung San Suu Kyi and over 50 of the elected MPs remained under arrest. As a sign of the NLD's desperation, in April the NLD's fourth-line leaders gave in to SLORC pressure and declared a new NLD leadership, headed by Ne Win's former comrade, Aung Shwe, without Suu Kyi and any of their disappeared colleagues.

The stage now appeared set for SLORC's next move, the declaration of a quiescent, but nominally 'civilian', administration, including some of its ex-BSPP favourites, to put its face to the National Convention and whatever constitution or new laws ensued. All real power, however, still remained with the army.

Political reform is undoubtedly coming to Burma. But short of another major upheaval, no one can predict its time-scale or shape.

An Outlook to the Future

Given the violence of Burma's political struggles over the past five decades, it is virtually impossible to make any accurate judgements about the country's future, whether about the NLD in the cities, the students who have lost over three years of their studies, or the ethnic insurgents still fighting in the countryside. The sad truth is that, despite the victories of people's power in Romania, Czechoslovakia and the countries of Eastern Europe, the experience of Burma has once again shown that repression all too frequently pays.

As Burma enters the 1990s, the situation has many close parallels with Ne Win's military caretaker administration of 1958-60 and, more especially, with the RC of 1962-74. Then it took 12 years for a new constitution to be introduced. During this time the military government went through various political motions but never once let go the reins of power. It imprisoned its political opponents, then called for discussion, proposed economic reforms but then tightened the *Tatmadaw*'s grip, fought insurgents and finally called for talks. The outcome, however, the *Burmese Way to Socialism*, had been long ordained.

This time it is the *Burmese Way to Democracy*. Its model is based on a hopeful blend of Indonesia and Thailand where, with a careful mixture of coercion and financial persuasion, army strong men in both countries have developed ostensibly 'democratic' political systems which have safely protected the military's interests. But in Burma's case, the same people (indeed many of the very same officers and commanders) who ruled Burma so disastrously for a quarter of a century under the BSPP are now claiming sole responsibility for introducing the new democracy system. With little trust in the abilities of their own people, they are using the same emergency powers and processes and there have been precious few changes to the civil laws. As SLORC officials make clear, the 1990 election has not produced a government, but a People's Assembly with vague powers and the military still the judge and jury on political reform.

If 80 year-old Ne Win were suddenly to die, most citizens believe the situation would change dramatically. Recent events in the Philippines and Haiti, however, have shown that overthrowing dictators such as Marcos and Duvalier is no guarantee of political reform. Indeed it may well be the easiest part of the process. Certainly in Burma, where senior officers have been loyal to Ne Win to a man, the regular rotation of military officers and constant MIS vigilance have prevented any powerful cliques forming from within the ranks of the defence services. Critics scour the different educational backgrounds of the military leadership and speculate on rivalries between the MIS wing under Khin Nyunt and military officers in the field, but all they find is a powerful bond to Ne Win.

In the twilight of Ne Win's rule, the door appears to be slowly opening. However, most of the burning political issues that have divided Burma for over 40 years (the insurgencies, the nationalities question, the economy, the balance of power between central and regional governments, the nature of free speech and democracy) are once again being left unresolved and have yet to be opened up for countrywide debate.

In 1988 and again with the 1990 election there has twice been the prospect of all parties coming together in what Aung San Suu Kyi called Burma's 'second struggle for independence' to discuss around the table all these issues peacefully in the light of the sufferings and experiences of the last 40 years. But this dream has evaporated along with the spilled blood of hundreds of Burma's young people. It is difficult to see the events of 1988-90 as anything other than a sad rerun of other tumultuous moments in the country's recent past (1948-50, 1962-4, 1974-6), as yet another generation of young students and political dissidents has failed in its protests and turned to armed insurrection against the central government. By the same token, the continuing predominance of the *Tatmadaw* in Burma's national life seems increasingly assured, for, taking advantage of the CPB's collapse, the army has pushed harder and further against the ethnic insurgents than ever before; these campaigns seem certain to continue in the 1990s.

In two short years the NLD has made an astonishing entry into Burmese politics and high optimism has been engendered by its victory in the 1990 election. But the army die-hards insist that any reforms must be instituted slowly and only with their complete approval. The arrest, torture and disappearance of political activists, which have cast a dark shadow over the country for many years, continue unabated; indeed the situation today is more repressive than at any time in the recent past.[48]

Great hopes are placed on Aung San Suu Kyi. She has reappeared like an avenging nemesis to haunt Ne Win with the memory of Aung San, the only truly unifying name in Burmese politics today. After the assassinations of her father and uncle (Than Tun), she more than anyone is aware of the hidden dangers and pitfalls of Burmese politics. She has repeatedly spoken of the need to combat fear after the violence of the last 40 years. In the weeks before her arrest, she turned her political attacks on Ne Win whom, she explained, her father had warned his comrades not to trust. 'My father didn't build up the Burmese Army in order to suppress the people,' she said.[49] 'Everybody knew from last year that the main culprit was Ne Win, but nobody seemed to have thought of mentioning his name,' she told the last Western journalists to see her.[50] Her detention, crude MIS propaganda and the implication of foreign allegiance through having a British husband have not so far sullied her name. They have merely added to her mystique. After Ne Win's ossified and repressive rule, her comparative youth in Burmese politics, her Western education and her international outlook all add to her appeal. Though cautioning against unrealistic expectations, with her calls for non-violence, patience and national unity she has struck a powerful chord in the country at large and used the 'Aung San' factor remarkably well. In a country as secretive and fear ridden as Burma, many citizens have taken heart from the election result to know that, two years after the democracy uprising was crushed, their neighbours and fellow countrymen cast their votes for the same ideals. That was the real victory of the NLD's campaign.

In its defence, SLORC has introduced some economic reforms. The results are already tangible in Rangoon and Mandalay, where roads have been widened and a mini building boom started after years of neglect. The unfamiliar names of Pepsi Cola and Amoco are starting to be heard and an open-door trade policy appears to have come to stay. But the road ahead is a rocky one. Unlike its UN stable-mates, Nepal and Chad, Burma did not collapse to become one of the world's ten poorest countries for simple economic reasons, but for age-old political ones which one day must be addressed. Virtually all foreign aid was cut off in 1988 and most governments make any resumption of aid conditional on political reform. With the exception of Iraq, no government has been more internationally condemned than Burma since 1988; these concerns peaked in a secret session at the United Nations in Geneva in March 1990, when the unusual step was taken of appointing a special rapporteur to investigate human rights abuses in the country.[51] The following month the US Senate unanimously passed legislation to prohibit the import of all products from Burma until the political situation improves. Now the great problems of currency revaluation, tough IMF austerity measures, the development of a new economic infrastructure and the transition from an agro- to an agro-industrial based economy, all lie ahead and will undoubtedly threaten the stability of whatever governments come to power over the next two decades. Inflation since 1988 is rampant, estimated at over 50 per cent in the first half of 1990 alone.

The money SLORC has generated so far has come from timber and oil, fishing and mineral concessions, and is largely 'signature' money for basic raw materials. This has relieved the regime's immediate crisis, but, as the destruction of Burma's last remaining forests, once the best preserved in Asia, has so graphically shown, in the short term will spawn little local development. The army has already set up a new military holding company, the Union of Myanmar Economic Holdings, with a paper capital of 10,000 million kyats (£1,000m at the official rate) and through whose hands many of the joint ventures are likely to be steered.[52] For veteran observers there is an uneasy sense of *déjà vu*; the company is a virtual replica of the Defence Services Institute of the 1950s, which grew rapidly to become the country's largest commercial institution by the time of the 1962 coup.

Allegations of army favouritism abound and the sons and daughters of senior officers have become the most immediate beneficiaries of the army's new 'get rich' philosophy. It is no coincidence that the army's main military operations since 1988 have been in south-east Burma, where it has wanted to free the way for the new fishery and timber businesses linked to the families of Sein Lwin and other senior army leaders. Local fishermen and villagers have been abruptly squeezed out. No such military resolve has been shown in the economic back-waters of the Shan State, where the illicit trade in opium and precious stones is thriving and lining the pockets of local officials and traders.

Much of the money SLORC has raised, including an astonishing $600 million for its embassy in Tokyo, has already been spent on the army, which is estimated to have gone up from some 190,000 to 230,000 men under arms since the coup.[53] The average citizen has no means of raising capital or developing contacts to take part in the new international and domestic trade. In fact, as in the 1930s and 1950s, the entrepreneurs who have so far done the best out of the new economic climate have been the Indian and Chinese communities which have their own banking and trading networks.

Perhaps the most alarming signpost to the future has been the complete collapse of the education system. For years many of Burma's best educated people (especially doctors and scientists) had been finding jobs abroad and leaving for exile. This exodus has turned into a flood since 1988. All universities and colleges of higher education have remained closed, while primary and high schools have repeatedly been shut down at the first sign of unrest. How Burma can hope to compete in the international economic community or train its own workers is unclear. A whole generation of students has lost its education since 1988 and, without properly qualified doctors, teachers and engineers coming through the system, yawning gaps are already beginning to appear in the economy. Amongst the present army leadership (who are virtually all career soldiers who have come up in combat through the ranks) there is a distinctly xenophobic, anti-intellectual bias and few ministers are equipped to perform the jobs they are appointed to do. They came under an embarrassing international spotlight in a much criticised SLORC submission to a UN meeting of LDCs in Paris in September 1990. Surprisingly taking the 1980s as a continuous political whole, the SLORC report praised the government's health and education records, but failed even to mention the 1988 anti-BSPP uprising, the 1990 election, the closure of schools or the imprisonment of the victorious NLD leaders. At no point did the enormity of the present crisis, or indeed the desperation of Burma's appearance at an LDC meeting, appear to have sunk in.[54]

Meanwhile, in the countryside the insurgencies continue. It is difficult to believe that anyone, after so many years of hardship and fighting and despite SLORC's belligerent words, could think in terms of a quick military solution. The experiences of racial conflicts around the world (from Sri Lanka to Ethiopia and Ireland) have shown that after years of lying dormant, these can always metamorphose into new political forms and directions. New Chin and Burmese insurgencies are already gathering pace. Moreover, in 43 years of conflict, organisations like the KNU and KIO have demonstrated a remarkable endurance and a consistent ability to escape from the brink of adversity. Whatever their weaknesses (and they have many) the ethnic forces of the NDF have long since shown that they are not merely the narrow racist forces the government has so often portrayed them to be. Behind their struggles are genuine national aspirations, which have yet to find a proper platform in the land that has become modern Burma.

And yet it is hard to escape the impression that the ageing leaders of the NDF, like Ne Win, Ba Thein Tin and the silver-haired veterans of the CPB and *Tatmadaw*, are caught in the same tragic time warp that has enveloped Burma since independence. The fierce battles being fought in the mountains today have their roots in the distant era of British rule and the campaigns of the Second World War. In 1958 the veteran Karen lawyer Saw Po Chit, a member of the 1946 Karen Goodwill Mission to London, caused an uproar at a meeting of KNU leaders when he warned: 'The way things are going we will spend longer in the wilderness than the lost tribes of Israel.' Over 30 years later his prediction has become alarmingly true. Already the veteran leaders of Kawthoolei are beginning to talk of the second 40 years of what they call the 'father to son' war.

On a more optimistic note, one of the younger KNU leaders privately told me: 'We are not like our fathers. We don't intend spending another 40 years in the jungles'. He predicts that in the next decade the ethnic minority struggles will find a new political platform in the cities. One of the most hopeful statements of future political intentions (little noticed at the time) came from the CPB's breakaway Wa leaders. In a placatory broadcast on their new radio station on 28 April 1989, just two weeks after their mutiny began, they issued an appeal addressed to the 'commanders and privates' of the *Tatmadaw*, 'to live together in friendship'.[55] While warning if the army attacked they would 'fight to the last man', they urged government troops to consider just why both sides were still fighting.

Perhaps here, in this war weariness, lies the key to the present crisis in Burmese politics and, if taken in the right spirit, the glimmer of hope of a peaceful solution. The continuing wars in Burma have not only brought the national economy to the brink of bankruptcy, but have wrought devastation on many of the country's ethnic minority regions. The Wa people, in particular, have suffered more than most. Since fighting between the CPB and the central government began in the Wa region in 1968, Maha San, leader of the Wa National Organisation, claims that as many as one in four of all ethnic Was may have died.[56] 'Every year the burden on the people has become heavier,' warned the Wa rebel radio station. 'The streams, creeks and rivers have dried up, while the forests are being depleted. At such a time what can the people of all nationalities do?'[57]

With the recent ceasefires in north-east Burma, which echo the KKY militia programmes of the 1960s, the ball is back in the army's court. But whatever the economic reforms, there will be little progress without political reform. With the repression continuing, young people are still fleeing to the jungles and new underground political cells are being formed. The hijacking of a plane *en route* from Bangkok to Rangoon in November 1990 by three Burmese students demanding the release of political prisoners was an act of increasing desperation. Without a political moratorium and a new Panglong, the conflicts will inevitably continue.

None the less, there is a new determination and spirit among the country's young students akin to that found among young people in South Africa and Eastern Europe. They were, after all, Ne Win's generation, brought up entirely under his rule. They were taught that the Burmese Army was their true parent and were thus all the more bitter about the brutality of the army's tactics. Something has undoubtedly clicked in the mould of Burmese politics. But whether the long hoped for change will come now through processes set in motion by the army (peaceably in the face of all adversity) or many years hence, is impossible to say. Many young students, having taken closer stock of the situation, say they are working now on a ten to fifteen year time-scale. They look back to the incredible hardships that faced the peasant supporters of Saya San in the 1930 anti-British uprising, the years of secret underground organisation that were needed by the *Dobama* movement of the 1930s, and the heroism of Aung San and the *Thirty Comrades* in the Second World War. By comparison, they say, their sufferings are only just beginning.

The last decade has seen the deaths of such veteran nationalist figures as Thakin Soe, Bo Yan Naing and Mahn Ba Zan. They remind themselves that another decade will see the eclipse of Ne Win, Ba Thein Tin, Bo Mya and the generation who began the civil war back in 1948. Rational voices argue for amnesties, discussion and peaceful evolution. For the moment, however, that is not the way of Burmese politics. A confused battle still continues between the army, the supporters of the democracy movement and the ethnic nationalists.

All claim to be representing the people's aspirations and to have the same objective, the development of Burmese democracy. If nothing else, Burma's tragic experience, after five decades of conflict, has amply demonstrated that one person's liberation struggle may well mean another's persecution. Amidst the high-flown rhetoric of patriotism and duty, few individuals from any community have been able to stand aside and remain truly neutral.

After so much bloodshed, then, it might be facile to expect an easy solution. But if any consolation is to be taken from the traumatic events of 1988-90, it has been the sight of Burma's young people, from all ethnic backgrounds, urgently talking together, whether in the cities, jungle or exile, to try and find a new solution to Burma's tangled problems without harking back to the legacy of the past. It is as if a spell has been broken and the country has awakened from a time warp.

A just solution to the ethnic minority cause has become a main priority. According to Moe Thee Zun, the ABSDF chairman:

> Federalism has become a life and death issue for our country. For over 40 years many parties in Burma have been fighting over this issue and a number of parties and even governments have fallen over it. We believe it has fallen to our generation to solve this problem now, and it is over this issue we shall succeed or fail.[58]

Their aspirations were summed up by a medical student from Rangoon, Zaw Oo, whose father is a Burmese Army officer:

What we now want is democracy. We don't want authoritarian one-party rule any more. We have all suffered so much. We believe that only a democratic government can end the 40-year civil war which has done so much damage to our country. And we believe that only a democratic government can bring real peace and harmony to all our peoples (from all ethnic races) and rebuild our failing economy.[59]

Hopefully the future lies in such hands.

Appendix: Millenarianism

Since independence a number of small millennial sects have been active amongst the rural Karen community in south-east Burma which, much to the embarrassment of the KNU, have often attracted more attention amongst Western academics in neighbouring Thailand than the Karen insurrection itself. The result has been some very lopsided studies of Karen ethnicity which greatly underplay the political significance of the Karen rebellion. By ignoring the decidedly 20th century form of the KNU movement and concentrating on such clearly esoteric phenomena they perpetuate the image of the Karens as a 'backward' tribal people. The best account is by Theodore Stern, '*Ariya* and the Golden Book: A Millenarian Buddhist Sect among the Karen' (*Journal of Asian Studies*, 27 (2), 1968, pp. 297-327).

Several such sects have been recorded over the last 150 years. In general they can be described as 'Animist' sects which borrow widely from Buddhist imagery and belief (especially the idea of the messianic figure of the *Cakkavatti*, or 'universal monarch', who will pave the way for the new order of the future (fifth) Buddha, *Arimetteya* (ibid.: 300), Christian prophesies of the 'Second Coming' and the Karen Legend of the Golden Book. They have usually been founded by messianic prophets who claim either to have in their possession the 'Golden Book' or who alone have the powers to read such a book when the White Brother returns. Their followers have come from virtually all Karen sub-groups and included Mons and Shans; most have been illiterate Animists. One exception is the *Maw Lay* sect, which still survives in the Maubin district in the Delta, whose followers apparently celebrate Buddhist festivals yet at the same time have built their own 'Christian' churches where they chant traditional Karen verses or *Htas*. But it should be noted that amongst Karens, just as amongst Mons and Burmans, there has often been a blurring of Buddhist and Animist belief and I, for example, have visited predominantly 'Animist' Sgaw villages in the Papun hills whose inhabitants none the less insist on describing themselves as Buddhists.

The two best-known sects today are the *Leke* (founded 1860), centred on the village of that name in the Kyondo district and noted for the famed 'chicken-scratch' script of their own Golden Book (in fact a hand-written school exercise book), and the *Telakhon*. The *Telakhon* is the only sect to have featured in the insurgency in any significant way. Also founded in the second half of the 19th century in the Kyain district by a prophet known as the *Phu Chaik* (Grandfather God/Buddha), by the early 1960s the *Telakhon* under the seventh *Phu Chaik* (an ethnic Pwo) had expanded to a movement several thousand strong in the eastern hills with an apparently complex system of village administration and ritualised worship, and had even spread across the border into Thailand.

The growing strength of this movement in the 1950s was to encourage the AFPFL government to try to turn this movement against the KNU. It was also in 1962 to encourage Western missionaries in Thailand, in conscious imitation of the

White Brother and Golden Book legends, to try and convert the movement to Christianity by approaching the *Phu Chaik* with leather-bound and gold-leaved Sgaw and Pwo versions of the Bible. These, however, turned out to be a disappointment since as *Telakhon* followers remember they did not explain, amongst other things, how to fix a car or radio. But the result of all this interest was to lead to a dramatic change in the *Phu Chaik*'s behaviour which became increasingly erratic. Apparently convinced that the age of *Arimetteya*, which according to one prophecy would come in his lifetime, had arrived he married, thus breaking the celibate traditions of the *Phu Chaik* line, and began trying to recruit KNU soldiers to attack government held towns as a demonstration that the *Telakhon* and not the KNU was the real Karen nationalist movement. This was finally to turn relations with the KNU sour. In 1967 the *Phu Chaik* ordered his followers, protected by special charms, to attack Kyaikto town after first warning, as a sign of their invincibility, the local Burmese commander. Not taking this threat seriously, the garrison suffered heavy casualties in the first attack, but in the second they were well prepared. Twenty-four of the *Phu Chaik*'s followers and six government troops were killed and the *Telakhon* soldiers retired in disarray. Shortly afterwards the KNU moved to put the movement down and the *Phu Chaik* was arrested and executed, along with his chief lieutenant, for allegedly murdering his wife. Today between 2,000 and 3,000 survivors of this sect linger on in the KNU 6th brigade/Thai border region where they are still waiting under two junior *Phu Chaiks*, apparently for the great *Phu Chaik*'s predicted return.

Information for this account has been supplied by several Karen pastors and informants, including Saw Tha Din, a former KNU leader who acted as the missionaries' intermediary, Benny Htoo, one-time KNU Eastern Division commander, who presided at the *Phu Chaik*'s trial, and Major Mu Tu, KNLA 6th brigade deputy-commander. These informants have described Stern's account as correct in all respects except one. The *Leke* expect *Ariya*, whom they are still awaiting, to be the same as *Y'wa* (God) whereas the *Telakhon*, who are more Christian influenced, believe *Ariya* to be the same as Christ.

Stern himself believes there is a 'religio-political' character to all such movements and a 'major source of millenarianism can be found in the Buddhist kingdoms which surrounded them'; as evidence, he quotes from one traditional Karen *Hta* which predicted the decline of the Mon, Burman and Siamese kings and the advent of a Karen king 'when the Karen will dwell within the great town, the high city, the golden palace' (ibid.: 300-4). He believes the same Buddhist prophesies and a belief in 'a divinely sent deliverer' were inherent in the uprisings of Burman and Mon *minlaung* pretenders, such as Smin Dhaw, in the 18th and 19th centuries, whom these Karen prophets presumably copied. Indeed one Karen-led *minlaung* rebellion against the British broke out in the Shwegyin hills in 1856. It is also possible that the fearsome Karenni chieftains who were 'legitimised' as *Sawbwas* by the Avan Court, probably at the end of the 18th century, were also consciously following, while outwardly Animists, the same Buddhist style and traditions of the Burman-Mon-Shan rulers in the valley kingdoms below.

And such millennial sects have not occurred only amongst the Karens. Similar movements have been identified amongst other hill peoples elsewhere in South-East Asia, such as the Khmu and Hmong in Laos. But perhaps the most striking example, as Stern points out, has also occurred in Burma amongst the Lahu of the Shan State where the *G'uisha* cult is identical in many respects to the *Y'wa* tradition of the Karens and has given rise to a succession of militant 'man-god' prophets (ibid.). This, in turn, led in the early 1970s to the remarkable outbreak of the local Lahu rebellion which has continued to the present day, still led by Paya Ja Oo, the son of one such ancient prophet, Pu Kyaung Lon (see Chapter 14). This cult, too, has in the past received the same missionary attention as the Karen *Telakhon*.

Lastly, it should be added, common to soldiers of all ethnic backgrounds in Burma has been a fascination with talismans, such as precious stones, sacred Buddhist, Animist or Christian relics or icons, and elaborate tattoos. Many soldiers go into battle covered in 'protective' imagery from a very mixed array of cultural and religious backgrounds.

Notes

Chapter 1

1   *The Guardian* (London), 26 July 1988.
2   Interview with Thu Yein, 28 Nov. 1989.
3   Rangoon Home Service, 19 July 1988 (henceforth RHS; see note following). The first, misleading Judicial Enquiry of 13 May also reported that 625 civilians were arrested during the March disturbances of whom 484 had since been released.
4   Ibid., 22 June 1988. Student leaders dispute this version and say as many as 100 people died that day. RHS is Burma's official state radio and is monitored by several news agencies abroad, including the BBC's *Summary of World Broadcasts* (henceforth *SWB*) and the Bulletins of the *Foreign Broadcast Information Service* (Washington) which both publish English translations. In this account I have used the BBC version for reference and where I have quoted from their translations give the publication date in full.
5   *Bangkok Post*, 29 June 1988.
6   *The Guardian* (London), 5 Aug. 1988.
7   RHS, 9 Aug. 1988; interview with ex-BSPP official Khin Maung Shwe, 29 Nov. 1990.
8   Interview with Bassein schoolteacher, Sun Men, 20 Jan. 1989.
9   RHS, 10 Aug. 1988.
10 RHS, 19 Aug., in BBC, *SWB*, 23 Aug. 1988.
11 Ibid.
12 Interview with Khine Saw Tun, Information sec. of the Rangoon Bar Council, 23 Nov. 1989.
13 Interview with Maung Phone Ko, chm. of Moulmein strike com., 1 February 1989. See also, M. Smith, 'Dark Days in Burma', *The Anti-Slavery Society Reporter*, 13 (5) 1989: 70-9.
14 RHS, 24 Aug. 1988.
15 *Far East Economic Review* (henceforth *FEER*), 7 July 1983, 5 Jan. 1984.
16 Interview with Winn Moe, 29 Jan. 1989; Moe Thee Zun, 29 Nov. 1989. For an interview with Min Ko Naing, see *Asiaweek*, 28 Oct. 1988. There also briefly existed another much smaller student front, the All Burma Students Democratic Association, led by Min Zeya, an ethnic Mon law student, which had similar aims and objectives.
17 Interview with Zaw Tun, ABFSU rep. to the GSC, 31 Jan. 1989. This picture has been confirmed in interviews with dozens of strike leaders from other towns across the country including Tavoy, Moulmein, Mudon, Paan, Toungoo, Taunggyi, Mongpai, Bassein, Henzada, Prome and Mandalay. Typically the strike com. leaders were respected local citizens, rather than students, such as Maung Maung Lwin (Mongpai), a headmaster; Nai Kelasa (Mudon), a monk; and Dr Myint Cho (Paan), a general practitioner. Many workplaces also had their own strike committees.
18 For Aung San Suu Kyi's own account of the influence of her father's memory, see *The Independent* (London), 12 Sept. 1988.
19 *The Guardian* (Rangoon), 30 Aug. 1988.
20 BBC World Service, 15 Sept. 1988.
21 Interview with U Nu, 2 Sept. 1988; *The Guardian* (London), 5 Sept. 1988.
22 See 'Voice of the People of Burma' (henceforth VOPB), 4 Sept., in BBC, *SWB*, 6 Sept. 1988.
23 One western mil. attaché alleged the CPB was behind the attack on the Min. of Trade building on 17 Sept. U Nu also confirmed the role of CPB supporters to me.
24 Those reportedly at the meeting included Ne Win and his three daughters Sanda, Thawda and Kyemon Win, Sein Lwin, Dr Maung Maung, Tun Tin, Kyaw Htin, Saw Maung, other members of the cabinet and 14 top mil. cdrs. But it is not known whether a later widely circulated version of this report, a copy of which is in my possession, is

completely genuine. It appears far too exact, leaving open the question of whether the original author was a genius or was working from leaked, inside information. The latter alternative appears the more likely. At any rate, this document was widely available at the time and played an important part in setting the political climate and is thus worth mentioning in full.

25 Ibid.
26 Ibid.
27 Ibid.
28 RHS, 26, 27 and 29 Aug. 1988.
29 *Bangkok Post*, 4 Feb. 1989.
30 *Associated Press*, 9 Sept. 1988.
31 Ibid. The AP correspondent Sein Win, a former ed. of *The Guardian* newspaper, had himself been arrested and imprisoned with his close friend, Aung Gyi, during Aug.
32 RHS, 10 Sept. 1988.
33 RHS, 11 Sept. in BBC, *SWB*, 13 Sept. 1988.
34 *The Guardian* (London), 12 Sept. 1988.
35 RHS, 13 Sept. in BBC, *SWB*, 15 Sept. 1988.
36 'Statement to the Nation by the Central Committee of the CPB', 10 Sept., VOPB, 17 Sept., in BBC, *SWB*, 19 Sept. 1988.
37 RHS, 18 Sept. in BBC, *SWB*, 19 Sept. 1988.
38 Terry McCarthy, *The Independent*, 19 Sept. 1988.
39 I reported several eyewitness interviews in the TV documentary, *Burma: Dying for Democracy* (Channel Four, UK), 15 March 1989. See also, Smith, 'Dark Days'. For a more detailed account, see Bertil Lintner, *Outrage: Burma's Struggle for Democracy* (White Lotus, London, 1990).
40 Sein Win, *Associated Press*, 19 Sept. 1988.
41 Interview with Min Lwin, Rangoon Medical Institute No.2, 29 Jan. 1989. Lwin helped carry away the wounded after seeing his friend, Zaw Lwin Htun, killed.
42 *Asiaweek*, 27 Jan. 1989.
43 For the army's account of the shootings see RHS, 19 Sept., in BBC, *SWB*, 21 Sept. 1988. This report suggests a considerable degree of armed resistance, sometimes led by monks; e.g. seven officers were allegedly kld. when a 1,000-strong mob attacked the Dala police station.
44 Smith, 'Dark Days', 72.
45 Interview, 4 Nov. 1988.
46 Interview with Skaw Ler Taw, 25 Oct. 1988. Large numbers of students/activists were recorded as passing through insurgent-held areas: from the NDF: 5,000 KNU, 2,000 KIO/SSPP, 1,300 NMSP, 1,000 PNO, 500 KNPP, 200 NUFA. From the CPB and its allies: 600, most of whom went to the KNLP and SSNLO. In addition, several hundred refugees fled secretly into Thailand or China and an estimated 800 to India. In the following months hundreds more continued to travel back and forth, while SLORC claimed over 3,000 were registered as returning.
47 Interview with Brang Seng, 27 Oct. 1988.
48 Winn Moe was elected VC; Than Win, former Pres. RUSU, Gen-sec.; Aung Naing and Ko Ko Oo, joint secs. A few other underground student cells briefly flourished, such as the Burma National Liberation Party, led by another ABFSU/Rangoon Univ. student, Maung Maung Kyaw, who visited Bangkok in early Nov., but surrendered the following year.
49 Interview with Ma Sein, 7 Oct. 1988.
50 Interview with U Nu, 13 Oct. 1988.
51 RHS, 14 Oct., in BBC, *SWB*, 17 Oct. 1988. The *Working People's Daily* of 22 Oct. described the BBC dispatches as 'a lot of crap and rubbish'. The main accusation centred on a mistaken BBC report, which stated that Mogok had been captured by the CPB. Journalists involved believe the BBC may have been deliberately fed misinformation.
52 See e.g. Brig-Gen. Khin Nyunt, *Burma Communist Party's Conspiracy To Take Over State Power* and *The Conspiracy of Treasonous Minions within the Myanmar Naingngan and Traitorous Cohorts Abroad*, (Guardian Press, Rangoon, 1989).
53 RHS, 30 Sept. in BBC, *SWB*, 3 Oct. 1988.
54 The first report was on 22 Sept. when three students, travelling with the NMSP, were

kld. in an ambush near Kawkareik. In early Nov. widespread publicity was given to the capture in battle of three armed Rangoon Univ. students who had joined the CPB in Tenasserim. The first ABSDF student to die was a Rangoon final year psychology student, Mahn Moe Kyaw Zan, beheaded by troops on 14 Nov. after capture near the Thai border.

55 RHS, 21 Oct. 1988. According to this report, in the previous three weeks there had been 83 battles in which 62 army personnel were kld. or missing and 110 wounded.

56 Insurgent battle claims generally contradict the army's figures. In the final Mae Tah Waw battle alone the KNU claims 56 govt. troops were kld. and 102 wounded. For the Mong Yang battle, see Ch.18.

57 Again no reliable figures of deaths exist. State radio released only spasmodic details: e.g. 29 Sept., ten 'looters' in Shwedaung Street, Rangoon; 5 Oct., 5 'looters' on the Rangoon-Syriam bridge; 23 Oct., 'dropout' at Mayangon high school; 3 Nov., three 'looters' at Shwedaung oilfield.

58 *Financial Times* (London), 12 Oct. 1988.

59 RHS, 4 Nov., in BBC, *SWB*, 7 Nov. 1988.

60 Interview with Moe Thee Zun, 29 Nov. 1989.

61 23 groups were represented at this meeting including the 11 parties of the NDF. Other key groups were the PPP of former Cabinet min., U Thwin, the Muslim Liberation Organisation and the overseas C'ttee for the Restoration of Democracy in Burma; see also Ch.20 and Chart 2.

62 Interview with NLD CC member, Nyo Aung Myint, 26 Nov. 1989. Myint was one of the few senior NLD leader to escape arrest. See also, Amnesty International, *Myanmar (Burma), Prisoners of Conscience; A Chronicle Of Developments Since Sept. 1988* (Nov. 1989).

63 *Working People's Daily* (henceforth *WPD*), 10 Jan. 1990.

64 Ibid.

65 Various edited versions and translations of Aung Gyi's letters are in circulation but no authorised copy exists. See also Ch.7, *n*.10.

66 *FEER*, 7 July 1988.

67 Interview, 23 July 1988.

68 RHS, 10 Aug. 1987.

69 This informant has requested anonymity. A clear example of Ne Win's superstition came in 1984 when, amidst great international embarrassment, he abruptly called off a state visit to France after a motorcycle outrider, guiding his entourage from the airport into Paris, fell off his motorbike. Ne Win told organisers his father had told him as a child, he must instantly leave any place where he was greeted by a bad omen.

Chapter 2

1 Interview with Maha San, Pres. of the WNO, 10 Jan. 1987.

2 *Census of India*, 1931, Vol.11, Burma, Pt.1: 202-3.

3 Ibid. 175-7, 202-4.

4 Ibid. 204; 'Observations by H.N.C. Stevenson on Karen Resolution, adopted 25 April 1946', 15 June 1946 in H. Tinker (ed.), *Burma: The Struggle for Independence, 1944-48* (HMSO, London, 1983) I, Doc. 566.

5 It is impossible to extricate any true ethnic sense from govt. published reports and figures. These are generally inaccurate calculations of local regional populations rather than racial breakdowns. But a figure of 1.9 m for the Karen population is one many Karens, including ex-BSPP officials, have told me was the BSPP's official working number for the 'Karen' population; Paos, Kayahs etc. were counted as separate races as part of what seems to have been a deliberate attempt to water down Karen numbers. Figures provided to me by the KNU Central Organisation Dept. give the following breakdown for the ethnic Karen population: Irrawaddy Delta and Pegu Yomas, 4 million; Tenasserim Division and territory east of the Rangoon-Mandalay highway, 2 million; Kayah and Shan States, 1 million. Under present conditions it is obviously impossible to evaluate the validity of these claims; see also *n*.7.

6 Figures supplied by officials of the SSPP, NMSP, ALP, RPF, CNF, KIO, PSLP and WNO. There are also large populations (in the hundreds of thousands) of Shans, Kachins and Palaung-Was in China and Chins (Mizos) in India, as well as small pockets of Mons in Thailand and Rakhines in Bangladesh. Again figures are unreliable and

this accounts for some of the historical confusion.

7 In mid-1990 e.g. the 4 underground 'nationality' movements were represented by the KNU, KNPP and KSNLF, PNO and SSNLO, and KNLP. The 1931 Census in fact identified 16 Karen sub-groups, numerically dominated by the Sgaw (37.8%), Pwo (35.6%) and Pao (16.5%). KNU leaders today in whose territory many of the smaller sub-groups live, claim to be able to identify over 20. The following sub-group classifications are still used in everyday Karen conversation (major habitation areas in brackets). Sgaw (Irrawaddy Delta, Pegu Yomas, eastern hills); Pwo (Irrawaddy Delta, Paan, Moulmein and Mergui); Pao (SW Shan State, Thaton, Toungoo); Kayah, Bre [or Kayow]-Mano, Yintale (Kayah State); Kayan, Yinbaw (SW Shan State, Kayah State); Paku, Gekho-Bwe (Toungoo, Kayah State); Gheba or White Karens (Pyinmana, Toungoo); Zayein or Black Karens (Central Shan State); Striped Karens (Central Shan State, Loilem, Mawkmai). The term Bwe is particularly confusing and is often used by Sgaw Karens as a general term for non-Sgaw hill Karen. There are also a number of even smaller Bwe, Bre or Sgaw related sub-groups still distinguished by the local population such as the Maw Nay Pwa, Tha Ler Pwa, Moh Pwa and Paleiki of Toungoo dist.

8 Michael Adas, *The Burma Delta. Economic Development and Social Change on the Asian Rice Frontier, 1852-1941* (Univ. of Wisconsin Press, 1974): 17.

9 N.J. Brailey, 'A Re-Investigation of the Gwe of 18th Century Burma', *Journal of SE Asian Studies*, 1 (2) Sept. 1970: 44.

10 Charles Backus, *The Nan-chao Kingdom and T'ang China's Southwestern Frontier* (Cambridge Univ. Press, 1981) 44-52. Reviewing this book in the *Journal of SE Asian Studies* (Sept. 1984) David Wyatt comments, 'That this myth, disproven and discredited half a century ago by Wilhelm Credner and others, lives on in contemporary works is an embarrassment, no less than is the compulsion Charles Backus feels to rehash the arguments in the work here reviewed.'

11 See e.g. Brailey, 'A Re-Investigation of the Gwe', 33-47; Victor B. Lieberman, 'Ethnic Politics in 18th-Century Burma', *Modern Asian Studies*, 12 (3) (1978): 468-9.

12 Ibid. The possibility of a Pao identity for the Gwe is most interesting, for there are several unexplained aspects to Pao history. Not only do the Paos live in two distinct areas of Burma in Thaton dist. in Lower Burma and the Shan State further to the north but, unlike other Karens, they are Buddhists with historical traditions of some antiquity. These suggest a long interrelationship with both the Mons and Shans. According to Pao legend, they fled to the Shan State in the face of an invasion of their territory in Thaton dist. by a Burman king. In the popular version of this tale told today, the Paos appear to have dated this flight back 900 years by appropriating the well-known story of the 11th century Mon king, Manuha (whom they claim was Pao), whose capital at Thaton was destroyed by Anawrahta and who was taken back as a prisoner to Pagan. It is possible that Pao legend keeps dim memory of such distant events, but by moving this migration to the 18th century, as the history of the Pao State of Hsihseng (Hsahtung) itself implies, and identifying the Pao with the 'Gwe' Karens, a great riddle in the history of the Karen peoples would be solved. As Brailey notes from the accounts of early British explorers, the same story of Karen migrations from Lower Burma into the eastern hills is told by the Kayah and Zayein (Sawngtung), and I have found the same story is familiar to the Kayans (Brailey, 'A Re-Investigation of the Gwe', 40-4).

13 This explanation was given to me by Mon villagers in the Three Pagodas Pass region in Jan. 1989. Likewise, they had a prompt explanation for another unidentified 'ethnic' term from the 18th century, 'Okpo', which has also confused historians. An 'Okpo', they say, is simply a place where bricks are made, and thus there are many concentrations of 'Okpo' villagers in different parts of the country.

14 For a particularly bitter argument see E. Nugent, 'Closed Systems and Contradiction: the Kachin in and out of History', in *Man*, Journal of the Royal Anthropological Institute, 17, 1982: 508-27 and the resulting corr. with E. Leach in *Man*, 18 (1) 1983: 191-206 and 18 (4) 1983: 787-8. Leach, who was the last western anthropologist to travel in the Kachin hills, describes Nugent's original article as 'fantasy'. As he explains, 'It was obvious to me in 1945 that there were huge gaps in our understanding of those societies, but political circumstances have made it impossible for either myself or anybody else to engage in anthropological research anywhere in the Kachin hills area during the

past 37 years, so the gaps have never been filled: but the "Kachin society" about which I wrote no longer exists, so they can now never be filled.' Leaders of the KIO today dispute this but it is a view with which I, based on my own travels, would largely agree. The wars of the last 50 years have brought about enormous change in virtually all traditional societies.

15 Charles Keyes, *The Golden Peninsula: Culture and Adaptation in Mainland SE Asia* (New York, MacMillan Publishing Co., 1977) 2-3. *The Gazetteer of Upper Burma and the Shan States* (5 vols. Rangoon, Supt., Govt. Printing and Stationery, 1900-1) compiled by Sir J.G. Scott and J.T.P. Hardiman at the turn of the century was to remain the basic ethnic/geographic handbook for govt. officers posted to Burma and still remains the starting point for most contemporary ethnic studies.

16 *Census of India*, 245.

17 Ibid; 174.

18 Ibid.

19 Edmund Leach, *Political Systems of Highland Burma* (G.Bell & Son Ltd., 1954).

20 F.K. Lehman, 'Ethnic Categories in Burma and the Theory of Social Systems', in P. Kunstadter (ed.), *SE Asian Tribes, Minorities and Nations* (Princeton Univ. Press, 1967) 100-1.

21 P. Hinton, 'Do the Karen Really Exist?' in Wanat Bhruksasri and J. McKinnon (eds), *Highlanders of Thailand*, (Kuala Lumpur, OUP, 1983) 155-68.

22 R.H. Taylor, 'Perceptions of Ethnicity in the Politics of Burma', *SE Asian Journal of Social Science*, 10 (1) 1982: 7. For a contrasting view see J. Silverstein, *Burmese Politics: The Dilemma of National Unity* (New Brunswick: Rutgers Univ. Press, 1980) 6-25.

23 Lieberman, 'Ethnic Politics in Eighteenth-Century Burma', 466-7.

24 As well as ALP units, there are Arakanese (both Muslim and Buddhist/Rakhine) volunteers serving with the KNU. e.g. in Jan. 1986 I was travelling in KNU-controlled areas in Tavoy dist. when 5 Arakanese deserters from the Burmese Army arrived at a KNU base. After brief retraining they were sent out on patrol with KNU units. Units of the NMSP and the WNO have also taken part in pitched battles in the defence of KNU territory. Since 1985 joint NDF battalions have also been in operation on different fronts across the country.

25 Min. of Information, *Burma's Fight for Freedom* (Rangoon, 1948): 92.

26 Pantanaw Win Thein, 'Heroes from the Hills', *Forward*, 15 Aug. 1966: 4.

27 RHS, 12 Feb., in BBC, *SWB*, 14 Feb. 1985.

28 Daw Ni Ni Myint, *Burma's Struggle against British Imperialism 1885-1895* (The Universities Press, Rangoon, 1983): 156-8.

29 *WPD*, 4 Oct. 1988.

30 Michael Aung Thwin, 'British "Pacification" of Burma: Order Without Meaning', *Journal of South East Asian Studies*, Sept. 1985: 258.

31 'Communique of the Revolutionary Council', SSIA, 1959 (Copy in my possession).

32 The Govt. of Kawthoolei, *The Karens and their Struggle for Independence* (KNU Publishing, 1984): 2-3.

33 AIO, *Hidden Colony* (Advanced Arakanese Comrade Publishing) 1 (1) Sept. 1985.

34 Declaration by the CPA (n.d.) (Copy in my possession).

35 Speech of U Ne Win, chm. BSPP, RHS, 11 Dec., in BBC, *SWB*, 15 Dec. 1979.

36 F.K. Lehman, 'Burma: Kayah Society as a Function of the Shan-Burman-Karen Context', in J. Steward (ed.), *Contemporary Change in Traditional Societies* (Urbana, Univ. of Illinois, 1967): 1-104.

37 Chao Tzang Yawnghwe, *The Shan of Burma: Memoirs of an Exile* (Institute of SE Asian Studies, 1987): ix. Yawnghwe incorrectly records as 1.3m the 1931 Census figure (p.203) of 1,037,406 for 'Tais' (Shans).

38 See Dorothy Woodman, *The Making of Burma* (London: The Cresset Press, 1962): 11. 'The convenient thesis that Burma is a happy little country geographically self-contained and psychologically uninterested in its neighbours, does not correspond with the facts of history.' Woodman's account, largely written from British sources, remains the fullest published account of the annexation of British Burma.

39 IMTFE Exhibit 628, *Tentative Plan for Policy toward the Southern Region*, 4 Oct. 1940, quoted in W.H. Elsbree, *Japan's Role in SE Asia Nationalist Movements, 1940 to 1945* (Cambridge, Mass., 1953): 17.

40 In fact, of Khun Sa's several Chinese-speaking lieutenants only his longtime right-hand
    man Chang Tse-chuang (a Manchurian) was actually born in China. Several of the
    CPB's Shan State cdrs. also speak Chinese and the CPB's radio station frequently
    broadcasted in Chinese. Distinguishing 'Chinese' identity in Burma presents many dif-
    ficulties. The 1931 Census recorded 193,594 Chinese inhabitants in Burma but this is
    most certainly an underestimate. During the 1950s a figure of 600,000 was more
    commonly mentioned. The 1931 Census identified three major Chinese ethnic sub-
    groups, Fukienese, Cantonese and Yunnanese, of which the Yunnanese were the
    largest. The Yunnan border has always been the most indistinct and during 1986
    another joint border inspection was completed. With a rugged geography and even
    more diverse array of peoples than the Shan/Kachin States, Yunnan similarly remained
    largely beyond central control until recent decades and was the scene of frequent local
    rebellions, notably the Panthay rebellion of the mid-19th century. Yunnanese Muslim
    traders had established caravan routes through to Siam long before the British arrival in
    Burma. Even today such pony caravans continue down to the Thai border. But such in-
    cursions from Yunnan were not always peaceful; e.g. a British Intelligence report for
    1938 describes an attack on 13 May on Mong Yang in the Kengtung substate by a 64-
    strong gang of 'Chinese' dacoits in which 4 people were kld. and 6 wounded. Monthly
    Intelligence Reports 1937/8 Shan States (India Office Records [henceforth IOR]:
    M/5/50, B (I) 18.
41 Interview with A.N. Phizo, 11 Sept. 1986.

Chapter 3
1   Dorothy Woodman, *The Making of Burma* (ref: Ch.2, *n*.38): 122. This campaign was
    even criticised in the British Parliament of the time and a scathing attack was launched
    in the pamphlet, *How Wars are got up in India*, by the MP, Richard Cobden.
2   Sir Charles Crosthwaite KCSI, *The Pacification of Burma* (London: Edward Arnold,
    1912): 21.
3   Woodman, *The Making of Burma*, 270-4.
4   'Letter from the Govt. of India to the Sec. of State', Simla, 19 Oct. 1886, No. 52, Public
    (India Office Records [henceforth: IOR]).
5   H.N.C. Stevenson, 'The Case for Applied Anthropology in the Reconstruction of
    Burma', *Man*, 2, Jan.-Feb. 1945: 5.
6   See M. Adas, *The Burma Delta* (ref: Ch.2, *n*.8): 58. These figures include the totals for
    both rice and paddy, i.e. unhusked rice. The area under rice cultivation showed the
    same remarkable increase, expanding from 700,000-800,000 acres to nearly 6m acres
    over the same period.
7   Sir Herbert Thirkell White, *A Civil Servant in Burma* (London: Edward Arnold, 1913):
    288-91. See also Edith L. Piness, 'The British Administrator in Burma', *Journal of
    South East Asian Studies*, 14 (2) Sept. 1983: 372-8.
8   Ultimately, under the 1935 Act there were 132 seats in the House of Reps. of which 12
    were reserved for Karens (of Ministerial Burma), 8 for Indians, 2 for Anglo-Burmans
    and 3 for Europeans. A number of other seats were reserved for various commercial
    and special interest groups. Frank Trager has calculated it was thus possible for ethnic
    Burmans to win 95 of the 132 available seats, *Burma: From Kingdom to Republic* (Pall
    Mall Press, London, 1966): 52.
9   'Memorandum by the Govt. of Burma on the Representation of Minorities', 10 Nov.
    1932 (IOR: M/1/13, P&J 126 B), para. 22. 'Moreover, the interests and needs of this
    section of the community do not appear to us materially different from the Burmese
    who live in the same areas. Further, we are opposed to the extension of the system of
    communal electorates unless a strong case is made out.' An appeal for communal rep-
    resentation on religious grounds by a Muslim leader, U Aung Thin, was also turned
    down on the same basis with the addenda that the Muslim community, identified as
    'Zerbadis' (116,000) from mixed Burman-Muslim unions, Arakanese Muslims includ-
    ing Kamans and Myedus (59,000), and 'India Muslims' (1931 Census: 396,504), was
    'too scattered' and that it might cause divisions from both the Muslim community else-
    where in the India Empire and the Indian 'Hindu' (1931 Census: 570,953) community
    in Burma (para.21).
10 J. Silverstein, *Burmese Politics: The Dilemma of National Unity* (ref: Ch.2, *n*.22): 30-2.
11 M. Aung Thwin, 'British "Pacification" of Burma' (ref: Ch.2, *n*.30): 245.

12 Burma Gazetteer for Henzada District, 1915: 29-30. See also the *Imperial Gazetteer of India*, 4, 1885: 182-3, which calculated the 'pure' Mon (Talaing) population (i.e. Mon-speaking) for British Burma as 154,553 but calculated the population of 'mingled Burmese and Talaing parentage' as even larger, at 177,939. This group, however, spoke only Burmese.

13 *Census of India* (1931): 176-7. See also J.S. Furnivall, *Colonial Policy and Practice* (New York Univ. Press, 1956): 116-21, 157-8.

14 In the May 1930 riots the death toll was officially estimated at 120 kld. and 900 wounded, but most observers believed this was an underestimate. Unlike the 1930 riots, which were confined to Rangoon, the disturbances of July/Aug. 1938 spread into most towns and dists. of Lower Burma and there were also a number of serious incidents reported in Upper Burma. The final casualty figures in the *Final Report of the Riot Enquiry C'ttee*, (Govt. of Burma, Rangoon, 1939) were calculated as 204 kld. and over 1,000 injured. It was the Indian community which came off very much the worse in all these clashes.

15 'Report on the Rebellion in Burma', Presented by Sec. of State for India to Parliament, June 1931 (HMSO): 13-14.

16 Furnivall, *Colonial Policy and Practice*, 184.

17 H. Marshall, *The Karens of Burma* (Burma Pamphlets: 1945): 37-8.

18 D.M. Smeaton, *The Loyal Karens of Burma* (Kegan Paul, Trench and Co., London, 1887): 201, 221-6.

19 In the 19th century Mrs Mason, the wife of one of the most important of the early missionaries, F. Mason, even believed that she could recognise in the patterns of various Buddhist artifacts and the dresses of Karen women 'the language in which God spoke to Adam' and founded a cult which split from the main Toungoo mission. Mason himself was suspended for several years until he renounced his wife's teachings. See Theodore Stern, *'Ariya* and the Golden Book: A Millenarian Buddhist Sect among the Karen', *Journal of Asian Studies*, 27 (2) 1968: 297-328.

20 Corr. of Dr Vinton quoted in Smeaton, *The Loyal Karens*, 8-19.

21 *KNDO Insurrection* (Rangoon, Govt. Printing & Stationery, 1949): 5-6. The insurrection was blamed on the 'prolonged politico-religious propaganda by a section of the Sgaw Karen Christians'. Given the relatively small size of the Christian Karen community, such claims need careful analysis. But without doubt accounts by missionaries such as Alonzo Bunker's *A Tale of the Making of the Karen Nation*, 1902, expressed in highly biblical terms, did little to lessen the racial temper. Provocatively (p.229), he described the Karens as the Hebrews 'ready to defend their new faith with their lives' against 'the dominant race... the Burmans... idolaters and extremely proud', who regard the Karens 'as did the Egyptians their Hebrew bondman': 'After the Deliverer came, the parallel was more marked. This being the relation of the two races, the Burmans were very reluctant to see the Karens pass out of their power. They were accustomed to say, "The Karens are dogs. Everyone knows they are a base and cowardly race".'

22 The (US) Baptist Church in Burma e.g., in 1962 recorded some 180,000 Karen, Kachin and Chin members, but only 5,341 Burman members, 3,500 Shans and Paos, and less than 1,000 Mons, all of whom are also predominantly Buddhist. Maung Shwe Wa, *Burma Baptist Chronicle* (Univ. Press, Rangoon, 1963): 268; for the best published account of the spread of Christianity in Burma see also, H.G. Tegenfeldt, *A Century of Growth: The Kachin Baptist Church of Burma* (William Carey Library, California, 1974).

23 A. Bunker DD, *Sketches from the Hills* (Fleming H. Revell Co., 1910): 104-8.

24 Quoted in F.R. Von Der Mehden, *Religion and Nationalism in SE Asia: Burma, Indonesia, the Philippines* (Madison, Univ. of Wisconsin Press, 1963): 191.

25 *The Guardian*, 19 Sept. 1987.

26 See e.g., speech of KNU Pres., Bo Mya, on Armed Forces Day, 2 Aug., 'Radio Kawthoolei', in BBC, *SWB*, 4 Aug. 1983.

27 Amongst the plethora of reports from the era of British rule, different reasons are advanced at different times for the lack of British interest in the development of the frontier areas. One reason was undoubtedly military. Vast numbers of troops would have been needed to bring under control and police all the outlying hill dists. Another was financial. The expenditure entailed would have been vast and for little immediate return. But one of the clearest statements of official British attitude was contained in

the 'Memorandum by the Sec. of State for India, Burma Excluded Areas', 29 Nov. 1933, by the Joint C'ttee on Indian Constitutional Reform (IOR: M/1/123). This suggested the ultimate reason was the sheer scale of the ethnic differences, as the British saw it, between the peoples of hills and plains: 'It is the absence of common outlook and aspirations which is perhaps the main factor militating against the assimilation of the backward tracts in the hills in the political institutions of the plains. The history of the relations between the backward tracts and the plains is one of opposition and hostility... Such feelings of antipathy die slowly in remote places; and the inhabitants of the backward tracts are still devoid of any real sense of community, political or otherwise with the plains' (p.4).

28 E.g. a 9-page 'Memorial from the Council of Karen Elders and the Karen National Association of Salween District, Papun' (IOR: M/1/33) was sent to the PM on 27 Feb. 1935 objecting to the continued 'exclusion' of the Salween dist. under the 1935 Act. Noting that in over 100 years of British rule no governor or chief commissioner had ever visited the dist., the Memorial concluded (p.6), 'We respectfully submit that there is no justification whatever to set half of the Province of Burma on the path of progressive realisation of self government while leaving out another half of it from the scope of the Reform.' The Salween dist. is today a major centre of the KNU insurrection. The KNA for Toungoo dist., which was arbitrarily divided by the reforms, also sent its objections; see *n.*48.

29 See e.g. *The Times* (London), 11, 17 Oct. 1933, and a confidential memo report on the 'Boundary between Burma and Assam', 1 Nov. 1933 (IOR: M/1/33).

30 Two Shan *Sawbwas*, Sao Hkin Maung of Mong Mit and Sao Shwe Thaike of Yawnghwe, did finally reach London, but they came against the wishes of the gov., Sir C. Innes, apparently by getting permission from his deputy while he was away. (IOR: M/1/68, Minute Paper P&J (B) 396, 27/9/33). In London they presented a 23-page pamphlet, 'Memorandum of the Federated Shan States by their Representatives', drawn up by a meeting of Shan chiefs in Taunggyi on 7 Sept. 1930. This set out the case for the independence of the Shan States. Claiming they had not been sufficiently consulted on constitutional matters in the past they now wanted (p.2), 'To present to the government the ultimate aim and ideal of the Shan States to attain to the dignity and status of an independent state under the Crown with the same constitution as the Indian States.' British officials were equally unenthusiastic about Shan representatives attending the Joint Select C'ttee meetings in 1933. One official claimed experience at the 1930 Conf. had shown Shan leaders to be 'most susceptible to pressure exerted on them by more adroit Burmans.' (Letter Monteath to Sir H. Stephenson, IOR: ibid.) In fact, and perhaps somewhat ambiguously, Sao Shwe Thaike was to become the first pres. of Burma at independence in 1948.

31 Stevenson, 'The Case for Applied Anthropology', 2-5.

32 For different accounts see Crosthwaite, *The Pacification of Burma*; Myint, *Burma's Struggle against British Imperialism* (Ref: Ch.2, *n.*28); and Sao Saimong Mangrai, *The Shan States and the British Annexation*, (Data Paper: No.57, SE Asia Program, Cornell Univ., Ithaca, New York, Aug. 1965).

33 For a detailed account of the early nationalist movement see A.D. Moscotti, *British Policy and the Nationalist Movement in Burma 1917-1937* (The Univ. Press of Hawaii, 1974): 17-68. Also Silverstein, *Burmese Politics*, 34-46. The 'footwear controversy' was over Westerners continuing to wear shoes in the precincts of Buddhist Temples without apparent regard for Buddhist custom and belief.

34 Ibid.: 38.

35 *Forward*, Dec. 1985: 26.

36 Trager, *From Kingdom to Republic*, 50

37 Ibid.

38 In 1856 a serious rebellion under a Karen *Minlaung* with 1,500 armed followers broke out in the Salween-Shwegyin hills, and in 1892 another *Minlaung* uprising occurred amongst the Kayan and other Karen sub-groups along the restive Karenni-Mongpai borders. Meanwhile guerrilla resistance continued in the Karenni hills into the 1890s even after the deposition of Sawlapaw, the most powerful of the Karenni chieftains. There were also problems in the British Army, and in 1899 one Karen battalion had to be disbanded for 'insubordinate conduct' (Crosthwaite, *The Pacification of Burma*, 131).

39 Dr San C. Po, *Burma and the Karens* (Elliot Stock, London, 1928): 66.
40 Great Britain, Govt. of India Act, 1919, app. N: 82 as quoted in Silverstein, *Burmese Politics*, 45.
41 Ibid.: 46. See also Po, *Burma and the Karens*, 6-10.
42 Ibid.: v, 81.
43 Ibid.: 79-83.
44 Ibid.: 80.
45 E.g. this was the verdict of the colonial govt. in one report in 1933: 'We doubt whether identity of interests between Burmans and Karens exists at present and if it does exist no harm will be done by giving Karens a little over-representation.' 'Memorandum by Govt. of Burma on the Representations received from the Representatives of Political Parties and Minorities', 1933, (IOR: M/1/120) para. 5.
46 Decypher of telegram from chief sec. to govt. of Burma home and political depts, to Sec. of State for India, 24 May 1935 (IOR: M/1/33).
47 Statement of People's Party, published in 'Memorandum by Govt. of Burma' (see *n*.45).
48 'Memorial from the Toungoo Branch of the Karen National Association to Gov. of Burma', 13 March 1935 (IOR: M/1/33); see also, *n*.28.
49 J.L. Leyden, 'The Karen Problem in Relation to Frontier Areas Administration', 28 June 1947 (IOR: M/4/3023). The leader of the Salween chiefs, Maung Shwe, was very much a traditionalist Sgaw hillman and, perhaps inspired by the KNA's activities on the plains, was to try to build his own nationalist movement in the Papun hills which combined traditional aspects of Christianity, Animism and Millenarianism. Calling himself 'Pu Kwe Kaw' (Honest Man), he built a monastery at Kler Doe Kya village called 'Wey Maw Kaw' (Kingdom of Heaven) where he conducted ceremonies which villagers today describe as a mixture of 'religion and nationalism'. This was to bring him into conflict with other local headmen and his death was engineered during the Japanese occupation, allegedly by another well-known headman, Saw De Ghai, later assassinated by the KNU.
50 H.N.C. Stevenson, 'Relation of the Karenni States to Burma', 24 June 1946, (IOR: M/4/3025): 7-8. For examples of the form of Sanad granted to the Karenni *Sawbwas* and *Myosas*, see C.U. Aitchinson (ed.), *A Collection of Treaties, Engagements, and Sanads relating to India and Neighbouring Countries* (Calcutta, Govt. of India, 1909) II: 85-9.
51 Interview with Nai Shwe Kyin, 22 Jan. 1985.
52 For the rise of the ANC, see U Aung Zan Wai, *Memoirs* (Rangoon, 1972, unpublished), 15-40; for U Seinda and the Auwadasariya Organisation, see Ch.4, *n*.88.
53 *Forward*, 15 Aug. 1966; Vumson, *Zo History* (Aizawl, Mizoram, 1986): 41.
54 Thein Pe Myint, 'The World Peace Camp and Burma', *Political Experience in the Revolutionary Period* (Rangoon, Shwe Pyi Tan, 1956): 535-6. The early slogan of the *Dobama* was 'Burma is our country; Burmese literature is our literature; Burmese language is our language. Love our country, raise the standards of our literature, respect our language', as translated in Silverstein, *Burmese Politics*, 39.
55 For the rise of the *Dobama* movement, see Jan Becka, *The National Liberation Movement in Burma during the Japanese Occupation Period (1941-1945)* (Dissertationes Orientales 42, Prague, 1983): 34-43; Khin Yi, *The Dobama Movement in Burma (1930-1938)* (Ithaca: Cornell Univ., SE Asia Program, 1988).
56 Khut Daung, *The Student Movement and Civil War in Burma* (extracts printed by Mahachon Publications, Bangkok, 1988): 80.
57 Ibid.: 81.
58 For a list of *Nagani* publications see D. Guyot, 'The Political Impact of the Japanese Occupation of Burma', Ph.D., mimeo. (Yale Univ., 1966): 14-15. Also see J.S. Thomson, 'Marxism in Burma', in F. Trager (ed.), *Marxism in SE Asia* (Stanford, 1959): 21-3 and R.H. Taylor, 'The Burmese Communist Movement and its Indian Connection: Formation and Factionalism', *Journal of SE Asian Studies*, 14 (1) 1983: 97. Marxist tracts published included selections from *Das Kapital* translated by Thakin Nu. Other publications included Marxist-inspired writings by several young Thakins, including Nu, Thein Pe and Soe. One of the best known was Ba Hein's *The Capitalist World*, which began with introductions by Thakins Soe and Than Tun. For Oo Kyaw's role in London in alerting the Thakins to Marxist political thought see B. Lintner, *The Rise and Fall of the Communist Party of Burma* (Ithaca: Cornell Univ, Southeast Asia

Program, 1990): 5.
59 Taylor, 'The Burmese Communist Movement', 96.
60 Becka, *The National Liberation Movement*, 40-1. Thakin Mya, later chm. of the Socialist Party, was the first Pres. of ABPO.
61 Personal corr. with CPB chm., Ba Thein Tin, June 1988.
62 Becka, *The National Liberation Movement*, 42.
63 Taylor, 'The Burmese Communist Movement', 98.
64 Ibid. For the unsuccessful exploits of Wu Wei Sai, a communist agent sent from Shanghai to Rangoon in May 1929, see Lintner *The Rise and Fall*, 5.
65 Taylor, 'The Burmese Communist Movement', 99. Thein Pe also mentioned another Thakin, Kyaw Sein, established contact with members of the British Communist Party in this period and set up his own Marxist study group, but they appear to have had no particular influence. Thein Pe's highly personalised 'Critique of Communist Movement in Burma' (n.d., 1966-73?), which, in the absence of other accounts, has been used as a standard reference on the early CPB years, is reproduced in Klaus Fleischmann (ed.), *Documents on Communism in Burma* (Hamburg, Institut fur Asienkunde, 1989): 222-48.
66 Becka, *The National Liberation Movement*, 60, 302.
67 The second time was in Aug. 1944 and though he soon left again because of what he described as Thakin Soe's 'sectarianism', Aung San admitted in 1946, 'I have still a genuine interest in Communism and the Communist Party.' *The Burman*, 9 March 1946.
68 Ba Maw, *Breakthrough in Burma: Memoirs of a Revolution, 1939-46* (Yale Univ. Press, 1968): 62-3. There are two scholarly English-language accounts of the national liberation movement's growing contacts with Imperial Japan; Becka, *The National Liberation Movement*, 51-76, which interprets events from Burmese sources from the perspective of the young nationalists, and Won Z. Yoon, *Japan's Scheme for the Liberation of Burma: the Role of the Minami Kikan and the 'Thirty Comrades'* (Ohio Univ., Papers in International Studies, SE Asia Series, No.27) which demonstrates from Japanese sources how the situation was manipulated to Japanese advantage.
69 Ba Maw, *Breakthrough in Burma*, 114-6.
70 Aung San, *Burma's Challenge* (p.1), reprinted in J. Silverstein (ed.), *The Political Legacy of Aung San* (Data Paper no.86, Ithaca, Cornell Univ. SE Asia Program, 1972).
71 Yoon, *Japan's Scheme*, 10-11; Becka, *The National Liberation Movement*, 59.
72 Ibid.: 64-5.
73 Ibid.: 63.
74 For a discussion see ibid.: 67, 305.
75 Ibid.: 68.
76 For a copy of this 'Blueprint' see *The Guardian* (Monthly), IV/3, 1957: 33-5.
77 Yoon, *Japan's Scheme for the Liberation of Burma*, 22-3.
78 Maung Maung, *Burma and General Ne Win* (Asia Publishing House, 1969): 81.
79 Becka, *The National Liberation Movement*: 76.

Chapter 4
1 War Cabinet Paper, 'Policy in Regard to Reconstruction in Burma after Re-occupation', 7 Aug. 1942, Memorandum by the governor of Burma, Sir R. Dorman-Smith, reprinted in H. Tinker (ed.), *Burma: The Struggle for Independence, 1944-48* (ref: Ch.2, n.4) I, Doc.1.
2 *Misconduct of Chinese Troops in Burma*, Defence Dept., Govt. of Burma, Simla, 1943 (IOR: M/3/856): 29. Marked 'Most Secret', the report details incidents involving Chinese troops across much of NE Burma. 'Locusts describes them in one word' (p.71). The average Chinese soldier was poorly armed and fed and largely left to fend for himself. Concluded S.C. Pollard of the Burma Frontier Service in Kengtung dist., which was handed over by the Japanese to the Siam govt.: 'Traditionally pro-Siamese and anti-Chinese sentiments were greatly fostered by the presence of Chinese troops and the senseless arrests and persistent thefts in which these indulged. They were more afraid of the Chinese than the Japanese' (p.3).
3 See Becka, *The National Liberation Movement* (ref: Ch.3, n.55): 333-4. There has been some speculation over the actual date and location of the AFO's founding meeting. But it seems certain that it was at the meetings held at Pegu, 4-7 Aug., that the principles

and objectives of the AFO/AFPFL were first drawn up, and these were subsequently reported at a series of follow-up meetings in Rangoon. However, it was not until March 1945 that the scale of the AFPFL's org. became widely apparent.

4   There are considerable variations in estimates of Japanese casualty figures inflicted by the AFPFL. See ibid.: 238, 352-3, for a discussion of claims from AFPFL sources. These estimates vary from 8,000 to over 20,000 kld. The CPB today calculates a figure of 'almost 20,000' (see *n.* 11). British estimates put them at much less; in his final report Adm. Lord Mountbatten calculated them as between 600 and 700 kld. *Report to the Combined Chiefs of Staff by the Supreme Allied Commander, South-East Asia, 1943-45* (London, 1951): 145. This discrepancy can partly be explained by casualties inflicted by ethnic minority forces working with the allies, who, while it can be argued were part of the anti-fascist resistance, did not actually work with the AFPFL.

5   No original copy of this manifesto appears to have survived, though it is still widely referred to today. Thein Pe, it seems, called it the 'Myingyan Manifesto'. The only printed version available is that of Tin Mya, *Myawaddy Magazine*, 13 (3) Rangoon 1964: 165; see Becka, *The National Liberation Movement*, 53, 299.

6   Personal corr. with Ba Thein Tin and Kyaw Mya, June 1988. This meeting, however, though influential was clearly very small. One of the participants, Tin Mya (who places Nyaungchaung, the Congress village, in neighbouring Kyaiklat township) in his popular, serialised memoirs, *Bone Bawa Hma Phyin* ('A Life in the Commune', in Burmese, *Myawaddy Magazine*, 1964-71), recorded just 7 people as having attended. Thus, according to Kyaw Mya, some CPB veterans would prefer to date the 1939 founding meeting as the 1st Congress and the 1944 congress as a party or CC meeting.

7   For an autobiographical account of his travels see R.H. Taylor (ed.), *Marxism and Resistance in Burma 1942-5: Thein Pe Myint's Wartime Traveller* (Athens, Ohio Univ. Press, 1984). See also Thein Pe (Myint), *What Happenened in Burma* (Allahabad, 1943).

8   The AFO divided Burma (i.e. Burma Proper) into 10 resistance zones with a mil. cdr. and political adviser in each. In many zones officials who later turned out to be leading communists predominated. Besides Ba Htoo, important communist mil. cdrs. included Kyaw Zaw (zone 4), today CC member of the CPB, and Ye Htut (zone 6). Leading communist political advisers included Thakin Soe, later Red Flag CPB leader, in zone 2 in the eastern Lower Delta whose mil. cdr. was Ne Win; Thakin Ba Thein Tin, present chm. of the CPB, in Moulmein dist. (zone 5); and Thakin Chit, later vice-chm. of the CPB, in zone 4. It was in the entirely communist-controlled zones, zone 4 which covered Pegu-Shwegyin and Thaton, and zone 6 which included Pyinmana-Meiktila and Toungoo, that the heaviest casualties were inflicted and which, significantly, were later to become major centres of the CPB insurrection. Than Tun himself was appointed as the AFPFL's liaison officer with the British Army. Initially the AFPFL Supreme Council consisted of nine members, Aung San, Ne Win and Let Ya from the BNA, Thakins Soe, Than Tun and Tin Mya from the CPB and Thakins Ba Swe, Kyaw Nyein and Chit from the PRP. In the following months the Council's composition was to fluctuate but the three principal spokesmen remained the same: Aung San, Cdr. BNA, Thakin Soe, Pres., and Than Tun, Gen-sec. For a detailed analysis of above see Becka, *The National Liberation Movement*, 222-3, 354 who draws heavily on the accounts of Tin Mya, *The Headquarters of the Anti-Fascist Revolution and Ten Zones of Resistance* (in Burmese), (Rangoon, 2nd ed., Aug. 1968), and *Bone Bawa Hma Phyin.*

9   See A.S. Kaufman, *Birma, Ideologia i Politika*, Moscow, 1973; Becka, *The National Liberation Movement*, 240, 354.

10 Than Tun, *People's Age*, 4 (36/7) 14 March 1948.

11 See e.g. VOPB, 29 March, in BBC, *SWB*, 5 April 1979.

12 'The Humble Memorial of the Karens of Burma to His Britannic Majesty's Secretary of State for Burma', Rangoon, 26 Sept. 1945, in Tinker, *Burma: The Struggle*, I, Doc.286.

13 Burma Intelligence Bureau, *Burma During the Japanese Occupation*, I, Oct. 1943: 23-8. See also Ian Morrison, *Grandfather Longlegs: The Life and Gallant Death of Maj. H.P. Seagrim* (London, Faber and Faber, 1947): 69-73, 183-201.

14 General Smith Dun, *Memoirs of the Four Foot Colonel* (Cornell Data Paper, No. 113, Ithaca, SE Asia Program, Cornell Univ.): 63.

15 Interview with Saw Tha Din, 23 Dec. 1985.

16 Quoted in letter, 'Sir Reginald Dorman-Smith to Lord Pethwick-Lawrence', 31 Jan.

1946 (IOR: M/4/3023) in Tinker, *Burma: The Struggle*, I, Doc.384.

17 Interview with Saw Tha Din, 23 Dec. 1985. According to Tha Din, Col. Suzuki at first refused to believe him and said he would only investigate his claims if two of the KNA delegation accompanying Tha Din agreed to go along with him. These, he warned, he would execute if Tha Din's claims turned out to be false. Five, however, immediately volunteered and once Suzuki saw for himself what was taking place, he moved quickly to stop the violence.

18 Burma Intelligence Bureau, *Burma During the Japanese Occupation*, 25-6.

19 Morrison, *Grandfather Longlegs*, 193-201.

20 Ibid.: 164.

21 'Press Release: KNU for Reuter', 25 June 1947, in Tinker, *Burma: The Struggle*, II, Doc.413.

22 *Forward*, 15 Aug. 1966; Vumson, *Zo History* (ref: Ch.3, *n*.53): 154-79.

23 For an account of Naw Seng's wartime bravery, see Ian Fellowes-Gordon, *The Amiable Assassins* (London, Robert Hale Ltd., 1957): 117.

24 Yawnghwe, *The Shan of Burma* (ref: Ch.2, *n*.37): 84.

25 Becka, *The National Liberation Movement*, 180, 337.

26 In July 1945 the strength of the British Burma Army was calculated as 22,061 of which the ethnic composition was (officers in brackets) Indian and Gurkha 13,500 (65), Chin 3,000 (7), Kachin 2,000 (3), Karen 2,000 (33), Burman 200 (3). The remainder were largely British and Anglo-Indian officers and GCO's. Working with the Burma Army were various guerrilla units of which Karen/Karenni forces, estimated at some 12,000 strong, were by far the largest. The BNA was calculated as 11,480 on the eve of the AFO uprising of which possibly 1,000 were Delta Karens. There were also innumerable guerrilla forces and various Shan and Kachin local forces. For the Arakanese resistance no reliable figures exist but guerrilla forces are generally estimated to have been several hundred strong. For British forces, see Supreme Allied Cdr., 15 July 1945, in *Burma: The Struggle*, I, Doc.224. The BNA figure comes from D. Guyot, 'The Political Impact' (ref: Ch.3, *n*.58): 394.

27 'The Blue Print for Burma', July 1944, in *Burma: The Struggle*, I, Doc.38.

28 'Burma: A Statement of Policy by His Majesty's Govt.', May 1945.

29 Lt-Gen. Slim, Memo, 'Burma National Army', 15 May 1945, in *Burma: The Struggle*, I, Doc.144. General Stopford of the XIIth Army later cabled from Singapore warning against the arrest of Aung San (ibid., Doc.490).

30 Mountbatten conceded in April 1945, 'As regards the BDA and the AFO, they have risen before it was clear to them that British forces would, or could, come to their rescue. And if it can be said that they are rising for their own ends, and not for the love of us, I think it would be unrealistic on our part to suppose that the people of any nation engage in war except in their own interests, however praise worthy these may be.' ('Draft Paper on Policy for Military Administration of Burma', 5 April 1945, Supreme Allied Command, in ibid., Doc.116.)

31 Trager. *From Kingdom to Republic* (ref: Ch.3, *n*.8): 63.

32 Hugh Tinker, *The Union of Burma* (OUP, 1957): 17.

33 Resolutions passed at the meeting called for the ending of mil. rule, the formation of an integrated Burma Army to include troops from all ethnic races, and the immediate formation of a provisional govt. pending the election of a Constituent Assembly. For an official account of the events of this period see Min. of Information, *Burma's Fight for Freedom* (Rangoon, 1948); AFPFL, *From Fascist Bondage to New Democracy: The New Burma in the New World* (Rangoon, Nay Win Kyi Press, n.d.).

34 Interview with Saw Hla Pru, ex-APLP, 17 Jan. 1987.

35 Tinker, *Burma: The Struggle*, I: xxxiv.

36 Becka, *The National Liberation Movement*, 258.

37 A. Buxton, *The New Statesman and Nation*, 9 Oct. 1948.

38 Becka, *The National Liberation Movement*, 170-3.

39 Ibid.: 260-1; Thein Pe, 'Critique of Communist Movement in Burma' (ref: Ch.3, *n*.65): 235.

40 R. Taylor, 'The Burmese Communist Movement and its Indian Connection' (ref: Ch.3, *n*.58): 108. The defectors included his closest wartime comrades, including Thakin Tin Mya (who later rejoined the White Flags), Daw Saw Mya, cdr. of the BNA Women's Forces, and Tun Sein. For lists of the way the Red Flag-White Flag leaderships divided

in this period, see Klaus Fleischmann, *Die Kommunistische Partei Birmas* (Hamburg, Institut fur Asienkunde, 1989): 387-9, 401.
41 Than Tun, *People's Age*.
42 Thein Pe Myint, *Political Experience in the Revolutionary Period* (ref: Ch.3, *n.*54): 442.
43 *New Times of Burma*, 30 Oct. 1946.
44 *The Burman*, 3 Nov. 1946.
45 Ba Tin (*aka* Goshal), *On the Present Political Situation in Burma and Our Tasks*, photocopy in my possession; see Ch.6.
46 *The Communist Daily*, 8 April 1947.
47 Memorandum, Top Secret, 'Communism in Burma since Aug. 1946', Sept., 1947, Burma Office (IOR: M/4/2535).
48 Ibid.
49 Ibid.
50 Interview with H.A. Stonor, 3 Jan. 1989.
51 Clearly all such speculations need the most thorough investigation. But Saw's claim that the weapons found in the lake behind his house, which directly implicated him, had been deliberately planted there were at first supported by several other non-AFPFL leaders, including U Ba Pe, who visited the Anglo-Burman journalist Max McGrath and told him they believed that they, too, were going to be framed. Interview with Max McGrath, 15 March 1987. McGrath, who reported on the trial and was later attached to U Tin Tut, Min. of For. Affairs, believed Saw never had a fair trial.
52 Maung Maung, *Burma and General Ne Win* (ref: Ch.3, *n.*78): 91-2.; see also *n.*74, Ch.3 *n.*67.
53 Ba Tin, *On the Present Political Situation*.
54 'The Humble Memorial of the Karens of Burma', see (ref: Ch.4, *n.*12.
55 *Rangoon Liberator*, 8 Nov. 1945. The 5 signatories of the KCO declaration included three men later to become leaders of the 'nationalist' KNU movement, Saw Tha Din, Saw Ba U Gyi and Thra Tha Htoo, and two who became prominent KYO supporters of the AFPFL, Mahn Ba Kin and Mahn Ba Khaing.
56 Ibid.
57 'Resolution adopted by Mass Meeting of the Karens', 25-27 April 1946, *Burma: The Struggle*, I, Doc.463.
58 See e.g., 'Record of Meeting on Frontier Areas', 7 Feb. 1947, in Tinker, *Burma: The Struggle*, II, Doc.274. At this historic EC meeting with the British Labour govt. rep., Arthur Bottomley, on the eve of Panglong, the two Karen EC members, Saw Ba U Gyi and Mahn Ba Khaing, said 'not a single word'. The other three EC members present, Aung San, Thakin Mya and Tin Tut, did all the talking.
59 In London Saw Tha Din, the last surviving member of the mission, says it was made absolutely clear to them by Arthur Henderson, under-sec. of state for India and Burma, there 'would not and could not' be any British support for an independent Karen State; interview 23 Dec. 1985.
60 *New Times of Burma*, 16 Dec. 1946.
61 'Circular issued by Karenni Ministers' (translation), Loikaw, 26 June 1947, *Burma: The Struggle*, I, Doc.417. On July 25 U Bee Tu Re, 'President of the United States of Karenni', passed on to the gov. the Constitution of the new State (IOR: M/4/3023).
62 'Appreciation of Panglong Conf. by the Kachin Elders'. Appendix C, Gov. of Burma Despatch, No.14, 30 April 1946 (IOR: M/4/2811).
63 H.N.C. Stevenson, 'Political Discussions at Panglong', Appendix D, in ibid.
64 Ibid.
65 'Kachin Elders', in ibid.
66 'Observations by H.N.C. Stevenson on Karen Resolution, adopted 25 April 1946', Rangoon, 15 June 1946, *Burma: The Struggle*, I, Doc.566.
67 'Study of Karen demands by D.B. Petch' (Extract), Rangoon, 31 Dec., 1946, *Burma: The Struggle*, II, Doc.154. Petch also tried to put these views to Burman leaders. Dr Ba U was incensed when he was approached. He replied, 'Though the Scotch and the Welsh have been demanding Home Rule for years, you have refused to give it to them. What you suggest would cause trouble between the Karens and the Burmans. I am glad to know there are very few Englishmen like you.' Dr Ba U, *My Burma* (New York, Taplinger, 1959): 196.

68   Telegram, 10 Downing Street to India Office, 20 April 1946 (IOR: M/4/3025).
69   Letter of H.N.C. Stevenson to H.A. Stonor, 9 Nov. 1981 (copy in my possession).
70   In Nov. 1947 the Burma Office persuaded the *Daily Mail* newspaper not to publish an
     article on the Karen situation by the Revd J.W. Baldwin, a long-serving, Seventh-Day
     Adventist missionary in Burma. Arthur Henderson, the sec. of state, called it a 'highly
     tendentious and somewhat inflammable statement' (Telegram, Sec. of State to Gov., 15
     Nov. 1947: IOR M/4/2736). Baldwin was one of the handful of British who stayed on
     to join the Karen rebellion. But perhaps the most curious example of news suppression
     concerned an incident in the Karenni States when on 19 Oct. Saw Nge Du, the *Myosa*
     of the Bawlake substate, apparently signed a declaration at a mass meeting in Loikaw
     withdrawing the agreement of Bawlake to join the new Karenni State in the future
     Union. This would undoubtedly have held up the accession of the Karenni States to the
     Union, and set off a hurried cover-up from Parliament back in London before U Nu
     managed to persuade Saw Nge Du to change his mind (see: IOR M/4/3025).
71   L.B. Walsh-Atkins, 'Karenni States: Proposal for Incorporation in British Burma',
     Burma Office Note, 4 Oct. 1945 (IOR: M/4/3025).
72   Letter of H.N.C. Stevenson to P.G.E. Nash, 15 Feb. 1947, *Burma: The Struggle*, II,
     Doc.286.
73   H.N.C. Stevenson, 'Economic Relations between the Frontier Areas and the Plains of
     Burma', Appendix E, Gov. of Burma Despatch, No.14.
74   Aung San, 'A Blueprint for a Free Burma', as quoted in Maung, *Burma and General Ne
     Win*, 291. The surviving literature of Aung San's speeches and writings is small and
     what his eventual attitude to any number of questions after independence would have
     been must remain conjecture. Up until his death the CPB still retained some hope he
     would rejoin them. But one of the best indications of his attitude to the minority ques-
     tion was his 'Address at the Convention held at the Jubilee Hall Rangoon 23rd May
     1947' and printed in J. Silverstein (ed.), *The Political Legacy of Aung San* (ref: Ch.3,
     n.70). Here he suggested using Stalin's definition in *Marxism and the National and
     Colonial Question* (London, 1942) to distinguish between a nation and a national
     minority. The constitution would establish varying degrees of autonomy for Burma's
     minorities depending on how closely they fitted Stalin's criteria for nationhood: 'A
     Nation is a historically evolved, stable community of language, territory, economic life,
     and psychological make-up manifested in a community or culture' (ibid.: 8). In Aung
     San's view only the Shans could be classified as a nation. For the other minorities to
     qualify for full national minority rights they should in theory form at least 10% of the
     total population.
75   A.A. Bernova and N.N. Cheboksarov, 'Ethnic Processes in South-East Asian Coun-
     tries', in *Ethnocultural Processes and National Problems in the Modern World*
     (Moscow, Progress Publishers, 1981): 275, who quote V.I. Lenin 'What the 'Friends of
     the People' Are and How They Fight the Social-Democrats', *Collected Works*, I
     (Moscow: Progress Publishers, 1977): 129.
76   Letter of H.N.C. Stevenson to Sir Hubert Rance, 20 Jan. 1947, *Burma: The Struggle*, II,
     Doc.208. Commenting on one of the last reports Stevenson submitted on a tour through
     the Kachin hills in late 1946, D.T. Monteath commented: 'This is the report of an offi-
     cer defending, by illustration, the plans he had formed for carrying out a policy of
     educating the hill tribes to a standard at which they could hold their own with the more
     sophisticated Burman and so secure equitable terms for amalgamation, in fact the
     White Paper policy. In the meantime Mr. Stevenson was at pains to put the FAA
     between the FA people and the Burmans, to protect the former from the latter. Where
     he fell down was, I think, that he regarded the Burman too much as the enemy; there
     are one or two incautious phrases indicating this attitude to which he perhaps gave
     incautious expression in public. He was a partisan not an interested broker.' (Burma
     Office Note B/F & FA 1004/47: IOR: M/4/2805).
77   Sir Hubert Rance to Lord Pethwick Lawrence, Telegram, 8 Nov. 1946, *Burma: The
     Struggle*, II, Doc.97.
78   House of Commons Debates, Vol.431, cols.2343-5, in ibid., Doc.147.
79   Telegram, Sir Hubert Rance to Lord Pethwick-Lawrence, 2 Jan. 1947, ibid., Doc.157.
80   Burma Office, 'Communism in Burma'. Than Tun denounced the agreement as a
     'compromise' in a document, *Present Political Situation*, because there was 'no imme-
     diate declaration of independence.' He also noted 'British troops would not be with-

drawn' and 'the monopolistic "Projects" would not be touched.' The CPB carried on a series of strikes which paralysed Rangoon throughout much of Feb. Thakin Soe also bitterly denounced the Atlee-San talks; 'Aung San may parley with the British Imperialists, but the people's revolution against British imperialism and its hirelings in Burma will go on. Aung San's day of reckoning will come (sooner than many people expect) and then we will take him as a prisoner to be tried by the "People's Tribunal" for betraying his country's cause.' Mocking Aung San's threat to stage an uprising if the talks failed, Thakin Soe claimed the people's revolution had already started in Toungoo, Pegu and Arakan against 'imperialists and their allies of the Aung San type' (Reuters, 7 Jan. 1947).

81 Memorandum, Pres., Bhamo Kachin District Council to the Executive Council, Federated Shan States, contained in telegram, Director, Frontier Areas Administration to Sec. of State for Burma, 11 Jan. 1947, *Burma: The Struggle*, II, Doc.176. The Executive C'ttee of the Council of Federated Shan States cabled the director, FAA from Lashio, Dec. 30 1946, contained in telegram, Director, FAA to Sec. of State for Burma, 2 Jan. 1947, in ibid., Doc.156.

82 According to British figures, 22 people were arrested, of whom 18 were hospitalised. The building was cleared only after the use of tear gas (telegram, Gov. to Sec. of State, 21 Jan. 1947: IOR: M/4/2535). Reuters, 23 Jan. 1947, put the casualty figures much higher, at 264, and the number of demonstrators at 4,000.

83 Telegram, South East Asia Land Forces to Min. of Defence, 14 Jan. 1947, *Burma: The Struggle*, II, Doc.181.

84 Telegram, Sir Hubert Rance to Lord Pethwick-Lawrence, 18 Jan. 1947, in ibid., Doc.203.

85 Proceedings of meeting held at 10 Downing Street, 20 Jan. 1947, in ibid., Doc.209.

86 *The Times* (London), 14 Jan. 1947.

87 For a background account of the meetings at Panglong seen through British eyes see 'Note by John Leyden on the Panglong Conf.', 20 Feb. 1947, *Burma: The Struggle*, II, Doc.294; for a highly confusing attempt to try and shed light on some of these arrangements, see Gen. Saw Maung, *WPD*, 10 Jan. 1990.

88 For a discussion of the 1947 Constitution, see Silverstein, *Burmese Politics* (ref: Ch.2, n.22): 185-205.

89 The APLP, sometimes also known as the Arakan People's Freedom League, grew from the earlier 'Central Auwadasariya Organisation' formed by U Seinda in 1940 at Kya Emdaung village, Kyaukpyu. During the Second World War U Seinda then merged forces with another nationalist cell led by the monk, U Pyin-nya Thi Ha, who had also been involved in the earlier formation of the Arakan National Congress. However, the entry of the BIA into Arakan during the war, veteran APLP leaders say, considerably confused the political direction of the nationalist movement. Arakan became a hotbed of underground activity during the Japanese occupation and the main route for allied intelligence officers, mainly working in the Muslim community, and communist organisers making their way to and from India. After the successful uprising by the BNA-backed ADA against the Japanese in Jan. 1945, U Seinda's armed followers, estimated at some 3,000-strong, stayed behind in the forests of Myebon, An, Munbra and Kyauktaw townships, and launched sporadic attacks on British units.

90 U Aung Zan Wai, *Memoirs* (ref: Ch.3, n.52): 140-41.

91 Ibid.: 164.

92 Ibid.

93 Bonbauk Tha Kyaw, *My Journey in the Revolution* [in Burmese] (copy in possession of AIO, n.d.): 276-8; *Weekly Intelligence Summary*, No.16, 19 April 1947, in 'Law and Order, Arakan' (IOR:M/4/2503).

94 In ibid., Minute Paper, B/C 1235/47, 12 Aug. 1947.

95 U Aung Zan Wai, 'Report to the Govt. Advisory C'ttee headed by Sir Ba U' (Abridged, 1961).

96 'Law and Order, Arakan', Minute Paper, B/C 1011/1947, 9 June 1947; Reuters, 3 June 1947.

97 E.g., British intelligence reported this demand was made at a meeting of 1,000 supporters of the Muslim Jamaitut-Ulma in Maungdaw on 19 April. *Weekly Intelligence Summary*, No.19, 10 June 1947.

98 See e.g., 'Marshall Shwin to the PM (via Gov.)', 16 June 1947, *Burma: The Struggle*, II,

Doc.402, which includes the signatures or thumbprints of 1,441 Karens from Shwegyin dist. (IOR: M/4/3023).

99   'The KNU to the PM (via Gov. of Burma)', 17 Feb. 1947 (IOR: M/4/3023), *Burma: The Struggle*, II, Doc.291 and 'Resolutions passed by the Karen Council of Action', 22 Feb. 1947, ibid., Doc.300.

100 Dun, *The Four Foot Colonel*, 85.

101 Testimony of Saw Marshall Shwin, Pres., Shwegyin Karen Association, *Frontier Areas Committee of Enquiry* (henceforth *FACE*), Part II, 126-34. 'It would be much better if the Frontier peoples alone decided for themselves.' Marshall Shwin today claims his full testimony was not included in the final report. Interview, 15 March 1988.

102 Ibid; M. Smith, 'Burma and World War II', *Cultural Survival*, 13 (4) 1989: 5.

103 According to Shwin, when he asked Sankey why he had not contradicted the testimony of the highly suspect Saw Lu Lu delegation, Sankey replied, 'They told me that if I said or did anything contrary to the interests of the AFPFL they would have me liquidated.... If I had given a negative answer, I would have been denied the privilege to fight.'

104 Testimony of Sao Maha, Chief of Mongmon, Northern Wa State, *FACE*, Pt. II, 39. When asked what constitutitonal reforms they desired they replied, 'None, only more opium.' *Burma: The Struggle*, II: 883.

105 J.L. Leyden, 'The Karen Problem in Relation to Frontier Areas Administration', 28 June 1947, *Burma: The Struggle*, II, Doc.421.

106 *FACE*, 150.

107 Ibid.: 159 and 165.

108 *Sunday Times*, 22 June 1947, as quoted in *Burma: The Struggle*, II: 610. Rees-Williams wrote: 'The Karens are equally at variance politically: the Animist Karens have no interest in the constitutional issue, the Buddhist Karens are inclined to side with the Burmans, while the Christian Karens, who are about 25% of the whole, and the educated ones at that are divided among themselves into two groups, one of which supports Aung San and the other is against him.' In fact, 8 different Karen delegations put forward statements to the *FACE*: the KNU, Shwegyin Karen Association, Salween dist. KNA, Toungoo Karens and the Central Karen-Taungthu (Pao) C'ttee of Thaton, which all supported the KNU; the KYO which asked for a Karen State 'federated to Burma'; Lu Lu's Salween delegation; and a Karenni-Mongpai team which demanded the right of secession for an enlarged Karen-Karenni State to include all Karens east of the Sittang River, but made final agreement on joining the Union conditional on Burma being accepted into the British Commonwealth. Shwin puts this confusing performance down to the short time the KNU had to prepare.

109 Interview with Saw Tha Din, 23 Dec. 1985.

110 Leyden, 'The Karen Problem in Relation to Frontier Areas Administration'.

111 Dun, *The Four Foot Colonel*, 84.

112 'Proposal to form a Karen Autonomous State within the Federation of Burma and to have minority rights of the Karens safeguarded by statute', n.d., submitted by the KYO to Dir. FAA, and passed to London 16 July 1947 (IOR: M/4/3023). For the Karen State the KYO demanded the inclusion of half of Toungoo dist. including the Pyinmana hill tracts, 60% of Amherst dist., and the entire Salween and Thaton dists. with the Sittang River marking the westernmost border. The estimated area of this state was 15,738 sq. miles with a Karen population of just over 600,000 and a Burman population of 225,152.

113 Telegram, Gov. of Burma to Sec. of State for Burma, 24 May 1947 (IOR: M/4/2503).

114 Interview with Nai Shwe Kyin, 22 Jan. 1985.

115 After the war Mon nationalist leaders, headed by Mon Po Cho, had initially joined with the AFPFL to argue the case for a Mon state, but realising it was not even on the AFPFL agenda, Po Cho's 'United Mon Association' (est. 9 Nov. 1946) boycotted the 1947 elections. Nai Shwe Kyin, however, stood (unsuccessfully) with 5 other Mon candidates on the grounds that, unlike the Karens, there were no reserved seats for the Mon community at all.

116 Interview with Mika Rolly, 25 Jan. 1987. 'Brigadier' Rolly, another early leader of the Karen insurrection, was Sankey's closest aide and adviser.

117 Telegram, R.E. McGuire to Sir Gilbert Laithwaite, 22 Sept. 1947.
118 Corr. between the Earl of Listowel and Thakin Nu, 7 Sept. 1947, *Burma: The Struggle*, II, Docs. 511, 513.
119 Interview with Skaw Ler Taw, 17 March 1988.
120 'Minutes of the Karen Leaders' Conf. sponsored by the KNU', 3-4 Oct. 1947 (IOR: M/4/3023).
121 Saw Po Chit, *Karens and Karen State* (KNU, Thathanahita Press, Rangoon, 1947): 1-8.
122 *New Times of Burma*, 20 Nov. 1947. On 28 Oct. 200 guerrillas also attacked Myebon town and on 11 Nov. another 400-strong guerrilla force clashed with the army near Kyauktaw.

Chapter 5

1   *Bangkok Post*, 15 Feb. 1988.
2   H. Tinker, *The Union of Burma* (ref: Ch.4, *n*.32): 312.
3   'Memorandum by the Sec. of State for India, Burma Excluded Areas', 29 Nov. 1933 by the Joint C'ttee on Indian Constitutional Reform (IOR: M/1/123).
4   Sao Saimong Mangrai, *The Shan States and the British Annexation* (ref: Ch.3, *n*.32): 101-45.
5   See Ch.3, *n*.38; Appendix A.
6   Telegram, Gov. of Burma to Gov.-Gen. of India, 18 May 1940, (IOR: M/3/982).
7   'Monthly Report of the Assistant Resident Loikaw for the month of May 1947' (IOR: M/4/3023).
8   Tinker, *The Union of Burma*, 4.
9   Sec. of State for India, 'Report on the Rebellion in Burma', (1931).
10 J.F. Cady, *A History of Modern Burma* (Cornell Univ. Press, 1958): 309-13.
11 Ibid.: 317
12 Becka, *The National Liberation Movement* (ref: Ch.3, *n*.55): 37, 293.
13 *Forward*, 15 Oct. 1968.
14 Morrison, *Grandfather Longlegs* (ref: Ch.4, *n*.13).
15 See Field-Marshall Sir William Slim, *Defeat into Victory* (Cassell, London, 1956): 142-3, 499, for a synopsis of British guerrilla tactics, still largely in use by the KNU today; see also, M. Smith, 'Burma and World War II' (ref: Ch.4, *n*.102).
16 T.R. Gurr, *Why Men Rebel* (Princeton Univ., 1971): 13, 177-92, 341. For an interesting analysis of Gurr's study through an examination of Shan rebellions along the Siam border at the turn of the 20th century see A. Ramsay, 'Modernisation and Reactionary Rebellions in Northern Siam', *Journal of Asian Studies*, 38 (2): 283-97.
17 See *n*.5. In 1692 the chronicle for the Shan State of Mongpai records a successful uprising by local Karen 'tribes', predominantly Kayan, in which the ruling Shan *Sawbwa* was kld. and his administration overthrown. Four years later a punitive expedition sent by the Avan king was repulsed, effectively establishing Mongpai's independence for the next 60 years and, it would appear, acting as an inspiration to other rebellious Karen sub-groups in the hills in the 18th and 19th centuries, notably the Karenni.
18 The SSPP, PNO, SSNLO, PSLO, WNO, TRC, KNLP, LNO, KIO as well as the various ex-CPB breakaway Wa, Kokang and Shan factions (see Chart 1).
19 E.J. Hobsbawm, *Bandits* (Penguin Books, 1972): 18.
20 Ibid.: 17-40.
21 Ibid.: 23, 40.
22 Max McGrath, *Asahi* (English language), 23 Feb. 1957, which includes an account of the activities of some of these gangs.
23 *The Daily Telegraph* and *Morning Post*, 18 Jan. 1961.
24 Interview, 23 July 1988.
25 Interview, 7 Jan. 1986.
26 For a rare contemporary study of the *Tatmadaw* see Tin Maung Maung Than, 'Burma's National Security and Defence Posture', *Contemporary SE Asia*, 11 (1) June 1989: 40-60.
27 See e.g. *Bangkok Post*, 6 Aug. 1985, for a BSPP report of more than 9,000 insurgents kld. and 10,000 captured or surrendered in a 4 year period. In a 14-month period in 1958/9, e.g., the *Tatmadaw* put insurgent losses at 1,872 dead and 1,959 wounded against 520 govt. dead and 638 wounded. Govt. of the Union of Burma, *Is Trust*

Vindicated? (Min. of Information, Rangoon, 1960): 31.
28 VOPB, 2 Feb. 1978.
29 KIO, 'Policy Statement' (1987); *WPD*, 28 Nov. 1988.
30 Ibid., 10 Jan. 1990.
31 Ibid.

Chapter 6
1   See e.g. CPB 'Third Party Congress Political Report' in VOPB, 23 March, in BBC, *SWB*, 28 March 1986.
2   Than Tun, *People's Age*, 4, 14 March 1948.
3   For his own version of the events of this period see a reprint of selected speeches in, U Nu, *Towards Peace and Democracy* (Min. of Information, Rangoon, 1949): 10-29.
4   The decision not to join the Commonwealth is generally dated by historians to the vote by the Constituent Assembly on 16 June 1947 to form the new Union of Burma as an 'Independent Sovereign Republic'. This followed earlier reflections along the same lines by Aung San. But even this decision some observers have linked to communist pressure; see e.g. Tinker, *The Union of Burma* (ref: Ch.4, *n*.32): 26.
5   Thakin Ba Tin (*aka* Goshal), *On the Present Political Situation in Burma and Our Tasks* (mimeograph, copy in my possession); see also *n*.10.
6   Ibid.
7   Ibid.
8   Other policies Ba Tin advocated included a 40-hour day and improved workers' conditions and rights; the 'self-determination' of national minorities and 'full autonomy' for the principal nationalities including the Arakanese; and a new constitution to guarantee 'full freedom and democracy'.
9   Ibid.
10 Much of the information on the CPB's early history was given to me in personal corr. with the CPB chm., Thakin Ba Thein Tin, during 1988-90, henceforth Corr. with Ba Thein Tin. Ba Thein Tin has been a CPB CC or Politburo member since the earliest wartime days of the CPB. Bertil Lintner has speculated that the absence of copies of Ba Tin's thesis on the CPB side has meant the document might not be authentic (Lintner, *The Rise and Fall*, ref: Ch.3, *n*.58: 13). Ba Thein Tin does not support this view. The distinctive language of the writing exactly echoes and paraphrases the speeches of Than Tun and other CPB and CPI leaders of the time. Ba Tin's public disgrace and execution in 1967 probably accounts for the lack of references to the document today, and it is also quite likely, given the chaos in 1948-52, that the document only had a limited circulation. None the less, detail by detail, the thesis exactly sets out and predicts CPB history during 1947/8, and the main doubt must be whether Ba Tin was the sole author or his name is a cover for someone else.
11 G.N. Overstreet and M. Windmiller, *Communism in India* (Univ. of California Press, Berkeley, 1959): 269-74. However, though during 1948 the CPI's confrontation with the Nehru govt. frequently turned to violence, the CPI leadership, apparently recognising Nehru's popularity, eventually settled for a policy which can best be described as 'brinkmanship'.
12 See e.g. Govt of the Union of Burma, *Is it a People's Liberation?* (Min. of Information, Rangoon, 1952): 8-9; Ruth T. McVey, *The Calcutta Conference and the SE Asian Uprisings* (Cornell Univ., 1958): 1-24.
13 See e.g. R. Butwell, *U Nu of Burma*, (Stanford Univ. Press, 1969): 96.
14 Corr. with Ba Thein Tin.
15 See e.g. CPB Politburo, 'Political and Social Report', VOPB, 25 Dec. 1979, in BBC, *SWB*, 7 Jan. 1980, for a commentary blaming the growing incidence of venereal disease in Burma on foreign tourists and for a long list of the other undesirable effects of decadent 'capitalist' culture in the country.
16 Thein Pe Myint's *Wartime Traveller* (ref: Ch.4, *n*.7): 208-18.
17 Ibid.: 298.
18 Trager, *From Kingdom to Republic* (ref: Ch.3, *n*.8): 99.
19 'Zhdanov Report to Communist Parties' Information Conf., 1947' quoted in Ba Tin, *On the Present Political Situation*.
20 Ibid; see also *n*.22.

21 See e.g. Overstreet and Windmiller, *Communism in India*, 259, 268.
22 Than Tun, *People's Age*. Though encouraged by the CCP successes in China, Than Tun warned these in themselves were 'not enough' unless supported by other communist victories in the region, particularly in Burma.
23 Ibid.
24 Govt. of the Union of Burma, *Burma and the Insurrections* (Rangoon, 1949): 41. Two members of the Yugoslav Communist Party were also reportedly in attendance. See also *WPD*, 14, 15 Nov. 1988, for the disillusioned account of a former CPB cadre, Soe Tun Ni.
25 Nu, *Towards Peace and Democracy*, 123; Tinker, *The Union of Burma*, 35. The AFPFL govt. of 1948-50 and the highly factionalised party it became in the 1950s was always a coalition, consisting of an ever-changing alliance of different political parties, unions and mass orgs. Besides the Socialist Party and the PVOs, other members in 1948 included the ABPO; the TUC(B); the Burma Muslim Congress; the Women's Freedom League; and the KYO.
26 Govt. of Burma, *Burma and the Insurrections*, 17-8.
27 Tinker, *The Union of Burma*, 35.
28 Ibid.
29 Trager, *From Kingdom to Republic*, 100.
30 Ibid.
31 For the full text of the Programme see Nu, *Towards Peace and Democracy*, 92-7 and 106-38. The Programme was approved by the Yellow Band PVOs and the Socialist Party, but next to Nu much of the credit for authorship of the Programme has gone to the above-ground communist, Thein Pe Myint.
32 Ibid.: 94.
33 Govt. of Burma, *Burma and the Insurrections*, ibid.: 8, 45-7.
34 Thein Pe Myint, *Political Experience During the Revolutionary Period* (ref: Ch.3, *n*.54): 453; see also *n*.38.
35 Govt. of Burma, *Burma and the Insurrections*, 22.
36 Thein Pe, *Political Experience*, 455; Maung Maung, *Burma and General Ne Win* (ref: Ch.3, *n*.78): 205: see also *n*.88.
37 Tinker, *The Union of Burma*, 36.
38 Ibid. At this stage reorganisation of the wartime PBF, PVOs and Allied Forces was still not complete and the Burma Army continued to be structured along racial lines. There were 5 ethnic Burman battalions known as the Burma Rifles, the 1st, 3rd, 4th, 5th and 6th, and a mixed race battalion, the 2nd, which also included some Gurkhas. The 1st, 3rd and some of the 6th were to join the CPB. There were also three ethnic minority regiments, the Karen, Kachin and Chin Rifles, each of which consisted of three battalions. All three Karen Rifles and the 1st Kachin Rifles joined the insurrections, while one battalion of the Chin Rifles retd. into the hills. This summary, however, takes no account of the UMPs and numerous auxiliary police and local militia forces, such as the *Sitwundan*, formed during the same period.
39 Dun, *The Four Foot Colonel* (ref: Ch.4, *n*.14): 83.
40 Ibid.: 86.
41 Ibid.
42 Ibid.
43 Information about the early activities of the KNDOs has been provided by a number of KNDO veterans, including Lt.-Col. Tha Paw, KNDO Dep-Cdr., Mika Rolly, an underground operative liaising between the Karen Rifles and the KNDOs, and Edmund Take, first KNDO cdr. of the Moulmein-Mergui region.
44 For a detailed chronology of desertions and attacks as seen through govt. eyes from 2 July 1948 to 26 June 1949, see *KNDO Insurrection* (Rangoon, Dir. of Information): 31-45.
45 Dun, *The Four Foot Colonel*, 52.
46 Interview with Saw Maw Reh, 18 March 1988; *New York Times*, 27 Aug. 1948.
47 Rolly has repeated the details of this story to me several times in a long series of interviews in the years 1984-90.
48 Ibid; interviews with Saw Tha Din, 22 Jan., 23 Dec. 1985.
49 Thein Pe Myint, *Political Experience*, 454-5.
50 See, e.g. Col. T. Cromarty-Tulloch, 'The Karens in the War in Burma', *Asiatic Review*,

1946: 248-50.
51 *The Times* (London), 22 Sept., 20 Nov. 1948.
52 See, Ch.4, *n.*70.
53 In fact in 1980 when Rolly resurrected the issue in an article, 'The Loyalty of the Karens' (13-page mimeo. in my possession), in which he described the handing back of Moulmein as 'an act of idiocy', he was briefly expelled from the KNU.
54 Interview with H.A. Stonor, 10 Aug. 1988.
55 *The Daily Telegraph*, 25 Sept. 1952. It was Stonor, in fact, who discovered Tulloch's embezzlement of funds from a young Karen student and called in the police.
56 Annexure A, 13 Nov. 1948, *Report of the Regional Autonomy Enquiry Commission* (Govt. Press, Rangoon, 1952).
57 Ibid.
58 Nu, *Towards Peace and Democracy*, 151.
59 Tinker, *The Union of Burma*, 38.
60 Much of the information on the KNU in this account is taken from a long series of interviews and corr. with Skaw Ler Taw, an ex-headmaster and Force 136 officer from Toungoo, between 1984 and his death in 1989. One of the KNU's leading ideologues, Skaw Ler Taw was secretary at many of the KNU's most critical meetings (including with the CPB, *Tatmadaw*, BSPP and CCP) over a 40-year period, and was still head of the KNU Information Dept. at the time of his death.
61 Nu, *Towards Peace and Democracy*, 212-13.
62 Ibid.
63 Myint, *Political Experience*, 453-4. Also closely involved in the formation of the *Sitwundans* was the dep-premier and For. Min., U Kyaw Nyein, who visited Britain in Nov. to try and obtain arms for this new force; *The Times*, 2 Feb. 1949.
64 *The Nation*, 22 Dec. 1948; Tinker, *The Union of Burma*, 38-9.
65 Reuters, 6 Jan. 1949.
66 *The Nation*, 16 Jan. 1949.
67 Tinker, *The Union of Burma*, 39.
68 For two eyewitness accounts of the events leading up to the battle of Insein, see the statements of Saw Bellay and Saw Po Tu in Dun, *The Four Foot Colonel*, 70-7.
69 Tinker, *The Union of Burma*, 40.
70 Dun, *The Four Foot Colonel*, 73-4.
71 U Nu, *Saturday's Son* (New Haven: Yale Univ. Press, 1975): 173; Dun, *The Four Foot Colonel*, 53-4.
72 Ibid.
73 Dun, *The Four Foot Colonel*, 56.
74 See Ch.8.
75 Other important towns that fell under rebel control at different stages during 1949 and early 1950 were: Tharrawaddy (White Flag CPB); Nyaunglebin, Taunggyi and Meiktila (KNU); Kyaukpyu, Sandoway, Chauk and Thayetmyo (PVO or RBA); and Buthidaung (*Mujahid*). For a more complete list and dates see Tinker, *The Union of Burma*, 44-5.
76 *The Times*, 25 Oct. 1956, 26 June 1958. Unlike other parts of Burma, towns in Arakan were usually governed by a coalition of rebel forces, including the CPB (White Flag and Red Flag), PVOs and U Seinda's APLP.
77 *The Nation* (Rangoon), 16 Sept. 1952.
78 The higher estimate was provided to me by a former Reuters correspondent Max McGrath, an Anglo-Burman, who covered both the battles of the Second World War and the insurrections in the 1940s and 1950s from Rangoon. Another more conservative estimate, which relies largely on U Nu's calculations, puts civilian deaths at 22,000 and mil. and govt. personnel at 5,700, and the displaced refugee population at 3m (Butwell, *U Nu of Burma*, 98). It is both McGrath's and my belief, based on our own observations of the fighting, that successive governments have deliberately underestimated casualties. In many outlying rural areas no casualty records have ever been kept at all. This practice was to get much worse under the BSPP.
79 U Nu, *From Peace to Stability* (Min. of Information, Rangoon, 1951): 134; Tinker, *The Union of Burma*, 48.
80 Many such reports were complete misinformation and were clearly calculated to confuse, still causing amusement amongst insurgent leaders who, reported dead or on the

point of surrendering, are still very much alive in the 'liberated zones' today. As a result it is virtually impossible to build up any kind of accurate picture of the insurgencies from the govt. side or press reports alone, as too many academics have tried to do. Again the situation was to get far worse after the 1962 coup.

81 Tinker, *The Union of Burma*, 300-1.
82 *FEER*, 7 July 1988; Trager, *From Kingdom to Republic*, 163.
83 See Ch.8, *n.*43.
84 Yawnghwe, *The Shan of Burma* (ref: Ch.2, *n.*37): 112.
85 Tinker, *The Union of Burma*, 43: Trager, *From Kingdom to Republic*, 113.
86 Ibid.; *The Times*, 4 April 1949.
87 For an overall summary of the development of Burma's foreign policy, see Tinker, *The Union of Burma*, 337-78.
88 There have been continuing rumours, frequently repeated by those close to the events of 1948, that Ne Win himself once considered joining his friend, Bo Po Kun, in the PVO rebellion. According to this theory only his rapid promotion due to the army mutinies and defections of 1948/9 prevented this. There would, however, appear to be no firm basis for this story. But it might be interesting to speculate what might have happened if the attempts by the generals, Smith Dun and Zeya, in mid-1948 to block his appointment as Defence Min. had succeeded. Within a year Dun had been ousted and Zeya had joined the CPB insurrection (see Thein Pe, *Political Experience*, 455). Still the best account for the rise of mil. rule in Burma and a broad contemporary analysis is Josef Silverstein, *Burma: Military Rule and the Politics of Stagnation* (Cornell Univ. Press, 1977): 44-51 and 80-119.
89 AFPFL, *From Fascist Bondage to New Democracy: The New Burma in the New World*, 30, as quoted in Silverstein, ibid.: 45.
90 Ye Yint Min Gaung, *WPD*, 4 Oct. 1988.

Chapter 7

1 Another significant exception, like Burma, is Malaysia. Here the British did stay on and the CPM launched a sustained armed challenge to the reimposition of colonial rule. However the CPM's supporters were largely ethnic Chinese and, crucially, the CPM failed to win much support from the Malayan majority.
2 In his presidential address U Nu caused consternation amongst the AFPFL's Socialist Party supporters when he claimed: 'Largely on hearsay and a cursory reading, we at one time impetuously and loudly claimed that Marxism was the same as Buddhism. We are very remorseful for having made such ill-considered and unfounded claims' (*The Times*, 30 Jan. 1958). Though he had helped set up the Socialist Party in 1945 and often packed his Cabinet with Socialist Party comrades, U Nu had not in fact been a member of any party since he became Prime Min. in 1947.
3 U Ba Swe, *The Burmese Revolution* (Rangoon, People's Literature House, 1952): 13-14, 17. According to Swe, Marxism 'occupies the lower plain', Buddhism 'the higher'.
4 Ibid.: 13-14, 17, 19, 33.
5 John S. Thomson, 'Marxism in Burma', in F. Trager (ed.), *Marxism in SE Asia: A Study of Four Countries* (Stanford Univ. Press, 1959): 37.
6 Tinker, *The Union of Burma* (ref: Ch.4, *n.*32): 68.
7 Ibid.: 72.
8 43 seats to the AFPFL's 162 in the 250 seat Chamber of Deputies, and apparently none (after initially being accredited 5) in the 125-seat Chamber of Nationalities. Again the poll was small (only two-fifths of eligible voters actually did so) and was severely disrupted by violence. Later no two sets of figures issued on the election result actually tallied. Significantly much of the dissatisfaction expressed at the time at the AFPFL's obstructive behaviour came from ethnic minority parties, such as the conservative ANUO, which briefly allied itself with the NUF. Other parties which won seats include the United Hill People's Congress, the All Shan States Organisation, the Kachin National Congress, the UNPO and various other ethnic independents. For a full discussion of the election, see Geoffrey Fairbairn, 'Some Minority Problems in Burma', *Pacific Affairs*, 30 (Dec. 1957): 299-311.
9 Ibid., see also Ch.8, *n.*29.
10 'Letter of Aung Gyi', 9 May 1988, to former RC members (copy in my possession).
11 Ibid. U Chit Hlaing was attributed authorship of the 'political terminology'. Both Chit

Hlaing and U Saw U, another former CPB supporter, had written for the pro-army magazine, *Myawaddy*, in the 1950s and were regarded as sympathetic to the *Tatmadaw*. Besides *Tatmadaw* hardliners such as Bo Tin Pe, other important influences Aung Gyi mentions on the development of the *Burmese Way to Socialism* include Ko Ko Gyi's notes from the seven-day courses in socialism he conducted when the Socialist Party was formed in 1945, the army's study of the experiences of Yugoslavia, and a miscellaneous cast of characters including U Ba Nyein from the NUF, Bo Htein Lin, an ex-rebel PVO leader, and Thein Pe Myint, the former CPB Gen-Sec. From the army Tin Pe, who replaced Aung Gyi as Ne Win's closest confidant in 1964, was ordered by Ne Win to study politics, Col. Kyaw Soe administration, and Col. Than Sein social welfare. Aung Gyi is disparaging about their abilities, describing how Tin Pe had to send to the army library for a trailer load of 'leftist' books. Aung Gyi himself grew increasingly disillusioned and left the army on 19 Feb. 1963 and was later imprisoned on three different occasions.
12 Corr. with Ba Thein Tin. See Ch.6, *n*.10.
13 Ibid.
14 Ibid.
15 For the PA's changing org. in the early 1950s, see e.g. K. Fleischmann, *Die Kommunistische Partei Birmas* (ref: Ch.4, *n*.40): 178-82, who relies on Burmese press reports for details.
16 CPB cdrs. were more successful in some areas than others in building a united PA, but by the late 1950s a loose national network had been established: 'Upper Burma Division' (Mandalay-Magwe) under such local officials as Thanmani Maung Maung, Bo Yan Aung and Ahlawarka; the 'Central Burma Division' (Yamethin-Pyinmana) under Thakin Pe Tint; Shan State (North and South) under Thakin Tin Tun, Bo Soe Maung and Bo Kyin Maung; 'Northern Division' (Katha-Pinlebu-Kachin State) under Myo Myint and Maran La Dee; 'Central Headquarters' under Than Tun and the Politburo, then mostly in the 'NW Division' (Pakokku-Minbu-Lower Chindwin) under Dr Nath, Rajan and Bo Sein Tin; 'Lower Burma Division' (Toungoo-Shweygin-Pegu) under *Yebaw* Mya; 'Tenasserim Division' under Tun Sein; Delta Division under Tun Kyi and Soe Than; Arakan Division under Kyaw Mya and Maung Tu. Again, see Fleischmann, ibid.: 391-4, for name lists of the CPB's changing High Command.
17 Interview with Mika Rolly, 26 Jan. 1987; see also Ch.8 for the way the KNU handled this problem.
18 Lenin in his 1902 classic, *What is to Be Done?* (Progress Publishers, Moscow, 1947), argued that given the limitations (in class consciousness etc.), the ever changing objectives of intellectuals and the different social democratic, peasant and trade union orgs., the historic aims of the proletariat could not be entrusted to their leaders who pursued largely economic goals. Therefore a disciplined revolutionary org., the Communist Party, would have to be formed to ensure continuity and a stable party org. to lead the revolution. Consisting at first of intellectuals and workers, this party would also at first probably have to be small and secretive, but in time, as professional revolutionaries, class distinctions within the party would disappear. At the same time the party would rapidly have to step up efforts to expand its influence among the masses and recruit new members from all sections of society (the army, trade unions, peasants etc.) but mostly from the urban and rural proletariat. It was a strategy the Bolsheviks successfully pursued in Russia. But to a background of 'armed struggle' in conditions which were most similar to Burma, the 'United Front' theory was most clearly developed by Mao Zedong in China in several classic works. See e.g., Mao Tse-Tung, 'The Question of Independence and Initiative within the United Front', 'On New Democracy', and 'Current Problems of Tactics in the Anti-Japanese United Front', in *Selected Works of Mao Tse-Tung* (Foreign Language Press, Beijing, 1975) II.: 213-17, 339-82, 421-30.
19 Trager, *From Kingdom to Republic* (ref: Ch.3, *n*.8): 107. These figures include troops with formal mil. training, but it is impossible to calculate true 'insurgent' numbers. Virtually every village, whether under insurgent or govt. control, had its own defence units and by 1953 the KNU alone claimed to be call on 20,000 men under arms.
20 White Flag CPB, 6,000; Red Flag CPB, 1,800; PVOs, 15,000; KNU, 12,000; *Mujahid*, 2,000; KMT, 7,000 (*The Nation*, 16 April 1953).
21 Trager, *From Kingdom to Republic*, 107.
22 See *n*.18.

23 Mao Tse-Tung, 'On New Democracy', 358-61.
24 Mao Tse-Tung, 'The Question of Independence', 215. For a more general summary of
    the 'United Front' strategy employed by communist parties in Asia based upon the
    Maoist/Chinese model, see Robert A. Scalapino, 'Communism in Asia', in *The
    Communist Revolution in Asia: Tactics, Goals and Achievements* (Prentice Hall Inc.,
    New Jersey, 1969): 18-25, 41-6; and John Girling, *People's War: the Conditions and
    the Consequences in China and South East Asia* (Allen and Unwin, London, 1969): 83-
    96.
25 Thomson, 'Marxism in Burma', 43.
26 Ibid.
27 Prominent 'national' trade union leaders who went underground with the CPB included
    Thakin Chit, Ba Tin, Mukarjee and Rajan of the ABTUC, Thakin Zin of ABPO and Ko
    Ko Lay of the Ministerial Services Union.
28 Various colourful but often wildly inaccurate stories about Thakin Soe's marital and
    extra-marital affairs have circulated in Burma for years. According to former Red Flag
    comrades, it was his affairs with his colleagues' wives which caused most resentment.
    According to these sources, he married six times. While working at the Burma Oil
    Company before the war he married two sisters whom he divorced when he went
    underground. During the anti-fascist resistance he then married a young Rakhine girl,
    Ma Khin Si, whom he also divorced shortly afterwards to marry Ma Hnin May, a Red
    Flag EC member. Both Thakin Soe and Hnin May were captured in 1948, but Soe was
    released a few months later from Tharrawaddy gaol by the White Flags. In 1952 he
    moved his HQ to Upper Burma and from there he persuaded by letter the Red Flag
    Cdr. of the Delta region, Gen. Aung Min, who, like Hnin May, had been arrested, to let
    him marry his wife, Ma Ngwe Zan, on the grounds that both were denied their basic
    'human rights'. Then in 1964 Ma Ngwe Zan and Politburo member, Gen. Kyaw Win,
    were sent into Rangoon on a secret peace mission and after both failed to return he
    married Kyaw Win's wife, Ma Khin Su. This, however, does not claim to be a final
    authoritative version of events, which perhaps would be more fitting of a Hollywood
    movie script.
29 See e.g. 'Voice of Malayan Revolution', 28 Aug. 1975 in BBC, *SWB*, 1 Sept. 1975 for a
    somewhat outdated analysis of Thakin Soe by the CPM.
30 Corr. with Ba Thein Tin.
31 *The Times*, 11 Nov. 1955; much of the information in this account comes from former
    Red Flag cadres and communist activists in Arakan whose reminiscences in interviews
    with me between 1986 and 1989 largely corroborate each other. The main informants
    have been Maung Han, who was attached to the Central Red Flag GHQ from 1954-60,
    Shwe Tha and Thein Pe, today of the CPA, and Maung Sein Nyunt and Kyaw Than Oo
    of the ANLP.
32 Ibid. In 1962 the Red Flags were able to set up a new base area in Myebon-An, but at
    the time of the CPA split, Red Flag armed strength had already fallen very low; in
    Sittwe dist. there were just 60 armed cadres (led by Maung Han), in Buthidaung, 50,
    and in Kyauktaw, just 40.
33 Ibid; Fleischmann, *Die Kommunistische Partei Birmas*, 141.
34 Govt. of the Union of Burma, *Is Trust Vindicated?* (ref: Ch.5, *n*.27): 19, 34.
35 *Burma Weekly Bulletin*, 2 June 1960; *The Nation*, 11 June 1960.
36 Ibid., 10 May 1960. Another reminder of the close personal nature of the civil war
    could be seen in even this tragic incident. Thakin Soe was political adviser in the
    Japanese Resistance to the local *Tatmadaw* Cdr., Kyaw Myint, who now had the
    responsibility of hunting down the Red Flags in the area. These, in turn, were led by
    another of Kyaw Myint's wartime colleagues, Myint Aung.
37 John H. Badgely, 'The Communist Parties of Burma', in Scalapino (ed.), *The
    Communist Revolution in Asia*, 318.
38 Thakin Pe Htay, *Marxism and the Renegade Krushchev* (Rangoon, 1962). Former Red
    Flag members also confirm the high priority given to literary publications in such up-
    country rural areas as Arakan where Shwe Tha and Thein Pe were members of under-
    ground cells putting out Red Flag propaganda through local Youth Front publications.
    But most books, like the more common White Flag publications, were political
    homilies, thinly disguised as romantic novels.
39 Held at the Red Flags GHQ at the 'Volley Ball Camp' near the Kochaung stream,

Myebon Township, Arakan.

40 Badgely, 'The Communist Parties of Burma', 318.

41 Tinker, *The Union of Burma*, 66-7. The 'Yellow' PVO Cabinet min., Bo Sein Hman, e.g., was kld. by a stray bullet while leading aerial strikes on White Band PVO positions near Tharrawaddy in April 1949.

42 *The Times*, 24 Jan. 1956.

43 *The Nation*, 25 Aug. 1958; John H. Badgley, 'Burma's Political Crisis', *Pacific Affairs*, 31 (1958): 346.

44 Thein Pe Myint, *Political Experience* (ref: Ch.3, *n*.54): 461-2.

45 See e.g. Govt. of the Union of Burma, *Is It a People's Liberation?* (ref: Ch.6, *n*.12): 30, for a White Flag, Red Flag, PVO and local KNU agreement from March 1951 published in the CPB HQ's 'Red Star' magazine.

46 *The Nation*, 10 Oct. 1952; Fleischmann, *Die Kommunistische Partei Birmas*, 159-60, 405-6.

47 See Fleischmann, *Documents on Communism* (ref: Ch.3, *n*.65) for a collection of statements from Tripartite meetings, reprinted from *The Nation*, 136-45.

48 Ibid.: 138.

49 Interview with Shwe Tha, 17 Feb. 1987.

50 Despite historic antagonisms between the Vietnamese majority and the region's 'hill tribe' minorities, through the 1940s and into the early 1950s the Vietminh were militarily very dependent on their base areas amongst the mountain peoples of the north. Hundreds of Tho (Nung) and Muong were enlisted into the Vietminh Army and several gained important political positions. Likewise in Laos, from the early 1950s until the eventual communist victory in 1975, ethnic Hmong forces under Lo Faydang provided a vital backbone of support for the Pathet Lao.

51 *NCNA*, 28 April 1969.

52 Than Tun, *People's Age*, VI, 14 March 1948.

Chapter 8

1 Nu, *Towards Peace and Democracy* (ref: Ch.6, *n*.3): 201.

2 Tinker, *The Union of Burma* (ref: Ch.4, *n*.32): 41-2.

3 The belief, rightly or wrongly, that they were about to be executed has been expressed to me by several of those released, including Aung Than Lay, today KNPP VC, who wrote an account of his internment in *The Karenni Journal* (Karenni Foreign Affairs Publishing, 1986) 5: 12-15.

4 Tinker, *The Union of Burma*, 42.

5 Ibid.

6 Interview with Mika Rolly, 22 Jan. 1987.

7 Maung Maung, *Burma and General Ne Win* (ref: Ch.3, *n*.78): 217.

8 *The Times*, 23 May 1949.

9 Interview with U Soe Aung, 20 March 1988.

10 *The Times*, 21 May 1949.

11 Reuters, 16 June 1949.

12 Details of these talks were recorded by former participants in a document, Ginjaw Komiti, *How the KIO was formed: A Brief History* (in Jinghpaw) (Jan. 1983, copy in my possession).

13 Tinker, *The Union of Burma*, 47.

14 'Minutes of the Kawthoolei Congress', 17-19 July 1950 (KNU Archives Dept.).

15 Interview with Skaw Ler Taw, 17 March 1988.

16 'Minutes of the Kawthoolei Congress'.

17 According to govt. reports, two Britons travelling with Ba U Gyi were also kld. in the ambush, Capt. Vivian whom the KNDOs had released from Insein gaol and a mysterious Mr Baker. KNU leaders deny Vivian (who later returned to the UK) was with the party, but agree a man calling himself Baker was. Various theories have been put forward about his identity. He described himself as a former Supt. of Police in Burma. Others believe he had been sent by Cromarty-Tulloch which would perhaps account for Ba U Gyi's intended journey to Bangkok.

18 *The Times*, 23 Aug. 1950. For a contrasting view see the reply of Lord Listowel in *The Times* of 25 Aug. who, while not doubting Ba U Gyi's sincerity, accused him of 'obstinacy' and of 'gambling on the fighting qualities of the Karens', thus ignoring U

Nu's 'fervent desire for a negotiated agreement'.
19 Interview with Skaw Ler Taw, 17 March 1988.
20 For a discussion of Karen ethnicity, see Ch.2.
21 Interview with Skaw Ler Taw, 17 March 1988.
22 See Ch.2, *n.36*; Tinker, *The Union Of Burma*, 75.
23 W. Hackett, 'The Pao People of the Shan State' (Ph.D thesis, Cornell Univ., 1953). One of the few anthroplogists to have conducted field-studies inside Burma since independence, Hackett estimated the Pao population in the Shan State in 1953 at 260,000 and expanding fast (p.13). For his eyewitness description of the early Pao rebellion, see 468-92, 528-40. Unlike Hla Pe, when volunteers from the estimated 50,000 Paos in Thaton dist. took up arms, most joined the KNU.
24 U Nu, 'Speech of 5 Oct. 1951', in *Burma Looks Ahead* (Min. of Information, Rangoon, 1953): 14.
25 Ibid.
26 Silverstein, *Burmese Politics* (ref: Ch.2, *n.22*): 197-8.
27 Tinker, *The Union of Burma*, 386.
28 Ibid.: 74.
29 Silverstein, *Burmese Politics*, 219.
30 Interview with Bruce Humphrey-Taylor, 12 June 1988; G.S. Seagrave, *My Hospital in the Hills* (New York, Norton, 1955): 119.
31 Interview with Skaw Ler Taw, 18 March 1988. These words have been remembered and never forgotten by veteran KNU leaders.
32 *The Times*, 9 May 1957.
33 Interview with Skaw Ler Taw, 18 March 1988.
34 Ibid.
35 Interview with U Soe Aung, 13 Jan. 1985.
36 Interview with Skaw Ler Taw, 18 March 1988.
37 Ibid.
38 Ibid.
39 *The Times*, 23 May 1955.
40 Interview with Skaw Ler Taw, 18 March 1988.
41 The hill Karens comprise over a dozen different sub-groups. By contrast in the Delta, though most KNU leaders were Christians, most Karens are Buddhists from the Pwo and Sgaw families: see Ch.2, *n.5, 7*, for a note on the Karen population.
42 Interview with Mika Rolly, 23 Nov. 1984.
43 Govt. of the Union of Burma, 'Kuomintang Aggression in Burma', *Burma Weekly Bulletin*, 6 May 1953; Tinker, *The Union of Burma*, 345-8.
44 *The Times*, 6, 21 April 1953.
45 The MPF was formally established on 27 March 1953 with its GHQ at Anankwin village, 30 miles west of Three Pagodas Pass, by an amalgam of three rebel Mon factions working with the KNU. The first included followers of Nai Shwe Kyin, who had earlier been imprisoned by the AFPFL. They moved up from Moulmein to Kawkareik immediately after the insurrections began and were not reunited until Kyin's release in late 1951. The second force was led by by Nai Aung Tun in Thanbyuzayat, and the third by Nai Non Lar, with its HQ at Mokenin village on the borders of Ye-Lamaing.
46 Interview with Skaw Ler Taw, 14 Jan. 1985.
47 See *Burma Weekly Bulletin*, 25 Nov. 1953, for an account of this shambolic withdrawal, described by several eyewitnesses as 'phoney'. Many of the KMT 'troops', as the photos show, were in fact Shan children, press-ganged into service to make up the numbers.
48 Tinker, *The Union of Burma*, 55-6.

Chapter 9
1 In Dec. 1949 e.g. the Chinese leader, Liu Shao-chi, in his opening address at the Asian and Australasian TUC in Beijing publicly commended the communist parties of Burma, Vietnam, Malaya and Indonesia for their 'correct' decision to wage armed struggle.
2 Girling, *People's War* (ref: Ch.7, *n.24*): 180.
3 See e.g. *NCNA* in Thai, 7 Nov. 1985. Soviet and US 'hegemonism' has always been a particular target of CCP leaders.

4   B. Lintner, *FEER*, 4 June 1987.
5   Ibid. In the USSR a number of cadres also reputedly met Stalin.
6   Ralph Pettman, *China in Burma's Foreign Policy* (Australian National Univ. Press, 1973): 5.
7   For a discussion see Pettman, ibid.: 20-1, who also mentions the possibility that Chinese leaders were seeking Kachin territory to 'bottle up' the rebellious Khambas in eastern Tibet and at the same time open up a road into Nagaland.
8   Tinker, *The Union of Burma* (ref: Ch.4, n.32): 373; *The Times*, 30 June 1954. The visit even coincided with the army's capture of a CPB stronghold near Katha.
9   Alfred McCoy, *The Politics of Heroin in SE Asia* (Harper Torchbooks, New York, 1972): 315.
10 See e.g., V. Thompson and R. Adloff, *Minority Problems in South East Asia* (Stanford Univ. Press, 1955): 28-31; R. Butwell, 'Communist Liaison in SE Asia', *United Asia*, 6, 1954: 146-51. For the exploits of one disillusioned Kachin communist, Maran La Dee, who crossed into China in the 1950s, see *The Nation* and *The Guardian*, 6 Nov. 1959.
11 Pettman, *China in Burma's Foreign Policy*, 20.
12 See the account of the Soviet defector, A.U. Kaznacheev, *Inside a Soviet Embassy: Experiences of a Russian Diplomat in Burma* (Lippincott, Philadelphia, 1962) for the clever methods used to bring sympathetic 'anti-capitalist' stories about developments in Burma into the Burmese press. The Soviet Embassy also used to supply Marxist literature to BWPP supporters and student groups.
13 *Pravda*, 19 Jan. 1953, as quoted in Trager, *From Kingdom to Republic* (ref: Ch.3, n.8): 225.
14 See e.g. Maung Maung, *The Guardian* (monthly), Oct. 1956: 36.
15 *The Times*, 7 Dec. 1955.
16 Corr. with Ba Thein Tin, see Ch.6, n.10. Only with the benefit of hindsight after the Soviet-China split did the CPB for a number of years accuse Soviet leaders of trying to impress their 'revisionist' ideas on them. 'This gang of renegades put forth this theory as early as 1954, before the 20th congress of the CPSU. In fact, as early as in 1954, these renegades had attempted to undermine Burma's armed revolution to make the CPB renounce the road of seizing political power by armed force and take the parliamentary road, namely, the road of capitulation to the bourgeoisie.' Statement of the CC of the CPB, 22 April 1970, in *NCNA*, 4 May 1970.
17 Girling, *People's War*, 24.
18 Ibid.
19 For an interesting account of the impact of this speech on the escalating conflict in Laos, which was most likely the real focus of Krushchev's concern, see Marek Thee, *Notes of a Witness: Laos and the Second Indochinese War* (Random House, New York, 1973): 19 ff. In a distinction much misunderstood by US analysts, Krushchev defined three kinds of war: 'world wars', 'local wars' (as between neighbours) and 'wars of liberation or popular uprisings'. Thee argues it was in fact a 'passionate' plea for coexistence in the light of the social and political advances of the 20th century. Indeed following the 1962 Vienna Accord, Krushchev appeared to reject any active Soviet role in SE Asia. Only in 1965, after he was ousted, did Brezhnev reverse Soviet policy in the region.
20 Gabriel Kolko, *Vietnam: Anatomy of a War, 1940-75* (Unwin Paperbacks, 1987): 64. Mao Zedong's doubts over Krushchev's advocacy of a 'peaceful transition to Socialism' were first voiced at a meeting of communist parties in Moscow in Nov. 1957. Tactically, the Chinese delegation, which was led by Mao, agreed that the policy might make sense but in a memorandum warned that any expectation of winning power by a parliamentary majority might 'weaken the revolutionary will of the proletariat'. For a discussion see Girling, *People's War*, 25-6, who quotes a later CCP denunciation of 'Krushchev's revisionism' from 1964 which claimed that violent revolution is a 'universal law of proletarian revolution'. See also *n.*16.
21 Corr. with Ba Thein Tin.
22 See e.g. *The Times*, 20 Nov. 1953 for the report of the ambush of the Mandalay-Maymyo train, allegedly by CPB guerrillas, in which 15 people were kld. and 23 injured; ibid., 26 March 1955, for the mining of another train west of Mandalay which resulted in another 30 deaths; ibid., 15 Aug. 1955, for the dynamiting of a bus, with a police escort, near Tavoy which kld. 37 passengers; and ibid., 16 Sept. 1955 for the

freeing of 134 prisoners from Nyaung Oo gaol in central Burma in a CPB raid. CPB leaders say such targets were 'military'.

23 *The Guardian*, 10, 12 Sept. 1959. For the White Flag's seven Politburo members, Thakins Ba Thein Tin, Tin Tun, Than Myaing, Zin, Chit, Htay and Ba Tin, the reward was set at 50,000 kyat, the same as for the Red Flag Politburo members, Kyaw Win and Nyunt Win. Again there were no takers. For dist. organisers the fee was usually 5,000 kyat.

24 Most of the CPB's leaders (like Aung San, U Nu and Burma's other young leaders) had been almost 'professional' revolutionaries in the national liberation struggle for over a decade by the time Burma's independence arrived in 1948; Ba Thein Tin, e.g., who passed exams to enter Rangoon Univ., had been a full-time *Dobama* worker before joining the CPB in 1939; Ba Tin had been a full-time CPB trade union organiser in Rangoon; while Ye Htut, Yan Aung and Thet Tun were wartime army officers. Strikingly, too, 8 of the 9 Socialist Party members of the AFPFL Cabinet in 1955 were former students at Rangoon Univ. (Tinker, *The Union of Burma*, 63).

25 *The Guardian* (monthly), Oct. 1956: 36.

26 Ibid., and Govt. of the Union of Burma, *Is it a People's Liberation?* (ref: Ch.6, *n.*12): 13.

27 Lin Piao, 'Long Live the Victory of People's War', *Peking Review*, 3 Sept. 1965.

28 In a document dated 17 March 1955 9 junior CPB leaders listed a number of Than Tun's alleged 'errors': going into rebellion without proper preparation; at first supporting the Nu-Atlee agreement and the terms of Burma's independence; promising victory within two years; thinking the CPB could fight its way towards China to find a new springboard; alienating the PVOs and other brother rebel groups; and 'exploiting racialism' by working with the KNU (*The Guardian*, monthly, Oct. 1956: 36).

29 *The Statesman* (Calcutta), 27 March 1955.

30 *WPD*, 19 Nov. 1988.

31 Corr. with Ba Thein Tin. See also *n.*16. Attending the meeting were Politburo members, Thakins Than Tun, Ba Tin, Tin Tun, Chit, Zin, and *Yebaw* Htay; CC members Dr Nath, Thakin Tin Mya, Col. Myo Myint, Maj. Tin Ye, Maj-Gen. Ye Htut; and Regional C'ttee members, Cols. Pu and Arlawaka, Maj-Gen. Soe Maung and Sein Tin. The CC meeting was followed up at the end of the year by a Senior Commanders Conf. to develop the new line attended by 20 senior officers on the Yaw River, Pakokku dist.

32 Geoffrey Fairbairn, 'Some Minority Problems in Burma', (ref: Ch.7, *n.*8): 300.

33 *The Times*, 4 Jan. 1957.

34 Ibid., 22 Aug. 1958.

35 Nyunt, *Burma Communist Party's Conspiracy* (ref: Ch.1, *n.*52): 71-6.

36 This informant, then a student at Rangoon Univ., had the job of ferrying CPB cadres from the countryside around Rangoon. The son of an AFPFL Cabinet min., he has requested anonymity.

37 The BWPP, like the CPB, also operated a Politburo system, and made little effort to disguise its support for the international communist movement. Indeed in 1989, when one of the BWPP leaders, Thakin Chit Maung, was interviewed in Rangoon for a TV programme I was working on, he sat beneath pictures of the hammer and sickle, Ho Chi Minh and other leading communist figures. He, however, refused to be drawn on questions of political ideology: 'This is the time for the struggle for democracy,' he said, laughing. *Burma: Dying for Democracy* (ref: Ch.1, *n.*39).

38 See e.g. *The Nation*, 11, 12 Sept. 1954, 8 Aug. 1960; also Ch.7, *n.*8.

39 See e.g. Nyunt, *Burma Communist Party's Conspiracy*.

40 Khut Daung, *The Student Movement and Civil War in Burma* (ref: Ch.3, *n.*56): 85.

41 *The Times*, 5 Oct. 1953.

42 For more detailed accounts of the student movement, see Josef Silverstein, 'Burmese and Malaysian Student Politics', *Journal of SE Asian Studies*, March 1970: 3-9; Tinker, *The Union of Burma*, 207-9.

43 *The Times*, 19 Oct. 1956.

44 For a study of Burmese-language publications in the 1950s, see John Badgley, 'Intellectuals and the National Vision: the Burmese Case', *Asian Survey*, 9 Aug. 1969: 598-613.

45 The importance of this recruiting system cannot be underestimated, and was explained

in a series of interviews with the CPB cadres, Shwe Kyaw Aung and Tun Win, 18-20 Feb. 1987, whose experiences, 20 years apart, exactly mirrored one another. Shwe Kyaw Aung organised CPB cells in govt. depts. in Rangoon in the 1950s; Tun Win, having joined a 'Marxist-Leninist-Mao Zedong thought' group at Rangoon Univ. in 1970, organised a CPB cell in Myohaung, Arakan, after graduation in 1972 where he was an accountant in a govt. cooperative dept. His main tasks were 'propaganda; to send necessary goods to the party in the forest if they asked; to persuade people not to join the *Tatmadaw*; and to try and interest people in Marxist-Leninist-Mao Zedong thought.' To this end he set up a secret library in his office. It was, he says, highly dangerous work but added, 'Each person must organise. If you are a teacher you must organise teachers; if you are a farmer, you organise farmers.' In 1975 he finally went underground as a full party member where he worked until 1986 in the CPB Arakan Province c'ttee's propaganda dept.

46 Other future insurgent leaders at Rangoon Univ. who grew up in this period included Chao Tzang Yawnghwe and Seng Haan of the SSPP, Pungshwe Zau Seng of the KIO, and numerous second-line leaders from the KNU, NMSP and Rakhine insurgent groups. Another student leader, who like Sai Aung Win later joined the CPB, was Sai Noom Pan, cdr. of the CPB's 768 brigade in the 1980s, who was wounded in July 1962 when troops fired at students on the univ. campus.

47 Corr. with Ba Thein Tin.

48 *The Times*, 16 June 1956.

49 For a summary of these operations based on govt. claims, see Fleischmann, *Die Kommunistische Partei Birmas* (ref: Ch.4, *n*.40): 235-6.

50 See e.g. *WPD*, 19, 20 Nov. 1988.

51 *The Times*, 27 Jan. 1958. This was, in fact, before the official announcement of the amnesty. Interview with former APLP member, Maung Sein Nyunt, 23 Feb. 1987.

52 *The Times*, 7 May 1958; interview with PNO pres., Aung Kham Hti, 29 Nov. 1984.

53 *The Nation*, 11 May 1958.

54 Interviews with former MPF leaders, Nai Shwe Kyin and Nai Non Lar, pres. and vice-pres. of NMSP, 18 Jan. 1989.

55 Ibid. The PNO e.g. claims still to have documentary evidence that its four basic demands (to end feudalism, rehabilitate the Pao region, legalise the PNO, and recognise a Pao 'autonomous state') were agreed by the army; subsequently, it claims, the govt. acted on only the first three of these demands; see *n*.52. In the MPF's case an eight-point accord was reached.

56 VOPB, 15 June, in BBC, *SWB*, 17 June 1986. The CPB, in what appears to be an arbritrary set of figures, puts the 'revolutionary' losses at 2,000 'Karens', all 5,000 PVOs, 1,000 from the PNO, more than 1,000 from the MPF, and 500 from the APLP in Arakan.

57 Ibid.

58 *Bangkok Post*, 12 April 1954.

59 Interview with Skaw Ler Taw, 14 Jan. 1985; Marshall Shwin, 11 Jan. 1985.

60 'Record of the Second National Congress'. An incomplete copy of this report, with several pages missing, has been made available to me.

61 Ibid. Another demand was 'Freedom of Religion'.

62 See Ch.8., *n*.45.

63 Usually going by the name 'Karenni National Organisation', in the early 1950s the Karenni resistance movement had consisted of a fluctuating number of village militia and armed volunteers, several hundred strong, who enjoyed widespread support across the state. The KNO leader, the young Kyebogyi *Sawbwa*, Sao Shwe, worked closely with the KNU and, for a time, the KMT. His plan, however, was always to establish a single, statewide Karenni front and in 1956, echoing the KNUP, plans for the KNPP were first drawn up. His premature death that year caused a leadership crisis. His wife Katareen, his first successor, was unable to control the situation and surrendered. The former KNU adviser, Tawplo, a skillful mil. cdr. who shared the KNUP's left-wing views, then took over the leadership but in 1958 was assassinated by one of his own men. In 1959 the KNPP's next choice, Me Aee, was kld. by govt. troops and his successor, Sao Shwe's former lieut., Saw Maw Reh, who had led the 1949 capture of Mawchi, was wounded and forced to surrender. In 1960 the next appointee, Po Kyan, also surrendered. Finally, later that year, Saw Maw Reh returned underground and has

led the KNPP ever since, in the 1970s briefly handing over the leadership to Hte Buphe and, more recently, to Plya Reh.

64 Interview with Saw Maw Reh, 18 March 1988; Tha Kalei, 17 July 1990; Nai Shwe Kyin, 18 Jan. 1989.

65 Two prominent KNU leaders who gave this reason for their surrenders were Saw Ba Lone, pre-war education sec. 1940-1, and Kyaw Sein, ex-industries sec.; see e.g. *The Nation*, 28 Sept., 22 Nov. 1959.

66 *The Times*, 27 March 1958; see also ibid., 21 Dec. 1957, for an attack on Thaton by a 200-strong force from the KAF 5th brigade.

67 The ABKO e.g. ran a campaign for a new population census, Karen proportional representation in the Union Parliament and the right of secession for the Karen State and re-demarcation of its borders (*The Nation*, 29 Nov. 1960). See also Ch.10 for the fate of U Pe Nyunt, clean AFPFL MP for Bilin, who in May 1959 went underground and joined the KNU.

Chapter 10

1 *The Times*, 7 Oct. 1958; finally, only on 7 Dec. 1989, in a letter to Gen. Saw Maung (copy in my possession) which led to his being placed under house arrest, U Nu explained that the only difference between the army's 'plans to seize power' in 1958 and 1962 was that on the first occasion he knew about it and was thus able to arrange an orderly transition 'in order to safeguard the honour of the army'.

2 *The Times*, 26 March, 10 April 1958.

3 Ibid., 1 Nov. 1958; Tinker, *The Union of Burma* (ref: Ch.4, *n*.32): 60.

4 Ibid.: 91; Silverstein, *Burma: Military Rule* (ref: Ch.6, *n*.88): 62-5.

5 See Ch.7, *n*.2.

6 Sein Win, *The Split Story* (*The Guardian*, Rangoon, 1959): 44-7.

7 Ibid.: 67-72; *New Times of Burma*, 31 Oct. 1958; *The Guardian* (monthly) Aug., 1958.

8 Win, *Split Story*, 67.

9 Ibid.: 75. 'Clean' AFPFL delegates claimed troops stationed in Sandoway, Hanthawaddy, Moulmein and Toungoo were colluding with the 'stable' faction.

10 Ibid.: 73-81. Win believed the appointment of Bo Hmu Aung, a popular war-hero, as the new Min. of Defence after the AFPFL split was also an attempt by Nu to curry favour with the mil. Aung, however, had been away from the army too long and had been superseded by a new generation of officers.

11 *The Nation*, 29 Sept. 1958. It is only fair to add that Sein Win's final verdict on the events of 1958 was that the army takeover was not a coup but that the army 'was un-doubtedly ready and fully prepared to strike back if it was struck' (p.90).

12 Trager, *From Kingdom to Republic* (ref: Ch.3, *n*.8): 177.

13 Even by his own eloquent standards, U Nu's speeches in Parliament that day were highly ambiguous. While denying there had been any coup, he also denied the AFPFL had been 'converted to communism'. But then, in apparent contradiction, he chose to add that so great was the 'fear and suspicion' in the army of a communist takeover, aggravated by the success of his 1958 'peace drive', that the 'only solution was to rein-force the authority of the C-in-C', Ne Win. Mil. officers, he said, already stung by the denunciations of clean AFPFL leaders, were now having difficulty controlling their units (*The Times*, 29 Oct. 1958). That day there were also rumours of a PCP plot to assassinate Ne Win.

14 *FEER*, 7 July 1988.

15 Silverstein, *Burma: Military Rule*, 79; for Aung Gyi, see Ch.7, *n*.10.

16 Ibid.: 77.

17 Trager, *From Kingdom to Republic*, 182.

18 Silverstein, *Burma: Military Rule*, 79.

19 Tinker, *The Union of Burma*, 61.

20 *The Nation*, 9 Jan., 30 July 1960.

21 Interview with Shwe Kyaw Aung, 18 Feb. 1987. A Coco Island deportee, Aung went into the 'liberated zones' on his release and is still an underground party organiser today.

22 *The Nation*, 20 Nov., 8 June 1959; *The Guardian*, 13 Sept. 1959; *WPD*, 14, 15 Nov. 1988.

23 Fred Von Der Mehden, 'Burma's Religious Campaign Against Communism', *Pacific*

Affairs, 33, Sept. 1960: 290-9.
24 Ibid.: 295; *Burma Weekly Bulletin*, 30 April 1959: 12-13.
25 *FEER*, 22 Sept. 1988.
26 Interviews e.g. with Revd Kelasa of the Mudon strike centre, 20 Jan. 1989, and Revd
    Ashin Kimazara, chm. of the All Burma Young Monks Union, 31 Jan. 1989. In Nov.
    1988 the ABYMU officially joined the insurgent DAB. According to the Revd
    Kimazara: 'Burma should be a very peaceful land, but the conditions have changed
    because of a tyrannical govt.... The monks work with the people but the govt. oppresses
    the people. The people love democracy and they love peace, so now we have to try and
    topple the govt.'
27 Quoted in Von Der Mehden, 'Burma's Religious Campaign', 298-9.
28 Ibid. A copy, from govt. sources, of the CPB's 'Party Line on Religion', dated to 1952,
    is reprinted in Fleischmann (ed.), *Documents on Communism* (ref: Ch.3, *n*.65): 129-30.
29 Govt. of the Union of Burma, *Is Trust Vindicated?* (ref: Ch.5, *n*.27): 27.
30 Ibid.: 19-34.
31 Ibid.
32 *Burma Weekly Bulletin*, 28 May 1959.
33 Interview with B. Humphrey-Taylor, 15 May 1988.
34 Interview with Skaw Ler Taw, 29 Jan. 1989.
35 *The Times*, 1 Feb. 1957.
36 Interview with Skaw Ler Taw, 8 Dec. 1985.
37 Interview with Nai Shwe Kyin, 22 Jan. 1985.
38 Despite efforts by the KNU to persuade the Chin Rifles to join their insurrection, the
    Chins had in the main stayed loyal to the Union (see Vumson, *Zo History*, ref: Ch.3,
    n.53: 207-11). The CNVP, though not formed until 1956, was declared as early as 1953
    by a group of students, farmers and Burma Rifles veterans in Daik-u dist. of the Pegu
    Yomas. Led by Saline Tha U (later kld. in action), Bo Khan and Saline San Aung, the
    CNVP demanded a separate Chin State from an expanded Chin Division and
    'autonomous regions' for Chin communities in other parts of the country.
39 *Burma Weekly Bulletin*, 2 June 1960: 37.
40 Govt. of the Union of Burma, *Is Trust Vindicated?* 19, 34.
41 *The Times*, 12 Jan. 1960.
42 Interview with Skaw Ler Taw, 9 Dec. 1985.
43 Ibid.
44 Ibid.
45 Silverstein, *Burma: Military Rule*, 71.
46 Ibid.: 79.
47 Maung Maung, *Burma and General Ne Win* (ref: Ch.3, *n*.78): 273.
48 Trager, *From Kingdom to Republic*, 198.
49 *The Times*, 26 Sept. 1961; *The Daily Telegraph* and *Morning Post*, 18 Jan. 1961.
50 Ibid.
51 *The Guardian*, 5 July 1960.
52 Ibid., 16 Nov. 1960.
53 See e.g. *The Times*, 21 Dec. 1959, quoting the Oct. 1959 issue of the Soviet monthly,
    International Affairs, which cited 'Indian sources'; see also Ch.11 for the KNU's con-
    tacts with the KMT and Thailand.
54 McCoy, *The Politics of Heroin in SE Asia* (ref: Ch.9, *n*.9): 135.
55 *The Times*, 23 Feb. 1961.
56 Ibid.
57 McCoy, *The Politics of Heroin in SE Asia*, 134-5.
58 See e.g., *The Nation* (Rangoon), 25 Nov. 1960 and *The Guardian* (Rangoon), 28 Dec.
    1960, 22 March 1961.
59 Ibid., 26, 29 March 1961.
60 *The Nation*, 31 March 1961.
61 *The Guardian*, 31 March 1961.
62 Ibid., 1 April 1961.
63 *The Times*, 25 April 1961.
64 *The Guardian*, 6 April 1961. At Leke newly built barracks which could accommodate
    KAF 500 troops were found.
65 Ibid.

66 Prominent amongst these were the *Mahadevi* of Yawnghwe, Princess Hearn Hkam, wife of the former Union Pres. Sao Shwe Thaike; Dr Ba Nyan; Sao Sai Mong; Jimmy Yang, the MP for the Kokang substate; and the Rangoon Univ. students, Sai Tun Aye and Sai Hla Aung. The best account of the rise of the Shan nationalist movement remains 'An Outline of the Political History of the Shan State from World War II to the Present', released by the SSA in 1965; reprinted as an appendix to *Proposal to Control Opium from the Golden Triangle and Terminate the Shan Opium Trade* (US Govt. Printing Office, 1975), which is a transcript of hearings at the House of Reps Subc'ttee on International Relations, 22-23 April 1975.

67 *The Nation*, 4 Dec. 1959.

68 Ibid., 4 Dec. 1959; *The Guardian*, 8 Dec. 1959, 1 March 1960; *Burma Weekly Bulletin*, 18 Feb. 1960.

69 Interview with Khun Kya Nu, 18 Jan. 1985. Later pres. of the SSPP, he puts the total armed strength of the different Shan factions in the 1960s at a maximum 8,000. However, from the very beginning the Shan movement was, as today, very fractured and into the early 1960s, while the KMT was still very active locally, the situation remained highly confused. But during 1960-2, at least, the main rebel groups were the SSIA, set up by the student leaders, Khun Thawda, Sai Tun Aye and Sai Hla Aung which broke away with the 'Tangyan-hero' Bo Maung from the *Noom Suik Harn* in 1960 and was active mostly in Mong Mit, Hsenwi, Hsipaw, Mong Yai, Mong Hsu and the north; the SNUF, led by a former White Flag CPB, Mo Heing (*aka* Gon Jerng), in Lawksawk, Taunggyi, Hopong, Loilem and the SW; the TNA, headed by the former *pongyi*, U Gondara (*aka* Sao Gnar Kham), in Kengtung in the east; remnants of the *Noom Suik Harn*, led by Saw Yanda, in the south along the Thai border; and a local militia force headed by Bo Dewaing in Mong Yai in the north. All followed the same strategy of trying to build up local rebel forces into regular battalions, but with only limited success.

70 *The Nation*, 27 Dec. 1960.

71 Other Rangoon Univ. alumni included Chao Kyaw Tun of the Mong Yai ruling family, whose father Chao Naw Mya also joined the uprising; Sai Tun Aye; Sai Hla Aung; Sai Myint Aung; Sai Pan and Hso Ten (*aka* Sai Kyaw Sein). A look at their subsequent careers reveals the many hardships they faced: Khun Thawda, after heading a joint Shan delegation to the 1963 peace talks and surviving several MIS assassination attempts, retd. into Thailand in 1968; Chao Kyaw Tun, kld. in action, 1961; Sai Tun Aye, surrendered 1962, joined Khun Sa/Gon Jerng's TRC in 1985; Khun Kya Nu, retd. as SSPP pres. in 1976, today a gems trader in Thailand; Sai Myint Aung, kld. in action in 1979 while acting pres. of SSPP; Sai Pan, briefly succeeded Sai Myint Aung as SSPP pres., assassinated 1983, reputedly by Khun Sa's gunmen; Sai Hla Aung, surrendered 1983 while pres. of SSPP; and Hso Ten, today CC member of SSPP and leader of a 1989 breakaway faction. Other prominent Shan leaders of the period included Khun Maha, ed. of the *Khitthit Shan Pye* journal (reportedly died 1990 with TRC); Khun Pung of the Hsenwi ruling family (later died in an accidental grenade explosion); Sai Kyaw Zam whose father was chief sec. to the Hsewni *Sawbwa* (today with TRC). U Gondara was assassinated in 1964.

72 The *Duwa* Lawan Li and U Zantha Sin, and the KNC pres., the *Duwa* Zau Lawn. See e.g. *The Guardian*, 3, 11, Dec. 1960. The first two were even accused of leading a crowd of over 4,000 demonstrators who stoned a train bringing U Nu's State Religion Com. to Myitkyina at the end of 1960.

73 *The Nation*, 3 Jan. 1961.

74 *Burma Weekly Bulletin*, 19 Oct. 1961.

75 See e.g. J. Silverstein, 'The Federal Dilemma in Burma', *Far Eastern Survey*, July 1959, 28 (7) 97-105; J. Silverstein, 'Politics in the Shan State: The Question of Secession from the Union of Burma', *Journal of Asian Studies*, Nov. 1958, No.28: 43-57.

76 Interview with Aung Kham Hti, 29 Nov. 1984.

77 *The Guardian* (monthly), May 1955: 18.

78 *The Nation*, 22 April 1959.

79 Silverstein, 'The Federal Dilemma', 104-5.

80 *The Nation*, 22 Dec. 1960; see also Ch.9, *n*.67.

81 *The Nation*, 16 and 31 Dec. 1960.

82 *Burma Weekly Bulletin*, 27 April 1961.

83 *The Nation*, 27 Oct. 1960.
84 Interview with e.g. former pres. of RPF, Jaffar Habib, now deceased, 14 Jan. 1986; interviews with ethnic Rakhine and Rohingya (Muslim) villagers along Naaf River, Feb. 1987; *The Nation*, 18 and 19 Jan. 1960.
85 U Aung Zan Wai, 'Report to the Govt. Advisory C'ttee headed by Sir Ba U, 1961' (abridged).
86 Ibid.
87 Interview with Maung Sein Nyunt, Pres. ANLP, 23 Feb. 1987; interview with Thein Pe and Shwe Tha, CPA CC, 19 Jan. 1986.
88 Yawnghwe, *The Shan of Burma* (ref: Ch.2, *n.*37): 119.
89 U Aye Soe Myint, Karen; Sama *Duwa* Sinwa Nawng, Kachin; and U Zahre Lian, Chin (ibid.).
90 'Memorandum Submitted by the Constitution Revision Steering C'ttee; Shan States; 22 Feb. 1961' (copy in my possession).
91 *The Times*, 3 March 1962.
92 *The Guardian*, 8 March 1962.
93 Ibid.
94 *Burma Weekly Bulletin*, 21 June 1962.
95 Interview with Saw Maw Reh, KNPP pres., 19 March 1988. The only contacts the KNPP had with Sao Wunna's men were unofficial trading deals between govt. and insurgent-held areas.
96 For a poignant account of his loyalty to the Union, see Yawnghwe, *The Shan of Burma*, 146.
97 Interview with Sao Hkun Hkio, 24 Feb. 1990.
98 Yawnghwe, *The Shan of Burma*, 119
99 Silverstein, *Burma: Military Rule*, 80.
100 *The System of Correlation of Man and his Environment*, as quoted, ibid.

Chapter 11

1 Silverstein, *Burma: Military Rule* (ref: Ch.6, *n.*88): 80.
2 According to Silverstein, the army's moral justification for the coup was that since cdrs. were party to Aung San's decision to enter politics, they maintained the right to intervene 'in time of national crisis' (ibid.: 80-1).
3 See Robert Taylor, *The State in Burma* (C. Hurst, London, 1988); and e.g. Taylor, *International Herald Tribune*, 8 Feb. 1989, which was copied and circulated to foreign govts. by Burmese embassies abroad.
4 Doubts over the fairness of the 1973 referendum are still voiced. Some 95% of the eligible 14,760,036 electorate reportedly voted of whom 90% gave their approval for the Constitution. Many voters complained of BSPP intimidation and ballot-rigging. None the less, in the ethnic minority Kayah (Karenni) State still only 71% of voters were recorded as giving their consent, in the Kachin State only 68%, and in the Shan State just 66%; 168 members of the Voting Com. were also reported kld., wounded or missing in insurgent attacks (Silverstein, *Burma: Military Rule*, 134).
5 Ibid.: 81; Govt. of Burma, RC, *The Burmese Way to Socialism* (Min. of Information, Rangoon) published 30 April 1962 and *The System of Correlation of Man and his Environment*, 18 Jan. 1963.
6 U Ba Than, *The Roots of the Revolution* (Min. of Information, Rangoon, 1962).
7 Silverstein, *Burma: Military Rule*, 103.
8 BSPP, 'Address Delivered by Gen. Ne Win, chm. of the BSPP, at the Opening Session of the 4th Party Seminar on 6 Nov. 1969' (Central Press, Rangoon): 28-9.
9 Much of the army's paranoia in 1978 over the Muslim question in Arakan was stirred up not so much by *Mujahids* or Bengali immigrants, but by the alleged involvement of the former Bangladesh mil. attaché in Rangoon, Col. Amin Chowdury, in this 'Arakanese liberation' plot, which was to have been begun by the assassination of BSPP leaders in Rangoon (see e.g. RHS, 22, 23 Sept. 1977). Four men, led by Mahn Ngwe Aung, who, as a member of the KNU, later led the 1982 attack on the Rangoon Broadcasting Station (he had been released under the 1980 amnesty) were brought to trial for their role. A fifth man, Kyaw Hla, who escaped, has confirmed most of the details of the plot to me (Interview, 3 Dec. 1984). Today Kyaw Hla heads the Muslim Liberation Organisation (formerly ALO), a DAB member, with small armed units active in KNPP

and KNU territory.

10 *FEER* Yearbook, 1966.
11 *The Times*, 9 July 1962.
12 Interview e.g. with Thamain Tun, 23 Jan. 1989.
13 Interview with Khine Saw Tun, 1962 RUSU EC member, 26 Nov. 1989. According to Tun, by 1964 he and Min Swe were the only two EC members who had not gone underground. Ba Swe Lay and Hla Kyi, e.g., had joined the CPB in the Delta, Ko Thet and Tin Tun in the Pegu Yomas, and Aung Tha Kyaw, Tha Doe and Kyaw Hlaing (the son of former AFPFL Min., Nyo Htwan) in Arakan. Others who joined the CPB included Thein Tun, Nyan Tun, Kyaw Khin, Hla Shwe and Soe Win, son of U Hla, the *Ludu* ed. Within a few years most had died in battle, through purges or from malaria. Tun, a lawyer who later became a member of the Rangoon Bar Council, joined the insurgent ALP after the 1988 democracy uprising. Other student leaders from the 1962 generation still politically active in the late 1980s included Maj. Sai Tin Pe with the SSPP, Sai Aung Win who joined a breakaway faction from the CPB in 1989 before surrendering, and Hla Shwe who co-founded the People's Progressive Party in 1988 and was subsequently arrested.
14 Interview with Dr Marta, present-day KNU CC member, 5 Oct. 1989.
15 'Letter of Aung Gyi' to former RC members (ref: Ch.7, *n*.10). A 'Crisis C'ttee' was established, including Cols. Kyaw Soe, Hla Han, Saw Myint, Than Sein from the RC, U Ba Aye from the Police and Bo Sein Lwin, 4th Burma Regiment, from the 'Kamayut front' near the campus.
16 For a graphic eyewitness account see Yawnghwe, *The Shan of Burma* (ref: Ch.2, *n*.37): 10-11.
17 Quoted in John Badgely, 'Burma's Zealot Wungyis: Maoists or St Simonists', *Asian Survey*, 5, Jan. 1965: 56.
18 For the later account of a White Flag student activist, see Ch.9, *n*.45; for a Red Flag supporter see Aye Saung, *Burman in the Back Row*, (Asia 2000, 1989).
19 James F. Guyot, 'Burma in 1988', *Asian Affairs* (Institute of SE Asian Studies, Singapore, 1989): 113.
20 See Ch.7, *n*.11.
21 Interview with Ven. U Rewata Dhamma, 18 Sept. 1989.
22 Trager, *Burma: From Kingdom to Republic* (ref: Ch.3, *n*.8): 402. Some 400 of those imprisoned were from the two AFPFL factions and over 2,500 from the NUF. The rest were mostly students, *pongyis* or 'economic criminals'; as of May 1965, only 1,900 had been released.
23 Silverstein, *Burma: Military Rule*, 117-18. Three reports were submitted. The majority report urged a retention of the 'federal' 1947 Constitution with new ethnic states where necessary; the minority report also suggested a federal system but under a one-party socialist state; U Nu, on the other hand, attacked the legitimacy of the RC and wanted all political restrictions lifted, the release of all political prisoners and the reconvening of the dissolved Parliament to vote on Ne Win as Pres.
24 *The Times*, 23, 27 March, 29 April 1965.
25 The army's version of the parley was produced in a brochure, *Internal Peace Parley (Historical Documents No.1)* (Rangoon, 1963); see also, e.g. *WPD*, 20 Nov. 1988, which was later republished in a 1989 *WPD* book of 'Collected Articles'. Amongst those who took part whom I interviewed or questioned are: from the KNUP/NDUF, Skaw Ler Taw, Than Aung; from the NMSP/NDUF, Nai Shwe Kyin; the KNPP/NDUF, Saw Maw Reh, Bo San Lin; the KRC, Mika Rolly; the KIO, Zau Mai; the SSIA-SNUF, Chao Tzang Yawnghwe, Khun Kya Nu; the CPA, Thein Pe; and the CPB, Ba Thein Tin.
26 Interview with Nai Shwe Kyin, 18 Jan. 1989.
27 Interview with Zau Mai, 22 Nov. 1984.
28 *Forward*, 7 Dec. 1963.
29 A copy of this letter, dated 7 Aug. 1963, is contained in a long KNUP document, *The Report on the Talks with the RC* (1963, KNU Archives). Ne Win also wrote a personal letter to another veteran Karen cdr., Saw Thein, who had served with him in the 4th Burma Rifles.
30 Interview with Nai Shwe Kyin, 18 Jan. 1989. Other NDUF dinner-guests with Ne Win on 30 Sept. 1963, including Skaw Ler Taw of the KNUP, also remembered these

words.
31 *Forward*, 7 April 1964.
32 *WPD*, 20 Nov. 1988.
33 *The Guardian* (monthly), Dec. 1963.
34 Interviews with Shwe Tha and Thein Pe (*aka* Soe Ni), CPA, 19 Jan. 1986; Zau Mai, KIO, 22 Nov. 1984. For the Shan talks see Yawnghwe, *The Shan of Burma*, 14-17. There was disagreement within the Shan nationalist movement over the 'federal' offer to the RC and many Shan armed opposition leaders wanted only to talk of secession.
35 KNUP, *Report on the Talks*.
36 Corr. with Ba Thein Tin (ref: Ch.6, *n*.10).
37 KNUP, *Report on the Talks*.
38 *Forward*, 7 Dec. 1963.
39 Ibid., 22 Nov. 1963; interview with Skaw Ler Taw, 14 Jan. 1985.
40 VOPB, 14 June, in BBC, *SWB*, 17 June 1981. The KNUP accused the *Tatmadaw* of 5 specific operations during Sept. and Oct., in Bassein, Pyapon, Kyaunggon, Ingabu and the Pegu Yomas (KNUP, *Report on the Talks*).
41 *Forward*, 15 Oct. 1968.
42 *WPD*, 20 Nov. 1988.
43 Ibid.
44 Interview with Khine Saw Tun, 23 Nov. 1989. Tun, as an Ethnic Students Federation rep., was selected to welcome the marchers on campus and cites the number of bags of rice they distributed as proof of the vast numbers of peace protesters, something the army has always denied.
45 Interview with Nai Non Lar, 18 Jan. 1989, who was not released until 1973, three years after the Pao leaders, Hla Pe and Kyaw Sein. Young peace activists were also locked away for long periods; e.g., Nai Pe Thein Zar, a student rep. on the Peace C'ttee from Moulmein College, was held without trial for 7 years (Interview, 24 Nov. 1989).
46 Interview with M. Rolly, 27 Jan. 1987.
47 See Ch.9, *n*.10.
48 Interview with Skaw Ler Taw, 14 Jan. 1985.
49 Ibid.
50 *Forward*, 7 April 1964.
51 Interview with Skaw Ler Taw, 14 Jan. 1985.
52 Amongst the insurgent leaders Rolly met were the Palaung leader, Hso Lane, and the Shan, Sai Pan, both of whom later became prominent figures in the SSPP (interview, 26 Jan. 1987).
53 Minutes of the 'Kawthoolei National People's Congress', 24 April 1963. The list of the 13 remaining KRC members, given in order of seniority in the Minutes, reflects the KNUP's later influence on the KNU movement; present or last positions in brackets. Mahn Ba Zan (d. 1981, KNU hon. adviser), Kaw Htoo (d. 1972, KNUP chm.), Skaw Ler Taw (d. 1989, KNU CC member), Mahn Mya Maung (d. 1985, KNU CC member), Kyin Pe (kld. in action 1968, KNUP Gen-Sec.), Tin Oo (6th brigade chm., KNU CC member), Maung Maung (KNU CC member), Than Aung (KNU vice-pres.), Maj. Baldwin (missing in action, 1967), Padoh Ba Thin (KNU Gen-Sec.), Sa Myo Thwe (surrendered), Ohn Pe Nyunt (assassinated 1964), Tamla Baw (KNLA vice-Chief-of-Staff, KNU CC member).
54 Ibid.
55 *Forward*, 22 March 1964.
56 Ibid., 7 April 1964.
57 Ibid., 22 April 1964.
58 Interview with M. Rolly, 27 Jan. 1987.

Chapter 12
1 *The Times*, 12 Feb. 1964.
2 Interview with Muhammad Jafar Habib, 14 Jan. 1986.
3 ANUO fizzled out in 1971 and was largely superseded by the KIO-trained AIO and KNU-backed ALP. Bo Kra Hla Aung resurfaced in 1988 during the democracy uprising and at a mass public meeting on 22 Aug. in Sittwe, joined by a number of other former insurgent leaders, he warned students to be ready for armed struggle since it would be the next 'decisive' step.

4 Interviews with Shwe Aye, KNLP chm., 19 July 1990; Saline Myu Aye (*aka* U Paung), former ZNF CC, 29 Jan. 1987 (see also *n*.50); interview with Khun Sa, 19 Jan. 1987. Angered by the demonetisation, Khun Sa, a local govt. militia leader, crossed sides to join a local Shan insurgent cdr., Bo Dewaing, who had fought in the 1959 Tangyan battle. The two men, however, soon fell out and in 1966 Khun Sa crossed back to the govt. KKY side and fought against Dewaing, who was forced to flee south. From this point on the distinction between the SUA as a 'rebel' force or a 'KKY' force has frequently been blurred.

5 See Ch.16, *n*.25.

6 See Ch.5, *n*.29.

7 'Communiqué of the Shan State War Council', 27 May 1964 (copy in my possession). TNA and NSH reps. also attended this founding meeting but refused to join the SSA.

8 Interview with Mai Ban Sein, PSLP, 18 March 1988; Chao Nor Far, 20 Jan. 1987.

9 *The Guardian*, 18 Aug. 1968; *Forward*, 15 May 1969; interview with Maha San, 10 Jan. 1987

10 Interview with Aung Kham Hti, Pres. PNO, 29 Nov. 1984; Tha Kalei, chm., SSNLO, 19 July 1990.

11 Nai Non Lar, NMSP vice-pres. until his death in 1989, spent nearly 10 years in gaol; Nai Aung Tun, min. of Mon Affairs under U Nu, was imprisoned for 5. Interviews with Nai Non Lar and Nai Shwe Kyin, 18 Jan. 1989; Bo Thi Ha, 22 Dec. 1985.

12 Tinker, *The Union of Burma* (ref: Ch.4, *n*.32): 61.

13 *NCNA*, 26 Nov. 1967.

14 Quoted in the *Yearbook on International Communist Affairs* (Stanford: Hoover Institution Press, 1968): 66.

15 McCoy, *The Politics of Heroin in SE Asia* (ref: Ch.9, *n*.9): 318-22.

16 There is no independent corroboration for these figures because troops allegedly took away the bodies of all the casualties, dead or alive. Rakhine nationalists list this as the fourth mass killing by govt. troops in Arakan since independence: 1952, over 100 villagers kld. at Tawpanzun village, Kyauktaw; 1954, several dozen suspected sympathisers of U Seinda's APLP massacred at Magigone village, Manaung; and 1956, all male villagers and a number of female inhabitants at Sanrey and Akazar villages, Pauktaw.

17 D. Murray, 'Chinese Education in SE Asia', *China Quarterly*, 20, Oct.-Dec. 1964: 79.

18 Interview, 10 Oct. 1989.

19 Pettman, *China in Burma's Foreign Policy* (ref: Ch.9, *n*.6): 37.

20 Ibid.: 36.

21 See e.g., *NCNA*, 15 Aug. 1967. These reports were backed up with anxious articles about the safety of Chinese aid workers in Burma and their 'proletarian' friendship with Burmese workers.

22 *NCNA*, 15 Aug. 1967.

23 *China Pictorial*, Sept. 1967.

24 *Peking Review*, 35, 25 Aug. 1967. The first CPB CC statement came as early as 28 June and was broadcast by *NCNA* on 1 July denouncing the 'cruel persecution' of the mil. govt. and grieving 'for the blood of our Chinese brothers'.

25 *The Guardian*, 29 Oct. 1967.

26 *WPD*, 20 Nov. 1988.

27 Those able to attend were Thakins Than Tun, Zin, Chit, Ba Tin, Pu and Mya, Bo Zeya and *Yebaws* Htay and Aung Gyi from the Central HQ staff, and Thakin Tin Tun (Shan State) and Soe Than (Delta); the absentees were Thakins Ba Thein Tin, Than Myaing and Pe Tint (China), Dr Nath (NW Division), Kyaw Mya (Arakan), Myo Myint and *Yebaw* Toke (Northern Division), Tun Shein (Tenasserim) and Yan Aung (sick).

28 *NCNA*, 28 April 1969.

29 *Peking Review*, No.47, 17 Nov. 1967.

30 See, 'Problems of Strategy in Guerrilla War against Japan' and 'On Protracted War', in *Selected Works of Mao Tse-Tung* (ref: Ch.7, *n*.18): 79-194.

31 VOPB, 18 May, in BBC, *SWB*, 23 May 1975.

32 *Peking Review*, 3 Sept. 1965. For e.g. of Than Tun paraphrasing Mao's strategy, see *NCNA*, 28 March 1968, on the 20th anniversary of the CPB insurrection.

33 *NCNA*, 28 April 1969.

34 Statement of the CPB CC, *NCNA*, 28 April 1969.

35 The second course in Feb. 1966 was attended by 37 people, including 7 former student leaders. The rest were senior functionaries of whom 4 later defected to co-author *The Last Days of Thakin Than Tun* (in Burmese) (Myayabin Press, Rangoon, 1969), *Yebaw* Mya (sec. Pegu Yoma Division), *Yebaw* Ba Khet (Office Supt., CPB HQ), *Yebaw* Tin Shein (dist. c'ttee, Tharrawaddy dist.) and *Yebaw* Saw Hla (dist. c'ttee, Toungoo).

36 *WPD*, 20 Nov. 1988

37 Some former communists have suggested that it was rather the Beijing returnees who 'chose' Zin and Chit as the leaders of their 'proletarian' movement (esp. after Than Tun's death) since they were regarded as politically less imaginative. By contrast, they regarded the 'intellectuals', Ba Tin and Htay, as being too individually motivated and internationalist in their outlook. However, while the split did develop along these lines, this theory wrongly downplays the political leadership of Zin and Chit, both of whom were highly experienced party organisers.

38 *Forward*, 15 Oct. 1968.

39 Ibid.

40 See e.g. *The Guardian*, 5, 11, 26 June 1968.

41 For the RC's version see *The Guardian*, 25-30 Sept. 1968. Maung Mya was an ethnic Chin and former *Tatmadaw* soldier before defecting to the CPB; the govt. has always maintained he acted alone. However, in the mid-1970s KNU officers became suspicious when a man answering to his description approached them and asked for help in forming an underground force to fight the BSPP. Under questioning they say he confessed to his past identity and, believing he was now on a second assassination mission, they decided to take no chances and executed him.

42 See Ch.9, *n*.25.

43 *Peking Review*, 13, 28 March 1969.

44 VOPB, 18 May 1975 in BBC, *SWB*, 23 May 1975.

45 *NCNA*, 14 Aug. 1967.

46 Ibid., 15 Aug. 1968.

47 Ibid., 27 April 1969.

48 'Political Report of the CPB CC', presented to the Third National Congress, VOPB, 15, 29 June, 5 July, in BBC, *SWB*, 17 June 1986 and ff.

49 For a discussion, see 'Political Report of the Politburo', VOPB, 2, 11 Dec. 1979.

50 Contrary to claims in Rangoon that the Chin hills have been 'insurgent free' there have been numerous attempts to set up Chin liberation movements over the past 4 decades. Most have failed due to a combination of 3 main factors, the diversity of the over 40 ethnic Chin sub-groups, and the remoteness and poverty of the region, which has caused many young Chins to volunteer to serve in the *Tatmadaw*. For the CNVP see Ch.10, *n*.38. A small Chin National Liberation Party was established in the early 1960s by Chin Ba Maung amongst the northern 'tribal' Chins and remained close to the Red Flag CPB. An equally small Chin Liberation Front, led by Peter Ba Cho and allied to the CPA, was also active in the southern Arakan Yomas in the 1960s. For failed attempts to set up Mizo/Chin fronts with Pakistani aid on the Indian border, see Vumson, *Zo History* (ref: Ch.3, *n*.53): 227-37. Several small groups have also been trained by the KIO, the earliest being the Chin Independence Army, formed in the early 1960s by Bo Phil Maung, a *Tatmadaw* defector. However, after returning to the northern Chin State this group disintegrated following Maung's assassination, allegedly by a govt. agent, Hkan Kan Hkup, who rather in the manner of Than Tun's assassin, Maung Mya (who approached the KNU), approached the KIO in 1976 to request training for his own rebel group. Recognised and denounced by other Chin troops with the KIO, he was executed. Perhaps the best known Chin org. internationally has been the ZNF, formed in 1964 by a group of Christian Chins from the north, led by Han Khan Tan, Peter, William and 'Jimmy' Thang Za Dal, who planned to return to the Tiddim-Falam area after training with the CNVP's Karen ally, the KNUP. Many, however, of the first 40 ZNF recruits, including Han Khan Tan, were kld. in action, and only in 1972 was the ZNF reformed as a small cell in KNPP territory by Thang Za Dal and the former CNVP member, U Paung. Here the ZNF was for a time overshadowed by the CDP of Mang Da Laing, a former Chin MP, who joined U Nu's PDP scheme in the early 1970 to build up the NULF (see Ch.14). With the NULF's eclipse, William, a Saline Chin and the most experienced Chin rebel cdr., joined the ALP on their fateful 'long march' north in 1976/7 where he and half the force met their deaths. See also *n*.62.

51 Most of the information in this passage and in the preceding paragraph on the NW Division was supplied to me in interviews and corr. with Arakan CPB leaders between 1987-90, including Politburo member, Kyaw Mya; CPB prov. sec., Saw Tun Oo and provis. c'ttee member, Kyaw Maung.

52 Interview with Kyaw Maung, 18 Feb. 1987.

53 Interview with Tun Win, 19 Feb. 1987.

54 Interview with Maung Sein Nyunt, 23 Feb. 1987.

55 Interview with U Khine Maung, dep-cdr. of the 1972 expedition, 18 Jan. 1986; interview with U Kyaw Hlaing, 2 Feb. 1989. The first team was helped by the insurgent NSCN, led by Muivah, and both were partly guided by agents of the MNF of Laldenga along the India border. Tun Shwe Maung surrendered in 1980 after complaints by his men when he took a second wife and Kyaw Hlaing took over the party leadership. Others say Maung never really recovered from the death of his brother on the 1977 March.

56 Interview with ALP sec., Khine Myo Min, 13 Jan. 1985; CC member, Na Na Ni, 18 Jan. 1986. Both men were captured. Khine Myo Min was badly wounded and Na Na Ni received the death penalty. Both, however, were released in the 1980 amnesty and immediately returned to the jungles.

57 Though it was Red Flag defectors, led by Kyaw Zan Rhee, who founded the CPA, the idea was first mooted in 1961 by another popular Rakhine nationalist, U Saw Maung. His life-story reads as a poignant illustration of Burma's endemic insurgencies. A former cdr. in the ADA, he then went underground again in 1948 with the PVOs as an aide to his wartime chief, Bo Kra Hla Aung. Having surrendered with the PVOs in 1958, in 1960 he joined the White Flag CPB, taking mil. charge of Kyauktaw township. Shortly afterward, he argued with White Flag leaders over the question of sending local funds to White Flag GHQ in central Burma and defected from the party with 30 troops, briefly using the new name, 'CPA'. In 1961, however, he was arrested on the way to hold secret talks with another former ADA leader, the Ven. U Pyin-nya Thi Ha, who was then the legal head of govt. in the Arakan Division, and took no part in the formation of the present-day CPA. After his release in 1963, he joined the underground ANUO of his longtime mentor, Kra Hla Aung, before joining the CPA in 1968. In the 1973 split, he sided with the 'nationalist' Maung Han faction against Kyaw Zan Rhee. Finally in 1979, nearly 4 decades after he began life as a soldier, he was kld. in action by the *Tatmadaw* near Paletwa.

58 For my own account of a journey along Arakan's borderlands and interviews with CPA leaders, see *Inside Asia*, 9, July-Aug. 1986.

59 The CPA's gen-sec., Shwe Tha, e.g. attended the RNA conference at Kawmoorah in KNU territory in May 1973 and later spent some months with the NMSP, even being held responsible for the NMSP's 1981 split (see *Focus*, Jan. 1982). It is a charge he absolutely denies. The CPA, which continues to denounce the Chinese occupation of Tibet, also for many years did not get on with the rival ANLP of Maung Sein Nyunt which, while avowedly Marxist, takes a more pro-Chinese position. The ANLP, which grew out of U Seinda's defunct APLP, remains more of a peasant and farmers' party.

60 See e.g. *Forward*, Aug. 1978, and contrast this with the welcoming tone for the returnees in *Forward*, March 1979; for a documented account, including photographs, of Muslim allegations of army atrocities see *Genocide in Burma against the Muslims of Arakan*, (Rohingya Patriotic Front, 11 April 1978, copy in my possession): see also, *Inside Asia*, for the continued persecution of Muslims and rebel Muslim organisations.

61 RHS, 28 Jan. 1974.

62 Interestingly, following the MNF's 1987 peace accord with the Indian govt. there has been greater cross-border political interest in the struggle of their Chin cousins and, in particular, the latest Chin insurgent force, the Chin National Front, headed by John Khaw Kim Thang. The CNF became the 11th member of the NDF in March 1989. Arms and finance remain a perennial problem, but by mid-1990 100 CNF guerrillas had completed training with the KIO and they appeared to enjoy free access along the unpoliced Mizoram border.

63 Interview with Kyaw Maung, 18 Feb. 1987. The CPB's full 'Constitution on Membership and Organisation' was broadcast on the VOPB, 10, 19 Feb., in BBC, *SWB*, 16, 25 Feb. 1980.

64 See e.g. *NCNA*, 28 March 1968.

65 Tinker, *The Union of Burma*, 68.
66 Interview with Thein Pe, 19 Jan. 1986.
67 Interview with Kyaw Maung and Tun Win, 18 Feb. 1987.
68 Ibid., Kyaw Maung.
69 *NCNA*, 14 Aug. 1967.
70 VOPB, 29 Jan., in BBC, *SWB*, 2 Feb. 1980.

Chapter 13
1 The new CC line-up was: Thakin Zin, chm.; Ba Thein Tin, VC (Beijing); Thakin Chit, sec.; Pe Tint (Beijing); Aung Gyi; Thakin Pu; Myo Tint; Kyaw Mya (Arakan); Soe Than (Delta); *Yebaw* Mya (Pegu); Thakin Tin Tun (Shan State); Tun Sein (Tenasserim); *Yebaw* Toke (North Burma); Dr Nath (NW Division). Mil. cdrs: Bo Aung Pe (Delta); Bo Pone Kyaw (Pegu Yomas); Bo Thet Tun (NW Division); Bo Myo Myint (North); Bo Kyin Maung, Bo Soe Maung (Shan State); Bo Aung Myint (Central Burma); Naw Seng, Than Shwe (NEC). Subsequent careers: Ba Thein Tin, Kyaw Mya, Myo Myint and Kyin Maung are present-day Politburo members; Than Shwe retd. after the 1985 Congress; Thet Tun surrendered in 1980. The following were kld. in action: Dr Nath, 1968; Aung Gyi, Myo Tint, Soe Maung, 1969; Tin Tun, 1970; Aung Pe, 1973; Toke, Thakins Zin and Chit, Pone Kyaw, 1975. Of the others, Pu died of natural causes in 1969, Soe Than was purged and Mya surrendered the same year; Naw Seng died in a mysterious hunting accident, 1972; Tun Sein was replaced by U Saw Han before the major party reorganisation of 1975, and Bo Aung Myint is variously reported as having died or been kld. in 1969; Pe Tint of cancer in 1990.
2 Interview with Khwan Mong, former SSPP CC, 20 Nov. 1984.
3 VOPB, 6 Oct. 1978. No data exist on when the custom finally died out, but if it still existed in the 1960s Wa leaders insist it was exceedingly rare.
4 *The Guardian*, 2 March 1968.
5 'Radio Peace and Progress', 2 March 1974, quoted in the *Yearbook on International Communist Affairs* (ref: Ch.12, *n.*14) 1975: 300.
6 Ibid., 1977: 258.
7 *NCNA*, 31 Oct. 1967.
8 Ibid., 13 Nov. 1967.
9 Ibid., 17 Nov. 1967.
10 Interview with Zau Mai, KIO vice-pres., 22 Nov. 1984.
11 'Agreement on the Formation of a United Front between Reps. of the CC of the CPB and KIO', 15 Jan. 1968. Copy in my possession.
12 See e.g., *NCNA*, 22 Nov. 1967.
13 See e.g., ibid, 8 June 1967.
14 For a succinct account of the NEC build-up see Bertil Lintner, *FEER*, 4 June 1987, which he later elaborated with maps in *The Rise and Fall* (ref: Ch.3, *n.*58).
15 For the Pawng Yawng rebellion see Ch.8.
16 This undated report, appended to the CPB-KIO treaty of 1968 (see *n.*11), was apparently written for the benefit of Thai and US intelligence officers to whom it was circulated.
17 Ibid.
18 VOPB, 9 Nov. 1972.
19 *FEER* Yearbook, 1972: 113.
20 Pettman, *China in Burma's Foreign Policy* (ref: Ch.9, *n.*6): 41.
21 VOPB, 15 Aug. 1971.
22 Ibid., 29 Nov. 1973. For the Wa reaction, see Ch.16.
23 M.C. Tun, *FEER*, 14 Jan. 1974.
24 Ibid.
25 VOPB, 15 July 1974.
26 RHS, 25 March 1973.
27 VOPB, 25 Aug. 1974.
28 Ibid., 18 Oct. 1973.
29 Ibid., 25 Aug., in BBC, *SWB*, 29 Aug. 1974.
30 *WPD*, 20, 21 Nov. 1988.
31 Interview with Zau Mai, 22 Nov. 1984.
32 Interview with Thamain Tun, 22 Jan. 1989.

33 See e.g., *FEER*, 9, May 1975; and Jeffrey Race, 'The War in Northern Thailand', *Modern Asian Studies*, 8 (1) 1974: 85-112, for an account of how low-level communist infiltration from Vietnam, via Laos, in the mid-1960s led within a few years to the build-up of the CPT in north Thailand and the napalm-bombing of ethnic Hmong hill tribe villages by the Thai Air Force in response.

34 See e.g. the speech of San Yu, gen-sec. of the BSPP, RHS, 26 Jan. 1976.

35 For a discussion, see Sir Robert Thompson, *Defeating Communist Insurgency: Experiences From Malaya and Vietnam* (Chatto and Windus, 1966); G. Kolko, *Vietnam: Anatomy of a War, 1940-75* (ref: Ch.9, *n*.20): 131-7.

36 See e.g. *Forward*, 1 April 1969; and the editorials in *Loktha Pyeithu Nezin*, 14 Feb. 1975 and *Botahtaung*, 18 May 1978.

37 *FEER* Yearbook, 1968: 121.

38 Brig. San Yu, *Forward*, 1 May 1969.

39 Pop Buell, quoted in Don Schanche, *Mister Pop* (David McKay Co., 1970): 294-5.

40 Identical allegations have been made to me by villagers from very different areas of Burma: Tenasserim, Karen State, Shan State, Mon State, Kachin State, Arakan State and the Delta, caught up in offensives many years apart. See also Amnesty International, *Burma: Extrajudicial Execution and Torture of Members of Ethnic Minorities* (London, May 1988). In the army's defence, the only 'excuse' for the callous scale of this violence against civilians can be that, rather as US soldiers found in Vietnam, in the dense, malaria-ridden forests and mountains of SE Asia, it impossible to distinguish friend from foe. Unable to speak local languages and dialects, predominantly Burman prisoners and *Tatmadaw* deserters have described to me the mounting fear and anger in their units as they sustained a steady toll of casualties through mine attacks, sniper fire and the occasional ambush by a largely unseen enemy. Outwardly friendly villagers are often the only local inhabitants they see for months on end. They say it thus takes only one insurgent attack for even the most well-intentioned soldier to regard all villagers as supplying intelligence and recruits to their enemy's side.

41 Interview with Pah La Hai, 14 Jan. 1987. Details of these allegations from Shwegyin and Thaton were documented in a report prepared for the London-based Anti-Slavery Society, 'Human Rights in Burma: Situation Report presented to the For. Affairs C'ttee of the House of Commons by the ASS, 5 March 1987'.

42 The pictures plus interviews with survivors and relatives of the victims were shown on Channel 4 News (UK) 19 Dec. 1989.

43 Interview with Col. Aye Myint, 18 July 1990.

44 *Peking Review*, 12 Jan. 1968.

45 For a synopsis of PA activities in early 1968 (not including the NEC), see *NCNA*, 15 Aug. 1968.

46 The CC represented all the KNUP brigade areas and was augmented by 10 'candidate' members at its annual meetings. From the CC, 4 party administrative bureaux were set up, each headed by a Politburo member. At the Second KNUP Congress of 26 March 1963 (which was, in fact, the last full KNUP Congress until the 'final' Congress of Sept. 1975), the CC appointed: party chm., Mahn Ba Zan, ed.; Kyin Pe, organ. and propaganda; Mya Maung, land and econ.; Kaw Htoo, mil. The 5th Politburo member was Skaw Ler Taw, then KNUP gen-sec. Of the 25 full and candidate CC members elected in 1963, 4 have since died, 8 were kld. in action, one was assassinated, 3 surrendered (one of whom, Saw Tun Aye, was subsequently executed by the KNU), one eaten by a tiger, one has retd. and 7 are still on the KNU CC today.

47 *Forward*, 1 Feb. 1970.

48 Ibid., 15 July 1969. These accounts were meticulous and revealed, e.g., 40,176.60 kyat went on mil. expenses, the single largest item on the budget, 35,000 kyat to settle the previous year's debts, 12,000 on remittances to the Delta divisional HQ, and 2,194 kyat on medicine; the KRC figure comes from 'ts former gen-sec., Skaw Ler Taw.

49 *Peking Review*, 36, 3 Sept. 1969.

50 Interview with U Soe Aung, 13 Jan. 1985

51 *Forward*, 15 June 1969.

52 Ibid., 15 March 1971.

53 Ibid.

54 Ibid., 1 May 1971.

55 RHS, 8 Dec. 1973, 8 Jan., 1974. Other key CPB organisers lost in this period included

the former army capt. and Beijing returnee, Bo Ba Nyunt, and the PA cdr. for Yedashe, Bo Tun Tha, who were captured, and Hla Aung and Kyin Aung, chm. and sec. of the Waw township unit, who were both kld.

56 Interview with Skaw Ler Taw, 8 Dec. 1985; indeed the SSWC's rep. at the founding meeting, Hso Ten, was imprisoned by the *Mahadevi* on his return and held for some time under the threat of death.

57 Ibid; interviews Bo San Lin, 9 Dec. 1985, Saw Maw Reh, 18 March 1988; Tha Kalei, Shwe Aye, 19 July 1990.

58 VOPB, 1 April 1973.

59 Ibid., 11 Nov. 1973.

60 Ibid., 20 Jan. 1974.

61 Ibid., 21 July, BBC, *SWB*, 24 July 1974.

62 Ibid., 15 Aug., BBC, *SWB*, 21 Aug. 1974.

63 *Yebaw* Mya et al., *The Last Days of Thakins Zin and Chit* (in Burmese), (Myayabin Press, Rangoon, 1976).

64 RHS, 20 March 1975; *Forward*, 1 May 1975.

65 Ibid.

66 Ibid.

67 Ibid.

68 See RHS, 12 April 1973, for Operations *Suzaga* and *Sinbyudaw* in which 1,800 suspected 'economic' and 'political' saboteurs were arrested.

69 Stories are legion of the ways in which army officers benefited from the black market trade. This could be by simple pay-offs and taxes collected by up-country cdrs. in the war zones, or by reselling on the black market imported goods which they were allowed to buy at subsidised prices in Rangoon. Cdrs. in NE Burma, in particular, were heavily involved in the black market in precious stones and one highly reliable informant frequently witnessed officers on their return from duty visiting the 'opium warlord' Khun Sa in Rangoon in the mid-1970s after his release from gaol, who was one of their main brokers. Jade from the Kachin State and rubies from the Shan State were easy to transport and highly profitable. But it is Ne Win himself, through his contacts in Switzerland, who is reputed to have made the greatest fortune.

70 *WPD*, 12 July 1974.

71 RHS, 8 June 1974.

72 *FEER*, 11 July 1975.

73 RHS, 22, 23 June 1974; VOPB in BBC, *SWB*, 12 June 1974.

74 Silverstein, *Burma: Military Rule* (ref: Ch.6, *n.*88): 143.

75 Ibid.

76 *Loktha Pyeithu Nezin*, 14 Dec. 1974.

77 Interview with Tun Aung Gyaw, 30 Jan. 1989.

78 Silverstein, *Burma: Military Rule*, 143.

79 Interview with Ye Myint Soe, one of those publicly accused, 22 March 1982; *FEER*, 11 July 1975.

80 *The Observer* (London), 31 March 1974.

81 RHS, 3 April 1976; interview with Tun Aung Gyaw, 30 Jan. 1989, who was also arrested and imprisoned for 5 years.

82 *Forward*, 1 Dec. 1970.

83 Interview with Shwe Tha, 21 Feb. 1987.

84 Ibid.

85 Ibid. The CPA's leading ideologue today, Shwe Tha was formerly with the Red Flags.

Chapter 14

1 *San Francisco Chronicle*, 19 Oct. 1970.

2 Interview with Bo Mya, 12 Jan. 1987.

3 Interview with Tin Maung Win, 7 Nov. 1987. According to Win, Aung Gyi and his student allies had adopted what they called a 'five fingers plan' to organise amongst 'the 5 key sections of Burmese society' (army, students/youth, Buddhist clergy, farmers/workers, and civil servants). Win, who had been educated at both Rangoon and Georgetown universities (in the US), was in charge of the youth movement.

4 *FEER Yearbook*, 1966.

5 R. Butwell, 'U Nu's Second Comeback Try', *Asian Survey*, 9 (11): 869.

6   See e.g., ibid.
7   Ibid.: 870-1 (For the IUAB proposals, see Ch.11, *n*.23)
8   Ibid.: 872.
9   'Letter of Aung Gyi', 9 May 1988, see Ch.7, *n*.10.
10 Ibid.
11 Ibid.
12 Butwell, 'U Nu's Second Comeback Try', 872. According to Butwell, after U Nu's arrest Gandhi almost cancelled one visit to Rangoon over Ne Win's refusal to guarantee her access to see him in detention.
13 Interview with Max McGrath, 20 Nov. 1987. Ironically McGrath had been imprisoned and deported by U Nu in 1960.
14 Ibid.; Butwell, 'U Nu's Second Comeback Try', 873.
15 Ibid.
16 Ibid.
17 Interview with J. Silverstein, 20 July 1990. Several PDP veterans then in malaria-ridden jungle camps remember a 'Mr Camel', who they were told was a wealthy Canadian sympathiser, visiting them on an 'inspection' trip in the company of Bo Let Ya and Law Yone prior to the deal being arranged. Aung Din (*aka* Eddie Myint), former PA to Bo Let Ya, believes $4m was eventually raised from a variety of such sympathetic Western sources (interview 23 April 1990).
18 I own a large collection of English-language documents on insurgent groups in Burma, from 1963 to the present-day, prepared by one Thai-Burmese intelligence group working for US intelligence agencies and Thai Border Patrol Police. In most respects they are accurate, and include reports on all rebel orgs., their troop-strengths and base areas, eyewitness accounts of historic meetings, profiles of key leaders, their relations with both the CPB and CPT, and even a translation of CPB letters intercepted in Karen CPT villages in Thailand. I have also frequently met Thai officers from various agencies in rebel-held areas and on two occasions (1982 and 1987) Americans, who, requesting anonymity, admitted their 'intelligence' identities; see also *n*.37.
19 McCoy, *The Politics of Heroin in SE Asia* (ref: Ch.9,*n*.9): 339. After interviewing Young, whom he described as one of U Nu's fund-raising 'assistants', McCoy believed Burma's 'future was mortgaged to the hilt' because of the number of mineral and oil concessions the PDP had promised Western investors.
20 Interview, 31 Jan. 1987. Now retd. but still living in the region, this well-placed informant has requested anonymity.
21 Interview with Tin Maung Win, 7 Nov. 1987. U Win died in the hills near Thaton and was buried in the forest. When one month later a *Tatmadaw* unit went to try and exhume his body, they were ambushed by the KNU and an army capt. and 5 soldiers were kld.
22 Interview with David Zaw Tun, 5 Jan. 1986.
23 Interview with Saw Maw Reh, 18 March 1988.
24 McCoy, *The Politics of Heroin in SE Asia*, 340.
25 *Forward*, 15 May 1970; see Ch.12, *n*.50, for Chin history.
26 See Ch.2, *n*.7 for Karen sub-groups.
27 For a scathing attack on Bo Mya ('Nga' Mya, 'Bandit' Mya), see *The Guardian* (Rangoon) 19 Sept. 1987.
28 Like many other Animist Karens, Mya's birthdate was never recorded, so 20 Jan. 1927 was chosen by the KNU for his birthday celebrations which are treated with great pomp and ceremony in Kawthoolei each year.
29 Morrison, *Grandfather Longlegs* (ref: Ch.4, n.13): 159-60.
30 Much of the information in this account comes from a series of interviews with Bo Mya in the years 1985-90 and with Pu Nah Moo on 30 Dec. 1985. Nah Moo had trained with the British Army in India and served with Col. Wingate before parachuting into the Papun hills with Col. Peacock. After the rebellion began, Nah Moo became a KGB council member and was Mya's commanding officer in the Hlaingbwe battalion.
31 See e.g., *The Nation*, 30 March 1961.
32 Interview with Bo Mya, 12 Jan. 1987.
33 *The Times*, 26 June 1954.
34 See Ch.13, *n*.48.
35 In the course of many journeys through KNU-held territory I have never found the

slightest evidence of poppy cultivation or heroin refining. This contrasts sharply with the situation in the Shan State to the north and even across the border in Thailand. The KNU has often enforced the death penalty for drug trafficking and the only opium or heroin I have seen has been seizures by KNU customs officers. In remote areas of Tavoy-Mergui, however, where the KNU, the *Tatmadaw*, the CPB and various Burman and Mon insurgent groups still vie for control, there is some marijuana cultivation by local villagers which KNU dist. officers claim they have been powerless to stop.

36 In the mid-1960s Benny Htoo, KNLC Defence Min., estimates regular KNLA troop strength in the east at some 3,000 men under arms: No.1 brigade, 1,000, Nos.2 and 3, 300 each, No.6, 600 and No.7, 700; interview, 23 Dec. 1985.

37 Until his death in 1989, Skaw Ler Taw kept a copy of his letter. Some of this advice, he claimed, came from US missionaries who were beginning to take an interest in the Karen struggle. In this period he remembered being shown a letter in which one missionary urged Bo Mya to expel 'the leftist leaders' (interview, 18 March 1988). Since this time a number of US and Australian missionaries (largely Seventh Day Adventist, Pentecostal or Baptist) have worked in Karen villages along the border and helped set up a number of health and educational projects in KNU-controlled areas. Most missionaries would appear to me, at least, to be non-political and with little influence, but several are believed by KNU leaders (in at least one case correctly) to have been reporting to the CIA.

38 Interview with Benny Htoo, 23 Dec. 1985.

39 Interview with Col. Marvel, 31 Dec. 1985.

40 Interview with Saw Ba Lone, 26 Dec. 1985.

41 In the late 1950s Mahn Ba Zan sent down Spurgeon Pu from Shwegyin with 300 troops to set up a KNUP dist. org. amongst local Karen villagers. This KNUP force had some contact with White Flag CPB units on the plains, but problems with local villagers persisted. Lin Htin, the NMSP and NLC also had designs on the area and Pu was eventually assassinated, apparently by a group of his own men. Thus into the late 1960s KNUP/KNLC control of the area had remained very tenuous.

42 Patriotic Youth Front Radio, 27 June 1970.

43 Ibid.

44 Interviews with Nai Shwe Kyin and Nai Non Lar, 18 Jan. 1989.

45 McCoy, *The Politics of Heroin in SE Asia*, 340.

46 Ibid.

47 Ibid.: 341-2.

48 Interview with Chao Tzang Yawnghwe, 24 Nov. 1984.

49 The SSPP-PYF statement was broadcast on PYF Radio, 30 Jan. 1973, BBC, *SWB*, 3 Feb. 1973.

50 *FEER*, 12 Dec. 1970.

51 Ibid., 8 Jan. 1972.

52 NULF Radio, 8 Dec. 1973. Beginning with Bo Yan Naing's initial 300-strong NLC force near Three Pagodas Pass in 1969, by 1971 PDP veterans estimate 4,000 PLA recruits had gathered in various PLA camps around the pass, another 4,000 under U Thwin in the Mae Sot area of Thailand from where they scattered out to various KNU bases along the border, and another 2,000 between Ranong and the Mawdaung Pass in the far south. NULF Radio usually broadcast from a hidden location near the confluence of the Salween and Moei rivers.

53 See e.g., RHS, 30 Dec. 1972, for a summary of PLA attacks reported by the *Tatmadaw*.

54 *The Guardian*, 19 Sept. 1987.

55 U Nu's resignation speech was broadcast on NULF Radio, 7 April, BBC, *SWB*, 8 April 1972.

56 Interview with Tin Maung Win, 7 Nov. 1987.

57 Interview with Khun Okker, 9 Jan. 1987.

58 Interview with Bo Aung Din, 23 April 1990.

59 See Ch.13, *n*.80.

60 Interview with Ye Myint Soe, 3 June 1982.

61 Interview with Col. Marvel, 31 Dec. 1985. According to Marvel, his instructions were only to disarm the PDP remnants; he did not expect a battle. Indeed Bo Let Ya had just been negotiating with Col. Oliver, cdr. of the KNU's 10th battalion, to move up to Three Pagodas Pass to start a new joint force with the KNU. Yan Naing, however,

insisted on fighting and Let Ya, despite KNU warnings, decided to stay with him. After the battle, the KNU found documents showing that Let Ya had also been in contact with CPB cadres in the area. Unlike Yan Naing, who returned to Rangoon in 1980, Let Ya appears to have had little intention of surrendering.

62 'Joint Communiqué by the KNPP, SSPP, KNLP and KNU', 2 May 1973, reproduced in *Proposal to Control Opium from the Golden Triangle and Terminate the Shan Opium Trade* (ref: Ch.10, *n.66*): 23-4.

63 FNDF, *Communiqué No.1*, 28 May 1975 (copy in my possession).

64 The groups that attended but did not join were the NMSP (which finally joined in 1982), SUA, SURA and ANLP.

65 KNU, *Policy and Rules and Regulations of the Karen National Union* (KNU Publishing, 1974). These regulations, approved by the 1974 Congress, were published in both Karen and Burmese-language editions and are today used as a handbook by KNU teachers and administrators throughout Kawthoolei.

66 Interview with Skaw Ler Taw, 18 March 1988.

67 *FEER*, 27 Feb. 1976. Most estimates put the CPT's armed strength at its peak in 1979/80 at 12,000 men under arms. Many of these were ethnic minority hill farmers, mostly Hmong in Thailand's far north, but there were also a significant number of Karens and Mons. From this point, however, CPT stength declined dramatically; see e.g., ibid., 9 Jan. 1986.

68 KMT activities were overseen by the 'Bor Kor 04' office set up in 1975 by Gen. Kriangsak Chommanand under the Thai Supreme Command; see *Focus*, Feb. 1982: 23-4. Both the CPB and CPT broadcast news of fighting with the KMT; see e.g. 'Voice of the People of Thailand', 29 Nov. 1977, BBC, *SWB*, 12 Dec. 1977, for a report of one CPT-KMT battle in Chiang Kham dist. KMT 'volunteers' later even took part in the Thai Army assault on the great CPT stronghold on Khao Khor mountain in 1981 (*FEER*, 8 May 1981). For the decline of KMT and SUA relations with Thailand from 1982, see Ch.16 including *n.61*.

69 Interview with Tin Maung Win, 7 Nov. 1987. The others banned were Hanson Kya Doe and Zali Maw.

70 *FEER*, 25 June 1976.

71 *The Observer* (London), 16 May 1976.

72 See Ch.7, *n.24*.

73 *FEER*, 25 June 1976.

74 Ibid.

75 KNU Central Standing C'ttee, 'Statement by the KNU to the Entire People', 15 Aug. 1986.

76 Interview with Mika Rolly, 25 Jan. 1987.

77 When asked why they took no action, one KNU officer replied, 'They have perhaps 100 men operating along the border near here. We could attack them, but what good would it do us? This is a guerrilla war. Even ten men with guns could cause us a a lot of harm.'

78 See e.g., *Bangkok Post*, 2 Dec. 1982, 18 Feb. 1983.

Chapter 15

1 *NCNA*, 20 May, in BBC, *SWB*, 22 May 1975.

2 VOPB, 3 July 1975.

3 *Peking Review*, 22, 30 May 1975.

4 Ibid.

5 Statement of the CPB on 55th anniversary of CCP, as quoted in the *FEER*, 4 June 1987; *NCNA*, 28 July 1977.

6 See e.g. VOPB, 4 Oct. 1984 for an adulatory report on China, the land 'wreathed with successes' which, under the CCP's leadership, today 'wins gold medals at the Olympics'.

7 *WPD*, 13 Nov. 1975.

8 *Pravda*, 14 April 1975, as quoted in the *Yearbook on International Communist Affairs*, 1976 (ref: Ch.12, *n.14*): 249.

9 *NCNA*, 10, 30 Sept. 1977 as quoted in ibid., 1978: 224.

10 See e.g. Bertil Lintner, *FEER*, 4 June 1987.

11 Copy in my possession.

12 The full list, their original base areas and their subsequent careers (* indicates pre-1968
    traveller to China): *Politburo*: Ba Thein Tin* (Tavoy), Pe Tint* (Pyinmana), Khin
    Maung Gyi*, Myo Myint (*aka* U Aung) (Pegu Yomas), Kyaw Mya (Arakan), Kyin
    Maung (Shan State), Tin Yi (*aka* Ne Win)*; All, with the exception of Pe Tint, who
    died in 1990, were still Politburo members in early 1991 and were believed to be in
    exile in China. *Full CC*: Soe Kyi (Pegu Yomas) kld. in action, 1975; Saw Han (Tavoy);
    Zau Mai* (Naw Seng group, ethnic Kachin) 1989 mutineer; Taik Aung*, retd. 1985
    Congress; Pe Thaung*; Hpalang Gam Di* (Naw Seng group, ethnic Kachin) retd.
    1985; Ye Tun (Pyinmana); Thet Tun (NW Division) surrendered 1980; Than Shwe*,
    retd. 1985; plus two more (never named) from the Delta and the NW Division.
    Candidate CC: Kyin Pyaing, retd. pre-1985; Soe Thein*, arrested by 1989 mutineers;
    Soe Lwin and Aye Hla (Tavoy); San Thu*; Sai Aung Win (ethnic Shan) 1989
    mutineer, surrendered 1990; Tun Myint (*aka* Mya Min, Pyinmana); Maung Maung
    Sein, retd. 1985; Ye Din* (*aka* Tun Lwin); Than Lwin Tun, died pre-1985; Thein
    Aung, retd. 1985; Aye Ngwe*; plus two more to be named from Delta (never named)
    and Arakan (Saw Tun Oo). In 1990 Saw Han, Aye Hla and Soe Lwin were still active
    in the CPB's last Tavoy-Mergui base areas and Saw Tun Oo in Arakan, while virtually
    all the other CC members listed above, unless otherwise specified, had moved to
    China.
13 VOPB, 17, 18 May, BBC, *SWB*, 23 May 1975.
14 Ibid.
15 For typical talks on agriculture, see VOPB, 10 Nov. 1977; oil, 27 Nov. 1977; a com-
    parison between Burma and China, 29 Jan. 1976; students, 6 April 1976; and the PA,
    12 June 1977.
16 VOPB, 10 Aug., BBC, *SWB*, 13 Aug. 1976.
17 Ibid.
18 VOPB, 17, 18 May 1975.
19 'Politburo Report', 1 Nov. 1978, broadcast VOPB, 1 Jan. 1980. Interviews with
    villagers in the Tenasserim Division have confirmed the essential details of this report.
    Under Soe Lwin and Saw Han, who organised the Divisional C'ttee, came two dist.
    c'ttees under Aye Hla, pol. sec., and U Boe Sein, Mil. cdr., in Tavoy; and Tin Oo, pol.
    sec., and Bo Ba Lwe, in Mergui.
20 Interview with Saw Lionel, 26 Jan. 1985. U Boe Sein was shot and crippled and his
    wife and family kld. in the Thayetchaung operation. Because of the diversity of the
    ethnic races in the region the CPB has always picked its staff with care. For many years
    the CPB's liaison officer in the Division was Tun Kyi, a Burmese- and Karen-speaking
    Mon Christian, a very rare combination!
21 VOPB, 18 May 1975.
22 RHS, 28 June 1975.
23 Interview with Maj. Zaw Bawn, 26 Jan. 1987.
24 VOPB, 1 Jan. 1980.
25 *Yearbook on International Communist Affairs*, 1979: 225.
26 *WPD*, 18 July 1980.
27 Over 2,000 political dissidents were reported as surrendering in a three month period in
    1980, mostly from the PDP, but this list also included 136 CPB insurgents from Arakan
    and 145 members of the Kokangese Shan State Revolutionary Army of Lo Hsi Ming,
    brother of Lo Hsing-han, who was released from gaol.
28 The *Tatmadaw*, too, has frequently resorted to guerrilla tactics. At 4 a.m. on 29 April
    1986 army commandos raided a CPB camp I visited, killing 4 CPB troops, including a
    veteran wireless operator, Bogri Tin Maung, who was beheaded.
29 Interview with Twan Aung Cho, 17 Feb. 1987; *WPD*, 7 Nov. 1986.
30 VOPB, 26 May 1978; BBC, *SWB*, 21 March 1979.
31 VOPB, 25 July 1978.
32 See e.g. VOPB, 29 Sept. 1987, for an 'incomplete' report of 80 govt. troops kld. or
    wounded in skirmishes during Aug. and early Sept.
33 VOPB, 12 Dec. 1977.
34 Ibid., 2 Feb. 1978.
35 Ibid., 6 Jan. 1980.
36 Politburo Report, ibid.
37 *The Guardian*, 27 March 1978; VOPB, 14 April 1978.

38 *Botahtaung*, 19 May 1978.
39 *Los Angeles Times*, 10 Aug. 1980.
40 VOPB, 13 Jan. 1980.
41 Interview with Khun Sa, 19 Jan. 1987.
42 *Weekend Telegraph* (London), 10 March 1967.
43 For a discussion see e.g. M. Smith, *Inside Asia*, Sept-Oct 1985, 5: 7-9, and United States General Accounting Office, *Drug Control: Enforcement Efforts in Burma are not Effective* (USGAO, Washington, 1989). In 1975 the Shan proposals were investigated by the US House of Reps; see *Proposal to Control Opium from the Golden Triangle and Terminate the Shan Opium Trade* (ref: Ch.10, *n.*66).
44 McCoy, *The Politics of Heroin in SE Asia* (ref: Ch.9, *n.*9): 343.
45 *FEER*, 4 June 1987.
46 Corr. with Ba Thein Tin (ref: Ch.6, *n.*10).
47 Interview with U Khine Maung, 19 Jan. 1986.
48 In addition to the Politburo (minus Kyaw Mya) those who attended were Zau Mai, Hpalang Gam Di, Soe Thein, Tun Lwin, Than Lwin Tun, Thein Aung, Ye Tun, Than Shwe, Mya Min, San Thu, Aye Ngwe, Maung Maung Sein and Sai Aung Win.
49 Several copies of the Politburo report, transcribed from the VOPB, have been printed. See e.g. Charles B. Smith, *The Burmese Communist Party in the 1980s* (Institute of SE Asian Studies, Singapore, 1984).
50 Corr. with Ba Thein Tin.
51 VOPB, 24 Feb. 1980.
52 Ibid., 18 March 1980.
53 Ibid.
54 Ibid., 11 Dec. 1979.
55 On the CPB side were Ba Thein Tin, Pe Tint and Ye Tun; on the BSPP side were Ne Win, For. Min. U Lay Maung, and BSPP sec. U Than Hlaing (VOPB, 14 June 1981).
56 Interview with Brang Seng, 27 Jan. 1989. The night before leaving Ne Win had even hosted a dinner at Govt. House attended by the KIO leaders Brang Seng, Zawng Hkra and Tu Jai.
57 VOPB, 14 June 1981.
58 VOPB, 29 June 1981.
59 Ibid.
60 Ibid., 14 June 1981.
61 Corr. with Ba Thein Tin.
62 The KIO's official statement on the breakdown of the talks was broadcast on the VOPB, 12 July 1981.
63 Corr. with Ba Thein Tin; interview with Brang Seng, 27 Jan. 1989.
64 VOPB, 10 July 1981.
65 Ibid., 11, 18 April 1983.

Chapter 16

1 Interview with Skaw Ler Taw, ex-KNUP Politburo member, 30 Jan. 1989.
2 *NCNA*, 28 April 1969.
3 Interview with Kyaw Maung, 18 Feb. 1987.
4 Interview with Kyaw Hlaing, 2 Feb. 1989.
5 Interview with Khwan Mong, 20 Jan. 1987.
6 *The Guardian*, 17 Feb. 1970, reproduced in Fleischmann, *Documents on Communism* (ref: Ch.3, *n.*65): 177-9.
7 Ibid.
8 Handwritten copy (in Burmese), dated 21 Jan. 1971, in my possession.
9 Ibid.
10 Interview with Skaw Ler Taw, 30 Jan. 1989.
11 *Peking Review*, No.13, 28 March 1968.
12 An exploratory party set out in 1968 but, finding its way blocked, turned back. The following year a senior cadre, Richard Tin Lin, and a 20-man party under CC member, Aye Han, travelled up by different routes to try and find a way through. Both eventually met up in Yunnan Province where they met Naw Seng shortly before his death. On their way back, Aye Han's party was ambushed by govt. troops in the Shan State and Han disappeared in flight, presumed murdered by robbers in the Ye Ngan area.

13 Information on the Dawna team and the KNUP's other missions to China has been sup-
     plied in a series of interviews in the years 1984-90 by a number of veterans of these
     journeys, including Skaw Ler Taw, Richard Tin Lin and Thamain Tun of the KNU and
     Khwan Mong of the SSPP.
14 Interview with Skaw Ler Taw, 15 Jan. 1985.
15 Ibid.
16 Ibid.
17 Ibid.
18 Ibid.
19 Interview with Abel Tweed, 1 Dec. 1984.
20 Interview with Zau Mai, 22 Nov. 1984.
21 Interview with KIO chm., Brang Seng, 12 Nov. 1987.
22 Interview with Naw Lon, ex-KIA soldier at Tam Ngop, 6 Jan. 1986.
23 Interview with Brang Seng, 12 Nov. 1987.
24 VOPB, 21 Jan., in BBC, *SWB*, 24 Jan. 1977.
25 From the beginning the KIO used the British 'brigade and battalion' system. At the
     KIO's 1st Congress at Nbaba village near Bhamo in 1964, it was decided to divide the
     founding 'Model' brigade into two brigades, North and South. Then at a CC meeting in
     1972 at the KIO's GHQ at Ronkong in the southern 'Triangle' region, it was decided to
     divide again into the present system with 4 brigades, the 1st in the north; 2nd west; 3rd
     east; and 4th south in the Shan State. In 1978 the KIO GHQ was moved from the 1st
     brigade area to its present location near Pajao on the Chinese border in the 3rd brigade
     area. Interview with Col. Zau Seng, 7 Dec. 1985.
26 See e.g., E.R. Leach, *Political Systems of Highland Burma* (ref: Ch.2, *n*.19).
27 This is the SSA's final brigade org. from the late 1970s. But over the years there have
     been frequent changes in SSA mil. structure, esp. in the 1960s, and other special
     battalions have been created. For a vivid, personalised account of life with the SSA, see
     Yawnghwe, *The Shan of Burma* (ref: Ch.2, *n*.37).
28 Quoted in *Yebaw* Mya et al., *Last Days of Thakin Than Tun* (ref: Ch.12, *n*.35): 804.
29 SSA GHQ, *Burma's Changing Situation and the Position of the SSA*, 10 June 1968; see
     also Ch.13.
30 Interview with KIO member, Jem Lomethong (13 Jan. 1986), who was told this by the
     Mahadevi herself at a meeting in Bangkok.
31 Yawnghwe, *The Shan of Burma*, 27-8.
32 Ibid.
33 A copy of this proposal and the following KIO-PSLO-SSPP agreement was reproduced
     in *Proposal to Control Opium from the Golden Triangle and Terminate the Shan
     Opium Trade* (ref: Ch.10, *n*.66). The PSLO is referred to by the name Palaung National
     Front.
34 Interview with Mai Ban Sein, 18 March 1988.
35 Interview with Gon Jerng, 20 Jan. 1987.
36 Ibid.
37 On a visit to Pieng Luang in 1984 in the last days of this extraordinary pact, I observed
     that opium and heroin were both easy to purchase. KMT and SURA soldiers and their
     families lived in satellite villages in the hills on both sides of the border around the
     market town of Pieng Luang which, daily crowded with hundreds of traders and
     colourful hill tribe villagers, was booming. Even more remarkably, a Thai army col.
     was giving training to SURA troops, while I was introduced to a Burmese police
     officer from Mong Hsat!
38 See Ch.15, *n*.43.
39 McCoy, *The Politics of Heroin in SE Asia* (ref: Ch.9, *n*.9): 318-31.
40 Interview with Skaw Ler Taw, 30 Jan. 1989.
41 Interview with Tha Kalei, 20 July 1990.
42 VOPB, 13 Dec. 1973.
43 Interview with Tha Kalei, 20 July 1990.
44 Interview with Aung Kham Hti, 29 Nov. 1984; Khun Okker, 9 Jan. 1986.
45 Interview with Tha Kalei, 20 July 1990.
46 See Ch.2, *n*.12.
47 Aung Kham Hti's PNO faction was not represented at the 1976 NDF meeting, but the
     ex-PDP follower, Khun Ye Naung, attended under the name of the Union PNO and

was appointed NDF vice-pres. Aung Kham Hti immediately objected and Khun Ye Naung was left with little choice but to join the PNO. The following year he surrendered.

48 Interview with Khun Zani Zet, 21 Nov. 1989. PNO-SSNLO areas often overlapped. But while SSNLO efforts were largely concentrated around Hsihseng and along the Shan-Kayah State borders, the PNO tried to set up 4 administrative areas, the Northern (between Laikha and Taunggyi), the Western (between Palaw and Pekon), the Central (Taunggyi to Hsihseng), the Eastern (Mawkmai to Thai border).

49 Asked about the future of the SSNLO, Tha Kalei replied, 'I've lost two brothers, two sons and so many officers and men in these long years fighting. I can't betray them by negotiating or surrendering to the *Tatmadaw*. Sometimes we've had large numbers, sometimes small, but we've never disappeared. As long as the *Tatmadaw* try to run the country the people will revolt. The important thing is that we keep the right goals. As long as we do this, the people will support us. We will never be defeated.'

50 Interview with Khwan Mong, ex-SSPP CC member, 26 Jan. 1987.

51 Interview with Khun Kya Nu, 18 Jan. 1985.

52 Interview with Khwan Mong, 26 Jan. 1987.

53 These events were dramatically captured by the British film makers, Adrian Cowell and Chris Menges, in their remarkable opium trilogy, *The Opium Warlords* (Central Television, UK), and saw the transition of the local KKY leader, Lo Hsing-han, from govt. cdr. to rebel chief to convict after the BSPP ordered the KKY units to disband in 1973. The SSA's proposals to sell the opium harvest, which won backing from the KIO, PSLO, Lo Hsing-han and SUA, eventually went before the US Congress but were rejected; see *n.33*.

54 After going underground with 800 KKY followers in 1973, Lo Hsing-han briefly joined with the SSA before being lured into Thailand and arrested. He was then deported to Rangoon, lending credence to the belief that he was only detained because he knew too much about official involvement in the drugs trade. His force was then taken over by his brother, Lo Hsing-min and, in 1976, they joined up with the remnants of Jimmy Yang's KRF to form the Shan State Revolutionary Force at Doi Lamg. In the 1980 amnesty, however, they all surrendered after Lo Hsing-han was released.

55 Interview with Khun Kya Nu, 18 Jan. 1985; and Tzang Yawnghwe, 24 Nov. 1984.

56 *Communiqué*, 25 May 1976, Office of the EC, SSPP (copy in my possession).

57 VOPB, 30 Jan., in BBC, *SWB*, 2 Feb. 1977.

58 Ibid.

59 Interview with Khun Sai, SSPP CC, 12 Jan. 1985.

60 VOPB, 4 March, in BBC, *SWB*, 8 March 1983.

61 *Bangkok World*, 22 Feb. 1985; *The Nation* (Bangkok), 29 Dec. 1985. In 1984 the Bor Khor 04 office, responsible for liaising with the KMT, was replaced with a new army task force, codenamed 327, responsible for overseeing the integration of these 'Chinese refugees' as they officially became known.

62 Interview with Khun Sa, 19 Jan. 1987.

63 See e.g. *The Observer* (London), 16 July 1989.

64 Interview with Gon Jerng, Khun Sa, 20 Jan. 1987.

65 Ibid.

66 In 1984 the SUA even exploded a bomb in Gen. Li's Chieng Mai compound, setting off another spate of rival killings. For a note on Chinese ethnicity, see Ch.2, *n.40*.

67 VOPB, 23 March 1986.

68 Interview with Saw Maw Reh, 18 March 1988.

69 Interview with Abel Tweed, 1 Dec. 1984.

70 Interview with Saw Maw Reh, 18 March 1988.

71 Interview with Johnnie Soe, ex-KNPP CC member, 16 June 1982.

72 Interview with Abel Tweed, 28 Jan. 1987.

73 Interview with Saw Maw Reh, 18 March 1988; Nya Maung Me, 20 July 1990.

74 Interview with Johnnie Soe, 16 June 1982. According to Soe, there were three conditions: the KNPP should help the KMT '93rd Division' as far as possible; the KNPP should put as much jade business as possible the KMT's way; the KNPP must remain anti-communist.

75 Interview with Abel Tweed, 28 Jan. 1987.

76 Interview with Nya Maung Me, 20 July 1990.

77 RHS, 19 Sept. 1988; interviews with Nya Maung Me and Shwe Aye, 20 July 1990.
78 Interview with Saw Maw Reh, 19 July 1990. On this basis the KNPP did not join the DAB.
79 Interview with Khun Pang, LNO CC member, 11 Jan. 1986.
80 Ibid.
81 Ibid.
82 Interview with Khun Okker, 9 Jan. 1986.
83 Sao Saimong Mangrai, *The Shan States and the British Annexation* (ref: Ch.3, *n*.32): 271.
84 Interview with Maha San, chm. WNO, 10 Jan. 1986.
85 Ibid., and interview with Moses King, a Wa agent recruited by the CIA, 21 July 1990; McCoy, *The Politics of Heroin*, 301-31.
86 *Forward*, 15 May 1969; interview with Maha San, 10 Jan. 1986.
87 Ibid.; interview with Maj. Khun Mung, WNO, 7 Dec. 1985.
88 Interview with Maha San, 10 Jan. 1986.
89 Ibid.
90 Interview with Padoh Lay Wee, KNU rep. to the NDF, 17 March 1988.
91 Interview with Khine Saw Tun, 20 Nov. 1989, member of an NDF delegation which met with the breakaway Wa faction in July 1989.
92 Interviews with Shwe Aye and Tha Kalei, 18 July 1990; for Karen population, see Ch.2, *n*.5, *n*.7.
93 Shwe Aye, ibid.
94 Ibid.
95 Ibid.

Chapter 17

1   Corr. with Kyin Maung, 10 Feb. 1990.
2   Ibid.
3   This breakdown was supplied to me by Bertil Lintner of the *FEER* in Dec. 1989, one of only three Western travellers reported to have visited the CPB's NEC; for the account of his journey, see B. Lintner, *Land of Jade* (Kiscadale, Edinburgh, 1990).
4   Interview with Johnnie Soe, 21 March 1982.
5   VOPB, 9 Aug., in BBC, *SWB*, 13 Aug. 1981.
6   Ibid.
7   Ibid., 3 Sept. 1982.
8   VOPB, 3 Dec. 1982; interview with Shwe Aye, 20 July 1990.
9   VOPB, 25 Feb. 1985.
10 Ibid., 24 March 1984. These details have been confirmed by the KIO.
11 Ibid., 23 March 1986.
12 See e.g. *Botahtaung* (in Burmese), 30, 31 May 1988.
13 *FEER*, 10 Feb. 1987.
14 *NCNA*, 4 May 1985.
15 *SE Asia Digest*, No.4, 23 June 1989.
16 Ibid.
17 Ibid.
18 SLORC Press Conf., Rangoon, 27 Oct. 1989.
19 Corr. with Ba Thein Tin (ref: Ch.6, *n*.10).
20 Ibid.
21 VOPB, 6 Jan. 1980.
22 Ibid.
23 Ibid., 22 Jan. 1980.
24 *FEER*, 28 May, 4 June 1987. See also Lintner, *Land of Jade*, 109-299.
25 The full CC list: *Politburo*: Ba Thein Tin, Pe Tint, Khin Maung Gyi, Myo Myint, Kyaw Mya (Rakhine), Kyin Maung, Tin Yi. *CC*: Kyaw Zaw, San Thu, Soe Thein, Sai Aung Win (Shan), Hpalang Gam Di, Zau Mai (Kachin), Tun Lwin, Pe Htaung, Tun Myint, Ye Tun, Aye Ngwe, Aye Hla, Saw Han, Soe Lwin (Tenasserim), Kyaw Myint, Tun Tin, Saw Ba Moe (Karen), Tint Hlaing, Kyauk Ni Lai, Pauk Yo Chang (Wa), Mya Thaung, Li Ziru (Chinese). A six-man mil. com. was also established under Ba Thein Tin, including Tin Yi (Chief-of-Staff), Kyaw Zaw (Deputy), Zau Mai, Pe Tint and Myo Myint.

26 I have interviewed one student leader involved in the seizure of the Min. of Trade building who has been named by SLORC as being 'CPB'. While not denying his CPB label nor the presence of many 'very secret and very clever CPB sympathisers' in the democracy movement, he is categoric that the CPB 'was not involved' in this particular attack. Interview, 31 Jan. 1989.
27 See Ch.1.
28 Nyunt, *Burma Communist Party's Conspiracy* (ref: Ch.1, *n.*52): 4.
29 e.g. VOPB, 4 Oct., in BBC, *SWB*, 7 Oct. 1987.
30 Khin Nyunt, Press Conf., 5 Aug. 1989.
31 *Asiaweek*, 27 Jan. 1989.
32 Interview with Nyo Aung Myint, CC member of NLD, 26 Nov. 1989.
33 Nyunt, *Burma Communist Party's Conspiracy*, 43.
34 Ibid.: 22.
35 Corr. with Kyin Maung.
36 I separately interviewed two students who claimed to be connected to this cell, including one Khin Nyunt accused by name. Both requested anonymity given the immense dangers they and their colleagues now face, but their highly cautious replies do corroborate one another and provide a convincing explanation of the true degree of the CPB's involvement. See *n.*26.
37 Ibid.; for Khin Nyunt's list of who MIS thinks were the leaders of this cell, coordinated by Dr Zaw Min who lived in the RIT compound, see Nyunt, *Burma Communist Party's Conspiracy*, 7, 84.
38 Interview with Moe Thee Zun, 28 Nov. 1989.
39 Nyunt, *Burma Communist Party's Conspiracy*, 42.
40 Ibid.: 33-4.
41 Ibid.: 3, 43.
42 The others listed were the chm. of Burma's Film Society, Aung Lwin, the ex-newspaper ed., Win Tin, Moe Thu and Chan Aye.
43 See *n.*26.
44 Interview with Aung Khaing, 3 Dec. 1989. Significantly, after the coup, like most other student activists, Aung Khaing did not contact the CPB, but made his way to KNU-territory to join the ABSDF.
45 The PPP was another resurrected party from the 1950s and 1960s, which had been part of the above-ground parliamentary NUF and most of whose leaders had been imprisoned by Ne Win in 1958-60 and again in 1963.
46 Interview with Maung Maung Lwin, 24 Nov. 1989. A former *Tatmadaw* officer, BSPP member and headmaster from Mongpai, Lwin led a group of 250 students who met with Shwe Aye and Tha Kalei on their flight to the jungles. Another group of 250 students followed behind them. Lwin eventually continued on to the Thai border, but most of his students agreed to go with the KNLP-SSNLO since they offered the immediate prospect of arms and training. Young people from peasants' backgrounds were invited to join the SSNLO and the more 'intellectual' students to join the KNLP since the KNLP chm., Shwe Aye, was himself from Rangoon Univ. while the SSNLO leader, Tha Kalei, was an ex-farmer. In 1989 100 of these CPB-trained students returned to KNLP-SSNLO territory as the DPA; interviews with Shwe Aye and Tha Kalei, 20 July 1990.
47 Interview with Moe Thee Zun, 28 Nov. 1989.
48 Interview with Revd Ashin Kimazara, 23 Nov. 1989.
49 Corr. with Kyin Maung; Nyunt, *Burma Communist Party's Conspiracy*, 67, 77-9.
50 Corr. with Kyin Maung.
51 Ibid.
52 Ibid.

Chapter 18
1 VOPB, 4 Sept. 1988. Earlier in the year the CPB had appeared more closely informed about events in Rangoon. This was because after the March killings a number of very clear eyewitness reports had reached Panghsang and were publicised on the VOPB, e.g., VOPB, 19, 21 May 1988.
2 Corr. with Ba Thein Tin (ref: Ch.6, *n.*10).
3 Ibid.

4   RHS, 2 Oct. 1988; corr. with Kyaw Mya, 15 Oct. 1988.
5   Corr. with Ba Thein Tin (copy of statement in my possession).
6   Ibid.
7   Interview with Shwe Aye, 20 July 1990. For details of this meeting in which Ba Thein Tin, in an implicit criticism of China, rejected the idea of becoming 'revisionist', see Lintner, *The Rise and Fall* (ref: Ch.3, *n*.58) 45.
8   Interview with Col. Zau Seng, 2 Dec. 1989.
9   Corr. with Kyaw Mya, 23 March 1989.
10 Ibid.
11 Quoted in BBC, *SWB*, 21 April 1989.
12 Ibid.
13 Corr. with Kyaw Mya, 12 May 1989.
14 Ibid.
15 Ibid.
16 Nyunt, *Burma Communist Party's Conspiracy* (ref: Ch.1, *n*.52): 59-63.
17 *FEER*, 1 June 1989.
18 Eyewitness evidence of large-scale Kokangese involvement in heroin production since the ceasefire is overwhelming. Travellers reported heroin refineries freely operating in border towns and villages such as Mong Ko, Hpong Seng and Mong Hom, allegedly with the encouragement of Brig. Maung Tint, who visited Kokang in June 1989. The refiners were all well-known Chinese-Kokangese entrepreneurs, including Hung Lau San, Wi Sang and Liu Go-chi. The heroin they refined appeared on the market under the brand-names 'Triple-K', 'Triple-Star', 'Triple-9' and 'Triple-5', and soldiers from the 99th LID were widely accused of involvement in trafficking. Encouragement by army officers for farmers to increase opium cultivation was also reported in the Putao area of the Kachin State, Namhsam and Lashio districts of the northern Shan State, and around Mong Hsat in the south.
19 *Report: NDF Delegates to Wa State*, 14 June-8 Aug. 1989 (copy in my possession).
20 Ibid. The 'Wa' faction also included ethnic leaders from other nationalities, including the former Kachin CC member, Zau Mai.
21 Message: Maha San (WNO) to NDF sec., 24 Nov. 1989 (copy in my possession).
22 Interview with Brang Seng, 19 July 1990. Within a year of the mutiny the Kokang group had set up business offices in Tachilek, Taunggyi, Lashio and several other towns in the Shan State, which appeared to be dealing with both sides in the civil war. Lo Hsing-min e.g. met KIO Chief-of-Staff Zau Mai in Nov. 1989 near Shweli to ask permission to transport timber from a SLORC concessionary area near Bhamo through KIO territory to China; the KIO refused.
23 Interview with Home Office spokesman, 11 April 1990.
24 Corr. with Kyaw Mya, 5 Jan. 1990.
25 Interview with Shwe Aye, 18 July 1990.
26 Ibid. According to Aye, Ba Moe had only 50 troops under his command, and the DPA's student leader, Peter, just 20 after the SSPP arrested another 30-strong DPA column returning from the north.
27 Corr. with Kyaw Mya, 26 July 1990.
28 Statement of the CPB, 'On National Conf.', 15 Aug. 1990.
29 Ibid.
30 VOPB, 14 June, in BBC, *SWB*, 17 June 1981.

Chapter 19
1   See e.g., *WPD*, 6 Dec. 1988.
2   NDF, 'Statement Issued by the 3rd Plenary Central Praesidium Meeting', 30 Oct. 1984.
3   For the KNU, the decision to seek a 'Federal Union' represented a considerable compromise. Just two months earlier Bo Mya had issued a declaration announcing 'to the world the independence' of the 'Republic of Kawthoolei' (Govt. of Kawthoolei, 'Proclamation of Independence', 19 Aug. 1984).
4   *The Nation* (Bangkok), 4 Feb. 1988.
5   'Statement by the KNU and NDF to the For. Affairs C'ttee of the House of Commons', 5 March 1987.
6   *Focus*, January 1982.
7   On 19 Nov. 1985 delegations headed by Bo Mya and Gon Jerng met in Chieng Mai to

discuss ways of ending territorial conflicts in the Shan State between NDF allies of the KNU and the TRC. Both sides agreed to work for a peaceful solution, but disagreed over the rights of other ethnic minorities within their respective territories. Gon Jerng held that 'nation and country' must be synonymous in the case of the Shan State, whereas Bo Mya replied, 'We don't use the expressions "Nation, country, culture and religion" like the TRC. In our fundamental laws we say, "Every man without discrimination as to race, religious beliefs or social class enjoys the right to live in Kawthoolei."' In reply Gon Jerng queried, 'Doesn't the name KNU imply the goal of a Karen nation and Karen country?' ('Talks Between TRC and KNU', 19 Nov. 1985; copy in my possession). Rather more surprisingly, in Dec. 1987 Bo Mya went to Mong Mai in the SW Shan State to meet Khun Sa who had now merged his SUA with the TRC. Discussion was over general regional developments and trade (esp. jade). At the end of the meeting both parties issued a joint anti-narcotics statement.

8   KNU, 'Statement by the KNU to the Entire People', 15 Aug. 1986.
9   Interview with U Soe Aung, 20 March 1988.
10 Interview with Bo Mya, 18 March 1988; Brang Seng, 27 Jan. 1989.
11 B. Lintner, *Land of Jade* (ref: Ch.17, *n.*3).
12 See *n.*7.
13 RHS, 2 Oct. 1978.
14 *FEER*, 8 Oct. 1982.
15 *Bangkok Post*, 31 March 1983.
16 The Education Min. e.g. arranges training classes for teachers from across Kawthoolei each March but has little money to distribute to the dists. Each dist. also runs its own courts and prisons. Only in cases of serious banditry are senior judges sent from GHQ to sort out local difficulties.
17 Buddhist KNLA 1st brigade troops, in particular, reject repeated *Tatmadaw* accusations since 1986 that they have attacked Buddhist temples in the Thaton area. They admit there have been a number of gun-battles at religious sites but claim that these have only been because troops from both sides tried to visit the temples at once. For an entertaining account of life in a remote community in Tavoy-Mergui which KNU officers regard as something of a 'Karen Siberia', see J. Falla, *True Love and Bartholomew* (CUP, 1991).
18 See e.g. *Bangkok World*, 1 Dec. 1983.
19 See e.g. *FEER*, 5 April 1984.
20 Interview with Capt. Say Do, 14 Dec. 1985. Allegations that the *Tatmadaw* has frequently shot suspected black marketeers in SE Burma are commonplace; e.g. 45 year-old Maung Po Ta, an ethnic Shan tin miner from Akalaw village, Kyain, claims in Aug. 1985 he survived a firing squad after being arrested with 3 friends in the forest near Chaung zone. Tied closely together, his 3 friends, Maung Yi (Burman), La Than (Shan) and Ta Tha (Mon) were kld. but Maung Po Ta himself miraculously survived, shielded by his friends' bodies as they fell on top of him. Interview, 22 Dec. 1985.
21 *Bangkok Post*, 22 April 1988.
22 During the unprovoked *Tatmadaw* attack on Sikkaya village (Ch.13), angry Thai soldiers guarding the Karen refugees told me they would instantly shoot any Burmese soldier who crossed into Thailand.
23 Amnesty International, *Burma: Extrajudicial Execution and Torture of Members of Ethnic Minorities* (ref: Ch.13, *n.*40): 3.
24 Ibid.: 67.
25 Interview with Capt. Say Do, 14 Dec. 1985.
26 RHS, 8 Oct., in BBC, *SWB*, 11 Oct. 1985.
27 *The Nation* (Bangkok), 15 March 1987.
28 AFP in English, 8 Nov. 1987.
29 *WPD*, 4 Jan. 1988.
30 *The Nation* (Bangkok), 4 Feb. 1988.
31 *Botahtaung*, 30, 31 May 1988

Chapter 20
1   Interview with Skaw Ler Taw, 18 March 1988.
2   Interviews with U Nu, 2 Sept., 13 Oct. 1988.
3   Brig.-Gen. Khin Nyunt, *The Conspiracy of Treasonous Minions* (ref: Ch.1, *n.*52): 107.

4   Ibid.
5   Interview with Moe Thee Zun, 29 Nov. 1989.
6   Expecting arrests, several other parties split into different fronts in this period to try
     and avoid martial law restrictions and broaden the spread of their movements.
7   One such interview was broadcast in March 1989 in the British TV programme,
     Burma: Dying For Democracy (see Ch.1, *n*.39).
8   Interviews with U Nu, 2 Sept., 13 Oct. 1988.
9   Letter of U Nu to Gen. Saw Maung, 7 Dec. 1989 (copy in my possession).
10   Undated letter (copy in my possession).
11   Nyunt, *The Conspiracy of Treasonous Minions*, 169, 231.
12   Ibid.: 115-6.
13   Interview with Moe Thee Zun, 29 Nov. 1989.
14   Ibid.
15   Scenes from the students' lives were screened in *Burma: Dying For Democracy*.
16   DAB Press release, 19 Nov. 1988.
17   See e.g., *Burma: Dying For Democracy*.
18   *Bangkok Post*, 24 Feb. 1990.
19   *FEER*, 22 Feb. 1990.
20   These same figures were given to me by KNU forestry offices in the 6th brigade, 10th
     and 20th battalion areas. *The Nation* and *Bangkok Post* during 1989/90 also carried
     near daily articles on the timber trade with a plethora of different statistics, some of
     which were taken up by Western newspapers and ecological groups. In reality, the
     trade was quite out of control, with timber illegaly cut in Thailand e.g. also being
     stamped 'Burma Teak', and nobody could get a total picture of what was really going
     on. For different accounts, see *FEER*, ibid; *Financial Times* (London), 21 June 1990.
21   Interview with Zaw Ye and Nay Myo, 7 Dec. 1989.
22   Interview with Dr Thaung Htun, 28 Nov. 1989.
23   Interview with Moe Thee Zun, 29 Nov. 1989.
24   See e.g. Amnesty International, *Myanmar: Prisoners of Conscience and Torture*, May
     1990.
25   ABSDF, *Dawn News Bulletin*, 2 (5) March 1990.
26   Ibid.
27   Interview with Saw Ba Lone, 25 Jan. 1989.
28   As with the elections of the 1950s, there were some disparities in the published election
     results. This was partly due to the delay in their release but also to the number of inde-
     pendents. I have used the incomplete results distributed by Burmese Embassies abroad.
     For background reports on the election build-up, see International Human Rights Law
     Group, *Report on the Myanmar Election* (Washington, 27 May 1990); Article 19,
     World Report 1991 (UK Libraries Association).
29   Interview with Maj. Walter, 20 July 1990.
30   The KIO later distributed videos of the 8 Feb. 1990 attack by the KIA 253 battalion,
     supported by the ABSDF 701/2 battalions, on a 100 truck convoy near Myitkyina in
     which 30 trucks were set ablaze and 20 govt. troops kld. (copy in my possession). In
     continuing fighting with the KIA 3rd brigade during July, the KIO reported over 300
     govt. fatalities, including porters, in the Sadon area.
31   *SE Asia Digest*, 7 July 1989.
32   Bo Mya, 'Open Letter to Saw Maung', 30 Nov. 1989 (copy in my possession).
33   Ibid.
34   See Ch.1, *n*.63.
35   Interview with Brang Seng, 3 March 1990.
36   A notable exception to this view was the only Western diplomatic team to visit, a par-
     liamentary delegation from West Germany, which was briefly allowed in the previous
     Feb. After a meeting with SLORC officials which it described as 'angry' and 'heated',
     the delegation predicted the election would be 'manipulated', but presciently warned
     that the vote might still go against the mil. and cast doubts on whether the regime
     would accept such a result. BBC, Burmese Service, 27 Feb. 1990.
37   For a typical speech by Saw Maung, see RHS, 27 March, in BBC, *SWB*, 2 April 1990;
     for a speech by Khin Nyunt, where he refers to NLD leaders as 'slaves in our country',
     see RHS, 29 April, in BBC, *SWB*, 2 May 1990; for the NUP's campaign speech, see
     RHS, 8 April, in BBC, *SWB*, 11 April 1990.

38 Interview with Nyo Aung Myint, 1 Dec. 1989.
39 *Bangkok Post*, 13 July 1990.
40 *The Nation*, 30 July 1990.
41 Interview with Aye Myint, 19 July 1990.
42 *The Nation*, 29 July 1990.
43 Interview, 13 July 1990.
44 Interview with Brang Seng, 17 July 1990.
45 BBC, World Service, 9 Sept. 1990.
46 See e.g. RHS, 23, 24 Oct. 1990.
47 Ibid., 18 Oct. 1990.
48 Evidence of these torture allegations was screened in a TV documentary I worked on in early 1991, *Forty Million Hostages* (BBC 1, UK, 10 Feb. 1991). See Amnesty International, *Myanmar: 'In the National Interest'* (Nov. 1990).
49 *Christian Science Monitor*, 13 June 1989; for another speech, see e.g. *Asiaweek*, 21 July 1989.
50 Channel 4 News (UK), 10 Aug. 1989.
51 A plethora of reports was presented to the UN Human Rights Com. by various govts and NGOs (collection in my possession). For detailed published reports, see e.g. *n.*24, 28, and Asiawatch, *Human Rights in Burma* (New York, 1990). The damning report of the rapporteur was finally delivered in Feb. 1991.
52 *Financial Times*, 23 Feb. 1990.
53 *Burma Alert*, 5, May 1990. The official sale price for the Tokyo Embassy was $236m; much of the rest is presumed to have been used for secret arms purchases.
54 Govt. of the Union of Myanmar, *Country Presentation*, (UN LDC Conf., Paris, Sept. 1990).
55 Quoted in BBC, *SWB*, 2 May 1989.
56 Interview with Maha San, 10 Jan. 1986.
57 BBC, *SWB*, 2 May 1989.
58 Interview with Moe Thee Zun, 16 July 1990.
59 Interview with Zaw Oo, 19 Jan. 1989.

INDEX

Abi 348, 349, 358
Academy for the Development of National Groups 324
Ai Hsiao-hsu 351, 352-3, 380
Akha 29, 32, 39, 41, 64, 250, 255, 323, 325, 344, 362, 364, 377, 393
Alaunghpaya 32, 101, 197, 199
Albania 201, 236, 301
All Burma Karen Organisation 174, 194
All Burma Peasants Organisation 56, 106, 122, 125-6, 175-6
All Burma Trade Union Congress 56-7, 69, 106, 119, 122, 125-6, 128, 163, 183, 188
All Burma Young Monks Union 16, 372
ABFSU, ABSDF, ABSU, see student fronts
All Nationalities Peoples' Democratic Front 381
Alliance for Democratic Solidarity Union of Burma 20, 405-6
Amnesty International 16, 397
Anawrahta 32, 36, 101, 197, 419
Animism 33, 44, 91, 144, 152, 281, 348, 393, 426-8
Anglo-Burmans/Indians 42, 114, 270
Anti-Fascist People's Freedom League: 20, 29; freedom struggle 60-86; in government 96, 101, 102-3, 105-8, 120-5, 127, 129, 136, 141, 144, 157-62, 167-8; composition of 70, 107, 124, 176; leaders 66-7, 88, 160, 176, 198; on minorities 73-4, 110, 112, 115-6, 118, 124, 146-8, 186, 244; split in 1950: 122-3; split in 1958: 123, 176-9; clean/stable 176-7, 180, 186-7, 194, 203-4; post-1962: 196, 292, 370-1, 383, 403
Anti-Separationist League 50, 53
Arakan: 28, 40, 43, 79-84, 114-5, 119, 217, 225, 275; rebellion in 44, 61-2, 64, 66, 71, 87, 90, 93, 96, 99, 106, 109, 125-6, 129-33, 135-6, 160, 173, 182, 184, 238-46, 308-10; State 3, 30-1, 37, 82, 124, 169, 176, 194, 200, 244, 288
Arakan Defence Army 64, 219
Arakan Independence Organisation 28, 36, 239-42, 245, 272, 308-9, 324, 330, 332
Arakan League for Democracy 240, 412, 417
Arakan (Muslim) Liberation Organisation 400
Arakan Liberation Party 182, 239-40, 245, 294, 359, 386
Arakan National Congress 53, 80
Arakan National Liberation Party 130, 182, 194, 219, 239, 245, 308-9
Arakan National United Organisation 163, 176
Arakan People's Liberation Party 80-1, 87, 119, 127, 129, 133, 135, 168, 176, 194, 239
Arakanese: 30, 34-7, 46, 51, 53, 75-6, 84, 202, 241, 244-5, 323; population 30, 239, 241; see also Muslims, Rohingya
Arunachal Pradesh 157

arms for democracy (1958) 167-9, 177, 184, 336
Asia Foundation 191, 201, 276
Asian Socialist Conference 121
Assam 40, 46, 332, 388
Attlee, Clement 75, 77, 87
Attlee-Aung San agreement 77-8, 83, 84
Aung, Bo Hmu 8-9, 21, 89, 107, 178, 270, 291-3, 297, 305, 309, 370, 403-5
Aung, U 20, 405
Aung Din 291, 293, 402
Aung Gyi, Brig. 8-9, 13-15, 21, 25, 39, 121, 124, 134, 176-7, 179, 186, 188-9, 196, 201-3, 212, 274-5, 366-9, 378, 414, 416
Aung Gyi, Yebaw 104, 156, 164, 208-9, 229, 231-2, 234, 236, 238, 261, 268
Aung Kham Hti 37, 193, 337-9, 359
Aung Lin, Bo 81, 129
Aung San 54-9, 61, 63, 65-71, 77-8, 88; memory of 6, 18, 23, 29, 36, 90, 144, 211, 218, 234, 368, 406, 419, 421, 424; on Army 109, 197-9, 384; on CPB 57-8, 71, 238; on minorities 34, 63, 73, 76-8, 80-5; on Ne Win 305, 421
Aung San Suu Kyi 9-10, 13-15, 17, 21-3, 177, 201, 366-9, 378, 382, 384, 401, 403-4, 407, 410-12, 414-5, 417-21
Aung Shwe, Brig. 9, 21, 168, 186, 403, 419
Aung Than 20, 180, 368, 370
Aung Thein Naing 166, 232, 234
Aung Tun, Nai 169, 187, 211
Aung Win, Sai 166, 253, 340, 377
Aung Zan Wai 53, 80-2, 135, 194
Ava 27, 32, 35, 36, 40
Aye Ko, Col. 263, 315, 319, 330, 364
Aye Myint, Col. 261, 415
Aye Ngwe 105
Ayu'tia (Siam) 397

Ba Hein, Thakin 54, 56-8, 164
Ba Khet 166, 211, 232-3
Ba Maw, Dr 50, 52, 57-8, 60-1, 63, 91-3, 116
Ba Moe, Saw 329, 365, 377-8, 381
Ba Nyein 123, 134, 162-3, 177, 203-4
Ba Pe 50, 70, 88
Ba Sein, Thakin 55, 58, 78, 93, 116, 274
Ba Swe 45, 54, 57, 69, 81, 103, 122-3, 130, 158, 162, 165, 167-9, 174, 176-7, 187, 192, 203-4, 273
Ba Swe Lay 166, 202
Ba Than, Oliver 114
Ba Thein Tin: 56, 70, 89, 104-6, 125-6, 129, 159, 167, 367, 374-5, 423-4; ideas of 229, 235-6, 246, 304-7, 316-8; in China 156, 161, 212, 226-7, 235, 247-50, 267, 303, 313, 377, 380; in peace talks 208-10, 318-19; on minorities